twisted from the ordinary

twisted from the ordinary

Essays on
American
Literary
Naturalism

Edited by Mary E. Papke

Tennessee Studies in Literature, Volume 40

THE UNIVERSITY OF TENNESSEE PRESS
Knoxville

Letters from the Edith Wharton Collection at Beinecke Library reprinted by
permission of the Estate of Edith Wharton and the Watkins/Loomis Agency.

Excerpts from THE STREET by Ann Petry copyright 1946 by Ann Petry. Copyright © renewed 1974 by Ann Petry. Reprinted by permission of Houghton
Mifflin Company. All rights reserved.

"Is American Literary Naturalism Dead? A Further Inquiry" by Donald Pizer
originally appeared in *American Literary Naturalism: Recent and Uncollected
Essays* (Bethesda, MD: Academia Press, 2002). It is reprinted here by permission of the publisher.

Copyright © 2003 by The University of Tennessee Press / Knoxville.
All Rights Reserved. Manufactured in the United States of America.
First Edition.

This book is printed on acid-free paper.

LIBRARY OF CONGRESS CATALOGING-IN-PUBLICATION DATA

Twisted from the ordinary: essays on American literary naturalism/
edited by Mary E. Papke.—1st ed.
     p. cm.—(Tennessee studies in literature; v. 40)
Includes bibliographical references and index.

ISBN 1-57233-223-9 (cl.: alk. paper)

1. American fiction—20th century—History and criticism.
2. Naturalism in literature.
I. Series.

PS374.N29 T89 2003
813'.50912—dc21   2002152532

Contents

V IRTUALLY EVERY MAJOR TEXT ON LITERARY NATURALISM SINCE ÉMILE
ZOLA'S MANIFESTOES INTRODUCES ITS ARGUMENT BY OFFERING AN OVER-
view of the philosophical foundations and aesthetic characteristics that would
mark a work of fiction as naturalistic. I will not here rehearse again the longstanding and ongoing debates over the definition of literary and philosophical naturalism; for such discussions, one can easily turn to the set of critical
analyses and overviews repeatedly cited in the essays presented here—notable
studies by, among others, Donald Pizer, June Howard, Lee Clark Mitchell,
Walter Benn Michaels, Paul Civello, and Donna Campbell. Despite disagree-
ments about what criteria determine whether or not a literary work should be
considered naturalist, most scholars and students of American literature do
acknowledge both the slippery nature of any such taxonomic gesture and the
equally suspicious concreteness of genre categorizations. Yet all would also
agree upon the moral weightiness of naturalism's claims, our continued need
to come to terms with its visions.

The curious evolution and essential difference of naturalism from early
nationalist and transcendentalist literature is something we recognize almost
intuitively from even the most cursory glance at the literature in question. We
do not, for example, confuse the many invocations of religiously sanctioned
racial differences in James Fenimore Cooper's Leatherstocking Tales for the
scientist racial determinism evident in Frank Norris's *McTeague* or mistake
Cooper's disquisitions on masculine and feminine natures as synonymous with
the gender and genetic determinism revealed in such different works as Mary
Wilkins Freeman's "Old Woman Magoun" and Stephen Crane's *Maggie*. Similarly, the glorified nation-building through war celebrated in so many early
American texts is one century later the subject of radical deconstruction by
Ambrose Bierce and, again, Stephen Crane, once more a celebration, if one
can call it that, of warrior instincts but for a very different reason. In naturalist works, the Enlightenment dream of inevitable progress and belief in human

perfectibility, of natural and positive balance among all elements of creation, seemingly turns into nightmare. For our own psychological and ontological security, we learn early on to recognize the assaultive threat of naturalism, its full-out attack on narrative and philosophical coherence, on meaning and the means through which we structure our moral lives. Naturalism was from its first appearance and remains to the present moment eminently recognizable and exceedingly resonant.

American literary naturalism, as the contributors to this volume illustrate, is a post-Enlightenment philosophical and aesthetic movement, the foundations of which are based on the materialist, scientistic determinism reflected most spectacularly in the social science theories of Auguste Comte and Hippolyte Taine; the primal evolutionary and economic theories of Charles Darwin, Herbert Spencer, and Karl Marx; later, the psychological and philosophical theories of Sigmund Freud, Friedrich Nietzsche, and Henri Bergson; as well as the literary counterparts to these theories, most notably the work of Émile Zola and, in America, his disciple Frank Norris. Naturalist works are profoundly concerned with the powerful influence of heredity and environment upon character, the role of chance and free will in the struggle for survival in an increasingly industrialized, urbanized capitalist state. The confluence of particular scientific discoveries, historical events, and capitalist demands and the consequent elaboration of a complementary necessitarian philosophy affected the making of the naturalist movement, the first concentrated showing of which appeared in America in the 1890s. That naturalism in America seems to have erupted spontaneously during this period should not blind us to its deep affinities with frontier, gothic, romance, transcendental, and sentimental literature. What so clearly differentiates naturalist works is the social construction of its authors, their recognition of a particular set of economic, social, psychological, and natural pressures upon individuals that constrain, propel, determine, in short, for particular reasons consonant with the new scientistic thinking and its various often unvoiced but nevertheless complex agendas.

The equally charged agendas of American naturalist writers and critics are the subject of this volume's essays. Each essay, of course, establishes at its outset the critical company it keeps. In that way the essays focus on literary production of both authors and critics, interrogating in unique fashion a set of broader metanarratives, including the marking out of naturalist territory, for example, and the making of a critical field and particular reputations, naturalism's own cultural capital. The essays focus our attention on the artists of the real ranging from those writing just before the 1890s, what is called the classic period, to those artists producing the latest configurations that command real estate in the self-referential world of the postmodern, naturalist fiction written at the turn into the new millennium. These primary literary works have their foundations in sentimentalism and realism, naive and critical alike, in melodrama and in the grotesque, in the narcissistic and the masochistic, in scenarios of profound cultural and individual crisis. The volume also addresses the making of a complementary canon of literary critics of American naturalism, these critics shaping the concepts by which and the forms in which we recognize literary naturalism in ways almost as important as do the fictional writers themselves. The literary and critical canons are significantly reconfigured in that the essays offer not only new interpretations of standard texts and the ever-evolving narrative of naturalism, but they also offer new ways of approaching naturalist texts—through various theoretical moves such as the lens of Foucault's work, for example, or with careful attention paid to nativist racialist theories, to the performative nature of naturalist fiction, to the search for authenticity in the age of mechanical reproduction, even to the relevance of selfish gene or chaos theory to the study of literature.

Why another study of naturalism now? Perhaps the more pressing question to ask is this: in what type of moral work does American literary naturalism engage? As a new graduate student, I was firmly warned off studying the naturalists; my mentors considered their work so powerfully depressing as potentially to cause one to do violence to one's self. Surely, I thought, literature effecting such drastic results warrants serious attention. The immense power of naturalist texts—to repulse, to shock, to unsettle profoundly one's conceived notions of self, freedom of will, and moral value—lies in their transgressiveness. The naturalists take virtually every signifier of meaning and of order, even the order of language itself, and unmask its utter fragility. Particularly unsettling is the bleeding away of sharp limits, the order and ordering of boundaries which we believe are absolutely necessary to moral life and self-recognition. Naturalism continuously shatters the boundaries between pain and pleasure, the pure and the impure, the human and the animal, the ecstatic and the abject. Naturalist works rewrite repeatedly negative rites of passage, a movement toward liminality as stasis or self-annihilation, worst-case scenarios, as it were, for some one character or group. This continual deconstruction of boundaries always already rendered permeable and therefore dangerous, this move toward self-loss or the disclosure that self is merely delusion can be quickly illustrated. In Hamlin Garland's "Up the Coolly," for instance, the land of milk and honey, the literal makings of Howard's first meal upon his return home, is upon closer inspection a land only of sweat and mud, the men's clothes as stained with the grass and earth as are the hides of the animals, as if the earth is slowly swallowing them all. The farmers are no better, as the story's most memorable image implies, than flies trapped in a pan of molasses, seduced by the promise of sweet sustenance, now doomed to die after useless, prolonged suffering. Here as in Rebecca Harding Davis's "Life in the Iron Mills," the struggle for survival of the fittest has already been decided, and those who work hardest have lost, the dilettantes and the privileged in fancy suits and fur coats having won by virtue of luck or birthright. Mary Wilkins Freeman's "Old Woman Magoun" and Stephen Crane's *Maggie* offer us the disturbing spectacle of beautiful infantilized young women doomed by virtue of their beauty and the particular circumstances of their birth. Lily and Maggie are made abject, the one killed so that she might escape her genetic/gender fate, the other also seduced by the blandishments of romance, no matter how debased these be, and so sent on her death walk by her accession to sexuality. The pure masculinity available to alpha-male Mitchell in "Life in the Iron Mills" but not to worker-artist Hugh "Molly" Wolfe is not, however, a defense against universal indifference or the aleatory nature of life as we see in Crane's "The Open Boat" or in Upton Sinclair's *The Jungle*; indeed, such masculine posturing is unmasked by the time of John Steinbeck's "Flight" as perhaps little more than a death wish, one easily satisfied by a grotesque set of events just this side of self-suicide. Similarly, while in *Sister Carrie* Carrie's ability to perform versions of femininity helps her achieve success, more typically in naturalist works we see recapitulated the self-abjection of extreme masochistic femininity, the steady and exceedingly painful movement toward death that, ironically, seems to provide the only meaningful experience of life force for the central women characters, as it does, for instance, in the early work of Evelyn Scott or the very recent novel *Suspicious River* by Laura Kasischke or, most notoriously, for Maria Macapa and Trina in *McTeague*. In turn, while McTeague, the quintessential naturalist character, at first frightens himself when he suddenly becomes an other self in the presence of the anaesthetized Trina, he later succumbs to his primal and animal drives, most memorably illustrated in his worrying of Trina's finger bones, his act the symbolic eating away simultaneously at his own human selfhood. His life serves as a powerful reminder of the classic naturalist trajectory, a walk into the valley of death with no promise of succor or salvation despite one's initial good intentions, meager expectations, or capacity for love. The naturalist plot of decline or defeat—its focus on abnormal and pathological economies of desire; its intense scrutiny of the powerful determinants of gender, race, class, and gender; its seemingly absolute refusal of sustained empathy for and dismissal of moral responsibility toward others—is unmistakable.

Naturalism calls into serious question, then, the humanist values upon which community is based. Its journey into the liminal, the transgressive, the pornographically violent, and the morally bankrupt seduces and repels us, for while we might recognize, even acknowledge the ideological, biological, psychological constraints it limns so graphically, we simply cannot accept that we live in a purely naturalist world. The naturalist's achievement is to imagine that world for us in so shocking a fashion that we are moved to respond in horror "Not that." For all its seeming pessimism, passivity, and self-destructiveness in the face of cultural crisis, naturalism depends upon the romantic hope that we will not simply settle for the spectacles of suffering or supreme indifference it presents with such visceral intensity. Naturalism thus asks us to refuse the hand dealt to us by our histories—if not to call for a new deck, since there isn't any other, then to reimagine the rules of the game and the order of play.

The following essays are ordered by their primary subject matter and so mirror chronological developments in the expression of naturalism in literature. Sara Britton Goodling investigates, for instance, the interstices between sentimentalism and naturalism, rereading the formative moments of naturalist agenda(s) as already present in selected works by Rebecca Harding Davis and Elizabeth Stuart Phelps. This discussion of a nascent naturalism is complemented by William Dow's elaboration of performative naturalism, "a staging of the inaccessible" rather than a transparently mimetic representation of reality in naturalist literature. Focusing on the major works of Stephen Crane and Frank Norris, Dow, like Goodling, also grounds his theory in a close reading of Davis's "Life in the Iron Mills." Robert Dowling's essay reconceptualizes the effect of Crane's best-known work through a detailed look at Bowery history and culture, arguing that in *Maggie* a vitiated Bowery culture performs Victorian codes of behavior and respectability, the cost of which cooptation of rebellious individualism is seen clearly in the life and fate of the beautiful but doomed protagonist.

The next group of essays, centered on the works of Frank Norris, takes theories of performance and self-cooptation further in the dialogue that each essay opens with various theorists of very different forms of community. Daniel Schierenbeck, for example, uses Michel Foucault's theory and analysis of the clinical gaze to focus upon authorship, naturalism, and the normative agenda of nativism in Norris's own theoretical writing and in his seminal *McTeague.* Hildegard Hoeller also rereads *McTeague* to uncover an economy markedly different from that of the market, that of the anti-gift—the perversion, that is, of the gift economy on which community, however small, depends. Adam H. Wood's examination of *The Octopus* also focuses on the effects of material considerations on communities of workers, demonstrating that Norris's romanticization of historical events and his reification of the material processes of market economy that determine the fate of the farmers animates the form of ideological myth construction necessary to early-twentieth-century capitalism.

While Wood describes the erasure of actual laborers and of human agency in *The Octopus,* Laura Hapke turns our attention to issues of gender and class as well as the more than curious erasure of racial diversity in Theodore Dreiser's novels of the working class. Revisiting the seductive city plot but one inscribed with a new racial dimension markedly different from that seen in the work of Crane, Norris, or Dreiser, Nancy Von Rosk rewrites race into naturalism in her essay on Paul Laurence Dunbar's *The Sport of the Gods,* the title of which work alone broadcasts Dunbar's investment in naturalist plots and philosophies. Brannon W. Costello looks at another non-traditional naturalist, Henry James, who in his *The Wings of the Dove* also reveals his close engagement with issues of determinism and agency central not only to naturalism but to early modernism as well. James R. Giles's postcolonial reading of Jack London's complex and contradictory imperialist agenda in *The Call of the Wild* similarly pays close attention to the seductive call to freedom London offers, a freedom that even now proves in this Nietzschean superdog tale to be so appealing to readers despite its immense cost in terms of civilized morality. David K. Heckerl's piece on London's *The Sea-Wolf* is an interesting companion piece to Giles's essay, offering as it does a trenchant critique of liberalism and the issue of individual agency through its analysis of Wolf Larsen, the embodiment of economic man in that he argues that self-preservation necessitates immoral behavior and, consequently, immoral behavior effects a maximization of self-authenticity.

The next few essays introduce us to contemporary debates concerning the increasing value of high art in the age of mechanical reproduction and conspicuous consumption. Barbara Hochman, for instance, details how such naturalist writers as Frank Norris and Edith Wharton were profoundly cognizant of the cultural capital implicit in sophisticated reading habits, as is readily seen in their many intertextual references and scenes involving high culture; this intense awareness was, Hochman goes on to argue, absolutely necessary in light of their attempts to enhance their own cultural standing through the making of "Literature." Donna Campbell traces the literary relationship between Edith Wharton's *The House of Mirth* and David Graham Phillips's *Susan Lenox,* the former now considered a classic, the latter now virtually forgotten but considered by Wharton a masterpiece of naturalism. Lilian R. Furst, in turn, delimits the search for and acquisition of the authentic, rather than the copy, in Wharton's *The Custom of the Country* as well as the different valuations and uses of the real and the original in a naturalist text. Katherine Joslin's essay on Jane Addams's *The Spirit of Youth and the City Streets* argues persuasively that authentic naturalism might best be found not only in Zola's literary prescriptions of science bearing down on the literary but in the inverse product, imaginative expression married to science, a naturalist literature of heightened observation and exposure intent on reform, a product of the true experimental moralist—such as Addams herself.

The last essays take us firmly by the arm and drag us into modernism and postmodernism, belying the received idea that naturalism died out, gruesomely, no doubt, at the turn of the century. The preceding essays on James, Wharton, Phillips, and Addams clearly suggest that such is simply not the case. The remaining essays make that case solidly. Tim Edwards, for example, revisits some of the elements discussed in early essays—the domestic sphere, female embodiment, and moribund Victorian moral conventions—to investigate the naturalism at the heart of Evelyn Scott's *The Narrow House*. Like Edwards, Kecia Driver McBride illustrates the value in rereading naturalism through the lens of feminism, in her case offering a close materialist feminist reading of Ann Petry's *The Street* and focusing in particular on the prison house of language that entraps the protagonist in terms of race, gender, and class as well as the commodity culture which holds out the promise of escape and self-fulfillment but, in the end, offers only devastating self-delusion and self-loss. Both Scott and Petry imagine searing violence against the self in their works; and in the case of Petry, we see the constant threat of violence against women, children, and those who are unable to fortify themselves against an immoral, racist, sexist, morally bankrupt world. The violence typical of a naturalist work is especially evident in Lana A. Whited's analysis of four true-crime novels—William Faulkner's *Light in August,* James M. Cain's *The Postman Always Rings Twice,* Richard Wright's *Native Son,* and Meyer Levin's *Compulsion,* novels in which acts of murder are overdetermined by factors of class, race, religion, sexual appetite, psychological damage, and cultural dysfunctionality.

The last three essays in the volume ask where and what naturalism is now. While many of the essays in the volume incorporate the work of theorists ranging from Zola to Pizer, Foucault to Althusser in their analyses, Mohamed Zayani takes as his subject matter theory itself—chaos theory, to be precise—and what its philosophical constructs might have to offer to our understanding of naturalism. He demonstrates in particular the importance of inconsistency and indeterminacy to naturalism, here through a brief look at Norris's *Vandover and the Brute*. Philip Gerber is also interested in new understandings of naturalism—if not its inconsistencies, then its constants—directing our attention to the possible impact of research in genetics on our reading of determinism. If Philip Gerber offers us a broad overview of naturalist works ranging from Zola to Proulx and touching upon, notably, the work of Dreiser, Anderson, Steinbeck, O'Hara, and Tom Wolfe, then Donald Pizer, the preeminent critic of American literary naturalism, shares with us the latest word in naturalism in his discussion of the work of three postmodern writers—Raymond Carver, Paul Auster, and Don DeLillo—and their indebtedness to determinist philosophies and naturalist devices and techniques. The last three essays take us, then, into twenty-first-century American literary naturalism.

Acknowledgments

I WOULD LIKE TO MAKE A FEW ACKNOWLEDGMENTS OF HELP BEYOND THE CALL OF DUTY. FIRST, I WOULD LIKE TO THANK BOTH NORMAN SANDERS and Dorothy Scura who in their capacities as chairs of the Tennessee Studies in Literature Board urged me to try my hand at a volume. The Hodges Trustees of the Department of English at the University of Tennessee generously supported my research on the project through the John C. Hodges Better English Fund. The Hodges Fund; the College of Arts and Sciences; and the Exhibit, Performance, and Publications Expense Fund of the University of Tennessee awarded me matching grants to assist with production costs, and for that I am most grateful. Don Cox commiserated with me about the many difficulties of editing such a volume, even as he worked in a seeming whirlwind on his own. D. Allen Carroll gently shepherded the volume through the review process and was always encouraging, ever ready to help. I would also like to thank the two readers who gave detailed assessments of the essays and most helpful suggestions for the last revision of the volume. Leanne Hinkle, with the greatest of patience and calm, led me through the intricacies of various word processing programs and most ably assisted me in the preparation of final copy. Chuck Maland, Nancy Goslee, and Bill Larsen heard about my project and heard about my project and heard about my project and were never anything but supportive. Finally, as always, I want to acknowledge the immeasurable help and comfort given to me on a daily basis by Allen Dunn. Without him, I would still be something, but I certainly wouldn't be quite as satisfied.

The Silent Partnership

NATURALISM AND SENTIMENTALISM IN
THE NOVELS OF REBECCA HARDING DAVIS
AND ELIZABETH STUART PHELPS

—*Sara Britton Goodling*

> Nothing remains to tell that the poor Welsh puddler once lived, but this figure of the mill-woman cut in korl. I have it here in a corner of my library. I keep it hid behind a curtain,—it is such a rough, ungainly thing. Yet there are about it touches, grand sweeps of outline, that show a master's hand. Sometimes,—to-night, for instance,—the curtain is accidentally drawn back, and I see a bare arm stretched out imploringly in the darkness, and an eager, wolfish face watching mine: a wan, woful face, through which the spirit of the dead korl cutter looks out, with its thwarted life, its mighty hunger, its unfinished work. Its pale, vague lips seem to tremble with a terrible question. "Is this the End?" they say,—"nothing beyond?—no more?" Why, you tell me you have seen that look in the eyes of dumb brutes,—horses dying under the lash. I know.
>
> —"Life in the Iron Mills," 1861

AT THE CLOSE OF "LIFE IN THE IRON MILLS," REBECCA HARDING DAVIS'S NARRATOR STANDS AT THE WINDOW OF AN UPPER ROOM IN THE HOUSE the Wolfes, a family of factory workers, once occupied. Formerly a collection of "kennel-like rooms" rented to half-a-dozen families (5), the house has been reclaimed by the middle class and transformed into a seemingly secure domestic space. Scattered around the room are "homely fragments" that confirm this transformation: a "half-molded child's head" and a sculpture of Aphrodite suggest love and motherhood; a "bough of forest-leaves" represents the taming and aestheticization of the natural world; an angel statue on the mantel introduces Christianity and moral authority (3, 34). The narrator's own idleness as she tells her story and the artistic tasks that await her are privileges of class that establish her economic security.[1] And her ability to articulate the Wolfes' frustration and oppression, her frequent assertions that "I know," establish her sympathetic but superior relationship to her tale.

The apparently secure position of this privileged sentimental narrator is precarious, however, for her home is located in the midst of the marketplace.[2] Her back window looks out over a "dirty" yard that is hemmed in by a "narrow brick-yard, strewed with rain-butts and tubs." Her front window looks out onto muddy streets through which the laborers "creep" on their way to and from "the great mills." She need not, or perhaps cannot,[3] go down into "the fog and mud and foul effluvia." Her class status protects her from this. But she cannot prevent the masses from entering her home. She hears their voices. She smells their tobacco. The air of her room is "thick, clammy with the breath of [these] crowded human beings." It is polluted as well by the smoke that is the breath of the mills. Even the wings of her angel statue are "covered with smoke, clotted and black." And lurking in the corner, partially concealed by a curtain, is the korl woman. Devoid of beauty or grace, carved from the refuse of the mills, this ugly, naked female body brings the "massed, vile, slimy lives" of the mill workers into the very room the narrator occupies, contaminating her domestic space with their hunger, sexuality, oppression, and exhaustion— contaminating, that is, sentimentalism with naturalism (3–4).

Located in "the borders of a Slave State" in 1861 (13), "Life in the Iron Mills" is written in the shadows of a great war, and it tells of the battle that raged between industrialism and domesticity, between the wage slave and his or her masters. The text is also a battlefield on which American literary naturalism and American sentimentalism struggle. Davis's project in "Life in the Iron Mills" is clearly sentimental; her text foregrounds female sympathy as it encourages readers to identify with and extend compassion to the industrial poor. It is only through the language of naturalism, however, that the story of the industrial poor can be told, and so naturalism and sentimentalism continually confront each other in this text. Sentimentalism's sympathy and optimism soften the naturalistic brutality of the Wolfes' story, in the same way the narrator's curtain conceals the korl woman. But just as this curtain is sometimes "accidentally drawn back," revealing a bare, imploring arm and a questioning face, naturalism's pessimistic determinism interrogates and challenges sentimentalism's "great hope" (4). This interrogation continues in other sentimental novels of the 1860s and 70s, in particular Davis's own *Margret Howth: A Story of To-day* (1862) and Elizabeth Stuart Phelps's *The Silent Partner* (1871).

How can this be? Naturalism this early in the century? Naturalism in texts written by women? Naturalism alongside sentimentalism? The suggestion will seem strange to those who accept the conventional definition of American literary naturalism—that it is a phenomenon of the 1890s, a European import, and a male genre; that it is sordid and dark, scientific and amoral;

that its characters are bestial and its narrators detached. For the sentimental novel, written "by, for, and about women" (Tompkins 125), is set in the middle-class home rather than the tenement, and focuses on the family and domesticity, not the alienation of the individual in an industrial society. While naturalist narrators approach their tales with irony, distancing themselves and their readers from their texts, sentimental narrators display sympathy, inviting their readers' engagement with their texts. While naturalist authors construct a godless universe controlled by powerful, unfeeling forces, sentimental authors present a world governed by moral laws and a merciful God.

The differences are striking, but sentimental texts are nevertheless peculiarly suited to be the birthplace of American literary naturalism for several reasons. First, sentimentalism's political project of boundary crossing, its desire to "effect connections across gender, race, and class" lines (Samuels 6), allows for the introduction of the kinds of monstrous, racialized, lower-class characters who people the landscape of naturalism. Prostitutes, drunks, disabled "freaks," madmen, and abusive husbands all make their appearance in sentimental texts. Second, sentimentalism's assertion that identity is dependent on the condition of the body introduces naturalism's fear of embodiment and biological determinism. As Karen Sanchez-Eppler states, "sentimental fiction constitutes an intensely bodily genre" (26). As a result, in sentimental fiction, "the recognition of ownership of one's body as essential to claiming personhood is matched by the fear of being imprisoned, silenced, deprived of personhood by that same body" (33). Third, sentimentalism's detailed description of material conditions —its effort to reproduce those conditions so accurately that its readers will be able to understand and experience characters' suffering—not only anticipates naturalism's journalistic style but also introduces naturalism's social and economic determinism. Philip Fisher, for instance, recognizes this in his reading of *Uncle Tom's Cabin,* for he notes that Stowe's portrayal of the material conditions of slavery leads readers to conclude that her characters' lives have been determined by the underlying economic system (122–26).

Finally, and most importantly, sentimentalism's uneasy marriage of reformism and resignation anticipates naturalism's inconsistency, its failure to sustain the pessimistic determinism that allegedly forms its ideological core. For the past fifty years, theorists of American literary naturalism have struggled to understand and account for naturalist authors' inability to produce a work of "pure" naturalism.[4] According to naturalist philosophy, human beings are devoid of free will and are acted upon by powerful forces which they can neither fully understand nor resist. The purpose of a naturalist text is to reveal the workings of these forces by describing, in an unimpassioned, scientific way, their effects upon the novel's characters. But few, if any, novelists actually achieve this ideal. Instead, they invest their characters with too much dignity, tell their stories with too much emotion, and slip into something which, as described by Malcolm Cowley, sounds remarkably like sentimentalism. "[M]ost of the naturalists are tender minded," Cowley says. "The sense of moral fitness is strong in them; they believe in their hearts that nature *should* be kind, that virtue *should* be rewarded on earth, that men *should* control their own destinies" (328). Naturalists thus taint their pessimistic determinism with impulses toward reform.

Similarly, sentimentalists seem to taint their reformism with an attitude of resignation. While sentimental narratives present benevolence as a "defining human virtue" (Howard, "Sentimentality" 70) and encourage readers to respond with compassionate action on behalf of the oppressed, they also suggest that submission, *not* an effort to change one's circumstances, is the proper response to suffering. Sentimental heroines rarely move beyond the confines of private, domestic space, and most of the action of sentimental novels takes place in the human heart (Tompkins 150). So while these heroines perform the kind of sympathetic identification with the oppressed that is encouraged in readers (Hendler 686), they, like Davis's narrator in "Life in the Iron Mills," do not take action to bring about change. Justice, these novels suggest, is found only in the next world. The injustice of this world must simply be endured. In its subject matter, its thematics, and its marriage of reformism and determinism, sentimentalism thus anticipates naturalism,[5] a claim I will illustrate with close readings of both Davis's *Margret Howth* and Phelps's *The Silent Partner.*

Margret Howth is a young woman who goes to work as a bookkeeper in a mill in order to support her aging mother and blind, narcissistic father. Realizing that her former lover will soon own the mill, Margret is encouraged by Dr. Knowles, a family friend, to find her true life's calling, something "higher" than marriage, motherhood, or caring for her parents (70). He urges her to join him in establishing a utopian community of social outcasts—immigrants, former slaves, and prostitutes. But an apocalyptic fire in the mill injures her lover, and he recalls his devotion to Margret as he recovers his health. The novel ends with the discovery of oil on the Howths' otherwise barren land, and we are left to assume that the two young lovers will live happily ever after.

In contrast, the heroine of *The Silent Partner,* Perley Kelso, is the daughter of a wealthy manufacturer and, at the novel's opening, is engaged to the son of her father's business partner. But when her father dies, crushed by a train, Perley moves to Five Falls, the fictional New England town where her father's mills are located, and becomes interested in her father's business and employees. There, she befriends Sip Garth, a mill girl, and Sip's deaf-mute sister Catty. Although Perley's request to be named partner in the mills is summarily dismissed by her fiancé and his father, Perley nonetheless finds purposeful work to do in Five Falls. She breaks her engagement, retreats from "Society," and devotes herself to improving the life of the mill people, particularly that of Sip and Catty.

Summarized in this way, neither text seems a likely candidate for the earliest naturalist novel in America. In their subplots, however, we find greater evidence of these texts as naturalism's progenitors. June Howard suggests that in some naturalist texts, characters are constructed according to a variety of generic codes that are determined by the characters' class status: middle-class characters are sentimental, lower-class characters are naturalistic (*Form and History* 175–76).[6] Davis and Phelps anticipate this class/genre dualism. Margret and Perley are for the most part typical sentimental heroines,[7] but both befriend lower-class characters who inhabit worlds far different from their own. As Margret and especially Perley enter these worlds, they encounter naturalistic characters whose lives are determined by the powerful forces of biology and environment.

In *Margret Howth,* one such group of characters is presented to readers in a sort of naturalistic tableau. To reveal the life of the underclass in an industrial society, Dr. Knowles takes Margret to a run-down house on the edge of town. Anticipating Charles Child Walcutt, who saw in naturalism "the jungle at our back door, full of creatures who do not answer to the social norms" (130), Knowles calls this place "a bit of hell: outskirt" (149). Margret finds herself in one dark room

> swarming with human life. Women, idle trampers, whiskey-bloated, filthy, lay half-asleep, or smoking, on the floor, and set up a chorus of whining begging when [Margret and Dr. Knowles] entered. . . . In the corner slept a heap of half-clothed blacks, going on the underground railroad to Canada. Stolid, sensual wretches, with here and there a broad, melancholy brow, and desperate jaws. . . . "So much flesh and blood out of the market, unweighed!" (150–51)

While Davis assures us that this is "human life," these "creatures" can only whine, beg, and lie prostrate in alcohol or sleep-induced stupor. Their bodies, whether bloated or black, bear the marks of poverty, unemployment, and slavery. The escaped slaves have little hope of reaching freedom. The "swarm-ing," directionless women will drink themselves to death, as has one who already lies dead in their midst.

Anticipating naturalism's objectivity and amorality, Knowles refuses to fault this mob for their condition, saying to Margret, "'Can they help it? Think of the centuries of serfdom and superstition through which their blood has crawled'" (151). In pointing to their helplessness in his attempt to defend them, Knowles also anticipates naturalism's dehumanization of the lower classes. His excusing them of moral responsibility robs them of moral agency. Incapable of making right choices, they are incapable of assuming meaning-ful social roles. Knowles thus asserts their worthlessness even as he tries to convince Margret to join him in his charitable venture, urging her to a life of reform even as he presents these lives as "unreformable."

If initially Knowles blames the condition of these people on historical determinism—years of poverty and enslavement—eventually he turns to bio-logical explanations. For after failing miserably in his effort to educate the children of the "dregs" he concludes, ". . . there's a good deal of an obstacle in blood. I find difficulty, much difficulty . . . in giving to the youngest child true ideas of absolute freedom, and unselfish heroism" (187). Knowles suggests that for these characters, as Lars Åhnebrink writes of Émile Zola's, "the out-come of life was usually hopeless sorrow, sometimes stolid resignation; often there was no other end than annihilation" (Åhnebrink 28).

This fleeting glimpse Davis gives us into a naturalistic underworld is less significant, however, than the more fully developed naturalistic portrait she pro-vides in the person of Lois, a friend of Margret's whom Walcutt might recognize as one of his "little monsters" (129).[8] Lois's monstrous body is emphasized from the first. She is introduced as "hopelessly crippled" (54), and we are told that "some deformity of her legs," probably caused by a vitamin deficiency, "made her walk with a curiously rolling jerk" (55). Her head is "misshapen" as well, and her face scarred (168). As if to accentuate her crippled body, Davis also gives her a damaged huckster's cart—a cart that "went jolting along in such a careless, jolly way, as if it would not care in the least, should it go to pieces any minute just there in the road"—as well as a disabled donkey who is "bony and blind of one eye" (53). She is a creature whom "Nature had thrown impatiently aside as a failure, so marred, imperfect, that even the dogs were kind to her" (64).

Her damaged body is matched by a damaged brain. Though the nature of her mental disability is unclear, its source is unquestionably the mill. She had worked in the mill for only nine years, but she tells Margret, "'T seemed longer to me 'n 't was. 'T seemed as if I'd been there allus,—jes forever, yoh know'" (68). She goes on to say:

> "I kind o' grew into that place in them years: seemed to me like as I was part o' th' engines, somehow. . . . 'T got so that th' noise o' th' looms went on in my head night 'n' day,—allus thud, thud. 'N' hot days, when th' hands was chaffin' 'n' singin', the black wheels 'n' rollers was alive, starin' down at me, 'n' th' shadders o' th' looms was like snakes creepin',—creepin' anear all th' time." (68–69)

The sexual imagery of this passage and Lois's suggestion that she had become a part of the machinery of the mill indicates that she is a product of industry. She was forced by her health to leave the mill at age sixteen, but not before the "slow years of ruin" had "eaten into her brain" (69). And so she still fears the mill, recognizing it as a threatening presence in her life:

> The mill,—even now, with the vague dread of some uncertain evil to come, the mill absorbed all fear in its old hated shadow. Whatever danger was coming to them lay in it, came from it, she knew, in her confused, blurred way of thinking. It loomed up now, with the square patch of ashen sky above, black, heavy with years of remembered agony and loss. . . . Her crushed brain, her unwakened powers, resented their wrong dimly to the mass of iron and work and impure smells, unconscious of any remorseless power that wielded it. (170–71)

In Lois's eyes, the mill is "a monster that kept her wakeful with a dull mysterious terror" (171). This monstrous place in part produced her monstrous body.

While Lois suggests both the destructive power of industry and the restrictive nature of embodiment, it is not only against these forces that she struggles, for as in "Life in the Iron Mills," *Margret Howth* is "written from the border of the battlefield" (3), and so surrounding industry is slavery. As the child of a former slave, Lois struggles against "all the tainted blood in her veins of centuries of slavery and heathenism [that are] trying to drag her down" (69). And just as she has been "ruined" by industry, her father, Joe Yare, has been ruined by slavery. Though he is a thief and an escaped convict, we are warned against judging Joe too harshly. He says in his own defense, "'Who taught me what was right? Who cared? No man cared fur my soul, till I thieved 'n' robbed; 'n' then judge 'n' jury 'n' jailers was glad to pounce on me.'" (166). Davis adds,

> There was not much in the years gone to soften his thought, as it
> grew desperate and cruel: there was oppression and vice heaped
> on him, and flung back out of his bitter heart. Nor much in the
> future; a blank stretch of punishment to the end. . . . What if he
> were black? what if he were born a thief? what if all the sullen
> revenge of his nature had made him an outcast from the poorest
> poor? Was there no latent good in this soul for which Christ died,
> that a kind hand might not have brought to life? (167)

Through Joe, naturalism confronts the social gospel of sentimentalism. In
keeping with sentimentalism, Davis suggests that Joe is innately good and lays
the responsibility for his behavior on the "absence of a kind hand" to bring that
goodness to life. Instead, a mysterious "wrong done to his soul in a day long
past" rankles in Joe and drives him to add arson and attempted murder to his
long list of crimes (168). Davis uses Joe to warn readers about the consequences
of their own apathy, but society is not solely to blame, for Davis also points to
Joe's race, suggests that he was "born" into vice, and indicates that he had
inherited a sullen, revengeful soul. Joe shares Lois's "tainted blood," and, like
Knowles's wretches, struggles against both heredity and history.

Though she shares his blood, Lois does not share her father's moral
corruption. Like Crane's Maggie, she is able to rise above her surroundings, to
recognize and create beauty from filth.[9] To a degree, Lois transcends naturalism, particularly in her redemptive death. Late one night, Joe sets a fire in the
mill in an attempt to kill the mill owner, Stephen Holmes, who has threatened
to return Joe to prison. Lois sees the fire, realizes her father is responsible,
breathes in deadly fumes while rescuing Holmes, and dies as a result. Her
sacrificial death inspires Holmes's mercy and secures a second chance for her
father. But Davis still insists that the sins committed by and against Lois's father
are visited on the daughter. It is Joe who sets the fire that kills Lois, and Davis
declares that the wrong done to Joe was "a wrong done to both . . . *irreparable,*
and *never to be recompensed*" (168; emphasis added). Using the language of naturalism, Davis indicates that both Lois and Joe are shaped and destroyed by
biological and environmental forces much more powerful than they.

In *The Silent Partner,* Phelps continues this naturalistic investigation of
the effects of "blood" and industry on the lower classes. Like Davis, her conclusions are bleak. Drawing her story from the pages of the Report of the
Massachusetts Bureau of the Statistics of Labor,[10] Phelps describes with almost
journalistic precision the stifling atmosphere of the mills, the smelly dampness
of the tenements, and the inadequacy of the mill workers' food and clothing.

This detailed documentation of urban and tenement life will become a standard of literary naturalism. Like Davis, Phelps also portrays the mill machinery as monsters and describes their power not only to silence the mill girls by "crunching" their songs (75–76) but also to crush the body of a young boy whose clothing gets caught in their "teeth" (170). And as in Davis, the monstrous mills produce monstrous people. Phelps suggests this partly through references to the animalism of the lower classes. One child laborer crawls up the stairs on his way to work "on 'all fours,' so much, so very much, like a little puppy!" (212). Another lies "curled up like a skulking dog" on the steps of a building (118). Phelps also points to the disfigured bodies of the mill workers, the "peculiar bleached yellow faces" of many of the mill women (119), the dyed yellow hands of the mill men (166), and the tendency of some workers, in the heat of the mills, to turn "black" as the blood gathers in their faces (232).

Catty, one of the mill women befriended by Perley Kelso, provides the most striking example of monstrosity. Her body has been destroyed by industry. Deafened by the great wheels of the mills while still in the womb, deformed by her labor, eventually blinded by a disease she contracts while picking cotton, Catty is both senseless and "repulsive" (96). She hears nothing but the noise of the great wheels of the mills which constantly "beat about in her head" (96). Her speech resembles the "snarl" of "an annoyed animal" (150). And she is "[a]n ugly girl,—a very ugly girl," so ugly, in fact, that Phelps describes her to readers as though she were an exhibit in a traveling freak show: "Look at her; it is a very loathsome under lip. Look well at her; they are not pleasant eyes" (88). "Walled up and walled in from that labyrinth of sympathies, that difficult evolution of brain from beast, the gorgeous peril of that play at good and evil which we call life" (86), Catty is hardly human.

Her behavior is as monstrous as her body. She drinks, she runs wild in the streets, and, Sip, Catty's sister, tells Perley, "worse," suggesting sexual promiscuity (84). Sip insists that Catty is not to blame, for she has had no one to teach her right from wrong (197), but Phelps suggests that Catty is nonetheless "corrupt," even beyond redemption. Describing Catty's death scene, Phelps writes:

> It was too late for dear love to touch her. Its piteous call she could not hear. Its wrung face she could not see. Her poor, puzzled lips moved as if to argue with it, but made no sound. Type of the world from which she sprang,—the world of exhausted and corrupted body, of exhausted and corrupted brain, of exhausted and corrupted soul, the world of the laboring poor as man has made it,

and as Christ has died for it, of a world *deaf, dumb, blind, doomed,* stepping confidently to its own destruction before our eyes. (277–78; emphasis added)

Through Catty, Phelps links damnation with disability, conflates both with poverty, and locates their source in industrialization.

Even more powerful than industry, however, is the economic discourse of the mills. Borrowing from Davis's "Life in the Iron Mills," Phelps develops the idea expressed by Kirby, a visitor to the mill, that workers would be better off if they could be reduced to machine-like hands, untroubled by thoughts, ambitions, and emotions. "'If I had the making of these men,'" says Kirby, "'these men who do the lowest part of the world's work should be machines,—nothing more,—hands. It would be kindness. God help them! What are taste, reason, to creatures who must live such lives as that?'" Addressing the mill employees, Phelps echoes Davis's text, saying, "Hayle and Kelso label you. There you are. The world thinks, aspires, creates, enjoys. There you are. You are the fingers of the world. You take your patient place. The world may have need of you, but only that it may think, aspire, create, enjoy" (71). The mill owners, exercising their class privilege, have developed a discourse that assigns physicality to the lower classes and reserves disembodiment for the wealthy.[11] In *The Body in Pain,* Elaine Scarry explains that "to be intensely embodied is the equivalent of being unrepresented" (201) while disembodiment is associated with power, voice, and control. This discourse of "heads" and "hands" thus insures the disempowerment and voicelessness of the mill workers.

Catty provides graphic visual representation of this discourse, for she is all "hands." Her "long, lithe, magnetic fingers" are her defining feature (86). The other mill employees, however, are equally embodied and therefore disempowered. Phelps makes this evident when the workers threaten to strike in response to a wage reduction. She writes:

There is something noteworthy about this term "strike." A head would think and outwit us. A heart shall beat and move us. The "hands" can only struggle and strike us,—foolishly too, and madly, here and there, and desperately, being ill-trained hands, never at so much as a boxing school, and gashing each other principally in the contest. (245)

As defined by the ruling economic discourse, the "hands" lack reason, emotion, voice, and discipline. They are violent, foolish, and self-destructive. Like

Catty, they are rendered senseless by industry and are powerless to change their situation.

The powerlessness, poverty, and embodiment of Davis's and Phelps's naturalistic characters introduce many of the fears to which later naturalists were said to be responding in their work: fear of physicality and a resulting vulnerability to biology and environment; fear of helplessness in the face of powerful social and economic forces. In order to defuse the fears these characters embody, Phelps and Davis, like later naturalists, deliberately distance them from readers. In later naturalist texts, this distancing is accomplished largely through irony. As Cowley explains, "There is something superior and ultimately tiresome in the attitude of many naturalists toward the events they describe. Irony—like pity, its companion—is a spectator's emotion, and it sets a space between ourselves and the characters in the novel" (332). Phelps and Davis do not employ the same kind of irony. Their narrative stance tends to be sentimental and therefore engaging. But their sentimental appeals for sympathy, forgiveness, or rescue on behalf of their characters place readers in an equally "superior" position.

Later naturalist authors also distance characters from themselves and their readers by conflating brutishness with physical, moral, racial, and economic "deviance." Their characters, who are poor, weak, and unsophisticated to begin with (Pizer 86), are frequently described using such racially charged terms as primitive, slime, savage, brutal, and instinct (Cowley 319). Naturalist authors often project images of violence, sexuality, and drunkenness onto their characters as well (Howard, *Form and History* 79), resulting in the absolute alienation of these characters from naturalism's white, middle-class, able-bodied Christian readers. Phelps and Davis anticipate these distancing techniques in their novels, demonstrating through their portrayals of Catty and Lois how the fears invoked by naturalism could be neutralized.

Davis heaps "deviance" onto Lois. Physically and mentally disabled, part African American, and "wretchedly low in the social scale" (54), Lois is thoroughly debased. Even her soul, Davis tells readers, is "lower, it might be, than ours, lay closer to nature, knew the language of the changing day, of these earnest-faced hills, of the very worms crawling through the brown mould" (65). According to Jean Pfaelzer, this passage demonstrates Emerson's influence on Davis, for Lois is a nature scholar who can "read" God in her surroundings and so know Him directly (71). But Davis may also be demonstrating the influence of Darwinian theory, for even before the American publication of *The Origin of Species* in 1860, people began using Herbert

Spencer's evolutionary theory to establish racial hierarchy.[12] Davis's assertion that Lois's soul is "lower" than "ours" certainly engages such a hierarchy and assures readers of their privileged racial position. Her suggestion that Lois "lay" closer to nature invites images of prostration before a higher order of beings. Lois's ability to understand the language of the "worms crawling through the brown mould" implies that she cannot walk erect, that she belongs to a "primitive" species, and that she is mired in dirt. Lois's debasement—social, physical, mental, and racial—arouses in everyone, including readers, "an undefined sense of pride in protecting this wretch whose portion of life was more meagre and low than theirs" (77). She lends readers confidence, making them feel strong, wise, capable, and white.

Catty is even more distanced from readers, for as was mentioned earlier, Phelps compounds Catty's disabilities and poverty with immorality. Phelps also draws more heavily than Davis on Darwinian views of race and class, for as Rosemarie Garland Thomson suggests, Catty is animalistic, even simian in appearance (576).[13] Catty's "low forehead," the "dull stoop" of her head, her "thick, drooping upper lip," and her "long, lithe, magnetic fingers" suggest racial "inferiority" even as they qualify her for display as a "missing link" (86). In fact, she closely resembles the subject of P. T. Barnum's "What Is It?" exhibit put on display in New York in 1860. The subject of this exhibit was a mentally handicapped African American man. Rather than identify him as such, Barnum invited audiences to decide for themselves what "it" was. No viewer, however, seemed to question "its" racial origin; indeed, every newspaper account discussing the exhibit assumed "it" must be African (Cook 152). A major reason for this was the man's low forehead, which was considered distinctly African. In Barnum's words, "The upper part of the head and the forehead in particular, instead of being four or five inches broad, *as it should be, to resemble that of a human being,* is Less Than Two Inches!" (qtd. in Cook 148). Though she is never identified as African American, Catty's low forehead, "ape-like" fingers, and "thick" lips distance her from white readers. "Walled up and walled in" from society by her physical, moral, social, and racial "deviance" (86), Catty, like Lois, assures readers that she is the "monster," not them.

In *Margret Howth* and *The Silent Partner,* however, the effort to distance readers from naturalistic characters such as Lois and Catty is complicated by a sentimental movement toward sympathy, identification, and reform.[14] Philip Fisher explains that the sentimental novel "depends on experimental, even dangerous, extensions of the self of the reader." Sentimental authors extend normalcy and normal states of feeling to people to whom these traits have been denied, and in so doing, they extend full humanity to "others" (98). Readers of these novels are thus encouraged to look beyond the bodies of characters, the outward markers that differentiate us from them, and to identify with people from other social categories. In fact, sentimentalism attempts to transcend the body and biological markers altogether, locating identity elsewhere—in "the (feminized) heart"—thus denying the importance of external differences (Clark 22). As Shirley Samuels says, readers of sentimental novels are asked to make "connections across gender, race, and class boundaries" (6). This sentimental project is achieved in varying degrees in the works of Davis and Phelps, but its influence is always evident, and the result is a movement toward identification with naturalistic characters who are at the same time distanced from readers in all the ways described above.

As noted earlier, however, Davis and Phelps prefigure naturalism even in this sentimental moment. June Howard explains that though brutish characters are clearly represented as "others" in naturalist works, they are always reflections or doubles of the author's white, middle-class self, demonstrating the precariousness and fragility of the secure position that naturalist authors attempt to establish for themselves and their readers (*Form and History* 101). Donald Pizer also notes that distance between the self and other, author and character, is seldom sustained in naturalism:

> *Compassion* for the fallen, *hope* of betterment for the lot of the oppressed, bitterness toward the *remediable* which lies unremedied —all the *emotions* which derive from a writer's sense that he is not a dispassionate observer of a scientific process but instead an imaginative presence infusing dignity and a sense of tragic potential into what he observes—create a living *engagement* between artist and subject matter that results in a fullness and complexity of expression rather than an emotionally sterile portrait of "forces at work." (20, emphasis added)

Using the vocabulary of sentimentalism, Pizer explains that naturalist authors frequently fail to adhere to the role of objective observer, and as they cease to be spectators, characters cease to be spectacles and become more fully human. As this happens, barriers between self and other are broken down, and the forces that work on "them" are seen as forces that work on "us."

In *Margret Howth*, this movement toward identification arises at the very end of the novel when Lois reveals emotional and sexual desires that tie her to readers, particularly female readers. From her deathbed, Lois observes the interaction of a young neighborhood couple, Jenny and Sam. They are to be married soon, and Jenny has come to show Lois her wedding dress:

> The poor deformed girl lay watching them, as they talked. Very
> pretty Jenny looked, with her blue eyes and damp pink cheeks;
> and it was a manly, grave love in Sam's face, when it turned to
> her. A different love from any she [Lois] had known: better, she
> thought. It could not be helped; but it *was* better. After they were
> gone, she lay a long time quiet, with her hand over her eyes. For-
> give her! she, too, was a woman. (258)

Davis's insistence that "she, *too*, was a woman" indicates her belief that in this
one emotion, if in no other, readers might find some way to identify with
Lois, an otherwise "otherized" character. The absence of a man's love and the
loneliness of a spinster can be understood by all women, those with blue eyes
and pink cheeks as well as those with "black" blood and "crooked" legs.[15]

In *The Silent Partner,* Phelps also encourages her readers to identify
with naturalistic characters through their shared understanding of spinsterhood. Unlike Lois, Sip has opportunity to marry—the night watchman for
Hayle and Kelso proposes to her. But Sip refuses him, saying, "I'll never bring
children into this world to be factory children, and to be factory boys and
girls, and to be factory men and women, and to see the sights I've seen, and to
bear the things I've borne. . . . They'd never get out of the mills. It's from
generation to generation. It couldn't be helped. I know. It's in the blood"
(287–88). Naturalism is evident even in this sentimental moment, for Sip's
statement confirms the power of industry, conflates social and biological
determinism, and sees no solution to oppression but voluntary extinction.
Still, Phelps follows this statement by inviting readers to recognize Sip's
humanity: "Sip had . . . a 'large share of human nature,' and she loved Dirk,
and she led a lonely life. She was neither a heroine, nor a saint, nor a fanatic
. . ." (290). She was simply a woman, Phelps implies, with emotions, desires,
and tears that Phelps's readers can understand.

Perley can understand, and she models the sympathy Phelps desires from
her readers. Perley shares Sip's singleness, choosing not to marry a devoted
man and a "good" match because he does not share her interest in reform. Sip
and Perley share other ties as well, for both women lost their mothers as children, and their fathers were both crushed by machinery. Their shared enslavement to the ruling economic discourse, however, ties them most closely
together, for the discourse of "heads" and "hands" that so powerfully determines Sip's and Catty's existence also determines Perley's. As a member of the
moneyed classes, Perley is a "head," but the label is far from empowering. It
has essentially disabled Perley by denying her the use of her hands. From the

first, Phelps draws our attention to Perley's white, creamy, listless hands. She tells us, in fact, that Perley's hand has "—rings" and in doing so, immediately indicates her powerlessness (10). As Judith Fetterley says, "The hand might have had fingers—strong capable ones, or weak listless ones, or nervous restless ones; instead it has '—rings,' and in having '—rings' it is had" (19). Perley's hands are not her own, and they bear the mark of male domination in the form of a ring.

Phelps again indicates the powerlessness of Perley's hands later in the novel when Perley requests to be made a partner. Mr. Hayle treats her request with condescension and quickly dismisses it as foolish, but Perley's fiancé Maverick, junior partner in the mill, drifts away from the conversation, ignoring her request altogether, and studies her hands. He draws the conclusion that "Story,[16] the next time he was in the country, should make a study of a hand upon squares of gray and green" (56). Later in the conversation, he occupies himself by "making little faces on Perley's pink, shell-like nails with the pencil" (60). Through these seemingly idle actions, Maverick demonstrates his conviction that Perley's hands are incapable of employment and her body unfit for the kind of work she desires. Perley's hands are "tied" (141) by a fiancé who, whenever she expresses a desire for an occupation, "fold[s] her two hands like sheets of rice-paper over his own, with an easy smile" (13); and by a discourse that aestheticizes her hands, making them objets d'art rather than useful, powerful parts of her body. This "disability" establishes a bond between Perley, Sip, and Catty that challenges the barriers of race, class, and embodiment.[17]

Phelps and Davis thus encourage the kind of sentimental identification between characters and readers that often complicates naturalism. However, they consummate this impulse toward identification by providing their naturalistic characters with sentimental endings not found in later naturalist texts.[18] In so doing, they seem to lose sight of their naturalistic vision. Like Little Eva's in *Uncle Tom's Cabin,* Lois's death in *Margret Howth* is steeped in Christian symbolism: she dies to save her father from the consequences of his sin (starting a fire in the factory); she runs through hellish flames to rescue a man who does not deserve her mercy, for he has shown no mercy to others; she forgives her father for his sin and begs for forgiveness on his behalf (211). Her Christlike sacrifice is justly rewarded, for as she dies, "a strange calm, unknown before, stole over her face; her eyes flashed open with a living joy." Davis assures us, "The cripple was dead; but *Lois,* free, loving, and beloved, trembled from her prison to her Master's side in the To-Morrow" (262). Lois does not share Little Eva's beauty, but she does share her frailty, her childlike faith, and her triumphant parting.

As noted above, Catty's death scene is more problematic than Lois's, for Phelps implies that Catty may be beyond redemption. At the end of the novel, however, Phelps counters this implication by suggesting that Catty, like Lois, has found freedom and wholeness in death, for somehow she has found a voice:

> Passed into the great world of signs, the deaf-mute, dead, grew grandly eloquent. The ring of the flood was her solemn kiss. The sunshine on the kitchen floor tomorrow would be her dear good-morning. Clouds and shadows and springing green gave her speech forever. The winds of long nights were language for her. Ah, the ways, the ways which Catty could find to speak. . . ! (279–80)

Through death, Catty becomes a "head," a disembodied voice who is "eloquent," "solemn," and "dear." She is purified through her alignment with nature and nature's God (292). She is a character with whom readers might identify after all.

In *Sensational Designs,* Jane Tompkins argues that this sort of sentimental ending enacts a theory of power in which the innocent victim is granted the capacity to change the world through her redemptive death (128–30). In contrast, naturalism's pessimistic determinism does not allow for innocence, redemption, or change, and the naturalist novel generally ends in despair. However, Davis and Phelps give us glimpses of naturalism even in their sentimental endings, for they imply that there is no way out for their naturalistic characters but through death. They offer hope of a great hereafter, but they suggest that the here and now cannot be changed, and in their texts, little does change for their naturalistic characters. "Life in the Iron Mills" takes place thirty years after Hugh Wolfe's death, but the ironworkers still creep through muddy streets, and the korl woman's question remains unasked and unanswered. Nothing has changed. At the end of *Margret Howth,* "poor old Knowles" is "bewildered at the inexplicable failure" of his charitable cause. He "doubts everything in the bitterness of wasted effort," and Davis acknowledges the bleakness of her text, saying, "My story is but a mere groping hint? It lacks determined truth, a certain yea and nay? It has no conduit of God's justice running through it, awarding apparent good and ill? I know: it is a story of To-Day" (264). Nothing can change for Knowles's "wretches" until "To-Morrow."

In *The Silent Partner,* Perley tries to take Sip out of the mills by finding her a new occupation, but Sip fails as a cook, a nursemaid, a waitress, a seamstress, a clerk, and a printer, and returns to her loom. "'I told you it was no use,'" Sip says to Perley. "'It's too late. What am I fit for? Nothing. What do

I know? Nothing. I weave; that's all. I'm used to that. I'm used to the noise and the running about. I'm used to the dirt and the roughness. . . . It's too late. I'm spoiled. I knew I should come back. My father and mother came back before me. It's in the blood'" (199–200). Perley can establish libraries, relief societies, schools, lectures, and reading rooms for the mill's employees (133), but she cannot counter the forces of history and heredity. So nothing changes for Sip, and nothing changes for the mill hands—not in this world anyway.

　　Davis and Phelps suggest that reform is desirable, but in the depiction of their lower-class characters, they imply that "it's too late." This tension between reformism and determinism, hope and despair, is the tension of naturalism. In the texts of Davis and Phelps, sentimental hope generally triumphs over naturalistic despair. In later naturalist texts, despair is often the victor. The struggle, however, is the same, and its birthplace is the sentimental novel.

NOTES

1. There has been some debate concerning the gender of Davis's narrator. Some critics choose to read the narrator of "Life in the Iron Mills" as male—see, for example, Jane Atteridge Rose. Kirk Curnutt insists that the narrator's gender cannot be determined and that Davis deliberately creates an androgynous storyteller (150). Like the majority of Davis critics, however, I read the narrator as female. Though Davis never refers to the narrator as "she," Davis surrounds her with symbols of domesticity and motherhood—the child's head, the angel on the mantelpiece. Davis's narrator also possesses the peculiarly feminine trait of sympathy, and she demands of her readers that they, too, sympathize with the plight of the Wolfes and temper their judgment of the Wolfes' actions with mercy, another feminine trait. The narrator's identification with Deb, the korl woman, and the feminized Hugh Wolfe provides further evidence of her own femininity. Finally, the narrator tells her story while standing at her window, looking out—a typical pose for a female subject in the paintings and illustrations of the time.
2. See Mark Seltzer's discussion of the marketplace in "Life in the Iron Mills" in "The Still Life."
3. Jean Pfaelzer suggests that Davis's female narrator is trapped in her domestic space, which is as "defined" and "enclosed" as the hovels of the ironworkers. "Unlike a roaming male narrator," Pfaelzer writes, "this woman is physically constrained by her gender. . . . Hence, although the narrator boasts that her 'eyes are free to look deeper' (5), Davis surrounds her with images of containment and repression" (28). Although Pfaelzer argues against a naturalistic reading of "Life in the Iron Mills," her discussion of the narrator acknowledges naturalistic images of entrapment and imprisonment in Davis's text.
4. June Howard notes that for the past fifty years, naturalism has consistently been associated with pessimistic determinism but that the "next most frequently made observation about naturalism must surely be that it is *not* pessimistic determinism" (*Form*

and History 36). Critics often find inconsistency in naturalist texts, a failure to follow through with the naturalistic agenda. This failure has been accounted for in many ways. Malcolm Cowley feels that American naturalists were too "tender-minded" and could not conceal their personal grief and anger in their texts (328). Charles Child Walcutt insists that no one could produce a coherent naturalist text, for the act of writing is "an exercise of creative intelligence which in itself denies what [the novelist] may be saying about the futility of life and the folly of man" (29). He also locates the source of naturalism's inconsistency in American transcendentalism. Donald Pizer and Lars Åhnebrink find traces of the romantic spirit in naturalist texts, particularly in the American naturalists' refusal to concede that life is meaningless. "While the naturalist novel does reflect a vast skepticism about the conventional attributes of experience," Pizer writes, "it also affirms the significance and worth of the seeking temperament, of the character who continues to look for meaning in experience even though there is probably no meaning" to be found (24). June Howard, on the other hand, looks not to the literary traditions that preceded American naturalism but to the historical moment that produced it. She identifies the antinomies of "this moment of naturalism"—the 1890s—as "human effort and determining forces," or "the human and the brutal" (*Form and History* 69). According to Howard, the contemporary philosophical struggle between these concepts is embodied in the pages of naturalist texts, resulting in a form defined by dynamic opposition rather than consistent adherence to a single concept, such as pessimistic determinism.

5. For at least a half-century, readers of Davis have hailed her as a pioneer in the development of American literary realism and naturalism. In 1951, for example, Bernard Bowron claimed that Davis "pioneered in . . . the literature of industrialism, critically concerned with contemporary social problems, which would ultimately give rise to American naturalism" (qtd. in Yellin 274). Sandra Gilbert and Susan Gubar in *The Norton Anthology of Literature by Women* write of "Life in the Iron Mills," "Some six years before the French novelist Émile Zola began publishing what were called 'naturalistic' novels, a thirty-year-old Virginian had brilliantly dramatized the socioeconomic implications of environmental determinism" (903). And Sharon Harris, in *Rebecca Harding Davis and American Realism,* examines in more depth the role Davis played in ushering in the age of realism and naturalism in American letters. (See also Jean Pfaelzer, "Rebecca Harding Davis: Domesticity, Social Order, and the Industrial Novel," *International Journal of Women's Studies* 4 [1981]: 234–44.) These readers do not, however, look beyond Davis to posit a broader relationship between sentimentalism and naturalism. Rather, they view Davis's industrial texts as remarkable anomalies of mid-nineteenth-century American women's literature.

Those scholars who have begun to examine the connections between sentimentalism and naturalism rarely reference Phelps's work. In *Hard Facts,* for example, Philip Fisher discusses the conflation of sentimental and naturalistic motifs in *Uncle Tom's Cabin* and argues that naturalism grows out of both sentimentalism and regionalism—another female literary tradition of the American nineteenth century. Donna Campbell, in *Resisting Regionalism,* offers a more thorough defense of this latter claim, arguing that American male naturalist authors deliberately defined themselves against what they viewed as overly feminine regionalist writing even as they borrowed significantly from the tradition. A lengthy study of the relationship between sentimentalism and naturalism, particularly in the industrial fiction of Davis, Phelps, and their contemporaries, thus remains to be done.

6. In *Form and History in the American Novel*, Howard claims that most naturalist novels contain a variety of competing narrative strategies, including the "domestic formula," or sentimentalism. However, she does not see sentimentalism as a starting point for American naturalism. Rather, she presents sentimentalism as either a crutch that naturalists sometimes "fall back on" (177) or a set of conventions against which naturalists define themselves: "In naturalism the conventionalized image of the domestic space becomes an enclave that can never seem wholly safe, for it is penetrated by the very impulses that are attributed to the wild man outside the campfire and is only tenuously independent of the pitiless economic jungle that looms outside the hearth" (181).

7. The typical sentimental heroine is a genteel, white, liberal, sympathetic orphan. As Glenn Hendler explains, she is also "feminine: other oriented, selfless, and emotionally tied to those who have helped her or who need help" (686). She models for readers the sympathy and identification that sentimental texts encourage. At the end of the novel, she is rewarded for her behavior with marriage or an equally intimate familial relationship.

8. In discussing the characters of Frank Norris's novels, Walcutt writes, "The assemblage of big and little monsters creates a sense of sociological extremes—of people or creatures who have to be in a new dimension of Darwinian thought rather than in the established frames of social conformity and orientation" (129).

9. In *Margret Howth*, Lois is said to possess an artist's sense. She is a "born colourist" who arranges the contents of her cart as though arranging colors on a canvas (110). Like Hugh Wolfe in "Life in the Iron Mills," Lois's artistry allows her to "rise above the level of her daily life" (94). The respite that her art provides, however, is temporary. She, like Hugh, is still mired in drudgery.

10. Phelps's note at the beginning of *The Silent Partner* reads, "I desire it to be understood that every alarming sign and every painful statement which I have given in these pages concerning the condition of the manufacturing districts could be matched with far less cheerful reading, and with far more pungent perplexities, from the pages of the Report of the Massachusetts Bureau of the Statistics of Labor, to which, with other documents of a kindred nature, and to the personal assistance of friends who have 'testified that they have seen,' I am deeply in debt for the ribs of my story."

11. For a discussion of the relationship between class and embodiment in Davis's "Life in the Iron Mills," see Mark Seltzer's *Bodies and Machines*.

12. For a discussion of the influence of theories of evolution on nineteenth-century American literature, see Ronald Martin's *American Literature and the Universe of Force* and Richard Hofstadter's *Social Darwinism in American Thought*.

13. Phelps makes several direct references to Darwinian theory in her 1882 novel *Doctor Zay*. Her heroine both refers to Darwin's theory of natural selection (98) and recommends that another character read one of Darwin's books on plant life (103).

14. In her afterword to *Margret Howth,* Jean Fagin Yellin traces the inconsistencies of the novel to its publishing history and contends that were it not for James Fields's insistence that Davis make her text less "gloomy" (289), *Margret Howth* would have presented a darker, more evenly sustained vision of industrialism and the underclass. Yellin finds the published novel's conclusion "hard to accept," for it attempts an "impossible transformation from scarcity to abundance" and an "equally impossible transformation from a narrative that presents itself as a self-conscious critique of conventional fiction to a narrative that presents itself within fictional convention" (286, 292). One wonders how much more naturalistic *Margret Howth* might have been had Davis not been required to make her text less despairing.

15. Davis makes a similar appeal to readers in "Life in the Iron Mills," suggesting that Deb Wolfe's look of "apathy" and "vacancy," a result of her unreciprocated love for Hugh, should be familiar to all women. Davis writes, "One sees that dead, vacant look steal sometimes over the rarest, finest of women's faces,—in the very midst, it may be, of their warmest summer's day; and then one can guess at the secret of intolerable solitude that lies hid beneath the delicate laces and brilliant smile" (9).

16. The reference is to William Westmore Story, nineteenth-century American sculptor.

17. In *The Silent Partner,* Phelps's use of the body of the wage slave to highlight the oppression of wealthy white women is similar to feminists' and abolitionists' use of the body of the slave woman. For a discussion of the slave body in feminist and abolitionist texts, see Karen Sanchez-Eppler's *Touching Liberty,* pp. 15–48.

18. According to Glenn Hendler, sentimental texts end either in marriage or in the restoration of the family. Often this involves a redefinition of the traditional family unit in which blood ties matter less than truly sympathetic relationships (686–87). Davis ends *Margret Howth* with Margret's marriage. Phelps concludes *The Silent Partner* by establishing a kind of sisterhood between Sip and Perley.

Works Cited

Åhnebrink, Lars. *The Beginnings of Naturalism in American Fiction.* Cambridge: Harvard UP, 1950.

Campbell, Donna M. *Resisting Regionalism: Gender and Naturalism in American Fiction, 1885–1915.* Athens: Ohio UP, 1997.

Clark, Suzanne. *Sentimental Modernism: Women Writers and the Revolution of the Word.* Bloomington: Indiana UP, 1991.

Cook, James W. "Of Men, Missing Links, and Nondescripts: The Strange Career of P. T. Barnum's 'What Is It?' Exhibition." *Freakery: Cultural Spectacles of the Extraordinary Body.* Ed. Rosemarie Garland Thomson. New York: New York UP, 1996. 139–57.

Cowley, Malcolm. "Naturalism in American Literature." *Evolutionary Thought in America.* Ed. Stow Persons. New Haven: Yale UP, 1950. 213–333.

Curnutt, Kirk. "Direct Addresses, Narrative Authority, and Gender in Rebecca Harding Davis's 'Life in the Iron Mills.'" *Style* 28 (1994): 146–68.

Davis, Rebecca Harding. "Life in the Iron Mills." *A Rebecca Harding Davis Reader.* Ed. Jean Pfaelzer. Pittsburgh: U of Pittsburgh P, 1995. 3–34.

———. *Margret Howth: A Story of Today.* New York: Feminist Press, 1990.

Fetterley, Judith. "'Checkmate': Elizabeth Stuart Phelps's *The Silent Partner.*" *Legacy* 3.2 (1986): 17–30.

Fisher, Philip. *Hard Facts: Setting and Form in the American Novel.* New York: Oxford UP, 1985.

Gilbert, Sandra, and Susan Gubar. *The Norton Anthology of American Literature: The Tradition in English.* New York: Norton, 1985.

Harris, Sharon. *Rebecca Harding Davis and American Realism.* Philadelphia: U of Pennsylvania P, 1991.

Hendler, Glenn. "The Limits of Sympathy: Louisa May Alcott and the Sentimental Novel." *American Literary History* 3.4 (1991): 685–706.

Hofstadter, Richard. *Social Darwinism in American Thought, 1860–1915.* Philadelphia: U of Pennsylvania P, 1945.

Howard, June. *Form and History in American Literary Naturalism.* Chapel Hill: U of North Carolina P, 1985.

———. "What Is Sentimentality?" *American Literary History* 11.1 (1999): 63–79.

Martin, Ronald. *American Literature and the Universe of Force.* Durham: Duke UP, 1981.

Pfaelzer, Jean. *Parlor Radical: Rebecca Harding Davis and the Origins of American Social Realism.* Pittsburgh: U of Pittsburgh P, 1996.

Phelps, Elizabeth Stuart. *Doctor Zay.* New York: Feminist Press, 1987.

———. *The Silent Partner and "The Tenth of January."* New York: Feminist Press, 1983.

Pizer, Donald. *The Theory and Practice of American Literary Naturalism: Selected Essays and Reviews.* Carbondale: Southern Illinois UP, 1993.

Rose, Jane Atteridge. "Reading 'Life in the Iron Mills' Contextually: A Key to Rebecca Harding Davis's Fiction." *Conversations: Contemporary Critical Theory and the Teaching of Literature.* Ed. Charles Moran and Elizabeth F. Penfield. Urbana: NCTE, 1989. 187–99.

Samuels, Shirley, ed. Introduction. *The Culture of Sentiment: Race, Gender, and Sentimentality in Nineteenth-Century America.* New York: Oxford UP, 1992. 3–8.

Sanchez-Eppler, Karen. *Touching Liberty: Abolition, Feminism, and the Politics of the Body.* Berkley: U of California P, 1993.

Scarry, Elaine. *The Body in Pain: The Making and Unmaking of the World.* New York: Oxford UP, 1985.

Seltzer, Mark. *Bodies and Machines.* New York: Routledge, 1992.

———. "The Still Life." *American Literary History* 3.3 (1991): 455–86

Thomson, Rosemarie Garland. "Benevolent Maternalism and Physically Disabled Figures: Dilemmas of Female Embodiment in Stowe, Davis, and Phelps." *American Literature* 68.3 (196): 555–86.

Tompkins, Jane. *Sensational Designs. The Cultural Work of American Fiction, 1790–1860.* New York: Oxford UP, 1985.

Walcutt, Charles Child. *American Literary Naturalism: A Divided Stream.* Minneapolis: U of Minnesota P, 1956.

Yellin, Jean Fagin. Afterword. *Margret Howth: A Story of Today.* New York: Feminist Press, 1990. 271–302.

Performative Passages

DAVIS'S *LIFE IN THE IRON MILLS,*
CRANE'S *MAGGIE,* AND NORRIS'S *MCTEAGUE*

—William Dow

S TRIPPING AWAY GENERIC PRECONCEPTIONS, STEPHEN CRANE'S *MAGGIE* (1893) AND FRANK NORRIS'S *MCTEAGUE* (1899) CREATE A SYMBIOTIC RELA-tionship between, on the one hand, journalism and the transparently mimetic and, on the other, the author's new consciousness of the reader and what I call a "performative naturalism." By this term, I mean a naturalism that comes into direct conflict with the traditional notion of representation, if representation is defined as a mimetic rendering of a pre-given reality. Naturalism, in this mode, becomes more a staging of the inaccessible than an explanation of origins, tak-ing the form of both performance and semblance, fiction and "truth." The new journalism of the late nineteenth century, of which Crane and Norris were avid participants, provided a discursive space that was fruitfully ambiguous in genre and truth status. Thus it is not surprising that for both writers this space led to performative techniques in their fiction—particularly evident in their showcase "realist-naturalist" works, *Maggie* and *McTeague*—techniques whose meanings include a giving over of the author's ability to discover and interrogate reality to spectacle, showmanship, and representation.

Crane and Norris began their careers as journalists, editorialists, and sketchists. Crane wrote for newspapers throughout his career, even after the publication of *The Red Badge of Courage.* Indeed, from the publication of his first sketches to his early death, Crane produced a voluminous amount of journal-ism, including sports writing, travel essays, war correspondence, and feature articles on New York City (Robertson 4). By the time *Maggie* was published, the young Crane was deeply immersed in his association with mass-circulation newspapers. Norris, too, was a reporter for the new press syndicates, "the lat-est technological instruments for the making and marketing of collective responses" (Levenson 155). Like Crane, Norris began his journalistic career early, writing for such journals and newspapers as *The Wave, The San Fran-cisco Chronicle,* and *Harper's Weekly.* "From writing fiction to reporting to preparing advertisements," Joseph McElrath writes, "Norris appears to have served a full apprenticeship" (15).

The popular and literary audiences for whom Crane and Norris wrote and tried to reach were not only virtually indistinguishable for both authors; such audiences were closely connected to what and how they wrote. That is, their portrayals of the American city—New York in *Maggie,* San Francisco in *McTeague*—express the wish to demystify the city and depict its "most iniquitous" parts (Talmage 71) and to do so in performative ways. Crane and Norris occupied a kind of middle ground, writing as observers of the city, perceiving it as obscure and undecipherable but hoping to formalize its passing moments into precise physical performances. Their naturalism constitutes the action of performance directed towards the reader as witness: a witness to the implicit truths claimed in both works and to literary naturalism as synecdoche, a synecdoche that attempts to reconstruct Crane's and Norris's perceived "worlds." An appeal to such a reader, or more specifically to the spectator-reader-witness, commingled with Norris's and Crane's blurring of high and low culture to push them towards a new realist-naturalist aesthetic while further separating themselves from a Howellsian realism.[1]

Through a performative approach, I will be examining some of the ways in which Crane and Norris render their sense of the surfaces and depths of American life.[2] I discuss naturalism in *Maggie* and *McTeague* as a form whose task was to make fiction not so much a source of symbolic, mimetic, or transcendental truths but of its own truth. Under this view, naturalism is inextricably linked with Crane's and Norris's specific perceptions of the American city, mass culture (including American forms of elite and popular "performance"), and emerging industrial capitalism. My purpose is to trace the interaction of naturalism with its own struggles for definition, ontological meaning, and perspective in *Maggie* and *McTeague,* focusing most specifically on the performative and its reformulation into the ironic and paretic.

My second objective is to bring Rebecca Harding Davis's *Life in the Iron Mills* (1861) into dialogue with *Maggie* and *McTeague* to show how the performative can be seen to coincide with the birth and rise of naturalism in the United States. Preceding Zola's first "naturalistic" novels by some six years, *Life* not only challenges the "traditional theories of the influences behind the movement from realism to naturalism"; it can be seen as putting into question many of the features contained in "a work of pure naturalism," as it has recently been called (Harris 7–8). *Life's* narrator aims at something not yet accessible to consciousness; she wishes to create a world that has not yet been identified. Consequently, whatever is represented in the text is meant less to define the world than to indicate a performed world. The term performative naturalism, I will argue, usefully highlights the constructed nature of all these fictional enterprises.

LIFE IN THE IRON MILLS: NATURALISM WITH A THEATRICAL HEART

Published thirty-two years before *Maggie* and thirty-eight years before *McTeague,* Rebecca Harding Davis's *Life in the Iron Mills* uses performative strategies of persuasion to induce the reader to believe that it refers to the "real." The fictiveness of *Life*, however, as in many "naturalistic" works, is shaped as much by the logic of the narrative as by that of the subject. *Life's* logic, as is indicated in the novel's subtitle, "The Korl Woman," centers on an aesthetic object, a mill-woman cut in korl. The narrator depends on the understanding of the most intimate subjectivity, the emotions and reactions produced in response to an aesthetic object. On his tour of the mill with Kirby, Doctor May and others, Mitchell, in the performatively resonant "amphitheatre of smothered fires," suddenly discovers the korl woman: "Mitchell started back, half-frightened, as, suddenly turning a corner, the white figure of a woman faced him in the darkness,—a woman, white, of giant proportions, crouching on the ground, her arms flung out in some wild gesture of warning" (31). Significantly presented in the middle of the novella, the sculpture prompts Mitchell and the other "visitors" to engage in their "pocket," "heart," and "head" argument (36–39). As in Crane and Norris, "truth"—social, political, psychological—can be understood most fully when it is filtered through some performative act or, in the case of *Life,* the korl woman, "[c]hipped to some purpose" (32), expressing "[o]ne idea: there it was in the tense, rigid muscles, the clutching hands, the wild, eager face, like that of a starving wolf's" (32).

Within the artistic frame of the novella, Davis is "concerned with the nature of the artist as restricted by humanity and environment" (Morrison 245), although I would add that, like Norris and Crane, she can only approximate what Wolfe, as an "artist," is groping toward. The narrator does not "dare" to make her meaning any "clearer, but will only tell [her] story" (14); she therefore constantly urges the reader to "loo[k] deeper into the heart of things" (21). She can only create a drama of the approximate, the ineffable: "I can paint nothing of this, only give you the outside outlines of a night, a crisis in the life of one man" (23)—and fill it in with performative renderings. She cannot completely explain what she describes but can only make a "tragic story out of it" (50).

In so doing, Davis stresses the part played by the emotions in the reading process: her words invite us not so much to think about and judge as to feel into or become—to realize a complex experience given in language. She, like Norris and Crane, is dissatisfied with all definite formulations, be they concepts, metaphors, or larger formal structures. Instead, she, like the authors of *Maggie* and *McTeague,* resorts to using grotesque devices—in the character of Deborah, with her "ghastly" face, "blu[e] lips," and physical deformities (16). And she relies on melodramatic renderings, as in the case of Hugh's death or Deb's religious "rescue." Davis's melodramatic language aspires to a purity that severs it from referentiality: "There is no need to tire you with the long years of sunshine, and fresh air, and slow, patient Christ-love, needed to make healthy and hopeful this impure body and soul" (63). As suggested here, all knowledge claims must pass through the funnel of individual consciousness. If, however, the performative sometimes seems to threaten the production of new knowledge, its very persistence reveals it as an inventive mode of knowledge and "truth" in its own right. Or, as Iser has argued in *The Act of Reading,* "What the language says is transcended by what it uncovers and what it uncovers represents its true meaning" (142).

The narrator wishes to establish an aesthetic mode of truth that sets the reader's mind into motion and induces a fuller receptivity so that aesthetic judgments are not confined to the cognitive faculties but, rather, to a more complete "sensibility." Davis advocates the part played by the body and emotions in the reading process: "This is what I want you to do. I want you to hide your disgust, take no heed to your clean clothes, and come right down with me,—here, into the thickest of the fog and mud and foul effluvia. I want you to hear this story" (13). Here it is clear that the narrator wishes the reader to take part in the performative rendering of the tale by "listening" to it; she wishes to unify the reader's sensibilities with those of the suffering characters (e.g., Hugh, Deb, Janey).

Through the "direct shock of poetic intensity" (Eliot 200), a heightened theatrical rendering ("the curtain . . . drawn back"), and a series of dramatically composed questions (e.g., "Has the power of its desperate need commanded the darkness away?" 65), the narrator concludes her tale. She returns us to the aesthetic object:

> Nothing remains to tell that the poor Welsh puddler once lived,
> but this figure of the mill-woman cut in korl. I have it here in a
> corner of my library. . . . Sometimes,—to-night, for instance,
> —the curtain is accidentally drawn back, and I see a bare arm

stretched out imploringly in the darkness, and an eager, wolfish
face watching mine: a wan, woful face, through which the spirit
of the dead korl cutter looks out. . . . (64)

Staged, the korl woman appears as something that by nature is intangible.
This staging, however, should not be interpreted as primarily a process of
completion. Rather, the staged life (i.e., here in the performative object) defies
completion, for there is no final limit to what might be possible. Multivalent,
the korl woman cannot be reduced to one meaning. Each middle-class visitor
to the iron mill interprets her differently.

Thus, this final representation of the korl woman becomes a mode that
functions to its maximum effect when, as ways of revealing the world, the
knowledge and experience the novel posits come to the limits of their usefulness. The performative denies such limits. This is why *Life* can usefully be
understood in terms of a performative struggle with the world the novella
describes, in which a kind of derealization precedes representation. As a prom-
ontory indicator of *Maggie* and *McTeague, Life* manages to make its case precisely in the combination of these aesthetic and social contingencies.

Of course like most fictions *Life* can produce realities; it, after all, dwells
on the "commonplace," insisting, for example, that class oppression has resulted
in a tragic joke: "You call it an altogether serious thing to be alive: to these men
it is a drunken jest, a joke,—horrible to angels perhaps, to them commonplace
enough" (12–13). Yet, if *Life* emphasizes its participatory relation to the environmental conditions that it represents, it emphasizes as well an internal and
irreducibly performative distance from those conditions. For instance, by her
insistent use of direct address and present verb tenses, the narrator engages in
an (almost) antagonistic and always performative dialogue with the reader, at
once pushing the reader away from and implicating her in the story:

What do you make of a case like that, amateur psychologist? (12)

You may think it a tiresome story enough, as foggy as the day,
sharpened by no sudden flashes of pain or pleasure. (13)

I will tell you plainly that I have a great hope; and I bring it to you
to be tested. (14)

You, Egoist, or Pantheist, or Arminian, busy in making straight
paths for your feet on the hills, do not see it clearly,—this terrible
question which men here have gone mad and died trying to
answer. (14)

> You laugh at it? Are pain and jealousy less savage realities down
> here in this place I am taking you to than in your own house or
> your own heart,—your heart, which they clutch at sometimes? (23)

Here the performative extends into the interior of the narrative, precisely in
the relationship between the narrator and reader; or, more specifically, in the
narrator's staging of the various identities she imagines her readers possess.
Life is, as Mark Seltzer has noted, not only "part of what it represents" but
also "*about* what it represents" (468). The reading of it is more an act of creation (signaled in the narrator-"you" relationship) rather than reception.
Accordingly, Davis's characters emerge less as an identity than as the impossibility of an identity (e.g., Hugh's "thwarted life" as an artist) or the poten-
tiality of an identity (e.g., Deb's middle-class redemption at the end of the
text). They therefore cannot be read merely metonymically or mimetically.
Instead, the meaning of Davis's aesthetics lies foremost in its "staging," its
new figuralizations, and in its reliance on processes of mediation as opposed
to mimetic acts.

MAGGIE AND *MCTEAGUE*: THE CITY
AS PERFORMATIVE MYSTERY

While focusing, like Davis, on the "commonplace," Crane and Norris engaged
in their own stagings and broadenings of discursive contexts. What is staged
in *Life's* mill town, "saturated" in the mystery of "fog and grease and soot"
(12), finds its parallels in *Maggie* and *McTeague.* In *Maggie* the wish for the
commonplace, for the demystification of urban spaces and social distances,
coexists with the wish not to explain mystery but to use it as a kind of surro-
gate experience for explanation. As Alan Trachtenberg has argued,

> By the end of the century spatial barriers appeared threatening
> and intolerable, and in the rhetoric of reformers the idea of mys-
> tery itself was the veil that hid the sight of the lower orders and
> their quarters from the "public," the readers of newspapers and
> the payers of taxes for whom the slums were par excellence an
> "elsewhere" shrouded in awe and fear. (140)

To preserve the city's mystery while seemingly revealing or explaining it,
Crane and Norris relied on performative techniques. Crane, for example,
tried to convey physical landscapes equivalent to his perceptions of the subjective lives of his characters. He suffused his story with so much subjectivity

that even the "objective" narrative renders it (Levenson 159). His New York is thus filled with windows that "uprear [their] forms amid squat, ignorant stables" (3), shadows of "grey ominous building[s]" (4), "gruesome doorways" which give up "loads of babies to the street and gutter" (6), and tenements that "quive[r] and crea[k] from the weight of humanity stamping about in its bowels" (6). These perceptions come not only from the narrator but also from Jimmie, Mary, Maggie, and the "chorus" of tenement dwellers, who see and express in the dense, impenetrable city their own sentiments and fears. It is a city that breathes, falls, and performs according to such perceptions.

Crane's city descriptions overflow with a hyperbolic, over-insistent roar of outrage and mockery to create a landscape of "hysteria and hallucination" (Walcutt 67). From Jimmie's impassioned defense of his "honor of Rum Alley" (3), characterized by such phrases as "circles madly," "furious assault," "barbaric trebles," "triumphant savagery," and "taunting oaths," to Maggie's walk to the "final block" in which "[the] structures seemed to have eyes that looked over her, beyond her, at other things" (53), Crane insists on performative conveyances and expressions (e.g., "infantile orations" 168) that do not necessarily advance the exploration of his subject or the "sociological thesis" that is so often attributed to him.

In this way, Crane constantly makes us aware of the narrator as a conveyor of performances: at one moment adopting a mock-heroic stance ("The mother and the son began to sway and struggle like gladiators" 29); at another ironically undercutting a character ("Maggie perceived that Pete brought forth all his elegance and all his knowledge of high-class customs for her benefit" 23); and yet at still another employing such attention-getting locutions as "the girl of crimson legions" (53), "the doorful of eyes" (48), "words of wind-demons" (13), and a "blue policeman turned red" (15). The language startles, calls attention to itself rather than to what it describes, and aims for impact and effect.

McTeague's urban portrayals similarly attempt to demystify the city while working to preserve its mystery. Norris's Polk Street, for instance, at first offers the fixed perspective of predictability, sameness, and stability of a world in which apparently little can go wrong. "Day after day," from the bay window of his "Dental Parlors," McTeague sees "the same panorama unroll itself":

> This little army of workers, tramping steadily in one direction, met and mingled with other toilers of a different description— conductors and "swing men" of the cable company going on duty; heavy-eyed night clerks from the drug stores on their way home to sleep; roundsmen returning to the precinct police station to

make their night report, and Chinese market gardeners teetering past under their heavy baskets. The cable cars began to fill up; all along the street could be seen the shop keepers taking down their shutters. (4)

But "an out-of-the-ordinary world, not familiar to the civic experience of most novel readers" (Levenson 168), surfaces once Trina and McTeague move for the second time. The perspective shifts: the window now looks out into "a grimy maze of back yards and broken sheds" (188). Taking us into the interior of their room, Norris presents a mysterious world where seemingly anything can occur:

> The one room grew abominably dirty, reeking with the odors of cooking and of "non-poisonous" paint. The bed was not made until late in the afternoon, sometimes not at all. Dirty, unwashed crockery, greasy knives, sodden fragments of yesterday's meals cluttered the table, while in one corner was the heap of evil-smelling, dirty linen. Cockroaches appeared in the crevices of the woodwork, the wall-paper bulged from the damp walls and began to peel. (188)

Situated in such an environment, Trina and McTeague live in their own withdrawn psychic spaces, possessed by the mysterious feelings, desperation, and degeneracy the city engenders.

Each character in *McTeague,* like each in *Maggie,* is self-deceived, estranged from all others, and occupies a world of his or her own, a world most conducive to performative renderings. The performative quality of *Maggie* and *McTeague* makes us see the elementary forms that link our own subjectivity with the world of originary experience. Performance offers its own metaphysical philosophy of the world: truth becomes an active construction of scenes put on "stage" by the author's eye rather than something that has to be uncovered. Truth, rather than a pre-given reality, becomes the subject of representation, but a subject that involves the reader in the stagings and enactments of the text.

PERFORMATIVE UNREALITY AND STRUCTURE

The world in *McTeague* and *Maggie* is obviously different from the one it refers to, for the performative world must differ from any extratextual existence. This theatricalization of reality is signaled early in *Maggie* when, for example, "the babe [Tommie] sat on the floor watching the scene, his face in contortions like that of a woman at a tragedy" (7) or when the tenement house hall "fill[s] with interested spectators," intent on seeing the fight between Mary and Jimmie (30), or in the scene in which Mary "reeled and swayed in the middle of the room, her fierce face convulsed with passion, her blotched arms raised high in imprecation" (32). And throughout the text it is signaled by the narrator's rendition of "eerie or spectral effects" as in a "great green-hued hall" (56), "pale green snow storms" (27) and suggestions of "artificial illumination or stage lighting" (Halliburn 57): "An old woman opened a door. A light behind her threw a flare on the urchin's quivering face" (9).

Within this world, the performative structure of *Maggie* is most clearly suggested by the three theatrical scenes that chart Maggie's demise. The purpose of such an unreality is to overstep what is known as the realistic given and to create a world that is never totally deceptive nor totally dependable, a world which occupies a dramatically charged middle ground. Each of the three scenes signals Maggie's further descent into apparent "moral" decay and her dependency on Pete. In the first scene in which Maggie is drawn to Pete, who "displayed the consideration of a cultural gentleman who knew what was due" (22), he performs for her, and she appropriately perceives him as bringing "forth all his elegance and all his knowledge of high-class customs for her benefit" (23). At one moment "gracious and attentive" and at another aggressive and imperious, regarding "with eyes of superiority the scene before them" (22), Pete is seen by Maggie as a "knight," and she recognizes in him an air of "distinguished valor" (38), a figure "looming like a yellow sun" (26).

Crane, however, sets Pete's performative stance in the reality of the music-hall public and thereby brings us back to the Bowery: "the vast crowd had an air throughout of having just quitted labor. Men with calloused hands and attired in garments that showed the wear of an endless trudge for a living. . . . The great body of the crowd was composed of people who showed that all day they strove with their hands" (22). But the narrator stops short of explanation, of "naturalistic" causes and effects, for the novel's impact, its most prominent feature, serves to appropriate—and eventually subsume—these elements.

This venue's audience, like Maggie herself, experiences what the narrator calls a "transcendental realism. Joy always within, and they, like the actor, inevitably without" (27). The performative unreality incites Maggie and the rest of the audience to "hu[g] themselves in ecstatic pity of their imagined or real condition" (27). Crane suggests here that his novel can best be conceived as a "mode of impacting" in which "the indefinability of our world is inscribed into it" (Iser 267). The impact that the narrator strives for never loses sight of its situational condition or function; but at the same time his objects of representation, going far beyond any pre-given state, serve as material from which something new and unexpected is formed.

In the second theatrical scene, the hall, more tawdry and ominous than the first, is of "irregular shape" in which a ballad singer sings "in the inevitable voice of brass" (38). While "men at other tables regarded [Maggie] furtively" and "gray-headed men, wonderfully pathetic in their dissipation, stared at her through clouds" (39), she "confined her glances to Pete and the stage" (39). This time, however, Maggie does not wish to become part of the performance, yet for most of the male spectators she is a part of it. She cannot escape it, though she wishes to do so and actually makes the decision (one of her rare decisions) for Pete and herself to leave the hall. This is not just a scene as played in ordinary life, nor is it one that unfolds and the reader merely watches; rather, like so many scenes in *Maggie,* it is both an ongoing event and a happening for the reader, enabling and encouraging direct involvement in the scene and, indeed, in the staging itself.

In the third music-hall scene, there are "twenty-eight tables and twenty-eight women and a crowd of smoking men" (42); the hall is even seedier and coarser than the first two. The smoke is "thicker," the "rumble of conversation" is replaced by a "roar" (42), and confusion is everywhere. Crane turns up the performative volume.

But, most importantly, this scene makes transparent Crane's gestures towards joining semblance and performance. "Valiant noise was made on a stage at the end of the hall by an orchestra composed of men who looked as *if* they had just happened in" (42). The "mere boy" who has accompanied Nellie into the hall "smiled again as *if* resolved to wait patiently" (45), during which time "he exterminated a number of cocktails with a determined air, as *if* replying defiantly to fate." In the following chapter, Maggie has "a shadowy look that was like a sardonic grin, as *if* some one had sketched with cruel forefinger indelible lines about her mouth" (48, my emphases throughout). Similar to the effect of such words as "perceived" (43), "apparently" (43), and "assumed" (44) found in this third scene, "as *if* " suggests that the textual world is to be viewed not as a reality but as if it were a reality. And so such words and locutions imply that the text is not meant to denote the world but a world enacted. Hence in disclosing itself, *Maggie* signals that everything is only to be taken as if it were what it seems to be, to be taken—in other words—as performance.

Similarly, the narrator of *McTeague,* remaining in the third person, resorts to enactment and semblance. He repeats the word "perhaps," for instance, as he describes McTeague's reasons for drinking: "Perhaps his nerves were naturally too dull to admit of any excitation; perhaps he did not really care for the whiskey, and only drank because Heise and the other men at Frenna's did" (172). The narrator self-consciously uses the expression "no doubt" when identifying "the famous Uncle Oelbermann" in the reception scene in chapter 9 (93), and he expresses further uncertainty when describing Marcus, who "*appeared* to contemplate in ecstasy the framed photograph of McTeague and Trina in their wedding finery" (144, my emphasis). Norris's language in *McTeague,* like Crane's in *Maggie,* repeatedly emphasizes that representation is not an act of mimesis because mimesis presupposes a given and verifiable reality. *McTeague* and *Maggie* are most urgently concerned instead with the reality their narrators directly engender.

McTeague, too, has its music hall act. At San Francisco's Orpheum in chapter 6, Trina and McTeague witness a rapid and illogical sequence of acts, which fluctuate from low comedy to high sentimentality, resonating with the organized incongruities of the novel itself:

> First was an overture by the orchestra, after which came "The Gleasons, in their mirth-moving musical farce, entitled 'McMonnigal's Courtship.'" This was to be followed by "The Lamont Sisters, Winnie and Violet, serio-comiques and skirt dancers." And after this came a great array of other "artists" and "specialty performers," musical wonders, acrobats, lightning artists, ventriloquists, and last of all, "The feature of the evening, the crowning scientific achievement of the nineteenth century, the kinetoscope." (55)

The narrator tells us in the course of his description that "[t]he performance went on," signaling that the act, paralleling the function of the three music-hall scenes in *Maggie,* is a microcosm and metaphor for the rest of the novel (58). Director as well as actor, the narrator offers a series of different performances and perspectives that take precedence over conveying any doctrine, epistemology, or social criticism.

Norris pays tribute to his performative objective by minutely describing his characters' corpses and disfigurements, by "staging" their deaths. Trina finds Maria brutally murdered, "show[ing] a fearful gash in her throat under her ear. All the front of her dress [is] soaked through and through" (177). Zerkow's corpse is discovered "floating in the bay," clenching in his hands "a sack full of old and rusty pans, tin dishes . . . [,] tin cans, and iron knives and forks" (180). Trina and Marcus both lose fingers (196, 242), and their murders are described in Norris's usual inflated tragicomic tones. McTeague's murder of Trina takes place "offstage" and, as the narrator implies, is so terrible it can only be summarized. For Mac's murder of Marcus, Norris resorts to "blatant melodrama," parodying the western formula story (Hug 219). Variously and often negatively interpreted by Norris commentators, these stagings, like those in *Maggie,* are integral to the novel's structure.

While *Maggie* and *McTeague* are often considered as naturalistic texts, such a description overlooks the complexity of their naturalism, which depends upon staged performance and, as in *Life,* potential alternatives to concrete historical determinations: "I can paint nothing of this, only give you the outside outlines, . . . whatever muddy depth of soul-history lies beneath you can read according to the eyes God has given you" (*Life* 23). Both novels suggest that what is staged is the appearance of something that cannot become manifest or completed, that cannot admit to any final limits. Thus, as part of an access to an infinity of possibilities, both novels posit their own theory of subjective truth rather than pointing to any particular truth to be "naturalistically" disclosed.

TOWARDS A NOVELISTIC THEATRICALITY: MELODRAMA AND THE GROTESQUE

I. The Melodramatic

In *Maggie,* Crane "aim[s] at accuracy and not compassion," as Trachtenberg has pointed out, but the story in order "to become a complicated piece of parody written with a serious regard" (145) largely relies on a performative naturalism. Thus, much in *Maggie* suggests, as part of this aim, the melodramatic: shock; terror; violence apparently for its own sake; stereotyped characters; a plot revolving around malevolent intrigue and violent action; mawkish sentiment; and so on. But in *Maggie,* Crane represents melodrama critically and subverts it for his own performative purposes. In so doing, he tries to show that the city, its poverty and social problems are fit subjects for his kind of fiction.

From the beginning of *Maggie,* then, the narrator puts his characters and readers in the role of spectator, presenting his subjects in planned disproportion and satirizing the expected moral ending and material success. Melodramatic images are foregrounded in different versions of the actual melodramas Pete and Maggie witness: plays in which "the brain-clutching heroine was rescued from the palatial home of her guardian, who is cruelly after her bonds, by the hero with the beautiful sentiments" (27). The narrator significantly focuses on the perceptions of Maggie and those of the "loud gallery" who see "the hero's erratic march from poverty in the first act, to wealth and triumph in the final one, in which he forgives all the enemies he has left" (27). A spectator, "seeking out the painted misery" for the comfort it eventually brings, "Maggie always departed with raised spirits from the showing places" (28). "[She] conceives of the possibility that her life could resemble what she sees on stage," as David Halliburn has noted, "and the reader conceives of the possibility that what she sees on stage could resemble her life" (49).

The melodramatic descriptions also take such conventional forms as Maggie's perceiving in Pete "the beau ideal of a man" (19) and she "vaguely tr[ying] to calculate the altitude of the pinnacle from which he must have looked down upon her" (19); or, representing Maggie's last chance for redemption (51), the clergyman who cruelly refuses to help her; or Mary's convulsive weeping over Maggie's "worsted boots" (57). Crane presents these melodramatic moments simultaneously as effect and perspective through which the reader can glimpse the narrator's views and motivations.

Adopting a similar position, Norris creates perspectivistic moments in which the reader can glimpse the artificiality of what the narrator is doing (and, paradoxically, his genuineness). For this purpose, Norris's use of the (mock or ironic) melodramatic often comes in the form of questions. For instance, when McTeague has "caught" Trina "in his huge arms" and his "sexually determin[ed]" drives awaken, the narrator asks: "And yet, was it to be feared? Was it something to be ashamed of? Was it not, after all natural, clean, spontaneous?" (50). Trina, too, appears to be caught in this sexual "spell," though "[s]he had not sought it, she had not desired it." The narrator asks, "Was it a blessing? Was it a curse? . . . Why should it all be?" (51). Similarly, he previously interrogated the aftereffects of Trina's "concession" to McTeague: "Was there something gone from Trina now? Was he not disappointed in her for doing that very thing for which he had longed? Was Trina the submissive, the compliant, the attainable just the same, just as delicate and adorable as Trina the inaccessible?" Here, in his use of the melodramatic, Norris gestures towards his performative aim, which is to show how Trina and the other major characters indicate a presence of the "inaccessible." The narrator then goes on to challenge the inevitable "result" of sexual pursuit: "With each concession gained the man's desire cools; with every surrender made the woman's adoration increases. But why should it be so?" (48).

As in *Maggie,* the melodramatic in *McTeague* spills over from the stage into the lives of the characters. However, in *McTeague,* it most often depends upon the narrator's voice, not character perception or expression, as in the infamous pant-wetting scene at the Orpheum:

> But at this moment a dreadful accident happened to Owgooste; his distress reached its climax; his fortitude collapsed. What a misery! It was a veritable catastrophe, deplorable, lamentable, a thing beyond words! For a moment he gazed wildly about him, helpless and petrified with astonishment and terror. Then his grief found utterance, and the closing strains of the orchestra were mingled with a prolonged wail of infinite sadness. (61)

Here Norris's portrayal of "low-brow" culture conflates with the melodramatic. Incorporating such levels of taste in his use of popular culture in the America of the nineties, Norris makes the melodramatic an integral part of his performative documentation.

The melodramatic for both writers serves as a counter and a certain kind of defiance to the often made claims that the naturalistic novel, particularly in its late-nineteenth-century manifestations in England and the United States, bordered on what critics of the eighties and nineties were calling the "pathological novel," or what H. M. Stutfield, for example, characterized as a literature that is concerned with an external expression of an obsessional interiority, a literature that thrives on "super-subtlety," "microscopic self-examination," "morbid pessimism," and which "expresses itself in the worship of ugliness, the minute and almost exclusive delineation of what is gloomy and squalid in life" (112). Melodrama in *McTeague* functions primarily as a parodic and comedic overlay to the kind of naturalistic world Norris describes in "Zola as a Romantic Writer" (1896) in which "[characters] must be twisted from the ordinary, wrenched out from the quiet, uneventful round of every-day life, and flung into the throes of a vast and terrible drama" (309–10), a world he later creates but simultaneously critiques in *McTeague.* In Crane, the melodramatic shifts the emphasis from individual pathologies to mass public taste in that the melodramatic, like *Maggie* itself, "is a vision of what typically happens rather than a report on what actually happens" (Ziff 109). Crane and Norris recognized the rising power of the new mass readership and the marketplace; at the same time, both wished to guard their artistic integrity, which they felt was being threatened by the repressive philistinism of commercialism and by the material conditions of the production and distribution of fiction. An essential part of their literary agenda was to train a melodramatic optic on the naturalistic text.

II. The Grotesque

The category of the grotesque, for Crane and Norris, amounts to the semi-comic, the hellish, and the wondrous, and, like the melodramatic, points to a mocking of working- and middle-class tastes. Crane often joins his descriptions of public entertainment with those of the grotesque. For instance, in the first theatrical scene, a "small fat man" "began to roar a song and stamp back and forth before the foot-lights, wildly waving a glossy silk hat and throwing leers, or smiles, broadcast. He made his face into fantastic grimaces until he looked like a pictured devil on a Japanese kite" (24). The "finale" of this same scene shows the dancer "f[alling] into some of those grotesque attitudes which were at the time popular among the dancers in the theatres uptown" (23). After seeing this melodrama, Maggie wonders if "the culture and refinement she had seen imitated" was done so "grotesquely by the heroine on the stage" (28).

Norris's use of the grotesque is inconsistent, as is his codifying of the deterministic "passions" of his characters, but this use largely fulfills his performative purpose: to change "common people" and occurrences into the "extraordinary, imaginative, grotesque even."[3] Seemingly confirming Zola's advice in Le roman experimental—"notre seule force véritable est dans la méthode" (10:39)—the narrator offers, for example, little reason for McTeague's loss of sexual passion for Trina (107). After chapter 10, McTeague's sexual animality (and its grotesque manifestations) is never mentioned again. Similarly, Norris does not explain why McTeague suddenly begins to "have ambitions" after losing his sexual interest in Trina and "relaps[ing] to his wonted stolidity" (109, 108). But Norris consistently adheres to Zola's idea that "[p]our un savant expérimentateur, l'ideal qu'il cherche à réduire, l'indéterminé, n'est jamais que dans le comment" (10:38). Norris concentrates much less on knowing the "origin" of nature than on delineating the "mechanism" of nature. His often grotesque representations of characters' "passions" do not result from bridging differences and cannot be conceived in merely mimetic terms but instead continually defer the quest for origins.

For both authors, the grotesque takes the form of an overflow or some kind of temporary validation of excess. Authorial imagination produces aberrations (madness, hallucination in McTeague; blood-filled violence, war "heroics" in Maggie) and strange configurations of feelings. What limits these imaginative soarings is that they are temporary, creating for the reader distinct perspectivistic moments. The interplay of such moments results in a staging of what was unavailable to the reader and indeed what can remain cognitively unfathomable. The portrayal of the visible in both novels occurs as a series of performative acts.

PERFORMATIVE: TOWARDS THE TYPE

Crane's and Norris's concern with the grotesque and its theatrical potential can be explained partially by the fact that in *Maggie* and *McTeague* characters cannot throw off their performative roles. On the contrary, the performative draws the character away from individuation toward the type. Indeed, a character's exterior may be all that the reader will be offered, and the character's private self may be indistinguishable from his or her public self.

This performative alignment is particularly evident in *Maggie,* signaled by the use of stereotypical words or phrases to designate characters. Thus following Pete's abandonment of her, Maggie is called "a girl of the painted cohorts" (52). The young man who accompanies Nell to the "hilarious hall" remains nameless; the narrator simply describes him as "the mere boy" (43, 45, 46). In chapter 18, Pete is repeatedly called "the man" (53–54) and Nellie "the woman of brilliance and audacity" (55–56). The Rum Alley tenement house characters are labeled as "spectators" (30).

Crane closes *Maggie* in a performative flurry in which Maggie becomes what such stereotypical descriptions of her have been leading towards—a theatrical exhibit:

> Through the open doors curious eyes stared in at Maggie. Children ventured into the room and ogled her, as if they formed the front row at a theatre. Women, without, bended toward each other and whispered, nodding their heads with airs of profound philosophy. A baby, overcome with curiosity concerning this object at which all were looking, sidled forward and touched her dress, cautiously. . . . (48)

Pacing back and forth, Maggie's mother, "expounding like a glib showman at a museum," "wheel[s] suddenly and point[s] with dramatic finger" (48). The stage metaphors and images continue as Maggie, rejected by her family and the tenement "crowd," leaves the apartment, followed by eyes that are strangely like a spotlight, "sending broad beams of inquisitive light into the darkness of her path" (48).

In chapter 17, Maggie makes her final appearance and exit, appropriately enough just as "[t]wo or three theatres emptied a crowd upon the storm-swept pavements" (51). Maggie then walks away from "the glowings of the stage . . . [,] a place of forgetfulness" (51), to where "[a] concert hall gave to the street faint sounds of swift, machine-like music, as if a group of phantom musicians were hastening" (52). She passes a "tall young man," another of Crane's types, who suddenly discerns that "[Maggie] was neither new, Parisian, nor theatrical" (52) before she goes into "the blackness of the final block" (53).

Norris, too, relies on performative types such as the "Other Dentist" (193) and the "Indian" (220), but his types are usually multiple and contradictory. For example, in the few pages spanned by the initial "dental parlor" scene, McTeague, who has figured earlier as a "draught horse" (2), is presented alternatively and in quick succession as "an over-grown boy" and "a crude primitive man"; Trina is in rapid turns called a "bourgeoisie," a "girl," "innocent and confiding, almost infantile," and a "boy, frank, candid, and unreserved" (14–15). At one moment McTeague appears to be mechanistic, a virtual embodiment of habit and rigidity (1), but soon after he is full of unpredictable aberrations and obsessions (18). Trina is by turns portrayed as doll-like and naive (13), "blindly persistent, with the persistency of a girl who has made up her mind" (15), and completely "frightened" and helpless (19). Through such depictions, the narrator can appear to merely observe and chronicle his character's motivations and actions—though he might do so "indignantly" or through apathy, bafflement, irony, or in contradictory or self-questioning "realistic-naturalistic" explanations.

It is a matter here, then, of wiping out the illusion of certainty—inherent in these multiple descriptions and portrayal of types—that what is suggested by the appearance actually exists. Consequently, semblance takes over, revealing itself as a form of mediation between truth, or a consciousness of truth, and that which is withheld from consciousness. Crane's and Norris's types further contribute to the understanding of semblance as presupposing a reality on which it depends but which it always must go beyond since it cannot arrive at reality itself.

CRANE AND NORRIS AS PERFORMATIVE STYLISTS

Following Rebecca Harding Davis, Crane and Norris appear to have remained immune from many of the assumptions of realist-naturalist thinking but probed such assumptions deeply enough so as to bring out their inconsistencies and contradictions. Crane's style, for example, was a contradiction in itself: "a radical challenge to a central tenet of realism—that the appropriate style for fiction is plain and literal" (Colvert 15–16). At the same time, he claimed that he simply wished to describe how "environment is a tremendous thing in the world and frequently shapes lives regardless" (*Letters* 14). To several reviewers of the mid-1890s, *Maggie* seemed full of "oddities," "petty tricks," an exhibit of "ironic self-consciousness" (Bell 30), sated with "hollow sentimentality" and "lurid melodrama" that turned Crane into "a caricaturist without humor" (Bright 152). What must be recognized here, however, is that *Maggie* is an implicit critique of conventional naturalism and realism, exposing the reductiveness of Howellsian theory, which excluded all "realisms" that did not aim to generate "a reality unmediated by language, accessible to the reader," that did not signify "a direct transmission of 'real life' in which style remains transparent" (Bell 133). Crane's performative style can largely explain the causes for these negative reviews, advance the argument of Crane as a doubtful realist-naturalist—too intrusive, too literary, too artful—and encourage us to disengage *Maggie* from the traditional view of literary naturalism.

Like Crane, Norris can be seen as taking a position that hinges not on his efforts to evoke "transparency" but on his talent as a performative stylist. As William E. Cain puts it, Norris "seems more intent on exhibiting and intensifying the scene than decrying it" (201). But for what purpose? Following Crane, Norris, I would argue, is aiming to make visible the contingencies and instabilities upon which *McTeague* depends. The intention, then, of Norris's experimentation, his "self-division" and "ambivalent attitudes" (Cain 201) is to reveal the meanings of "natural phenomena," the forces behind human culture and urban mystery that he can only approximate in *McTeague*.

As a performative stylist, Norris deploys semantic instability to conceal and simultaneously reveal his point of view. Specifically, the narrator does not submerge or efface authorial presence from the text but instead provides a multileveled performative vision of reality in which he juxtaposes characters' interpretations with his own and thereby rules out consensus. The pervasiveness of viewpoints, whereby the characters' perspective is supplemented, even supplanted, by the narrator's (and vice versa), is especially characteristic of the performative in *McTeague*. In the novel's first six chapters, for instance, Norris gives us three separate points of view. The first or second sentence of each chapter, by containing the name of a particular character, clearly indicates the governing viewpoint: the events in chapters 1 through 2 are first related through McTeague's eyes; in chapter 3, Maria's perceptions take over; in chapters 4 and 5, the point of view shifts back to McTeague; and in chapter 6, events filter, in the beginning, through Trina's perceptions. This shifting corroborates the fact that Norris's experiments originate in our responses to his constructed world more than to the tangible world itself.[4]

Not surprisingly, the performative came to be the visceral, spiritual essence of Crane's and Norris's aesthetic—within which *Maggie* and *McTeague* are presented less as a means of explaining than as circumstantial narratives of responses and reactions. It is of course simply impossible for any writer to avoid issues of performance, as every testing for the conventions and frames for presenting a text can find language "performing." But the performative, particularly in the "naturalistic" text, makes conceivable the extraordinary possibilities of human beings, who precisely because they do not seem to have a determinate nature can be represented in almost unlimited ways. Finally, unlike most formalistic approaches that deny any connection between literature and the world and any distinction between fictional and factual narratives, the performative signals the need of realist-naturalist texts to maintain some point of contact with the world while, at the same time, distancing itself from it—a need that guarantees that their relation to that world will not be purely one of opposition.[5]

The performative certainly challenges the "totalizing" capacity of naturalism, evidenced already in *Life,* as it asserts its value and meaning against the possibility and existence of the recorded or represented. For Davis, Crane, and Norris, naturalism is most valuable when it is more expressive than representational, focusing on performed actions rather than mimesis, and making judgments for "truth" a matter of active construction rather than a comparison with an *a priori* reality. Conceiving of these three writers as performative rather than representational stylists can help us recontextualize the commonly held critical notion that naturalism has no place in current literary theory, invigorate discussion of these "naturalists" as prose stylists, and revise our notions of literary naturalism.

NOTES

1. For an incisive discussion of elite and mass culture in nineteenth-century America, see Robertson, pp. 2, 17, 20, and 44–45.
2. The issue of performative meaning is capacious. I am indebted here to, among others, H. P. Grice, "Meaning," *Philosophical Review* 66 (1957): 377–88; Randall Knoper, *Acting Naturally: Mark Twain in the Culture of Performance* (Berkeley: U of California P, 1995); Elizabeth Freund, *The Return of the Reader: Reader-Response Criticism* (London: Methuen, 1987); Steven Mailloux, *Interpretive Conventions: The Reader in the Study of American Fiction* (Ithaca: Cornell UP, 1982); Douglass Oliver, *Poetry and Narrative in Performance* (Carbondale: Southern Illinois UP, 1986); and Wolfgang Iser, *Prospecting: From Reader Response to Literary Anthropology* (Baltimore: Johns Hopkins UP, 1989).

   The meanings of the performative on which this essay particularly draws include the notion that inaccessible realities can only be penetrated by staging them, by performing what is withheld. In Wolfgang Iser's words, "what can never become present to ourselves and what eludes cognition and knowledge and is beyond experience can enter consciousness only through feigned representations" ("Do I Write" 313). There is in this approach an interconnection of author, text, and reader to be conceived as an "ongoing process that produces something that had not existed before" (Iser, "Play" 325). There is also a direct conflict with the traditional notion of representation, if representation is defined as a mimetic description of a presupposed reality. This non-mimetic theory of literature points to, as Winifred Fluck has argued, the special place of the literary text: "if literature is not to be justified by truthful representation, the source of its special potential must be derived from the fact that it is, by definition, different and thus ideally suited to counter dominant ways of world making" (197). Instead of operating as a mirroring instrument, literature in this model serves to disturb preconceived cultural constructions of identity, invoking what otherwise cannot become present.

3. Norris, "Zola as a Romantic Writer," 309–10. Here Norris is putting forth his ideas on Zola's naturalism, arguing that "what counts" is Zola's world of "big things; the enormous, the formidable, the terrible" (310).

4. Aesthetically, for Norris and Crane, changing perspectives are part of the phenomenon Randall Knoper describes: "[N]ineteenth-century theater and novels were imbued with each other, novelists in particular writing for an audience in tune with stage conventions, echoing theatrical values of melodrama, burlesque, variety, spectacle, 'situation,' and 'effect,' and rehearsing a preoccupation with performance and role-playing" (9).

Although this is not the place to trace the rich social history of American forms of elite and popular "performance," it is relevant to note that *McTeague* and *Maggie* certainly have roots in the nineteenth-century performative traditions—in such entertainments as Shakespearian plays, traveling shows, minstrelsy, and music halls. Norris and Crane frequently subordinated their skills of discovering and interrogating reality to those of show and spectacle, intermingling mimicry and mimesis, the performative and informative.

5. The performative meaning in *Maggie* and *McTeague* never constitutes the *entire* meaning. As Ellen Spolsky puts it, "[p]erformative meaning will never provide enough meaning to satisfy, will never make consultation of the context unnecessary. The consultation of the context *will* provide additional meaning; it will not, however, cancel performative meaning" (421). Performance and its effects in both works do not prevent their authors from realizing their investments in reference and essence.

WORKS CITED

Bell, Michael. Introduction. *The Problem of American Realism: Studies in Cultural History of a Literary Idea*. Chicago: U of Chicago P, 1993.

Benfey, Christopher. *The Double Life of Stephen Crane*. New York: Alfred A. Knopf, 1992.

Bright, Edward. "A Melodrama of the Streets." *Illustrated American* 20 (11 July 1896): 94.

Cain, William. "Presence and Power in *McTeague.*" *American Realism: New Essays.* Ed. Eric J. Sundquist. Baltimore: Johns Hopkins UP, 1982. 199–214.

Colvert, James. "Stephen Crane and Postmodern Theory." *American Literary Realism* 28.1 (Fall 1995): 4–22.

Crane, Stephen. *Maggie: A Girl of the Streets.* Ed. Thomas A. Gullason. New York: Norton, 1979.

———. *Stephen Crane: Letters.* Ed. R. W. Stallman and Lillian Gilkes. New York: New York UP, 1960.

Davis, Rebecca Harding. *Life in the Iron Mills, or The Korl Woman.* New York: Feminist Press, 1972.

Eliot, T. S. "Dante." *Selected Essays.* New York: Harcourt Brace Jovanovich, 1978.

Fluck, Winifred. "The Search for Distance: Negation and Negativity in Wolfgang Iser's Literary Theory." *New Literary History* 31.1 (Winter 2000): 175–210.

Gullason, Thomas A. "The Prophetic City in Stephen Crane's 1893 *Maggie.*" *Modern Fiction Studies* 24.1 (Spring 1978): 129–37.

———. "Tragedy and Melodrama in Stephen Crane's *Maggie.*" *Maggie: A Girl of the Streets.* By Stephen Crane. Ed. Thomas A. Gullason. New York: Norton, 1979. 245–53.

Halliburn, David. *The Color of the Sky.* Cambridge: Cambridge UP, 1989.

Harris, Sharon M. "Rebecca Harding Davis: From Romanticism to Realism." *American Literary Realism* 21.2 (Winter 1989): 5–19.

Hug, William J. "*McTeague* As Metafiction? Frank Norris' Parodies of Brett Harte and the Dime Novel." *Western American Literature* 26 (1991): 219–28.

Iser, Wolfgang. *The Act of Reading: A Theory of Aesthetic Response.* Baltimore: Johns Hopkins UP, 1978.

——— "Do I Write for an Audience?" *PMLA* 115.3 (May 2000): 310–14.

———. "The Play of the Text." *Languages of the Unsayable.* Ed. Sanford Budick and Wolfgang Iser. New York: Columbia UP, 1989. 325–39.

———. *Prospecting.* Baltimore: Johns Hopkins UP, 1989.

Knoper, Randall. *Acting Naturally: Mark Twain in the Culture of Performance.* Berkeley: U of California P, 1995.

Levenson, J. C. "*The Red Badge of Courage* and *McTeague*: Passage to Modernity." *American Realism and Naturalism.* Ed. Donald Pizer. New York: Cambridge UP, 1995. 154–77.

McElrath, Joseph R. *Frank Norris Revisited.* New York: Twayne, 1992.

Morrison, Lucy. "The Search for the Artist in Man and Fulfillment in Life—Rebecca Harding Davis's *Life in the Iron Mills.*" *Studies in Short Fiction* 33.2 (Spring 1996): 245–53.

Norris, Frank. *McTeague: A Story of San Francisco.* Ed. Donald Pizer. New York: Norton, 1977.

————. "Zola as a Romantic Writer." 1896. *McTeague: A Story of San Francisco.* Ed. Donald Pizer. New York: Norton, 1977. 308–10.

Robertson, Michael. *Stephen Crane, Journalism and the Making of Modern American Literature.* New York: Columbia UP, 1997.

Scholes, Robert. *Structural Fabulation: An Essay on the Fiction of the Future.* South Bend: U of Notre Dame P, 1975.

Seltzer, Mark. "The Still Life." *American Literary History* 3 (1991): 455–86.

Shulman, Robert. "Realism." *Columbia History of the American Novel.* Ed. Emory Elliott. New York: Columbia UP, 1991. 160–88.

Spolsky, Ellen. "The Limits of Literal Meaning." *New Literary History* 19 (1988): 421–22.

Stutfield, Hugh M. "The Psychology of Feminism." *Blackwood's* 161 (1897): 112.

Talmage, Thomas De Witt. "From *The Night Sides of City Life.*" *Maggie: A Girl of the Streets.* By Stephen Crane. Ed. Thomas A. Gullason. New York: Norton, 1979. 71–75.

Trachtenberg, Alan. "Experiments in Another Country: Stephen Crane's City Sketches." *American Realism: New Essays.* Ed. Eric J. Sundquist. Baltimore: Johns Hopkins UP, 1982. 138–54.

Walcutt, Charles. *American Literary Naturalism: A Divided Stream.* Minneapolis: U of Minnesota P, 1956.

Ziff, Larzer. *The American 1890's: Life and Times of a Lost Generation.* New York: Viking, 1966.

Zola, Émile. *Oeuvres complètes.* Ed. Henri Mitterand. Paris: Cercle du livre précieux, 1966–69.

Stephen Crane and the Transformation of the Bowery

—Robert M. Dowling

IN THE LATE SEVENTEENTH CENTURY, A RURAL PATH KNOWN AS BOWERY LANE (FROM THE DUTCH WORD *BOWERIJ*, OR FARM) WAS PUT TO USE AS THE main postal route from New York to Boston. The lower mile of this, situated in the heart of Manhattan's Lower East Side, became known simply as the Bowery. Due to its heavy commercial traffic and proximity to immigrant neighborhoods, the Bowery rapidly swelled into a celebrated urban boulevard, rivaling the already famous Broadway to its west. And with the construction of the Great Bowery Theater in 1826, the Bowery and thereabouts became New York's theatrical center, both on the stage and off. The area was packed to the point of bursting with cheap theaters, burlesque shows, dance halls, brothels, basement-level dives, and beer halls that seated up to two thousand patrons. It competed with Broadway, but did not cater to a Broadway crowd; it was notoriously flamboyant and alive with action; it was the epicenter of working-class culture and openly advertised itself as such, basing its appeal on picaresque urban experience and melodramatic spectacle.

By 1871, the year Stephen Crane was born, the Bowery as it was known worldwide had all but vanished. And with the construction of the Third Avenue elevated train seven years later, the boulevard was transfigured beyond recognition. The sun was blocked out by the tracks, and the streets were showered with hot oil and coal. By 1893, the year Crane published the vanity edition of his first novella, *Maggie: A Girl of the Streets,* the Bowery was already the infamous Bowery, once again conspicuous but now for alcoholism, poverty, homelessness, and crime. The streets were filled with hoboes and rival gangs. The number of prostitutes drew sailors by the thousands. The area was no longer a bastion of republicanism, and its inhabitants were continually being inveigled into accepting an oppositional system of social behavior. They were helpless in a cycle of cultural prostration seemingly indefinite in origin. As T. J. Jackson Lears postulates in "The Concept of Cultural Hegemony," "most people find it difficult, if not impossible, to translate the outlook implicit in their experience into a conception of the world that will directly challenge the hegemonic culture" (596). For the majority of New Yorkers grappling with the city's process of industrialization and urbanization, challenging the dominant culture was as unimaginable as the act of cultural absorption was subconscious. The indisputably dominant Victorian culture, distinguished by an allegiance to the cult of respectability and traditionally associated with Broadway and Fifth Avenue, had effectively wiped out its working-class counterpart on the East Side.[1]

Late-nineteenth-century New York Bowery culture was also one obsessed with consumption. Ironically, this consumer culture, such as might be found in New York's theaters, dance halls, and museums, proved far more effective for bringing urban "low life" into the "respectable" fold than did the evangelical moral reform efforts of the 1860s, '70s, and '80s. It is within this atmosphere that *Maggie*'s tragic protagonists reside. But the cultural space *Maggie* occupies signals less a beginning than an ending; the richness of antebellum Bowery culture was stifled by its incorporation of Victorian codes of behavior, and Crane renders his characters prostrated by the contradictory effects. Though Crane does give lip service to the new consumer culture, he does not present it as a vehicle for personal individuation and cultural dissent. Those processes, on the Bowery at least, were vestiges of a former time. *Maggie,* in short, is not a story of rebellion but of conformity.

Victorian culture in New York was in its infancy when the Bowery's cultural and physical boundaries began to define themselves. The tensions that emerged were clearly contingent upon a mutual exigency of identity as related to cultural politics. Richard Butsch, in his "Bowery B'hoys and Matinee Ladies," acknowledges that "middle- and upper-middle class Americans wished to distinguish themselves from the uncultivated working class at the very time when the working class was politically ascendant, at least rhetorically" (385). As a result, a Gramscian "war of position" clearly took place, a conflict for cultural hegemony rather than state power, in which codes of behavior were the primary mechanisms of attrition. Proper social markers for Americans with "respectability" included certain clothes, levels of education, and speech patterns, along with many other codified social graces. These were all learned behaviors, however, and adoptable by the "vulgar" masses. The codes then became increasingly rarified and more difficult to interpret and adopt. Once firmly established, middle-class New Yorkers became obsessed with protecting the status of Victorian respectability, at the expense of the indecorous rabble. To ensure social order, however, they eventually condoned the proliferation of respectable morals and manners in order to regulate satisfactorily the behavior of the working class. By the 1890s, the Victorian ideology had become so entrenched in New York's social consciousness that the notion of respectability would have a sizable effect on the actions and value structure of the very working-class culture that initially despised it.

One of the finest commentaries on the cultural transformation of the Bowery in this context has been furnished by, of all people, Henry James. While slumming in the neighborhood of the Bowery at the age of sixty, following his return to the United States in 1904, James attended a theater performance that closely resembled the fictional space constructed by Stephen Crane a decade earlier. James observed there a "vertiginous bridge of American confectionery," which he identified as a bridge that transverses the gap between the Victorian codes being enacted on the stage and the level of the audience's assent. He speculated that these "almost 'high class' luxuries, circulating in such a company, were a sort of supreme symbol of the promoted state of the aspirant to American conditions" (196). The most fascinating dramatic action for James was not what was taking place on the stage but rather the unwritten dialogue between the audience and the notions of respectability the theater and, more importantly, the society at large was selling: "Nothing (in the texture of the occasion) could have had a sharper interest than this demonstration that, since what we pretend to do with them is thoroughly to school them, the schooling, by our system, cannot begin too soon or pervade their experience too much. Were they going to rise to it, or rather fall from it—to our instinct, as distinguished from their own, for picturing life?" (199). James observed a new social lesson, one diametrically opposed to what Walt Whitman had referred to in *Democratic Vistas* (1871) as "great lessons of nature," lessons of unique culture expression. "Were they to take our lesson submissively," James asks, "in order to get with it our smarter traps and tricks, our superior Yankee machinery?" (199). Venues of popular entertainment such as the one James described, ones boldly sworn to elevating Bowery life, did not answer Whitman's call in *Democratic Vistas* for "variety and freedom" but enforced, as James attested, "blank conformity to convention" (198).

If one takes into account this transformation of Bowery culture over the nineteenth century, Stephen Crane's central characters in *Maggie*—Jimmie, Maggie, and Pete—can be viewed as fragmented relics of a culture drowned out by rampant urban American growth and its effects on New York culture in the form of middle-class Victorianism. This essay addresses the place of Crane's writings in the cultural history of the Bowery, then, rather than their place in literary history. It has been argued that Crane's knowledge of New York and the Bowery culture he represents is secondhand, taken from Jacob

Riis and the mass of Methodist moral reform tracts that abounded during that period (Benfey 63). Crane scholars find it difficult, however, to nail down precisely how well Crane may or may not have known the district. Regardless, Crane's novella is charged with a social energy that corresponds significantly with the Bowery and its past. Though Crane may have begun to conceptualize *Maggie* in Syracuse, before he had experienced Manhattan life to any substantial degree, in every chapter there exist salient references to the city's signature "respectable" culture and how it was both loathed and emulated by many of the Bowery's inhabitants.

Victorians themselves are not meant to be portrayed here as hobgoblins or bugaboos. Crane himself certainly points to no group or individual as inherently evil; his characters are products of a naturalistic environment that is beyond rational action. As a likable character from Crane's sketch "An Experiment in Luxury" wisecracks, "Nobody is responsible for anything. I wish to heaven somebody was, and then we could all jump on him" (*Crane* 550). Though there was no doubt a very real cultural conflict between vying groups, there is an aura of inevitability in the effect of urbanization on the Bowery, whether it be at the hands of Victorianism or some other cultural force. What immediately follows is a brief narrative account of the development of the historically resonant subculture from which Crane and others have drawn for their portraits of New York life, the Bowery B'hoys and G'hals. Following that, I will demonstrate how the novella *Maggie,* along with some of his other New York writing, illustrates the means by which that singular culture was suppressed.

While still a teenager, actor Frank Chanfrau ate regularly at the Broadway House, a small eatery on Grand Street in the middle of Manhattan's Lower East Side. At lunch one afternoon, Chanfrau overheard a boisterous young man howl to the waiter, "*Look a heah! Gimme a sixpenny plate ev pork and beans, and don't stop to count dem beans . . . !*" This was Mose Humphreys, a printer at the *New York Sun* and one of the "fire boys" of the mid-1830s. Over a decade later, the playwright Benjamin A. Baker would catch wind of Chanfrau's comical mimicking of the then famous Bowery B'hoy's style of speech. Baker promptly composed a dramatic sketch for Chanfrau to perform on the popular stage. They showed it to William Mitchell, the proprietor of a Lower East Side venue, Mitchell's Olympic Theater. Mitchell criticized the play or, more specifically, Baker's writing, remarking that "the characters are good, but what a bad piece!" Months later, coming up short for a new idea, he consented to let Chanfrau give Baker's play, then entitled "New York As It Is," a trial performance (Brown 284).

When Chanfrau first strolled onto the stage with a swagger and a sneer, the clamorous audience plunked into a hushed silence. This might have been discomfiting for Chanfrau since they generally greeted their favorite actor with lusty applause, but the fact is, as drama historian Allston T. Brown notes, the audience "didn't recognize Chanfrau. He stood there in his red shirt, with his fire coat thrown over one arm, the stovepipe hat . . . drawn over one eye, his trousers tucked into his boots, a stump of cigar pointing up from his lips to his eye, the soap locks plastered flat on his temples, and his jaw protruded into a half-beastly, half-human expression of contemptuous ferocity" (284). Chanfrau ripped the cigar from his mouth, spat on the stage, and bellowed, "*I ain't a-goin' to run wid dat mercheen no more!*"[2] The audience was no longer silent. As reported in the *New York Herald* the next day (April 18, 1848), the crowd "climbed up to the stage boxes, and all seemed bent on genuine frolic. The police and officers connected with the theater were rendered powerless. . . ." A mob of people pushed in from the street, but at length the police got it under control. They "hereupon commenced to clear the front of the stage amid the most deafening cheers," the *Herald* continues, "and some of the B'hoys were to be seen springing forward on the heads of their different groups of friends, from the stage, whom they joined in the pit, amid continued laughter" (qtd. in Buckley 392).

Under its new name, "A Glance At New York In 1848," the play was performed for forty-eight consecutive nights, selling over forty thousand tickets, making it, up to that point, the most popular play in American history (Buckley 392–93). William Dean Howells later admitted to being wholly beguiled by its reception: "Some actor saw and heard things spoken with the peculiar swagger and whopperjaw utterance of the B'hoy of those dreadful old days . . . and he put them on stage and spread the poison of them all over the land, so that there was hardly anywhere a little blackguard boy who did not wish to act and talk like Mose" (*Criticism* 271). Though this response appears to be criticism by a hopeless traditionalist, Howells appreciated the impact the play had on his own consciousness: "Other things have come and gone," he grants, "things of Shakespeare, of Alfieri, of Cervantes, but those golden works of a forgotten dramatist poet remain with me" (*Criticism* 271). The Baker sketch was, in short, an unintentional power play of cultural credibility. The Mose character empowered the "lower million" with both a defiant attitude and a comic voice. The B'hoy thereafter became a widely known dramatic presence on the American stage, and the stage was one of the most influential cultural vehicles of the time.

William Dean Howells rightly observes that Jimmie Johnson, Maggie's younger brother, was "an Ishmaelite from the cradle, who, with his warlike instincts beaten back into cunning, is what the B'hoy of former times has become in our more strenuously policed days" ("New York" 154). Indeed, there are numerous traits shared by Crane's characters and the B'hoys and G'hals of the old Bowery. Pete, for example, is described as having "an enticing nonchalance," with his hair "curled down over his forehead in an oiled bang" and a red scarf tied around his throat (25), while Maggie, like her G'hal counterparts, is a seamstress infatuated with the theater.[3] If we recall Chanfrau's performance while reading the following scene from *Maggie*—Crane's dramatic introduction of the character Pete—the comparability between stage and fictional characters is even more vivid: "Down the avenue came boastfully sauntering a lad of sixteen years, although the chronic sneer of an ideal manhood already sat on his lips. His hat was tipped with an air of challenge over his eye. Between his teeth, a cigar stump was tilted at the angle of defiance" (8). The analogy Howells proffers likening Crane's Jimmie to the B'hoys is, then, perhaps even more applicable to Pete, who will ultimately contribute to Maggie's metamorphosis from seamstress to street walker. At the same time, Crane makes Jimmie an admirer of fire engines, which seems to testify to the author's intent to evoke Bowery history, as the B'hoys were extreme in their fascination with fire fighting. "A fire engine," Crane remarks, "was enshrined in [Jimmie's] heart as an appalling thing that he loved with a distant dog-like devotion. They had been known to overturn street-cars" (23). To the B'hoys, fighting fires was a contact sport. Any activity, including socializing with their female counterparts, the G'hals, was immediately broken off by the sound of a distant fire signal. Those familiar with the Lower East Side would know at that point to keep their heads about them.

The B'hoy became recognizable as a distinct type in the popular consciousness of mid-nineteenth-century New York at a time when the establishment of urban "types" was vital to the evolution of the city's identity (Buckley 359). But much like the case with the rich and visible New York gay culture in the 1920s (Chauncey 335), the famed Bowery B'hoys of the 1840s attracted too much press in the eyes of the dominant culture and faced a subsequent backlash.

For instance, reporting on May 12, 1849, directly after the Astor Place Riots for *The Home Journal,* journalist N. P. Willis complains of the personal affronts men of "good society" had to endure at their hands: "If the English tragedian wishes to see the company that he offends, he has only to follow the well-dressed idler down the Bowery and observe the looks he gets from Mose and the soap-lockery as he goes along. . . . Let but the passive aristocratic party select a favorite, and let there be but a symptom of a handle for the B'hoys to express their dissent and the undercurrent breaks forth like an uncapped hydrant" (qtd. in Buckley 296). Not surprisingly, the negative feeling was mutual. A B'hoy character in popular novelist Ned Buntline's *The G'hals of New York* (1850) is seen railing in disgust against the Victorian lack of respect for his position in society. Complaining to his sister about their bad financial luck, their father having lost a substantial fortune, he is dumbfounded by the general lack of compassion they confront each day on the street: "Gas! Will our rich 'quaintances recognize us in our rags as they used to do when we were proud and dressed like them? Will they even speak to us? No! They turn from us as though they thought we were going to rob 'em; and if you meet 'em in the street, they turn their eyes another way and hurry past you as if you had the small pox, and they were afraid o' ketchin' it!" (16). Parodying the B'hoys' irreverence in *The B'hoys of New York* (1848), one of Buntline's characters, a newspaper editor self-styled as "THE B'hoy of New York," decides to change the title of a proposed article on lewd female exhibitionism from "SHAMEFUL" to "Chaste And Beautiful Representations Of Ancient Statuary" in order to, he vociferates, "Give the Puritans a dash!" (11–15).

Invoking these antebellum subalterns allows us to bring Crane's cryptically impressionistic images of Bowery culture into focus. American authors had certainly appropriated the characteristics of the B'hoys well before Crane. Both Melville and Whitman, for instance, discovered in the B'hoy a refreshingly American articulation. Indeed, the character Henry Jackson in Melville's *Redburn* is described as dressing like a Bowery B'hoy (Reynolds, *Beneath* 285), and Whitman biographers Gay Wilson Allen and David S. Reynolds have attributed many of the characteristics of Whitman's "I" in *Leaves of Grass* to the B'hoy. "[Whitman's] whole persona," Reynolds argues, "wicked rather than conventionally virtuous, free, smart, prone to slang and vigorous outbursts—reflects the B'hoy culture" (*Walt* 155). Nineteenth-century reviewers labeled Whitman the "Bowery B'hoy of Literature," and Whitman used "Mose Velsor," the name most commonly associated with the B'hoys in the popular press, as a pseudonym for many of his newspaper articles (Reynolds, *Walt* 105, 103). Whitman's choices characteristically disregarded the period's increasingly virulent modes of cultural discrimination.

As a protective rather than a purely egotistical measure on the part of the Victorian middle class, the dissemination of Victorian culture was enforced in all conceivable media. The most powerful aspect of Crane's Bowery writing in general, and *Maggie* in particular, is his ability to recognize this phenomenon in urban American culture. The results of a half-century's worth of cultural incorporation are transparent in Crane's characters and prose. Crane's fragmented style simulates the fragmented consciousness of Bowery dwellers at this point in the district's history. Though Crane's Jimmie is delivered to the audience as an urban Huckleberry Finn, if more violent in nature, his self-esteem is far less developed than it at first appears. His B'hoy-like mannerisms are heightened by his overcompensation in the face of cultural defeat. And the social arenas in which the characters interact demonstrate to what extent the culture at large is responsible.

In his sketch "An Experiment In Luxury" (1894), Crane cogently provides us with his take on cultural dissemination. While dining at his wealthy young friend's house, his narrator reflects on the derisive view of the very rich by the Christian middle class and their complementary condescension toward the very poor:

> Indicated in this light chatter about the dinner table there was an existence that was not at all what the youth had been taught to see. Theologians had for a long time told the poor man that riches did not bring happiness, and they had solemnly repeated this phrase until it had come to mean that misery was commensurate with dollars, that each wealthy man was inwardly a miserable wretch. And when a wail of despair or rage had come from the night of the slums *they had stuffed this epigram down the throat of he who cried out and told him that he was a lucky fellow. They did this because they feared.* (556, italics mine)

What is being taken to task here is the age-old custom of the church's designation of the poor as unfortunates and the rich as selfish, unhappy mongers. "'And, in the irritating, brutalizing, enslaving environment of their poverty,'" the narrator's friend insists, the poor "'are expected to solace themselves with these assurances . . .'" (549). The "youth," as the focalizer of the story is called, is surprised by how functional and happy the wealthy family is. Further, there is no inherent love for the poor in the espoused vision, he learns; the espousers are simply terrified of the "other half" confronting their situation on their own terms.

This parable suggests the Victorian fear of a consumer class with access to and control over any and all consumable products. If the Bowery culture as epitomized in the antebellum years was being drummed out of existence because of what Victorians perceived as the threatening nature of subcultural activity, the culture of the Gilded Age's nouveau riche is equally condemned.

The wealthy host in "An Experiment in Luxury" confidently sums up his position on the issue: "'it is impossible for me to believe that these things equalize themselves; that there are burrs under all rich cloaks and benefits in all ragged jackets, *and the preaching of it seems wicked to me*'" (549, italics mine). Both the B'hoys and the barons, in other words, were being demonized by the popular media of the time.

This cultural posturing and antagonism was a manifestation of the city's developing consumer culture, which Keith Gandal describes as providing "a sort of moral inspiration" (13) to slummers exploring the Bowery. For the Bowery population itself, however, acculturation served as a dampening force rather than a liberating one. In Pete's courtship of Maggie, for instance, he escorts her to a number of amusements that had burgeoned throughout the city to accommodate a growing body of consumers with increasingly standardized tastes. These include music halls, dance halls, theaters, dime museum freak shows, the Central Park Menagerie, and the Metropolitan Museum of Art. Crane's ironic observations of Victorian melodrama in particular, both toward the culture that creates it and the culture that buys into it, demonstrates that, in Miles Orvell's words, "if the stage is not 'realism' then by implication the novella *Maggie,* which tells these truths, is realism" (129). Crane portrays the theater as offering "an atmosphere of pleasure and prosperity," which "seemed to hang over the throng, born, perhaps, of good clothes and two hours in a place of forgetfulness" (70). As Maggie for the first time blissfully takes in the emollient scenes on stage, "no thoughts of the atmosphere of the collar and cuff factory came to her" (33). Happiness is thus equated with distractions and vicarious experience, a historical transformation that might be seen as the inception of the future culture of television, video games, and the Internet.

Throughout Crane presents Maggie's continual fall into the world of fantasy as a manifestation of cultural coercion. Maggie idealizes Pete, an actor in life who adheres to a bogus self-image of respectability. She is duped into trusting the facade. The fiction of the stage begins to distort the very reality it loosely represents, and the characters seem to comprehend each other only in melodramatic terms. When Maggie falls, her neighbors envision her as the Eve-like character that Crane designs her to be, and children "ogle her as if they formed the front row of a theatre" (65). Similarly, George Kelcey in Crane's second Bowery novella, *George's Mother* (1896), is overwhelmingly jealous of Maggie's attentions towards Pete, both of whom make appearances in the later novella. Like Pete, George aspires to be both Bowery tough and chivalric gentleman. And, like Maggie, George sees his beloved through the lens of popular drama. In his daydreams, George superimposes Maggie's form onto the mass-produced images of staged melodrama, and with a nod to the contributions of photography, he places the couple "in scenes which he took mainly from pictures[;] this vision conducted a courtship, strutting, posing, and lying through a drama which was magnificent from glow of purple" (236).

The standard venue for impressing young ladies on the Bowery was, indeed, the theater—and the paramount theatrical form in both *Maggie* and the New York it represents is the moral-reform drama. Initially developed by Moses Kimball and P. T. Barnum for museum theaters, moral-reform dramas were deliberately designed to address the needs of a middle class attentive to Protestant standards of decency (Butsch 383). If the theater had been a primarily working-class space in the opening decades of nineteenth-century New York, by the 1860s it drew a decidedly Victorian audience that determined its content and conduct. Middle-class values, as a result, were simultaneously acted out on the stage and absorbed by the audience. The consequent metamorphosis of theatrical space seems paradoxical in that consumption and respectability, previously oppositional paradigms (Butsch 375), were now inextricably intertwined. It is by showing how these oppositions play off of one another that Crane's work and its sociological contribution is brought into crystalline clarity. The mimetic nature of the exchange between buyer and seller, for instance, is made remarkably comprehensible. The central thematic irony of *Maggie* has been identified as "the self-righteous condemnation of a woman who is good by the very society responsible for her downfall" (Brennan 64), but there remains some question why this would be true historically. It is important to expose the origins and nature of this type of cultural dialectic, not just its manifestations, especially since foolish inconsistency seems to be the central aspect of Crane's *Maggie*.

Maggie Johnson is, among other things, used as a control in the Zolaesque experiment of looking at the New York popular theater as a means of understanding both the issue of class cultural consciousness and the popularized understanding of womanhood. For instance, each time Maggie exits the theater, she

> departed with raised spirits from the showing places of the melodrama. She rejoiced at the way in which the poor and virtuous eventually surmounted the wealthy and wicked. The theater made her think. She wondered if the culture and refinement she had seen imitated, perhaps grotesquely, by the heroine on the stage, could be acquired by a girl who lived in a tenement house and worked in a shirt factory. (37)

Crane is being ironic, perhaps even cruel here, in describing the exaltations of his heroine in this way, but his analysis of class aspiration nevertheless rings true. Most New Yorkers were complicit in this culture of conformity; they had been nurtured to accept "refinement" as the ultimate state of being. Contemplating her suitor, rendered pretentious by the narration, Maggie observes instead that he "was extremely gracious and attentive. He displayed the consideration of a cultured gentleman who knew what was due." In addition, she "perceived that Pete brought forth all his elegance and all his knowledge of high-class customs for her benefit. Her heart warmed as she reflected upon his condescension" (31). While she is dreamily imaging a fantasy constructed by a culture at odds with her own, Pete is, in one of the few truly funny scenes of the book, chivalrously badgering the wait staff: "'Say, what deh hell? Bring deh lady a big glass! What deh hell use is dat pony?'" (31).

The theater scenes in *Maggie* demonstrate with subtle accuracy the trend towards what Richard Butsch calls the "taming" of the Bowery theatergoer. In contrast to Whitman's lusty descriptions of early Bowery dramatic performances in which the audience and the players interacted to create one large performance that transcended the limits of the play itself, the theatergoers of Maggie's world give themselves fully to one-way, passive entertainment. Refinement in late Victorian New York had become the status quo in the theater, if it had not yet completely taken hold of the music hall. The mores imposed on Victorian women in the streets of New York—to avoid eye contact, to dress down so as not to attract attention, to maintain emotional self-control, and so on—were swiftly transferred to the theater. Emotive expressions such as anger and laughter were no longer tolerated. Often dress codes were established, and hissing, drinking, eating, arriving late, and leaving early were forbidden at most venues.

In short, the proliferation of middle-class etiquette effectively "feminized" the theater, concurrently making it a feminine space while rejecting the fervent audience participation that had attracted its original audience. Proprietors increasingly changed the atmosphere of their venues to accommodate this new cult of middle-class female respectability, and they quickly came to understand that women, as Ann Douglas has argued, had gained supremacy over consumer culture (7). In 1866, for example, *The Spirit Of The Times,* a gentleman's magazine, complained that many men succumbed to the "bore of attending dull or even good performances for the sole purpose of escorting their Mary Janes" (qtd. in Butsch 392–93). Walt Whitman, in his nostalgic essay "The Old Bowery," poetically, though perhaps too sentimentally, mourns this refinement of the theater experience: "So much for the Thespian temple of New York fifty years since [the 1830s and 1840s], where 'sceptered tragedy went trailing by' under the gaze of the Dry Dock youth, and both players and auditors were of a character and like we shall never see again" (1216).

In Pete and Maggie's music hall as well, the reader is brilliantly introduced to the penetration of Bowery tastes by Victorian culture in the later decades of the nineteenth century. The crowd contains, Crane writes, all of "the nationalities of the Bowery," who "beamed upon the stage from all directions" (30). In the spirit of radical democracy, a singer appeals to the Irish workers in attendance by describing in one of her songs "a vision of Britain annihilated by America, and Ireland bursting her bonds." The climax of the performance is "The Star-Spangled Banner"; when the song begins, "instantly a great cheer swelled from the throats of this assemblage of the masses. There was a heavy rumble of booted feet thumping the floor. Eyes gleamed with sudden fire, and calloused hands waved frantically in the air" (32). Crane calls attention to this display of old Bowery behavior by smartly commencing with a dancer "attired in some half-dozen skirts," causing Maggie to wonder "at the splendor of the costume" and to lose herself "in calculations of the cost of the silks and laces" (31). For the finale of that part of the show, the dancer "fell into some of those grotesque attitudes which were at the time popular among the dancers in the theatres up-town, giving to the Bowery public the phantasies of the aristocratic theatre-going public, at reduced rates" (31–32). During all this, the audience is being attended to by little boys with "costumes of French chefs" selling "fancy cakes"[4] under gilded chandeliers, a spectacle substantiating the "vertiginous bridge of American confectionery" Henry James reports (30). Among the performers, a pair of girls listed as sisters—for rather obvious reasons of propriety—sing a duet "that," Crane ironically puts in, "is heard occasionally at concerts given under church auspices" while dancing in a way "which of course can never be seen at concerts given under church auspices" (32). The continuous and telling juxtapositions of old Bowery and new Victorian culture are thus served up to his readers just as Crane's boys in French chef hats serve up sweets to the fictional laborers.

Material consumption is not the only proselytizing mode we see in *Maggie*. In one scene involving a Protestant missionary, Crane brings the proverbial horse out from under the blanket. Jimmie Johnson is strolling past a mission church on the Bowery when he has an epiphany that calls to mind Stephen Dedalus on The Strand. The revelation is one that allows him to "clad his soul in armor." Inside the mission an evangelical preacher is sermonizing to a Bowery audience. In his sermon condemning sin, he addresses the crowd in "yous." It simply never occurs to him to use the first person plural. His grammar is, of course, restricted by the boundaries of permissible discourse. The sermonizer is a saved man and the audience damned because they have not yet been fully acculturated into what is perceived as the only tolerable cultural paradigm—the Victorian, the Christian, the respectable. The philosopher animadverts a system that has no viable alternative. Jimmie, however, feels that he personifies an alternative culture inconceivable to this minister and his flock. The dialectical nature of the episode is clear to Crane: "A reader of words of wind-demons might have been able to see the portions of a dialogue pass to and fro between the exhorter and the hearers" (20). Jimmie stands alone in this crowd, a minority oppositional voice.

Maggie Johnson, in turn, somewhat dislocated in the Bowery world, is a figure under the gaze of her tenement's "philosophers," characters Crane assigns to deliberate over the nature of their condition. The young Maggie's initial deferment of Bowery behavior stumps them: "none of the dirt of Rum Alley seemed to be in her veins. The philosophers, up-stairs, down-stairs, and on the same floor, puzzled over it" (24). How is it, they ask themselves, that a girl born and raised on the Bowery could have escaped the then perceived stigma of Bowery existence? In many ways, this is the most self-reflexive point in the book. Crane himself is directly questioning his own motives for making Maggie such an anomaly. The novella, though singled out by many critics as the most artfully constructed Bowery tale ever written because of its combined expressionistic and realistic aspects, provides an acceptable heroine for mass consumption. Had the heroine been the more G'hal-like Nell, the street-smart but ultimately loathsome friend of Pete's, no one would have read her death as tragic; in fact, few middle-class readers would have bought the book at all.

Crane makes the final scene of Maggie's degradation palatable to his audience—the middle-class reader—by recycling the tragic circumstances of a girl who blossoms in a mud puddle, then meets a fateful death. In the 1893 edition, Maggie is killed by her client, a "huge fat man in torn and greasy garments" who "laughed, his brown, disordered teeth gleaming under a grey, grizzled mustache from which beer-drops dripped" (72). The grotesque man follows her until they stand together: "At their feet the river appeared a deathly black hue" (72). In the D. Appleton edition, which appeared three years later, Crane suggests that Maggie commits suicide, a trope of the Victorian melodrama: "She went into the blackness of the final block. . . . At the feet of the tall buildings appeared the deathly black hue of the river" (144). He made these changes to appease his more respectable readership, to expose the hypocrisy of the Bowery characters, and because he himself was equivocating. By having Maggie commit suicide, Crane could both punish her as a fallen woman and allow her to achieve redemption by contrition, thereby allowing the book to end on a sentimental note. Additionally, because Richard Watson Gilder, the editor of *Century Magazine,* was appalled by the dialogue in Crane's first *Maggie,* for the 1896 edition, D. Appleton and Company subsequently forced Crane to edit out all of its unseemly language before they would agree to publish it (Wertheim iv). Crane submitted to constant concessions of this kind throughout his career, as did many writers defer to the moral standard of the Victorian world of publishing. The book market was not dissimilar, then, to the theater in regard to censorship and gentrification.[5]

The son of a Methodist minister, Crane himself held contradictory views on the dogma of "respectability." He was especially ambivalent about prostitution: he had not, for instance, pressed charges on Doris Watts, a prostitute who tried to blackmail him; he testified in court on behalf of Dora Clark, a prostitute who was arrested in his company; and he probably married Cora Stewart, a seasoned madam. But, as Laura Hapke asserts, "Crane never resolved his ambivalence about the unchaste woman, a tension between idealization and condemnation which his work on prostitution embodies" (67). Crane could not fully accept, or fully deny, that a prostitute could survive society's imposed and enforced judgments. Nevertheless, he himself propagated the cultural construct that he openly rejected.

The overwhelming force of the sentimental and the respectable unleashed in the novella are not only the product of determining institutions—the church, the family, and the community—but the grotesque imposition of middle-class mores onto the slum's inhabitants. No other aspect of the novella is as much a testament to Crane's genius. Each of the primary characters in the novella contributes to Maggie's fall. Each takes the side of popular morality over familial and neighborhood ties. In one scene, even Jimmie consciously broods over whether or not to forsake his sister in favor of his position in society:

> Of course [he] publicly damned his sister that he might appear on a higher social plane. But, arguing with himself, stumbling about in ways that he knew not, he, once, almost came to a conclusion that his sister would have been more firmly good *had she better known why.* However, he felt that he could not hold such a view. He threw it hastily aside. (57, italics mine)

In a similarly self-reflexive moment, it "occurred to him to vaguely wonder, for an instant, if some of the women of his acquaintance had brothers" (43). Jimmie does not forgive or help his sister when she turns to prostitution, but he is incapable of explaining to himself why. Indeed, his actions run counter to his own constructed identity. His Bowery self is clearly weaker than the identity that has been constructed for him by the "well-dressed men . . . of untarnished clothes" he so ardently deplores (21).

A brief glance at *George's Mother* provides us with another telling example of this process of cultural discrimination and assent. The book, a kind of chronologically contiguous sequel to *Maggie,* is a study of a young man from the country who is caught between three major cultural strains on the boulevard. One is his mother's moralistic devotion to the church and her constant appeals to him to attend mass with her; another is the alluring but violent and drunken life of the street and the friendships he rapidly acquires there; the last is a group of older drinkers who have Victorian aspirations but are far too dissipated to achieve respectability. All are essentially conformist alternatives. No one social group satisfies George, who longs to fit in but despairs when the options are presented to him. Crane explicitly reveals George's reluctance to join his mother at the local church: "In his ears was the sound of a hymn, made by people who tilted their heads at a prescribed angle of devotion. It would be too apparent that they were all better than he. When he entered they would turn their heads and regard him with suspicion. This would be an enormous aggravation, since he was certain that he was as good as they" (224). His actual uncertainty on this point is made clear in the unconscious slip in the second sentence. That is, he is unconvinced of his own equal standing with those he criticizes. Maggie faces a similar dilemma when she attends the theater. In fact, virtually all of Crane's major characters question their personal standing when they enter the various theaters of social construction.

Maggie's almost last word in the novella is the enigmatic utterance "Who?," a question that remains, at least superficially, unanswered in the text. To address that question, I will again draw from T. J. Jackson Lears who writes as follows:

> To resort to the concept of cultural hegemony is to take a banal question—"who has power?"—and deepen it at both ends. The "who" includes parents, preachers, teachers, journalists, literati, "experts" of all sorts, as well as advertising executives, entertainment promoters, popular musicians, sports figures, and "celebrities" —all of whom are involved (albeit often unwillingly) in shaping the values and attitudes of society. (572)

For Henry James, this exchange was realized in the popular theater he visited but not limited to it. James thinks of the "odd scene [at the theater] as still enacted in many places and many ways, the inevitable rough union in discord of the two groups of instincts, the fusion of the two camps by a queer, clumsy, wasteful social chemistry" (199).

This "wasteful social chemistry" brewed in New York as a result of the governing society's desire to bridle the effects of rampageous urban expansion. Unlike many European cities, New York in the nineteenth century promoted itself as a city free from economic class distinctions. In some ways I believe this was true and that the actual conflict was fought over cultural legitimacy and representation. Though Victorian and Bowery culture may have coexisted for a time in New York, Victorianism rapidly came to determine the values, sentiments, and prejudices of civil society on the Bowery, as well as throughout the city. If we accept Alfred Kazin's assertion that "the surest thing one can say about Crane is that he cared not a jot which way the world went" (68), it is equally true, as Hamlin Garland acknowledges, that Crane's *Maggie* "grew out of intimate association with the poor" (2). Describing Jimmie Johnson, Crane cuts a figure not unlike his own: "On the corners he was in life and of life. The world was going on and he was there to perceive it" (20). The Bowery which Crane presents so powerfully in *Maggie* is one that draws from a very real historical process: the modernization of slum dwellers whose cultural consciousnesses—specifically in regard to Bowery culture as it survived over the decades—conflicted with and were ultimately determined by nineteenth-century American Victorianism.

NOTES

1. I admit that "Victorian" is a highly unstable category, but I do not want the argument here to be obfuscated by semantics. I am using the term "Victorian" to identify the culture of middle- to upper-middle-class American Protestant moralism that manifested itself in a cult of "respectability" in the middle of the late nineteenth century.
2. "Mercheen" is Bowery dialect for a fire engine.
3. All references to Crane's work refer to the Library of America edition, unless otherwise noted in the citation. The "oiled bang" and "red scarf" constituted a fashion statement remarkably similar to the B'hoys' "soaplocks," long locks of hair that hung in front of their ears and were slicked down with bear grease or soap, and their penchant for wearing red shirts and scarves.
4. Butsch reports that "the indulgent nature of matinees and 'cream cakes' distinguished it from the museum theater as a 'woman's place' and indicated that it was an early facet of the culture of consumption" (390).
5. Significantly, the graphically violent, sexual, politically dissident, and wildly popular novels of the so-called "city mysteries" group of the 1840s and 1850s, led by George Lippard, Ned Buntline, John Vose, and George Thompson, among many others, have no substantial corollaries in the 1890s.

WORKS CITED

Benfey, Christopher. *The Double Life of Stephen Crane: A Biography.* New York: Alfred A. Knopf, 1992.

Brennan, Joseph X. "Ironic and Symbolic Structure in Crane's *Maggie.*" *Maggie: A Girl of the Streets.* By Stephen Crane. Ed. Thomas A. Gullason. New York: Norton, 1979. 173–84.

Brown, Allston T. *A History of the New York Stage: From the First Performance in 1732 to 1901.* 1903. Vol. 1. New York: Benjamin Blom, 1964.

Buckley, Peter George. "To the Opera House: Culture and Society in New York City, 1820–1860." Diss. SUNY–Stony Brook, 1984.

Buntline, Ned. *The B'hoys of New York.* New York: Dick and Fitzgerald, 1848.

———. *The G'hals of New York.* New York: Dewitt and Davenport, 1850.

Butsch, Richard. "Bowery B'hoys and Matinee Ladies: The Re-Gendering of Nineteenth-Century American Theater Audiences." *American Quarterly* 46.3 (Sept. 1994): 374–405.

Chauncey, George. *Gay New York: Gender, Urban Culture, and the Making of the Gay Male World, 1890–1940.* New York: Basic Books, 1994.

Crane, Stephen. *Crane: Prose and Poetry.* Ed. J. C. Levenson. New York: Library of America, 1984.

———. "An Experiment in Luxury." 1894. Crane, *Crane: Prose and Poetry* 549–57.

———. *George's Mother.* 1896. Crane, *Crane: Prose and Poetry* 213–77.

———. *Maggie: A Girl of the Streets.* 1893. Crane, *Crane: Prose and Poetry* 5–78.

———. *Maggie: A Girl of the Streets.* New York: D. Appleton, 1896.

Douglas, Ann. *The Feminization of American Culture.* 1977. New York: Avon, 1978.

Gandal, Keith. *The Virtues of the Vicious: Jacob Riis, Stephen Crane, and the Spectacle of the Slum.* New York: Oxford UP, 1997.

Garland, Hamlin. Manuscript note concerning Stephen Crane's *Maggie.* Signed and undated. Two pages. Berg Collection of English and American Literature. New York Public Library. Astor, Lennox, and Tilden Foundation.

Hapke, Laura. *Girls Who Went Wrong: Prostitutes in American Fiction, 1885–1917.* Bowling Green: Bowling Green State U Popular P, 1989.

Howells, W. D. *Criticism and Fiction and Other Essays.* New York: New York UP, 1959.

———. "New York Low Life in Fiction." 1896. Rpt. in *Maggie: A Girl of the Streets,* by Stephen Crane. Ed. Thomas A. Gullason. New York: Norton, 1979. 154–55.

James, Henry. *The American Scene.* 1907. Bloomington: Indiana UP, 1968.

Kazin, Alfred. *On Native Grounds: An Interpretation of Modern American Prose Literature.* 1942. New York: Harcourt Brace, 1995.

Lears, T. J. Jackson. "The Concept of Cultural Hegemony: Problems and Possibilities." *American Historical Review* 90 (June 1985): 567–93.

Orvell, Miles. *The Real Thing: Imitation and Authenticity in American Culture, 1880–1940.* Chapel Hill: U of North Carolina P, 1989.

Reynolds, David S. *Beneath the American Renaissance: The Subversive Imagination in the Age of Emerson and Melville.* 1988. Cambridge: Harvard UP, 1995.

———. *Walt Whitman's America: A Cultural Biography.* 1995. New York: Vintage, 1996.

Wertheim, Stanley, ed. *The Merrill Studies in* Maggie *and* George's Mother. Columbus: Charles E. Merrill, 1970.

Whitman, Walt. *Poetry and Prose.* Ed. Justin Kaplan. New York: Library of America, 1996.

Is There a Doctor in the House?

NORRIS'S NATURALIST GAZE OF CLINICAL
OBSERVATION IN *McTEAGUE*

—*Daniel Schierenbeck*

T WO DISTINCT TRENDS IN *McTEAGUE* CRITICISM HAVE DEVELOPED OVER
THE LAST fiFTY YEARS: ON THE ONE HAND, ONE STRAND OF CRITICISM
stresses the naturalism of *McTeague* and points out how this novel exemplifies
certain characteristics of that literary movement; on the other hand, the opposite strand of criticism stresses the aesthetics and form of *McTeague* and
chooses to avoid reading this novel in a naturalist frame.[1] I would argue, however, that in striving for dominance in this critical conversation—in trying to
establish an exclusionary discourse of *McTeague* criticism—many critics have
overlooked points of synthesis between the naturalism of *McTeague* and its
aesthetics and form. One point of synthesis that I will highlight is the function of the gaze in *McTeague*. Using Foucault's analysis of the clinical gaze
from *The Birth of the Clinic* and linking it to his theories of discourse, I will
explore how *McTeague* may be read as a representation of Frank Norris's attitudes toward professional authorship, naturalism, and nativism.[2] By analyzing Norris's use of the naturalist gaze of clinical observation, I contend that
McTeague not only highlights the privileged position of the naturalist author,
but it also portrays the normative vision of this position, which projects immigrant Americans as sites of abnormality and disease whose removal from the
labor force of society then becomes naturalized.

Norris's attitude toward professionalism can be seen as early as his application to Harvard, wherein he pronounced his aim "to be thoroughly prepared
for a literary profession" (qtd. in Heddendorf 680). As David Heddendorf
points out, this view of professionalism was enhanced by his working with
L. E. Gates: "Writing under the instructional critic of this kind, Norris fed
convictions that would mark his own criticism a few years later" (680). Part of
Norris's concern with professional authorship stems from his recognition of
the power of that position: "He who can address a hundred thousand people
is, no matter what he may be, in an important position" (88).[3] Norris also views
the novel as "one of the most important factors of modern life" (96), and since

the novel has this powerful presence, he argues that people "turn to him [the novelist] the moment he speaks, and what he says they believe" (96). Furthermore, as Norris argues, "because it [the novel] is so all-powerful to-day, the people turn to him who wields this instrument with every degree of confidence" (95). Even as he recognizes the authority of the professional author, however, Norris also expresses his fear about a lack of proper training for authors. For example, in "Novelists of the Future: The Training They Need," he contends that novelists "go fumbling and stumbling along in this undisciplined fashion, governed by no rule, observing no formula, setting themselves no equation to solve" (11).

This recognition of the importance of the authority of the professional author and the concern with how that authority could be regulated is also registered in Norris's aesthetics. At this time in American culture, Burton Bledstein argues, "words rather than face-to-face or direct human contact became the favorite medium of social exchange" (65). Bledstein notes that "a riot of words and a crisis of confidence alarmed a society which began placing its faith in professional persons. . . . Legitimate authority now resided in special spaces, like the courtroom, the classroom, and the hospital; and it resided in special words shared only by experts" (78–79). Norris seems to recognize the import of this crisis of words, and so his naturalist aesthetics are informed by a desire to professionalize, and thus legitimize, authorship by turning to the expert language of science and medicine.[4] Indeed, as Bledstein points out, professionals often appealed to science for their authority (83), and their appeal to that authority, along with the impressive instruments of their specialization, helped them to seem a trustworthy, institutionalized group. It is also significant that in developing his naturalist aesthetic, which in turn establishes the claim to professional authorship, Norris particularly relies on the clinical scientific gaze.[5] For example, he declares that the true writer of historical fiction "will see the . . . man beneath the clothes, and the heart beneath both" (87). Norris felt that part of the inadequacy of realism was its surface observation: for him, the realist novel as an "instrument" (95) is a blunt tool that does not probe deeply enough. Therefore, in his "A Plea for Romantic Fiction," Norris argues for what he calls the power of true Romance: "Can we not see in it an instrument, keen, finely tempered, flawless—an instrument with which we may go straight through the clothes and tissues and wrappings of flesh down deep into the red, living heart of things?" (75). "To Romance," he claims, "belongs the wide world for range, and the unplumbed depth of the human heart, and the mystery of sex, and the problems of life, and the black, unsearched penetralia of the soul of man" (78). In his definition of professional authorship, Norris thus demands a scientific method which is accomplished through the probing nature of clinical observation.[6]

Norris's emphasis on clinical observation in his naturalist aesthetics, as well as their connection to his concern about the status of the author, can be traced in part to Émile Zola's "The Experimental Novel." In this essay, Zola founds his argument for the importance of the experimental method and its application to the novel on the work of the physiologist Claude Bernard. Zola uses a scientific treatise as a model because of the similarities he sees between literature and medicine: "What determined my choice, and made me choose 'L'Introduction' as my basis, was the fact that medicine, in the eyes of a great number of people, is still an art, as is the novel" (1). For Zola, the significance of Bernard's work is his fight against this perception of medicine as an art and his ability "to put medicine in a scientific path" (1). Zola contends that the same shift can be achieved for literature: "Since medicine, which was an art, is becoming science, why should not literature also become a science by means of the experimental method?" (18). The parallel work of the novelist and the doctor is emphasized throughout this essay, and he depends upon a facile substitution of each profession for the other to make this point: "It will often be but necessary for me to explain the word 'doctor' by the word 'novelist,' to make my meaning clear and to give it the rigidity of a scientific truth" (1). Thus, Zola does not simply draw a parallel between the work of the novelist and the doctor, but he also bolsters his arguments about literature by instantiating them within a scientific discourse. Accordingly, he writes, "I intend on all points to intrench myself behind Claude Bernard" (1). Zola also employs clinical metaphors, arguing that naturalist works "experiment on man" and "dissect piece by piece this human machinery" (14). This dissection is necessary for the doctor and the novelist to achieve the purpose of the experimental method: "to study phenomena in order to become their master" (13) and thus "to make one's self the master of life in order to be able to direct it" (14). Therefore, through the experimental method, the naturalist author accedes to the powerful position of being able "to be the master of good and evil, to regulate life, to regulate society" (15). Given the importance of Zola's influence on naturalist aesthetics in general, and on Norris in particular, it is not surprising, then, that in his own aesthetics Norris places a great deal of emphasis on the clinical gaze, for observation and experiment are the hallmarks of the experimental method.

The similarities between the doctor and the novelist and the concerns about how these professions may be viewed also suggest the ways in which Foucault theorizes the relationships between medicine, professionalism, and the gaze in *The Birth of the Clinic*. Foucault's analysis opens up the possibility of seeing the clinical gaze in Norris's aesthetics as more than just a literary inheritance from Zola; indeed, it allows us to see the discursive relations between medicine, professionalism, and literature as well as the importance of the power of the gaze to the establishment of a discursive practice.[7] An especially relevant chapter in Foucault's work is "The Lessons of the Hospital," in which he examines the dispute over the control of the discourse of medicine between university faculties and the Royal Society in late-eighteenth-century France. As Foucault points out, after the French Revolution, leaders in France tried to open up medicine as a free practice, hoping that by virtue of this free competition "quacks would disappear" (72). Eventually, the medical societies were successful in establishing standards of professionalism, and the medical profession became "defined by qualifications and protected by laws" (73). Foucault analyzes the debates over the practice of medicine and finds the essential point of dispute: "all these discussions had . . . the merit of revealing what the real question was [—] . . . the very meaning of the medical profession and the privileged character of experience that it defines" (78). This "privileged character of experience" was defined in large part by the clinical gaze, for the major innovation of the medical profession that arose from these debates was the requirement of a clinical test in which a candidate would examine a patient from his bedside and would then expound upon the character of the species of the disease as well as its treatment. The result was a defining of the terms of medical professionalism with the use of the gaze. The clinical gaze was figured as "a gaze that was at the same time knowledge, that was master of its truth, and free of all example" (81). Thus, the professional doctor's speech (his *enonce*) is given power through its being imbedded in the enunciative modality of his profession. That is, the power of the doctor is institutionalized by the merit of the profession, which in turn is defined by the diagnostic gaze.

Foucault's account of this crisis in the medical profession in France and the resulting innovation of the clinical gaze bears a striking resemblance to Norris's concern over professionalization and his emphasis on clinical observation in carving out an aesthetic that defines professional authorship. Indeed, Norris's attitude toward the position of the professional author may be likened to Foucault's concept of the enunciative modality: just as the doctor speaks from a position of power with a particular discursive practice, so does the professional author. Through its use of anatomical metaphors, Norris's naturalist aesthetic presents the same probing gaze of the physician, and these metaphors resound with the superiority of the medical gaze that can search into the depths of the human body in order to find explanations for life. More-over, by using metaphors borrowed from scientific and medical analysis, Norris is able to establish more firmly the credentials for the literary profes-sional by positing them as already established by previously institutionalized discursive practices. Because of the enhanced power of this position, however, Norris, like the medical faculties in Foucault's account, seeks to exclude those who are not properly trained. I would suggest, then, that Norris's aesthetics similarly fashion an exclusionary discourse, which is also limited to those who employ the clinical gaze. Further, Norris's fascination with light and darkness in his aesthetics also reveals significant characteristics of another type of gaze. In "The Eye of Power," Foucault describes the gaze of the Rousseauian dream: "It was the dream of a transparent society, visible and legible in each of its parts, the dream of there no longer existing any zones of darkness" (152). How-ever, this dream of a transparent society, of a gaze that gives light to everything, has also within it the seeds of the Benthamite Panopticon; Norris's gaze can thus also be seen as a will to power and knowledge.[8]

It is telling that many of the issues that are reflected in Norris's critical essays are also dramatized in *McTeague*. As Heddendorf points out, "McTeague's particular social status raises the issue of professionalism in this novel and in Norris's self-image as an author" (678). McTeague, the false den-tist, can be seen as an example of someone who practices a profession without the requisite knowledge or training. In our first glimpse of McTeague's office, we can see that he has all the trappings of the profession. He decorates his "Dental Parlors" with signs of his profession such as the "back numbers of 'The American System of Dentistry'" (6–7) and "the seven volumes of 'Allen's Practical Dentist'" (7).[9] Though McTeague has the ornaments of profession-alism, his training (or lack thereof) and his actions reveal that he is unqualified as a professional. We learn early on that McTeague's mother was "filled with the one idea of having her son rise in life and enter a profession" (5–6), and when a traveling dentist stopped by, she found her opportunity. Norris goes on to describe the haphazard method of McTeague's training: "He had learnt it after a fashion, mostly by watching the charlatan operate. He had read many of the necessary books, but he was too hopelessly stupid to get much benefit from them" (6). Here, not only does Norris emphasize McTeague's stupidity, but he also demonstrates that McTeague did not complete the institu-tionalized training required of a professional and so through him suggests "the threat of incompetence that professionalism seeks to exclude" (Heddendorf 680). Though Norris may not, echoing Zola, be arguing for a substitution of the "dentist" with the "novelist," given the important conjunctions among medicine, literature, and professionalism for Norris, the description of McTeague and his lack of training appears strikingly similar to Norris's characterization of other novelists whose methods he disparages. Though they attempt to practice within the field of professional authorship and have all the trappings of a professional author, they also lack the requisite training and methods and thus should be excluded from their profession.[10]

Not only does McTeague lack the training necessary to becoming a professional, but he also lacks the requisite clinical/scientific gaze that defines professionalism in medicine (as well as in naturalist fiction). For instance, as McTeague tries to apply a clinical gaze to his patient Trina, Norris demonstrates McTeague's inability to identify and articulate a medical diagnosis. McTeague's observations are hedged with probability; he cannot come up with a firm diagnosis but must settle twice for prefacing his response with a shaky "I guess" (18). A further indication of his lack of the professional/clinical gaze occurs after he puts Trina under. Once she is unconscious, McTeague's gaze is not one of scientific knowledge and analysis, but it becomes a perverse gaze. McTeague in this instance becomes the grotesque epitome of the pretender who does not have a professional gaze, the one who clearly represents the dangers of an unqualified professional.

The many different descriptions in the novel of McTeague gazing stupidly help to cement the impression of McTeague as one who may apprehend the visible but is unable to analyze it scientifically or to express it well. In *Birth of the Clinic,* Foucault argues that one important element of clinical observation was the ability to translate the visible form of disease into language—the combination of "visible symptomatology" (112) and "verbal analysis" (112). McTeague is first of all apparently incapable of a correct analytical scientific gaze. That is, he is repeatedly described as having "gazed" or "gazing stupidly" (51, 56), "looking stupidly" (84, 133, 150, 154), "gazing vaguely" (133), or as possessing an "unseeing gaze" (150) or an "ox-like gaze" (213). Like the realist authors Norris disliked, McTeague "never questioned himself, never looked for motives, never went to the bottom of things" (108, see also 187). McTeague is also unable to formulate his thoughts in language. In fact, one of the striking weaknesses that McTeague demonstrates throughout the novel is his inability to grasp or master language. After Trina wins the lottery, we are told of McTeague that "speech failed him" (75); when Trina pleads for him to love her, "McTeague would stammer something, gasping, and wagging his head, beside himself for the lack of words" (79); when Marcus confronts him at the bar, "his lips moved, but he said no word" (82). Furthermore, at different points in the novel, other characters are able to bewilder and overcome McTeague merely with a plethora of words (116, 168, 187).

McTeague's lack of a professional/medical gaze along with his linguistic limitations indeed constitutes one of the reasons for his downfall. His emergence as a professional, since it was not embedded in the discursive practice of the medical profession, was built on tenuous grounds. Heddendorf sees *McTeague* as an ambivalent criticism of professionalism; for him, "the baleful significance that the gold tooth comes to have in the novel corresponds to Norris's own misgivings about professionalism" (683). However, by examining *McTeague* within the framework of Norris's critical essays and the concept of the professional/medical gaze, I would argue that Norris instead consistently shows the dangers of pretending to be a professional without the requisite training and knowledge. McTeague is a lower-class type who tries unsuccessfully to instantiate himself within the position of the medical field; however, we can see that any *enonce* that McTeague utters is imbedded in a false enunciative modality. Similarly, in Norris's view, any who present themselves as speaking from the site of professional authorship, of discursive mastery, but who do not meet the requisites of the scientific gaze must be regarded with caution and in some cases even be excluded from this practice.

This notion of professionalism and the responsibilities of authorship is also demonstrated through the minor characters of this novel. Marcus Schouler is a person who, like McTeague, is "a bungler" (11), in his case in his profession of dog surgery. His training is similar to McTeague's: "Marcus's knowledge of the diseases of domestic animals had been picked up in a haphazard way, much after the manner of McTeague's education" (11). Marcus is also a pretender in other ways, for he "was continually making use of the stock phrases of the professional politician" (12), though he is not himself a professional politician. Like McTeague, he repeatedly wants the authority of professionalism without going through the requisite training, going so far as to dream "of a cowboy's life and [seeing] himself in an entrancing vision involving silver spurs and untamed broncos" (100). Later, he realizes to some degree this "former vision of himself" (236) and actually becomes a rough type of cowboy, but when he tries to act as a professional law enforcer, the ideal westerner, he dies in the desert. Marcus's favorite expression is "outa sight" (32, 40, 70), and this expression may serve in important ways to explain his death. Marcus tries to attain professional status merely by envisioning himself in a position of authority, but without proper training, without proper insight, he is quickly rendered "out of sight." He is another member of the non-professional class finally excluded because of his inadequacies from the position of authority of professionalism.

Maria and Zerkow and Grannis and Miss Baker also act out the danger of placing authorship in the wrong hands.[11] As Donna Campbell notes, Maria

Macapa, with her stories of the gold dishes, may be the "most notable story-teller" (45) in *McTeague*. Maria thus acts in the position of author when she repeats her description of the gold plate several times throughout the novel (30, 39, 74–75). Her "accurate" and "almost eloquent" (30) narration causes Zerkow to imagine vividly the gold plate: "he fancied he could see that wonderful plate before him, there on the table, under his eyes, under his hand, ponderous, massive, gleaming" (75). Eventually, this "recital had become a veritable mania with him" (75), and this "hallucination" (136) eventually leads to both Maria's and Zerkow's deaths. Maria does seem to possess something of the naturalist gaze of accuracy and detail; however, she does not aspire to the responsibility of a professional. Campbell argues that "Maria's sordid death suggests the destructive powers of imagination, both in her concocting the story and in Zerkow's believing it" (45). I would add that by presenting this story over and over again to "the eye of his [Zerkow's] perverted mind" (136), Maria simply does not function adequately as a responsible professional novelist in that the story controls her and not she it. Again we see the power of fiction and possibly the dangers of listening to a naive author.

Finally, Miss Baker also creates fictions—in her case, about Grannis. She imagines him as "the younger son of a baronet" (14), and the absurdity of this fiction is quickly pointed out by the narrator: "It was preposterous to imagine any mystery connected with Old Grannis. Miss Baker had chosen to invent this little fiction, had created the title and the unjust stepfather from some dim memories of the novels of her girlhood" (14). Though her fictions do not lead to any particular disaster for the couple, they do serve a point. Throughout most of the novel, Grannis and Miss Baker continually avoid the gaze of face-to-face contact. Even when they are brought together—and it "seemed as if a malicious fate persisted in bringing the two old people face to face at the most inopportune moments" (123)—they are always "avoiding each other's gaze" (69). Grannis and Miss Baker learn about each other through observation, but it is only partial; they keep their doors cracked for some semblance of observation, but their vision is necessarily fleeting. Further, their romance is twice described as "the long retarded romance of their commonplace and uneventful lives" (99, 182). By portraying their superficial observation, their non-naturalist gaze, and by describing their romance as "commonplace and uneventful," Norris clearly links the authorship of Grannis and Miss Baker in terms of their banal romance with the mundane realists' project, for he also describes the Howellsian realist novel as "the commonplace tale of commonplace people" (71). Ultimately, Grannis and Miss Baker, realist novelists of their own lives, fade away because they do not possess the naturalist gaze necessary to the professional field of authorship Norris prizes and in which he hopes to dominate.[12]

Though *McTeague* may be read as reflecting Norris's attitudes concerning professional authorship as a necessarily exclusionary discursive practice, of greater significance is the way in which the use of the gaze allows Norris to give nativist claims greater authority by connecting them to the discourse of professionalization. By investing his naturalist gaze with an emphasis on scientific description and analysis, as well as by positing that type of description and analysis as a necessary professional tool, Norris's naturalist gaze assumes a great normative power. Reading Norris further in terms of Foucault's analysis, I would argue that through its focus on observation and diagnosis, Norris's naturalistic gaze objectifies its characters as sites of disease and abnormality and creates a normative structure which can support a nativist structure of thought.

One important problem that Foucault raises concerning the use of clinical observation is its objectification of the subject of the gaze. Indeed, Foucault observes that this objectification is "the most important moral problem" (83) that is raised by clinical observation. He asks, "by what right can one transform into an object of clinical observation a patient whose poverty has compelled him to seek assistance at the hospital?" (83). With the sanctioning of clinical observation, the patient "was now required to be the object of a gaze, indeed a relative object, since what was being deciphered in him was seen as contributing to a better knowledge of others" (83). Under the clinical gaze of medicine, the patient becomes an object—specifically an object that is important only for its demonstration of a particular disease. As Foucault points out, "If one wishes to know the illness from which he is suffering, one must subtract the individual" (14). Though the institution of medicine may have democratic aims behind it, at the same time the power it enacts through its clinical gaze helps turn it into an institutional power that objectifies its subjects and so proves itself profoundly undemocratic.

Since the clinical gaze reveals the disease by objectifying the subject, such a gaze is also invested with the normative powers granted to the profession of medicine itself. Foucault notes this important shift in the medical agenda:

> Medicine must no longer be confined to a body of techniques for curing ills and of the knowledge they require; it will also embrace a knowledge of *healthy man*, that is, a study of *non-sick* man and a definition of the *model man*. In the ordering of human existence it

> assumes a normative posture, which authorizes it not only to dis-
> tribute advice as to healthy life, but also to dictate the standards
> for physical and moral relations of the individual and of the soci-
> ety in which he lives. (34)

According to Foucault, "the prestige of the sciences of life in the nineteenth century, their role as model, especially in the human sciences, is linked originally
not with the comprehensive transferable character of biological concepts, but,
rather, with the fact that these concepts were arranged in a space whose profound structure responded to the healthy/morbid opposition" (35). Thus, what
results is the binary of the normal and the pathological: the definition of health
and normality is defined through its opposition to the diseased and pathological.[13] In "The Politics of Health in the Eighteenth Century," Foucault points
out that the basis of this transformation in medicine "has to do with the preservation, upkeep, and conservation of the 'labour force'" (171). The prospect of a
body being healthy or unhealthy, normal or pathological, draws a distinction in
the labor force "between the more or less utilisable, those more or less amenable
to profitable investment . . . and with more or less capacity for being usefully
trained" (172). Therefore, Foucault concludes, "the biological traits of a population become relevant factors for economic management, and it becomes necessary to organise around them an apparatus which will ensure not only their
subjection but the constant increase of their utility" (172). The apparatus of the
clinical gaze thus becomes important as a means of social control rather than
just a reflection of concern for public health.

The gaze of Norris's naturalism, like the gaze of clinical observation,
structures a discourse of healthy/morbid opposition, for part of Norris's aesthetic is the focus of his naturalistic gaze on the abnormal. Recall that he admires
"Romance" more than realism, and "Romance" "is the kind of fiction that
takes cognizance of variations from the type of normal life" (76), while "Realism is the kind of fiction that confines itself to the type of normal life" (76). In
"Zola as a Romantic Writer," Norris argues in perhaps his most often-cited
passage this radically particular focus of the naturalistic gaze: "The naturalist
takes no note of common people, common in so far as their interests, their
lives, and the things that occur in them are common, are ordinary. Terrible
things must happen to the characters of the naturalistic tale. They must be
twisted from the ordinary, wrenched out from the quiet, uneventful round of
every-day life, and flung into the throes of a vast and terrible drama that works
itself out in unleashed passions, in blood and in sudden death" (71–72). Though
Norris claims a belief in democratic fiction (the Rousseauian dream of the

light-giving gaze), he nevertheless focuses on the lower classes as objects that are important primarily for their exhibition of a particular disease or abnormality. By concentrating on the uncommon, the diseased members of society, Norris's naturalistic gaze then becomes a normalizing force; he is able to define normality by representing to us abnormality in *McTeague,* these observations backed by the authority of his professionalism.

For example, in *McTeague,* the gaze of Norris's naturalism presents the primary characters of the novel through excessive external and physical description, which focus continually objectifies the characters and presents them as abnormal. From the beginning description of McTeague, for instance, we are shown his "monstrosity": Norris describes McTeague as a "young giant" with a "huge shock of blond hair" and "immense limbs" (6). He goes on to describe his "enormous" hands (6), which Norris often links to "wooden mallets" (6), and his head as "square-cut, angular" (6), his jaw as "salient, like that of the carnivora" (6). At once, the narrative gaze focuses on McTeague's abnormality, his grotesque body, which is matched with a "stupid" (6) mind. Norris then reiterates these descriptions in order to strengthen our perception of McTeague as something abnormal (106). Trina, in contrast to the giant McTeague, is described in terms of extreme diminution. She is "very small and prettily made" (17), though she is invested with overly luxurious hair, which Jennifer Boyd argues may be evidence of Norris's characterization of her "as the *femme fatale*" (53). When we see these two characters through the narrative gaze, however, we can almost at once diagnose them as sites of disease and the pathological. While Miss Baker exclaims in a positive manner "What a pair!" (69), with our trained eyes (or eyes trained by the narrator) we can see the ignorance behind her statement and can prognosticate the fatal consequences. The clinical observation of Norris's naturalism places the reader not in the position of a judge hearing a case but in that of a doctor (or social architect) who is forced to diagnose and treat unhealthy and pathological lives.[14]

Besides presenting excessive and repetitive external description of the primary characters, Norris also restricts the amount of psychological motivation in his characters, which action again helps to objectify them as sites of disease and abnormality. Oftentimes throughout the novel, when we expect some psychological explanation of a character's actions, we instead encounter a series of diagnostic questions. For example, after McTeague's battle with the brute within and his "sexualization" of Trina, we find this passage: "Why could he not always love her purely, cleanly? What was this perverse vicious thing that lived within him, knitted to his flesh?" (22). Likewise, after Trina kisses McTeague, the narrator presents rhetorical questions rather than offering psychological analysis: "Did she love McTeague? Difficult question. Did she choose him for better or for worse, deliberately, of her own free will, or was Trina herself allowed even a choice in the taking of that step that was to mar her life?" (53). Examples of this type of narrative method run throughout *McTeague* (see 65, 83–84, 93, 95, 103, 185, 215). By failing to give the reader a full vision into any one character's motivations, feelings, and thoughts, the narrative gaze limits our vision to the symptoms of disease in each character's case, from which presentation we are to draw our conclusions. The focus on external description and the diagnostic promptings of these rhetorical questions highlight the objectification of these characters and the responsibility of the reader to find the correct diagnosis for the characters' disease(s): we are not looking for an explanation for the characters' actions in their psychology except insofar as we can define their disease and abnormality.

A final way that Norris's narrative method objectifies its characters and projects them as interesting only in terms of their diseases is through the enforced spectatorship to which he subjects them. The narrative action always points out the windows in each of the dwellings in which McTeague and Trina live. Boyd argues that the descriptions of the ever smaller residences mirror their "social and moral degeneration" and that Trina and McTeague's lack of space "not only reflects character, it also defines it" (45). I would add that the windows throughout *McTeague* create what June Howard calls "recurrent images of blocked action and enforced spectatorship" (114). For example, as the narrator tells us, "Day after day, McTeague saw the same panorama unroll itself. The bay window of his 'Dental Parlors' was for him a point of vantage from which he watched the world go past" (9). McTeague later shares this view with Trina (141), and Trina also gazes out the window by herself (104). As Ron Mottram argues, "the image of the member of an audience watching an unrolling panorama or an unrolling strip of film, unable to change its course or to stop it, is appropriate to Norris's conception of the world and is represented in McTeague standing at the window" (578). However, the window also serves as a point of separation; McTeague, and to some extent Trina, is able to look out the window, but since he is immobilized, he becomes objectified.[15] That is, the bay window is also looked into throughout *McTeague,* not least of all, figuratively, by the reader. Before McTeague and Trina are married, Trina glances upward at McTeague through the window (92–93). This experience is so significant that later in the novel Trina recalls it in vivid detail (189–90). Trina and McTeague are also married in front of the bay window of the photographer's rooms (91). After they are married, Trina gazes into her own home: "At times she passed the flat and looked up at the windows in her home. . . . Occasionally in the windows of the 'Parlors' she beheld McTeague's rounded back as he bent to his work" (110). Norris's repetitive mention of Trina's looking up at the window helps to reinforce and re-assert the presence of the objective naturalist gaze and to contrast it with the view of the objects of this gaze. David Guest also notes that there are "a number of . . . scenes in which the narrator describes characters unaware of being observed" (39) and argues that this narrative method "facilitates diagnoses" and helps "reinforce our sense that the narrator is both objective and omniscient" (39). I would emphasize that when we see Trina gazing into windows at her husband, we are reminded of the diagnostic quality of the narrative gaze: Trina's limited view of McTeague and their abnormal life is juxtaposed with the objectifying description of the all-seeing and strangely controlling naturalist gaze.

Besides the objectification of its subjects through abundant physical description and a lack of psychological motivation, Norris's clinical gaze at times even gives us overt diagnoses of the characters' disease. For example, the narrator traces McTeague's actions to his genetic makeup. After he asks several questions about McTeague's actions toward Trina while she is in the dentist chair, the narrator gives us a diagnosis: "Below the fine fabric of all that was good in him ran the foul stream of hereditary evil, like a sewer. The vices and sins of his father and of his father's father, to the third and fourth and five hundredth generation, tainted him. The evil of an entire race flowed in his veins. Why should it be? He did not desire it. Was he to blame?" (22). Norris here clearly shows that his narrative method in this novel is not meant to explain the psychological motivations of McTeague but to present a case study of a "tainted" class of individuals. In the same manner, Norris describes Trina's case study in terms of heredity: "A good deal of peasant blood still ran undiluted in her veins, and she had all the instinct of a hardy and penurious mountain race—the instinct which saves without idea of consequence—saving for the sake of saving, hoarding without knowing why" (78–79). He also describes Trina's greed in clinical terms: "It was a passion with her, a mania, a veritable mental disease" (196). We can thus observe Trina's degeneration as the symptomatology of her disease. Similarly, Zerkow is presented as a stereotypical Jew whose disease is revealed rather clearly: "It was impossible to look at Zerkow and not know instantly that greed—inordinate, insatiable greed—was the dominant passion of the man" (28). In a less detailed fashion, Norris traces "the veritable mania" (75) of Zerkow and his subsequent actions as following the natural course of a virulent disease. The emphasis on genetic determinism in naturalism, indeed, breaks no new ground; at the same time, by projecting genetic determinism in immigrants through the clinical observation of his naturalism, Norris is able to elucidate a normative structure of healthy and diseased—in this case, it seems, in order to present the downfall of immigrants as a natural and naturalized process.[16]

Norris's depiction of the characters in this novel as diseased and abnormal objects, useful primarily for their demonstration of the disease of immigration itself, helps to instantiate Norris's nativist impulses within a normative structure. As Foucault writes, "description, in clinical medicine, does not mean placing the hidden or the invisible within reach of those who have no direct access to them; what it means is to give speech to that which everyone sees without seeing—a speech that can be understood only by those initiated in true speech" (115). The "true speech" that understands the nature of McTeague's disease is the discourse of nativism, for even as Norris's descriptions of the characters objectify them, his focus on their abnormality reveals the disease of immigration. In a particularly nativist manner, the gaze of Norris's naturalism seeks to define its lower-class characters as pathological or unhealthy, and the particular descriptions given offer readers initiated in nativism the opportunity to see the characters' disease as the genetic determinism of immigrants. As Hugh Dawson points out, "Norris structures his character [McTeague] upon just those traits that nativist ideology had long taught were the 'race impulses' of the Irish" (36) and thus his "physical features, psychology and—most conspicuously—his highly distinctive name mark McTeague as stereotypically Irish-American" (34). Likewise, Trina and Marcus Schouler are marked by their German background, Maria Macapa is of Central American descent, and Zerkow is a Polish Jew, with only Grannis and Miss Baker presented as "pure" Anglo-Americans. Jared Gardner contends that through his creation of a "criminal immigrant 'type'" (55) in the character of McTeague, Norris is able to link the genetic determinism of naturalism with Lombrosian theories of criminology which "were founded upon a disease model of criminality coincident with an unprecedented wave of immigration" (54) and used to support nativist thought. Though Guest argues that these Lombrosian theories of criminology that *McTeague* uses also produce a normative structure since they "perform cultural work by naturalizing socially constructed concepts of criminality and normalcy" (23), I would argue further that the normative structure of Norris's clinical gaze also provides a way for Norris to normalize the nativist view of the diseased nature of immigrants and their necessary eventual extinction.

Since Guest sees *McTeague* as participating "in the naturalizing of the power to incarcerate" (24), his emphasis on the way the gaze operates is focused on how it depends upon an opposition between normal and abnormal to naturalize "a discourse of penal power" (44). I see the clinical gaze operating in a similar manner but with different results. By establishing a heightened objectivity and speaking from a position of institutionalized power, the clinical gaze is able to normalize notions of healthy and diseased and thus can be used to support a nativist project. Foucault writes, "analysis and the clinical gaze also have this feature in common that they compose and decompose only in order to reveal an ordering that is the natural order itself" (94). In the same manner, Norris's naturalistic gaze examines the disease of immigration in order to reveal the natural order. By elaborating the degenerative disease within his immigrant characters, Norris demonstrates that they are not utilizable as part of the working labor force. As Gardner puts it, "ultimately, in the immigrants' failure to reproduce and in their violent self-destruction, an innate confidence in natural selection is at work in Norris's conclusion. He falls back on his teacher's [Le Conte's] confidence, believing finally in the tendency of evolution to kill off the degraded races populating San Francisco" (59). McTeague's death at the end, therefore, does not only normalize penal power, but it also normalizes the extinction of that part of the labor force that is unhealthy and dangerous to the whole capitalist system. Moreover, since Norris's views are imbedded within the discourse of professional authorship, they take on heightened authority. Like the trained surgeon who can spot a disease, isolate it, and remove it through surgery, Norris is able to remove the "tainted" races of new Americans by naturalizing their degeneration and death. Perhaps then, American labor can be restored to its healthy state.

I would argue that examining the use of Norris's naturalist gaze to support a nativist discourse in *McTeague* is vital because it helps unfold the larger nativist project at work in his writing. Though the complexities and depth of Norris's nativism have not been fully explored, one of the most revealing and pervasive links to nativism throughout his writings is his persistent "Anglo-Saxonism."[17] As John Higham points out, there were two trends in the Anglo-Saxon tradition of nativism in the 1890s: "One was defensive, pointed at the foreigner within; the other was aggressive, calling for expansion overseas. . . . [O]ne warned the Anglo-Saxon of a danger of submergence, while the other assured him of a conquering destiny" (144). The aggressive trend, with its confidence in its "powers of assimilation" (Higham 145) was linked with and indeed justified imperialist projects; the defensive trend, responding to recent shifts in the sources of immigration and to scientific theories of race, became concerned with the ultimate efficacy of Anglo-Saxon assimilation and consequent fears of the Anglo-Saxon promise being corrupted by the new immigrants. Dawson and Gardner's studies of *McTeague* provide good analyses of the defensive posture, especially fears concerning assimilation, but Norris's writings take part in both trends of the Anglo-Saxon tradition of nativism.

Evidence of Norris's connections to the aggressive tradition of Anglo-Saxon nativism can be seen in his first published novel, *Moran of the Lady Letty,* in which work Ross Wilbur is able to discover his Anglo-Saxon race impulses through his contact with the Viking figure Moran, and who in the end is able to defeat a gang of Chinese pirates before going off to Cuba. In "The Literature of the West," "A Neglected Epic," and "The Frontier Gone at Last," Norris also celebrates the destiny of the Anglo-Saxon race in its conquering and civilizing of the West and in its new project of turning eastward in an imperialistic project.[18] *The Octopus* continues this celebratory notion of the Anglo-Saxon spirit through Magnus Derrick, who embodies the spirit of "the Forty-niner" (204), which for Norris was the modern representation of the Anglo-Saxon, and through the portrayal of Cedarquist's plans to ship wheat to the Orient: "We'll carry wheat into Asia yet. The Anglo-Saxon started for there at the beginning of everything and it's manifest destiny that he must circle the globe and fetch up where he began his march" (446). Finally, since the resurgence of the aggressive and imperialistic version of Anglo-Saxonism received much of its impetus from the Spanish-American War and gained popularity through the writings of Rudyard Kipling, Norris's praise of the victory of Cuba in terms of Anglo-Saxon destiny and his admiration of Kipling need more attention for their nativist and racialist implications.[19]

In the tradition of the more defensive version of Anglo-Saxon nativism, Norris sets up the differences between "true Americans" (the Anglo-Saxons) and the immigrant Americans. In setting up these differences in several *Wave* sketches, "Among Cliff-Dwellers," "Japan Translated," and "Cosmopolitan San Francisco," Norris espouses the Anglo-Saxon notion of race-forming but also expresses doubts whether some immigrants will be able to be fully assimilated. This doubt of the efficacy of assimilation is then coupled with scientific aspects of race theory and emerges as a fear of the degeneration of the Anglo-Saxon race in "A Case for Lombroso," in which work a girl of "red-hot, degenerate Spanish blood" degrades an American lover (*Apprenticeship* 1:129).[20] The heightened distances between Anglo-Saxon Americans and immigrants and the implicit fear of degeneration is also evident in the famous scene in *The Octopus* of the slaughtering of the rabbits: "The Anglo-Saxon spectators round about drew back in disgust, but the hot, degenerated blood of Portugese, Mexican, and mixed Spaniard boiled up in excitement at this wholesale slaughter" (345). Though the eugenics movement and its connection to nativism gains more prominence after Norris's death, the elimination of immigrants in *McTeague,* and even the drowning of the Jew in the shipwreck in *Vandover and the Brute,* can be read as part of the larger fabric of Anglo-Saxon nativism that Norris exhibits throughout his writings.

Though I have attempted to elaborate the connection of naturalism and nativism in *McTeague* and have sketched some further evidence of nativism throughout Norris's writings, there is a need to investigate further the extent to which the nativist and racialist project is inherent to naturalist aesthetics.[21] As Howard contends, the "investigation of naturalism . . . doubly entails an investigation of its historical moment—as the condition of its production and as the source of discourses embedded within the works" (ix). Indeed, the resurgence of a nativist discourse in the 1890s and its adoption of Darwinian race theories is not merely coincidental to the rise of naturalism and its determinist philosophy but part of its very fabric. Though the historical work of critics such as Gardner and Dawson is important and needs to be extended to more of the works of Norris and other naturalists, I would argue that it can also be supplemented with a closer examination of naturalist aesthetic theories. By examining naturalist aesthetic theories more closely in light of such historical and social movements as nativism and professionalism, we can continue to unmask the complex discursive practices of naturalist authors and gain a more fully historicized understanding of this most penetrating form of fiction.

NOTES

I would like to thank Gina Rossetti for her valuable comments and advice on this essay. I am also grateful to the anonymous readers for their insightful suggestions.

1. For more "classic" naturalist readings, see Lars Åhnebrink's *The Influence of Émile Zola on Frank Norris* and *The Beginnings of Naturalism in American Fiction;* John Conder's *Naturalism in American Fiction;* William Dillingham's *Frank Norris: Instinct and Art;* W. M. Frohock's *Frank Norris;* Ernest Marchand's *Frank Norris;* Donald Pizer's *The Novels of Frank Norris;* and Charles Walcutt's *American Literary Naturalism.* For naturalist readings that take into account the historicity of the genre, see June Howard's *Form and History in American Literary Naturalism* and Walter Benn Michaels's *The Gold Standard and the Logic of Determinism.* The most prominent "anti-naturalist" or aesthetic readings are Jennifer Boyd's *Frank Norris: Spatial Form and Narrative Time;* Suzy Bernstein Goldman's "*McTeague* and the Imagistic Network"; Joseph Gardner's "Dickens, Romance, and *McTeague*"; Don Graham's *The Fiction of Frank Norris;* Barbara Hochman's *The Art of Frank Norris Storyteller;* Joseph McElrath's "The Comedy of Frank Norris's *McTeague*"; and Ron Mottram's "Impulse toward the Visible." For a fuller description of *McTeague* scholarship, see Charles Crow's "Gnawing the File," which uses the categories of "anti-naturalist" and "neo-naturalist" (1).

2. David Heddendorf provides insightful analysis of Norris's attitude toward professionalism in *McTeague,* but he does not link it to Norris's naturalist aesthetics. Furthermore, Heddendorf contends that in *McTeague* Norris displays an ambivalent and contradictory attitude toward professionalization, which, in turn, reflects "the paradoxical quality of professionalism" (683); I claim that Norris is arguing more positively for the authority of professionalization. Though Jennifer Boyd and Ron Mottram have both looked at the spatial and pictorial qualities of *McTeague,* they have not examined the larger implications found in the concept of the gaze, nor have they connected the gaze to Norris's naturalism. Boyd sees Norris "linking the creation of visual art with the creation of fiction" (45), and she concentrates on how Norris creates spatial form within the temporal medium of narrative. She argues, for instance, that "throughout the novel, structure reinforces plot; spatiality dictates action; and repetition, parallelism, and pictorialism serve to counter the linear progression of the narrative" (44). Mottram sees photography as an important part of the "aesthetic reference" of *McTeague* (574), and he goes on to link the visual qualities of Norris's writing to his interest in photography and the early motion picture. Also, June Howard has examined spectatorship and the gaze in the naturalistic novel, but she has not applied this concept extensively to *McTeague*; and while David Guest does look at observation in the narration of *McTeague,* he concentrates mainly on aspects of penal power. Howard shows how observation and the gaze help to separate "the Other" (or "the Brute") from the narrator, and she explains how this separation is part of the form and ideology of naturalism. Her chapter on "Naturalism and the Spectator" deals primarily with *Sister Carrie.* Guest links "the diagnostic gaze of surveillance" (36) primarily with the discourse of penal power and relies on Foucault's theories of the panopticon. I, however, will be working with Foucault's theories of clinical observation and the medical gaze. (On Foucault and naturalism, see also Irene Gammel's *Sexualizing Power in Naturalism,* a study of Theodore Dreiser and Philip Grove that examines the genre through Foucault's "history of sexuality" [6]). Finally, though Hugh Dawson and Jared Gardner discuss the nativism in *McTeague,* they do not explore the connection between Norris's nativism and his naturalist aesthetics.

3. All quotations from Norris's critical essays are from *The Literary Criticism of Frank Norris,* ed. Donald Pizer.

4. Howard also discusses the connections between professionalism, science, and naturalism and concludes that "naturalism not only manifests structural affinities with professionalism in general and professionalizing social sciences in particular, but offers itself as a kind of social science. It concerns itself with objective facts conveyed by an objective researcher" (140).

5. Pizer (*Theory and Practice* 120–23) argues that Norris's definition of naturalism consists of a combination of what Norris termed realism and romance, but I would point out that Norris often conflates the terms "romance" and "naturalism." For example, Norris refers to Zola as a Romantic writer (71, 76), but he also describes him as a naturalist (71). In his "Plea for Romantic Fiction," Norris describes what we would call (and I think Norris would call) naturalism. Therefore, when I describe Norris's attitude towards naturalism and toward romance, I use both terms to designate the same type of literature.

6. See also David Guest's commentary on "A Plea for Romantic Fiction," in which he links Norris's "imagined omniscient gaze" (36) and the narrative vision in *McTeague* with surveillance and police work (36–37). The imagery that Norris employs in delineating his aesthetic could also be described as very phallic. Though Norris did admire some female local color writers, I think that he was trying also to exclude women from the discourse of naturalism. In "Why Women Should Write the Best Novels: and Why They Don't" (*Literary Criticism of Frank Norris* 33–36), Norris argues that a woman cannot write as good a novel as can a man because she is shut off from and is therefore unable accurately to describe "real life" (36).

7. David Shumway points out that Foucault does not heavily theorize the notion of the medical gaze in *Birth of the Clinic*. However, it is clear that he was thinking of issues such as enunciative modalities and the power of discursive practice, which later become more fully theorized in "The Eye of Power," "The Discourse on Language," and *The Archaeology of Knowledge*.

8. For a discussion of how Norris's gaze can be seen as more fully related to the Panopticon, see Guest's analysis of the gaze (34–42).

9. All quotations from *McTeague* are from the Norton critical edition (1997), edited by Pizer.

10. For example, in "The True Reward of the Novelist," Norris attacks the imitation of good historical fiction as "the perversion of a profession, the detestable trading upon another man's success" (84). He derides these authors as non-novelists because they "are business men" (84), and he views them as "content to prostitute the good name of literature for a sliding scale of royalties" (84). In Norris's view, then, these authors should be excluded from the profession.

11. Donna Campbell argues that by using these different stories, "Norris explored the problems inherent in the convergence of three late nineteenth-century literary movements: realism, naturalism, and local color fiction" (41). While Campbell concentrates on "the theme of storytelling" (46) and Norris's representation of local color fiction, I want to emphasize the attitudes toward naturalism and professional authorship that these stories represent.

12. Campbell contends that the Grannis and Miss Baker plot represents local color fiction and thus fades away because "neither the old couple, their story, nor local color fiction has anywhere else to go" (47). However, since Norris uses the adjective "commonplace" to describe both their relationship and Howellsian realism, I contend that they represent the larger category of realism. In fact, they enact the "drama of a broken teacup" (76), which Norris describes as a typical scenario of realism in "A Plea for Romantic Fiction" and "Zola as a Romantic Writer."

13. It is interesting to note that in this section Foucault offers further explanation for such changes in nineteenth-century medicine. He writes that this medicine "formed its concepts and prescribed its interventions in relation to a standard of functioning and organic structure, and physiological knowledge—once marginal and purely theoretical knowledge for the doctor—was to become established (Claude Bernard bears witness to this) at the very centre of all medical reflexion" (35).

14. Ian Watt, in his discussion of Defoe in *The Rise of the Novel*, uses this image of the judge and quotes Hazlitt's observations on Richardson: "It is like reading evidence

in a court of Justice" (34). In "The Experimental Novel," Zola uses the metaphor of the judge to describe the position of the author rather than the reader: "We novelists are the examining magistrates of men and their passions" (6).

15. In my use of the term "separation," I am also drawing upon Howard's insightful commentary concerning the narrative strategies of naturalism: "The aesthetic ideology and documentary project of naturalism link it to other practices like sociology that depend on the separation of the object of knowledge and the knowing subject, the transparency of perception and language, and the self-sufficient authority of fact" (147).

16. For a thorough analysis of genetic determinism and degeneration in *McTeague,* especially in relation to Cesare Lombroso and Max Nordau, see William Dillingham's *Frank Norris* (74–79, 113–14) and Pizer's *The Novels of Frank Norris* (52–63). Though Jared Gardner expands upon Pizer's work by connecting Lombrosian theories of criminology and naturalist theories of genetic determinism with the discourse of nativism, and though he does touch upon the idea of immigrants as diseased, he does not expand upon the idea of immigration as disease and how it is normalized through Norris's use of the clinical gaze. The importance of Norris's use of the clinical gaze to reveal the diseased nature of immigrants can be seen in its reflection of the immigration law of 1891 in which "persons suffering from a loathsome or contagious disease" (qtd. in Higham 100) were barred admission to America. The treatment of the death of immigrants as a part of genetic determinism becomes prominent in nativist thought in the 1890s and 1900s and later is linked to eugenics as nativism combined with the scientific discourse of Darwinism in order to present its own racial theories with a heightened objectivity and believability (see Stuart Anderson's *Race and Rapprochement* [28–36], Gardner [52–57], John Higham's *Strangers in the Land* [133–36; 149–57], Hofstadter's *Social Darwinism in American Thought* [146–73], and Howard [85–86]).

17. For historical accounts of Anglo-Saxonism, see Anderson's *Race and Rapprochement* (11–61), Thomas Gossett's *Race: The History of an Idea in America*, Higham's *Strangers in the Land* (131–93), Hofstadter's *Social Darwinism in American Thought* (146–73), and Howard Mumford Jones's *The Theory of American Literature* (79–117). Higham's study is especially useful because he connects Anglo-Saxonism to nativism. Brief accounts of Norris's Anglo-Saxonism can be found in Anderson (59–60), Chase's *American Novel* (198), Dillingham (55–58), Gossett (198–227), Howard (96), Marchand's *Frank Norris* (132–35), Pizer's introduction to *The Literary Criticism of Frank Norris* (99–103), and in Larzer Ziff's *The American 1890s* (250–74). None of these accounts examines the full breadth of Norris's Anglo-Saxonism and its racial implications, nor do they account fully for its connections to nativism. Dawson and Gardner do connect nativism and Anglo-Saxonism, but they do not relate Norris's nativist tendencies to his naturalist aesthetics.

18. In "The Literature of the West" Norris describes the "scattering advance line of . . . Anglo-Saxons" (106) who conquer the West. He laments the fact that "the Forty-niner" (106), an Anglo-Saxon hero and "blood brother to Roland and Grettir the Strong" (107), has not received epic treatment. "A Neglected Epic" continues this theme and claims that the hero of the American West "died that the West might be subdued, that the last stage of the march should be accomplished, that the

Anglo-Saxon should fulfill his destiny and complete the cycle of the world" (121). In "The Frontier Gone at Last," Norris speculates on what will happen now that the Frontier, "the place of poetry of the Great March" (111), is gone and the "race impulse" (113) to conquer remains: "March we must, conquer we must, and checked in the Westward course of empire we turned Eastward and expended the resistless energy that by blood was ours in conquering the Old World behind us" (113).

19. In his account of Norris's Cuban adventures, Franklin Walker records Norris's reaction to American victory: "Santiago was ours—was ours, ours, by the sword we had acquired, we, Americans, with no one to help—and the Anglo-Saxon blood of us, the blood of the race that has fought its way out of a swamp in Friesland, conquering and conquering, on to the westward, the race whose blood instinct is the acquiring of land, went galloping through our veins to the beat of our horses' hoofs" (199). For Kipling's influence on Anglo-Saxonism and imperialism, see Anderson (57–58), Gossett (202–3), and Pizer (*Literary Criticism* 20–23, 101). In light of Kipling's connections to Anglo-Saxonism and imperialism, Norris's question "*A qui le tour*, who shall be our Kipling?" (30) in "An Opening for Novelists" takes on serious implications.

20. For Norris's *Wave* sketches, see *The Apprenticeship Writings of Frank Norris,* ed. Joseph R. McElrath Jr. and Donald K. Burgess. In "Among Cliff-Dwellers," Norris describes these residents as "a queer, extraordinary mingling of peoples" (1:262) and speculates that "in a few more generations the Celt and the Italian, the Mexican and the Chinaman, the Negro and the Portugese, and the Levantines and the 'scatter-mouces' will be merged into one type. And what a curious type it will be" (1:264–65). Norris's confidence in assimilation is further shaken in "Japan Translated" where he argues that "we hope to have a good deal of America some day, when all these nationalities become merged into one, but we are busy race-forming just now and are rather elemental yet" (2:59). Finally, in "Cosmopolitan San Francisco," Norris refers to the immigrant population of the city as a confusion of races and an "agglomerate rather than conglomerate" (2:210), and he is especially concerned with the difference of the Chinese, which he fears makes them difficult to assimilate. Gardner also provides a discussion of the fears of assimilation in "A Case for Lombroso" and "Among Cliff Dwellers," as well as pointing out these fears in "A Defense of the Flag," "Thoroughbred," and other early *Wave* sketches (55–56).

21. For the connection between nativism and modernism, see Michaels's *Our America.* He uses the term "nativist modernism" to "suggest the structural intimacy between nativism and modernism" (2) and argues "that the great American modernist texts of the '20s must be understood as deeply committed to the nativist project of racializing America" (13).

WORKS CITED

Åhnebrink, Lars. *The Beginnings of Naturalism in American Fiction.* Cambridge: Harvard UP, 1950.

———. *The Influence of Émile Zola on Frank Norris.* Cambridge: Harvard UP, 1947.

Anderson, Stuart. *Race and Rapprochement: Anglo-Saxonism and Anglo-American Relations, 1895–1904.* East Brunswick, NJ: Associated UP, 1981.

Bledstein, Burton J. *The Culture of Professionalism: The Middle Class and the Development of Higher Education in America.* New York: Norton, 1976.

Boyd, Jennifer. *Frank Norris: Spatial Form and Narrative Time.* New York: Peter Lang, 1993.

Campbell, Donna M. "Frank Norris' 'Drama in a Broken Teacup': The Old Grannis–Miss Baker Plot in *McTeague.*" *American Literary Realism* 21 (1993): 40–49.

Chase, Richard. *The American Novel and Its Tradition.* Garden City, NJ: Anchor, 1957.

Conder, John J. *Naturalism in American Fiction: The Classic Phase.* Lexington: UP of Kentucky, 1984.

Crow, Charles. "Gnawing the File: Recent Trends in *McTeague* Scholarship." *Frank Norris Studies* 13 (1992): 1–5.

Dawson, Hugh. "McTeague As Ethnic Stereotype." *American Literary Realism* 20 (1987): 34–44.

Dillingham, William B. *Frank Norris: Instinct and Art.* Lincoln: U of Nebraska P, 1969.

Foucault, Michel. *The Archaeology of Knowledge & The Discourse on Language.* Trans. A. M. Sheridan Smith. New York: Tavistock, 1972.

———. *The Birth of the Clinic: An Archaeology of Medical Perception.* Trans. A. M. Sheridan Smith. New York: Vintage, 1975.

———. "The Eye of Power." *Power/Knowledge: Selected Interviews and Other Writings, 1972–1977.* Ed. Colin Gordon. Trans. Colin Gordon, Leo Marshall, John Mepham, and Kate Soper. New York: Pantheon, 1980. 146–65.

———. "The Politics of Health in the Eighteenth Century." *Power/Knowledge.* New York: Pantheon, 1980. 166–82.

Frohock, W. M. *Frank Norris.* Minneapolis: U of Minnesota P, 1968.

Gammel, Irene. *Sexualizing Power in Naturalism: Theodore Dreiser and Philip Grove.* Calgary: U of Calgary P, 1994.

Gardner, Jared. "What Blood Will Tell: Hereditary Determinism in *McTeague* and *Greed.*" *Texas Studies in Literature and Language* 36 (1994): 51–74.

Gardner, Joseph H. "Dickens, Romance, and *McTeague.*" *Essays in Literature* 1 (1974): 69–82.

Goldman, Suzy Bernstein. "*McTeague* and the Imagistic Network." *Western American Literature* 7 (1972): 83–99.

Gossett, Thomas F. *Race: The History of an Idea in America.* New ed. Oxford: Oxford UP, 1997.

Graham, Don. *The Fiction of Frank Norris: The Aesthetic Context.* Columbia: U of Missouri P, 1978.

Guest, David. "Frank Norris's *McTeague*: Darwin and Police Power." *Sentenced to Death: The American Novel and Capital Punishment.* Jackson: UP of Mississippi, 1997. 21–44.

Heddendorf, David. "The 'Octopus' in *McTeague*: Frank Norris and Professionalism." *Modern Fiction Studies* 37 (1991): 677–88.

Higham, John. *Strangers in the Land: Patterns of American Nativism, 1860–1925.* New York: Atheneum, 1963.

Hochman, Barbara. *The Art of Frank Norris, Storyteller.* Columbia: U of Missouri P, 1988.

Hofstadter, Richard. *Social Darwinism in American Thought, 1860–1915.* Philadelphia: U of Pennsylvania P, 1945.

Howard, June. *Form and History in American Literary Naturalism.* Chapel Hill: U of North Carolina P, 1985.

Jones, Howard Mumford. *The Theory of American Literature.* Ithaca: Cornell UP, 1965.

Marchand, Ernest. *Frank Norris: A Study.* Stanford: Stanford UP, 1942.

McElrath, Joseph R. "The Comedy of Frank Norris's *McTeague*." *Studies in American Humor* 2 (1975): 88–95.

Michaels, Walter Benn. *The Gold Standard and the Logic of Naturalism: American Literature at the Turn of the Century.* Berkeley: U of California P, 1987.

———. *Our America: Nativism, Modernism, and Pluralism.* Durham: Duke UP, 1995.

Mottram, Ron. "Impulse toward the Visible: Frank Norris and Photographic Representation." *Texas Studies in Literature and Language* 25 (1983): 574–96.

Norris, Frank. *The Apprenticeship Writings of Frank Norris, 1896–1898.* Ed. Joseph R. McElrath Jr. and Douglas K. Burgess. Vols. 1 and 2. Philadelphia: American Philosophical Society, 1996.

———. *The Literary Criticism of Frank Norris.* Ed. Donald Pizer. Austin: U of Texas P, 1964.

———. *McTeague: A Story of San Francisco.* Ed. Donald Pizer. 2nd ed. New York: Norton, 1997.

———. *The Octopus: A Story of California.* Ed. Kenneth S. Lynn. Cambridge, MA: Riverside, 1958.

Pizer, Donald. *The Novels of Frank Norris.* Bloomington: Indiana UP, 1966.

———. *The Theory and Practice of American Literary Naturalism.* Carbondale: Southern Illinois UP, 1993.

Shumway, David. *Michel Foucault.* Boston: Twayne, 1989.

Walcutt, Charles C. *American Literary Naturalism: A Divided Stream.* Minneapolis: U of Minnesota P, 1956.

Walker, Franklin. *Frank Norris: A Biography.* New York: Russell & Russell, 1963.

Watt, Ian. *The Rise of the Novel: Studies in Defoe, Richardson, and Fielding.* Berkeley: U of California P, 1962.

Ziff, Larzer. *The American 1890s: Life and Times of a Lost Generation.* New York: Viking, 1966.

Zola, Émile. "The Experimental Novel." *Émile Zola: The Naturalist Novel.* Ed. Maxwell Geismar. Montreal: Harvest House, 1964. 1–32.

McTeague

NATURALISM, LEGAL STEALING, AND THE ANTI-GIFT

—*Hildegard Hoeller*

American Naturalism . . . is realism . . . infused with pessimistic determinism.

—Donald Pizer, 1965

WHAT MAKES FRANK NORRIS'S *MCTEAGUE* SO PESSIMISTIC? THIS ESSAY WILL ARGUE THAT NORRIS'S NOVEL, BOTH ITS ECONOMIC AND NATU-ralist bend, is centrally concerned not with gold and greed but with the tragic and complex relations between gift exchanges and market exchanges. While I agree with other economic readings that gold is a central symbol in the novel, my reading suggests that the fall from gift exchange through market exchange into the lethal realm of what I call the anti-gift is even more important to our understanding of the novel's economic and naturalist concerns. I coin the word anti-gift to describe a process in which characters, in a perverse mirroring of gift communities as gift theorists describe them, deplete rather than augment the gift cycle and where their bonds to each other are deadly rather than friendly and fertile. Norris's novel depicts such a perversion of the gift. While Norris's characters are initially bound to each other by gifts, once driven by a greed derived from capitalist thinking, they begin to deplete the gift cycle by turning gifts into profit rather than circulating them; they legally steal from, rather than give to, each other. These legal thefts, I will argue, ultimately lead to the bestial violence and murders in the novel.

This perverse and deathly realm of the anti-gift is the opposite of a functioning, fertile gift community, and it is always coexistent with both the gift and the market economy; more so, it is contained within the logic of both because the former allows and the latter propels and motivates the anti-gift. It is in these complex and dangerous relations between gift and market exchanges that Norris gives "life on its lowest levels" "the moral complexities and ambiguities that Milton set his fallen angels to debating" (Pizer 87). The deterministic pessimism of Norris's naturalism lies in his brutal depiction of the fact that the gift cannot defend itself against a rising capitalism that fractures communities and stresses self-interest; the perversions of the anti-gift are nothing but a logical extension of the market thinking when it enters the private realm of gift-giving. *McTeague* shows us how humans turn into beasts because they violate the gift through legal stealing and end up living in the hellish space of depletion rather than abundance, barrenness rather than fertility, enmity rather than friendship. In depicting this perverse realm of the anti-gift—the structural opposite of the gift community gift theorists describe—Norris sees the end of the gift, of human dignity, friendship, love and joy, and the beginning of an unlivable, monstrous realm of perversion and murder that, he warns us, is inevitable in light of the rise of capitalism.

Consider that the three major plotlines in the novel—McTeague's relationship to Marcus, the dentist's marriage to Trina, and the relationship between Maria and Zerkow—are all explicitly about this motion from gift to commodity exchange and to anti-gift and murder. McTeague's friendship with Marcus is initiated through a gift exchange: McTeague offers his services as a dentist to Marcus free of charge. When Marcus asks McTeague to treat his cousin Trina, the dentist does so. Then McTeague falls in love with Trina, and Marcus sacrifices his own romantic interest in Trina to his friend. Marcus also uses the power of gift-giving in his heroic self-aggrandizement about his sacrifice and in his constant insinuations that McTeague owes him. But the situation becomes violent only when Trina wins the lottery. Marcus's behavior changes as he now *claims* that McTeague owes him—even for spending a night at his house—while McTeague responds that he has nothing to give to Marcus. The dentist cannot understand how and why the rules have changed. A deadly struggle between the two men ensues from here and ends only at the very end of the novel in Death Valley when both men die chained to each other.

Trina's relationship to McTeague runs a parallel course. It, too, begins with gift exchange and then turns deadly. First, McTeague treats Trina's teeth for free. Then, later, Trina gives McTeague her gift of the great golden tooth. After this gift, she slowly begins to steal from him and from her family and friends. She elicits gifts and withholds them from further circulation, or she asks McTeague to give to a third party and secretly keeps the gift. Her miserliness—a result of the lottery win and the hole the gift of the golden tooth leaves—compels her to deplete what could be an abundant circle of gift-giving by taking gifts out of that circle and turning them into commodities; like Marcus, she turns common gifts—such as food or a tea offered during a visit—into profits for herself by refusing to reciprocate and by counting the gain. Because of this miserliness, this legal stealing, McTeague ultimately murders Trina.

Legal stealing is also at the heart of the third and equally lethal plot of the novel: that of Maria Macapa and the Jewish character Zerkow. Maria legally steals—turning gifts into commodities—consistently throughout the novel. She asks others whether they have things to spare that they could give her and then turns them into commodities by bringing them to Zerkow's junk shop. In her case, too, Norris links such theft to murder. Maria gives life to a sickly child, but both Zerkow and she are too miserly to support and feed it, and it quickly dies. Later Zerkow kills Maria.

Norris's final scene stresses the importance of these plots of deathly depletion of the gift cycle. At the culmination of their rivalry Marcus and McTeague face each other in Death Valley with no water and an abundance of gold. They fight, and Marcus dies in the process of the fight; McTeague remains shackled to his dead companion. This final scene shows the poisonous, lethal potential of the anti-gift and the terrible deathly bondage that comes along with it. The abundance of gold—the legacy of Trina's lottery win, which turned the gift exchange between the two men into its opposite—ironically highlights the dearth of life in Death Valley. In Death Valley we see the realm of the anti-gift most clearly: a realm that is the opposite—a terrible parody—of the fertile gift community gift theorists describe.

The gift has always been associated with narrative. In his great essay on the gift, Marcel Mauss notes how the gifts exchanged amongst people in the South Seas have names, "personality, a past and even a legend attached to them" (Mauss 22). Furthermore, the key terms of discussions of gift economies, such as gift, obligation, bond, community, sacrifice, marriage, inheritance, and others, are terms eminently suited for the study of narratives. Indeed, these terms tend to center most narratives. It is thus readily apparent that the central terms of gift economic theory are important for the understanding of narrative.

In Marcel Mauss's view, there is no such thing as a "pure" or disinterested gift; for him gifts are obligations. Although some philosophers, notably Jacques Derrida, continue to define the gift as precisely that which is disinterested, the notion of the gift economy depends upon the obligation to give, receive, and repay (Mauss 37–41). That sense of obligation is what makes an economy—an ongoing system of exchange—possible. The obligatory nature of gift exchange not only creates community, Mauss believes; it joins discrete communities into a larger pattern of circulation.

Significantly, gift economies are not barter economies; that is, the pattern of exchange most typical of gift economies is circular. As Lewis Hyde notes in his inspired discussion of the *Kula* circle made famous by Malinowski's study of Trobriand gift exchange, the circle of gift exchange is equivalent to the social body (Hyde 16–18). My gift to you passes out of sight as you pass it on.

A return gift comes from someone else—as though "from around the corner" (Hyde 16) or "out of the blue." The common expression "what goes around, comes around" expresses perfectly the mixture of strangeness and inevitability that characterizes the gift economy.

You give to me, but I give to someone else. Your return will come from yet another person. Gift economies are a way of talking about a network of non-barter, non-monetary relationships based on complex and often indirect social obligations. The simple employer/employee relationship wherein labor is exchanged for money or the landlord/tenant relation in which living space is rented for money or a share of the crops are not gift economies; they are "economic" in the standard sense. Gifts, on the other hand, cannot be valued in money. Money is never quite a gift. A money gift is very welcome, no doubt, but what one buys with it does not feel like a gift; it feels like one commodity among others. What we receive must be rendered to someone—again and again—and not simply returned to the giver. That is the essential structure of the gift economy. A gift is never "pure" because to receive a gift is to entangle oneself in a web of obligation called a community. This is one reason why both Mauss and Derrida note the gift/poison connection by punning on the German word for poison, "Gift."[1] Compensation is even more important and, of course, more problematic in a relationship in which money is not involved. Lovers exchange gifts, not money. Marriage itself, no matter how encumbered with very real financial or property considerations, is regarded as a gift exchange, with the father "giving away" the bride in a vestigial display of patriarchal largesse.

Gift-giving, Hyde theorizes, is a fertile practice, as the circulation of the gift tends to increase it and to build community. That, too, distinguishes it from the capitalist market economy, which is both alienating and profit-oriented but not self-generating. A deal leaves no sense of obligation and thus no ties. A gift, on the other hand, creates both the impulse to give again and a sense of obligation towards the giver. And the most fundamental gift is the gift of life, which gets circulated and augmented as generations mature. The gift community is thus fertile, bonding, and circular; society governed by market exchange is based on scarcity, alienation, and self-interest.

Hyde's treatment of the gift emphasizes this distinction, even opposition, between gift and market exchanges. Norris, on the other hand, devotes his novel to understanding that these two economies always coexist; his novel relentlessly pursues the complexities, possibilities, and implications of this co-existence. Seeing that within the market logic the gift can be seen as a waste, and that the gift itself by its nature allows itself to be turned into profit, Norris shows us a world where in a deadly collaboration the two logics annihilate his characters. To describe this phenomenon and to characterize the true pessimism of Norris's naturalism, I have coined the terms *legal stealing* and *anti-gift*. Norris points us to the realms gift theorists have avoided: the realm of the anti-gift, in which the gift circle is exploited through legal stealing and, as the result, the community is turned into its perverse opposite. It is neither fertile and bonding as the gift economy demands, nor strictly alienated as capitalist orders normally are; rather, characters are strangely and lethally bonded to each other in their market-driven exploitation of their gift relations.

Norris's novel could not be more explicit in using Trina's lottery win to depict the fall of the friendship between McTeague and Marcus as a fall from a friendly gift exchange to its deathly opposite—the anti-gift. The unlikely friendship between McTeague and Marcus Schouler grew out of a gift exchange. The two men frequented the same "coffee joint" (10) and lived in the same flat; further, "on different occasions McTeague had treated Marcus for an ulcerated tooth and refused to accept payment. Soon it became to be an understood thing between them. They were pals" (10). Norris's narrative makes it almost formulaically clear that it is the gift-giving (the refusal of payment) that creates the friendship ("they were pals").

True to the spirit of gift exchange, the circle widens after that when Marcus asks McTeague to treat Trina, his love interest, who has fallen from a swing and knocked out her front tooth. McTeague begins to treat Trina as a favor to Marcus, but soon he develops desire for his patient. While McTeague struggles with his animal desires for her, a courtship develops between the two; later, the dentist proposes. After some struggle, Trina accepts. When McTeague confesses to his friend his passion for Trina, Marcus recognizes both that his friend's love for Trina is greater than his own and that there is an opportunity for a noble sacrifice. He 'gives' Trina to his friend and gains appreciably thereby:

> The sense of his own magnanimity all at once overcame Marcus. He saw himself as another man, very noble, self-sacrificing; he stood apart and watched this second self with boundless admiration and with infinite pity. He was so good, so magnificent, so heroic, that he almost sobbed. Marcus made a sweeping gesture of resignation, throwing out both his arms, crying, "Mac, I'll give her up to you. I won't stand between you." There were actually tears in Marcus' eyes as he spoke. There was no doubt he thought himself sincere. At that moment he almost believed he loved Trina conscientiously, that he was sacrificing himself for the sake of his friend. The two stood up and faced each other, gripping hands. It was a great moment; even McTeague felt the drama of it. What a

fine thing was this friendship between men! The dentist treats his friend with an ulcerated tooth and refuses payment; the friend reciprocates by giving up his girl. This was nobility. Their mutual affection and esteem suddenly increased enormously. . . . Nothing could ever estrange them. Now it was for life or death. (35)

The two men enjoy the sentimental narrative of their own friendship and the bonds Marcus's gift creates. Their friendship is "increased enormously" through Marcus's noble gift—a gift that reminds one of the father's giving away the bride. Indeed, Marcus himself is transformed by his sacrifice into a new man, a man of "boundless," "infinite," "magnificent," "heroic" qualities, a "good" man. The sacrifice between the two men brings abundance and transformation. And this exchange is moving, even to the coarse McTeague. Indeed, Norris draws a distinction between McTeague's natural participation in gift exchange and Marcus's artificial role in it.[2]

Because of this distinction, however, as soon as Norris's "god-from-the machine" (89) gets to work in the form of Trina's winning lottery ticket, the noble friendship between the two men turns lethal. Marcus now abandons this second noble self and translates his earlier generous gesture from the logic of the gift to that of the market; as a result, he turns from friend to foe. Marcus attempts to turn his sacrifice, now with a price tag attached to it, into debt and regrets fully the "loss" he incurred by giving up Trina. Norris makes this translation quite clear. At first, joy abounds at this "non-[sensical]" event (65)—this gift out of nowhere—of Trina winning $5,000 in the lottery: "She was to possess five thousand dollars. She was carried away with the joy of her good fortune, a natural, spontaneous joy—the gaiety of a child with a new and wonderful toy" (65). Norris thus depicts Trina's joy as "natural" and childlike. Indeed, everybody considers the win a gift and enjoys it enormously: "Anything was funny at a time like this. In some way every one of them felt elated. The wheel of fortune had come spinning close to them. They were near to this great sum of money. It was as though they too had won" (66). The joy is "natural" and abundant, and it reaffirms community.

It even builds community. The two shy old people Old Grannis and Miss Baker are finally thrown together and turn from strangers to friends because of the festivities: "They were strangers no longer; they were acquaintances, friends. What an event that evening had been in their lives!" (72–73). The lottery is couched in mythical terms as a great "charity" in the service of a more just and egalitarian society: "Invariably it was the needy who won, the destitute and starving woke to wealth and plenty, the virtuous toiler suddenly found his reward in a ticket bought at hazard; the lottery was the great charity, the friend of the people, a vast beneficent machine that recognized neither rank nor wealth nor station" (67–68). The lottery creates joy as long as it is perceived as a gift "out of the blue," a benign regulator of the social body that brings back to those deserving and in need what they need to be human.

Only Marcus acts against this "natural" response and exhibits a "sudden unaccountable mirthlessness" (67). The narrator asks "what was the matter with Marcus?" and notes that "at moments he seemed singularly out of temper" (67). Then, suddenly, the engagement of Trina and the dentist is announced. As everyone congratulates the couple and wishes them good luck, Marcus becomes increasingly upset: "'He's lucky enough already,' growled Marcus under his breath, relapsing for a moment into one of those strange moods of sullenness which had marked him throughout the evening" (69–70). When he is finally alone, Marcus gives vent to his anger:

> He took a couple of turns up and down the yard, then suddenly in a low voice exclaimed, "You fool, you fool, Marcus Schouler! If you'd kept Trina you'd have that money. You might have had it yourself. You've thrown away your chance in life—to give up the girl, yes—but this"—he stamped his foot with rage—"to throw five thousand dollars out of the window—to stuff it into the pockets of someone else when it might have been yours, when you might have had Trina and the money—and all for what? Because we were pals. Oh, pals is all right—but five thousand dollars—to have played it right into his hands—God damn the luck!" (76)

Comparing gift and market exchanges (being pals versus gaining $5,000), Marcus furiously renounces his friendship since he perceives it as the cause for his business loss. In a vague way he believes that McTeague has legally stolen from him. Now that the gift is connected to money and commodity exchange, the earlier gift transaction seems a foolish loss rather than a magnanimous gesture, a miserable theft rather than a noble sacrifice.

From here on, Marcus tries to regain his loss and claim his share of the lottery wins. But in his interactions with McTeague, Marcus's newfound and perverse market logic confuses the dense dentist. For instance, Marcus demands from McTeague the four bits entrance fee he paid for McTeague and Trina at the picnic they enjoyed together. Furthermore, he suggests that McTeague also owes him for a night's lodging he had offered and requests that his friend pay him the market rate of half-a-dollar that would have been charged elsewhere. McTeague offers compensation, but Marcus's response worries him: "'I don't want your damn money,' shouted Marcus in a sudden rage, throwing back the coin. 'I ain't no beggar'" (80). At the end of this scene, McTeague is rendered "miserable," totally at a loss at how he had "offended his pal" (80). He does not understand that Marcus is trying to retroactively transform gift relations into money relations. He now claims debt where gifts were previously exchanged. Marcus does not ask for the money from the lottery win but literally translates a friendly loan into debt and an act of hospitality into a tenant-landlord relationship.[3] The dentist is dumbfounded, confused, and "distressed" by this change of logic. At first he operates in both exchange systems—he gives Marcus the money he owes and tells him that he is "obliged" (80)—but then he realizes that an "account" needs to be squared and that he does not want Marcus to be "out anything on [his] account" (80). But, of course, the friends can never square the debts and entanglements their gift relation has created between them. Marcus's recognition of this problem is precisely what enrages him. He knows he has no real right to claim the $5,000; so instead, he translates a gift gesture (letting McTeague stay overnight) into a market transaction (renting accommodations for a night) and "charges" McTeague the market rate equivalent to his gesture of hospitality. Yet, in the next second he recognizes the falsity of this claim by refusing to take "charity" from his friend as if he were a beggar.

While Marcus feels wronged, then, he cannot really understand within which logic he might have been wronged. He is furious because he has been "played for a sucker long enough" (80); and his rage is so enormous because it is ultimately unanswerable. Marcus finally demands some of the money: "It's my due. It's only justice" (83). As he tells the barkeeper in McTeague's presence, "he stole away my girl's affections, and now that he's rich and prosperous and has got five thousand dollars that I might have had, he gives me the go-by. He's played me for a sucker." He then asks McTeague, "do I get any of the money?" "It ain't mine to give," answers McTeague; and then, "No, you don't get any of it" (83). Infuriated by what Marcus understands to be a legal theft, Marcus breaks McTeague's pipe and then throws his jackknife at his former friend, barely missing his head, but Marcus leaves the bar before the fight escalates: "Death had stooped there for an instant, had stooped and passed, leaving a trail of terror and confusion" (84). McTeague finds the whole incident "inexplicable" (84).

Through the influence of market values, and in the unutterably confusing realm between market and gift, a friendship has tumbled from noble sentiment and abundant warmth to terror, confusion, and the threat of death. Norris dramatizes this transformation by juxtaposing it with the abundance of the gift. McTeague storms out to pursue Marcus. When he does not find him in his flat, he returns to his own and stumbles on a package. Coming seemingly out of the blue as true gifts do,[4] it is a birthday present from Trina—the big golden molar he has so ardently desired: "It was the Tooth—the famous golden molar with its huge prongs—his sign, his ambition, the one unrealized dream of his life; and it was French gilt, too, not the cheap German gilt that was no good" (85). Later, when McTeague hears Marcus returning to his flat, "he could not reinstate himself into the mood of wrath wherein he had left the corner grocery. The tooth had changed all that. What was Marcus Schouler's hatred to him, who had Trina's affection? What did he care about a broken pipe now that he had the tooth? Let him go" (86). When Marcus comes to his room, however, he finds it broken open by McTeague and exclaims, "How do I know how many things he's stolen? It's come to stealing from me, now, has it?" (87). Whereas, placated by the gift, McTeague returns from hatred to affection, Marcus remains furious, believing that the legal theft of his girlfriend—what he once saw only as the acceptance of a gift—and stealing in its more usual sense go hand in hand. To Marcus, McTeague is a thief through and through.

The dentist, on the other hand, finds tremendous comfort in his new gift, the enormous tooth. During the night he awakes many times worrying about the tooth just being a dream, "but he always found it—Trina's gift, his birthday present from this little woman—a huge, vague bulk, looming there through the half darkness in the center of the room, shining dimly out as if with some mysterious light of its own" (87). Thus for now, the dentist receives a tooth for a tooth, and so Norris introduces to us the idea that his novel takes place in the lethal space between gifts and commodities. The dentist naturally inhabits the space of gift exchange, unaware of any perversion of it. Marcus, on the other hand, does not. Instead, he comes to inhabit the realm of the anti-gift: bonded in rage to his friend/foe who appears to have legally stolen from him.

When Marcus connects legal stealing to stealing, he articulates a central theme in the novel. Norris explores this concept in depth in his character Maria, who has made both legal stealing and stealing the main occupations in her life; one leads to the other. Maria sets the deathly plot of the novel in motion through a form of legal theft, a "friendly" coercion, trying to get Trina to play the lottery:

> She stopped and drew a bunch of blue tickets furtively from her pocket. "Buy a ticket in the lottery?" she inquired, looking at the girl. "Just a dollar." . . . "Buy a ticket," urged Maria, thrusting the bundle toward Trina. "Try your luck. The butcher on the next block won twenty dollars the last drawing." Very uneasy, Trina bought a ticket for the sake of being rid of her. Maria disappeared. (16)

In Maria, Norris shows the most obvious example of someone exploiting the gray area between commodity and gift. Maria causes Trina to be "uneasy" and thus forces her to get rid of her through a market transaction. Maria forces this type of transaction precisely both because she is part of the community and she needs to be bought off. Trina cannot dismiss her as she might a stranger on the street, and Maria uses this fact and the uneasiness it creates; in a way she profits from Trina's wish to loosen the bond between herself and Maria, a coercion that relies on there being a bond in the first place.

Maria uses this technique throughout the novel, using her bonds to others as a way of forcing them to 'give' her what she wants. For instance, Norris shows us how Maria legally steals by soliciting 'gifts' and then turning them into commodities:

> Once every two months Maria Macapa set the entire flat in com-
> motion. She roamed the building from garret to cellar, searching
> each corner, ferreting through every old box and trunk and barrel,
> groping about on the top shelves of closets, peering into ragbags,
> exasperating the lodgers with her persistence and importunity.
> She was collecting junk, bits of iron, stone jugs, glass bottles, old
> sacks, and cast-off garments. It was one of her perquisites. She sold
> the junk to Zerkow, the rags-bottles-sacks-man, who lived in a
> filthy den in the alley just back of the flat and who sometimes paid
> her as much as three cents per pound. (23)

Norris's words "groping," "searching," and "ferreting" show how driven Maria is in her search to convert 'gifts' into commodities—to get them for free and then to sell them for a price. Maria exploits the community rather than existing within it; in that sense, she mirrors Marcus's alienation from the community after Trina wins the lottery. Both of these characters see in the community, and its gift bond, a possibility for profit or loss rather than circular fertility.

The relationship between Maria and Zerkow, in turn, is initially care-fully circumscribed in terms of business; they both insist on the market as their context, even though both operate at the very fringes of market society. When Maria turns her gifts and legal thefts into money, the negotiations are hard. Indeed, Zerkow himself is in the business of transforming a form of gift into money, selling junk that seems to have lost its commodity status. When Zerkow offers her a low price for the "gifts" Maria got from the people in the building, she shouts in indignation, "I might as well make you a Christmas present!" (16). Maria carefully polices the borders between commodity and gift even as she perversely exploits these.

Indeed, in his description of Maria's foray into McTeague's office, Norris shows how easily legal stealing and actual stealing go hand in hand. Maria pressures McTeague to give her some of his instruments, and, dazed as he habitually is, he finally yields: "'Yes, all right, all right,' he said, trying to make himself heard. 'It *would* be mean. I don't want them.' As he turned from her to pick up the box, Maria took advantage of the moment to steal three mats of sponge gold out of the glass saucer. Often she stole McTeague's gold, almost under his very eyes" (27). Stealing from him almost under his eyes suggests capitalizing on the unutterable boundary between gift and commodity, exploiting the moment of gift-giving which blurs the boundaries of possessions and rights. It is precisely this confusion that causes Marcus's unanswerable rage. Legal stealing is a terrible temptation, Norris seems to say; more than that, it brings out our worst instincts. When gifts and the market become conflated, the result is the terrible anti-gift—the exploitation and depletion of the gift rather than its regeneration and augmentation. This depletion of the abundant gift circle is initially legal and then turns illegal and finally lethal.

Frugality, too, is a form of legal stealing whenever there are gifts and bonds between people. Norris uses his character Trina, the miser, to exemplify this. From the beginning Trina holds onto her resources: recall her insistence in the beginning of the novel that McTeague not extract a dead tooth from her mouth but somehow preserve it. Yet, she turns truly miserly only after she wins the lottery and gives the large tooth to her husband. And her miserliness drives her to legally steal from others, more and more so, until her violations of the gift economy drive McTeague, in turn, to murder her. As soon as Trina wins the lottery—with the exception of the gift of the tooth—she begins to boycott the circulation of things in order to reap a profit from them. This boycott—this legal theft—is what turns the abundance of the lottery win into scarcity. Reacting to the lottery win not as a gift but as a fetish of kinds, Trina begins to cling to her $5,000 "with a tenacity that was surprising; it had become for her a thing miraculous, a god-from-the-machine . . . [;] she regarded it as something almost sacred and inviolable" (89). This sense is so strong it makes her perceive her gift of the tooth to McTeague as a loss, a hole or cavity that needs to be refilled. Trina's miserliness mirrors Marcus's feeling that his gift, Trina herself, is a loss he needs to recover. Indeed, the lottery win in the form of $5,000 compels both Trina and Marcus to re-see earlier gifts as losses; and they both try to restore these losses through legal stealing.[5]

Like Marcus, Trina begins to exploit gifts in the form of donations and hospitality in order to respond to the perceived loss. For example, when asked by her family for fifty dollars, Trina doesn't want to send the money: "'But fifty dollars is fifty dollars, Mac. Just think how long it takes to earn fifty dollars. Fifty dollars! That's two months of our interest'" (140). Trina's response shows both the tautology of money—unlike gifts it can only be understood in terms of itself—and the two ways to get it: working (industrial capitalism) and earning interest (finance capitalism). In both logics, a gift to the family is an incomprehensible and unjustifiable waste. But Trina does understand about community and therefore cannot outright deny her family help when they are in need. Instead, she responds to this dilemma by legally stealing:

> "I'll tell you what we'll do, Mac," she said to her husband; "you send half and I'll send half; we'll send twenty-five dollars altogether. Twelve and a half a piece. That's an idea. How will that do?" "Sure, sure," McTeague had answered, giving her the money. Trina sent McTeague's twelve dollars, but never sent the twelve that was to be her share. (141)

Trina thus exploits the gift community of marriage—a community in which one shares funds and extended family obligations—but she does so in order to "profit" by lying about her own share in this transaction. When McTeague asks her about it, she lies as she does later about the price of items she buys or the money they received from the sale of their goods (159). Every lie, every withheld gift to the community of their marriage, translates into a profit for Trina.

This rejection of family begins the separation of funds that fuels Trina's miserliness. She loses her ability to think in communal—even familial—terms. Later that becomes more obvious when McTeague cannot work as a dentist anymore and Trina wants to move them into a smaller room. McTeague refuses and reminds Trina of their marital gift community: "'Well, it's all in the family. What's yours is mine, and what's mine is yours, ain't it?' 'No, it's not; no, it's not; no, it's not,' cried Trina vehemently. 'It's all mine, mine. There's not a penny of it belongs to anybody else. I don't like to have to talk this way to you, but you just make me'" (151). McTeague responds as follows: "'You make me sick, you and your money. Why, you're a miser. I never saw anything like it. When I practiced, I never thought of my fees as my own; we lumped everything in together'" (152). Here again, Norris depicts McTeague as someone who naturally understands and even articulates the gift economies structuring his life; he assumes and condones that his fees move from market to gift exchange when he brings them home. And his response to Trina's perversion of these rules is an instinctive revulsion, a feeling of "sickness."

Trina, on the other hand, is more and more drawn into the sick realm of legal stealing, into the logic of the anti-gift. While McTeague's response is instinctual and organic, Trina's response is a logical, reasonable, self-interested exploitation of the gift economy within the logic of market exchange. Driven by this logic, Trina's legal stealing escalates throughout the novel. For example, "Trina still had her mania for family picnics, which had been one of the Sieppes' most cherished customs, but now there were other considerations" (126). Looked at through the eyes of the market, this gift-sharing custom is seen as a loss. Trina, who loves picnics, now worries about including others because it will incur a cost. In the same vein, Trina becomes increasingly scared of extending hospitality, while she seeks out the hospitality of others as a form of profit. For example, when Maria visits and suggests a cup of tea, Trina refuses to offer it:

> "No, no," cried Trina with niggardly apprehension; "no, I haven't got a bit of tea." Trina's stinginess had increased to such an extent that it had gone beyond mere hoarding of money. She grudged even the food that she and McTeague ate, and even brought away half loaves of bread, lumps of sugar, and fruit from the car conductor's coffee joint. She hid these pilferings away on the shelf by the window and often managed to make a very creditable lunch from them, enjoying the meal with the greater relish because it cost nothing. (164)

Norris here emphasizes the violations of gift-spheres (not only of friends but also of family and husband) involved in Trina's hoarding. In a perfectly logical mirroring of this, Trina pays visits as a form of profiteering: she "would go and call on Miss Baker on the floor below. The little dressmaker might ask her to stay for lunch, and that would be something saved" (172). Or she "would run over and see Maria; possibly she could have lunch there. At any rate, Maria would offer her a cup of tea" (174). Finally, she steals from herself and her husband, withholding food, lowering their standard of living, and forcing McTeague to walk in the rain rather than give him money for the bus fare (161). Of most importance is that Trina violates McTeague's human dignity when she makes it impossible for him to remain part of a community that depends on gift exchange: "What a humiliating position for Trina to place him in, not to leave him the price of a drink with a friend, she who had five thousand dollars" (163).

It is for this reason that McTeague begins to abuse Trina. Norris symbolically lets the violence begin on Thanksgiving (169). Then McTeague steals "her" money (190). Trying to reverse the alienation from the community Trina's miserliness costs him, McTeague squanders the money in order to have friends. But the city itself is too alienated a space to allow him to build a community: "He had spent her money here and there about the city in royal fashion, absolutely reckless of the morrow, feasting and drinking for the most part with companions he picked up heavens knows where, acquaintances of twenty four hours, whose names he forgot in two days, then suddenly he found himself at the end of his money. He no longer had any friends" (200). McTeague and Trina both are out of balance—their community and its natural gift flow destroyed by the lottery money and Trina's exploitative understanding of it.

Returning destitute and starving, McTeague finally kills his wife because she refuses to give a gift. The murder takes place during the Christmas season and on the day the kindergarten where Trina works celebrates Christmas and the New Year; it is, just like Thanksgiving, a day of gift exchange. Norris stresses that Trina herself has profited from the gift-giving season; her business of producing toys has boomed. "It's a good thing for me, " Trina reflects, that children "all have birthdays and Christmases" (188). When McTeague returns starving, Trina refuses to give him money for food, the most fundamental gesture of charity. In fact, she herself is appalled by her own refusal and reconsiders: "Miser though she was, Trina was only human, and the echo of the dentist's heavy feet had not died away before she began to be sorry for what she had done. 'I ought to have given him something. I wish I had; I *wish* I had,' she cried suddenly with a frightened gesture of both hands, 'what have I come to be that I would see Mac—my husband—that I would see him starve rather than give him money? No, no. It's too dreadful. I *will* give him some'" (199–200). She shouts after him, but it is too late. Trina herself understands that her humanity is at stake in her refusing to give McTeague food. Her husband sees the dreadfulness as well and in almost identical terms: "'She had five thousand dollars in that room, while I stood there, not twenty feet way, and told her I was starving, and she wouldn't give me a dime to get a cup of coffee. Oh, if I once get my hands on you!' His wrath strangled him" (200). His fury is fueled even more when he finds out that Tina has sold his concertina, which he now has to buy back: "Trina had sold his concertina—had stolen it and sold it—his concertina, his beloved concertina, that he had had all his life. Why, barring the canary, there was not one of all his belongings that McTeague had cherished more dearly" (202–3). Norris stresses McTeague's hating Trina for this legal theft of the concertina, an object he is attached to as he is to the bird, each possession offering him intangible pleasures of self-expression. The refusal to feed him and the theft and sale of the instrument both are unbearable, inhuman violations of the gift structures of human lives. And these violations against his humanity create the rage in McTeague that drives him to murder Trina.

It is therefore telling and keenly appropriate that he kills Trina on a gift-giving holiday. Trina receives a dollar as a gift from one of the ladies (204),[6] and then, in response to her denying him even that, McTeague kills her and leaves her to die in a pool of blood (207), while he rescues the canary: "The canary would be days without food; it was likely it would starve, would die there, hour by hour, in its little gilt prison. McTeague resolved to take it with him. He took down the cage, touching it gently with his enormous hands, and tied a couple of sacks about it to shelter the little bird from the sharp night wind" (207). McTeague kills Trina, in other words, for refusing the gesture he now extends to the bird. The dentist's innate nature is gentle and caring. Trina's refusal to give him food when he was starving and shelter when he was freezing is inhuman, and his response to this inhumanity is grotesquely violent. Yet, he immediately resumes caring human behavior, giving the bird what Trina refused to him. He gives till the end of the novel and at great risk of his own life. Norris makes clear, then, that McTeague killed Trina because she refused the most fundamental gift and thus lost her own humanity and threatened McTeague's. Trina's murder, in a sense, serves to put an end to legal stealing and to restore the gift community.

The novel contains several other murders, each of which is a result of miserliness and legal stealing. In a way, the two misers Maria and Zerkow "legally" murder their child by neglecting to give, as Trina refused McTeague, the simple, fundamental gifts of nurturing. Thus, the death of this child is the perverse opposite of McTeague's care for the canary and its survival. Later, Zerkow murders Maria and then kills himself because Maria cannot remember the story about the golden dishes that Zerkow needs to live and that he expected to get for free for the rest of his marriage. The story Maria tells of the golden dishes is at the core of the gift relations between the two misers in that when Maria tells the story, Zerkow offers her a drink. But this is, from the beginning, also a perversion of gift relations since Zerkow marries Maria to be able to get this story for free and as often as possible. He never circulates the story further; indeed his miserliness, which causes the death of his child, prevents the tradition from going on. When Maria loses the story, cannot remember it anymore, Zerkow kills her and himself. The story, that of Maria's family, is yet another hint by Norris about one of the fundamental gifts that build community—the gift of tradition, inheritance of meaning and recirculation of meaning. In the story of Maria and Zerkow, we see how miserliness brings an end to two gift cycles: that of the gift of life and that of the gift of tradition and inheritance.

Finally, Norris leaves no doubt that McTeague's murder of Marcus is a result of legal stealing. In retaliation for McTeague's 'theft' of Trina, Marcus legally steals from McTeague when he reveals to the world that the dentist does not have a license. Yet, even then Marcus cannot get over the loss of the $5,000 he associates with his gift of Trina to *McTeague*. When he joins the search party for McTeague, he explains his interest in—his deathly, relentless obsession with—finding McTeague not in terms of Trina's murder but in terms of this loss: "'This thing's a personal matter of mine—an' that money he got away with, that five thousand dollars, belongs to me by rights'" (237). Till the last moment, when both men realize that they are dead men because they are without water in the middle of Death Valley, they still struggle over the $5,000 that caused their enmity in the first place. When McTeague tries to take the money with him, Marcus's rage is refueled: "'Hold on,' exclaimed Marcus with rising aggressiveness. 'Let's talk about that. I ain't so sure about who that— who that money belongs to.' 'Well, I *am,* you see,' growled the dentist. The old enmity between the two men, their ancient hate, was flaming up again" (242–43). Marcus, like Trina, is driven by a compelling force that lies between gift and market exchange. Even in this last scene he cannot quite claim the money as his own and is left with a feeling of injustice that cannot be eradicated. He is driven by the same unutterable forces—unutterable at least when facing McTeague—that propelled him in the beginning of the novel. Unable to let gifts circulate and to trust such circulation, he is caught in the mistake of trying to recover the "loss" of his initial gift, a loss he felt to be depleting rather than augmenting his life only when it got a price tag. This poisonous feeling of friendship, revenge, and rage makes Marcus lock McTeague to his dying body. The two enemies/friends die in the deathly scarcity of Death Valley—a space symbolic of the scarcity of the realm of the anti-gift even within the presence of abundance. Nearly all of the characters in the novel kill friends and family, and all do so as a result of legal stealing—the type of legal stealing, Norris emphasizes, that corrodes the gift community, poisons it into its opposite, and murders human life and dignity.

As Walter Benn Michaels writes,

> One could, perhaps, best describe naturalism as a working-out of a set of conflicts between pretty things and curious things, material and representation, hard money and soft, beast and soul. But this doesn't mean that the naturalist writer is someone who has chosen the beastly side of these dichotomies (the side literary history ordinarily associates with naturalism) or even that he is someone who

has chosen with any consistency either side. The consistency—indeed, the identity—of naturalism resides in the logics and their antithetical relation to one another, not necessarily in any individual, any text, even any single sentence. (173)

Comparing his own definition of naturalism to those of Pizer and Richard Chase, both of whom assert "Norris's commitment to the 'strength of man's animality'" (173), Michaels clarifies in a footnote that his "own point is not so much to quarrel with these characterizations as to suggest an understanding of naturalism in which their negations would also have a place" (173). My own essay contributes to both of these strategies of approaching naturalism. It takes its fundamental definition of naturalism as a form of "pessimistic realism" that is concerned with man's animality from Pizer, and it is inspired by Michaels's interest in locating naturalism within economic questions.

Pizer argues about *McTeague*:

Norris believed that the source of . . . violence beneath the surface placidity of life is the presence in all men of animal qualities that have played a major role in man's evolutionary development but which are now frequently atavistic and destructive. Norris's theme is that man's individual family heritage (alcoholic degeneracy in McTeague's case) can combine as a force towards reversion, toward a return to the emotions and instincts of man's animal past. McTeague is in one sense a "special case" of reversion, since his degenerate parents in part cause his atavistic brutality. He is also, however, any man caught up in the net of sex, and in this second aspect of man's inherited animal nature Norris introduces a tragic element into McTeague's fall, an element that contributes to the novel's thematic tension. (89)

There is no doubt that Norris links McTeague's atavistic nature to his sexual awakening, to his degenerate parents, and to his race.[7] However, the trigger for the lethal violence, the atavistic brutality, between the characters is the legal stealing certain characters pursue, the mingling of the gift and the market economy. Animal nature itself is not aggressive; or, at least, the novel is consistently uncertain about that.[8] The narrator makes contradictory statements about the dentist's nature. For example, in the beginning of the novel we read that "McTeague's mind was as his body, heavy, slow to act, sluggish. Yet there was nothing vicious about the man. Altogether he suggested the draft horse, immensely strong, stupid, docile, obedient" (6). Later he is described as a "gigantic, good-natured Saint Bernard" (79). But, even within a page, we also find contradictory remarks such as "to hurt Trina was a positive anguish for McTeague" and "suddenly the animal instinct in the man stirred and woke; the evil instincts that in him were close to the surface leaped to life, shouting and clamoring" (21). McTeague tries to struggle against that animal instinct, his sexual passion for Trina, but he loses. However, the infamous first kiss, gross as it is, and as much as it is a sign of his yielding to that animal instinct, is not evil but actually rather benign in effect, leading to the marriage between Trina and McTeague.

What make McTeague truly vicious are violations to the gift economy that structures the social body and gives humans dignity and humanity. Almost formulaically, Norris compares the fight between Marcus and McTeague to the animosity between two caged dogs in order to show that nature is not violent but that the enmity between the two men is. The dogs, who appear to hate each other, finally face each other, and, to everyone's surprise and disappointment, refuse to fight: "with all the dignity of monarchs they moved away from each other" (123). In this prelude to the fight between McTeague and Marcus, Norris makes clear that it is not natural to fight; the two dogs that seemingly hate each other in their cages choose not to once they are free. And, it is not natural instinct but rather the regret over the gift exchange from the vantage point of the market that precipitates the violence between the two men: "Never had the quarrel between the two men been completely patched up. It did not seem possible to the dentist now that Marcus had ever been his pal, that they had ever taken long walks together. He was sorry that he had treated Marcus gratis for an ulcerated tooth, while Marcus daily recalled the fact that he had given up his girl to his friend—the girl who had won a fortune —as the great mistake of his life" (124–25).

In a similar vein, Trina becomes self-destructively, violently miserly only when she abandons the rules of the gift economy. She herself sees the lottery as changing her: "'I didn't use to be so stingy,' she told herself. 'Since I won in the lottery I've become a regular little miser. It's growing on me, but never mind, it's a good fault, and anyhow I can't help it'" (119). The narrator concurs: "Trina had always been an economical little body, but it was only since her great winning in the lottery that she had become especially penurious" (107). The pessimism of Norris's naturalism is evident here: while it is not natural for Trina to be violently stingy—indeed, her enormous gift to McTeague might be read as her natural response to the abundance the lottery brings—her entrance into a world of money, speculation, investment (the market) makes her so. At the same time she grows obsessive, we see McTeague initially converting back to a gift economy in his relation to others. He spends all his money on making "friends" in bars. Later in the novel he shares his gold finds with his partner. There is a suggestion here that gift exchange—a peaceful, humane network of human relations—is part of human nature. Characters only abandon this humane behavior when they are seduced to think in market terms and so turn from giving to legal stealing, from a gift community to the perverse realm of the anti-gift. In this realm—an almost inevitable realm once one is seduced to exploit the gift through the logic of the market—elemental and horrible violence and atavism are unleashed. In a perverse defense of one's humanity—which can only exist within the realm of the gift—Norris's characters revert to the atavistic and destructive forces Pizer describes. In this impossible struggle, Norris indeed creates great tragedy.

In this essay, I suggest that we consider carefully this central theme, which Norris himself sets up as the key issue in the very beginning of the novel and which the novel pursues to its very end. The economic concerns of the novel cannot only be seen in its interest in gold but also in Norris's astute and complex view of the intermingling of gift and market economies.[9] While Michaels argues that seeing *McTeague* in light of the gold standard debate is useful but does not place the novel in a particular position in that debate, my reading of the novel's interest in gift and market economies reveals the novel's rather consistent—even forceful—theory about the relation of those economies. It is a key to Norris's naturalism: his "realism with a pessimistic determinism." Seeing the overwhelming logic of market exchange invade the lives of all his characters, and seeing at the same time the necessity of gift exchange for their humanity, Norris depicts an inevitable fall into the horrible space of the anti-gift. The gift makes us—even the carnivorous McTeague—human. But, by its very nature, the gift cannot defend itself against legal stealing, and so the market corrodes the gift and deprives us of human dignity. It is the nature of the logic of the market turned loose onto the realm of the gift—a realm wherein stealing becomes legal—that brings out the angry beast in us, according to Norris. In that hybrid space, the gift turns into its legal and finally lethal antidote, the anti-gift, which turns humans into angry bestial monsters, loyal friends into furious enemies, mothers into murderers, and life itself into a desert, a valley of death, a lethal, perverse realm of extraction, sterility, and hate. The anti-gift is Norris's foreboding vision of a capitalist twentieth-century America.

NOTES

Regarding the epigraph: Donald Pizer calls this "a traditional and widely accepted concept of American naturalism" (85) in his 1965 essay, "Nineteenth Century American Naturalism," reprinted in *The Theory and Practice of American Literary Naturalism: Selected Essays and Reviews* (Carbondale: Southern Illinois UP, 1993).

1. In *Given Time,* for example, Derrida remarks that "we know that as good, it can also be bad, poisonous (*Gift, gift*), and this from the moment the gift puts the other in debt, with the result that giving amounts to hurting, to doing harm" (12). Derrida takes this idea from Marcel Mauss's essay "Gift, Gift," which examines the relation between the English word *gift* (present) and the German word *gift* (poison).

2. Norris, for example, does not mention that Marcus ever reciprocated the gifts McTeague extended.

3. Technically, Marcus had simply lent the money he now reclaims from McTeague. Marcus told his friend at the time: "I'll pay for you and you can square with me when we go home" (44). But the issue had never come up again until this moment, when Trina's lottery win changes Marcus's attitude towards the dentist. Nonetheless, the incident shows again that Marcus never truly thinks in gift terms.

4. It is important in this context that the novel never reveals where this gift comes from and that the narrator does not know how it has been paid for.

5. Barbara Hochmann's article "Loss, Habit, Obsession: The Governing Dynamic of *McTeague*" has as its central argument that the "structure [of the novel] centers on the problem of personal loss and its implication for the self" (179). Hochmann argues that McTeague is not sufficiently able to adapt to change and to accept loss.

6. This detail once again betrays Norris's careful treatment of gift exchange. The money as gift is the gift gesture within an employer-employee relationship.

7. Hugh Dawson's article "McTeague as Ethnic Stereotype" elaborates on McTeague as an Irish American.

8. Many critics have noted this inconsistency; see for example, Ware, p. 45, Hochmann, p. 189.

9. For example, Thomas Ware's article "'Gold to Airy Thinness Beat': The Midas Touch in Frank Norris's *McTeague*" discusses the central symbolism of gold in the novel and its close relation to greed. While Ware notices many if not all the same moments analyzed in my essay, he comes to the conclusion that the "doctrine is simply that life, so abundant, so appealing in the daily satisfaction of physical needs, so promising, cannot be regenerated in the search of sterile wealth or anything which seems to represent it; 'gold' itself, scattered almost carelessly throughout the novel, comes in the end to be equated with insensitivity and death, even as it is, say, in Chaucer's 'Pardoner's Tale' or in the legend of Midas" (40). What gets lost in such a reading are the complexities of Norris's thinking about economic transactions as well as an account of the specific interest in what I have called legal stealing in this essay, an activity that structurally undergirds the novel and gives it its overwhelmingly pessimistic logic.

Works Cited

Dawson, Hugh J. "McTeague As Ethnic Stereotype." *American Literary Realism* 20.1 (Fall 1987): 34–44.

Derrida, Jacques. *Given Time: I. Counterfeit Money.* Chicago: U of Chicago P, 1992.

Hochmann, Barbara. "Loss, Habit, Obsession: The Governing Dynamic of *McTeague*." *Studies in American Fiction* 14.2 (Fall 1986): 179–90.

Hyde, Lewis. *The Gift.* New York: Vintage, 1983.

Mauss, Marcel. *The Gift.* New York: Norton, 1990.

————. "Gift, Gift." 1924. *The Logic of the Gift.* Ed. Alan Schrift. New York: Routledge, 1997. 28–32.

Michaels, Walter Benn. *The Gold Standard and the Logic of Naturalism.* Berkeley: U of California P, 1987.

Norris, Frank. *McTeague.* Ed. Donald Pizer. Norton Critical Edition. New York: Norton, 1997.

Pizer, Donald. *The Theory and Practice of American Literary Naturalism.* Carbondale: Southern Illinois UP, 1993.

Ware, Thomas C. "'Gold to Airy Thinness Beat': The Midas Touch in Frank Norris's *McTeague*." *Interpretations* 13.1 (Fall 1981): 39–47.

"The Signs and Symbols of the West"

FRANK NORRIS, *THE OCTOPUS,* AND THE
NATURALIZATION OF MARKET CAPITALISM

—Adam H. Wood

The best business you can go into you will find on your father's farm or in his workshop. If you have no family or friends to aid you, and no prospect opened to you there, turn your face to the great West, and there build up a home and fortune.
—Horace Greeley, 1841

We do not ride the railroad; it rides upon us. Did you ever think what those sleepers are that underlie the railroad? Each one is a man. . . .The rails are laid on them, and they are covered with sand, and the cars run smoothly over them. They are sound sleepers, I assure you. And every year a new lot is laid down and run over; so that, if some have the pleasure of riding on a rail, others have the misfortune to be ridden upon.
—Henry David Thoreau, 1854

WITH *THE OCTOPUS* (1901), FRANK NORRIS BEGAN TO NARROW HIS FOCUS ON THE FACTORS THAT "DETERMINE" THE CONDITIONS OF HUMAN EXISTENCE. Often concerned with the natural inadequacies of humankind—greed, avarice, alcoholism, genetic inevitability, etc.—in novels such as *McTeague* and *Vandover and the Brute,* with *The Octopus* Norris addresses, while under the veil of natural considerations, predominantly more material themes. This is not to suggest that material themes were completely new to Norris's work. Considerations of his novels have always noted his insertion of symbols of the material world (take, for example, the overbearing image of the tacky, gilded tooth in *McTeague*), but these symbols were always presented merely as signs of the characters' desires and failings and not of the *cause* of those desires and failings. *The Octopus,* for the first time in Norris's work, marks material considerations as the central influence on the characters within.

This shift from the Darwinian natural to the more material may, as many critics have argued, be traced directly to the volume and intensity of research Norris conducted when seeking out the story of *The Octopus:* the events leading to and resulting from the Mussell Slough shootout between the farmers of the central San Joaquin Valley and the Southern Pacific Railroad. Donald Pizer notes that Norris "devoted more time and effort to *The Octopus* than to any of his other works . . . compil[ing] several notebooks of newspaper clippings bearing on economic and social issues taken up in the novel" (*Novels* 121). The extent of Norris's investigation is not surprising, however, in consideration of the task he set out to achieve. "I think there is a chance for somebody to do some great work with the West and California as a background," Norris wrote to William Dean Howells in 1899; "My idea is to write three novels around the subject of Wheat . . . and in each to keep the idea of this huge Niagara of wheat rolling from West to East" (*Letters* 34). To complete such a massive task, Norris needed to understand not only the event of the shootout but the characters—both human and corporate—that were involved in the event and to recast these in terms of his creative project "with all the guts [he could] get into it" (*Letters* 48).

What Norris's research produced, I will argue, is the setting for the creation of the *myth* of the Mussell Slough incident and the California "background" found within *The Octopus.* In the text, we find Norris working to simplify his research and romanticize events in order to construct a novel that is largely historically accurate and yet riddled with ideological contradictions. This essay traces these fictional forms of contradictions to their historical source in the two central yet markedly non-human characters of the novel—the wheat and the railroad. Norris's artistic representations of these "signs and symbols of the West" (as the young poet Presley terms them, 47) as self-sufficient, reified entities work to articulate an already established cultural myth of the "naturalness" of the material process and conflict in the novel, the struggle to control political power. By reexamining the popular cultural attitudes towards the Californian wheat market and the overarching dependence on the railroad for the distribution of this vital crop, I will show that the contradictions of myth within *The Octopus* are indicative of the larger political contradictions within the socially Darwinistic historical climate of the early twentieth century. Read in this way, *The Octopus* may be viewed as a text which unconsciously reveals the process of myth construction inherent in the reification of the market of wheat as a natural phenomenon.

BETWEEN HISTORY AND MYTH: MUSSELL SLOUGH AND ITS REPRESENTATION

On May 11, 1880, a bitter conflict over land rights came to a bloody conclusion. That morning, United States Marshall Alonzo W. Poole arrived at Henry Brewer's ranch, Mussell Slough, with orders to evict Brewer from the land he had worked and cultivated for nearly a decade. With Poole that morning were the land's two new "legal" owners, Walter J. Crow and Mills D. Hartt. Expecting the arrival of the eviction notice, Brewer was not alone. At least a dozen of Brewer's fellow settlers—also to be evicted from their lands—had come to meet the marshall to deny the rights of the new owners to take their land. According to Oscar Lewis in his study *The Big Four,* an account of the Central Pacific Railroad, as the marshall moved to meet the group, "[a] spokesman for the farmers demanded that he delay dispossessing any of their numbers until the higher court had passed on the legality" of the seizure (393). The marshall, "who had no taste for his role" in the affair, submitted to the farmers' suggestion that he allow them to escort him "safely out of the county" (394). Crow and Hartt, however, were not to be so easily persuaded to abandon their right to the farmers' land. Crow, apparently the more volatile of the two, raised his shotgun and proceeded to fire, shooting one of the farmers in the face. The farmers then returned fire on Crow and Hartt. After the gunfire had ceased, eight men including Crow and Hartt lay dead scattered about the farm. Despite the horror of the battle, the remaining farmers and their families were only weeks later evicted from their land.

While land disputes were quite common in the vast landscape of California, the conflict at Mussell Slough was more complex than most. Brewer and the other farmers had been leasing their land from the Southern Pacific Railroad and expected eventually to buy the land outright at a cost of $2.50 to $10 an acre as initially quoted by the railroad. In order to cultivate the arid land, the farmers had united their capital and built an extensive irrigation system. While the irrigation system did improve the quality of their land and the abundance of their crops, it also made the land far more valuable for the railroad than the original quoted price. The railroad adjusted the cost to an outlandish $25 to $40 per acre and then demanded that ranchers either purchase their lands at the newly quoted prices or quit their improved land to make room for new purchasers. While the farmers initially felt that the railroad had simply forgotten their previous agreements and prices, they became increasingly aware of the reality of the situation as the railroad began advertising the land for public sale. Believing that legal maneuvers promised to correct the railroad's misdeeds, the farmers united and organized a Settlers' League, submitting their case to the Californian Congressional representatives. In late 1879, the case came to trial, but the farmers' limited legal resources were outdone by the railroad's expansive legal talent and, more importantly, the railroad's control over much of the politics of California by means of both legal and illegal financial support. The decision sided with the railroad, and the farmers were left to return to their land to prepare an appeal to the Supreme Court. Before the Supreme Court could make a decision, however, a United States Marshall arrived at Brewer's Mussell Slough with the land's new owners to enforce the original ruling (Lewis 354–90).

Crow and Hartt, the new owners of the land—including Brewer's—were not simply farmers who sought to make a living off of the land but were, instead, dummy purchasers. "They had come into the valley," Lewis records, "because the railroad had offered them free farms provided they were able to maintain possession of them against the settlers" (391). Confident that they could indeed "maintain possession" of the land, Crow and Hartt came prepared for resistance, and it was, surely enough, resistance they found. Despite the bloodshed at Mussell Slough, the railroad did eventually retake possession of the land, furthering its monopolistic hold over the wheat industry in California. What had appeared initially as a simple land dispute was, in actuality, one of the most hostile corporate takeovers in American history to date. The Southern Pacific now had hold over the whole industry and made the railroad the largest landowner in the entire state.

Most of this history, if not all, Frank Norris knew. As a novelist, Norris believed in the inescapable importance of research. Having spent two years as a *Wave* reporter, Norris surely understood the need for accuracy in reporting and recognized that in order to achieve accuracy, thorough research was essential. And while Norris is known to have spent a great deal of time doing research for his earlier novels, "firsthand research was required" for the construction of *The Octopus* (Pizer 118). Norris immersed himself in studying newspaper reports of the Mussell Slough incident, interviewing many of the major figures involved, as well as researching the economic dealings of the Southern Pacific Railroad. Norris's research familiarized him intimately not only with the events leading to, resulting from, and including the Mussell Slough massacre but with the major individuals involved.

However, despite Norris's research and the undeniable accuracy of certain aspects of the novel, *The Octopus* is not an historical novel. Much of the

shift from historical accuracy to fictional representation may be understood
in terms of Norris's naturalistic approach to fiction outlined in his discussion
of "Zola as a Romantic Writer." "The naturalist takes no note of common
people," Norris writes,

> common in so far as their interests, their lives, and the things that
> occur in them are common, are ordinary. Terrible things must
> happen to the characters of the naturalistic tale. They must be
> twisted from the ordinary, wrenched out from the quiet, unevent-
> ful round of every-day life, and flung into the throes of a vast and
> terrible drama that works itself out in unleashed passions, in
> blood, and in sudden death. (*Literary Criticism* 71–72)

The process of Norris's fictionalization of the events of Mussell Slough may
be seen to have taken two distinct yet inexorably related patterns. The first
pattern, reflecting Norris's contention that the naturalist "takes no note of
common people," is demonstrated by his simplification of history in his
reassigning of the class position of the farmers in the novel. While the farmers who actually resisted and ultimately lost to the railroad were predominantly working-class individuals—mostly immigrants who struck out West
seeking to support themselves and their families—Norris's farmers are, as
Pizer notes, "capitalists who have large investments in land and equipment
and who are competing with the railroad for the riches of the land" (120).
The second pattern, suggested by Norris's contention that the events of the
naturalist novel must be "twisted from the ordinary," deals with a specific
style of romanticization that works to draw attention away from just such a
simplification of history. Within *The Octopus,* the characters are provided a
certain grandiosity, and the events are portrayed in a style that Norris felt to
be "epic." Thus, Norris takes a story of industrial conflict—the working-
class farmers versus the industrial giant of the railroad—and provides it
with what he understood to be "the unplumbed depths of the human heart,
and the mystery of sex, and the problems of life, and the black, unsearched
penetralia of the soul of man" (*Literary Criticism* 78). By removing the "common people" and romanticizing the events of the novel at the price of the
actual historical conflict, Norris allows two distinctly non-human—and
thus reified—characters to come to the forefront of the novel: the wheat and
the train. It is only through the exclusion of the workers and the romanticization of events that these two reified characters are able to "control" the
events of the novel.

CULTIVATING A MYTH: THE LIFE OF THE WHEAT

The Octopus is not, then, a text about the individuals and events surrounding Mussell Slough; it is less about the characters who work the crops as it is about the crops that work the characters. Norris had conceived of it as only one of "three novels around the one subject of wheat" (*Letters* 34). In his letters to Howells, he elaborates his "idea": "First, a study of California (the producer), second, a study of Chicago (the distributor), third, a study of Europe (the consumer)" (34). *The Octopus, The Pit,* and the unwritten *The Wolf* were to comprise the story of the production, distribution, and consumption—the life cycle as it were—of one of the most precious of late-nineteenth-century commodities. His "epic" *The Octopus* opens just "after the recent hauling of the crop" and, in spite of the conflict and violence throughout the novel, ends with the cold reminder *"But the* Wheat *remained"* (3, 651). Norris presents the wheat as not a simple crop for cultivation but, rather, as "a concrete symbol of man's relationship to nature" (Pizer, *Novels* 117). It is the unique naturalist conception of "man's relationship to nature" that further empowers the grand symbol of wheat. Norris, at least partially subscribing to the naturalist "school" (a precarious term itself), championed the philosophy that humankind was determined (and usually pessimistically so) by the larger forces of nature. This philosophy builds on Zola's contention made years earlier in his *The Experimental Novel* that "there is an absolute determinism in the existing conditions of natural phenomena" of which humankind was just one. It is in this sense that Norris develops the wheat as a symbol for both a provider of wealth and as a power indifferent to those for whom it provides. The characters that populate the novel are secondary to the power of the wheat because they are subject to its power.

It is noteworthy, as June Howard asserts, that "the characters we *see* in *The Octopus* are agriculturists on a scale never attempted by the farmers who resisted the railroad at Mussell Slough" (121). Norris for the most part erases the largely immigrant farmer population and replaces them with "gentlemen ranchers, employers of farmhands who . . . scarcely get their hands dirty" (Howard 121). Interestingly, Norris may have unwittingly revealed his selectivity in choosing the characters who populate the novel. Reflecting, perhaps, Norris's lack of concern for the actual workers of the farms is the young poet Presley who, after meeting one of the immigrant workers (one of the very few glimpses the novel offers), shows little tolerance for the working class on the farms. Norris writes, "These uncouth brutes of farmhands and petty ranchers, grimed with the soil they worked upon, were odious to him beyond words. Never could he feel in sympathy with them, nor with their lives, their ways, their marriages, deaths, bickerings, and all the monotonous round of their sordid existence" (5). Thus, while Norris acknowledges the *presence* of the workers on the farms by presenting the emigrant Bismarck first, he quickly reminds the reader that it is not such individuals who are the focus of the story. These "petty" farmhands are insignificant in comparison to the great battle of capital embodied in the struggle for the control of wheat.

It should also be remembered that when Norris set out to create *The Octopus,* he sought to create a story that was, in his own words, "distinctly American" (*Letters* 34). In attempting to produce a story that was at once of California and yet "distinctly American," Norris would have been quite aware of not only what he conceived America to be but what his reading public would have conceived America to be.[1] A predominantly white, middle-class American reading public would be less likely to sympathize with the struggle of immigrant farmers in conflict with a white-run railroad. Again, there is a striking similarity between Norris's desire to write a story that is both honest to the story of California (the novel's subtitle) and America and the dilemma that Presley faces in his quest for his muse. In a lengthy passage that bears reproducing here, Norris writes of how Presley ponders his quest:

> But whatever he wrote, and in whatever fashion, Presley was determined that his poem should be of the West; that world's frontier of Romance, where a new race, a new people—hardy, brave, and passionate—were building an empire; where the tumultuous life ran like fire from dawn to dark, and from dark to dawn again, primitive, brutal, honest, and without fear. . . . He strove for the diapason, the great song that should embrace in itself a whole epoch, a complete era, the voice of an entire people, wherein all people should be included—they and their legends, their folklore, their fightings, their loves and their lusts, their blunt, grim humour, their stoicism under stress, their adventures, their treasures found in a day and gambled in a night, their direct, crude speech . . . —all this, all the traits and types of every community from the Dakotas to the Mexicos, from Winnipeg to Guadalupe, gathered together, swept together, welded and riven together in one single, mighty song, the Song of the West. (9–10)

Yet, despite the great length Norris goes to provide an all-inclusive list of the numerous "types of every community," *The Octopus* (and, we are led to believe, Presley's poem "The Toilers," too) is not about these people. At the same time, Norris seems to make a conscious effort to remind the reader that the "true" story of California is not to be found within *The Octopus.* What we find in the novel is, instead, a distinctly "whitewashed" American story. That is, once the workers (aside from extremely limited appearances) are erased from the novel, the image of the wheat can begin to take on new prominence. And, as the workers of the farms are ignored, so, too, is the work that wheat cultivation requires. Thus, Presley enters Los Muertos only "after the recent hauling of the crop" (3), after the workers and the work are effectively finished.

Norris, it seems, is aware of the ludicrousness of the proposition of a farm without workers. As we learn early in the novel, "[t]here had not been much of a crop to haul that year" (4). Magnus Derrick, the "owner" of Los Muertos, who "had hardly raised more than enough to supply seed for the winter's sowing" is purported to want in the coming year to work his land *without* the workers (4); as Bismarck tells us, "Mist'r Derrick gowun to farm der whole demn rench hisseluf der next yahr. No more tenants" (6). Responding to such an outlandish suggestion, Annixter tells Presley "'You give Magnus Derrick my compliments and tell him he's a fool'" (28). Annixter's contention about the impossibility of Derrick's maintaining his farm alone suggests Norris's awareness of the problematic of writing an "epic of wheat" without writing about the workers who are essential to the initial step of cultivation. That is, despite the novel's beginning *after* the harvest and thus being able to omit the workers, Norris consciously reminds the reader that there are, in fact, or, at least, have been workers. Readers, then, enter *The Octopus* much like Presley; they are aware that there must be workers, as evidenced by the lone Bismarck and the discussion of Derrick's prospects of working his land alone, yet what they witness, what they observe, is an atmosphere virtually devoid of anything beyond the trace of those workers because they are secondary to the story Norris sought to write. "Accuracy is the attainment of small minds," Norris tells us, "In fiction [accuracy] can under certain circumstances be dispensed with altogether. . . . To be true is the all-important business" (*Literary Criticism* 58).

With the workers carefully written out of the story, Norris is able to put his full powers to depicting the wheat itself—of which there seems an infinite supply. The power of the image of wheat in *The Octopus* is based largely on its sheer volume. Indeed, the Los Muertos setting is a sea of wheat; houses and their inhabitants are mere islands amongst the raging tide of grain. It is a landscape where "[f]rom the steps of the porch," Derrick observes, "the view to the southward expanded to infinity. There was not so much as a twig to obstruct the view. . . . The flat monotony of the land, clean of fencing, was broken by one spot only, the roof of the Division Superintendent's house . . ." (58). And while Derrick views the wheat before him strictly in terms of its market value as much as he did the gold mines he had worked previously, other characters feel the wheat to be much more sinister at its core. Derrick's wife, for example, is led to feel that "never for one moment since the time her first glance lost itself in the unbroken immensity of the ranches had she known a moment's content. . . . Los Muertos frightened her" (59). For Mrs. Derrick, the wheat is far more than a crop; it is something that "troubled her, and even at times filled her with an undefinable terror. To her mind there was something inordinate about it all; something almost unnatural. The direct brutality of ten thousand acres of wheat, nothing but wheat as far as the eye could see" (60). Mrs. Derrick's fears of "an undefinable terror" alert the reader that the wheat is, within *The Octopus,* far more complex than a mere staple. For Mrs. Derrick, the wheat possesses an agency beyond its place as "food of the people": it is "unnatural," "direct," and "brutal." In sharp contrast to the notion of wheat as simply a passive, natural crop to be cultivated, the wheat here is figured as being a power unto itself. Mrs. Derrick's remarks reflect what Carey McWilliams terms "the folklore of climatology" in his study *Southern California Country:* "In many cases . . . the size and rapidity with which things grew in Southern California conveyed a sense of unreality so overpowering as to make the visitors feel unhappy and profoundly disconcerted" (102). As a relative newcomer to California from "five hundred acres, neatly partitioned" in eastern Ohio, Mrs. Derrick senses an agency to the wheat beyond its "growing" that inspires "an undefinable terror."

Mrs. Derrick is not alone in her panic, though others have little trouble defining precisely what is to be feared about the wheat: *its market.* While Mrs. Derrick interprets her terror as a direct result of the wheat's multitudinous *self,* the farmers fear the wheat only in its function *as a commodity:*

> Magnus and the multitude of other ranchers . . . had no love for their land. They were not attached to the soil. They worked their ranches as a quarter of a century before they had worked their mines. To husband the resources of their marvellous [*sic*] San Joaquin, they considered it niggardly, petty, Hebraic. To get all there was out of the land, to squeeze it dry, to exhaust it, seemed their policy. When, at last, the land worn out, would refuse to yield, they would invest their money in something else; by then, they all have made fortunes. They did not care. "After us the deluge." (298)

The importance of wheat, then, for the farmers, has to do with wheat itself only insofar as the market of wheat affects them. Once that market "refuses to yield," they will seek out another market. There is no love for the land; there is instead a love for the commodity. Derrick and, we assume, the other farmers had set out to farm only after the promise of success had been made: "In a few years [California's] output of wheat exceeded the value of her output of gold, and when, later on, the Pacific and Southwestern railroad threw open to settlers the rich lands of Tulare county . . . Magnus had been quick to seize the opportunity and had taken up the ten thousand acres of Los Muertos" (64). The market of wheat entices the farmers, but not the wheat itself.

The market, however, is not always kind. The wheat market is in constant conflict with other markets, and the farmers know—as Norris would have—that any market can both create and destroy fortunes. Huddled around the ticker—"the most significant object in [Harran's] office"—the farmers "no longer felt their individuality, . . . a unit in the vast agglomeration of wheat land the whole world round" (53–54). As part of Norris's "Niagara of wheat," the farmers begin to associate the market with the wheat itself: the wheat that the farmers have unnaturally wrested from the land and transformed into market begins to renaturalize itself, for all the farmers, as a living market in the throes of perpetual peril. "Everything seemed to combine to lower the price of wheat," we learn:

> The extension of wheat areas always exceeded increase of population; competition was growing fiercer every year. The farmer's profits were the object of attack from a score of different quarters. It was a flock of vultures descending upon a common prey . . . cut and cut and cut. Everything, every element of the world's markets, tended to force down the price to the lowest possible figure at which it could be profitably farmed. (56)

In animating the economic conflict at the base of the events of the novel, Norris presents the wheat market as a natural phenomenon. It is a market animalized, full of fierce competition, attacks, and flocks of vultures. The wheat market is presented less as subject to the changes of the overall market and of capital than it is subject to every element of the natural world. The wheat market is, in fact, so natural as to be subject to predators. Norris's animalization of the wheat market works ironically to romanticize the wheat *itself* as the object of central concern in the novel; the wheat market thus moves to the forefront of the novel as an individual character subject to the laws of nature and to the style of naturalism.

The wheat market is, therefore, not simply the location for conflict or merely part of the California backdrop but, instead, the central motivator or agent for action within the novel. It is this romanticization of the market that leads Walter Benn Michaels to argue that "the subject of naturalism becomes the money economy so that the economy can become a subject" (178). For Michaels, this "ascription of interests to a money economy . . . is only a figure of speech or a mistake, personification or pathetic fallacy" in that it fails to consider the absent individuals who make up the economy: The economy is "made up of people, and it acts likes a person; but the person it acts like is not the people it is made up of" (178, 179). The romanticization of the wheat market results in a similar mythical construct, a market functioning as an individual independent of the individuals who actually effect its constitution.

The romantic personification of the wheat market is not, of course, limited to its fictional construction within *The Octopus*. The source for Norris's personification of the market may be traced directly back to its source in the *language* of the market itself. In researching the economy surrounding the Mussell Slough incident, Norris would have likely come across numerous references to the personification of wheat such as crop reports declaring that there was "AN EXCITED WHEAT MARKET" and that "Wheat [was] fairly active and a shade higher."[2] Like the discussion of wheat in the novel, popular presses encouraged the personification of the wheat market with the use of terms like "excited" and "active" to imply a wheat market that functions on its own. As in the novel, such a discourse ignores the process of wheat production and those who work to cultivate wheat, and is thus able to present the wheat based solely on its *market value*. Once transformed in such a way, the wheat is figured less as a simple natural crop (subject to strictly natural laws) as it is a commodity subject to mythically naturalized market laws. With the workers erased and the wheat given epic status, the conflict of the novel becomes less that between the farmers (and their phantom workers) and the railroad than between the wheat and the railroad or, more accurately, the conflict between the wheat market and the railroad market. And while many naturalist novels are noted for their attempts to diminish human agency, the degree of this diminishment within *The Octopus* is certainly striking.

CONTROLLING A MYTH: THE TIGHTENING GRIP OF THE RAILROAD

After declaring that "[t]he P. and S.W. is an Enemy of the State," Dyke, the one-time railroad engineer now turned farmer, tells a story about his young daughter, Sidney:

> Precious little I've ever told her of the railroad or how I was turned off, but the other day . . . along comes a through freight . . . and when it had passed, what do you suppose the tad did? . . . She goes

> to the fence and spits a little spit after the caboose and puts out her
> little head and, if you'll believe me, *hisses* at the train; and mother
> says she does that same every time she sees a train go by, and never
> crosses the tracks that she don't spit her little spit on 'em. (220)

Because Sidney doesn't actually understand the conflict the farmers have with the railroad—or, as Mrs. Dyke says, "What can she understand of the public franchises?"—it is likely that she is simply modeling her parents' behavior. Given Dyke's disdain for the railroad and Mrs. Dyke's belief that the railroad's practices are "not right," Sidney surely comprehends at least their hatred for the railroad. But, in that she doesn't understand the railroad for what it is—in the simplest terms, a corporation—she must hate the *train* itself; she spits her little spit at it.

What concerns Mrs. Dyke even more than the behavior of her little girl, "who's as sweet and gentle as can be in every other way," is the commonality of her daughter's sentiment. "She says the other little girls at school and the boys, too, are all the same way," Mrs. Dyke offers, ". . . it's all of them . . . and think of all the grown people who hate the [rail]road, women and men, the whole county, the whole State, thousands and thousands of people" (221). Sidney's "venomous" display reflects not only the feelings of her immediate family but more so a generalized sense of hatred in the community. Indeed, within the vast landscape of *The Octopus,* it is difficult to locate any support for the railroad outside of those who work for it. The railroad having offended, cheated, and stolen its way through California left most, if not all, Californians skeptical of its "workings." And one can verify that Norris is accurate in his replication of public opinion for the actual railroad in California; as Lewis notes, "the entire population of the Coast realized what power the [railroad] held over them . . . [;] the major share of virtually every business and industry on the Coast was diverted from its normal channel into the hands of the railroad and its controlling group" (365). For all intents and purposes, then, the people of California were, despite their hatred for it, completely subject to the railroad corporation and its business practices.

Near the beginning of the second book of *The Octopus,* Norris describes a map of the state of California, one that outlines not only property lines, but, more importantly, it outlines the "vast, complicated network of red lines marked P. and S.W.R.R." (288). Norris describes that throughout the map

> ran the plexus of red, a veritable system of blood circulation, com-
> plicated, dividing, and reuniting, branching, splitting, extending,
> throwing out feelers, off-shoots, tap roots, feeders—diminutive

little blood suckers that shot out from the main jugular and went twisting up into some remote county, laying hold upon some forgotten village or town, involving it in one of a myriad branching coils, one of a hundred tentacles, drawing it, as it were, toward that centre from which all this system sprang. . . . It was as though the State had been sucked white and colourless, and against this pallid background the red arteries of the monster stood out, swollen with life-blood, reaching out to infinity, gorged and bursting; an excrescence, a gigantic parasite fattening upon the life-blood of an entire commonwealth. (289)

As an image, the map Norris describes is quite provocative. Not only does it establish the conflict between the ranchers and the railroad, but it continues to articulate the notion of the naturalness, however grotesque, of such a conflict. The volume of animalistic language in this passage—from the descriptions of blood to the tentacles and the vampirism—works to present the railroad not as a threat to the ranchers' profits but, rather, as a threat to the land itself. It is a "monster," a "gigantic parasite" that is a predator on the "entire commonwealth."

The ascription to the railroad of predator status has led Michaels to argue that "Norris describes [the railroad] as if it were itself the consumer" instead of the distributor (185). This is important since if the railroad is perceived as the *consumer* of the wheat, it is granted mythical agency. That is, whereas it is actually the railroad *trust* that "devours" the farmers' profits, Norris presents the case as instead the inhuman railroad itself devouring the wheat, the "life-force." Presley at first believes the same: after a locomotive encounters a flock of Vanamee's sheep, he is initially disturbed by the "slaughter, a massacre of innocents [where] . . . to the right and left, all the width of the right of way, the little bodies had been flung; backs were snapped against the fence posts; brains knocked out." But while he initially perceives the railroad as "the galloping monster, the terror of steel and steam, with its single eye, cyclopean red, shooting from horizon to horizon," he will come to see it as "the symbol of a vast power, huge, terrible, flinging the echo of its thunder over all the reaches of the valley, leaving blood and destruction in its path; the leviathan, with tentacles of steel clutching into the soil, the soulless Force, the iron hearted Power, the monster, the Colossus, the Octopus" (50–51). Presley, in attempting to understand the hold that the railroad has over the farmers (and virtually every other aspect of the State), cannot avoid making certain mythical allusions as well as natural comparisons. The vastness of the railroad empire, with its tracks spreading across the nation, begins to take on the appearance of a grotesquely distorted octopus, tentacles outstretched, pulling everything in to be consumed.

Norris's choice of the animal he would use to represent the railroad was, in a sense, made for him. California presses had already likened the conquest of California by the railroad trust (termed "the big four" for its key figures) to the action of a monstrous octopus.[3] Interestingly enough, John R. Robinson, a former supporter of the railroad who turned sour and filed suit against it, had published a report on the railroad in 1894 entitled *The Octopus: A History of the Construction, Conspiracies, Extortions, Robberies, and Villainous Acts Of the Central Pacific, Southern Pacific of Kentucky, Union Pacific, and Other Subsidized Railroads.*[4] And, as Glen A. Love asserts, "[w]hether or not [Norris] saw Robinson's book at that time, he can hardly have missed it and the 'sensational' lawsuit against the Southern Pacific when he was gathering material for his *The Octopus* . . ." (1). Titles aside, even the language used in Robinson's work parallels the language within Norris's novel: for instance, Robinson writes, "For the past thirty years or more California has been in the grip of a monster corporation, powerful as it has been unscrupulous, criminal, venal, oppressive, unmerciful and autocratic. . . . This octopus is ever reaching out its tentacles, never ceasing in its efforts for supremacy and control" (qtd. in Love 2). That the language of Norris's work is similar to Robinson's is not to suggest that Norris "stole" the image of the octopus but, rather, that the octopus was an image that would have been readily recognized by Norris's intended audience.

Indeed, even before the publication of Robinson's text, the image of the railroad as octopus was clearly established. In an 1882 edition of *The Wasp,* political cartoonist Edward Keller published a cartoon entitled "The Curse of California."[5] Described as "the single most important cartoon in California history" (Salzman and Brown 30), the drawing depicts a large octopus, tattooed with the words "railroad monopoly." Each tentacle clutches a different object; ranging from the politics of California to the wheat export to the stage lines to—most importantly to this discussion—a dead farmer dangling just above a gravesite labeled "Mussell Slough." The octopus of the cartoon grins joyfully as it pulls its "acquisitions" closer to its mouth. And while it is likely that Keller himself was not the first to use the octopus image, he was the first to popularize its usage, making the symbol easily recognized and understood. A similar cartoon by James Swinnerton in 1896 reinforces the first while further identifying exactly what the railroad controlled: the eight arms of the octopus are extended, gripping the "honest vote," manufacturers, farmers, merchants, orange raisers, the press, Oakland, and San Francisco. The caption reads "This is the Monster California Must Destroy Now if Ever." What the cartoons articulate is, then, the popular perception of the railroad's acting not as a corporation in search of financial profit but, rather, as an uncontrollable monster rapidly devouring wheat, land, peoples, whole city-states; it is this popular myth that Norris extends in his novel. As with the wheat market, Norris animates the railroad as octopus by romanticizing its actions. In the sense that the railroad did, in fact, consume the bulk of the state by extending its "lines" to bring in fortune, it is only one more step to romantically equate it with a natural predator, one who indifferently *feeds off the people* and cannot be stopped. The actions of the railroad, naturalized in such a way as were those of the wheat market, become subject only to mythical natural laws. "Constantly this sort of thing must occur," Norris writes, "little industries choked out . . . [,] the air full of death rattles . . . [,] forgotten by every one but the monster who . . . with one tentacle grabbed a hundred thousand acres of wheat, and with another pilfered a pocketful of growing hops" (358). The naturalness of this conflict emerges in the language of necessity used by Norris: "This sort of thing must occur." The battle for survival in the wheat market and the railroad trust is as natural in *The Octopus* as is the battle for survival witnessed in nature.

Figured as a natural predator, then, the railroad (as octopus) begins to appear as if it functions of its own will, that it functions in spite of human interaction or intervention. This position, evident throughout the novel, is presented most forcefully by the railroad president Shelgrim. Responding to Presley, who has come to meet "the man whose power was so vast, whose will was so resistless, whose potency for evil so limitless," Shelgrim declares the following:

> "try to believe this—to begin with—*that railroads build themselves.* Where there is a demand sooner or later there will be a supply. Mr. Derrick, does he grow his wheat? The Wheat grows itself. What does he count for? Does he supply the force? What do I count for? Do I build the railroad? You are dealing with forces, young man, when you speak of Wheat and the Railroads, not with men. There is the Wheat, the supply. It must be carried to feed the People. There is the demand. The Wheat is one force, the Railroad, another, and there is the law that governs them—supply and demand. Men have only little to do in the whole business. Complications may arise, conditions that beat hard on the individual— crush him maybe—*but the Wheat will be carried to feed the people*

as inevitably as it will grow. If you want to fasten the blame of the affair at Los Muertos on any one person, you will make a mistake. Blame conditions, not men." (576)

There is an interesting logic to Shelgrim's assertion, a logic that stems from Shelgrim's endorsement of the naturalness of the conflict. Using the actual naturalness of the wheat—that it does grow itself (though, crucially, it does not *cultivate* itself)—Shelgrim is able to posit the railroad as natural: The railroad also builds itself. There is the seemingly natural law of supply and demand which dictates the "conditions" of the conflict between "ungovernable forces," and men, Shelgrim asserts, "have little to do in the whole business." Thus, despite Presley's argument that Shelgrim "control[s] the road," Shelgrim confidently replies, "I can *not* control it. It is a force born out of certain conditions and I— no man—can stop it or control it" (576). The power of the octopus is, Shelgrim would have us believe, beyond the realm of human comprehension: it, in turn, like the wheat, is totally indifferent to those who would try to control it.

But despite Presley's capitulation to such an account—"he could not deny it . . .[;] it rang with the clear reverberation of truth" (576)—there is obviously a problem with Shelgrim's position. While it may, in fact, be true that wheat does grow itself (in that it would grow regardless of human presence), it is certainly not true that the railroad builds itself. As is well known, the bulk of the railroad line in California was laid by a predominantly Chinese workforce. But, because we enter *The Octopus* once the majority of rail track has been laid, Norris can again erase the workers. Norris is then able to present the railroad as extending its lines naturally as the stretching tentacles of a monster beyond control. Similar to the construction of the wheat as functioning of its own agency, the history of the railroad is simplified by the absence of its workers, allowing for the construction of the myth of the railroad as an autonomous predator, another non-human life force.

THE POLITICS OF MYTH, THE MYTH OF POLITICS

Once Presley buys in to the myth of the railroad as natural predator, he no longer lays the blame for the shootout with the ranchers on the railroad. For Presley, there is something to Shelgrim's contention that men are not to blame but, rather, forces and conditions. Men are simply present—caught up in a sense—amidst the naturalness of the conflict:

Forces, conditions, laws of supply and demand—were these the enemies, after all? Not enemies; there was no malevolence in Nature. Colossal indifference only, a vast trend toward appointed

goals. Nature was, then, a gigantic engine, a vast cyclopean power,
huge, terrible, a leviathan with a heart of steel . . . crushing out the
human atom standing in its way. . . . (577)

In this the most direct statement within the novel about the form that nature
takes, Norris inverts the relationship between nature and economy. The "laws of
supply and demand"—terms from economic theory—are naturalized here resulting in an inversion of the general concept of nature. It is by this inversion that
Norris is able to posit economic "law" as natural—without malevolence—while
asserting that nature is, in fact, a gigantic engine. Thus, nature is commodified,
hence denaturalized, as we saw in the case of the wheat, while the market, the
grand symbol of what "the twentieth century will be," is reified, hence naturalized. The simplification of history and the romanticization of objects results in the
naturalization of the market and therefore any and all actions taken to control the
market. Again, human agency is profoundly qualified.

If this is the case—that the natural has been denaturalized and the unnatural naturalized—then the ultimate conclusion that Presley reaches near the
close of the novel is, for him at least, justified. In considering the power of the
wheat, the predatory nature of the market, and the events resulting in the Los
Muertos slaughter, Presley comes to realize that "[m]en were nothings, mere ani-
malculæ, mere ephemerides that fluttered and fell and were forgotten between
dawn and dusk" (634). Men, it is suggested, because they are subjected to the nat-
ural(ized) processes of the market, are secondary, in the last instance, according
to the laws of nature. Given this, Presley, in seeking "the explanation of existence," comes to understand that "[m]en were naught, death was naught, life
was naught; FORCE only existed—FORCE that brought men into the world,
FORCE that crowded them out of it to make way for the succeeding generation,
FORCE that made the wheat grow, FORCE that garnered it from the soil to
give place to the succeeding crop" (634). Presley here internalizes the process of
naturalization inherent in the construction of the myth of the market.

Fredric Jameson addresses this process of naturalization and the inter-
nalization thereof in his work *Marxism and Form*. In discussing the commodification of produced objects and the reification of "matter which has
been invested with human energy and which henceforth takes the place of
and functions like human action," Jameson argues that these phenomena
result in the construction of a larger myth of capital (244):

The appearance is that of commodities and of the "objective" network of relationships which they entertain with each other and
which ultimately include within themselves the whole legal and

property system itself, as well as the economic modes of distribution and production: yet, paradoxically, this illusion of objective
reality forms the very existential fabric of our lives, which are
characterized by *belief* in this reified appearance ... and which are
wholly absorbed with the acquisition and consumption of commodities in general. (296)

In terms of *The Octopus,* with the commodification of the wheat and the
reification of both the wheat market and the railroad, Presley and many of
those around him are led to believe in the reality of "this reified appearance"
and, therefore, the naturalness of the capitalist system as a whole. The
"FORCE" that Presley feels to be at the center of existence is the force of market capitalism. But, through the naturalization of the market, the entire system of capitalism is itself naturalized: it becomes a system which functions
solely of its own will and in which "men are naught." Humankind, as Shelgrim attests, "have only little to do in the whole business."

It is because of the belief in the naturalness of the capitalist system that
Vanamee is led—despite the slaughter of the farmers and the railroad's acquisition of their land—to relate hopefully to Presley that "Evil is short-lived.
Never judge of the whole round of life by the mere segment you can see. The
whole is, in the end, perfect" (636). Considering the events of the novel—the
loss of life and land—it is a rather odd statement that Vanamee makes. How
is it that such an optimistic attitude can be adopted? How can the events of
the novel be reconciled in terms of a "perfect whole?" The answer, it seems,
for Norris stems from the fact that the system of capitalism remains intact:

> Men—motes in the sunshine—perished, were shot down in the
> very noon of life, hearts were broken, little children started in life
> lamentably handicapped; young girls were brought to a life of
> shame; old women died in the heart of life for lack of food. In that
> little, isolated group of human insects, misery, death, and anguish
> spun like a wheal of fire.
>
> *But the* WHEAT *remained.* (651)

That the wheat remains—and, of course, its market—is all that is required to
make the whole, in the end, perfect. Here, the ideology of capitalism unites
with the ideology of social Darwinism. Human existence is merely a matter
of social survival in the midst of the "forces" and "conditions" of a reified market capitalism. The ideology of early-twentieth-century capitalism—reinforced
by the "science" of social Darwinism—supports the belief that as long as the

market system prevails, those individual men who succeed or fail, live or die, are of secondary concern. It is the system that is to be believed in, not the men who are subject to it.

Readers having witnessed the atrocities animated in the novel, however, might find it quite difficult to accept this philosophy as perfect. The novel does, after all, encourage us to identify and sympathize with the plight of the farmers, even as types, and, further, to engage in the hatred of the predatory railroad. The sentiment that closes the novel, "the Truth . . . will, in the end, prevail," is less than totally convincing, particularly in the way the text attempts acknowledgement of any contradictions. What are we to do with this lingering uneasiness with Norris's epic?

One might, of course, accuse Norris of complicity with the ideology of market capitalism.[6] However, Norris's own political leanings were, as Michaels asserts, "contradictory and their commitments uncertain" (176). Perhaps a more profitable reading would acknowledge that the contradictions of the text are, at their source, contradictions of the ideology from which the text emerged. Such textual contradictions and irresolutions are, simply stated, cultural contradictions at their source. *The Octopus,* then, embodies the dominant ideology of market capitalism but, in fact, is not necessarily complicit with that ideology.

To illustrate this concept more clearly, let me return momentarily to Jameson. If the literary text is "a symbolic act, whereby real social contradictions, insurmountable in their own terms, find a purely formal resolution in the aesthetic realm" (*Political Unconscious* 79), then the text which fails (or refuses) to construct a "purely formal resolution," or, as is the case of *The Octopus,* constructs an obviously problematic resolution, provides a more accurate picture of the ideology from which it is created. Further, Jameson argues, "the literary work . . . as though for the first time, brings into being that very situation to which it is also, at one and the same time, a reaction" (82). In this sense, the formal resolution offered in *The Octopus*—that the whole is perfect—works to animate the ideological imposition of social Darwinism and the naturalness of market capitalism at the same time that it calls it into question. The textual contradiction present within the novel "brings into being" the cultural contradictions to which it responds; but by removing the individuals who produce, in the most basic sense, the wheat and the railroad, and by allowing the wheat and the railroad to come to the forefront of the novel, Norris allows the reader to see, in Louis Althusser's terms, "the *ideology* from which it is born, in which it bathes, from which it detaches itself as art, and to which it *alludes*" (222). Norris's "story of California" thus animates not the particular incident of Mussell Slough but the process of myth construction necessary to the conquest of California, the form of ideological myth construction required in early-twentieth-century capitalism. It is only by understanding this process of myth construction that the textual contradictions of *The Octopus* may be thoroughly historicized and understood as both inherent in the deterministic novel and, more crucially, indicative, perhaps critical, of capitalism's contradictory ideology of the "forces" and "conditions" that control humankind's fate.

NOTES

I would like to thank Audrey Goodman for her support and guidance of this project, from its early ideas to its present form.

1. As his numerous writings on the subject of the American audience suggest, Norris was quite aware of just who the mass reading public was. See, for example, Norris's writings on "The American Public and 'Popular' Fiction" as well as "Fiction Writing as a Business" in *The Literary Criticism of Frank Norris,* edited by Donald Pizer.
2. These two reports, both from the *New York Times,* are indicative of the entire stock-reporting media. The central discourse of the stock market is a stock's activity: what it does.
3. The "Big Four" were Collis P. Huntington, Leland Stanford, Mark Hopkins, and Charles Crocker.
4. Interestingly, the book was forced out of print by a largely railroad-financed publishing industry.
5. The two cartoons are available in Lewis's *The Big Four.* "The Curse of California" was originally published in *The Wasp,* San Francisco, 19 Aug. 1882. "This is the Monster California Must Destroy Now if Ever" was originally published in the *San Francisco Examiner,* 14 Dec. 1896.
6. For instance, Richard Allan Davison contends that "Norris became a friend of Collis P. Huntington (the very model for Shelgrim) [. . . and that Norris] felt that the capitalistic system with all its flaws did seem to work" (83).

WORKS CITED

Althusser, Louis. "A Letter on Art." *Lenin and Philosophy and Other Essays.* Trans. Ben Brewster. New York: Monthly Review, 1971. 221–27.

Davison, Richard Allan. "Frank Norris and the Arts of Social Criticism." *American Literary Realism* 14.1 (1981): 77–89.

"An Excited Wheat Market." *New York Times* 26 Sept. 1897: sec. 8:4.

Folsom, James K. "Social Darwinism or Social Protest? The 'Philosophy' of *The Octopus.*" *The Merrill Studies in* The Octopus. Ed. Richard Allan Davison. Columbus: Charles E. Merrill, 1969. 132–40.

Howard, June. *Form and History in American Literary Naturalism.* Chapel Hill: U of North Carolina P, 1985.

Jameson, Fredric. *Marxism and Form.* Princeton: Princeton UP, 1971.

——. *The Political Unconscious: Narrative as Socially Symbolic Act.* New York: Cornell UP, 1981.

Lewis, Oscar. *The Big Four: The Story of Huntington, Stanford, Hopkins, and Crocker, and of the Building of the Central Pacific.* New York: Knopf, 1955.

Love, Glen A. "The Other Octopus." *American Literary Realism* 14.1 (1981): 1–5.

McWilliams, Carey. *Southern California Country: An Island on the Land.* New York: Duell, Sloan, and Pearce, 1946.

Michaels, Walter Benn. *The Gold Standard and the Logic of Naturalism.* Berkeley: U of California P, 1987.

Norris, Frank. *The Letters of Frank Norris.* Ed. Franklin Walker. San Francisco: Book Club of California, 1956.

——. *The Literary Criticism of Frank Norris.* Ed. Donald Pizer. Austin: U of Texas P, 1964.

——. *The Octopus.* New York: Penguin, 1986.

Pizer, Donald. *The Novels of Frank Norris.* Bloomington: Indiana UP, 1966.

Salzman, Ed, and Leigh Brown. *The Cartoon History of California Politics.* Sacramento: California Journal Press, 1978.

"The State of Trade." *New York Times* 28 Aug. 1897: sec. 6:4.

Zola, Émile. "From *The Experimental Novel.*" *Critical Theory Since Plato.* Ed. Hazard Adams. Fort Worth: Harcourt Brace Jovanovich, 1992. 644–55.

No Green Card Needed

DREISERIAN NATURALISM AND
PROLETARIAN FEMALE WHITENESS

—Laura Hapke

O VER THE PAST FEW DECADES, SCHOLARS HAVE MOVED WELL BEYOND PREVIOUS PARADIGMS OF AMERICAN LITERARY NATURALISM IN GENERAL and Dreiser studies in particular.[1] The classic scholarship of the past drew the naturalist as an American Zola who dramatized the collision of environment and heredity with the America *idée fixe* of the success ethic. Dreiserian texts in particular were said to overlay this quasi-mechanistic model with both the primacy of desire and a compassion for the working poor. Now the cutting-edge scholarship includes recent deconstructions by Christophe Den Tandt, Walter Benn Michaels, and Amy Kaplan; and essay collections edited by James L. West as well as Miriam Gogol. Looking at Dreiser and his fellow naturalists and realists, Den Tandt finds that naturalism, "using the plurivocal approach to an unrepresentable social world" (xi), exists in a dialogic interplay with the romantic sublime. No less revisionist rereadings find *Sister Carrie, Jennie Gerhardt,* and other Dreiser texts to be consumerist narratives "embracing the ethos of capitalism which values excess over restraint" (Michaels, qtd. in Kaplan 142). The "new" Dreiserian naturalism is further viewed as an attempt to manage the contradictions of a society that prospers by marketing unfulfilled materialist desires (Kaplan 143) or, simply, as an account of the endless process and contradictions of a "convulsive" capitalism (Zayani 18).

Read within such contexts, *Sister Carrie*'s emphasis on monotony in an age of mechanical reproduction exists in tension with the restlessness, desire, and unsettledness that erupt in the novel's adulteries, strikes, and financial reversals. No Dreiserian character can experience contentment within a system that is inherently unstable and that exhibits such a twinned commodification of fantasy and lack of fulfillment.

In this startling shift of critical discourse, what remains curiously repressed is the issue of Dreiser's relationship to capitalism's "hard contract" (*Sister Carrie* 40). For different reasons, in all of these recent studies he remains the writer who allied himself with *Success* magazine, who ambivalently admired titans and financiers, and who sought far more to explain than to muckrake class stratification and ethnic, racial, and gender segregation. As a scholar with a focus on labor fiction, I reposition Dreiser and his taxonomy of paid work within a literary naturalism of social protest. As Carla Cappetti aptly notes, the decades after the McCarthy era saw the scholarly mainstream's denigration of naturalism as inherently "proletarian." Denied too was a straight line of influence from Dreiser to the proletarian authors, like Mike Gold (who praised Dreiser), James T. Farrell, Jack Conroy, and Nelson Algren, who lapsed into postwar obscurity and disrepute. To join a renewed labor studies conversation about literary naturalism as an early form of industrial realism, I (re)trace the Dreiserian intersection of capital and labor (Wixson 349), but rather than reinscribe the title characters of Dreiser's woman-centered early novels in the masculinist tradition of the proletarian bildungsroman, I build on the groundwork laid by Shelley Fisher Fishkin, Miriam Gogol, and others who have studied Dreiser's gendered presentation of turn-of-the-century workers. Recent surveyors of Dreiser bibliography have noted that the historical truth of Dreiser's accounts of working women's lives offers new possibilities in labor studies (Orlov and Gogol 15).

There is an added dimension, however, to a class and gender analysis of literary naturalism. As Mary Papke astutely observes, there are few black, Jewish, immigrant, or other minority writers readily accepted as naturalist, whereas Frank Norris, despite his hardly ambiguous white supremacist views and classism, is constantly invoked. Dreiser may not be as conscious of that agenda as Norris, but he certainly buys into it. Yes, this "labor Dreiser" widens the naturalist discussion of working-class experience but only by positioning white working people in a landscape of relative privilege (Lott; Roediger, *Wages;* Bernardi). Dreiser's racial-ethnic theories remain under-researched; it is my purpose here only to generate discussion and to place Carrie within a still-evolving American delineation of race and the "real" working class.

As a social-protest writer with a residual bitterness about his family's ethnic and economic marginalization, Dreiser intuitively understood the period distinctions between native-born workingmen and everyone else—racial-ethnic men and women in particular. His chapters on menial shoe-factory work as the only kind of job that an unskilled provincial young woman like Carrie can find rest squarely on a comprehension of the hierarchies in the labor movement of his day.

At the top was the "male and pale" skilled artisan who dominated the trade union movement in ways that still endure. This upper tier of the labor movement could even aspire to a bourgeois, pro-capitalist identity—but only as long as it confined its membership to native-born or Anglo-Saxon immigrant whiteness. The majority of ethnic workers were excluded from such affiliations and historically had little opportunity to profit from a labor-class version of acquisitive individualism in the industrial trades.[2] The skilled trades routinely ignored or opposed the job needs of recently freed blacks and newly arrived Slavic and Mediterranean immigrants,[3] and they were loud in vilifying the Chinese, perceived in most quarters as strikebreaking or otherwise wage-deflating emigrants (Miller 175, 195–99, 235n). And the skilled trades were unmoved by a federal Indian policy that turned detribalized Native Americans into reservation-based laborers. In white labor's name, workers demanded attention, forged a certain visibility, and pointed repeatedly to their exclusion from the American Dream (Freeman et al. 30; Montgomery, "Workers' Control"). At the same time, non-union craft workers, even in the increasingly militant carpentry, iron, and steel industries, applied the old artisanal ethic to industrial autonomy.[4]

New social historians have argued in their groundbreaking texts of history from the bottom up that these working-class privileges, as Daniel Bernardi notes, rest on "an ideology of race that positions 'whites' as normal and 'non-whites' as deviant and inferior" (105; Freeman et al.). A recent American Studies Association conference included a panel on "Repudiating Whiteness: The Politics of Passings and Trespassings" that addressed some of Dreiser's colleagues, the Midwestern expatriate Sinclair Lewis chief among them.[5] For students of actual Midwest labor racism, Rich Halpern's investigation of color hierarchies in the Progressive-era Chicago meatpacking industry and beyond is helpful, as is S. J. Kleinberg's survey of Pittsburgh's segregated working-class neighborhoods in the shadow of the steel mills. The most incisive work has been done on the "poor whites" of the American Southwest and West. In *The White Scourge*, Neil Foley finds such constituencies eager to hold on to "the whiteness of manhood" (12). Rather than be spurned as the "bad-gened whites" of eugenicist theory, they pride themselves on being the "purest whites" in Appalachia (6). Writing about the continued white rural sharecropping culture in Texas (where the Ku Klux Klan maintained a presence) prior to the Second World War, Foley posits that the "pore whites" clung to what they were not—black, Mexican, or foreign-born (7). If, at least in this regard, whiteness was a collective identity, sustaining it involved a posture of defiance in regions so impoverished that there were no jobs for either whites or people of color.

Elsewhere too, of course, during the last century's early decades, the racialized presence of African Americans shaped the American landscape whether in the many actual conflicts or the reinvented ones of Dreiser's industrial Midwest and Northeast. Jim Crow attitudes and laws dominated the late-nineteenth-century proletarian landscape; as late as 1898 the AFL suggested mass coloniza-tion of African workers (Roediger, *Wages* 141). It can be argued that blackness is the crucial if apparitional racial category in a novel like *Sister Carrie* so devoted to the progress of its lily-white heroine. With its focus on the ethnic workers who people Carrie Meeber's labor sub-world, this paper can only touch on the important issue of the black worker's place in the ethnic color hierarchy. Return-ing to Dreiser as an imaginer of the laboring classes for the quarter of a century between *Sister Carrie* (1900) and *An American Tragedy* (1925), we should now place these texts within the multiple and conflicting contests of naturalism, wage-earning women's history, and "whiteness studies."

The question, then, is whether Carrie (and to a lesser extent, the side-lined labor figure Roberta Alden) fits the "bad-gened" white trash definition of single womanhood—an uneducated lower-class woman toiling at a dead-end job and not averse to paid sexual encounters. Is Carrie doing what was commonly and nativistically called the "nigger work" that white men would not deign to do? Blacks and ethnic women were absent as yet from the factory floor in the late 1880s, as they still are in small-town America when Clyde Griffiths becomes Roberta's supervisor. Yet there is no doubt that the work-place was sweated labor of the lowest sort.

The phony eugenics at the core of both nativism and racism began its flowering as a dubious science around the turn of the century. Dreiser was born into the largest immigrant group in Chicago, but throughout his life, despite an attraction to High German "Kultur," he presented himself as an American narrator, distanced from the painful ethnicity of his early days. Though the Dreiser family was quite poor, his mother had middle-class aspirations. Ger-manic origins were not handicaps to skilled industrial work—the construc-tion, furniture, and cigar trades (the last a trade in which blacks occupied the lowest, segregated rung). Irishmen, on the other hand, may have ascended to foreman positions in the steel and railroad trades, but they were consistently presented in bestial images in the pages of American fiction—as Dreiser does in the unfinished *An Amateur Laborer*—their faces often smeared with slum or coal-mining dirt.[6] To an extent, the Germans handily joined others grouped by government surveys as "Caucasians": the Welsh, British, and Scandinavians were the aristocrats of the labor movement in the early union years.[7] This was the same period in which Dreiser was imagining the blue-collar lives of Carrie Meeber, her brother-in-law Sven Hanson, a railroad yard cleaner, and that "underworld of toil" characteristic of Chicago in the year 1889, when Carrie arrives there.

What is clear from the novel's outset is that, as Dreiser wishes us to know, Carrie exhibits neither "bold" nor "vulgar" (read oversexed) behavior, two marks of unprincipled lower-class white work, whether Appalachian or otherwise. In fact, Dreiser offers Carrie's whiteness as a given. When he writes about ethnics, he uses the familiar period labels—at their most extreme in a story written and published the same year he was finishing *Sister Carrie*, "Nigger Jeff," a lynching tale whose attitude is ambiguous at best toward the n-word. In contrast, Carrie occupies what David Roediger, a well-known scholar in the new "whiteness studies" field, calls a "sort of invisible norm" (qtd. in Newitz and Wray 3) rather than membership in a "racially marked group existing in relation to many other such groups" (Newitz and Wray, 5). It should be remembered, too, that as early as antebellum times the labor movement distinguished white man's labor from "nigger work" (Laurie 27).[8] Into that racist category they poured the various "Hunky" and East European constituencies flocking to steel mills and ethnically segregated company towns—of which Chicago was one. Furthermore, the stigmata of racial differ- ence were applied especially to Jews, whether upwardly mobile or not. A dar- ing new book by Karen Brodkin, *How Jews Became White Folks* (1998), locates this marginalization even as recently as the Second World War.

Carrie herself arrives in Chicago with no understanding of or interest in the remaking of a once white American working class (Takaki 311–24, 201–2; Freeman et al.). She seems to be oblivious to the fact that almost 800,000 new arrivals to the city are immigrants or their children. Not so Dreiser himself. As a proletarian wagon driver and cub reporter, Dreiser was a participant-observer of the "other half" well before he completed *Sister Carrie* in 1899. In the late 1880s and early 1890s, he was a veteran of five successive jobs, including bill col- lector for cheap curios and clocks. (It is no accident that a sign of the perpetual economic failure of Clyde Griffiths's father is his attempt at clock peddling in the Windy City.) The Chicago and Saint Louis business and factory districts walked wearily by a job-seeking young American girl surely had an ethnic presence in the 1880s, as Dreiser, who drove a laundry wagon for his Jewish employers, well knew. The influx of Jews was heavy enough by 1888 for the Hebrew Immigrant Aid Society to open a Chicago office (Cutler 56), and rela- tive ethnic "haves" like Dreiser's bosses could look back to a Jewish presence in the city of half-a-century. Dreiser's job also took him into the Slavic neigh- borhoods, "where people were . . . bustling over potatoes . . . and cabbage," and into the black ghettoized districts, where he negotiated with washerwomen (Lingeman 46). Blacks were routinely imported as strikebreakers in the meat- packing and heavy-industrial districts of the city, an anti-unionist tactic that

Dreiser would probably have known about. He certainly could not have missed the Jim Crow operative in Chicago's "Black Belt" (a grim herald of the bloody Race Riot of 1919). He witnessed racial violence, too, when in 1893 he covered a lynching near Valley Park, fifteen miles from Saint Louis, an event that inspired the story "Nigger Jeff" (Lingeman 67). Ethnic labor in the city space was also the subject of Dreiser's 1894 pieces written as a cub crime reporter in Saint Louis, Pittsburgh, and Allegheny (Lingeman 87), including "Fall River" (c. 1899), a piece on a Gorkyesque cross-ethnic post-strike Homestead.

Midwestern habitat was likewise crucial to the comprehension of immigrant oddity in the work of a major "local color" writer who was well known to mass audiences when Dreiser was still an unknown. When the regionalist author Hamlin Garland was dispatched to post-strike Homestead, he focused on the squalid communities surrounding it, ignoring both the steel-mill experience and the skilled "white" workers' dwellings a short distance from the mill, even those that housed the militant strikers of 1892 themselves. "To give these folk power would unchain strange beasts," he concluded of the newest ethnics (Garland).[9] Other visitors to the sullen Homestead further decried what they perceived as the squalor of the ethnic inhabitants (Dreiser, "Fall River"; see also *Sister Carrie,* 498–501).

The urban story successfully offered its hyperactive inner-city ethnics to Garland's middlebrow audience, to whom the working, marginal, and criminal poor, all embodied in the immigrant, were exotic (Giamo 54). Sharing with this book-buying readership a moralism about the metropolitan "lower orders" central to the genteel practitioners of so much pre-1890s portraiture, tenement authors never rejected class ascension or the rags-to-riches credo outright. The social Darwinism of their slum tales implicitly reasserted their own Protestant values. But like their bourgeois readers, they were fascinated by those who neither saw ambition as triumph over adversity nor engaged in the Franklinesque struggle upward. In tenement fare, the very disorder of ethnic laboring life is a tourist attraction.[10] The perceived descent into the immigrant city generates a taxonomy of types. Substituting eccentricity for aspiration, these tales "cloud the conditions and dynamics of poverty by an unfailing reduction to moral individualism, the picturesque, or the dangerous classes" (Giamo 32).

By 1895, a few years before beginning *Sister Carrie,* Dreiser had walked across City Hall Park and visited the infamous Mulberry Bend of Little Italy (Lingeman 94–95); his retrospective location of Carrie's story in Chicago in 1889 was overlaid with his understanding of the cross-ethnic, industrial Midwest and Northeast, both prior to and in the decade following that time. But it was also influenced by his colleague in the industrial Northeast, E. W. Townsend. The subject of Dreiser's hardly complimentary review in *Ev'ry Month* magazine, Townsend's approach was more anti-model than template for serious American writers, naturalistic or not (Dreiser, "Literary Shower"). Few authors put the Lower East Side laboring ethnic on parade, transforming the working and borderline poor into an exciting slum show, with more popular success than Townsend. He struck publishing gold in the early 1890s with the Chimmie Fadden stories. They were a regular feature of the *New York Sun* and in eponymous book forms sold 200,000 copies ("Edward W. Townsend Dies"). All that had repelled a Hamlin Garland about working people—their rough ways, lack of ambition, unrestrained emotion, and slangy inarticulateness—became the stuff of comedy in the person of the truculent Irish street kid Chimmie.[11]

If Chimmie's monologues and observations of the pretensions of the Four Hundred generate a comedy based on the unbridgeability of class gaps, he is as harmless as a stage Irishman. He peddles newspapers, hangs around the settlement house observing the Ladies Bountiful, and accepts tips from the rich for escorting them on saloon tours. "Mr. Paul often says t'me dat he's stuck on de Bow'ry" (177), he observes.[12] In all ways he is a sidewalk gamin asserting his class identity for humorous ends: "Listen. De old mug calls me 'a unregenerate heathen!' Did ye ever hear such langwudge?" (11). To milk the cross-class comedy, Townsend has Chimmie gain the patronage of a society employer, trading his newsie's route for a valet's post (103). But he remains the court jester, returning to his old haunts for new material.

Although Stephen Crane chose to satirize the shallowness of the Townsend model in *Maggie: A Girl of the Streets* (1893), he did not spare the ethnic subject in so doing, as the many anti-Irish passages in the novella demonstrate. Without undermining the nativist racialism of a Stephen Crane or a Frank Norris, Dreiser took another path. Dreiser's knowledge of working-class makeup is at odds with his decision to portray the working class as white. In other words, he fits naturalism to fashion, as did even the period's rare socialist texts, which preferred the skilled native-born or old immigrant worker to the unruly ethnic. For instance, Mrs. Nico Bech-Meyer's 1894 novel *Pullmantown* privileges a German machinist and an American-born carpenter. Both men doubt whether the unskilled new workforce can achieve political awareness.

Dreiser's choice, then, was between the nativist vision and the absent ethnic. If we consider Sven Hanson as the product of a narrow literary choice, we see that this American-born child of a Swede—as Dreiser is careful to note (12)—is a suspect type to be sure: hard to fathom and mean-spirited even though he is a white in the railroad yards, not an Irish or black. But his ambitiousness and parsimony separate him psychically from the Chicago and Homestead ethnics of the otherwise diverse period fare of Garland, Crane, and their contemporaries. What, then, is blue-collar whiteness, where is it, and how is Carrie its exemplar, even its goddess?

To answer: Carrie never steps out of a white work and leisure world. Even the derelicts are white—her father, the "flour-dusted miller," the "ragged men" in Chicago (145), the "rough, heavy-built" individuals (27) who eye her, Evans the barkeeper (125), and the "poorly-clad girls" (145). The hierarchy of mainstream, presumably non-ethnic whiteness is implicitly underscored by Dreiser's reference to the Irish coal heavers whom Carrie sees on her walk. "Irishmen with picks, coal heavers with great loads to shovel," are proletarians in contrast to other manual workers but also "Americans busy about some work which was a mere matter of strength" (145).

Carrie travels with few clothes but is never without the mantle of racial privilege, as a traveling salesman eyeing her on the train (blacks sat in different cars) attests. Compared to the many "swarthy" and racially suspect immigrant women flocking to the factory floor at the end of the nineteenth century, Carrie is as untarnished by nativist class prejudice as she is unaffected by class consciousness. Her own Americanness, particularly her name and her father's small-town Protestant background (that flour-dusted miller), propels her above the era's many greenhorn strugglers in the Darwinian clothing trades laborscape. Of course we know very little else about Carrie's genealogy, but its very blankness suggests an absence of ethnic ties: the homogeneity of the dominant culture.

Carrie's brief foray into shoe work is suggestive, too. Although by her time the pay had dwindled, shoe work was traditionally a Yankee daughter's trade, and the women in it had often been compared to the Lowell mill girls. By the early decades of the nineteenth century, native-born white women formed a significant portion of the region's workforce in textile New England, with Lowell, Massachusetts, the jewel in the region's manufacturing crown.[13] Moreover, well before the Civil War a female seamstress and laundress workforce was a fixture of shoe factories in New England, collar manufacturers in New York State, and the piecework clothing trade in New York City. Their hopes were evident in organizations like the Ladies' Shoebinders, the United Seamstress Society, and the New York Working Women's Labor Union (Blewett; Turbin; Stein, pts. 1 and 2; see also Siegel 81; Foner 139). Labor sparks even flew, thanks to the Daughters of Saint Crispin, among skilled shoe-factory workers at Lynn agitating before and after the Civil War (Blewett; Cameron, chs. 1–3; Levine, ch. 2).

Chicago, in turn, saw its women factory hands march two decades later, though not in the devolving shoe trades: more than two decades after the Civil War, Carrie's coworkers have, in Dreiser's rendering, clearly debased the principled rebelliousness of the Daughters of Saint Crispin. Yet even the most sex-obsessed girls on her shop floor are native-born, as witnessed by their slangy vernacular. However much her self-absorption walls her off from social or industrial solidarity with them, Carrie Meeber's experiences among female sewing machine operators in a Chicago shoe factory mirror those of the women of the less "political" workplace cultures carved from sweatshop toil: she resents the strictures on her freedom and the monotony of her work-day, and she longs for an unspecified lover to take her out of the fray. Only her timorous response to these experiences, evidenced by her initial fear of the masher Drouet, reinforces Dreiser's gentrification of her as a princess among workplace serfs. From the moment she enters the sex-segregated work site— the skilled male workers are spatially separated from the unskilled females— Dreiser focuses on her revulsion at the "common" woman she meets there (*Sister Carrie* 53). To her eyes, they are too familiar with the men, who joke and even touch them playfully. But if these implicitly promiscuous women realize the period's worst fears about the workplace—they are "free with the fellows and exchange . . . banter in rude phrases which at first shocked her" (53)—they are Yankees still: the girl at her left may have bad grammar and utter phrases like "Say . . . what jeh think he said?" (38), but she is slangily American through and through.

Furthermore, one can contextualize Carrie's reaction within that of the larger white male working-class society. Her innocent habit, for instance, of standing in the doorway of her brother-in-law's house in a white working-class neighborhood raises fears that she will be taken for a prostitute —evidence of the clinging to respectability that was fiercely evident in "border-line" neighborhoods like Van Buren Street.

Carrie's education may be scanty, but her grammar is good (note the correctness of her Dear John letter to Hurstwood later in the novel). She can navigate a white work world: she applies for shop and office jobs and takes factory work only as a last resort (256). The rare black women with clerical skills worked only for black-owned businesses, and Carrie could have beaten them out of the work had she even considered so doing.

The fact, then, that the two men in her life see her as "this lily" (146), and that her employers see her as "pretty," as prettiness is constructed in Dreiser's world—refined, "sweet-faced" (41), she carries herself as one who "felt that she should be better served" (41)—takes on more than clichéd meaning, as does the fact that as a coquette on the stage in New York she is appealing in the standard American girl mode of the time.

Only in later novels does another hardy young working woman—Jennie Gerhardt (German American rather than East European or Mediterranean) or upstate New York's Roberta Alden—profit from or fail in spite of the invisible privilege her racial identity provides. Reading *An American Tragedy* backward from our day, with its intensified focus on racial and gender inequalities in the naturalist text, one finds that Dreiser was here investigating fault lines in the workforce rather than collectivity.

This is particularly the case with his portrayal of female workers. The portrait of Carrie's spiritual cousin, Roberta Alden, in his novel *An American Tragedy,* is crucial for an understanding of the way Dreiser's leftist ideology collided with his racial attitudes. Roberta is somewhat of an anomaly at the Lycurgus Collar Factory: a non-ethnic factory hand. With her small-town Protestantism, work ethic, and at least more religious training than Carrie Meeber, she resembles those Yankee daughters who peopled the Lowell mills when the "lady of industry" ideology was developed by manufacturers in search of a cheap, tractable labor force. By the 1860s, all thought of Lowell ladies was gone: Irish and, later, Polish workers in Lycurgus were refashioning the morality and workplace culture of the mill. By the time *An American Tragedy* was written, Fordism had taken a viselike hold of assembly lines such as Roberta's. An unknown soldier in a womanly army at the Griffiths factory —one of the "old and weary-looking women who looked more like wraiths than human beings" (248)—she finds no gateway to opportunity, only a future marked by monotonous way stations in what she sees as the dreary journey from one low-level job to the next.

Whiteness once again complicates the matter of Roberta's abdication of ambition. This disappointed daughter of the shabby genteel (but too refined to be quite "poor white") would have settled for a "practical education" in bookkeeping on the lower rungs of white-collardom (246). Her derailed hopes are evident in the factory job she has to take. She becomes so fixated on marital instead of job-site ascension that she ducks training sessions at the home of a coworker for amusement park evenings with her lover, whom she hopes will marry her. Dreiser points to Roberta as one who rechannels her legitimate need for job advancement into an obsessive and Hollywood-fueled interest in wedlock. Viewed in the context of her white Protestant mainstream identity, however, her abdication of ambition reveals something else as well.

The woman from a WASP culture, even a downwardly mobile one, was figuring in period fiction more and more as a vestige. She felt neither at home among the factory oligarchs like the Griffithses nor ethnic or political kinship with the "bread and roses" marchers of venues like the ethnic Lawrence Textile Mill. No wonder that the conservative writer Winston Churchill, in the 1917 bestseller with which Dreiser may have been familiar, *The Dwelling Place of Light,* kills off the American-sounding Janet Bumpus, Roberta's pregnant predecessor. (Janet is a step up from Roberta; as an office worker, she catches the eye of the factory owner, but otherwise plot similarities abound.) Like Roberta after her, she is too ambitious to marry a mere, or non-white, factory hand, and too déclassé to form a part of an industrial elite.

What Marx called the vulnerability of the factory girl to the seduction of her capitalist employer—in Roberta's case, her manager—should not blind us to Roberta's sense of white entitlement. She is no less an ethnic snob than Clyde—even on death row he resents that a fellow prisoner is Chinese. Whatever awe she may have of Clyde in the Lycurgus social pecking order, she is certain of her moral and racial superiority to the girls with accents who work alongside her. However commonplace, even vulgar, Roberta begins to appear to Clyde, she projects her own status vulnerability onto the sensual, in-her-face Poles, Italians, and others who try to wring some joy out of monotony on the line.

Set against the "red scare" climate of the Sacco and Vanzetti 1920s, Roberta, a symbol of the white working class under siege, is as morally unattractive as the Griffiths clan, from the Aladdin-like Clyde to the snide Gilbert. A possessive investment in her own whiteness, replicated in countless period social surveys of the steel town, the dance hall, the department store, and the Lower East Side, is a crucial dimension of her character and one that has too long been overlooked in studies of "proletarian naturalism."

Roberta Alden's racial identity cannot protect her, however, from the murderous greed of a poor boy determined to climb up. Carrie Meeber, in contrast, moves completely from the hard times dominating the lives of white and non-white working-class people alike. Dreiser chose not to tell their New York story. Even if she had had to do sewing work for another decade after relocating to New York, she would never have been among the casualties of the Triangle Shirtwaist Fire, one of the city's worst industrial tragedies. A true workers' event, in contrast to Carrie's quicksilver movement up from and out of manual work, the fire martyred only the immigrant Jews and Italians whose allies would forge the "swarthy" ILGWU. Thus did Dreiser legitimize his lower-middle-class title character, protecting her from tainted associations with unionist ethnicity.

In a larger sense, this racialized vision disrupts Dreiser's association with the social-protest mode as much as does his ambivalent attitude toward monopoly capitalism. To be sure, by the 1930s Dreiser had enlarged his understanding of the disenfranchised among the white working class. He found proletarian whiteness to be no capitalist asset in his tour of strike-torn mining towns in Harlan County; in the next decade, he formally joined the Communist Party. Whatever his evolving vision of the "poor white" workingman, however, his enduring portraits of white workingwomen dissatisfied with their class position neither challenge nor, for that matter, indict the ideology of selective ascension central to the "success ethic." To the end of Dreiser's life, the competitively individualistic heroine Carrie, and her luckless alter ego Roberta, continued to pose troubling questions about his privileging of proletarian female whiteness.

NOTES

1. For an excellent summary of the "old" and "new" in Dreiser studies, see Miriam Gogol's introduction in Gogol (xvii). See also Orlov and Gogol.
2. Ostreicher argues for a "working-class subculture of opposition" (xv). Yet he defines the term in a way that suggests cooperation with one another rather than opposition to the capitalist way: "an interlocking network of formal institutions and informal practices based on an ethic of social equality."
3. Comments Ehrlich, "Throughout the later 1870s and well into the 1880s unskilled jobs were at a premium, and the continued influx of immigrant workmen only served to intensify this problem" (530). By 1865 there were three million immigrants in the United States, and four million African Americans.
4. Fixing output quotas themselves, in some cases they secured privileged positions without union rules or accommodation to employers (Montgomery, "Workers' Control" 489, 492).
5. "Repudiating Whiteness: The Politics of Passings and Trespassings," American Studies Association Conference, Detroit, 13 Oct. 2000. The University of Toronto hosted a conference titled "Defining Whiteness: Race, Class, and Gender in North American History" on Oct. 13–15, 2000.
6. In 1894, for instance, then Police Commissioner of New York City Theodore Roosevelt referred to the "Irish Race." A notable exception is Dreiser's McClure's essay, "The Mighty Burke" (1911), in which he praises an Irish foreman at the expense of his (Italian) crew.
7. For the argument that the Germans were no better regarded than the Irish, see Bernardi (105), although he is vague on the time period in the nineteenth century to which he alludes.
8. Laurie, Artisans into Workers 27. I found this common racist phrase of the day in an 1844 issue of the craft-connected periodical The Mechanic (Roediger, Wages 44).
9. Although a few hundred blacks lived in Homestead, Garland apparently did not "see" them. Garland's comment on "strange beasts" is quoted in Taylor (187). So, too, in The Workers (1898), the economics professor Walter Wyckoff, a participant-observer of manual laborers, both immigrant and native-born, spends more time describing their lodgings and customs than their work.

10. Good analyses of tenement tales and novels appear in Giamo (54–64) and in Trachtenberg.

11. On one level, Chimmie is the spiritual grandfather of the confrontational toughs of Depression-era gangster films like *Angels with Dirty Faces* (1938) and *The Public Enemy* (1931). On another, he is a clever update of the antebellum Mose figure, with an overlay of Elizabeth Oakes Smith's good-hearted newsboy.

12. A similar character appears in the popular cartoons of the period; see Woolf and Outcault.

13. On Lowell's centrality to women's labor history, see Dublin.

WORKS CITED

Bernardi, Daniel. "The Voice of Whiteness: D. W. Griffith's Biograph Films." *Race and the Emergence of U.S. Cinema*. Ed. Bernardi. New Brunswick, NJ: Rutgers UP, 1996. 103–28.

Blewett, Mary H. *We Will Rise in Our Might: Workingwomen's Voices from Nineteenth-Century New England*. Ithaca: Cornell UP, 1991.

Brodkin, Karen. *How Jews Became White Folks and What That Says About Race in America*. New Brunswick, NJ: Rutgers UP, 1998.

Butler, Elizabeth Beardsley. *Women and the Trades: Pittsburgh, 1907–1908*. 1909. Introduction by Maurine Weiner Greenwald. Pittsburgh: U of Pittsburgh P, 1984.

Cameron, Ardis. *Radicals of the Worst Sort: Laboring Women in Lawrence, Massachusetts, 1860–1912*. Urbana: U of Illinois P, 1993.

Cappetti, Carla. *Writing Chicago: Modernism, Ethnography, and the Novel*. New York: Columbia UP, 1993.

Couvares, Francis G. *The Remaking of Pittsburgh: Class and Culture in an Industrializing City, 1877–1919*. Pittsburgh: U of Pittsburgh P, 1984.

Cutler, Irving. *The Jews of Chicago: From Shtetl to Suburb*. Urbana: U of Illinois P, 1996.

Den Tandt, Christophe. *The Urban Sublime in American Literary Naturalism*. Urbana: U of Illinois P, 1998.

Dreiser, Theodore. *An Amateur Laborer*. 1904. Ed. Richard W. Dowell and James L. W. West III. Philadelphia: U of Pennsylvania P, 1983.

———. *An American Tragedy*. 1925. New York: New American Library, 1964.

———. "The Factory." 1910. *Theodore Dreiser: A Selection of Uncollected Prose*. Ed. Donald Pizer. Detroit: Wayne State UP, 1977. 175–80.

———. "Fall River." Unpublished manuscript, [c. 1899]. Theodore Dreiser Papers, Van Pelt–Dietrich Library, U of Pennsylvania.

———. *Jennie Gerhardt*. 1911. New York: Penguin, 1989.

———. "The Literary Shower." *Ev'ry Month* (1 Feb. 1896): 10–11.

———. "The Mighty Burke." *McClure's* 37 (May 1911): 40–50.

———. *Newspaper Days*. 1931. Ed. T. D. Nostwich. Philadelphia: U of Pennsylvania P, 1991.

———. "Nigger Jeff." 1898. *Free and Other Stories.* New York: Boni and Liveright, 1918. 76–111.

———. "Scenes in a Cartridge Factory." *Cosmopolitan* 25 (July 1898): 321–24.

———. *Sister Carrie.* 1900. Ed. James L. West et al. New York: Penguin, 1981.

———. "The Strike To-day." *Toledo Blade* [24 Mar. 1894]: 1, 6. *Sister Carrie: An Authoritative Text, Backgrounds, and Sources.* Ed. Donald Pizer. 2nd ed. New York: Norton, 1991. 417–23.

———. "Three Sketches of the Poor." *New York Call* 23 Nov. 1913: 10.

———. "The Transmigration of the Sweatshop." *Puritan* 8 (July 1900): 498–502.

Dublin, Thomas. *Women at Work: The Transformation of Work and Community in Lowell, Massachusetts, 1826–1860.* New York: Columbia UP, 1979.

"Edward W. Townsend Dies." *New York Times* 17 and 21 Mar. 1942.

Ehrlich, Richard L. "Immigrant Strikebreaking Activity: A Sampling of Opinion Expressed in the *National Labor Tribune,* 1878–1885." *Labor History* 15 (Fall 1974): 528–42.

Filippelli, Ronald L. "Fall River Textile Strikes of 1884 and 1889." *Labor Conflict in the United States: An Encyclopedia.* Ed. Ronald L. Filippelli. New York: Garland, 1990. 159–75.

———. "Homestead Strike." Filippelli, *Labor Conflict* 241–46.

Fishkin, Shelley Fisher. "Dreiser and the Discourse of Gender." *Theodore Dreiser: Beyond Naturalism.* Ed. Miriam Gogol. New York: New York UP, 1995. 1–30.

Foley, Neil. *The White Scourge: Mexicans, Blacks, and Poor Whites in Texas Cotton Culture.* Berkeley: U of California P, 1997.

Foner, Philip S. *Women in the American Labor Movement from Colonial Times to the Eve of World War I.* New York: Free Press, 1979.

Freeman, Joshua, et al. *Who Built America?: Working People and the Nation's Economy, Politics, Culture, and Society.* Vol. 2. New York: Pantheon, 1992.

Garland, Hamlin. "Homestead and Its Perilous Trades." *McClure's* 111 (June 1894): 3–20.

Giamo, Benedict. *On the Bowery: Confronting Homelessness in American Society.* Iowa City: U of Iowa P, 1989.

Gogol, Miriam, ed. *Theodore Dreiser: Beyond Naturalism.* New York: New York UP, 1995.

Greenwald, Maurine Weiner. "Introduction: Women at Work Through the Eyes of Elizabeth Beardsley Butler and Lewis Hine." Butler vii–xlvi.

Halpern, Rick. *Down on the Killing Floor: Black and White Workers in Chicago's Packinghouses, 1904–1954.* Urbana: U of Illinois P, 1997.

Kaplan, Amy. *The Social Construction of American Realism.* 1988. Chicago: U of Chicago P, 1992.

Kleinberg, S. J. *The Shadow of the Mills: Working-Class Families in Pittsburgh, 1870–1907.* Pittsburgh: U of Pittsburgh P, 1989.

Laurie, Bruce. *Artisans into Workers: Labor in Nineteenth-Century America.* New York: Farrar-Noonday, 1989.

Levine, Susan. *Labor's True Woman: Carpet Weavers, Industrialization, and Labor Reform in the Gilded Age.* Philadelphia: Temple UP, 1984.

Lingeman, Richard. *Theodore Dreiser: An American Journey.* New York: John Wiley, 1993.

Lott, Eric. *Love and Theft: Blackface Minstrelsy and the American Working Class.* New York: Oxford UP, 1993.

Michaels, Walter Benn. *The Gold Standard and the Logic of Naturalism: American Literature at the Turn of the Century.* Berkeley: U of California P, 1987.

Miller, Stuart Creighton. *The Unwelcome Immigrant: The American Image of the Chinese, 1785–1882.* Berkeley: U of California P, 1969.

Montgomery, David. "William Sylvis and the Search for Working-Class Citizenship." *Labor Leaders in America.* Ed. Melvyn Dubofsky and Warren Van Tine. Urbana: U of Illinois P, 1987. 3–24.

———. "Workers' Control of Machine Production in the Nineteenth Century." *Labor History* 17 (1976): 489, 492.

Newitz, Annalee, and Matt Wray. Introduction. *White Trash: Race and Class in America.* Ed. Newitz and Wray. New York: Routledge, 1997.

Orlov, Paul, and Miriam Gogol. "Prospects for the Study of Theodore Dreiser." *Resources for American Literary Study* 24.1 (1988): 1–21.

Ostreicher, Richard Jules. *Solidarity and Fragmentation: Working People and Class Consciousness in Detroit, 1875–1900.* Urbana: U of Illinois P, 1986.

Outcault, R. F. *"The Yellow Kid": A Centennial Celebration of the Kid Who Started the Comics.* Introduction by Bill Blackbeard. Northampton, MA: Kitchen Sink, 1995.

Peiss, Kathy. *Cheap Amusements: Working Women and Leisure in Turn-of-the-Century New York.* Philadelphia: Temple UP, 1986.

Pizer, Donald. "The Strike." Dreiser, *Sister Carrie,* ed. Pizer 416.

Roediger, David. *Towards the Abolition of Whiteness: Essays on Race, Politics, and Working Class History.* London: Verso, 1994.

———. *The Wages of Whiteness: Race and the Making of the American Working Class.* London: Verso, 1991.

Siegel, Adrienne. *The Image of the American City in Popular Literature, 1820–1870.* Port Washington, NY: Kennikat, 1981.

Stein, Leon, ed. *Out of the Sweatshop: The Struggle for Industrial Democracy.* New York: Quadrangle–New York Times Book Co., 1977.

Takaki, Ronald. *A Different Mirror: A History of Multicultural America.* Boston: Little, Brown, 1993.

Taylor, Walter Fuller. *The Economic Novel in America.* Chapel Hill: U of North Carolina P, 1942.

Townsend, E. W. *Chimmie Fadden*. 1895. New York: Garrett, 1969.

Trachtenberg, Alan. "Experiments in Another Country: Stephen Crane's New York City Sketches." *Southern Review* 10 (Spring 1974): 265–85.

Turbin, Carole. *Working Women of Collar City: Gender, Class, and Community in Troy, 1864–1888.* Urbana: U of Illinois P, 1992.

West, James L. W., III. Introduction. *An Amateur Laborer.* By Theodore Dreiser. Ed. Richard W. Dowell and James L. W. West III. Philadelphia: U of Pennsylvania P, 1983. xi–lv.

———, ed. *Dreiser's* Jennie Gerhardt: *New Essays on the Restored Text.* Philadelphia: U of Pennsylvania P, 1995.

Wixson, Douglas. *Worker-Writer in America: Jack Conroy and the Tradition of Midwestern Literary Radicalism, 1898–1990.* Urbana: U of Illinois P, 1999.

Woolf, Michael Angelo. *Sketches of Life in a Great City.* New York: G. P. Putnam's Sons, 1899.

Zayani, Mohamed. *Reading the Symptom: Theodore Dreiser, Frank Norris, and the Dynamics of Capitalism.* New York: Peter Lang, 1999.

Coon Shows, Ragtime, and the Blues

RACE, URBAN CULTURE, AND THE
NATURALIST VISION IN PAUL LAURENCE
DUNBAR'S *THE SPORT OF THE GODS*

—*Nancy Von Rosk*

W HEN HE DESCRIBES THE CONDITIONS THAT CONTRIBUTED TO THE
DEVELOPMENT OF LITERARY NATURALISM, DONALD PIZER REMINDS US
that "the 1890s were . . . distinguished . . . by a full realization of changes that
had occurred during the previous two decades—in particular, the rapid shift
from a predominantly rural, agrarian civilization to an urban, industrial society . . ." (17). Lee Clark Mitchell also attends to this "rapid shift" when he
explains why "social determinism fascinated" America's writers and why literary naturalism "thrived in a country so committed to personal liberty" (527).
"The answer," he writes, "lies at least in part in the rapid industrializing of
American society, which as never before displayed practices fully at odds with
its Republican ideals" (527). In *Form and History in American Literary Naturalism,* June Howard also emphasizes cultural transformation. "When Americans of the late nineteenth and early twentieth centuries voiced their thoughts
for contemporaries," she notes, "they often reported that they felt themselves
living in a perilous time, a period of change and uncertainty, of dislocations
and disorders. Naturalism is a literary form that struggles to accommodate a
sense of discomfort and danger" (ix). Amy Kaplan, meanwhile, views the
work of late-nineteenth-century writers as a "strategy for imagining and managing the threats of social change" (8). As these critics reinforce, naturalism
was a response to dramatic cultural change, and for their subject matter America's naturalists would repeatedly turn to the city where these changes were
most markedly felt and realized. Indeed, our most well-known naturalist
novels—*Maggie, McTeague,* and *Sister Carrie*—all situate their characters'
struggles within this new urban environment. As Richard Lehan notes, "The
city now organizes the means to satisfy biological needs and desires. The modern city has taken the place of the primitive jungle—re-presenting the old natural struggle in new urban terms" (60).

Yet, while the naturalists turned their attention to America's expanding
cities and the nation's underclass, and explored such subjects as poverty and

class conflict, their work is still marked by a curious absence. Naturalism took hold during the period known as the "racial nadir"—a period marked by the failure of Reconstruction and the beginnings of the African American urban migration. Moreover, African Americans and African American culture had been shaping America's popular urban culture for decades. Even though one could argue that in the 1890s, race was still America's greatest "discomfort," race is not an obvious concern for most naturalist writers, nor has race been a compelling element in much of the critical discussion of their work. Since most criticism has focused primarily on the works of a small group of white male writers—Crane, Norris, Dreiser, and London—our reading of the naturalist tradition has been limited.[1] When we turn, however, to Paul Laurence Dunbar's long neglected and overlooked novel *The Sport of the Gods,* we are able to see the racial dimension of the world literary naturalists were struggling to depict. An African American text which brings together the plantation tale and urban realism, Dunbar's novel is a unique and an especially important work of American literary naturalism.

DUNBAR'S PROJECT

Primarily recognized for his poetry, Dunbar's work as a novelist has not met with enthusiastic critical acclaim. His earlier novels have been described as "white" since all the characters are white and virtually no reference is made to the presence of black people (Revell 139). Dunbar has also been seen as a black writer who "sold out" to his white audience by writing in the plantation tradition—a genre that sentimentalized the Old South by depicting the relationship between a master and slave as a benevolent, paternal one. Robert Bone, for example, views *Sport of the Gods* within this tradition when he asserts that the novel "reiterates the plantation-school thesis that the rural Negro becomes demoralized in the urban north" (42). "Thus at the height of Post-Reconstruction repression," he writes, "Dunbar was urging Negroes to remain in the South where they could provide a disciplined labor force for the new plantation economy" (42). Recent criticism, however, has begun to revise such earlier judgments; indeed, critics have begun attending to the radical nature of *Sport of the Gods,* viewing the novel as Dunbar's protest work, as something distinctly different from what he had produced beforehand. Peter Revell, for example, emphasizes that *Sport of the Gods,* unlike Dunbar's other novels, is a "black" novel and one of the first significant contributions by African American writers to the art of the novel (139). He also believes that "the naturalism of *Sport of the Gods* . . . is an indication that Dunbar wanted and tried to extend his range and break free of the old forms" (171). Houston Baker views the novel as subversive; "from the outset," he writes, "one is alerted that Dunbar's text is a fiction whose implied goal is to avoid a monotonous iteration of traditional patterns of narrative" (130). Gregory Candela, in turn, points out that critics have not seen the irony in Dunbar's work. (71, 72). "Rather than place him outside black authors' march toward realism," Candela declares, "he should be placed in the vanguard as a novelist able to mix inflexible elements of melodrama with the consciousness of an ironic mask" (72). Critic Lawrence Rodgers also places Dunbar "in the vanguard." He credits Dunbar with creating a pioneer work of extreme importance—the "African American Great Migration novel." He sees Dunbar's work as initiating what may be found again and again in migration fiction—the centrality of southern folk culture (39, 54). Casey Inge, in another recent reading of the novel, believes it is "a reply to Post-Reconstruction domestic novels" (228). Rather than reading the novel as "buying into the legacy claimed by plantation literature," he contends, "we should understand the presence of the idyllic extended family of the plantation novel . . . as a challenge to the idealization of the family by many Post-Reconstruction African American novelists" (228). "Dunbar," he writes, "argues against relying upon domesticity as an emancipatory discourse" (228). Charles Scruggs also views Dunbar's work as breaking new ground since it concentrates on issues which will be especially important for later twentieth-century African American writers; as he puts it, "the city's moral ambiguity would become an ongoing black tradition" (50). "Already recognizable," he observes, "are the beginnings of mass culture and the ambiguous state of isolation in the city" (16).

This survey of critical commentary reinforces Dunbar's precarious and difficult position. It makes sense that some critics see him as the very embodiment of white middle-class values, while others see him as especially black, radically minded, and subversive. He inevitably had to be *both*; writing for a white audience, he would have to speak to that audience's values, yet for a black man in 1902, the very act of writing itself is radical and always potentially subversive. Indeed, Dunbar's critical reception emphasizes the doubleness of Dunbar as well as the doubleness of his project. In writing *Sport of the Gods,* Dunbar was examining not only what happens when a Victorian middle-class sentimental (white) culture collides with the new urban mass culture but also what happens when an African American family who subscribes to the values of this dominant culture encounters the new urban mass culture. Dunbar's work is thus a crucial text for understanding African American literature and history, and it is also an important work of literary naturalism, following in the tradition of writers like Dreiser and yet expanding the boundaries of that tradition in some remarkable ways.

Like Dreiser's *Sister Carrie* (1900), *The Sport of the Gods* (1902) focuses on the moral perils of the new urban metropolis. Both novels highlight the breakdown of the sentimental Victorian home and the lure of the city's new public spaces—the beginnings of "nightlife" and the mass entertainment industry. Yet while Dreiser creates an essentially "white" city, Dunbar shows us how the "color line" divides and maps urban space. Dunbar's text makes visible what had been for the most part invisible in the urban novels of the late nineteenth and early twentieth centuries—a viable black presence in northern American cities well before the Great Migration was under way. Here we find the vibrant realm of the African American—the ragtime and blues bar, the vaudeville stage and the boarding house. Moreover, Dunbar's theater is a racially mixed one, a theater which shows the wildly popular "coon" shows of the 1890s and early 1900s, a phenomenon that is never mentioned in Dreiser's work but is ubiquitous in turn-of-the-century American popular culture. As Dunbar's novel highlights for us, America's new urban popular culture was inextricably intertwined with blackness, or, rather, with what Americans imagined blackness to be.

Another important element of Dunbar's naturalism is the undermining of the period's popular plantation narrative. Rather than the benevolent patriarchal southern home where blacks are taken care of and protected by their white "father," the southern home in Dunbar's novel is a theater where lies are told and secrets withheld, a space as dangerous and as theatrical as any to be found in the urban north. The "comfortable" dependency the Hamiltons experience living down South on the "master's" estate is as problematic as the racist popular culture they will encounter in the city of New York. Indeed, the Hamiltons cannot move beyond that southern patriarchal "plantation"—even when they encounter the freer environment of the more liberal north, for the "genteel" white culture that betrays them knows no geographical bounds. This "overdetermined" white culture seems to close in on the Hamiltons even more insistently during their bid for opportunity and anonymity in New York City.

THE BEGINNINGS OF AFRICAN AMERICAN URBANIZATION AND THE RISE OF MASS CULTURE

Although scholars have generally referred to the Great Migration as beginning during World War I, significant numbers of African Americans were on the move long before this. As Laurence Levine observes, "There has been an unfortunate tendency to equate Negro migrations with the Great Migration to the North during the World War I period. In fact significant movement of Negroes began as soon as freedom made it possible" (263). In his analysis of black folk songs after emancipation, Levine draws our attention to the emphasis on movement and the predominance of the railroad (262). "The raw statistics of black migration north," he insists, "only begin to give a sense of the movement involved since so much of this was secondary migration. The route from the southern farm to the northern city was not necessarily direct but frequently was preceded by migration to a southern town or city" (263). Carole Marks also observes that many blacks moved to southern cities first and that "farm laborers set in motion between the 1890s and 1910 three migration streams. Although these were relatively small, they resulted in urbanizing 22% of the black southern population by 1910" (34). Thus, many of the migrants who arrived North were not rural agricultural workers but people who were, to a certain extent, socialized in urban mores much like the Hamilton family in Dunbar's novel.

While northern cities held a promising allure for southern blacks, black communities were only just beginning to form there, and life was especially harsh for these early urban pioneers. The Hamiltons arrive in a New York that has "an Afro-American community in the process of evolution, where black migrants . . . find pockets of black people but no localized sense of community," for turn-of-the-century Harlem was not yet the center of African American culture but, rather, an area for well-to-do white residents. (Scruggs 45). As Paul Revell notes, "New York's black population lived in a number of scattered blocks . . . not in a single area of predominantly black residence" (94). When the black population of the city expanded by 25,000 during the last decade of the nineteenth century, the primary area of concentration of black residents was the Tenderloin, from 20th Street to 53rd Street and San Juan Hill; "in these areas the black residents were usually concentrated in one or two densely populated blocks, set here and there in areas of white occupation, usually of first and second generation Irish and German immigrants" (Revell 94). This community "had many of the problems of later Harlem—overcrowding, drastically unhealthy and insanitary living conditions, and a rent system that operated unfairly" (Revell 94). As Kevin Gaines points out, "Real estate agents were often unconcerned with preserving the middle-class character of black neighborhoods and profited from the residential segregation that produced crowded slums. This, combined with municipal policies confining prostitution, saloons and gambling to black sections away from white residential and commercial areas, led elite blacks, among others to see a correlation between urbanization and moral chaos" (180).

In addition to grim living arrangements, work was often hard to come by in northern cities like New York. As Jacob Riis remarks in *How the Other Half Lives,* "Ever since the [Civil] war, New York has been receiving the overflow of the colored population from the southern cities. . . . Whether the exchange has been an advantage to the Negro may well be questioned. Trades of which he had practical control in his Southern home are not open to him here" (115). Indeed, according to Theodore Kornweibel, the northern city posed as many obstacles perhaps as its southern counterpart:

> Blacks were systematically barred from industrial jobs except as strikebreakers. Readily available employment was found only in low-paying servicing occupations or occasional unskilled labor where few prospects for advancement or security existed. . . . Blacks found themselves suffering under a job ceiling in which entrance into some professions and skilled trades was being increasingly curtailed . . . while opportunities for employment and subsequent upward mobility were being accorded non–English speaking immigrants. In trades where blacks had traditionally enjoyed good employment opportunities and sometimes near monopolies like barbering, catering, and waitering, they found themselves faced with organized and often successful attempts to force employers to discharge blacks and hire only whites. . . . The result was that by the turn of the century, in city after city of the North, the proportion of Blacks in unskilled or service occupations numbered 80 percent or more. (110)

Despite the harshness and limited opportunities of northern city life, these cities nevertheless still "symbolized . . . places to which one might escape the imprisonment of sharecropping and agricultural peonage" or places where one could "perhaps find greater prospects for political and social expression" (Kornwiebel 110). Eventually the city would become the hub for the black arts and entertainment industry. As Lewis Erenberg points out, "Many of the early hot spots in New York were run and frequented by blacks. Northern and southern cities allowed blacks to find a degree of neighborhood hegemony outside white society. For the first time, they had the opportunity to express aspects of their identities and their cultures, unmolested by white society. It was in the cities that blacks developed ragtime and jazz, for it was there they had a degree of personal freedom and also where they underwent a process of secularization" (22–23). Indeed, while New York City does not turn out to be "all the glory, all the wealth and all the freedom of the world" the Hamiltons imagine it will be, Dunbar nevertheless shows us a vibrant city where there seems to be less racial oppression and more freedom (78). Blacks and whites intermingle as "equals" at the Banner Club. Joe watches the black youths promenading in their "spruce clothes," walking the streets "so knowingly, so independently" (87). Mr. Thomas and Mrs. Jones enjoy dancing to ragtime, and Thomas's enthusiasm for New York is contagious: "It's the only town on the face of the earth. . . . We git the best shows here, we git the best concerts—say, now what's the use o my callin it all out—we simply git the best of everything" (90). Besides highlighting his enthusiasm for urban living, Thomas's speech is revealing in another sense. What Thomas emphasizes in his praise is New York's public amusements, the entertainment industry, the beginnings of mass culture. And it is this new urban culture which holds such contradictory meanings for the African American—a culture that, while promising new freedoms, would continue to enforce an insidious racism.

THE SPORT OF THE GODS

As the novel opens, the Hamiltons' lives seem to hold much potential. We learn that Berry Hamilton is an ambitious man who strives to better himself much like the urban heroes created by Horatio Alger: "He was one of the many slaves who upon their accession to freedom had not left the South, but had wandered from place to place in their own beloved section, waiting, working, *struggling to rise* with its rehabilitated fortunes" (2, my emphasis). Like Alger's hero, Ragged Dick, who carefully lays away his meager earnings in the savings bank, Berry too feels "the advantage of steady self denial" (Alger 105). What is stressed alongside the Hamiltons' industry and hard work is their loyalty to the Oakleys. Berry is described as "following" the example of his employer, Maurice Oakley (3). The Hamilton house is "replenished with things handed down from 'the house' . . . and with others bought from the pair's earnings" (3), and "flowers bloomed in the little plot in front and behind it; vegetables and greens testified to the housewife's industry" (4). Highlighting its reflection of white middle-class values, the Hamilton home is also marked by a gendered ordering of separate spheres: "Berry had time for his lodge and Fannie had time to spare for her own house and garden" (3). And while Fanny and Berry work hard, save their money, and view their home as a haven to be protected, their children are inclined to value a domesticity based on leisure, consumption, and display. Although this home which Kitty and Joe are born into is described as a "bower of peace and comfort," the narrator is quick to undercut this, for into this pastoral ideal enter materialistic desires.

Joe, we are told, is of a "cheerful disposition," yet he nevertheless "from scraping the chins of aristocrats came to imbibe some of their ideas and rather too early in life bid fair to be a dandy" (4). Later when the Hamiltons move to New York, Dunbar reminds us that Joe "had started out with false ideals as to what was fine and manly" (100). Kit, on the other hand, is spoiled by her mother since there was "nothing too good for her to wear," and she "had the prettiest clothes of any of her race in the town" (5). Indeed, Dunbar highlights how the family's love of finery and clothing, their aspiration to genteel theatrical manners is central to their identity. The morning after Francis's farewell dinner, the Hamiltons talk of "de way dem woman was dressed" and Joe "contented himself with devouring the good things and aping the manners of the young men whom he knew had been among last night's guests" (35). Significantly, Dunbar's narrator also describes these "doting" parents as "doing their duties and spoiling their children much as *white* fathers and mothers are wont to do . . . [;] what the less fortunate Negroes said of them and their offspring is not worthwhile" (6, my emphasis). Immediately, then, the Hamilton family is aligned with the "genteel" white family, but this genteel white family is morally bankrupt, and the Hamiltons' dedication to the Oakleys as well as their alienation from the "less fortunate Negroes" only heightens the bitterness of Dunbar's naturalist vision.

Although loyal to the Oakleys for so many years, the Hamiltons are banished promptly and efficiently when Berry is suspected of theft. Unlike Alger's hero, who is rewarded for adhering to traditional middle-class values, Berry Hamilton is punished, for his bank account only convinces Oakley of his guilt. Indeed, Dunbar shows us that the sentimental ties between these families is a fiction; the Oakley home is ultimately a theater wherein the dishonest and charming brother recently arrived from Paris can stage his own melodrama. Frank's finely cultivated urbanity, Dunbar suggests, prevents the Oakleys from seeing him clearly: "He had the face and brow of a poet, a pallid face framed in a mass of dark hair. There was a touch of weakness in his mouth, but this was shaded and half hidden by a full mustache that made much forgivable to beauty-loving eyes" (11). Just as the Oakleys cannot see beyond Frank's urbane charm, they ultimately cannot see beyond Berry's blackness. It is therefore easy for Frank to play the role of innocent victim while Berry is cast as the "depraved black man." Caught in this "master plot"—a white melodrama which needs a criminal—Berry resists this script to no avail, and his adherence to white middle-class values, his careful savings of his earnings, merely renders him all the more deviant.

Despite weak circumstantial evidence, Oakley insists on seeing Berry as a guilty man. Even Berry's desperate appeal and reminder—"[A]ftah de way I've put you to bed f'om many a dinnah, an' you woke up to fin' all yo money safe?"—cannot move Oakley, who prides himself on being a "hard-headed businessman" (45, 26). Responding vindictively, he even refuses to honor his brother's wishes to go easy on Berry: "He is gone and will never know what happens so I may be as revengeful as I wish, " he tells his wife. Both brothers, we learn, are liars and "do as they wish" when they believe no one is looking.

Dunbar then highlights how Berry becomes a scapegoat for both black and white communities. For the whites, this is a case to "review and comment on": "It had been long since so great a bit of wrong doing in a negro had given them cause for speculation and recrimination" (52). Those who have their doubts, like the detective and the Colonel, are either ignored or unwilling to voice their concerns in such a hostile environment. For the "gentlemen assembled in the Continental bar," "Berry was already proven guilty" (57). As disturbing as this judgment is, perhaps the reaction of the black community is even more so. When the accounts of the lodge Berry was a treasurer for are audited, the lodge members "seemed personally grieved when his books were found to be straight" (49). The A. M. E. church "hastened . . . to purge itself of contamination by turning him out" (49). Dunbar's narrator explains this rejection: "In the black people of the town the strong influence of slavery was still operative, and with one accord, they turned away from one of their own kind upon whom had been set the ban of the white people's displeasure . . . the safety of their own positions and firesides demanded that they stand aloof from the criminal" (50). The community's response, however, also reveals that the Hamiltons have "sinned" against their black brethren: "He wanted to dress his wife an chillen lak white folks, did he? Well he foun out he foun out" (51). "W'enevah you see niggahs gittin so high dat dey own folks ain good enough fu em, look out, " asserts another neighbor (52). When Maurice Oakley wonders where the Hamiltons will go, his wife assures him "oh some of their people will take them in" (79). She mistakenly assumes that the black community is united, but, as Dunbar shows us, class often divides those of the same race. Indeed, when Joe looks for work in a colored barbershop, he is ridiculed and turned away. With nowhere to turn, the Hamiltons look to New York—"a city that like Heaven . . . seemed the center of all the glory, all the wealth and all the freedom of the world" (78).

Dunbar's chapter detailing the Hamiltons' arrival in New York brings to mind the descriptions of opportunity, delight, and danger one finds in Dreiser's work. The opening paragraph of chapter 7 highlights the aesthetic delight to be found in the city—the seduction of the eye and the danger of succumbing to all this visual plenitude:

> To the provincial coming to New York for the first time . . . the
> city presents a notable mingling of the qualities of cheeriness and
> gloom. . . . If he have any eye at all for the beautiful he cannot help
> experiencing a thrill as he . . . catches the first sight of the build-
> ings of New York. . . . A new emotion will take his heart as the
> people hasten by him—a feeling of loneliness, almost of grief, that
> with all of these souls about him he knows not one . . . [;] after he
> has passed through the first pangs of strangeness . . . the real fever
> of love for the place will take hold upon him. . . . Then if he be
> wise he will go away. . . . But if he be a fool, he will stay and stay
> on until the town becomes all in all to him; until the very streets
> are his chums and certain buildings and corners his best friends.
> Then he is hopeless and to live elsewhere would be death. The
> Bowery will be his romance, Broadway his lyric . . . and he will
> look down pityingly on all the rest of humanity. (81–83)

This passage suggests that encountering the city for the first time is to experience a kaleidoscope of emotion. Further, if one has an "eye" for the beautiful, the city is the place for encountering visual delight, but in order to experience this, one must also experience the isolation and loneliness of the detached spectator. "After a while," however, one will adjust and be trans-formed. The spectator will be "happy" regarding the indifference of the crowd since one can now look and study that crowd better. Eventually, the passage implies, one will come to believe it is better to be a spectator than a partici-pant. The faces of the crowd will fade away so that the very streets will become one's "chums," and certain buildings and corners one's "best friends." In this way, the city becomes oddly depersonalized, and yet one can experi-ence a thrill of power through this detachment, "looking down pityingly on all the rest of humanity." While there is, then, an explicit recognition of the power one experiences in self-detachment and widening vision, there is even more wariness here of the power of the new urban space to shape the indi-vidual, to wrest the individual away from community. Perhaps Dunbar, more so than the other naturalists, sees urban space as especially deceptive—"if he be wise he will go away, any place," he writes. Although for the African

American the city may foster more dreams, hold more symbolic significance, it also harbors more threats, more obstacles, and less opportunity.

Not only were urbanized African Americans faced with a popular culture that celebrated and ridiculed "blackness," the "individualistic" orientation of city life was a dramatic contrast to traditional African American patterns of community. In their work entitled *Long Memory*, Mary Frances Berry and John Blassingame remind us of the important cultural differences between the white family ideal of middle-class America and the typical African American family:

> One of the major functions of the lower-class black family was to toughen its members to a world of systematic brutalization by the police, by businessmen, and by other facets of white caste restrictions. Lower-class culture helped to minimize the pain this involved. Within the family as in no other area of life, white America freed the black man to work out his response to systematic oppression. One mode of adaptation was the extended family. After slavery, the extended family was prevalent in the black community. Generally black households had twice as many relatives outside the immediate family as did white ones. Egalitarian in nature, the family was marked by flexibility of roles, informal adoption of children and care for the aged. Blacks seemed to have greater abhorrence for institutionalizing the aged than whites did. When aged blacks did not live with their children, several other members of the local community took responsibility for them. (85)

With the high value it places on privacy and individualism, the new urban culture would undermine such notions of family. Significantly, the Hamiltons never subscribe to this African American ideal. Well before their arrival in New York, Dunbar highlights that they adhere to a white middle-class ideal—an ideal that privileges individualism and privacy, for in their southern home, the family is "shut in upon itself," detached from the wider black community (61).

Once in New York the family's isolation and vulnerability becomes more obvious. Immediately upon arrival, the Hamiltons look for some community, a community they did not need when they worked for the Oakleys. They look for familiarity, "for some colored face," and they "finally [see] one among the porters who were handling the baggage" (84). Mr. Thomas, however, is a problematic figure, a kind of confidence man, and Dunbar's contradictory description highlights this: "He was exceedingly polite," yet "he looked hard at Kitty" (84). As Thomas guides them, the narrator emphasizes the family's naiveté, their inability to read the new urban environment. For instance, the boarding house Thomas leads them to seems "too much for their pockets"; they are surprised at its "apparent grandeur" (84). Even inside, the narrator notes, "The sight of hard gaudily upholstered installment plan furniture did not disillusion them, and they continued to fear that they could never stop at this fine place" (84). They learn, however, that the proprietor Mrs. Jones is "willing to come to terms with them" (84). Moreover, the boarding house reveals itself to be neither grand nor genteel, and though Mrs. Jones seems "gracious and home-like," the boarding house's difference from "home" will soon become dramatically clear (84). During their first evening, Mr. Thomas brings some beer and Mrs. Jones brings the glasses, and the "Rag time man came down" so that Mr. Thomas and Mrs. Jones could "two-step" (95). Offering Kitty and Joe beer, and encouraging them to come out and see the coon shows, Mr. Thomas and Mrs. Jones challenge the authority of Mrs. Hamilton who feels her notions of propriety are under siege. "Oh let em stay, a little beer ain't going to hurt em," urges Mrs. Jones, while Thomas claims, "they'll get out o that, all right if they live in New York" (93). As in *Sister Carrie,* and other urban naturalist works like *Maggie* and *McTeague,* there is no home which will function as a "haven" from the powerful forces of city life.

From the outset, then, this new urban culture works upon the sensibility of each family member and weakens family ties. Joe, for example, blindly embraces New York; his desires continually expand; like Dreiser's Carrie, the more he sees, the more he wants. He looks at the young fellows "dressed in their spruce clothes and he wondered with a sort of envy where they could be going. Back home there had been no place much worth going except church and one or two people's houses. But these fellows seemed to show by their manners that they were neither going to church nor a family visiting" (87). The nature of public life down South had been to reinforce domesticity and community; it was centered on the family and the church. Public life in New York, however, is not about family or church socials; it is about individual pleasure. This public life is characterized by a new theatricality and style, an emphasis on the visual, where promenading and being seen are most important. Like Carrie, Joe yearns to be a part of the spectacle. He wants to be looked at, and "things" seem to call out to him. He imagines himself "red-cravated" and "patent leathered," being admired by others (87). Like Carrie, Joe also quickly forgets his family and sees them as an impediment to his own success. He grows increasingly distant from his mother and sister, forgetting "to feel the natural pity for his father, toiling guiltless in the prison" (88). Eventually his family will be a burden that he must cast off, much as Carrie decides to cast off Hurstwood, but Joe's rejection of his family does not expedite any rise in his fortunes. He will instead end up like Hurstwood, for in Dunbar's city, cutting family ties can have only devastating consequences.

We sense the vulnerability of these family ties when Thomas takes the Hamiltons out to their first "coon" show, for this scene emphasizes that the generations within the family are dramatically at odds. This generation gap reflects a larger cultural division: traditional Victorian manners coming into conflict with a new urban mass culture. As Gaines has pointed out, many black leaders were "alarmed" at the impact of urbanization and mass consumer culture, and upper-class blacks tended to insulate themselves from the city's new realm of public amusements (179). Unlike the upper-class blacks, Mrs. Hamilton cannot insulate herself, though there is much in this popular culture which she too finds "alarming." Indeed, while Joe and Kitty enthusiastically embrace the popular "coon" show, their mother feels uncomfortable and out of place as she watches the performance: "At first she was surprised at the enthusiasm over just such dancing as she could see any day from the loafers on the street corners down home, and then . . . she laughed and applauded with the rest, all the while trying to quiet something that was tugging at her away down in her heart" (106).

This entertainment tugs at the very "white" Victorian values she holds dear, values which uphold a more definitive boundary between highbrow and lowbrow. Since the new urban mass culture calls those boundaries into question, Mrs. Hamilton wonders if she has been too much of a highbrow, if "she had always been wrong in putting too low a value on really worthy things" (106). Her ambiguous response to the show's portrayal of black culture may also remind her of her estrangement from the black community "down home." This caricature, this exaggeration of southern life to make the northerner laugh and feel superior, makes her uneasy as she has not yet completely embraced a northern urban identity. Neither rooted in the southern community nor at home in this new urban one, Mrs. Hamilton is not sure what to laugh at. There is also the very unsettling situation of having something familiar made into something spectacular. Familiar types from her former community become strange and unreal as they are now exaggerated and packaged for consumption. As Scruggs explains, "the coon show made the past more attractive by sentimentalizing it, while the packaging process called attention to the falsity of the spectacle" (46). This theatrical spectacle, then, is something alien yet something familiar, something that delights her and yet something that disturbs her, that keeps "tugging away at her heart." The inherent contradictions of the new entertainment are key: "But they could sing and they did sing . . . they threw themselves into it because they enjoyed it and felt what they were doing, and they gave almost a semblance of dignity to the tawdry music and inane words" (102).

Beginning with the antebellum minstrel shows, America's popular culture had consistently celebrated black culture at the same time that it ridiculed it. Eric Lott describes this inherent doubleness when whites would "black up" and portray African Americans as "the simultaneous drawing up and crossing of racial boundaries" (Lott 6). "Minstrel performers often attempted to repress through ridicule the real interest in black cultural practices they nonetheless betrayed—minstrelsy's mixed erotic economy of celebration and exploitation," what Lott terms "love and theft" (6). Lott also remarks that even in its early days, the emphasis of the minstrel show was on "spectacle rather than narrative. . . . Black figures were there to be looked at, shaped to the demands of desire; they were screens on which audience fantasy could rest, and while this purpose might have a host of different effects, its fundamental outcome was to secure the position of white spectators as superior controlling figures" (141). By the time we reach the end of the nineteenth century, however, the nature of blackface has changed. Unlike the case in the antebellum minstrel show when mostly whites would be "blacking up" and portraying African Americans for white audiences, blacks were now performing, portraying themselves for racially mixed audiences.[2] But the African American comedians, singers, and dancers who began to appear on the vaudeville stage in the middle 1890s were required to portray—in a more authentic fashion—the "darky" characters created earlier by white performers (Nasaw 54). As the entertainment industry packaged black entertainers for consumption, America's popular culture only continued to denigrate the black culture it seemed to acclaim. Further, as this "lowbrow" culture rises in popularity and more and more people—black and white—begin enthusiastically to "consume" it, the white cultural establishment becomes fraught with great anxiety. As Edward Berlin observes in his *History of Ragtime,*

> Ragtime's emergence in the 1890s coincided with new technical means of mass music communication—recordings and piano rolls—and a vastly expanded publishing industry . . . [;] these developments combined to alter drastically the nature and scope of popular culture; whereas regionalism continued to exist, it became possible to introduce trends on a nationwide basis, creating a degree of national homogeneity. Many of the nation's cultural leaders

158

looked on with horror as ragtime, the first recipient of the new music technology, engulfed the nation. They had envisioned the country's music life "maturing" along the supposedly well-ordered lines of European musical academicism. Instead they witnessed the intrusion of a music that stemmed not from Europe but from Africa. (32)

The indignation of cultural leaders, however, could not stop the public's demand for the new music. According to Berlin, "Ragtime's proponents were quite as outspoken as its critics. Ragtime, they claimed, was liked by most people, including European royalty and some notable European musicians; its rhythms were distinctive, unique and innovative; it was the only music characteristically American" (44).

In addition to the cultural debates within the white establishment, there were divisions within the black community. As Kevin Gaines notes, "many black intellectuals and leaders expressed alarm at the impact of urbanization, migration and the homogenizing forces of mass consumer culture on the black community" (179). These "new secular pastimes and attractions" meant "challenges to religious traditions of black leadership and authority" (179). Indeed, according to Bernard Bell, "one of the great American paradoxes Dunbar reveals in his novel is the Puritan and Victorian attitude of many blacks toward forms of folk music. To pre–World War I rural black southerners, especially those with middle-class ambitions, there were two kinds of ethnic music: the Lord's (spirituals) and the devil's (blues, ragtime, and jazz)" (73). Willie the Lion Smith, a jazz pianist, recalls that "back in those early days, churchgoing Negro people would not stand for ragtime playing; they considered it to be sinful. Part of that feeling was due to the fact that the popular songs you heard played around in the saloons had bawdy lyrics and when you played in a raggy style, folks would right away think of the bad words and all the hell-raising they heard about in the red-light district" (Levine 178). In his analysis of the black upper class, Willard Gatewood points out that plantation melodies and especially ragtime were "shunned" (192). Indeed, upper-class urban blacks tended to insulate themselves from the new world of public amusements and mass culture. Since blacks of all classes were often barred from places of social amusement frequented by whites, and many found black-owned establishments socially unacceptable because they encouraged indiscriminate mixing of all classes, upper-class blacks centered their social world in the home.

Dunbar, too, seems to see the rising mass culture as particular harmful to African Americans, yet as a writer for the black theater, Dunbar himself embodies the cultural divisions of his times. Dunbar, the son of former slaves, lived at the "margins of the black leisure class" (Gaines 189); "although he, as rising poet of the race, spent many social hours with the intellectuals of . . . black society, he would simultaneously bask in their attention while maintaining a fascination for 'low life' that others, particularly his wife Alice, would find abhorrent" (Gaines 184). In *Sport of the Gods,* the narrator may criticize the show, but he cannot help pointing out the importance the show has for the audience, the sense of power and pride it generates: "There were a large number of coloured people in the audience and because members of their own race were giving the performance, they seemed to take a proprietary interest in it all" (102, 101). And after criticizing the costumes of the performers, even the narrator admits, "But they could sing, and they did sing, with their voices, their bodies, their souls" (102). Dunbar's attitude towards the coon show and its "detestable ditties" was, according to Gaines, "understandably deeply ambivalent" (190). "New York cabaret life was a world that Dunbar knew intimately," Gaines goes on to say; "he saw value in blacks performing their own syncopated songs and dances for black audiences even while it galled him that they so avidly consumed the stereotyped entertainments that he believed were foisted on them" (190). Revell also comments on the difficulty Dunbar had in reconciling this contradiction—his career moving from appeasing the white establishment to increasingly chafing against it. For instance, "his contributions to musical comedy," Revell writes, "demonstrate an initial willingness to abide by the relatively degraded standards of the minstrel show and its early successors, and a later reluctance to contribute to this kind of production at all" (106).

Dunbar's increasing reluctance as well as his writing of *Sport of the Gods* may have been encouraged by the fact that these "degraded standards" became even more degrading by the end of the nineteenth century. Historian Rayford Logan has described this period as the "nadir" in race relations, and C. Vann Woodward points out that segregation in the South was a "creation of the late nineteenth and early twentieth centuries" (Blassingame 348): "Deprived of political power and the protection of law enforcement agencies, blacks faced a virtual reign of terror in the South . . . [;] between 1882 and 1900, there were 3,011 lynchings in the United States" (Blassingame 349). Influenced by the Social Darwinist movement, scientists in England, the United States, and South Africa tried persistently to "prove" that blacks were intellectually inferior to whites (351). An especially vicious racist atmosphere, therefore, combining with the improvements made in mass production ensured that the entertainment industry's portrayal of blacks became not only more insidious but more wide-reaching. In the 1890s, according to many scholars, America witnessed a "coon song craze," a "major pop culture phenomenon" (Dorman 450).[3]

David Nasaw declares that "it is impossible to overstate the popularity of black misrepresentations" during this era: "African American caricatures were a staple of the vaudeville bill; black musicals were playing on Broadway and touring the first class theaters of the country and coon songs were the hottest selling item in sheet music" (54). Popularity, however, does not nurture respect: "the intent to caricature and humiliate blacks was evident not only in the coon song lyrics but in the illustrations for the sheet music as well. The comic black figure had existed for a long time before the coming of the coon songs, but according to J. Stanley Lemons, 'the treatment of blacks in illustrations had presented them as humans'" (Nasaw 104–5). As Nasaw points out, this was not the case in "the sheet music of the 1890s that pictured them with animal features . . . [;] the sheet music showed blacks with big mouths, big ears, oversized hands and feet, and sloping foreheads (meant to indicate limited intelligence) . . ." (56). James Dorman argues that as we move away from the dandy of the antebellum minstrel show to the urban coon of the 1890s, we encounter a major negative shift in white perception of blacks (450): the coon song craze was a "necessary sociopsychological mechanism for justifying segregation and subordination" (466), and Dorman's analysis of the period's "coon" songs leads him to make some disturbing generalizations:

> Blacks began to appear as not only drunk and ignorant and indolent but also devoid of honesty or personal honor, given to drunkenness and gambling, utterly without ambition, sensuous, libidinous, even lascivious. Coons were in addition to all of these things, razor-wielding savages, routinely attacking one another at the slightest provocation. . . . The flashing steel straight razor became in the songs the dominant symbol of black violence while the coon himself became that which was signified by this terrible weapon. The subliminal message was clear: Blacks are potentially dangerous; they must be controlled and subordinated by whatever means necessary. (450)

That so many coon song writers and performers were black makes this industry even more insidious and problematic. Indeed, what Dunbar seems to stress throughout his novel is the profound self-destructiveness of the African American who must live and survive within America's deeply racist culture. At the end of the novel, Joe comes to embody the worst stereotype of the "coon"—drunken, vain, and violent—while his parents recall the "Uncle

Tom" stereotype as they return South to live "in back of the big house." As we see the Hamiltons first subscribe to the genteel plantation culture and later embrace the northern urban coon show, Dunbar shows us that they have no other cultural frame of reference within which to imagine themselves.

For the younger Hamiltons, the new urban theater is especially powerful in shaping their sensibilities. In the theater, Kitty becomes "enchanted" and Joe, too, is "lost, transfixed, his soul floating on a sea of sense" (104, 103). Bringing to mind the experience of Dreiser's Carrie, the theater calls up even more desires within Joe: "[I]t inspired him with a desire to work and earn money of his own, to be independent both of parental help and control and so to be able to spend as he pleased" (109). Single-minded and obsessive, Joe is determined to become part of the urban crowd, to be admired and popular. He wishes to secure employment so that Thomas will take him out, and Thomas does so but only to get closer to Kitty. When Thomas brings Joe to the Banner Club and tells the gang "He's got some dough on him. He's fresh and young and easy," and the men grow excited with the prospect of making some money, he tells them to "go easy" and not to frighten him off, to "make him believe that you've got coin to burn and that it's an honour to be with you" (111). Soon they all treated "the lamb" with "a pale, dignified, high-minded respect that menaced his pocket book and possessions" (113).

While Dunbar highlights the moral depravity of the Banner Club, he nevertheless gives us a portrait of an unusual community. As the works of Erenberg, Nasaw, and Berlin remind us, *both* blacks and whites were enthusiastically consuming "black" culture, particularly black music, at the turn of the century. Ragtime piano playing is a regular feature of the Banner Club as are "free" concerts which promote the latest "coon song," "Come Back to Yo Baby Honey" (123). The Banner Club is also a popular place for "slummers," or, as Dunbar puts it, "the curious who wanted to see something of the other side of life" (118). The white reporter Skaggs is "a constant visitor," and his lady friend Maudie "had a penchant for dancing to Rag-time melodies as only the 'puffessor' of such a club can play them" (118). Although the Banner Club is ostensibly a black club, Dunbar draws our attention to the heterogeneous nature of the crowd gathered there. The Banner Club's diversity and its many functions suggest both its vibrancy and importance. It is an "institution for the lower education of Negro youth. It drew its pupils from every class of people and from every part of the country . . . [;] it stood to the stranger and the man and woman without connections for the whole social life. It was a substitute—poor it must be confessed—to many youths for the home life which is so lacking among certain classes in New York" (117). Dunbar also stresses how the club's theatricality is self-conscious, for here everyone performs and the role-playing is acknowledged, necessary. Skaggs, for instance, is a "monumental liar" and must tell a story of growing up with "darkies" to explain why he associates with blacks—"the same old story that the white who associates with Negroes from volition usually tells to explain his taste" (121). Here Joe meets Hattie Sterling, a chorus girl who teaches him much "because it was her advantage to do so" (131). He, in turn, makes enough to "show her a good time," and "nothing could keep her from being glorious in his eyes—not even the grease painting which adhered in unneat patches to her face, nor her taste for whiskey in its unreformed state" (125). Dunbar thus emphasizes over and over again not only the theatrical nature of the city's public life but the enormous influence and power this life has over the individual.

Though the Hamilton family was divided well before they reached the city, the urban environment exacerbates those once subtle divisions. Soon Joe is not only distant from his family but feeling contempt for them. Instead of obeying his mother and watching out for his sister, he leaves his sister in the care of Thomas so that "the poison of the unreal life about her" begins to affect her character (130). "She had grown secretive and sly," Dunbar writes; "The innocent longing . . . she had expressed that first night at the theater was growing into a real ambition and she dropped the simple old songs she knew to practice the detestable coon ditties which the stage demanded" (130). Eventually Kitty will work alongside her mother in "sullen silence" (130). Even Mrs. Hamilton, in her despair, drifts "farther away from her children and husband and all the traditions of her life" (131).

Unlike Dreiser's work, wherein the past can be cut off, family left behind, and new identities created, the characters in Dunbar's work are ultimately unable to escape their past. Though they hide the fact that Berry Hamilton is in jail, this secret is revealed by their former neighbor Minty Brown when she visits New York. In his reading of the novel, Lawrence Rodgers sees the family's attempts to preserve their reputation after her arrival as a mark of their inability to read the city (53). "That Berry's prison sentence is regarded as a point of honor," he writes, "aptly illustrates how badly the family has misread the values of their new home" (53). I would argue, however, that Rodgers overlooks some important facts and that this secrecy illustrates something else. Rather than their "misreading" of the city, the family's attempts to "preserve their reputation" illustrate the dramatic divisions within the urban black community, divisions which show a sentimental Victorian culture coming into conflict with a more modern individualistic one. Only the Banner Club sees the family's "fugitive status" as "a point of honor." Mrs. Jones, on the other hand, responds just as Mrs. Hamilton fears she would. The family must leave, or as Mrs. Jones puts it, "it'll soon be all over town and tha'ud ruin the reputation of my house" (139). Kitty later informs Joe that "Minty's story had reached their employers and that they were out of work" (159). This division of values—the Club's disregard of propriety and reputation and Mrs. Jones's concern with it—exacerbates the divisions between Joe and his family. While his mother and Kitty are thrown out on the streets and out of work, he is embraced at the Banner Club, for Sadness "reads" the fugitive status of the Hamilton family in a very different way. According to Sadness, all are "suffering from fever" (147). Sadness tells Joe of his own family tragedy—the lynching of his father—and then reveals the tragic histories of other Banner Club regulars: Viola, who "killed another woman"; Barney, "indicted twice for pick pocketing"; and Poor Wallace who lost the money his father left him and knows "already how to live on others as they have lived on him" (147, 148). His talk makes Joe feel "wonderfully in it" (149). Here in the Banner Club, but not in other urban spaces such as Mrs. Jones's boarding house or the workplace, the father's supposed crime is not a mark of shame but a mark of solidarity with the other individuals of the club, with all those who have experienced racial oppression.

Within this context, then, it is interesting to consider Bernard Bell's assertion that Sadness is a "living embodiment of the blues" (73). "Instead of turning to the Bible, the bullet, or the bottle to cope with the searing experience of racism," Bell declares, "Sadness survives by plumbing the depths of his soul and affirming the resiliency of the human spirit. . . . Sadness has developed a tragicomic vision of life, which in the Afro American tradition affirms the redemptive power of suffering and humor" (74). The fact that Joe begins to feel "wonderfully in it" suggests that Sadness—who is described as "sadly gay"—does function as a "living embodiment of the blues" (145). According to Levine, "blues performed some of the functions for the secularized masses that religion did: it spoke out of a group experience; it made many individual problems—dislocation, loneliness, broken families, economic difficulties—seem more common and converted them into shared experiences" (Levine 235). Levine also maintains that while creating a "shared experience" for African Americans, the blues "represents a major degree of acculturation," a shift in African American culture towards a privileging of the individual. Levine points out that although the communal call and response form of earlier African American folk music—the work songs and the spirituals—may have remained in the blues form, it was the blues singer who responded to himself or herself either verbally or on an accompanying instrument (221). In this way, Levine argues, blues singing "signaled the rise of a more personalized individual-oriented ethos among Negroes at the turn of the century" (221):

> By the last decades of the nineteenth century, blues songs were increasingly common and it was not coincidental that a new emphasis upon the individual and individual expression was taking hold in black song at the very time Booker T. Washington's philosophy was taking hold among black intellectuals and the black middle class. The individualist ethos, always strong in the United States, was perhaps ideologically most persuasive in the decades before and after the Civil War. In the latter period especially, the nation was imbued with the notion that Man could progress according to the Horatio Alger model. . . . Freedmen had this message thrust upon them. . . . Negroes were being acculturated in a way that would have been impossible during slavery. (223)

It is this "individualist ethos," however, which Dunbar seems unable to embrace. Just as he shows us that believing individual virtue and hard work will always be rewarded is naïve through the example of Berry, he is also critical of the street wisdom of the Banner Club. Although Sadness's humor and revelations make Joe feel "wonderfully in it," Sadness's tragicomic view of life is essentially an urban one stressing an individual-oriented sensibility. Sadness himself is a performer who embodies an urban theatricality which stresses a conscientious fashioning of the self. Bell even argues that Sadness belongs to the "tradition of the confidence man" (74). As the narrator puts it, he is part of the class that lives "like the leech upon the blood of others" (150). So, while Dunbar shows us the solidarity of this group of eccentric individuals who seek refuge from a cruel world which has shut them out, he also cannot help moralizing on their tragicomic view of life, noting that it gives Joe a "false bravery" (149). And even Sadness cannot help sarcastically criticizing the isolation and loneliness of such extreme individualism as he describes the case of Wallace to Joe: "Wallace will live, eat, drink and sleep at the expense of others . . .until, broken and useless the poor house or the potter's field gets him. Oh it's a fine rich life my lad. I know you'll like it" (149). "Joe might have turned back," the narrator remarks "if he could only understand all that the man was saying to him. But he didn't" (149). Instead, Sadness's sarcasm is lost on Joe who begins to see the want of a "good reputation as an unpardonable immaturity."

While one might argue that Sadness is a blues figure, a survivor, Dunbar nevertheless sees Sadness as part of a "fraternity of indolence," wherein individuals ultimately look out only for themselves (150). While it seems Joe finds a community at the Banner Club, he really only finds solace in a bottle and eventually becomes such a pitiful drunk that Hattie no longer wishes to be seen with him. Joe, in turn, kills Hattie because he sees her as the cause of his downfall, and the Club which seemed to be a substitute family for Joe quickly forgets him: "[S]o Sadness and all the club with a muttered 'Poor devil' dismissed him. He was gone. Why should they worry?" (212). In the end, the club offers no solace, no authentic community; only the "mother heart" has room for grief and pain (214).

Like her brother who momentarily found a new freedom in New York before his eventual addiction and imprisonment, Kitty, too, must negotiate the contradictory elements of urban life. Though one could say she is the survivor of the family, the most successful, her success is treated ambiguously, bringing to mind the success Dreiser affords Carrie. Upon first entering the theatrical world, Kitty is a country innocent much like Carrie; unsure at first, she soon learns to play the role required of the chorus girl. She drinks the beer Hattie offers her although she does not like it and puffs on a cigarette. While Mrs. Hamilton feels her daughter is degrading herself, Kitty tells her mother that nowadays people think stage people are respectable. Moreover, she adds, "I'm doin it to help you" (167). Recalling the situation of Carrie when Hurstwood was unemployed and times were difficult, Kitty enters the stage to help out the family, but we see that eventually the younger members of the Hamilton family live ultimately for themselves alone. When her heartbroken mother speaks of marrying the "race horse man" out of desperation, Kitty thinks it will be "splendid" because "race horse men most always have money" and "you got to live for yourself now" (169). Thus, family becomes an impediment, an obstacle, and an individualist ethos prevails. At the end of the novel, Dunbar's description of Kitty's rise reinforces this: "From the time she went on the stage she had begun to live her own life, a life in which the chief aim was the possession of good clothes and the ability to attract the attention which she had learned to crave" (216). However, while Dreiser depicts Carrie's family life as oppressive, suggesting she has lost nothing in leaving her family behind, Dunbar suggests Kitty has lost much indeed, for he implies that her success will be short-lived and fragile, and unlike Dreiser, he expresses little sympathy towards his character.

In the end, the family is broken apart as the younger individuals within it look to their own fates. As Dunbar's tragic ending reinforces for us, an individual-oriented ethos is especially problematic for the African American who must live within a hostile culture, for family ties may be one's only safety net. His novel seems to stress the foolishness of subscribing to a white culture that privileges the individual but at the same time does not recognize the individual worth of an African American. With Joe in prison, Kitty wandering from show to show, and Berry and Fannie returned to their cottage down South, Dunbar's vision of the city seems especially hopeless and grim. But this pessimism is not directed only at urban life. While Joe and Kitty are criticized for abandoning family ties and embracing the extreme individualism of urban life, Dunbar suggests that Berry and Fanny have all along been maintaining sentimental ties to the wrong community. Now that Mr. Oakley is insane, his mind snapped from the burden of keeping Berry's innocence and his brother's guilt a secret, Leslie Oakley begs the Hamiltons to return South, to spend the rest of their days in "peace and comfort," since it was the only "amend she could make" (255). The Hamiltons return to their old cottage "as much to satisfy her as to settle themselves," yet even here at "home" the Hamiltons are pawns controlled by powerful forces; they are still the "sport of the gods," still obeying white orders. Dunbar leaves us with a particular chilling image to reinforce this: "Many a night they sat together with clasped hands listening to the shrieks of the madman across the yard and thinking of what he had brought to them and to himself" (255). Trapped in the past, constantly reminded of the horrors, the madness of slavery's legacy, the Hamilton home has become a nightmare—a scene of madness from which one cannot escape. At the end of Dunbar's novel, then, we are left with nowhere to go. Although he shows us the liberating potential of the new urban culture for the African American, in the end, Dunbar concludes that, like the southern genteel culture the Hamiltons left behind, the newer northern urban culture is also determined by the overwhelming power of white culture to define what it means to be an African American.

NOTES

1. The groundbreaking work of such recent critics as Elizabeth Ammons, Eric Sundquist, and Kenneth Warren are notable exceptions here. In her work on turn-of-the-century American literature, Ammons devotes chapters to Sui Sin Far, Anzia Yezierska, and Frances Ellen Harper to show how women writers across the spectrum of race, class and ethnicity were engaged with issues of power and literary experimentation. See *Conflicting Stories: American Women Writers at the Turn into the Twentieth Century* (New York: Oxford UP, 1991). In his monumental work *To Wake the Nations,* Sundquist reads white and black authors alongside each other to

reveal the interrelations between Anglo American and African American literary traditions. His work includes readings of Turner and Douglass, Melville and Delaney, Twain and Plessy, and Charles Chesnutt. See *To Wake the Nations: Race and the Making of American Literature* (Cambridge: Belknap-Harvard UP, 1993). Warren also explores the ways in which "the presence of Afro Americans has shaped . . . the meaning of American literature" (11). He examines, for example, the ways racial concerns shape James's aesthetic, and juxtaposes James with African American writers Frances Ellen Harper and W. E. B. Du Bois. See *Black and White Strangers: Race and American Literary Realism* (Chicago: U of Chicago P, 1993).

2. There were some black minstrel performers before the end of the nineteenth century—Ira Aldrich and William Henry Lane, for example. Also, William Wells Brown, in addition to lecturing, would perform blackface at antislavery meetings to gain financial and popular support. See Paul Gilmore's "'De Genuine Artekil': William Wells Brown, Blackface, Minstrelsy and Abolitionism," *American Literature* 69.4 (Dec. 1997): 743–80.

3. The term *coon* as a designation for black did not come into widespread use until the 1880s. Dorman notes American blacks had long been associated with the raccoon: "By ascription blacks loved hunting, trapping and eating raccoons. Moreover, the minstrel figure, 'Zip Coon' had come to be symbolically identified with blacks in general" (452). David Roediger, on the other hand, reminds us that what had once been a common word for "white country persons" had by the early twentieth century been transformed into a "racist slur" (97).

WORKS CITED

Alger, Horatio. *Ragged Dick and Struggling Upward.* New York: Viking-Penguin, 1985.

Baker, Houston A., Jr. *Blues, Ideology and Afro-American Literature: A Vernacular Theory.* Chicago: U of Chicago P, 1984.

Bell, Bernard. *The Afro American Novel and Its Tradition.* Amherst: U of Massachusetts P, 1987.

Berlin, Edward A. *Ragtime: A Musical and Cultural History.* Berkeley: U of California P, 1980.

Blassingame, John W., and Mary Frances Berry. *Long Memory: The Black Experience in America.* New York: Oxford UP, 1982.

Bone, Robert. *The Negro Novel in America.* New Haven: Yale UP, 1965.

Candela, Gregory. "We Wear the Mask: Irony in Dunbar's *Sport of the Gods.*" *American Literature* 48 (1976): 60–72.

Dorman, James. "Shaping the Popular Image of Post-Reconstruction American Blacks: The Coon Song Phenomenon of the Gilded Age." *American Quarterly* 40.4 (1988): 450–71.

Dunbar, Paul Laurence. *The Sport of the Gods.* New York: Arno, 1969.

Erenberg, Lewis. *Stepping Out: New York Nightlife and the Transformation of American Culture, 1890–1930.* Westport, CT: Greenwood Press, 1981.

Gaines, Kevin K. *Uplifting the Race: Black Leadership, Politics and Culture in the Twentieth Century*. Chapel Hill: U of North Carolina P, 1996.

Gatewood, Willard B. *Aristocrats of Color: The Black Elite, 1880–1920*. Bloomington: Indiana UP, 1990.

Howard, June. *Form and History in American Literary Naturalism*. Chapel Hill: U of North Carolina P, 1985.

Inge, Casey. "Family Functions: Disciplinary Discourse and (De)Construction of the 'Family' in *The Sport of the Gods*." *Callaloo* 20.1 (Winter 1997): 226–42.

Kaplan, Amy. *The Social Construction of Realism*. Chicago: U of Chicago P, 1988.

Kornweibel, Theodore, Jr. *In Search of the Promised Land: Essays in Black Urban History*. Port Washington, NY: Kennikat, 1981.

Lehan, Richard. "The European Background." *The Cambridge Companion to American Realism and Naturalism, Howells to London*. Ed. Donald Pizer. Cambridge: Cambridge UP, 1995. 47–73.

Lemons, J. Stanley. "Black Stereotypes as Reflected in Popular Culture 1880–1920." *American Quarterly* 29 (Spring 1977): 104–5.

Levine, Lawrence. *Black Culture and Black Consciousness: Afro American Folk Thought from Slavery to Freedom*. Oxford: Oxford UP, 1977.

Lott, Eric. *Love and Theft: Blackface Minstrelsy and the American Working Class*. New York: Oxford UP, 1993.

Marks, Carol. *Farewell—We're Good and Gone: The Great Black Migration*. Bloomington: Indiana UP, 1989.

Mitchell, Lee Clark. "Naturalism and the Languages of Determinism." *Columbia Literary History of the United States*. Ed. Emory Elliot. New York: Columbia UP, 1988. 525–45.

Nasaw, David. *Going Out: The Rise and Fall of Public Amusements*. New York: Basic Books, 1993.

Pizer, Donald. *The Theory and Practice of American Literary Naturalism*. Carbondale: Southern Illinois UP, 1993.

Revell, Peter. *Paul Laurence Dunbar*. Boston: G. K. Hall, 1979.

Riis, Jacob. *How the Other Half Lives*. New York: Dover, 1971.

Rodgers, Lawrence. *Canaan Bound: The African American Great Migration Novel*. Urbana: U of Illinois P, 1997.

Roediger, David. *The Wages of Whiteness: Race and the Making of the American Working Class*. New York: Verso, 1991.

Scruggs, Charles. *Sweet Home: Invisible Cities in the Afro-American Novel*. Baltimore: Johns Hopkins UP, 1993.

"Working" towards a Sense of Agency

DETERMINISM IN *THE WINGS OF THE DOVE*

—*Brannon W. Costello*

> If I am going to be drowned—if I am going to be drowned—if I am going to be drowned, why, in the name of the seven mad gods who rule the sea, was I allowed to come thus far and contemplate sand and trees? Was I brought here merely to have my nose dragged away as I was about to nibble the sacred cheese of life?
>
> —Stephen Crane, "The Open Boat"

> Why should a set of people have been put in motion, on such a scale and with such an air of being equipped for a profitable journey, only to break down without an accident, to stretch themselves in the wayside dust without a reason?
>
> —Henry James, *The Wings of the Dove*

I DO NOT MEAN TO SUGGEST, BY THE PAIRING OF THE ABOVE PASSAGES, ANYTHING SO SIMPLISTIC AS A READING OF HENRY JAMES AS A "TRADITIONAL" naturalist in the manner of Stephen Crane or Theodore Dreiser. I would, however, argue that we can hear in those two excerpts the echoes of an association that often goes unexplored. I would further argue that a close examination of James's treatment of the theme of determinism in *The Wings of the Dove* will not only reveal closer affinities between James and the naturalist writers than are commonly perceived but, more importantly, will also perhaps suggest a new way of understanding the relationship between determinism and agency, a controversial topic among scholars of naturalism.

Some of us may question whether James has a useful contribution to make to a conversation about a movement with which James's work is not conventionally aligned. That is, the theme of determinism has always seemed primarily the province of the naturalists, and critics do not make a habit of classifying James among them. Certainly, James does not seem the most logical candidate for such a classification. His repressed, internal, obsessively crafted novels have little in common, at first glance, with the lurid sex, sensational violence, and shoot-from-the-hip craftsmanship of the stereotypical naturalist novel. This division of James from any but the international or modernist movements has a long history. Early critic Stuart P. Sherman, for instance, labels James an "aesthetic idealist," his work in sharp contrast to the "barbarous naturalism" of Dreiser. Sherman argues that James regards the naturalists with "aristocratic contempt" and that he elevates "all experience to the aesthetic level." This strategy "deliver[s] Henry James from the riotous and unclean hands of the naturalists," who "go a-slumming in the muck and mire of civilization" (249). More recently, Lee Clark Mitchell has classified James as a "moral realist" who grants his characters autonomy, in sharp contrast to naturalist authors whose characters must always obey their strongest impulse (*Determined Fictions* ix). Moreover, James's persistent focus on the interior differs from the subject matter of most naturalists: Mitchell claims that the naturalists focused so much on the external because they "dismissed subjectivity as irrelevant to either character or event, and denied anything like the possibility of a free-standing self" (*Determined Fictions* 19).[1] Donald Pizer, in turn, has argued that James, along with William Dean Howells and Mark Twain, "maintained in varying degrees the ethical idealism of the pre-industrial, pre-Darwinian America of their youth" rather than adopting the more pessimistic views of late-nineteenth-century naturalist writers (*Twentieth Century* 3). Indeed, much of the criticism on James in general and *The Wings of the Dove* in particular clearly reflects this notion of James as an ethical or moral idealist: critics debate at great length who the actual "villain" of the piece is or which character bears responsibility for the events of the plot.[2] That so many critics take for granted the presence of a devious schemer in a work so suffused with the language of determinism illustrates the powerful, lasting influence of traditional categorizations such as those of Sherman and Pizer.

However, and even though he steadfastly refuses to consider James a naturalist, Pizer proposes a complicated, fluid definition of naturalism that potentially makes room for James. He claims that "there is no neat definition applicable to the movement in America, but rather a variable and changing and complex set of assumptions about man and fiction which can be called a naturalist tradition" (xi); moreover, he continues, "the genius of American naturalism . . . lies in the looseness and freedom with which American writers dealt with" (5) the example of French naturalist Émile Zola—a major influence on James.[3] One of the unifying traits in this loosely organized genre, what Pizer calls its "ideological core," is "a sense of man as more circumscribed than [is] conventionally acknowledged," as determined by heredity and environment (6); and, as John J. Conder summarizes, such "determinism plays a central role in American literary naturalism" (17). According to Pizer, for the naturalists "the feeling was that man was limited, shaped, conditioned—determined, if you will—and the search was for appropriate symbolic constructs to express this sense" (4). As June Howard observes, naturalist works focus not simply on the fact of determinism but also on the "characteristic opposition between human will and hereditary and environmental determinisms that both shape human beings and frustrate their desires" (40). Lee Clark Mitchell agrees, arguing that American literary naturalists primarily "are bound together by historical context and philosophical determinism," but he also notes that "naturalism is distinguished by . . . no specific technique or style" ("Naturalism" 545). The critics' portrayal of the naturalists as less an organized movement and more a group of diverse writers teasing out the implications of a determinist ideology for humankind and for fiction opens space for a reading of James as another writer involved in their shared endeavor.

Consider that while a recognition of determinism's centrality may have united the naturalists, the critics remain divided over what argument(s) the naturalists actually make about determinism and agency, and if, indeed, a deterministic worldview leaves any room for meaningful individual agency. A brief survey of some of the most famous contributions to this conversation will help us to understand better the contribution that I will claim James makes. Charles C. Walcutt, an early commentator on the naturalists, argues that naturalist novels operate on the idea that "natural laws and socioeconomic influences are more powerful than the human will" (20). However, he also claims that while an utterly determined naturalist character may have no capacity for agency, the naturalist novelist, by depicting the character's plight, moves those who read his work to find ways to overcome determinism and thus creates the possibility for agency: "The more helpless the character, the stronger the proof of determinism; and once such a thesis is established the scientist hopes and believes that men will set about trying to control the forces which now control men" (25). Pizer argues, partially in response to Walcutt, that "the naturalist often describes his characters as though they are conditioned and controlled by heredity, instinct, or chance. But he also suggests a compensating humanistic value in his characters or their fates which affirms the significance of the individual and of his life" (*Realism* 13). As he says elsewhere, naturalist fiction "affirms the significance and worth of the seeking temperament, of the character who continues to look for meaning in experience even though there probably *is* no meaning" (*Twentieth Century* 9). In other words, while Walcutt claims that the essential helplessness of naturalistic characters and the meaninglessness of their lives serve as an impetus for readers to realize their own potential for agency, Pizer claims that naturalist characters find meaning in their search for meaning, that they transcend their downtrodden, determined lives by adopting a hopeful attitude.

Conder, in turn, criticizes Pizer's theory as fundamentally beside the point because "it ignores the basic contradiction between freedom and determinism and focuses instead on the subordinate attitudes associated with these doctrines" (3). According to Conder, the concept of the "individually significant" in the determined world that Pizer proposes does nothing to enlighten or comment upon the tension between determinism and freedom, since a person may easily have significance without having freedom. Conder believes instead that American naturalism adheres to a model of determinism found in the theories of Henri Bergson, who argues "that man has two selves, one determined, one free; and that the freedom of the second self is beyond the confines of that determinism" (14). Conder claims we should not apply the principles of mechanistic determinism to the psyche because the psyche exists in "pure time," where the causal relationships of the physical world do not apply, and so "no external force alone can be said to be the sufficient cause of any single psychic state" (15). However, since individuals must live in a social, physical world, they develop "a social self . . . that usually conceals the self living in pure time. . . . That self's acts, too, are fully determined by society" (15–16). Thus, though people do have a measure of freedom, "free acts are rare because man is rarely in contact with the self capable of performing them" (16).

With these ideas in mind, we should look now to the handful of critics who have explored the possible similarities between James and the naturalists. Though these critics of course deal with the issue of determinism, they do not always place it at the center of their analyses. For instance, Lyall Powers's *Henry James and the Naturalist Movement* takes the connection between James and Zola as its focus. Powers discusses the influence on James of French realists and naturalists, and though he characterizes James as "uncomfortable with the ugliness and especially with the dirtiness" of much he read in Zola, he argues that many of James's works—notably *The Bostonians, The Princess Casamassima, The Tragic Muse,* and several shorter pieces—demonstrate most strikingly the influence of his French colleague (37). According to Powers, Zola's focus on "the important influence of heredity and environment in determining the intellectual and sensual nature of man" particularly struck James (20). For example, in the story "Lady Barberina," James gives great "attention to the heredity of its heroine and the related environment" (71). Moreover, Powers advances the theory that in that story what Jackson Lemon

"believes to be his exercise of choice is merely his acceptance of the determined line of action" (75), a claim that suggests that James has already begun
to complicate the relation between determinism and the possibility of agency.
Although Powers goes on to argue, through a brief reading of *The Ambas-
sadors,* that James continued to employ naturalist techniques in his "Major
Phase," he does not address the issue of how those later works deal with the
theme of determinism, one of the primary links between naturalist fiction and
The Wings of the Dove.

More recent critics have also investigated the naturalist elements of
James's work, in some cases specifically in *The Wings of the Dove.*[4] Perhaps the
most important of these for my study is Lee Clark Mitchell's "The Sustaining
Duplicities of *The Wings of the Dove.*" Mitchell argues that while Kate *seems*
to make choices freely, "the choices she makes appear after the fact unlike
choices at all" (187). For instance, she apparently offers to make a striking
material sacrifice for her father, but she does so knowing "that her father
would never risk defying his wealthy sister-in-law. Kate's pledge is simply a
ploy to embarrass him into a flat rejection. And yet she acts throughout *as if*
her choice were real, thereby making it seem that her offer might be
accepted" (187). Mitchell claims, then, that while Kate is "the woman who is
arguably least her own mistress and most constrained by circumstance," she
nevertheless enacts a performance that makes her seem free. However,
Mitchell does not fully develop this promising and intriguing idea. Rather, he
contends that the "radically contradictory set of assumptions about selfhood
and agency" that the novel apparently articulates is only one of the novel's
many unresolved paradoxes (209). Further, readers should "embrace" this
"discordancy" because to do otherwise "is finally to settle for a vision that is
sadly reduced" (210). Yet Mitchell is not done with the subject of Kate Croy
and her confrontation with determinism. In another essay from the same
period, he argues that "Kate is enmeshed in an elaborate web. She may seem
responsible for effecting the end of her relationship with Densher, but the
narrative voice remains troublingly divided" ("Naturalism" 532).

I would like to adapt and expand Mitchell's claims here. First, I would
question his statement that the "narrative voice remains troublingly divided,"
since to speak of any sort of overarching, unified narrative voice in this novel is
to lose sight of James's strategy for forcing the reader to view events from the
minds of individual characters. Instead, I propose that the division that Mitchell
perceives is actually between the fact of determinism and the fiction of agency
that characters must construct. My reading relates to and builds on Mitchell's
initial argument that characters with little control over their destinies can

nonetheless somehow perform agency, as well as on Powers's notion that the completely determined Jackson Lemon of "Lady Barberina" acts as though he believes himself free to choose. I contend that in *The Wings of the Dove,* James advances the theory that although individuals are inevitably determined—by biology, heredity, economy, gender, environment—they must behave as though they were free, for to do otherwise is to refuse the potential for meaningful engagement with the world and with others and to doom oneself to isolation and alienation. The model that I propose resembles both Pizer's in its emphasis on how a determined character reacts to and interprets her determinedness—though I would stop short of saying that any sort of positive "transcendence" occurs in *The Wings of the Dove*—and Conder's in its focus on the ways in which individual characters develop a sort of double consciousness when faced with a deterministic world, though while he sees that "free" inner self as always already existing, I would argue that in fact it is the "free" self that must be constructed by the individual subject. We think of this focus on consciousness as more characteristic of the modernists than the naturalists; the most intriguing aspect of James's project here, then, may in fact be his adaptation of a fundamentally naturalist philosophy to a modernist aesthetic.[5]

To understand how James develops his argument, we should first examine how he depicts the very different ways in which the novel's three main characters behave in the face of their determinedness. The novel opens, significantly, with Kate Croy's growing realization of the futility of individual agency, of the delusory nature of the belief that people completely control their own fates: when she goes to see her father, Lionel Croy, who has committed an unspeakable sin and doomed the family to poverty, she wonders "why should a set of people have been put in motion, on such a scale and with such an air of being equipped for a profitable journey, only to break down without an accident, to strand themselves in the wayside dust without a reason?" (21–22). Indeed, her entire doomed family has acted out an almost baroque plot of decline: in addition to her father's crime, she must contend with the death of one brother from typhoid fever "contracted at a poisonous little place . . . that they had taken for a summer," the death of her other brother "dreadfully drowned, and not even by an accident at sea, but by cramp, unrescued, while bathing," and her widowed sister's "unnatural marriage" to an unremarkable, unsuccessful man (55). Kate thinks of this chain of events as "the proof of the heaviness, for them all, of the hand of fate" (55). The loss of her former state of relative wealth and privilege forces her to consider her essential powerlessness, a condition determined by a combination of her economic status and her gender. She reflects that a "penniless girl" can do nothing, and she imagines that "she might still pull things round had she only been a man" (22–23). Lionel Croy drives the point home when he tells her that "we're not possessed of so much, at this charming pass, please to remember, as that we can afford not to take hold of any perch held out to us" (28). His declaration underscores their agency-less state not only through the use of economic language ("afford") but also through the animalistic connotations of "perch." But he need not remind her: we know that she flies to her aunt Maud Lowder after her mother dies because "there had been nothing else to do—not a penny in the other house, nothing but unpaid bills that had gathered thick while its mistress lay mortally ill" (34).

Though we can see clearly how circumscribed and determined Kate's choices are, we can also see in these early passages how she manages to create a sense of agency. At her father's, she attempts to keep from viewing herself as an inevitable inheritor of her family's legacy of doom: when she "show[s] herself . . . a face" in her father's mirror, she sees not only her physical form (over which she maintains a measure of control) but also that "after all she was not herself a fact in the collapse" (22), a distancing that allows her to preserve a sense of autonomy.[6] Indeed, one of the most aggravating conditions of her survival at her aunt's is the necessity to relinquish any semblance of control not only over her actions but also over her ostensible motivations: she accepts "with smothered irony other people's interpretations of her conduct. She often ended by giving up to them—it seemed really the way to live—the version that met their convenience" (34). However, that she accepts these interpretations with "smothered irony" suggests that she still manages to maintain an inner, personal illusion of her own agency. Although she truly has no other choice than to remain with her aunt, Kate does manage to create a sense of agency even though her position there makes her even more of an object, even less in control of her life. Indeed, even she thinks of herself as a commodity: "I am . . . on the counter, when I'm not in the shop-window" (169). Kate feels constrained to stay in this position—in the hopes of eventually receiving some money—because of her sense of obligation to her father and her sister: as she tells Merton Densher, "my position's a value, a great value for them both. . . . It's *the* value, the only one they have" (59).

Her consciousness of this responsibility leads Kate to place her "value" in circulation in Maud's social circle, to "work" their relationship (ostensibly) for eventual gain. However, though, as I noted above, critics often center their investigations on the question of who actually "works" whom and to what ultimate advantage, I would question the fundamental assumption of that type of reading. I would argue that for James "working" is not a system of meaningful exchange and social progress but is instead an elaborate construct in which individuals who have no agency can create the enabling illusion of it and, in some cases, even form a sort of community. This implication that the system of "working" has little meaning outside the small circle of workers is reinforced throughout the novel as characters conflate "work" with "play" or a "game." For instance, in the opening scene, Lionel Croy tells Kate (in connection with her decision to work Aunt Maud) that "the only way to play the game *is* to play it" (30). Merton Densher, in turn, reflects upon "the oddity . . . of their game" (196) in working Milly, and when he shares his ruminations with Kate, she says "of course it's a game" (198). Kate seems most in tune with the game's rules; when she visits Merton in Milly's rooms, she observes that "we can't again . . . play her *this* trick" (201). Near the end of the novel, Merton observes that "we've played our game and we've lost" (372), and Kate insists that she always did "play fair" with Milly (392). These passages suggest that the elaborate schemes of "working" that characters—primarily Kate—develop are really a sort of formal "play" that creates a sense of agency for characters but leaves the status quo essentially unchanged. Moreover, as Kate explains to Milly, "the worker in one connection was the worked in another; it was as broad as it was long—with the wheels of the system, as might be seen, wonderfully oiled." This constant reciprocal manipulation can potentially have a positive effect on interpersonal relationships, since, as Kate observes, "people could quite like each other in the midst of it" (116), and many such workers reach a "happy understanding" (116). Though I would certainly not want to portray this system as some sort of utopia, it does provide a way for determined people to interact as subjects rather than objects.

Kate's drive to create and maintain an inner, personal sense of her own agency in the face of determinism starkly contrasts with Milly Theale's attitude. In Milly we see an especially complex embodiment of the perplexing relationship between determinism and agency: though she should, by all rights, have more freedom to act than nearly anyone else in the novel, she is also curiously constrained by her illness and, strangely, by the very wealth that should make her free.[7] Though her privileged status would seem to place her, as Susan Stringham observes, in a position to look "down at all the kingdoms of the earth" and "choose among them" (87), her vaguely defined illness converts this multiplicity of possibility to a single, pre-determined inevitability: instead of surveying a wealth of choices, "it was as if they looked down from their height at a continent of doctors" (91).[8] Though these passages come from Susan's perspective, Milly later suggests that she takes much the same view of her condition: when she reports on Sir Luke Strett's prognosis, she says that "I can do exactly what I like—anything in all the wide world. I haven't a creature to ask—there's not a finger to stop me. *I can shake about till I'm black and blue*" (150, my emphasis). "Black and blue" of course connotes death, or at least physical harm, and "shake about" suggests a futile, useless movement without real progress in any direction. Milly realizes that her nominal freedom will still lead inexorably to death. Indeed, the theme of the inevitability of her death and therefore the uselessness of any action she might take recurs frequently in Milly's speech and thoughts. She makes up her mind to "let things come as they would, since there was little enough doubt of how they would go" (97). When Lord Mark takes her to see the Bronzino portrait, Milly reflects that the subject "was dead, dead, dead. Milly recognized her in words that had nothing to do with her. 'I shall never be better than this'" (137). She again expresses her resignation when she remarks that "one's situation is what it is. It's *me* it concerns. . . . Nothing can really help . . . It wouldn't make any real difference—it won't make any, anything that may happen won't—to any one" (147–48).

Indeed, Milly's economic privilege not only fails to save her from her determined end, but it even circumscribes her, limits her possibilities for identity and agency in very particular ways. Susan observes that "a princess could only be a princess," and this role represents "a perfectly definite doom for the wearer" (85). Moreover,

> it prevailed even as the truth of truths that the girl couldn't get away from her wealth. . . . it was in the fine folds of the helplessly expensive little black frock that she drew over the grass as she now strolled vaguely off. . . . She could not dress it away, nor walk it away, nor read it away, nor think it away, she could neither smile it away in any dreamy absence nor blow it away in any softened sigh. That was what it was to be really rich. It had to be *the* thing you were. (85–86)

Again, Milly concurs with her friend's analysis of her situation; she struggles to express this awareness of the similar functions of her poor health and her vast wealth to Susan in an early conversation in which "everything" and "it" seem to refer simultaneously to her material possessions and to her illness (90–91). Further, much as Kate's economic status determines her position in her social circles, Milly's wealth and grace determine her by making her a valuable commodity: "she was made for great social uses" (133). As an object for everyone's manipulation in their game of work, she feels that she and Susan "had just been caught up by the incalculable strength of a wave that was actually holding them aloft and that would naturally dash them wherever it liked" (109). She realizes that she is "in a current determined, through her indifference, timidity, bravery, generosity . . . by others; that not she but the current acted, and that somebody else was always the keeper of the lock or the dam" (166). Indeed, Milly perceives herself as determined by social rules even in simple conversation: she imagines her discussion with Lord Mark as moving along "lines immediately laid down [that] were . . . definite enough" (101) so that the characters come across less as individual agents and more as trains moving along tracks that lead to a prescribed destination.

Milly's reaction to her determined condition has little in common, then, with Kate Croy's creation of agency; in fact, she seems to enjoy, to crave, her position of powerlessness. She enjoys London society precisely because of the way that it offers her so few legitimate choices. When Susan warns her that "we move in a labyrinth," Milly replies with a "strange gaiety," "Of course we do! That's just the fun of it! . . . Don't tell me that . . . there are not abysses. I want abysses" (120). Milly's approval and appropriation of the labyrinth metaphor underscores her joy at a forced lack of genuine agency: the labyrinth constantly offers its wanderers essentially meaningless choices, for one may choose and choose all one wants, but all of the possible outcomes already exist, are already determined. Further, Milly's longing for abysses represents her desire never to escape this social labyrinth and never to have to accept agency or responsibility. She responds to her determinedness by completely abdicating responsibility and repudiating agency; she allows others to determine utterly her identity and her behavior. She initially rejoices when Sir Luke tells her that she should "not worry about anything in the world, that if [she'll] be a good girl and do exactly what he tells [her] he'll take care of [her] for ever and ever" (143), and, further, that she "must accept any form in which happiness may come" (149). However, she quickly finds his directive far too vague: she thinks that "he had beautifully got out of it," that "he should have talked to her all about what she might with *futility 'do'*" (155, my emphasis). Milly wants more specific guidelines, such as the ones that Eugenio, her primary servant in her Italian *palazzo,* provides. Eugenio "had brought home to her . . . the conception, hitherto ungrasped, of some complete use of her wealth itself, some use of it as a counter-move to fate. It had passed between them as preposterous that with so much money she should just stupidly and awkwardly *want*—any more want a life, a career, a consciousness, than want a house, a carriage, or a cook" (263). Unlike Kate, who conceives of her periodic acceptance of others' wills as a function of her own will, Milly thinks of this acquiescence as simply another way of avoiding having to act: she refers to her elegantly furbished abode as the "ark of her deluge" and reflects that "she would never, never leave it—she would engage to that; would ask nothing more than to sit tight in it and float on and on" (264).

Milly also takes greatest satisfaction in Kate's likening her to a dove, for "she found herself accepting as the right one, while she caught her breath with relief, the name so given her" (171). Doveliness, for Milly, somehow involves self-sacrifice and service to those who have shown her kindness. For instance, when she reports back to Mrs. Lowder that she can glean no evidence of Merton's presence from her conversation with Kate, Maud's praise of her as an "exquisite thing" gives "her straightaway the measure of the success she could have as a dove" (172). She then commits herself to accepting this identity, this pattern of behavior: "she studied again the dovelike," for she "should have to be clear as to how a dove *would* act" (172). Since acting like a "dove" involves somehow this willingness to help facilitate matters for her supposed friends, Milly behaves in accordance with Maud Lowder's suggestion that she and Merton might make a good match (a behavior further encouraged by her already existing attraction for him); indeed, she knows that she must like him even if they have both changed to the point of non-recognition. When she meets Densher again, she thinks that "she couldn't tell if he were different or not, and she didn't know nor care if *she* were. These things had ceased to matter in the light of the only thing she did know" (180), that "whatever he did or didn't Milly knew she should still like him—there was no alternative to that" (181). Thus, she pushes aside any consideration of whether or not they actually remain attracted to one another and adheres to a prescribed set of beliefs and actions, a strategy that serves only to facilitate the formation of their relationship on false premises. This reading may help us better understand Milly's part in the novel's end; though we may find it tempting to read her "willing" of the money to Merton as just that—an act of will, whether generous or devious— I would suggest that it actually demonstrates the depths to which Milly has sunk, the complete acceptance of her "dove" role. If, as I have claimed, we can see doveliness as a position that requires sacrifice and assistance for one's friends' plans, then we can read her bequest of the money—after she knows that that is what Kate and Merton desire—as completely determined by the position imposed on her by Kate. Milly's uncritical acceptance of every role forced upon her, with its prescribed behaviors, ensures that she will interact with others always as a thinking object, never as a subject.

If Kate and Milly represent two diametrically opposed responses to the fact of determinism, then Merton Densher stands caught between these two contrasting ideologies. Though the notably unprosperous newspaperman does not actively search for others to determine him, as does Milly, he generally strives to avoid even the suggestion that he might be responsible for anything that happens to him or to anyone around him. James initially describes him as a man who has no control even over his own limbs, a walking talking Cartesian split: the curious impression that he makes "was the accident, possibly, of his long legs, which were apt to stretch themselves; of his straight hair and well-shaped head, never, the latter, neatly smoothed, and apt into the bargain at the time of quite other calls upon it, to throw itself suddenly back and, supported behind by his uplifted arms and interlocked hands, place him for unconscionable periods in communion with the ceiling, the tree-tops, the sky" (46).

However different their perspectives might be, Merton's reaction to his situation in life has been determined, like Kate's and Milly's, in part by family history and heredity. His frugal father "had been, in strange countries, in twenty settlements of the English, British chaplain, resident or occasional, and had had for years the unusual luck of never wanting a billet." However, this steady work did not lead to economic prosperity, and "as his stipend had never been great he had educated his children, at the smallest cost, in the schools nearest; which was also a saving of railway fares" (71). This forced fragmentation of experience has fundamentally shaped Merton's identity: "he had been exposed to initiations indelible. Something had happened to him that could never be undone" (71). The Merton that emerges, then, rather paradoxically, is a person "in which the elements, the metals more or less precious, are so in fusion and fermentation that the question of the final stamp, the pressure that fixes the value, must wait for comparative coolness" (46); Merton later thinks of his shifting, uncentered nature as having a sort of "plasticity" (284). Kathleen Komar notes the ways in which the free indirect discourse used to represent Merton's thoughts reflects this lack of any unifying, motivating commitment: the section that introduces him "is marked not by discrete blocks of independent clauses, but rather by embedded, qualifying phrases and dependent clauses which cause the main clause to be disjointed and spread over several lines, thus reducing its impact" (477). For Merton, this decentered, unfixed nature does not signal greater possibility for agency but rather reflects his own reluctance or inability to risk any one particular course of action.

Merton's relatively unaffluent early life has also created in him a "private inability to believe he should ever be rich . . . [;] he saw himself remain without whether he married or not" (54–55). When Kate rebuffs one of Merton's requests to take him in his impoverished state ("Just as I am"), he reflects that "he had no more money just as he was than he had had just as he had been, or than he should have, probably, when it came to that, just as he always would be" (197). Similarly, he later thinks that "well as she certainly would look in pearls, pearls were exactly what [he] would never be able to give her" (304). The resignation, the acceptance of his undistinguished economic status as inevitable and unchallengeable (even in the midst of their "working" of Milly) that comes through so clearly in the language of these selections starkly contrasts with Kate's own refusal to surrender to her determined state. In fact, James prepares us for the disintegration of their relationship when he has Merton note how Kate seems fundamentally unsuited for poverty: when he and Kate go to visit Marian, Merton observes that while Kate "wouldn't have been in the least the creature she was if what was just round them hadn't mismatched her," his "natural, his inevitable, his ultimate home . . . wasn't at all unlikely to be as queer and impossible as what was just round them" (381).

Indeed, though Merton and Kate no doubt care deeply for each other, passages of the text clearly suggest that these essential differences in their individual natures doom their relationship to inevitable failure even before Milly Theale begins to complicate matters for them in earnest. When Kate goes to meet Merton at the train station in utter disregard for the possible loss of "value" to her family that an open show of affection might cause, she thinks that while she can occasionally behave in accordance with more lofty ideals, "to-morrow, inevitably, she . . . would become a *baser* creature, a creature of alarms and precautions" (187, my emphasis). The claim here that *at base,* at the fundamental, instinctual level, Kate's primary concerns are with her survival in a social jungle suggests a conflict with Merton's basic, idly idealistic desire for her to chuck all that and join him in poverty, a desire which he (and James) presents in a sexualized language that underscores its urgency and centrality for him: "his desires had grown . . . [;] he felt all the force of his particular necessity. . . . Their mistake was to have believed that they *could* hold out . . . against an impatience that, prolonged and exasperated, made a man ill" (189). Interestingly, he finds her most attractive when she acts least herself, an ill omen for their relationship: he finds it "prodigiously becoming to her" when she "forget[s] . . . to look about for surprises" (190). These passages make clear the ways that their hereditarily and environmentally determined natures stand in nearly complete opposition to each other, and, I would argue, so preclude any successful long-term partnership.

This tension becomes most clear when Kate and Merton begin their "working" of Milly Theale. Though such a plan might provide the illusion of agency required for them to further their own "happy understanding," Merton steadfastly refuses to accept any sort of responsibility, to claim even the illusion of agency. As Kristin King claims, Densher in fact "manipulate[s] scenes to create a sense of absent agency, of things happening without any particular action on anyone's part" (2). He tells himself that "he had himself as yet done nothing deceptive" and that "It was Kate's description of him, his defeated state, it was none of his own; his responsibility would begin . . . only with acting it out" (228). However, he quickly begins to realize the complications inherent in this position, for agency is not only constructed by his actions but also by other people's interpretations of them. He understands that the mere fact of his presence makes him complicit in the plan, makes him responsible. Ironically, Milly's misapprehension makes him an agent: "He saw it with a certain alarm rise before him that everything was acting that was not speaking the particular word"—that is, the truth about his relationship with Kate (228). Though he accepts himself as determined, he is continually pulled back to an image of his own agency that stems, paradoxically, from his refusal to act.

Merton reacts to this dilemma by thinking of the development of his and Milly's relationship not as a result of his complicit, active passivity, not as a part of a plan at all, but instead as brought about

> by a force absolutely resident in their situation and operating . . . with the swiftness of focus commonly regarded by sensitive persons as beyond their control. The current thus determined had positively become for him by the time he had been ten minutes in the room, something that, but for the absurdity of comparing the very small with the very great, he would freely have likened to the rapids of Niagara. An uncriticised acquaintance between a clever young man and a responsive young woman could do nothing more, at the most, than go. (229)

Thus, Merton clings to a view of their attachment as an inevitable result of their natural social positions as "clever young man" and "responsive young woman," as inevitable and unquestionable as a rushing river. As the plan progresses, his deterministic justifications become even more elaborate: "Something incalculable wrought for them—for him and Kate; something outside, beyond, above themselves, and doubtless ever so much better than they: which wasn't a reason, however—its being so much better—for them not to profit by it. Not to profit by it, so far as profit could be reckoned, would have been to go directly against it" (314). He even theorizes his inaction as a veritable social *law* for someone in his position, a strategy that allows him to remain passive for reasons other than complicity with Kate's plan: "The single thing that was clear in complications was that, whatever happened, one was to behave as a gentleman. . . . Three women were looking to him at once, and though such a predicament could never be . . . ideal, it yet had its immediate workable law. The law was not to be a brute" (285). Though neither Densher nor James offers a clear definition of the role of the "gentleman" versus that of the "brute," we can speculate with some confidence that since, as June Howard points out, the "brute," a recurring figure in the naturalist literature of the 1890s and early 1900s, most obvious in Frank Norris's *Vandover and the Brute,* often takes the form of the "savage" or "wild man" who suffers from an "incapacity for . . . self-control" (89), Densher's "gentleman" would be a creature of passivity and self-repression before action. Elsewhere, he figures his inaction as necessary to Milly's continued survival: since "he was mixed up in her fate, or her fate, if that should be better, was mixed up in *him,* so that a single false motion might either way snap the coil," the best course of action, for all concerned, "was to do nothing" (322). In perhaps the most striking example, when Lord Mark tells Milly about Kate and Merton's relationship, Merton reminds himself that "it wasn't a bit he who, that day, had touched her, and if she was upset it wasn't a bit his act" (329).

Yet, while he takes consolation in his determinedness, Merton also sees how his insisted upon lack of agency keeps him from having the sort of relationship with Kate that he wants, since if he assumes no responsibility for anything, he can take credit for nothing and therefore has no leverage to use to convince her to sleep with him. However, he adeptly manipulates the appearance of his agency so that he can seem to take credit for his presence in Venice with Milly without seeming to be involved with Kate's plot. He tells Kate that he "had been the first to know [Milly] . . . [;] he was not *there,* not just as he was in so doing it, through Kate and Kate's idea, but through Milly and Milly's own, and through himself and his own, unmistakably" (286–87). While he has gotten them that far on his own, he has told no lies (287), so he does not share any responsibility in the plan's negative aspects. Even this strategy, however, eventually works to allow him to erase his own sense of agency. He thinks of Kate's agreement to come to him as a "contract" with "special solidity," and that now "his equivalent office was to take effect" (313). Thus, he has, through his assertion of will, created a situation in which he has no real choice but to honor the "contract" by continuing with the manipulation of Milly.

Kate and Merton's relationship ultimately deconstructs itself—as was inevitable—in the final pages of the novel. Densher's shrugging off of agency, his tendency simply to be "still" so as to preserve a certain image of himself, has disastrous consequences for his relationship with Kate. When he and Kate discuss the probability that Milly, with dovelike determination, has willed a sum of money to him, the fact that she has done so *forces* him to face the reality of his agency in her manipulation. Densher has difficulty accepting this reality; it makes him "wince" when Kate tells him, "We've succeeded" (364).

However, rather than assume responsibility, take the money, and marry Kate, Merton again finds a way to figure himself as agency-less, albeit perhaps not in as neat a way as he would like: Merton decides that in his relationship with Milly, "something had happened to him too beautiful and too sacred to describe. He had been, to his recovered sense, forgiven, dedicated, blessed" (370). In seeing himself as forgiven, Merton is no longer accountable for any wrong he may have committed. However, he knows that this new condition, the only one that will allow him to maintain his image of himself, is predicated also on not accepting the money, the symbol of his complicity. A marriage to Kate with the money would represent an undeniable acceptance of agency, of responsibility, of the reality of his "brutishness" in working Milly Theale. Again he asks Kate to join him in this disavowal: "It's as I am that you must have me," he tells her (372). Merton's ultimate, final refusal even to imagine himself as a free subject, whether this be an accurate description of possibility or not, dooms him to isolation and alienation. When he receives the letter notifying him of Milly's bequest, he typically abdicates any agency: he tells Kate, "I'll abide by whatever you think of it" (392). Kate, also typically, chooses to act, even though she knows her action has no real meaning: she defiantly throws the letter in the fire but then tells Merton that he will "have it all . . . from New York" (394). She refuses Merton's offer at least in part because the way he makes it underscores his acceptance of determinism: he says, "I'm in your power. . . . You must surely feel . . . how you 'have' me" (401). Their hereditarily and environmentally determined fundamental differences in nature, we can see, are obviously incompatible, and their relationship reaches the inevitable end for which James has subtly prepared us.

What, then, can we make of this outcome in light of James's overall treatment of determinism and agency in the novel? Though James clearly, I think, favors Kate's performance of agency over Merton's acceptance of determinism, there is a limitation on how triumphantly we can read Kate's getting the money, since she does end up quite alone. Perhaps James means his ambivalent ending to underscore the necessity of not only constructing a sense of agency but also of doing so as a community, even of two, of forming meaning together. Whatever the case, *The Wings of the Dove* offers a unique contribution to the ongoing debate over how determinism and agency work in the naturalist novel; indeed, the model of determinism and agency that I argue James promotes here might even be seen as a precursor or transition into modernism, in which aesthetic movement the struggle to make sense of and overcome alienation within a world beyond the control of any individual figures prominently. In order for Kate Croy to survive in this wasteland, she cannot afford the luxury of a belief in individual agency or in transcendent meaning. Instead, she must accept the fact of her own determinedness and construct an ostensibly free public self, a self that can interact—that can "work" or "play"—with others and forge connections with them, even if those very interactions are governed by a complex web of determining forces. To choose to do otherwise—as Milly and Merton do—leads inevitably to alienation.

NOTES

1. That a narrative of interiority automatically denotes a free, undetermined subject is a claim that my argument implicitly questions and that Mitchell himself contradicts elsewhere, as we shall see.

2. For a typical example of this sort of criticism, see for instance Robert C. McLean, "'Love by the Doctor's Direction': Disease and Death in *The Wings of the Dove.*" McLean argues that Milly suffers from a mental, not physical, ailment, that "a sexually frustrated Milly Theale is the victim of her own warped mind" (130). McLean further claims that Milly schemes and maneuvers to win Densher's affections, and kills herself (via a plunge from the balcony of her Venetian abode) to spite Densher and Kate when she realizes that she will never have him. She jealously "smother[s] their capacity of the life of love and sexuality Milly herself was denied" (148). This essay interests me in particular because of the way that it seems to contradict itself when dealing with the issue of freedom and determinism: it seems curious that McLean can at one moment characterize Milly as a "victim" of repression but then at the next take her so thoroughly and unsympathetically to task for her actions. See also Duco van Oostrum, *Male Authors/Female Subjects: The Woman Within/Beyond the Borders of Henry Adams, Henry James, and Others.* Van Oostrum's chapter on *The Wings of the Dove* positions Merton Densher as not merely passive and weak but rather as actively "annexing and possessing" Kate and Milly: "He transforms his initial passive feminization into a violent masculine possession of women" (103). She asserts that while generous readers have argued that Merton achieves a new, "nonbinary" masculine identity that exists beyond traditional gender roles, his new masculinity "still defines itself in opposition to the female characters in the text, and actually remains entrenched in an oppressive cultural binary"; indeed, he "safely reduces [Milly and Kate's] differences and relegates them to a female sphere" (107).

3. Lewis Fried and Yoshinobu Hakutani concur with Pizer's claim that naturalism is a characteristically "loose" literary form: "However rigorously the formula [of the experimental novel] might be applied . . . it is nevertheless a personal and necessarily subjective activity. . . . There have been no two American writers alike in the use and interpretation of doctrine" (2).

4. Another related essay, though less central to my argument, is Ronald R. Janssen's discussion of money and materialism in the novel. Janssen argues that "James's novel represents, in a more civilized manner, the same erosion of relationships by materialism, greed, and ambition that one finds in such contemporary naturalist

novels as Frank Norris's *McTeague* or Theodore Dreiser's *Sister Carrie*" (163). He suggests, for instance, that Kate, "applying the deterministic logic she has learned from observing the behaviour of her own relatives, believes [Milly's] freedom to be based solely on her financial security" (165). However, Janssen further argues that "James's treatment assumes, in the end, a metaphysical dimension quite beyond the bounds of naturalistic fiction" (165); rather paradoxically, he claims that the novel is ultimately about Kate's choice between love and money, a choice that he sees as curiously free and undetermined.

5. Paul Civello has similarly argued for Ernest Hemingway as the prime example of a "modernist naturalist," for in his works "the self no longer *perceives* an order in the material world—for there is none—but *creates* its own." He continues by noting that "Hemingway . . . would transform the naturalistic novel by depicting a distinctly modern response—one in which the self creates its own order and meaning —to the naturalistic world of force" (3). Civello's discussion is compelling, and I have no desire to challenge the idea of Hemingway as modernist naturalist, but I would suggest that the synthetic approach that Civello identifies in Hemingway actually has its antecedent in James and his *The Wings of the Dove*.

6. Though she takes her reading in a different direction altogether, Kathleen Komar also discusses the "highly reflexive consciousness" indicated in the way that "the outward projection of [Kate's] vision is turned back upon herself" (474).

7. My concern here is primarily with the fact of Milly's illness, not with attempting to diagnose it. However, for such diagnostic speculations, see for example Caroline G. Mercer and Sarah D. Wangensteen, "'Consumption, Heart Disease, or Whatever': Chlorosis, a Heroine's Illness in *The Wings of the Dove*," and Adeline Tintner, "Inoperable Cancer: An Alternate Diagnosis for Milly Theale's Illness."

8. For a detailed reading of the Miltonic influence, see for instance Adeline Tintner, "Paradise Lost and Paradise Regained in James's *The Wings of the Dove* and *The Golden Bowl*."

WORKS CITED

Civello, Paul. *American Literary Naturalism and its Twentieth-Century Transformations.* Athens: U of Georgia P, 1994.

Conder, John J. *Naturalism in American Fiction: The Classic Phase.* Lexington: UP of Kentucky, 1984.

Crane, Stephen. "The Open Boat." *The Heath Anthology of American Literature.* Ed. Paul Lauter et al. 3rd ed. Vol. 2. New York: Houghton Mifflin, 1989. 608–24.

Fried, Lewis, and Yoshinobu Hakutani. *American Literary Naturalism: A Reassessment.* Heidelberg: Carl Winter, 1975.

Howard, June. *Form and History in American Literary Naturalism.* Chapel Hill: U of North Carolina P, 1985.

James, Henry. *The Wings of the Dove.* 1909. New York: Norton, 1978.

Janssen, Ronald R. "The Power of Possession: Money and Marriage in *The Wings of the Dove*." *The Magic Circle of Henry James: Essays in Honor of Darshan Singh Maini*. New York: Envoy, 1989. 160–67.

King, Kristin. "Ethereal Milly Theale in *The Wings of the Dove*: The Transparent Heart of James's Opaque Style." *Henry James Review* 21 (2000): 1–13.

Komar, Kathleen L. "Language and Character Delineation in *The Wings of the Dove*." *Twentieth Century Literature* 29.4 (1983): 471–87.

Mercer, Caroline G., and Sarah D. Wangensteen. "'Consumption, Heart Disease, or Whatever': Chlorosis, a Heroine's Illness in *The Wings of the Dove*." *Journal of the History of Medicine* 40 (1985): 259–85.

Mitchell, Lee Clark. *Determined Fictions*. New York: Columbia UP, 1989.

———. "Naturalism and the Language of Determinism." *Columbia Literary History of the United States*. New York: Columbia UP, 1988. 525–45.

———. "Sustaining Duplicities in *The Wings of the Dove*." *Texas Studies in Literature* 29.2 (1987): 187–214.

Pizer, Donald. *Realism and Naturalism in Nineteenth-Century American Literature*. Carbondale: Southern Illinois UP, 1966.

———. *Twentieth Century American Literary Naturalism: An Interpretation*. Carbondale: Southern Illinois UP, 1982.

Powers, Lyall. *Henry James and the Naturalist Movement*. East Lansing: Michigan State UP, 1971.

Sherman, Stuart P. *On Contemporary Literature*. New York: Henry Holt, 1917.

Tintner, Adeline. "Inoperable Cancer: An Alternate Diagnosis for Milly Theale's Illness." *Journal of the History of Medicine* 42 (1987): 73–76.

———. "Paradise Lost and Paradise Regained in James's *The Wings of the Dove* and *The Golden Bowl*." *Milton Quarterly* 17.4 (1983): 125–31.

Walcutt, Charles C. *American Literary Naturalism, A Divided Stream*. Minneapolis: U of Minnesota P, 1956.

Assaulting the Yeehats

VIOLENCE AND SPACE IN
THE CALL OF THE WILD

—James R. Giles

EARLE LABOR HAS DESCRIBED JACK LONDON'S CLASSIC 1903 NOVELLA *THE CALL OF THE WILD* AS A "WILD ROMANCE" (78), AND ONE OF THE MAJOR ingredients of its romanticism is a valorization of violence. The text's deceptive complexity arises, in large part, because London wants to celebrate the freedom inherent in a violent rejection of restraint, while also positing a binary opposition between "civilized" reason and "primitive" unreason. Not only is such an opposition doomed from the beginning, but the text's aesthetic power is tied to its inevitable collapse.

London's determination to argue for the superior rationalism of white "civilization" in *The Call of the Wild* is an integral part of his imperialist agenda. The plot of the novella, as its many readers know, follows the transformation of the protagonist Buck from northern California dog of leisure to invisible and consequently mythic "Ghost Dog," head of an Alaskan wolf pack. This transformation climaxes in Buck's savage attack on the Yeehat Indians, the narrative moment when violence overwhelms and deconstructs the text. The scene is disturbing in several ways, most importantly because its language exults in Buck's savage assault of the Yeehat Indians.

In the scene, London's defining binary opposition, already considerably undermined, collapses totally. The description of Buck's revenge against the Yeehats is condensed into one relentlessly graphic paragraph:

> The Yeehats were dancing about . . . when they heard a fearful
> roaring and saw rushing upon them an animal the like of which
> they had never seen before. It was Buck, a live hurricane of fury,
> hurling himself upon them in a frenzy to destroy. He sprang at the
> foremost man (it was the chief of the Yeehats), ripping the throat
> wide open till the rent jugular spouted a fountain of blood. He did
> not pause to worry the victim, but ripped in passing, with the next
> bound tearing wide the throat of a second man. There was no

withstanding him. He plunged about in their very midst, tearing, rending, destroying, in constant and terrific motion which defied the arrows they discharged at him. In fact, so inconceivably rapid were his movements, and so closely were the Indians tangled together, that they shot one another with the arrows; and one young hunter, hurling a spear at Buck in mid air, drove it through the chest of another hunter with such force that the point broke through the skin of the back and stood out beyond. Then a panic seized the Yeehats, and they fled in terror to the woods, proclaiming as they fled the advent of the Evil Spirit. (151–52)

On a purely visceral level, readers may well be impressed most by the breathless, cinematic effect of the paragraph. Buck's progress from Yeehat throat to Yeehat throat is narrated through a montage effect, which evokes countless classic Hollywood horror films juxtaposed with the more shameless film "epics" celebrating "the settlement of the west" and the coincidental massacre of the "savage" American Indians. The paragraph will be more or less troublesome depending upon the degree to which the severed jugular veins seem like genuine human jugular veins or merely dehumanized, if bloody, targets for Buck's rage.

Indeed, dehumanization is a central issue in London's text, which objectifies the Yeehats through narrative omission as well as commission. Critics have long noted their deus ex machina role. The Yeehats do not even appear in the novel until London produces them out of nowhere to murder John Thornton and thus reconcile Buck's dilemma of choosing between his love of Thornton, the rational representative of civilization,[1] and the accelerating appeal of "the call of the wild" (variously identified by London as "the primitive" and "the primordial"). London, of course, wanted, and could expect, his early-twentieth-century white readership to react to the scene by cheering Buck's bloody revenge because, after all, the Yeehats had killed Thornton, a more than sympathetic white male character.

A postcolonial perspective problematizes, if not negates, such an obvious and such a racist response. As Edward W. Said points out, white imperialists invaded the physical spaces of nonwhite peoples throughout the world and then redefined such spaces as belonging to the colonizing powers, thereby reducing native inhabitants to the status of bothersome "foreigners" who needed to be removed. Said says, "imperialism after all is an act of geographical violence through which virtually every space in the world is explored, charted, and finally brought under control" (225). Buck's attack on the Yeehats emblematizes the savage and violent assault of the "savage" colonial by the "rational" colonizer.

Before the Yeehats actually enter the text, the narration goes to some length to demonize them. Thornton, two human associates, and approximately seven dogs have gone in search of a "fabled lost mine, the history of which was as old as the country," but which "no living man had looted" (129). Initially, they find themselves alone in a mysterious and primitive space. But, as Buck senses on the day he tracks an ancient bull moose into the forest and observes an arrow protruding from his prey's side, the isolation of Thornton's party is about to end: "As he held on he became more and more conscious of the new stir in the land. There was life abroad in it different from the life which had been there throughout the summer. . . . He was oppressed with a sense of calamity happening, if it were not calamity already happened . . ." (149). London thus makes the indigenous Yeehats seem violent invaders of a (since the arrival of Thornton's party) "white space," who cruelly assault nature (the bull moose) itself. It is hardly surprising, then, when Buck, upon returning to camp, finds the rest of Thornton's party—men and dogs—lying dead, filled with arrows. In fact, Buck finds first the corpse of one of the dogs, "an arrow protruding, head and feathers, from either side of his body" and another dog "thrashing about in a death struggle." Only then does he notice the body of the man Hans, "feathered with arrows like a porcupine" (151).

London conveniently ignores several things in the above scenario. The space surrounding the lost mine is, of course, infinitely older than the white "history of the country," which is nevertheless all that London is concerned with. Temporarily abandoned when Thornton's party "discovers" it, it lies within the seasonal home of the Yeehats and thus is not "white" or even neutral space at all. The Indians' killing the bull moose in a hunting expedition is a mode of survival, and even their massacre of Thornton's party is an attempt to reclaim invaded space. Still, even if the reader should recognize the Yeehats' point of view, there seems little reason for them to kill the dogs, a consideration that London, in a text glorifying a dog, intends to weigh heavily with the reader.

Let us turn now from the Yeehats' slaughter of Thornton's party back to Buck's revenge. In the description of the spear that "one young hunter" has driven through the chest of another until it protrudes from his back, London enacts the imperialist paradigm and thereby gives rise to several layers of meaning, not all of them consistent. In the imperialist context, it is important to note that the fatal (and phallic) penetration is a consequence of almost burlesque proportions on the part of the Indians who are "so closely . . . tangled together" that they kill each other while trying to ward off the assault of the enraged Buck. The Yeehats' deadly, yet broadly comic, incompetence seems, then, a final turn of the screw in the text's dehumanization of them. It is bad enough that the Yeehats are "savages"; it is even worse that they are ridiculous savages. In fact, the implicit (il)logic of London's text seems to be that only "civilized" white men and dog-protagonists can profitably adopt savage behavior. The Yeehats' unnecessary killing of the sled dogs represents a gratuitous reversal of the dynamic of imperialism in which historically the white invader attacked and despoiled nature. At the same time, the logic and morality of imperialism would demand that they be punished in the most severe manner possible if for no other reason than their turning Hans into a very dead porcupine—i.e., they objectify him by reducing him to dead and no longer human matter. They, not the white men, pervert nature.

Moreover, London's textual logic implies that it is somehow "unnatural" for the Yeehats to defend their space from imperialist exploitation. Thornton and his associates are, after all, only interested in "discovering" gold in the lost mine region and returning with it to enjoy the luxuries of "civilization." Christopher Gair, in an essay on the doppelgänger motif in *Call of the Wild*, perceptively summarizes the central implications of London's treatment of the Yeehats:

> Of course, the passage reveals a great deal about London's representation practices, rather than telling us anything "accurate" about Yeehat culture. It suggests that the representation of the Yeehats as superstitious, aggressive, and incompetent is a strategic construction designed to conceal or justify the occupation of their land and the removal of their minerals by the Americans. (203)

It seems unarguable, then, that London is intent upon dehumanizing the Yeehats in order to justify the imperialist invasion, and appropriation, of their space for capitalist profit. They constitute, however, only half of the paradigm of dehumanization in the passage and, in many ways, the least interesting half. The other half is embodied in Buck, the savage aggressor. Not just in this scene but throughout the novel, one encounters in the characterization of Buck several levels of dehumanization—and, paradoxically, of something like its reverse. To state the obvious, Buck is a dog, not a human being. But, as London critics have long noted, both Buck and his mirror image White Fang are very "human" dogs and function, on at least some level, as heroic projections of their creator.[2] Thus, Buck is technically an animal with exceptional intelligence and the tastes of "a sated aristocrat" who is transformed by a brutal environment into a "dominant primordial beast," and the defining moment in this transformation is his attack on the Yeehats.

Long before the death of John Thornton, Buck has been hearing "the call of the wild" and feeling the pull of violence. Charles Watson provides the best summary of what the call entails: "[w]hat Buck seeks as an alternative to order and work is the deeper satisfaction of the irrational, the anarchic, and the demonic, symbolized by the hunt and the kill" (42). In his assault on the Yeehats, Buck surrenders completely to the violent, the irrational, and the demonic. More importantly, so does his creator. Undoubtedly without intending to, London has, in one graphic paragraph, succeeded in conveying the ugly, non-heroic reality of imperialism, as opposed to the idealism with which its defenders justified it. He realizes thereby a climactic moment in his initially reluctant but ultimately exultant descent into more than one level of a very different kind of "lost mine."

In short, London has Buck discard all civilized restraint and unleash deadly violence against the weak and vulnerable. The text describes Buck, after the assault on the Yeehats, as feeling "a great pride in himself" because "he had killed man, the noblest game of all, and he had killed in the face of the law of club and fang. He sniffed the bodies curiously. They had died so easily. It was harder to kill a husky dog than them" (153). There are obvious Nietzschean overtones to all this—Buck, the savage Superdog exterminating even the finest examples of a slave race.

Throughout the text, the application and connotation of the word "savage" has, not at all consistently, been evolving. The first dramatic shift comes in the last half of chapter 2, "The Law of Club and Fang," and is summarized by the famous title of chapter 3, "The Dominant Primordial Beast." Under the harsh tutelage of Francois and Perrault, Buck learns the necessity of discarding the lingering vestiges of a bourgeois morality in the Yukon. Specifically, he learns to steal food in order to avoid starvation:

> This first theft marked Buck as fit to survive in the hostile Northland environment. It marked his adaptability, his capacity to adjust himself to changing conditions, the lack of which would have meant swift and terrible death. It marked, further, the decay or going to pieces of his moral nature, a vain thing and a handicap in the ruthless struggle for existence. It was all well enough in the Southland, under the law of love and fellowship, to respect

private property and personal feelings; but in the Northland, under the law of club and fang, whoso took such things into account was a fool, and in so far as he observed them he would fail to prosper. (32–33)

On the surface, deterioration of civilized morality seems an undesirable thing. London could, moreover, count on a turn-of-the-century bourgeois reader indoctrinated by the sentimentalities of the Victorian novel accepting, without much introspection, his implicit equation of "private property and personal feelings" with "the law of love and fellowship." From a strictly rational perspective, the implied reader of this passage and of essentially the first half of London's text should perceive the disintegration of Buck's civilized self as a tragic diminution.

Instead, readers have traditionally been excited, even thrilled by, the pampered bourgeois dog's transformation into "dominant primordial beast." Buck becomes now the super savage freed from the restraints of civilization; and, in contrast to the Yeehats, he can handle it. Moral restraint seems now foolish, even suicidal; while savage assault on lesser creatures is valorized. Imperialism is implicitly advocated as escape, as joyously irresponsible freedom; once outside the artificial barriers of civilization that he of course erected, the white male can steal from and even murder "Yeehats" all over the world without hesitation or regret. "Exterminate the brutes," indeed.

In this complex dynamic, it is essential that *Call of the Wild*'s Yeehats be both incompetent savages *and* "the noblest game of all." The kind of freedom that London's text increasingly advocates demands that the ripped jugulars be those of human beings, even if of a lesser order than the white imperialists. More than London's probably unconscious admission that imperialism was a murderous game is involved here. Crucially, there is the appeal of a return to the primordial, of escape from bourgeois morality and restraint, a luxuriating in excessive, illegal activity, and, perhaps best of all, the abandonment of rationality.

Almost from the first, in fact, London's valorization of reason is problematic. The novella's opening paragraph does emphasize Buck's capacity for rational and abstract thought:

Buck did not read the newspapers, or he would have known that trouble was brewing, not alone for himself, but for every tidewater dog, strong of muscle and with warm, long hair, from Puget Sound to San Diego. Because men, groping in the Arctic darkness, had found a yellow metal, and because steamship and transportation

> companies were booming the find, thousands of men were rushing
> into the Northland. These men wanted dogs, and the dogs they
> wanted were heavy dogs, with strong muscles by which to toil, and
> furry coats to protect them from the frost. (1)

Here illiteracy seems the major hindrance to Buck's rationality and potential for abstract thought. Could he but read newspapers, *he would know* that he and potentially every other dog of his approximate physical type on the West Coast might soon become classic victims of biological and environmental determinism.

Shortly thereafter, the narrative voice retreats from such a strong affirmation of the cerebral side of Buck. After Buck witnesses the brutal killing of the friendly and trusting Curly by a full circle of dogs who fight as "wolfish creatures" (20), he is haunted by images of Curly's death: "The scene often came back to Buck to trouble him in his sleep. So that was the way. No fair play. Once down, that was the end of you" (22). Here the narrator adds a significant cautionary note: "Not that Buck reasoned it out. He was fit, that was all, and *unconsciously* he accommodated himself to the new mode of life" (33, italics mine). The narrator further stresses that the transformation is, to a significant degree, an atavistic reversal: "And not only did he learn by experience, but instincts long dead became alive again. The domesticated generations fell from him" (35).[3] Earlier in the same chapter, the text asserts that "an idea came to [Buck]." In a less than consistent manner, London's narrator seems to equate reason with Buck's lingering civilized self, and instinct or "unreason" with his emerging "primordial" self. In the description of Buck's rivalry with Spitz for leadership of the sled team, the narrator continues to posit a motivation for the central character that falls somewhere between the rational and the instinctual and, in fact, seems to contain elements of both: "[Buck] was pre-eminently cunning, and could bide his time with a patience that was nothing less than primitive" (48–49). Throughout the remainder of the novel, Buck's "primordial" side increasingly assumes dominance over his domesticated surface.

There are a series of defining moments in Buck's process of reverse evolution. After he hears the howls of the wolves prowling in the darkness that surrounds the central campfire (the darkness of madness or "unreason" that surrounds the reassuring light of reason), Buck's "primordial" nature demands release:

> All that stirring of old instincts which at stated periods drives
> men out from the sounding cities to forest and plain to kill things
> by chemically propelled leaden pellets, the blood lust, the joy to
> kill—all this was Buck's, only it was infinitely more intimate. He

> was ranging at the head of the pack, running the wild thing down,
> the living meat, to kill with his own teeth and wash his muzzle to
> the eyes in warm blood. (56)

Not surprisingly, the fight in which the once thoroughly domesticated dog physically destroys his rival comes soon. Even here, though, the animal's rationality does not give way completely: "He fought by instinct, but he could fight by head as well" (60).

A further challenge to Buck's domesticated veneer comes in dreams. In a passage that anticipates the appearance in 1907 of *Before Adam* and prefigures exploration of a deeper level of the text's metaphoric "lost mine," the dog dreams of an evolutionary ancestor of human beings:

> [This pre-human creature] uttered strange sounds and seemed
> very much afraid of the darkness, into which he peered continu-
> ally, clutching in his hand, which hung midway between knee
> and foot, a stick with a heavy stone made fast to the end. About
> his body there was a peculiar springiness, or resiliency, almost cat-
> like, and a quick alertness as of one who lived in perpetual fear of
> things seen and unseen. (71)

In this remote time, man's ancestor, in order to survive physically, could only fear a darkness that contained "great beasts of prey" (71). While no "great beasts of prey" (except those in human form) threaten modern, "civilized" man, Michel Foucault argues that imagination, which contains within it the truth of madness, perennially does. The darkness both frightens and calls out to Buck to leave the security of the campfire, the circle of light, and come and explore its hidden truth. London is being drawn inexorably downward toward the deepest recesses of the subconscious, toward a confrontation with that which, while buried, is never truly lost and which may erupt at any moment in irrational and even violent thoughts and action.

The "hairy man" reappears in a later dream of "this other world" in which "the salient thing seemed fear," and this time the dog follows obedi-ently at his heels as they explore a mysterious landscape that leads from "the beach of a sea" up into trees through which primordial man "travel[s] ahead as fast as on the ground, swinging by the arm from limb to limb, sometimes a dozen feet apart, letting go and catching, never falling, never missing his grip" (133–34). Now the "lost mine" has become vertical space extending into the treetops of a dream world, but despite its seductiveness, it remains just as frightening as it was before.

Ironically, or perhaps fittingly, it is the civilized effetes, Charles, Hall, and Mercedes, who set in motion the final stage in Buck's reversal to the primordial. It is their arrogance, their incompetence, their inexperience that almost destroy Buck and result in his rescue by John Thornton. Thornton briefly threatens to reverse entirely Buck's de-evolutionary process by awakening in him a new and thoroughly civilized emotion: "Love, genuine passionate love, was his for the first time" (106). The voices from the "darkness" continue to call to him, but his love for Thornton restrains him from answering them: "as often as he gained the soft unbroken earth and the green shade, the love of John Thornton drew him back to the fire again" (112).

But even Thornton is unable to drive the "hairy man" from Buck's memory, and soon the "dog" is running with a timber wolf that emerges mysteriously from out of the forest. During the running, the echoes of the primitive, the primordial, seem more liberating than threatening: "He had done this thing before, somewhere in that other and dimly remembered world, and he was doing it again, now, running free in the open, the packed earth underfoot, the wide sky overhead" (138–39). Even for a dog, though, civilization and good breeding are no easy things to throw off; and London delays for a brief time Buck's final surrender to the primitive and his own excavation of the deeper levels of the lost mine: "[Buck's] *cunning* was wolf cunning, and wild cunning; his *intelligence*, shepherd intelligence and St. Bernard intelligence . . ." (142, italics mine).

It is at this point that the Yeehat Indians step in to complete Buck's transfiguration and to set in motion the collapse of London's opposition of imperialist reason to savage violence and the disturbing climax of his "wild romance." It is most telling that London describes Buck as acting out of "passion" in his deadly assault of the Yeehats. Like his contemporary Frank Norris, London at times in his fiction celebrates the exultation found in surrender to violent passion. Both writers were fond of describing the liberating effects of atavistic reversals to violence by white characters on the frontier who thereby appropriate nonwhite space and thus, apparently without quite realizing what they were doing, dramatize the savagery of the imperialist program. After all, the "old instincts" periodically drive men "out from the sounding cities" to kill with impunity in the pure, silent space of the frontier. Murder is, then, instinctual, a barely submerged part of human nature, which happens to fit nicely with the imperialist agenda.[4] It must be said, though, that especially in the fiction of London, celebration of violent passion is not *always and solely* related to imperialism.

A crucial passage in *The Call of the Wild* for understanding London's ethos comes near the end of chapter 3, "The Dominant Primordial Beast," and describes Buck experiencing "an ecstasy that marks the summit of life, and beyond which life cannot rise":

> And such is the paradox of living, this ecstasy comes when one is most alive, and it comes as a complete forgetfulness that one is alive. This ecstasy, this forgetfulness of living, comes to the artist, caught up and out of himself in a sheet of flame; it comes to the soldier, war-mad on a stricken field and refusing quarter; and it came to Buck, leading the pack, sounding the old wolf cry, straining after the food that was alive and that fled swiftly before him through the moonlight. He was sounding the deeps of his nature, and of the parts of his nature that were deeper than he, going back into the womb of Time. He was mastered by the sheer surging of life, the tidal wave of being, the perfect joy of each separate muscle, joint, and sinew and that it was everything that was not death, that it was aglow and rampant, expressing itself in movement, flying exultantly under the stars and over the face of dead matter that did not move. (56–57)

When teaching *The Call of the Wild,* I always ask students if they really understand this passage, and most say they do. Some recall moments in which they have experienced, paradoxically often through strenuous physical exercise, feelings of liberation from the restraints of their bodies, and others talk about meaningful personal accomplishments that become more possible after momentary transcendence of the individual, isolated self. They are usually not troubled by the contradictions inherent in such readings of the passage and are, in fact, perceptive in not being so. London is, in fact, celebrating escape from the body and the isolated ego.

London's three illustrations of those feeling the power of "ecstasy" introduce more problematic, and ultimately more important, complexities and contradictions than are evident in his imperialism paradigm. There is the "artist" "caught up and out of himself" in a "sheet of flame" that apparently represents the creative process rather than the created artifact. A plausible reading of this seems to be that, for London, the most meaningful kind of art is possible only when the artist reaches a state of self-forgetfulness that borders on unconsciousness. Reason, not to mention revision, would seem irrelevant to this conception of the creative process. In fact, rational control is apparently a limitation that must be escaped. There is also Buck's "sounding the old wolf cry" and "of the parts of his nature that were deeper than he, going back into the womb of Time." One could hardly ask for a clearer indication that Buck is London's doppelgänger: by surrendering to a deep and timeless "nature," he has become an artist creating the ancient song of the wolves.

Perhaps most revealingly, there is, also, the "soldier, war-mad on a stricken field" and achieving a sense of profound aliveness by killing others. In the last half of the novella, echoes of Nietzsche and the late-nineteenth-century "cult of masculinity" British and American writers abound. To some degree, London, by largely excluding women from his text, minimizes the excessive chauvinism of the H. Rider Haggard school and, indeed, of some of his own fiction. But he certainly does not avoid association of the "war-mad" soldier with both the genuine artist and London's canine alter ego. The text's paralleling the soldier who kills to achieve ecstasy and the artist who creates to do so seems paradoxical, as if killing and creating are simply two manifestations of the same phenomenon. London is talking about something basic to the creative process even as he is asserting that preserving one's own life by killing the enemy in combat produces an ecstasy not unrelated to madness. The environment, the space, of combat is itself madness; but, now deep inside the lost mine, London is concerned with internal rather than external space, the kind of passion that Buck feels when he attacks the Yeehats. For London the ecstasy of creativity is, at least to some degree, assaultive, even murderous. And madly, joyously irrational. Art constitutes warfare against the ultimate enemy, death, and its defeat, even if only during the creative process, produces a kind of divine madness. For London, the graphic description of Buck's ripping open the throats of the Yeehats is an intoxicating affirmation of art's vanquishing of death. Murder is for him an instinctual passion that affirms the life of the murderer—all of which violence is easier to take if one can ignore the humanity of the enemy here, the Yeehats, which London's white readership, couched in imperialist doctrine, certainly did.

The Call of the Wild continues to attract readers (academic as well as general), and one assumes that most of them discover in it an appeal that transcends imperialist concerns. In the last analysis, the precise nature of this appeal may be elusive. Perhaps writing that appeals on a fundamentally irrational level cannot in fact be rationally analyzed; and, precisely in that context, two theoretical texts by two very dissimilar writers shed some light here. In the first, Frank Norris, in an essay called "A Plea for Romantic Fiction" and from his 1903 collection *The Responsibilities of the Novelist,* defends romanticism in fiction by redefining it. He first asserts that Romance "is the kind of fiction that takes cognizance of variations from the type of normal life.

According to this definition, then, Romance may even treat of the sordid, the unlovely—as, for instance, the novels of M. Zola" (280). He adds later that "to Romance belongs the wide world for range, and the unplumbed depths of the human heart, and the mystery of sex, and the problems of life, and the black, unsearched penetralia of the soul of man" (282).

Perhaps excessive violence in naturalism appeals precisely because it evokes something in the dark, "unlovely" souls of its readers. London, in *The Call of the Wild,* was not explicitly interested in exploring "the mystery of sex" but was most certainly interested in investigating the mystery of the human capacity for violence, the human capacity to kill. In this sense, Buck's assault on the Yeehats may well contain its saving truth, that human beings most easily feel ecstasy in violent action against those who, for whatever reason—imperialist aggression, the demands of warfare, racism, economic oppression—have already been dehumanized. London may also be telling us that we all sometimes envision others as "Yeehats," even if we do not attack them and rip open their jugular veins.

Writing approximately sixty years after Norris, Michel Foucault, in *Madness and Civilization,* suggests that the most memorable art comes precisely when rationality fails to suppress an underlying "unreason" or "madness." These revelatory moments in art, he further notes, manifest themselves in celebrations of violence: "For Sade as for Goya, unreason continues to watch by night; but in this vigil it joins with fresh powers. The nonbeing it once was now becomes the power to annihilate. Through Sade and Goya, the Western world received the possibility of transcending its reason in violence, and of recovering tragic experience beyond the promises of dialectic" (285). For whatever reasons, Foucault does not consider London or the other American naturalists here, but he might well have. In the graphic depictions of violence that crowd their texts, London and Norris especially dramatize the power of a suddenly overpowering unreason. Norris's "Romance" and Foucault's "madness" seem to have a great deal in common, then; and the collapse of London's celebration of imperialist reason in *The Call of the Wild* illustrates these related concepts in an especially interesting and complex way.

The essential movement in *The Call of the Wild* is from a celebration of rationality to unreason or "instinct" and, finally, to the mad violence of Buck's attack on the Yeehats. As London's alter ego, Buck both surrenders to and assaults the primitive forces of the night and thereby gives the novel its lasting power. London's uncritical imperialist morality allowed him to identify the Yeehats as primitive beings whose space had to be appropriated by the civilized white colonialist and who thus had to be gotten out of the way.

But a significant, and increasingly overt, thematic level of *The Call of the Wild* celebrates a violent, and fundamentally mad, reaction against all those forces outside the campfire of reason, such frightening manifestations of the imagination, of "the black, unsearched penetralia of the soul of man," as the "hairy man" swinging rapidly through menacing trees and a wolf pack led by a legendary Ghost Dog who leaves Indian hunters dead with their throats slashed. Whatever the problems the novel poses to consistent "rational" reading, it is this increasingly dominant and jubilant trope, this exploration of "the lost mine" of the subconscious that, in the end, constitutes London's "wild romance" and thereby guarantees its lasting appeal.

NOTES

1. By focusing on traditional gender roles, Jonathan Auerbach deconstructs the logic behind the Thornton characterization and the Thornton-Buck relationship, arguing that, at different points in the text, Thornton symbolically functions as "god the father," "male lover," and "wife" to Buck ("Congested Mails" 67–68).
2. Earl Wilcox, for instance, describes him as "an exceptionally wise dog" (93); James Glennon Cooper approaches the novel through "archetypal patterns" and argues that *"The Call of the Wild,* which was written almost directly from the unconscious, has all of the symbols and images of the Hero myth" (26); Andrew Flink creatively and convincingly reads the novel from an autobiographical perspective, arguing that, in writing it, London was responding to two traumatic personal experiences, the refusal of his biological father to acknowledge him and his incarceration in the Erie County (New York) Penitentiary as a vagrant; equally creative and persuasive is Earle Labor's mythic reading of the novel in which he argues that "London employs the lower animal as a symbol of man's unconscious brute impulses" and points out that "the buried impulses" examined in the novel "are essentially human, not canine, and . . . the reader identifies with Buck more profoundly than he realizes" (6–8). Recent readings take the idea of Buck's "humanness" in especially intriguing directions. Gair's doppelgänger interpretation is a Marxist approach to the novel that argues for a general "transformation of Buck from 'sated aristocrat' into 'dominant primordial beast'" and posits Buck's "inexhaustible capacity for change (capitalism's constant craving for newness and replacement)" as the key to his survival (199). In "'Congested Mails,'" Jonathan Auerbach, by emphasizing Buck's role as a mail carrier, reads the novel as a dramatization "of London's own struggle to gain recognition as a writer"; and, in *Male Call,* Auerbach focuses upon London's creation of a masculine persona as central to his enormous success as a writer and argues that *"The Call of the Wild* dramatizes London's own struggle to gain recognition as a writer" (88). Finally, in her perceptive and useful *The Call of the Wild: A Naturalistic Romance,* Jacqueline Tavernier-Courbin views Buck as a hero in the conventions of Western cultural romanticism: "Although not human, Buck is a romantic hero. Not only does he possess great romantic qualities such as courage, endurance, leadership, loyalty, a passionate ability to love, and a total disregard of danger in defending or avenging those he loves, but he is also gorgeous" (103).

3. London, in an essay entitled "The Other Animals," tried to clarify his ideas about canine thought processes. He wrote that "these dog-heroes of mine were not directed by abstract reasoning, but by instinct, sensation, and emotion, and by simple reasoning" (195). In *The Call of the Wild,* this attempt at a rather fine distinction breaks down the more overtly Buck becomes London's alter ego. He also stated in a letter that "[w]e know little or nothing about what dogs think. But then we may conclude from their actions what their mental processes might be, and such conclusions may be within the range of possibility" (*Letters* 381). In other words, we don't really know how dogs think, and thus the potential for creative interpretation is open.

4. June Howard's *Form and History in American Literary Naturalism* contains some perceptive insights into the relative importance of frontier and urban violence in frontier and urban naturalist texts.

WORKS CITED

Auerbach, Jonathan. "'Congested Mails': Buck and Jack's 'Call.'" *American Literature* 67 (Mar. 1995): 51–76.

_____. *Male Call.* Durham: Duke UP, 1996.

Cooper, James Glennon. "A Womb of Time: Archetypal Patterns in the Novels of Jack London." *Jack London Newsletter* 9 (1976): 16–28.

Flink, Andrew. "*The Call of the Wild*: Jack London's Catharsis." *Jack London Newsletter* 11 (1978): 12–19.

Foucault, Michel. *Madness and Civilization: A History of Insanity in the Age of Reason.* Trans. Richard Howard. New York: Random House–Vintage, 1988.

Gair, Christopher. "The Doppelgänger and the Naturalist Self: *The Call of the Wild*." *Jack London Journal* 1 (1994): 193–230.

Howard, June. *Form and History in American Literary Naturalism.* Chapel Hill: U of North Carolina P, 1985.

Labor, Earle. "Jack London's Mondo Cane: *The Call of the Wild* and *White Fang.*" *Jack London Newsletter* 1 (1967): 2–13.

London, Jack. *The Call of the Wild and Other Stories.* New York: Arcadia House, 1950.

_____. *The Letters of Jack London.* Ed. Earle Labor, Robert C. Leitz III, and I. Milo Shepherd. Vol. 1. Stanford: Stanford UP, 1988.

_____. "The Other Animals." *Revolution and Other Essays.* New York: Macmillan, 1910.

Norris, Frank. "A Plea for Romantic Fiction." *Criticism and Fiction by William Dean Howells / The Responsibilities of the Novelist by Frank Norris.* Cambridge, MA: Walker–de Berry, 1962.

Said, Edward W. *Culture and Imperialism.* New York: Random House–Vintage, 1994.

Tavernier-Courbin, Jacqueline. *The Call of the Wild: A Naturalistic Romance.* New York: Twayne, 1994.

Wilcox, Earl. "Jack London's Naturalism: The Example of *Call of the Wild.*" *Jack London Newsletter* 2 (1969): 91–101.

Advantage! What is advantage? And will you take it upon yourself to define with perfect accuracy in exactly what the advantage
of man consists of? And what if it so happens that a man's
advantage sometimes not only may, but even must, consist
exactly in his desiring under certain conditions what is harmful
to himself. . . . And if so, if there can be such a condition then the
whole principle becomes worthless. What do you think—are
there such cases?

—Fyodor Dostoevski

AMERICAN STUDIES, LIBERALISM, AND
THE QUESTION OF DISSENT

ALTHOUGH LIONEL TRILLING'S FORMALIST CONCEPTION OF THE LIBERAL
IMAGINATION HAS BEEN SERIOUSLY CHALLENGED BY 'MATERIALIST' CULTURAL
criticism based in considerations of race, class, and gender, his founding
premise—that "[i]n the United States . . . liberalism is not only the dominant
but even the sole intellectual tradition" (ix)—continues to define the context of
opposition for contemporary Americanists. Myra Jehlen, for example, grounds
her path-breaking work *American Incarnation* in the assertion that John
Locke's liberalism, particularly his doctrine of "self-possessive individualism"
(Jehlen 3), constitutes the "givens of the universe of American thought, the
subterranean foundation upon which statement, argument, decision, [and]
consciousness arose" (20). Lockean liberalism, she goes on to say, "organize[s]
American self-consciousness as grammar organizes speech" (21). More recently,
but with a shift in emphasis from Locke to Emerson, Cyrus Patell maintains
"that the problem with U.S. liberal ideology is its ongoing reliance on Emerson-
ian modes of thinking" (xiii). Emerson's core doctrine of self-reliance "crys-
talliz[es] . . . what might be called *the official narrative* of U.S. individualism"

(xiii), so much so that whether it is explicitly "[a]cknowledged or not, Emerso-
nianism is the ground upon which contemporary U.S. liberal theory is built"
(xv). Given the preoccupation with liberalism among Americanists from
Trilling to the present, it does indeed seem, as Cary Wolfe has remarked, that
"the study of American culture . . . is so intertwined with the foundational
assumptions of Liberalism that you have to wonder at times if it is possible to
do Americanist criticism and *really* talk about anything else" (124).

The perceived hegemony of liberalism in American culture raises the
crucial issue of whether American critics or authors ever truly dissent from,
or authentically oppose, the saturating medium of liberal ideology. Thus, a
primary theme of contemporary American studies is "complicity," which
focuses attention on how American writers routinely "undercut their own
often-dissenting criticism by implicit consent to nationalist [liberal] ideology" (Trachtenberg xi). Sacvan Bercovitch, perhaps the most prominent and
important Americanist writing today, concludes that "America's classic texts"
—literary and scholarly alike—invariably "represent the strategies of a triumphant liberal hegemony. Far from subverting the status quo, their diagnostic and prophetic modes attest the capacities of the dominant culture to
absorb alternative forms, to the point of making basic change seem virtually
unthinkable" (367). And yet, if by liberalism we mean the efforts of Trilling,
F. O. Matthiessen, Richard Chase, and others to defend "a sacred-secular
library of America set against the ideologies in America of racism, imperialism, capitalism, and patriarchy" (16), it follows for Bercovitch that deliberately *embedding* American letters in these "adverse facts of American history"
(12) opposes liberalism by subverting its "hermeneutics of transcendence" (4).
Such an approach, based in what Donald Pease calls "resistant materialities
[of] race, class, and gender" (3), envisions a post-national condition of American studies wherein previously excluded groups are moved "from the status
of objects of social regulation within the national [liberal] narrative into performative powers . . . able to change that narrative's assumptions" (4). An
especially vigorous mode of dissent from liberalism, then, finds expression in
the current widespread reorientation of American studies toward "stories
about those who are disenfranchised, marginalized, and brutalized by the
dominant [liberal] culture even as that dominant culture celebrates its basis in
the protection of individual rights" (Patell xviii).

The following essay on Jack London's *The Sea-Wolf* contributes to this
emerging critique of liberalism in American studies, but it does so in a manner that departs from the usual foundation in issues of race, class, and gender.
Bercovitch indicates the mode of criticism I pursue when he defines dissent as

"a form of protest conceived at the interstices of free-enterprise theory, and developed within the gaps or lacunae in the [liberal] principle of subjectivity" (346). Rather than abandon problems of individual agency in favor of broad sociological categories, the mode of dissent pursued here focuses attention on how London's novel exposes and exploits a serious weakness in the liberal conception of economic behavior. With the hypothetical aid of London's malevolent antihero, Wolf Larsen, I endeavor to show that Larsen's conduct challenges the presumed convergence of reason and morality embodied in liberal notions of 'economic man,' particularly in the behavioral logic of what analytic theorists refer to as "constrained preference maximization."[1] Supporting this logic is the opinion that an economic agent can best maximize his or her preferences, and thus his or her well-being, through agreeable participation in cooperative enterprise. Given an agent's overriding interest in self-preservation narrowly construed as economic well-being, it is rational to be moral, or at least to appear to be moral. As will be seen, Wolf Larsen's behavior pushes the logic of preference maximization to a point at which, breaching the *a priori* convergence of reason and morality, liberalism destroys itself according to its own logic. Wolf Larsen mobilizes the moral nihilism lurking in the soul of economic man, thereby restoring to view the 'state of nature' shadowing the bourgeois pursuit of security and comfort. Not only do rational and moral conduct *diverge* in Wolf Larsen's efforts of preference maximization, but the reader is forced to consider (contra liberalism) whether it is *rational to be immoral.*[2] Larsen's internal subversion of market society disturbs the belief, fundamental to the liberal logic of consumption, that rational behavior is moral (or at least cooperative) behavior.

Before engaging the details of London's *The Sea-Wolf*, I should say a bit more about how I intend to proceed on the topic of Wolf Larsen's dissent from liberalism. The first section of this essay explains and clarifies the idea that Larsen's dissent is *internal* to the behavioral logic underpinning liberal notions of rational economic agency. I then move to a consideration of how Thomas Hobbes, whose thought on reason and self-preservation informs these notions, might reply to the challenge of Larsen's moral nihilism. In the course of this dialogue between Hobbes and Larsen, the presence of Friedrich Nietzsche, whom London mentions on the first page of his novel, becomes especially significant. Ultimately, it is Nietzsche's idea of 'authenticity,' of remaining true to one's most cherished self-image even at the cost of self-preservation, that sustains Larsen's conduct against Hobbes's objections. Finally, I conclude the essay with a brief reflection on how London's imagination of Larsen contests Walter Benn Michaels's influential opinion that naturalist fiction, despite its dissenting intentions, tends to be "exemplary . . . not because it criticizes or endorses the culture of consumption but precisely because . . . it *exemplifies* that culture" (27). Although Larsen's behavior does indeed exemplify the liberal logic of economic behavior, the shocking manner of Larsen's complicity in liberalism belies Michaels's sense of benign neutrality.

MORAL NIHILISM AND ECONOMIC BEHAVIOR IN JACK LONDON'S *THE SEA-WOLF*

Let me begin by allowing London's Wolf Larsen to describe, or rather to assent to a description of, his nihilistic character. Larsen is the respondent in the following dialogue with the novel's first-person narrator, Humphrey Van Weyden:

> "Then you are an individualist, a materialist, and, logically, a hedonist."
> "Big words," he smiled. "But what is a hedonist?"
> He nodded agreement when I had given the definition.
> "And you are also," I continued, "a man one could not trust in the least thing where it was possible for a selfish interest to intervene?"
> "Now you're beginning to understand," he said, brightening.
> "You are a man utterly without what the world calls morals?"
> "That's it."
> "A man of whom to be always afraid—"
> "That's the way to put it."
> "As one is afraid of a snake, or a tiger, or a shark?"
> "Now you know me," he said. "And you know me as I am generally known. Other men call me 'Wolf.'" (72)

It gets much worse. Larsen is described as possessing "a strength we are wont to associate with things primitive, with . . . the creatures we imagine our tree-dwelling prototypes to have been—a strength savage, ferocious, alive in itself, the essence of life in that it is the potency of motion" (29). This superior physical capacity is complemented by a "tremendous mental or spiritual strength" which seemed to "lay behind, sleeping in the depths of his being" (32). With respect to Larsen's extraordinary natural endowment, the narrator concludes that there is "no measuring, no determining of metes and bounds, nor neatly classifying in some pigeonhole with others of similar type" (33).

Though he possesses no formal education, Larsen is remarkably intelli-
gent. An articulate proponent of a philosophical materialism based in the
works of Charles Darwin and Herbert Spencer, Larsen is also an astute reader
of Shakespeare, Browning, Poe, Tennyson, and De Quincey. But while Larsen
"possessed intellect to an unusual degree," we are reminded that "it was
directed solely to the exercise of his savage instincts and made him but the
more formidable a savage" (166). For example, Larsen's understanding of
Spencer and Darwin, enhanced by a harsh career at sea, issues in the austere
conviction that the "big eat the little that they may continue to move, the
strong eat the weak that they may retain their strength. The lucky eat the most
and move the longest, that is all" (52). Larsen's Malthusian view of nature's
economy regards "living [as] merely successful piggishness" (65):

> "Why, if there is anything in supply and demand, life is the cheap-
> est thing in the world. There is only so much water, so much earth,
> so much air; but the life that is demanding to be born is limitless.
> . . . Life? Bah! It has no value. Of cheap things it is the cheapest.
> . . . Where there is room for one life, she [nature] sows a thousand
> lives, and it's life eats life till the strongest and most piggish life
> is left." (64)

The value of human life being no exception to this rule, Larsen responds to
the prospect of a crew member's plunge from the ship's rigging by observing
that "[h]ad he fallen and dripped his brains upon the deck like honey from
the comb, there would have been no loss to the world. He was worth nothing
to the world. The supply is too large" (65). In light of such views, it is hardly
surprising that Larsen assigns himself the following 'utility' value:

> "This body was made for use. These muscles were made to grip,
> and tear, and destroy living things that get between me and life. . . .
> I out-grip them, out-tear them, out-destroy them. Purpose does
> not explain that. Utility does . . . Stability, equilibrium . . . Feet
> with which to clutch the ground, legs to stand on and to help with-
> stand, while with arms and hands, teeth and nails, I struggle to kill
> and not be killed. Purpose? Utility is the better word." (117)

The sheer magnitude of Larsen's person, sublime in its excessive physical and
mental force, accentuates his standing as "an individualist of the most pronounced type" (69). As the narrator observes, Larsen's "tremendous virility
and mental strength wall him apart" (69); his fellow seafarers are "more like

children to him . . . and as children he treats them, descending perforce to their level and playing with them as a man plays with puppies" (69).

Wolf Larsen is, in other words, the epitome of Richard Miller's moral nihilist: an individual possessed of extraordinary physical and mental capabilities who, consequently endowed with superior powers of self-protection, appears capable of maximizing satisfaction of whatever preferences he might have (see endnote 2). Larsen is himself aware of this superior natural endowment as expressed in his desire to remain "true to the promptings of the life that is in me" (122). In fact, Larsen's commitment to maximizing satisfaction of his excessive 'life-force' informs his rejection of moral conduct insofar as constraining his behavior would, as he puts it, "wrong . . . the life that is in me" (72). As Larsen sees it,

> "With immortality before me, altruism would be a paying business proposition. I might elevate my soul to all kinds of altitudes. But with nothing eternal before me but death, given for a brief spell this yeasty crawling and squirming which is called life, why, it would be immoral for me to perform any act that was a sacrifice. Any sacrifice that makes me lose one crawl or squirm is foolish— and not only foolish, for it is a wrong against myself and a wicked thing. I must not lose one crawl or squirm if I am to get the most out of the ferment." (73–74)

This passage exposes the novel's narrator as unreliable, indeed wrong, in his understanding of Larsen as a "magnificent atavism, a man so purely primitive that he was of the type that came into the world before the development of the moral nature" (85). On the contrary, Larsen, far from being "unmoral" (85), would appear to be an ethical egoist in the sense suggested by Nietzsche in *On the Genealogy of Morals*. For Larsen, as for Nietzsche, the problem with morality is that it "demand[s] of strength that it should not express itself as strength, that it should not be a desire to overcome, a desire to throw down, a desire to become master, a thirst for enemies and resistances and triumphs" (Nietzsche 45). From Larsen's perspective, it is wrong of morality to demand that he constrain his actions since stifling his "prerogative of roaring" (96) violates the essence of who he is. "One man cannot wrong another man," Larsen remarks; "[h]e can only wrong himself. As I see it, I do wrong always when I consider the interests of others" (72).

While Larsen's ethical egoism is questionable, he might have justified his beliefs and behavior according to the economic logic of preference maximization. Larsen could argue that insofar as moral behavior would impede maximization of his desires and interests, it would be irrational for him to act morally. We must suppose that Larsen's character is likely to manifest itself in extreme preferences, and that satisfaction of these preferences will require actions dedicated to bringing about extreme states of affairs. Acknowledging this possibility, however, obliges us also to recognize that the cooperative arrangements of market society actually *prohibit* Larsen's efforts to realize his authentic self. That is, it would be irrational for Larsen to engage in either cooperative or moral behavior precisely because in so doing he would fail to maximize satisfaction of those special desires and powers which constitute his authentic self. Indeed, Larsen must *deliberately destroy* the conditions of economic cooperation precisely in order to create those circumstances most conducive to maximizing satisfaction of his superior natural endowment. In destroying market society, Larsen acts rationally insofar as his actions have (for him) the positive consequence of bringing about a 'state of nature' enabling maximum satisfaction of his preferences. And since Larsen's society-destroying behavior is profoundly immoral, we come to the conclusion that Larsen *ought to act immorally in order to act rationally.* It is only by destroying the cooperative structure of market society that Larsen can bring about a state of affairs enabling optimal satisfaction of his extraordinary natural endowment, thereby fulfilling his desire to remain "true to the promptings of the life that is in me" (122).

To illuminate further the disturbing prospect of Larsen's immoral reasonableness, we need to consider Larsen's actions in terms of the 'choice situation' he confronts. While I have focused thus far on the sublime dimensions of Larsen's character, we must also take into account his economic role as captain of a hunting schooner bound for the seal-rich waters of the Bering Sea. As captain, Larsen is the coordinating authority for a division of labor—boat-steerers, boat-pullers (rowers), seal hunters, and deep-water sailors—whose collective economic success depends entirely on cooperative interaction. Since no individual can possibly fulfill all the functions required for success in such an enterprise, the success of each person is inextricably linked to the success of the group. As David Gauthier has remarked, we should think of the hunt as "participation in a co-operative activity . . . in which each huntsman has his particular role co-ordinated with that of the others, as the implementation of a single joint strategy" (*Morals* 166). As was suggested above, however, cooperation is a self-defeating choice for Larsen insofar as it obliges him to renounce satisfaction of his extraordinary powers. Larsen, in order to maximize satisfaction of these powers, requires the challenge of extreme experiences equal to his excessive character. To illustrate this point, consider Larsen's response to the onset of a particularly nasty gale:

> His face was stern, the lines of it had grown hard, and yet in his eyes—blue, clear blue this day—there was a strange brilliancy, a bright scintillating light. It struck me that he was joyous, in a ferocious sort of way; that he was glad there was an impending struggle; that he was thrilled and upborne with knowledge that one of the great moments of living, when the tide of life surges up in flood, was upon him. (127)

Such experiences "seemed the breath of his [Larsen's] nostrils, this carrying of life in his hands and struggling for it against tremendous odds" (138). These are the truly high times in Larsen's life, and it is only at such times that he is able to fulfill his extraordinary natural endowment.

Of course, the problem with natural phenomena such as gales is that Larsen has no causal control over their occurrence. Consequently, Larsen is confronted with a serious maximization problem insofar as the extreme circumstances conducive to optimal satisfaction of his preferences rarely occur. The pressing question for Larsen is this: how might he conduct himself so as to insure the *regular* occurrence of those circumstances conducive to maximizing satisfaction of his preference for violent struggle? A poor choice of action would be to maintain the economic structure of his environment as a cooperative endeavor for mutual gain. It would be irrational for Larsen to choose a cooperative strategy which has the consequence of minimizing satisfaction of his preferences or of impeding his desire to be true to the capacities of his authentic self. Moreover, if we invoke with David Gauthier the "traditional conception of morality as a rational constraint on the pursuit of individual interest" (*Morals* 2), we can only conclude that it would be irrational for Larsen to act morally. If morality is essentially about constraining one's behavior, and if constraining one's behavior is precisely what *does not* maximize self-interest, then one is rationally required to forgo moral behavior. Larsen does not choose morally, but in failing to choose morally he does choose rationally, for it is only by destroying the cooperative (market) structure of his environment that Larsen can regularize occurrence of those extreme circumstances conducive to ongoing satisfaction of his preference for violent struggle.

In effect, Larsen's actions transform a cooperative or civil environment into a Hobbesian 'state of nature' in which he can repeatedly maximize satisfaction of his preference for violent conflict. As no commentary can possibly do descriptive justice to the sundry brutalities perpetrated by Larsen, suffice it to say, in the terms of another of London's novels, that the "measure of [life] was the carnivorous ferocity displayed in injuring and marring fellow-creatures' anatomies" (*Martin Eden* 793). Traumatized by the spectacle of Larsen's ceaseless abuse of his crew, the narrator can only remark that "[a]s for myself, I was oppressed with nightmare. . . . Brutality had followed brutality, and flaming passions and cold-blooded cruelty had driven men to seek one another's lives, and to strive to hurt, and maim, and destroy" (101). Larsen is explicitly identified as the "cause" of this "carnival of brutality" (93), and many of the crew reciprocate Larsen's acts of violence. But reciprocation in kind is what Larsen most desires, since it is precisely in the extremities of violent struggle that he optimizes satisfaction of his extraordinary physical and mental force. One opponent in particular, the Irishman Leach, gains Larsen's admiration by raising the struggle to an especially gratifying level. As Larsen explains,

> "It gives a thrill to life . . . when life is carried in one's hand. Man is a natural gambler, and life is the biggest stake he can lay. The greater the odds, the greater the thrill. Why should I deny myself the joy of exciting Leach's soul to fever-pitch? For that matter, I do him a kindness. The greatness of sensation is mutual. . . . Really . . . he is living deep and high. I doubt that he has ever lived so swiftly and keenly before, and I honestly envy him, sometimes, when I see him raging at the summit of passion and sensibility." (121)

In terms similar to those elicited by his struggle with the forces of nonhuman nature, Larsen revels in the sublime satisfactions of mortal combat with other human beings. But whereas Larsen is unable to regulate the occurrence of gales, he can, by acting immorally, determine the frequency of violent struggle in his immediate environment. As a point of strategic preference maximization, Larsen dedicates himself to insuring that his fellow seafarers "never had a moment's rest or peace[:] . . . morning, noon and night, and all night . . . he devoted himself to making life unlivable for them" (119–20). Through ceaseless perpetration of all manner of psychological and physical abuse, Larsen causes the emergence of a 'state of nature' which facilitates everyday maximization of his special desires and powers. Such conduct is profoundly immoral, but given the special nature of Larsen's preferences his behavior seems entirely rational.

HOBBES VERSUS NIETZSCHE: REASON, AUTHENTICITY, AND SELF-PRESERVATION

As is well known, Thomas Hobbes's *Leviathan* is centrally concerned with how the institutions of civil society, based largely on contractual agreement, emerge from a hypothetical 'state of nature' in which material scarcity prompts "a condition of warre of every one against every one" (189). Approached atomistically, the central problem is to explain how (in David Gauthier's terms) a ruthlessly egoistic 'straightforward' maximizer acting in a state of nature metamorphoses into that 'constrained' maximizer whose mode of interaction expresses the cooperative commercial norms of civil society. Hobbes's own explanation of this dispositional transition derives from the tension between the 'Right of Nature,' which acknowledges the individual's unlimited "Right to everything; even to one anothers body" (190), and the first 'Law of Nature,' which is "a Precept, or generall Rule, found out by Reason, by which a man is forbidden to do, that, which is destructive of his life, or taketh away the means of preserving the same, and to omit, that, by which he thinketh it may be best preserved" (189). Thus, while Hobbes assumes an essentially nonmoral self who reasons that since "all the voluntary actions of men tend to the benefit of themselves . . . those actions are most Reasonable, that conduce most to their ends" (204), he also places an internal rational constraint (self-preservation) on the egoist's maximizing behavior.

In the Hobbesian view, a 'constrained' maximizer is predisposed to maximize satisfaction of only those preferences which, upon reflection as to future outcomes or consequences, will not compromise the fundamental concern for self-preservation. One obeys the first Law of Nature by prudently refraining from maximizing satisfaction of those preferences which run "against the reason of [one's] own preservation" (205). For "when a man doth a thing, which . . . tendeth to his own destruction, howsoever some accident which he could not expect, arriving may turne it to his benefit; yet such events [still] do not make it reasonably or wisely done" (204).[3] Hobbes's seminal point, preserved in Locke's liberalism, is that an agent's preference maximizing behavior is rational insofar as it does not imperil his physical well-being. However, when Hobbes considers those persons who "taking pleasure in contemplating their own power in the acts of conquest . . . pursue [it] farther than their security requires" (185), what prevents us from maintaining that such persons qualify as rational if maximizing satisfaction of their power of conquest overrides fear of personal injury and death? Perhaps *not* being able to maximize satisfaction of one's desire for power and dominion is, for certain persons, a fate worse than death. Indeed, the example of Wolf Larsen places considerable strain on Hobbes's claims for the binding power of self-preservation as an internal constraint on maximizing behavior.

Although Larsen pays little heed to the conflicting demand of the 'Law of Nature' as a sufficient constraint on the unlimited exercise of his 'Right of Nature,' he sometimes does acknowledge self-preservation as a strong internal constraint on his own "piggish" behavior. Consider Larsen's interpretive gloss on the maxim, observed by the preacher in Ecclesiastes, that "a living dog is better than a dead lion":

> "He [the Preacher] preferred the vanity and vexation to the silence and unmovableness of the grave. And so I. To crawl is piggish; but not to crawl, to be as the clod and rock, is loathsome to contemplate. It is loathsome to the life that is in me, the very essence of which is movement, the power of movement, and the consciousness of the power of movement. Life itself is unsatisfaction, but to look ahead to death is greater unsatisfaction." (91)

But if Larsen's overriding interest is indeed self-preservation, why does he act in a way that can only contribute to premature cessation of his "power of movement"? Under pressure of this Hobbesian question, Larsen's actions appear to be irrational. However, we must keep in mind that the immense satisfaction Larsen derives from confronting and causing extreme situations is intimately linked to Nietzschean questions of authenticity or truth to oneself. Clearly, Larsen's actions demonstrate an overriding preference in favor of maximizing his will to authenticity.[4] What Hobbes describes as "taking pleasure in contemplating [one's] own power in . . . acts of conquest" (185) ultimately overrides Larsen's desire to avoid bodily harm. While Larsen finds death "loathsome to contemplate" (91), the pleasure of "carrying his life in his own hands and struggling against tremendous odds" finally outweighs his fear of death (138). In Larsen's view, it is better to be a dead lion than a lion who, subordinating his true nature to a cowardly concern for mere physiological persistence, compromises his authentic being as 'king of the jungle.'

That Larsen might prefer to maximize satisfaction of who he is precisely by hazarding his own life is, for Hobbes, simply unimaginable. And yet, it is precisely the market logic of preference maximization that recommends the rationality of those persons who, like Wolf Larsen, prefer to realize their authenticity through acts of violence, even at the ultimate expense of their own lives. The Hobbesian injunction to preserve one's body at all costs is finally too narrow, for what if accommodating present circumstances simply to ensure bodily survival requires sacrifice of one's psychological sense of integrity or authenticity? For some persons, a concern for physical well-being is simply too weak a constraint on preference maximization, especially if preserving a cherished self-image overrides concern about continued physiological existence. As long as there are fates worse than death, self-preservation in the Hobbesian sense of mere organic persistence *does not* provide a sufficiently strong brake on the runaway logic of preference maximization. If preservation of one's body provides the only reason for why moral nihilists like Wolf Larsen should constrain their behavior, then perhaps we should look to other perspectives on economic reasoning for a possible critique of the moral nihilist.

WOLF LARSEN AND THE QUESTION OF DISSENT IN NATURALIST FICTION

As a singular instance of London's naturalistic conception of selfhood, Wolf Larsen seriously challenges Walter Benn Michaels's claim that representations of agency in naturalist fiction do "not exist in opposition to the marketplace but are produced and contained within it" (112). While I agree with Michaels that the marketplace produces Wolf Larsen's subjectivity, it is wrong to conclude that his dissent from market society is therefore contained or defused. Larsen's dissent evokes the "primal scene of Liberalism" as the state of nature (Wolfe 125), but Michaels's understanding of liberalism refuses to go deeper than the bourgeois civil order of private property and cooperative economic enterprise. Michaels's attenuated sense of the term "Lockean" limits liberalism to the "relentlessly bourgeois . . . story of the origin of property and, by the same token, of the origin of self" (10) when, in both Hobbes and Locke, the liberal self emerges in the state of nature *prior to* the origin of property. What Larsen's behavior restores to view is market society's origin in the state of nature, that nasty and brutish condition of egoistic warfare upon which the liberal economic order supervenes. Michaels's restriction of liberalism to the civil order of private property, corporations, and financial speculation elides the state of nature, a glaring omission given Michaels's interest in the logic and language of liberal economics. That the state of nature is an essential component of classical liberal thought is indisputable, but not a trace of this notion appears in Michaels's work.[5]

By contrast, Wolf Larsen is fluent in the language of the state of nature, and herein lies his radical dissent from market society. As explained at length in my interpretation of *The Sea-Wolf*, Larsen turns the liberal logic of preference maximization against itself, and thus against the market order it sustains, by returning this logic to its violent origins in the state of nature. Larsen's behavior recovers the genuine ground of dissent by setting preference maximization in the service of Nietzschean authenticity against the liberal belief that reason and cooperative economic conduct necessarily converge. Brutally corrosive of the liberal economic order, Larsen's actions occasion the *devolution* of market society toward its origins in the bloody conflict of 'each against all.' That Larsen's dissent is *internal* to market society is true insofar as the state of nature is germane to this society's self-understanding as elaborated in the thought of Hobbes and Locke. In Michaels's account of market society, however, the "state of nature has been forgotten or sanitized" (Mansfield xvi) and rational self-interest, initially a "recommendation of ferocious aggrandizement" (xxiv), is dissolved into a benign logic of complicity. It is London's Wolf Larsen who recovers those "violent movements of business" (Michaels 100) which, revealing the origin of liberal selfhood in the state of nature, reassert the dissenting force of naturalist fiction.

NOTES

1. According to this liberal view of economic agency, individuals typically seek to 'optimize' or 'maximize' satisfaction of their interests or 'preferences' by constraining their behavior—what is commonly called 'cooperation with others'—out of due regard for their own preservation or well-being. Cooperative behavior among individuals can and does evolve into more altruistic or 'other-regarding' forms of interaction, but for sober liberals like Hobbes and Locke this is hardly characteristic. Individuals engaged competitively in free-enterprise circumstances are essentially selfish or possessive, and will constrain their maximizing behavior only because the rational imperative of self-preservation requires it. Self-preservation is the liberal individual's overriding concern, and the effort to maximize satisfaction of a particular preference is rational only if it adequately secures an agent against significant harm. For a sufficiently detailed account of liberal notions of economic behavior, see David Gauthier, *Morals By Agreement* (Oxford: Clarendon, 1986); and also *Moral Dealing: Contract, Ethics, and Reason* (Ithaca: Cornell UP, 1990).

2. My sense of the disturbing convergence—embodied in London's portrait of Wolf Larsen—between liberal ideas of rational economic agency and moral nihilism derives in large measure from Richard W. Miller's recent work in moral philosophy. Miller describes the moral nihilist as a person "whose attitude of radical unconcern for others" (18) is *rational* if "three conditions are met. The choice would be to his own advantage. He does not care about its harmful effects on others, although these effects make it wrong. And his not caring is not unreasonable" (314). Possessed of "special desires and powers," the moral nihilist is "someone [who] greatly enjoys some activities requiring harm to others and [who] has sufficient self-protective power to forgo cooperation beyond a limited circle of potential allies" (94). Thus, given his superior self-protective power and the consequent likelihood of

consolidating personal advantage, the moral nihilist's harmful actions, although profoundly immoral, are nonetheless rational. Miller concludes that the possibility of such rational wrongdoers places a weighty "burden of proof on anyone who thinks that zero-degree of concern for people as such is incompatible with rationality" (92). Miller's emphasis on "advantage" and "self-protective power" clearly links the moral nihilist's behavior to liberal notions of preference maximization and self-preservation, and thus to core liberal assumptions about rational agency. Essentially, the moral nihilist challenges liberal faith in the convergence of rational and moral conduct by his extreme adherence to the liberal logic of preference maximization. Such is precisely the disposition, in my view, of London's Wolf Larsen. See Richard W. Miller, *Moral Differences* (Princeton: Princeton UP, 1992).

3. For relevant discussions of Hobbes's moral philosophy, see Gauthier, *Moral Dealing,* 11–23; Greg Baumgart, "Ethics and Its Amoral Justification in Hobbes," *Ratio* 23 (1981): 47–62; and Gregory Kavka, *Hobbesian Moral and Political Philosophy* (Princeton: Princeton UP, 1986).

4. In *The Will to Power,* Nietzsche suggests a notion of personal authenticity that overrides the desire to preserve oneself. Based on the premise that life "strives after a maximal feeling of power," an "accumulation of force," Nietzsche concludes that "nothing wants to preserve itself, everything wants to be added and accumulated" (368). Thus, it "can be shown most clearly that every living thing does everything it can not to preserve itself but to become more" (367). See Friedrich Nietzsche, *The Will to Power,* trans. Walter Kaufmann and R. J. Hollingdale (New York: Vintage, 1968). For an important general account of authenticity as the primary "hypergood" of modernism, see Charles Taylor, *The Malaise of Modernity* (Toronto: Anansi, 1992).

5. The weaknesses in Michaels's understanding of liberalism are also apparent in a brief aside on the extraordinary conduct of Herman Melville's Bartleby. In reply to Brook Thomas's claim that Bartleby's famous 'I prefer not to' subverts the liberal (Lockean) ideology of contract, Michaels objects that "[e]ven Bartleby-like refusals of the world remain inextricably linked to it—what could count as a more powerful exercise of the right to freedom of contract than Bartleby's successful refusal to enter into any contracts?" (19). What Michaels neglects to consider here is that Bartleby's exercise of his *right* to freedom of contract dissents radically from the fundamental *law* of possessive conduct as formulated by both Hobbes and Locke. This fundamental law holds that an agent's exercise of his or her right to freedom is *rational*—and thus convergent with the enlightened disposition of liberal economics —only if it conduces to the agent's physical well-being. From this Hobbesian-Lockean perspective, what Michaels calls Bartleby's "successful" (19) exercise of freedom of contract is actually a dismal failure of rationality insofar as his persistent 'I prefer not to' conduces to his own death. Relations of contract assume the uncoerced agreement of individuals seeking to preserve themselves through cooperative enterprise, and although Bartleby's refusal of this relation is indeed an exercise of freedom, the fact that this choice is self-destroying violates the fundamental premise of contract: the rational desire to preserve oneself.

Also, given Michaels's pointed criticism of external or 'transcending' notions of opposition, it is important to note that Bartleby's dissent from market relations *does not* presume his transcendence of them. On the contrary, Bartleby's conduct enacts an immanent critique of market society by opposing one fundamental tenet of the logic of consumption (the right to freedom of contract) to another fundamental tenet (the law of self-preservation). Bartleby's endorsement of this logic demands that he constrain his right of freedom in deference to the more fundamental concern for self-preservation, but this is precisely what—in the audacity of his dissent—he prefers not to do. Whether Bartleby is reflexively aware of the antagonism between right and law, and thus of the nature of his dissent, is really beside the point. Bartleby (much like Wolf Larsen) simply enacts this antagonism as the constitutive substance of his person and in so doing reveals a disturbing contradiction of interests internal to the behavioral logic of liberal society. Dissent does not necessitate, as Michaels would have us believe, an assumed Archimedean standpoint beyond market structures.

WORKS CITED

Bercovitch, Sacvan. *The Rites of Assent*. New York: Routledge, 1993.

Gauthier, David. *Moral Dealing: Contract, Ethics, and Reason*. Ithaca: Cornell UP, 1990.

——. *Morals By Agreement*. Oxford: Clarendon, 1986.

Hobbes, Thomas. *Leviathan*. 1651. Ed. C. B. MacPherson. Harmondsworth, England: Penguin, 1985.

Jehlen, Myra. *American Incarnation*. Cambridge: Harvard UP, 1986.

London, Jack. *Martin Eden*. New York: Library of America, 1988.

——. *The Sea-Wolf and Other Stories*. 1904. Harmondsworth, England: Penguin, 1989.

Mansfield, Harvey C. *Taming the Prince: The Ambivalence of Modern Executive Power*. Baltimore: Johns Hopkins UP, 1993.

Michaels, Walter Benn. *The Gold Standard and the Logic of Naturalism*. Berkeley: U of California P, 1987.

Miller, Richard W. *Moral Differences*. Princeton: Princeton UP, 1992.

Nietzsche, Friedrich. *On the Genealogy of Morals*. Trans. Walter Kaufmann and R. J. Hollingdale. New York: Vintage, 1989.

——. *The Will to Power*. Trans. Walter Kaufmann and R. J. Hollingdale. New York: Vintage, 1968.

Patell, Cyrus R. K. *Negative Liberties: Morrison, Pynchon, and the Problem of Liberal Ideology*. Durham: Duke UP, 2001.

Pease, Donald. "National Identities, Postmodern Artifacts, and Postnational Narratives." *boundary 2* 19.1 (1992): 1–12.

Trachtenberg, Alan. Foreword. *Beloved Community*. By Casey Nelson Blake. Chapel Hill: U of North Carolina P, 1990.

Trilling, Lionel. *The Liberal Imagination*. New York: Viking, 1950.

Wolfe, Cary. "Antinomies of Liberalism: The Politics of 'Belief' and the Project of Americanist Criticism." *Discovering Difference: Contemporary Essays in American Culture*. Ed. Christopher K. Lohman. Bloomington: Indiana UP, 1993. 123–46.

Highbrow/Lowbrow

NATURALIST WRITERS AND
THE "READING HABIT"

—*Barbara Hochman*

> Miss Stepney was not sufficiently familiar with the classic drama
> to have recalled in advance how bearers of bad tidings are prover-
> bially received.
>
> —*The House of Mirth*

TOWARD THE END OF THE NINETEENTH CENTURY, THE PROLIFERATION OF BOOKS AND READERS BECAME A MAJOR TOPIC OF DISCUSSION IN AMERI-can journals, newspapers, and elsewhere. Publishers, editors, reviewers and educators celebrated what they perceived as an unprecedented growth in the reading population. As Walter Besant put it, addressing the "Congress of Authors" in 1893, "A writer of importance in our language may address an audience drawn from a hundred millions of English-speaking people . . . [;] never before in the history of the world has there been such an audience" ("Congress of Authors" 29). Henry James struck a similar note in his essay on "The Future of the Novel": "The book, in the Anglo-Saxon world, is almost everywhere," he wrote (336). Others saw the reading explosion as a specifically American phenomenon. According to Frank Norris, "there [were] more books read in the United States in one year than in any other country of the globe in the same space of time" ("American Public" 126).

The vision of a mounting flood of books and readers triggered many questions about how and what to read. Reviews and literary essays encouraged cultivation of the "reading habit," stressing the benefits to be gained by devoting "even five minutes a day" to reading books (Richardson 45, 46).[1] Reading was celebrated as a boon to the individual and the nation. Some commentators saw the reading habit as a good thing in itself and emphasized that any and all reading was valuable. "Better bad books than no books," as Frank Norris put it ("American Public" 127). Other commentators, however, viewed the flood of printed matter with suspicion. Many stressed the importance of selectivity, urging that books must be "well-chosen" and properly read. Too many books and indiscriminate reading practices might pose a threat to tradition and what Edith Wharton called "the integrity of letters" ("Vice" 518).

All such discussions relied upon some image of the reader and the reading public as well as an idea of how "Literature" was being read—and should be read. This essay will suggest that many images of reading, projected in reviews and literary essays of the period, dovetail with related images in realist and naturalist fiction. Crane, Norris, Wharton and others took careful note of cultural debates about the "reading habit" and the growth of the reading public; they also knew that the cultural capital invested in a restricted group of "well-chosen" great books was on the rise. I will be focusing on two ways in which novelists engaged these issues within their work. Through intertextual references and scenes of reading, naturalist writers attempted to consolidate their own positions not only in a literary marketplace but also in a cultural hierarchy.

Naturalist writers entered a hotly contested literary "field" in which editors, reviewers, and educators debated what was to count as "Literature" and tried to shape contemporary reading practices.[2] *The Octopus* and *The House of Mirth* are rarely linked together in discussions of late-nineteenth- and early-twentieth-century fiction, but they provide illuminating evidence of the interplay between fiction and other sorts of literary discourse at the turn of the century. Edith Wharton and Frank Norris published their first fictional works contemporaneously, just when commentators were debating the pros and cons of the reading habit and, in the process, establishing a canon of "the best books." By tracing scenes of reading in the work of Norris, Wharton, and others, we can create a useful perspective on the way naturalism positioned itself in American literary culture.

Naturalist writers competed with historical romance and sentimental fiction in the literary marketplace, but they competed with a poetic and classical tradition for an enduring place in the literary pantheon. Intertextual references and scenes of reading in naturalist texts suggest that by invoking the ancient classics, on the one hand, and nineteenth-century "classics," on the other,[3] novelists of the period mapped out a set of coordinates in the cultural field and adumbrated what Robert Darnton has called a "protocol" for reading literature (157). This protocol drew on contemporary assumptions about literary value and aimed to modify both the extravagant contemporary reverence for certain books and the relatively low cultural status occupied by the novel itself. Before turning to *The Octopus* and *House of Mirth,* it will be useful to look more closely at the way books—especially "great books"—were represented in literary discourse at the end of the nineteenth century.

In 1893 James Russell Lowell published an essay in *The Century* entitled "The Five Indispensable Authors." Lowell suggested that only Homer was truly "indispensable." Like other cultural commentators of the 1890s, Lowell took the literary sophistication of his readers for granted; he also celebrated certain "classics" as repositories of intellectual, moral, and cultural value. For Lowell, as for many others, classics were "gospels in the lay bible of the race" (223). In this context the cultural position of contemporary novelists was insignificant at best.

The habit of reading, especially the habit of reading "Literature," acquired a class-marked cachet at the turn of the century. In the much quoted words of John Ruskin, commentators asked, "Will you gossip with your housemaid or your stable boy, when you may talk with queens and kings . . . [,] the chosen and the mighty of every time and place?" ("Reading and Education" 102).[4] Reading certain books was repeatedly associated with access to select society—it was to hobnob with the "chosen and the mighty." In a sense, such formulations suggested that books would open castle doors to everyone. Yet the notion that books are better company than "your housemaid or your stable boy" immediately qualifies the potentially democratic message by suggesting that "the reader" belongs to a world of privilege to begin with. The "best" books were figured as superior companions, "kings and queens," or "great men who are not in a hurry."[5] Social snobbery informs numerous formulations about the way one's books, like one's friends, reflect one's character and social standing. The ancients, in particular, were represented as the precious possession of an elite.

For Lowell, the democratic potential of the revolution created by print was nothing to celebrate: "It may well be questioned," he wrote, "whether the invention of printing, while it democratized information, has not also leveled the ancient aristocracy of thought. . . . When men had few books they mastered those few; but now the multitude of books lord it over the man" (223). Paradoxically, however, the very notion of "Five Indispensable Authors" not only suggested that everyone should and even could read classics. ("Plato or Virgil is waiting to talk to me," in the words of another discussion ["Desultory Reading" 943].) It also reinforced the increasingly popular notion that a comfortably manageable "short list" of "the best books" would foster cultural, social, and economic success.

The easy availability of the classics in particular represented both promise and threat, depending on one's position in the cultural hierarchy. "I sit with

Shakespeare, and he winces not," W. E. B. Du Bois wrote in a famous passage of *The Souls of Black Folk*; "Across the color line, I move arm in arm with Balzac and Dumas. . . . I summon Aristotle, Aurelius, and what soul I will" (Du Bois 87).[6] Like many contemporary scenes of reading, this one associates certain authors with literary culture, imagined as a lofty height, a "high Pisgah" (87). But for Du Bois to read Aristotle and Shakespeare had explicit political implications: it was to cross the color line, where not only could one "summon" the greatest of Western poets but (in a common trope of the period) one could also dismiss them, by closing the book.[7] To imagine books as available to all was to offer every reader the benefits of "conversation" with "the chosen and the mighty." To suggest that a reader could dismiss such distinguished company with impunity was to go a step further: it was to question the dominant position of "the great." Du Bois's vision of universal access and individual preference ("I summon . . . what soul I will") implied power and a kind of freedom that created a particular problem for commentators who, like Lowell, were eager to preserve hierarchical distinctions in both literature and society.

The only novelist who appears in Lowell's group of indispensable authors is Cervantes, who was (as Lowell emphasizes) Shakespeare's contemporary. At the end of the century, the novel as a genre was still suffering from what Harold Bloom has called "belatedness." In the 1880s and nineties, to be sure, an increasing number of voices were raised on behalf of fiction as a serious and meaningful literary form. Still, novels were rarely taught in schools, nor were they generally found on "recommended" lists of the "best books," even those in popular manuals.[8] When novels did appear in such contexts, they were almost never realist or naturalist works. In this sense Du Bois's inclusion of Balzac and Dumas in his scene of reading was almost as radical as his reference to the color line.[9]

Insofar as classic writers were widely perceived as the *sine qua non* of "true" culture, they could become a stick with which to beat mass circulation newspapers and magazines, as well as popular literature, including novels. Yet many commentators were uncertain about the place and especially the future of the classics in the contemporary United States. For the majority of readers, one typical editorial suggested, "Homer, Virgil, Dante, Shakespeare and Milton are shelved classics," revered, perhaps, but unread ("Editor's Study" 152). How, then, was their value to be conceptualized? "A Booke is the pretious [*sic*] life-blood of a master spirit; stored up to a life beyond life." Milton's words were inscribed in the portal of the main reading room of the New York Public Library when it opened its doors in 1911. The inscription valorized the idea of certain authors as "master spirits"; it was also a monument to the enduring vitality of their books. But how alive were the "classics" in late-nineteenth-century America?

"Soon I shall become a classic," a well-established author says, in an early Wharton story: "Bound in sets and kept on the top shelf . . . brr, doesn't that sound freezing?" ("Copy" 113). To represent the classics as dead and cold was to imply that the contemporary novel was alive and vital. But to debunk the classics was neither to neutralize their cultural value nor to acquire their stature. In order to vie with the classics for the status of "literature," naturalist writers had first to display their own familiarity with privileged texts and traditional tropes. Crane's Henry Fleming is disappointed when his mother says nothing about the imperative of returning from battle either with his shield or on it. Norris's Presley wanders through the San Joaquin Valley with a copy of *The Odyssey* in his pocket. If Norris, like Crane, provides an ironic perspective on the ancient author in the modern context, both novelists believed that some of the cultural capital invested in Homer, Dante, and Shakespeare could be transferred to their own account. Shelved classics, one commentator proposed, could still contribute to the support of "a general culture" if used by "the present masters in literature" ("Editor's Study" 152).

As if taking this advice, many naturalist writers devised a strategy of allusion that had multiple functions. First of all, classical references could establish an author's credentials as what Edith Wharton called a "born reader" ("Vice" 513), on comfortable terms with the texts of the Western tradition. Second, recurrent allusions, especially transient and understated ones, could serve as a covert invitation to a select group of readers—those who could pick up and appreciate the reference. (Evoking both Shakespeare and Stendhal, Edith Wharton ends an early essay on contemporary reading practices by referring to "The Happy Few" ["Vice" 521]). Nonetheless, such allusions signaled exclusivity only up to a point: they would not prevent a novel like *The Octopus* or *The House of Mirth* from being accessible to many readers who missed the scattered references entirely. They might even have a certain snob appeal for yet another group of readers—those who recognized that something "higher" was being referred to, though they might not know exactly what. One of the most popular fictions in America toward the end of the century was *Trilby* by the British novelist George Du Maurier. This book, peppered not only with classical references but with Latin phrases and French passages, could not have been as popular as it was if it had been read only by those fully comfortable with French and Latin.

But allusions to the classics could do more than signal the cultural level of the author and possibly the reader. They could also expose as misguided some contemporary and culturally typical uses of "the ancients." When Presley reads Homer for poetic inspiration in *The Octopus,* Norris suggests that the poet (unlike the naturalist novelist) is out of touch with reality. Many of the ancient motifs in *House of Mirth* take the form of decorative artifacts—the helmeted Minerva on Mrs. Penniston's ormolu clock and the gilded goddesses on the Welly Brys' ceiling (113, 140). Such trivialization of classical images could set in relief the more sustained and pointed uses of classics within the same text.

As novelists, both Norris and Wharton reaped undeniable benefits from the expansion of the reading public. As commentators, however, they represent two opposed approaches to the idea of the book/reading explosion. Norris celebrated it and, as we have noted, he expressed his conviction that even the reading of "bad books" would be for the best. "Something very like . . . a renaissance [has occurred]," Norris wrote, "and . . . 70,000,000 [people] have all at once awakened to the fact that there are books to be read. As with all things sudden, there is noticeable with this awakening a lack of discrimination" ("American Public" 126–27). Representing the reading public as a "great animal, . . . a great [hungry] brute . . . [,] a pachyderm" who, "once aroused" is ready to "devour anything," Norris stressed that public taste would gradually improve—the creature would slowly but surely turn from the "hay and twigs" to the "new-mown grass and fruit trees" (126–27). It is easy to see traces of Norris's own sense of cultural superiority in his image of the reading public as a pachyderm (and the idea of an "aroused . . . brute" has devastating implications throughout Norris's work). Still, Norris emphasizes here that both democracy and literary culture would be served by giving the omnivorous creature free rein.

Wharton's condescension toward what she saw as the indiscriminate reading practices of an expanding public is more evident than Norris's and reflects her conviction that she is a member of "true culture" herself. In an article evocatively titled "The Vice of Reading" (1903), Wharton voiced her misgivings about "that 'diffusion of knowledge' commonly classed with steam heat and universal suffrage in the category of modern improvements" (513). Her particular disdain is reserved for the "mechanical" reader who attempts to cultivate the "reading habit" by "read[ing] for just so many hours a day" (515). This misguided soul succeeds only in becoming "the slave of his bookmark" (516). He is directly opposed to the "born reader" who has a spontaneous rather than a deliberate approach to books and who appreciates the pleasures of "intellectual vagrancy" (including the "improvised chase after a fleeting allusion" [516]). By emphasizing the difference between a "wrong" and a "right" way to read, and by stressing both education and natural inheritance, Wharton (like Lowell) expresses doubts about the proliferation of books and readers.

Both *The Octopus* and *House of Mirth* are in dialogue with Lowell and other cultural custodians who contributed to what Lawrence Levine has called the sacralization of culture at the turn of the century. Classical allusions in naturalist texts acknowledge the privileged position of "the ancients" in American culture, but they directly challenge the assumption that "great books" should be deferred to as powerful "masters." Through intertextual references and scenes of reading, both *The Octopus* and *The House of Mirth* suggest an approach to the classics that is quite different from their appropriation as revered but often unread cultural icons.

Indeed, both novels satirize the fetishization of the book—especially the old, rarified book and its association with sublime moments. Norris and Wharton set out to integrate Homer, Aeschylus, and others into contemporary culture by asserting their right to recast classic texts within their own. At the same time, classical allusions bolster the novel's claim to a legitimate place in a more diversified tradition of literary culture than the one imagined by Lowell and others. Finally, as we shall see, in *The Octopus* as in *House of Mirth,* nineteenth-century European realism becomes a counterpoint to the ancients and part of an argument for an evolving, vigorous, hybrid tradition, rather than a pure and "aristocratic" literary line.

Norris repeatedly invokes Homer—both *The Iliad* and *The Odyssey*—as an image of value set in contrast to the spectacular and the commercial aspects of American culture: "The young Greeks sat on marble terraces overlooking the Aegean Sea and listened to the thunderous roll of Homer's hexameter," Norris writes; "But the youth of the United States learn of their epic by paying a dollar to see [Buffalo Bill's] Wild West Show" ("Neglected Epic" 120). There may be nostalgia for a lost oral tradition here, but Norris (unlike Presley in *The Octopus*) does not simply yearn for the heroism and romance of the past. Using the image of Homer to stress continuity rather than disjuncture, Norris designated the epic poet as the forebear of the contemporary fiction-writer.[10]

In "The Responsibilities of the Novelist," Norris describes the novel as an "all-powerful . . . instrument" for the "expression of modern life" (95) and associates it with another powerful "instrument"—Odysseus's bow. The modern novelist, Norris asserts, is the "favored one . . . into whose hands the gods have placed the great bow of Ulysses" (96). To elaborate the idea of this lineage, Norris invokes the same scene of *The Odyssey* that Presley reads in the first chapter of *The Octopus*: Drawing "his little tree-calf edition [of Homer] from the pocket of his shooting coat" (38), Presley immerses himself in the text and seems to derive spiritual sustenance and poetic inspiration.

Don Graham has suggested that Norris took Homer's poetic achievement as a kind of baseline for art drawn from nature: Presley's "aesthetic fails" because it is "derivative" (74). In this scheme of contrasts, the Homeric epic is allied with "real life," along the lines of Norris's well-known cry: "We don't want Literature, we want life" ("Opening" 30). While Norris surely identified Homer with nature and vitality, this association was not the only source of Homer's "power" for Norris. In late-nineteenth-century America a struggle was on to define what Homer represented and which writers (or readers) could claim the epic poet as their own.

Norris repeatedly invokes Homer in the first chapter of *The Octopus,* and throughout the novel he employs Homeric motifs, Homeric similes, and scenes of feasting, games, and battle. I suggest that by doing so, Norris lays claim not only to "nature" and primordial "life" but to culture. Like Lowell and others, Norris associated Homer with "true" literature. If Homer's position as a cultural icon could be used to discredit the novel, it also made him a significant resource in the battle for realism and naturalism.

The first chapter of *The Octopus* can be read as a meditation on the place of the novel in late-nineteenth-century America and as a protocol for reading *The Octopus* itself. The three central "heroes" of the novel, introduced in this opening chapter, are rather anomalous for a "naturalist" work. All are college graduates; two are poets (though Presley is only a "poet by training" [32]). In a sense, the third young man—Annixter—is the one most fit for the role of a hero. Like "headstrong Achilles" upon whom he is in some sense modeled (Lutwack 27–28; Machor 48), Annixter dies young, and violently. What repays closer attention in the present context, however, are Annixter's reading practices.

Annixter has "a deep respect [for] the man who could rhyme words," and therefore he has "great admiration" for Presley. Annixter believes "it [takes] brains to grind out a poem. It wasn't everyone who could rhyme 'brave' and 'glaive,' and make sense out of it" (25). Of course Annixter himself doesn't actually read poetry; in fact, he thinks there is "not much use in [it]" (25). But this only confirms his sense that poetry inhabits a higher realm. If not "everyone" can produce poetry, and not everyone can read it either, this is all the more proof that it must be an exalted form.

While Annixter believes that poetry is "high" literature, his preferred medium, like Norris's, is the novel. Throughout *The Octopus* Annixter reads (and rereads) *David Copperfield*. In fact, he thinks Dickens is the only novelist worth reading: "Everything else was a lot of lies" (25). Whether studying law or reading fiction, Annixter reads from the gut, "devouring, digesting" (25) (generally accompanied by a bag of prunes). Annixter is something of a comic figure, but his reading practices are instinctive and vital. Certain aspects of Norris's own style, moreover, reconfirm Annixter's taste for Dickens in particular. Dickens's poetics, as well as Homer's, are recalled and recast in Norris's use of "epic epithets," his habit of associating descriptive phrases with particular characters and repeating them verbatim each time the character appears.[11]

The figure of Annixter raises the question of what literature one should read and how to read it. Norris implicitly answers this question with the imperative to read nineteenth-century novels, and to read them intensively, for reality and "truth." If this formulation is a cliché of the realist and naturalist aesthetic, it gains resonance when we look more closely at the contrast between Annixter and Presley as readers. In the climactic moment of chapter 1, Presley seems to transcend himself and his surroundings by reading Homer. As Don Graham has shown, Presley's experience in this episode is elaborated through an array of intertextual echoes (68–75). By adding Keats's poem "On First Looking into Chapman's Homer" to the allusions in the scene, we uncover another facet of Norris's concern with modes of reading, and with the classics in particular.

Keats's poem links the experience of reading to a journey in "the realms of gold" (line 1). The climax of this "journey" is compared to the moment when Cortez "star'd at the Pacific—and all his men / Look'd at each other with a wild surmise— / Silent, upon a peak in Darien" (lines 11–14). For Presley, too, reading Homer is linked to a vision of new vistas and experienced on a hilltop: "As from a pinnacle, Presley, from where he now stood dominated the entire country" (38). What he sees, moreover, might be aptly described as "realms of gold": "Everything . . . was overlaid with a sheen of gold . . . swimming in a golden mist" (38). Under the influence of this vision, Presley is "drunk with the intoxication of mere immensity" (39). But just when Presley believes he is about to "grasp" the "inspiration" for "his epic" (39–40), the speeding passenger engine appears, and in one of the best-known scenes of *The Octopus*, "the iron monster" plows its way through a herd of sheep, creating a "slaughter, a massacre of the innocents" (41). This scene has often been read as an ironic exposure of Presley's poetic aspirations, and it surely has that effect. At the same time, the scene directly pits two ways of reading Homer against each other: Presley's and Norris's.

The locomotive shoots by Presley "with a roar . . . vomiting smoke and sparks; its enormous eye, cyclopean red, throwing a glare far in advance" (41).

The Cyclops is itself a Homeric image, one that refers the informed reader to the Cyclops episode of *The Odyssey* in which another implacable monster destroys sheep and vulnerable men. Norris's allusion, moreover, is reemphasized in the chapter's closing lines, when Presley again sees "the galloping monster . . . in his imagination . . . but [sees] it now as the symbol of a vast power" (42). The Homeric motif here represents power clearly enough, but this is not only the power of economic forces, machine culture, and social reality; it is also the power of literary tradition. Norris thus acknowledges Homer's influential cultural status while demonstrating his own mode of reading.

The incorporation of Homeric elements into *The Octopus* reflects Norris's respect for the cultural capital invested in the epic poet; Norris knew that "Homer" was a name to conjure with. But Norris did not see Homer as either an unapproachable idol or a source of "poetic inspiration"—and certainly not as a "shelved" classic. He believed that the classics and the turn-of-century novel could actively serve one another. They could only do so, however, if the ancients were approached with the kind of freedom which, according to Lawrence Levine, had characterized both producers and consumers of Shakespeare in the earlier part of the century—before the Bard became a high-cultural ideal to be approached (if at all) with awe.[12] Norris knew his Homer well; he could therefore adapt him freely. As a reader of Homer, Norris was what Certeau has called a "poacher"—borrowing, appropriating, and recasting. In "Reading as Poaching," Certeau imagines the reader as a traveler—like the speaker in Keats's poem, and like Presley. Certeau shifts the emphasis, however, from "just looking" to more active participation: "all readers . . . move across lands belonging to someone else, like nomads poaching their way across fields they did not write, despoiling the wealth of Egypt to enjoy it themselves."[13] The allusive texture of *The Octopus* implies that reading as a "poacher" is preferable to reading with reverence, whether informed or benighted.

In *The House of Mirth,* as in *The Octopus,* an implicit contrast emerges between the narrator's approach to "Literature" and the way it is read and used by the characters themselves. Wharton's heroine, Lily Bart, is said to be fond of "sentimental fiction" (36), but she is really not much of a reader. We never see her absorbed in a book. Still, her relation to printed matter repeatedly becomes a ground of Wharton's social commentary and a way of asserting the cultural status of the novel itself.

Although Lily rarely reads, she "prided herself on her broad-minded recognition of literature and always carried an Omar Khayam [*sic*] in her travelling bag" (68). To an "informed reader" Lily's "recognition of literature" is only mocked by her "Omar Khayam." Like some of the minor characters in *The Octopus* (Annie Derrick, Mrs. Cedarquist and her "salon"), Lily combines sentimentality and naiveté with a respect for "culture" that she but dimly understands. Like Presley, moreover, Lily associates literary or cultural value with something not only "higher" but also lost and "old." Thus, Lily is attracted by Selden's "reputed cultivation . . . which she felt would have had its distinction in an older society" (68).

In the upper-class world of *House of Mirth,* there are many "old" books and some libraries but few readers. In the library at Bellomont, for example, there are "shelves lined with pleasantly-shabby books," yet this library is "never used for reading" (61). One morning, as Lily roams through the house looking for Selden, she heads for the library, thinking that it might "have been resorted to by the only member of the party . . . likely to put it to its original use" (61). Lily's desire for Selden is heightened by his association with "culture" —and his general aura of inhabiting an amorphous "higher" sphere. Higher spheres and other transcendent forms, however, are the subject of recurrent irony in *House of Mirth,* as they are in *The Octopus.* Lily feels herself lifted "to a height apart," for example, when she goes to the opera looking exquisite in a new dress. But the narrator notes that if "Lily's poetic enjoyment of the moment was undisturbed by the base thought that her gown and opera cloak had been indirectly paid for by Gus Trenor, the latter had not sufficient poetry in his composition to lose sight of these prosaic facts" (122). The ironic opposition of "poetic enjoyment" and "poetry" with "prosaic facts" in this formulation exposes what Wharton sees as a characteristic misconception of poetic emotions, "higher" spheres, and elevated cultural forms.

The House of Mirth begins with Lily's visit to Selden's flat, where his "small library" (6) captures her imagination and is described in some detail. Lily is attracted to the "agreeable tones and textures" of his shabby volumes and "her eyes lingered . . . on them caressingly" (10). As the scene unfolds, she lifts "one book and then another from the shelves, fluttering the pages between her fingers [with] her drooping profile . . . outlined against the warm background of old bindings . . ." (11). At the end of the novel it is the image of Selden—*and* his books—that prevents Lily from committing the unethical act that might have restored her social standing. Having left her rooms with the intention of using Bertha's love-letters to neutralize her social power, Lily "seemed suddenly to see her action as [Selden] would see it. . . . She had a vision of his quiet room, of the bookshelves, and the fire on the hearth" (319–20). When Lily pays her final visit to Selden, "the library looked as she had pictured it. . . . [S]he recognized the row of shelves from which he had taken down his La Bruyère and the worn arm of the chair he had leaned against while she examined the precious volume" (321). The image of Selden's books accompanies Lily as she burns Bertha's love-letters—an act which she experiences as another "high moment" (328), but one that is the prelude (if not the trigger) for her death.

If the Gryce Americana—that collection of "rubbishy old books" (47)— means money and social standing to Lily, Selden's bookshelves and his "quiet" firelit room represent an aesthetic and moral ideal. Lily's grasp of the values suggested by the "precious volumes" is tenuous, however; Wharton thus raises a question about the place of "old books" in the moral and cultural life of both "Old New York" and turn-of-century America. *The House of Mirth,* like "The Vice of Reading," repeatedly stresses the difference between readers for whom books are like living creatures and readers for whom books are either fetishized objects or dead ones—"like fossils ticketed and put away in the drawers of a geologist's cabinet" ("Vice" 517). The novel directly engages the issue of reading through Lily's use of unread books (from *Omar Khayyam* to Selden's La Bruyère) and through the figure of the book collector—Selden as well as Gryce.[14] For Wharton, book collecting (like becoming a classic) is bound up with the idea of death.

In "The Vice of Reading," as we have noted, Wharton suggests that "the improvised chase after a fleeting allusion" is a primary pleasure of literature (516). Through its own fleeting allusions to Aeschylus, Shakespeare, Goethe, and other "classics,"[15] *The House of Mirth* proposes a way of relating to old books that is different from collecting them. Weaving a complex web of classical allusions (intertwined with more contemporary references), Wharton implies that classic texts can revitalize as well as deaden; it all depends on how they are read, digested, and deployed.

The "Furies" first enter Wharton's novel when Lily, having staved off Trenor's aggressive sexuality, recalls having once picked up "a translation of the *Eumenides* . . . in a house where she was staying." In an unusual move, Wharton suggests that Lily has read this ancient tragedy with enough care for her "imagination [to have] been seized by the high terror of the scene when Orestes, in the cave of the oracle, finds his implacable huntresses asleep and snatches an hour's repose" (156). After this point in Wharton's text, the idea of "the Furies [who] might sometimes sleep, but . . . were always there in the dark corners" (156) intermittently recurs, suggesting the inescapability of Lily's tragic entanglements (173, 178, 182, 311).[16] The recurrent image of the furies provides both the reader and Lily herself with a lens through which to focus Lily's experience.

Lily's own preoccupation with the furies is difficult to interpret. Her sense of herself as a tragic figure pursued by the avenging "huntresses" may encourage her to believe that it is better to die in an "exalted" state than to suffer the "dinginess" and compromises of the life she has come to. Just before Lily takes her lethal dose of chloral, she feels "an intense longing to prolong, to perpetuate the exaltation of her spirit" that has resulted from her "last moment with Lawrence Selden." Lily "dreaded to fall from that height" (333). It is possible to see Lily's use of Aeschylus as one more example of reading that is informed by a misguided conception of the sublime. Yet insofar as Wharton took Lily seriously as a "tragic" figure,[17] Lily's conceptualization of her life through the one text that fires her "imagination" might be designed to raise her above the passivity and drift of a typical naturalist character.

"In whatever form a slowly accumulated past lives in the blood," Wharton wrote toward the end of *House of Mirth*, ". . . it has the same power of broadening and deepening the individual existence, of attaching it by mysterious links to all the mighty sum of human striving" (336–37). The "slowly accumulated past" in this passage is generally taken to be the moral and social heritage that Lily lacks. It has been associated with the norms of "gentlemanly" behavior that (at the last minute) reassert their hold on Trenor when he is about to rape Lily; it has been related to the traditional image of motherhood that makes Lily respond so deeply to her final contact with Nettie Struther. Yet the passage also points to another "form" which a "slowly accumulated past" can take—literary heritage. Whether or not Lily herself benefits from seeing her life in a tragic perspective, the recurrent image of the furies encourages the reader to relate both Wharton's heroine and her novel to themes and genres of the past. Moreover, the final phrase of the passage, with its possible reference to *Faust*—the "mighty sum of human striving"— signals Wharton's concern with her own place in the Western tradition.

For Wharton, as for Norris, the idea of literary heritage was linked to that of cultural hierarchy; it raised the question of how the novel was to relate to the recognized "masters" of literature. But the *House of Mirth* is studded with allusions to fairytales and nineteenth-century novels as well as to the *Oresteia* and Shakespeare. As *David Copperfield* becomes a counterpoint to Homer in *The Octopus*, so Wharton positions her own text in relation to European realism as well as "classic" works.[18] The most sustained intertextual reference in *The House of Mirth* (apart from the motif of the furies) involves James's *The Portrait of a Lady*. In one richly allusive moment, for example, Lily's youthful desire to marry "an English nobleman with political ambitions and vast estates; or . . . an Italian prince with a castle in the Apennines and an hereditary office in the Vatican" (37) refers the informed reader directly to two of Isabel's suitors: Lord Warburton (literally "an English nobleman with political ambitions and vast estates") and Osmond who, though not an "Italian prince," resides in Italy and would surely have liked to be one.[19] (Osmond is also associated with the Pope, the chief resident of "the Vatican.")[20] In addition, the reference to the suitor with "a castle in the Apennines" alludes to a scene in which James's Isabel and Mme. Merle discuss the dreams of their youth (174–75). By invoking Eliot and James as well as Aeschylus and Goethe, Wharton encourages her reader to indulge in "the delights of intellectual vagrancy" and the search after a "fleeting allusion," while suggesting that the novel is not only the heir to a classic tradition but a form which might save that tradition from both frivolity and calcification.

Although the novel itself was still an upstart in literary culture at the turn of the century, its popularity was steadily increasing. But in the context of America's deepening cultural divisions, the novel's very popularity was another strike against it. Nina Baym has suggested that in the middle of the nineteenth century, the discourse of classical heritage was inseparable from the gendered division between "the novel" and "Literature." Writing about the popular women novelists of the 1850s, Baym notes that Fanny Fern, Marion Harland, and other women "were expected to write specifically for their own sex and within the tradition of their woman's culture, rather than within the Great Tradition. They never presented themselves as followers in the footsteps of Milton, and Spenser" (178). Drawing on Baym, Annette Kolodny suggests that the popular women novelists of the "feminine [1850s] . . . made a virtue of their . . . necessities by invoking an audience of [women] readers for whom aspirations to 'literature' were as inappropriate as they were for the writer" (152).

By the 1890s, however, the idea of a "Great Tradition" and the idea of "literature" had become both more sanctified and more widely accessible. Although the cultural respectability of the novel was far from that of classical drama or Homeric epic, its status had risen, along with its popularity. It was read by both men and women, despite its stigmatization as a "feminine" form. Naturalist writers in particular presented a direct challenge to the idea that the American novel was written with the "young girl" in mind.[21] Norris repeatedly called for "virile" fiction in his literary commentaries; but this was only an extreme formulation of a goal shared by Crane, Dreiser, Wharton, and others: the novel was to reflect the harsh realities of American life. It was also to be taken seriously as "Literature."

From the naturalists' point of view, the "power" of tradition (like that of the Cyclops) often seemed destructive, and they surely resisted the stranglehold of powerful "masters." Still, Norris, Wharton, and others also knew that they would not enter the canon by ignoring it. Norris could joke about his "immortul worruk" and the idea of the literary biographies that might be written about him one day (Walker 36, 41, 64–65). Still, neither he nor Wharton scorned the idea of Great Literature. Intertextual references to both the ancients and the moderns helped them to articulate that conception as they understood it: a "great tradition" with a place for turn-of-century naturalist writers.

NOTES

1. "Everybody has some time to read, however much he may have to do," Richardson insists. "Many a woman has read to excellent purpose while mixing bread, or waiting for the meat to brown, or tending the baby—simply reading a sentence when she could. Men have become well-read at the blacksmith's forge, or the printer's case, or behind the counter" (45–46). In the words of another essay, "The quantity of reading that may be done in a year by the employment of even small portions of time is surprising to those who have not observed the matter" ("Reading Habit" 60). As Joan Shelley Rubin notes, "the most famous predecessor" of the "middlebrow" institutions that flourished after World War I (book clubs, "great books" groups, radio programs, etc.) was Charles W. Eliot's "Five Foot Shelf of Books" designed in 1909 to "furnish a liberal education to anyone willing to devote fifteen minutes per day to reading them" (27–28). But the notion of making culture available in time-efficient, bite-sized pieces is already apparent in the 1880s and nineties.
2. On literary culture as a kind of force field, see Bourdieu.
3. Martin notes that "[f]ollowing the decline of instruction in Latin and Greek, Dickens, Cooper, Scott and their peers came to be known as 'classics'" (19). See also Hart, 183. Still, there were classics and Classics. On the shifting relation of books and "culture" at the end of the century, see Rubin, chapter 1, and Radway, chapter 4.
4. For another contemporary use of the same citation, see James Baldwin, 40–41. "When you have the opportunity to make the acquaintance of such as these," the passage continues, "will you waste your time with writers whom you would be ashamed to number among your personal friends?"
5. Rees, 83. By the same logic, of course, some books could be figured as inferior, even corrupting company. An analogous set of images represents certain works as rare dishes to be savored while comparing others to "opium or intoxicating liquors" (See Clarke, 674). On the class overtones of figuring some texts as conducive to intemperance and addiction, others as objects of "connoisseurship," see Glazener, 95–108.
6. As Kenneth W. Warren puts it, the passage "celebrates a possible high cultural transcendence of racial segregation" (267). On the differentiation of cultural levels in this period, see also Levine and Brodhead.

7. In his chapter on "The Reading Habit," Richardson cites Petrarch as follows: "I have friends whose society is extremely agreeable to me; they are of all ages and of every country. . . . It is easy to gain access to them, for they are always at my service and I admit them to my company and dismiss them from it whenever I please" (23). Baldwin cites the same passage in *The Booklover,* 10. Noah Porter, president of Yale, also used the imagery of books as people to be admitted or dismissed from a reader's "company" at will: "If instead of the deferential temper [that we ought to maintain toward an author] we are captious, critical and hard to be convinced or moved, we had better dismiss the author from our presence by closing his book" (51). On some implications of the trope of books as friends in nineteenth-century America, see my *Getting at the Author.*

8. Porter, for example, included such a list in his 1882 edition. See also Baldwin, or Abbott (113). Abbot's *Hints for Home Reading* represented just the kind of "democratization" that Lowell was attacking. Contributors included such distinguished men of letters as Charles Dudley Warner, F. B. Perkins, Hamilton W. Mabie, Edward Everett Hale, and Henry Ward Beecher. But the volume was part of a series of self-help books which included such titles as "What to Eat," "Till the Doctor Comes and How to Help Him," "How to Educate Yourself," "A Manual of Etiquette," and "Hints on Dress by an American Woman."

9. Du Bois's reference to Dumas here is complex in yet another way: as was widely known, Dumas himself was a mulatto.

10. On Norris's use of Homer, see also Lutwack, Vance, Machor, and Palladino-Craig.

11. On Norris's use of "epic epithets," see Lutwack, 26, and Palladino-Craig, 232–42. For a discussion of the Norris-Dickens connection, see Gardner.

12. Lawrence Levine emphasizes the difference between the "human Shakespeare who existed for most of the nineteenth century [and who] could be parodied with pleasure and impunity" and "the sacred Shakespeare who displaced him at [the century's] close" (74).

13. Certeau, 174. Like many other reading theorists and social historians, Certeau conceptualizes reading as an active appropriation of meaning, rather than as passive absorption. He does so in part to challenge the static model of a hierarchical culture which imposes meaning on "consumers." He thus raises questions about the nature of the power vested in a literary elite which establishes criteria for the "treasures" of literary meaning: "What then is the origin of the Great Wall of China that circumscribes a 'proper' in the text . . . and makes it the secret order of a 'work?' . . . This fiction condemns consumers to subjugation because they are always going to be guilty of infidelity or ignorance when confronted by the mute 'riches' of the treasury thus set aside" (171).

In the last twenty years, realist and naturalist writers themselves have often been seen to occupy positions of power from which, on the one hand, they legislate taste and, on the other, subordinate the populations they represent in their fiction. (See, for example, Glazener and Howard.) Although these charges are undeniable on one level, it is also worth noting that, for reasons of class or gender, naturalist writers themselves were often outsiders to "high" literary culture —as was their chosen medium, the novel.

14. Although Selden, unlike Gryce, would seem to read the books he owns, his way of using them is more akin to Presley's than to Norris's or Wharton's. Thus Selden's "Republic of the Spirit," the special realm that he encourages Lily to enter, is represented as an ethereal non-place. On the one hand, like the idea of "high" culture, it is (as Lily points out) "a close corporation" (74). On the other hand, it is a hazy ideal, appropriately expounded at Bellomont on another transiently illuminated hilltop.

15. Shakespeare is referred to several times in *House of Mirth*. "Does one go to Caliban for a judgment on Miranda," Selden reflects (142). Bellomont, the Trenor estate where Lily and Selden "had once met for a moment" (142), alludes to the aristocratic setting in *The Merchant of Venice*. As Maureen Howard has pointed out, the "Benedick" (the name of the bachelors' building where Selden lives, and which Rosedale owns) alludes to the "confirmed bachelor" of *Much Ado About Nothing* (139).

   Allusions to *Faust* in *House of Mirth* are more oblique than references to Aeschylus or Shakespeare, but they recur, especially in the form of the "two beings" who reside in Lily—"one drawing deep breaths of freedom and exhilaration, the other gasping for air in a little black prison-house of fears" (67; cf. 156, 174). The idea of "two selves in one breast" is central to Goethe's *Faust* and recurs as a sustained motif in *Age of Innocence*.

16. For a feminist perspective on what the "furies" meant to Wharton, see Ammons, 58, 189, 195–96.

17. In one much-quoted passage of *A Backward Glance,* Wharton notes that her challenge in writing *House of Mirth* was to explore the "tragic implication" and "dramatic significance" of a "frivolous society" by examining "the people and ideals" that it destroys. Her solution to this problem was her "heroine, Lily Bart" (207).

18. On the relation between *House of Mirth* and *Daniel Deronda,* see Seltzer (103–4) and Erlich (51–52). *Middlemarch* is directly invoked in *House of Mirth* as well. In one of her conversations with Selden at Bellomont, Lily suggests that "[m]oney stands for all kinds of things; its purchasing quality isn't limited to diamonds and motor cars" (74). Selden's response ("Not in the least; you might expiate your enjoyment of them by founding a hospital" [74]) is a direct and ironic reference to Dorothea's position at the end of *Middlemarch.*

19. "For all I . . . know he may be a prince in disguise," Ralph tells Isabel, "he rather looks like one, by the way—like a prince who has abdicated in a fit of fastidiousness and has been in a state of disgust ever since" (*Portrait* 214).

20. "'You seem to me to be always envying some one, [Isabel remarks to Osmond early in their relationship]. Yesterday it was the Pope; to-day it's poor Lord Warburton.'

   'My envy's not dangerous; it wouldn't hurt a mouse. I don't want to destroy the people—I only want to *be* them. . . . '

   'You'd like to be the Pope?' said Isabel.

   'I should love it—but I should have gone in for it earlier. . . .'" (*Portrait* 256)

21. H. H. Boyeson was one well-known spokesman for the destructive effects of the young girl on American literature: "The average American has not time to read anything but newspapers, while his daughters have an abundance of them at their

disposal, and a general disposition to employ it in anything that is amusing. The novelist . . . knows, in a general way what ladies like, and as the success of his work depends upon his hitting their taste, he makes a series of small concessions to it, which, in the end determine the character of his book. . . . The silence concerning all the vital things of life . . . I believe to be the most serious defect in the present American fiction" (qtd. in Åhnebrink 17). Cf. Norris, *Literary Criticism,* 28. For a challenge to the idea that women were the main novel-readers in the nineteenth century, see Zboray, especially chapter 11, "Gender and Boundlessness in Reading Patterns."

WORKS CITED

Abbott, Lyman, ed. *Hints for Home Reading: A Series of Chapters on Books and Their Use.* New York: G. P. Putnam's Sons, 1880.

Åhnebrink, Lars. *The Beginnings of Naturalism in American Fiction.* Cambridge: Harvard UP, 1950.

Ammons, Elizabeth. *Edith Wharton's Argument with America.* Athens: U of Georgia P, 1980.

Baldwin, James. *The Booklover: A Guide to the Best Reading.* 1884. Chicago: McClurg, 1898.

Baym, Nina. *Women's Fiction: A Guide to Novels by and About Women in America 1820–1870.* Ithaca: Cornell UP, 1978.

Bourdieu, Pierre. *The Field of Cultural Production: Essays on Art and Literature.* Ed. Randal Johnson. Cambridge, UK: Polity Press, 1993.

Brodhead, Richard. *Cultures of Letters.* Chicago: U of Chicago P, 1993.

Certeau, Michel de. "Reading as Poaching." *The Practice of Everyday Life.* Trans. Steven F. Rendall. Berkeley: U of California P, 1984.

Clarke, George. "The Novel-Reading Habit." *Arena* 19 (May 1898): 670–79.

"Congress of Authors." *Dial* 15 (16 July 1893): 27–32.

Darnton, Robert. "First Steps Toward a History of Reading." *The Kiss of Lamourette: Reflections in Cultural History.* New York: Norton, 1989.

"Desultory Reading." *Spectator* 1898 (24 Dec. 1898): 943–44.

Du Bois, W. E. B. *The Souls of Black Folk.* Greenwich, CT: Fawcett, 1961.

"Editor's Study." *Harper's Monthly Magazine* 103 (June–Nov. 1901): 152–54.

Erlich, Gloria C. *The Sexual Education of Edith Wharton.* Berkeley: U of California P, 1992.

Gardner, Joseph H. "Dickens, Romance, and *McTeague*: A Study in Mutual Interpretation." *McTeague.* By Frank Norris. Ed. Donald Pizer. New York: Norton, 1977. 361–77.

Glazener, Nancy. *Reading for Realism: The History of a U.S. Literary Institution.* Durham: Duke UP, 1997.

Graham, Don. *Frank Norris: The Aesthetic Context.* Columbia: U of Missouri P, 1978.

Hart, James. *The Popular Book: A History of America's Literary Taste.* New York: Oxford UP, 1950.

Hochman, Barbara. *Getting at the Author: Reimagining Books and Reading in the Age of American Realism.* Amherst: U of Massachusetts P (forthcoming).

Howard, June. *Form and History in American Literary Naturalism.* Chapel Hill: U of North Carolina P, 1985.

Howard, Maureen. "The Bachelor and the Baby." *The Cambridge Companion to Edith Wharton.* Ed. Millicent Bell. New York: Cambridge UP, 1995. 137–56.

James, Henry. "The Future of the Novel." 1899. *Theory of Fiction: Henry James.* Ed. James E. Miller. Lincoln: U of Nebraska P, 1972.

———. *The Portrait of a Lady.* New York: Norton, 1975.

Keats, John. "On First Looking into Chapman's Homer." *The Complete Poetical Works and Letters of John Keats.* Boston: Houghton, 1899.

Kolodny, Annette. "A Map for Rereading: Or, Gender and the Interpretation of Literary Texts." *The Captive Imagination: A Casebook on "The Yellow Wallpaper."* Ed. Catherine Golden. New York: Feminist Press, 1992. 149–67.

Levine, Lawrence. *Highbrow/Lowbrow: The Emergence of Cultural Hierarchy in America.* Cambridge: Harvard UP 1988.

Lowell, James Russell. "The Five Indispensable Authors (Homer, Dante, Cervantes, Goethe, Shakspere [*sic*])." *Century Illustrated Monthly Magazine* 47 (Nov. 1893– Apr. 1894): 223–24.

Lutwack, Leonard. *Heroic Fiction, the Epic Tradition and American Novels of the Twentieth Century.* Carbondale: Southern Illinois UP, 1971.

Machor, James L. "Epic, Romance, and Norris's *The Octopus.*" *American Literary Realism* 18 (1985): 42–54.

Martin, Jay. *Harvests of Change.* Englewood Cliffs, NJ: Prentice Hall, 1967.

Norris, Frank. "The American Public and 'Popular' Fiction" (syndicated, 2 Feb. 1902). Pizer 126–28.

———. "A Neglected Epic." *World's Work* (Dec. 1902). Pizer 119–22.

———. *The Octopus.* 1901. New York: Signet, 1964.

———. "An Opening for Novelists: Great Opportunities for Fiction Writers in San Francisco." *Wave* 16 (22 May 1897). Pizer 28–30.

———. "The Responsibilities of the Novelist." *Critic* (Dec. 1902). Pizer 94–98.

Palladino-Craig, Allys. *Heroic Resonance in the Canon of Frank Norris: His Use of Classical and Northern European Sources.* Diss. Florida State U, 1996.

Pizer, Donald, ed. *The Literary Criticism of Frank Norris.* New York: Russell and Russell, 1976.

Porter, Noah. *Books and Reading: What Books Shall I Read and How Shall I Read Them?* New York: Scribner's, 1882.

Radway, Janice. *A Feeling for Books: The Book-of-the-Month Club, Literary Taste and Middle-Class Desire.* Chapel Hill: U of North Carolina P, 1997.

"Reading and Education." *Dial* 16.2 (1895): 101–3.

"The Reading Habit." *Critic* (30 July 1892): 60.

Rees, J. Rogers. *The Diversions of a Book Worm.* New York: George J. Coombes, 1887.

Richardson, Charles. *The Choice of Books.* New York: Useful Knowledge, 1882.

Rubin, Joan Shelley. *The Making of Middlebrow Culture.* Chapel Hill: U of North Carolina P, 1992.

Seltzer, Mark. *Bodies and Machines.* London: Routledge, 1992.

Vance, William L. "Romance in *The Octopus*." *Critical Essays on Frank Norris.* Ed. Don Graham. Boston: G. K. Hall, 1980. 116–37.

Walker, Franklin. *The Letters of Frank Norris.* San Francisco: Book Club of California, 1956.

Warren, Kenneth W. "Troubled Black Humanity in *The Souls of Black Folk* and *The Autobiography of an Ex-Colored Man*." *The Cambridge Companion to Realism and Naturalism.* Ed. Donald Pizer. New York: Cambridge UP, 1995. 263–77.

Wharton, Edith. *A Backward Glance.* New York: Scribner's, 1964.

———. "Copy: A Dialogue." 1901. *Crucial Instances.* New York: AMS, 1969. 99–119.

———. *The House of Mirth. Edith Wharton: Novels.* New York: Library of America, 1985.

———. "The Vice of Reading." *North American Review* (1903): 513–21.

Zboray, Ronald. *A Fictive People: Antebellum Economic Development and the American Reading Public.* New York: Oxford UP, 1993.

The "Bitter Taste" of Naturalism

EDITH WHARTON'S *THE HOUSE OF MIRTH* AND
DAVID GRAHAM PHILLIPS'S *SUSAN LENOX*

—*Donna M. Campbell*

LTHOUGH EDITH WHARTON MIGHT HAVE SHUDDERED AT EDMUND
WILSON'S CHARACTERIZATION OF HER AS A "TREMENDOUS BLUESTOCK-
ing," the confident literary judgments she expressed in *The Writing of Fiction,
A Backward Glance,* and her letters nonetheless depict a critical sensibility
sharpened by immersion in the best of classic and contemporary literature (29).
One judgment, however, seems initially at odds with Wharton's usual insistence on the importance of form: her lavish praise for a naturalistic novel that
has largely been neglected by contemporary critics, David Graham Phillips's
Susan Lenox: Her Fall and Rise (1917). In 1921, after Sinclair Lewis wrote to
congratulate Wharton on winning the Pulitzer Prize, she responded, "Your
book [*Main Street*] and *Susan Lenox* (unexpurgated) have been the only things
out of America that have made me cease to despair of the republic—of letters"
(*Letters* 445). Critics such as Janet Beer Goodwyn and Cynthia Griffin Wolff
have framed Wharton's choice as exemplifying her wide-ranging reading in
American fiction, with Blake Nevius finding Phillips's work a New Woman
novel like *The Custom of the Country* (61) and Elizabeth Ammons an illustration of Wharton's thesis that "marriage enslaves women."[1] In *Edith Wharton's
Women: Friends and Rivals,* Susan Goodman observes that "Susan learns what
Lily suspects: not much separates the business of marriage from the business
of prostitution" (49).

Wharton's affection for and extensive comments about the book suggest
that it deserves a much fuller treatment in light of her own work, especially
The House of Mirth. As a novel of business, working-girl tale, social problem
novel, and naturalistic bildungsroman, *Susan Lenox* both incorporates and
debunks several popular genres in much the way that *The House of Mirth* blurs
the distinctions between conventional society novel and naturalistic exposé.
Moreover, as a retrospective commentary on *The House of Mirth, Susan Lenox*
suggested to Wharton possibilities for naturalism beyond the limited world of
"navvies and char-women," possibilities that allowed the frank investigation

of female sexuality in ways that Wharton had hinted at more circumspectly in "Bunner Sisters" and other works. In claiming *Susan Lenox* as a "neglected masterpiece," Wharton promotes the naturalistic novel as an artistically complex means to examine the nexus of sexual display, artistic identity, and economic power at the heart of early twentieth-century culture.

I

Although Cynthia Griffin Wolff notes in *A Feast of Words* that Wharton privately "recommended *Susan Lenox* (the unexpurgated version) to her friends" (365), the earliest of Wharton's published references to *Susan Lenox* occurs in the 1927 *Yale Review* essay "The Great American Novel." Praising Sinclair Lewis for "demolish[ing] the tottering stage-fictions of a lavender-scented New England, a chivalrous South, and a bronco-busting West," Wharton notes that he was nonetheless "not the first discoverer of Main Street":

> Over thirty years ago, Robert Grant situated "Unleavened Bread" in the same thoroughfare; and so, a little later, did Frank Norris his "McTeague," and Graham Phillips his "Susan Lenox"—and they were all, as it happens, not only "great American novels," but great novels. But they came before their time, their bitter taste frightened a public long nurtured on ice-cream soda and marshmallows, and a quick growth of oblivion was trained over the dreary nakedness of the scene they had exposed. (648)

Here as elsewhere, Wharton groups Phillips with his American contemporaries; the "thoroughfare" they share is the broad, bare highway of naturalistic representation that cuts through the "sentimental vegetation" of American regionalism. A few years later, Wharton incorporated much of the same material into chapter 7 of *A Backward Glance,* where the first of two references to *Susan Lenox* in that work appears. Although the manuscript version of the chapter does not include the passage, in the published version Wharton expresses her "great admiration for [Robert Grant's] early novel, 'Unleavened Bread,' which, with W. D. Howells's 'A Modern Instance,' was the forerunner of 'Main Street,' of 'Babbitt,' of that unjustly forgotten masterpiece 'Susan Lenox,' of the best of Frank Norris, and of Dreiser's 'American Tragedy'" (894). Discriminating here between the precursors of *Main Street* and other works of American realism, Wharton applies the term "masterpiece" only to Phillips's novel. She reiterates this judgment later in the book, stating her conviction that someday "that . . . neglected masterpiece, Graham Phillips's

'Susan Lenox'" will emerge from obscurity (960). In her correspondence, Wharton was not, of course, necessarily sparing in her use of the term "masterpiece." In one letter to John Hugh Smith, for example, she applies it to works as disparate as Anita Loos's *Gentlemen Prefer Blondes* and Lord Rosebery's *Napoleon* within the space of two short pages.[2] Her manuscript revision of the phrase from "great novel" to "masterpiece" in *A Backward Glance* suggests, however, an attempt to distinguish *Susan Lenox* in some way from the rest, to restore perhaps some of the critical attention, as opposed to notoriety, that she felt had been unjustly denied it.

These tantalizingly brief public statements merely hint at a much more complete explanation of Wharton's engagement with the book, an account that emerges from an unpublished exchange of letters between Wharton and Rutger Jewett, her senior editor at D. Appleton and Company, shortly after she first read the book during the summer of 1920. In the first letter, dated July 28, Wharton dispenses with routine publishing business before devoting this lengthy paragraph to the novel:

> I have just read Susan Lenox, which I came across accidentally. It is a great book, full of almost all the qualities I most admire in a novelist. I was not particularly interested in Phillips's early books, which seem to me a crude attempt to combine fiction with "social welfare"; and even in Susan Lenox there is far too much unnecessary moralizing and lecturing. But the tremendous vitality of the book survives even this drawback, and it remains, on the whole, the most remarkable novel I have read in a long time. I am told that it has been suppressed in America, and if this is so it is an interesting commentary on the fact that the police acts [*sic*] as our literary censors. If it is true that the book is out of circulation, could you unofficially help me to a copy? What a pity that poor Phillips died! May I suggest that when the next edition comes out (as of course it will before long, for such a senseless interdiction will certainly be raised), there should be a serious introduction by a man of letters somewhat more capable of understanding the book and situating it critically where it belongs in English fiction?

This passage answers old questions even as it raises new ones. First, its extensive praise dispels any suggestion that Wharton may have been using "masterpiece" in the qualified fashion implied by the subsequent words "of its kind." Moreover, it confirms, as *A Backward Glance* does not, both the approximate date of Wharton's introduction to this work and her long acquaintance with

Phillips's other novels, although it is not clear what other books of Phillips's Wharton may have read. The existing records of Wharton's library list a second printing of the first edition of *Susan Lenox* as the only novel of Phillips's she owned, an edition she marked with the following handwritten inscription: "Original unexpurgated edition. Given to me by R. B. Jewett September 1920."[3] However, her knowledge of Phillips's works dates to at least 1904. Although the letter itself is not extant, the letter book for Charles Scribner's Sons for that year contains summaries of letters to Wharton written by Edward L. Burlingame, editor of *Scribner's Magazine,* and William Crary Brownell, head of the book division at Scribner's. Writing to Wharton on 21 September 1904 about proposed titles for *The House of Mirth,* Burlingame responds to an apparent suggestion on Wharton's part of "The Cost" or "The Year of the Rose" for this work by noting that "*The Cost* has just been used as a title by David Graham Phillips,"[4] a reference that suggests their mutual acquaintance with Phillips's works.

In his August 16, 1920, response to Wharton's letter praising the work, Jewett echoes her judgment of *Susan Lenox* as a "great book" and caps Wharton's joke about police censorship with a brief anecdote proving that her point was "more true than [she] realize[d]." Wharton replied on September 13, thanking Jewett for sending her an unexpurgated copy of *Susan Lenox*:

> When I wrote you about the book I had no idea that an expurgated edition had been published. I confess that I regret it for it seems to me that your position would have been stronger if you had waited until intelligent public opinion compelled the withdrawal of the grotesque censorship. It is indeed a great book, and I wish the preface had been written by some one more worthy of introducing it to the world.

The writer so lacking in worthiness was the popular novelist Robert W. Chambers, whose own light romances Susan Lenox herself discards before turning to the meatier fare of Dickens and Balzac. He had been chosen for the task by Phillips's sister, Caroline Phillips Frevert, a personal friend of Chambers. Jewett goes on to explain the circumstances of the "grotesque censorship" in his September 30 reply: "Phillips' sister had charge of the Susan Lenox situation. She decided that it was much better to revise a few paragraphs in order to raise the blockade and enable the book to be sold in the open market." The "few paragraphs" Jewett mentions, however, amount to over a hundred pages of excised passages, and the "expurgated" version became a standard reprint edition, followed even in the 1977 Popular Library and

Southern Illinois University Press editions which claim to be "unexpurgated." (Of modern editions, only the two-volume 1968 Gregg Press edition reprints the unexpurgated 1917 text.)

The closest contemporary to Phillips and the best person to write the preface, in fact, might well have been Wharton herself, and the letter may be Wharton's oblique attempt to hint at this to Jewett. Although his life and his path to authorship differ from Wharton's in many respects, in his themes and subjects Phillips resembles his more famous counterpart. Born to a well-to-do Indiana family in 1867, Phillips attended Asbury College, now DePauw University, before transferring to Princeton in 1885. Beginning in 1890 as a journalist for the *New York Sun,* Phillips became a highly paid writer for the *New York World* in 1893, where, as the paper's London correspondent in 1897, he covered the Greek-Turkish confrontation at Velestinos also recorded by correspondents Stephen Crane and Richard Harding Davis.[5] Phillips gained even greater fame for his pieces in George Horace Lorimer's *Saturday Evening Post,* but his journalistic career reached its pinnacle with his articles advocating political reform, notably one groundbreaking series for Hearst's *Cosmopolitan* magazine: "The Treason of the Senate." Part Progressive-Era reform tract, part popular journalism, "The Treason of the Senate" ran from March through November 1906 and immediately caused a sensation. After the appearance of the first article, an attack on Chauncey Depew, the "railroad senator" from New York, Theodore Roosevelt denounced Phillips and the entire muckraking school of journalism in "The Man with the Muck-Rake," the speech that gave the movement its name. Shaken by the attack, Phillips, who had begun writing novels beginning with the pseudonymously published *The Great God Success* in 1901, now turned to writing fiction for a living. Between 1901 and his death in 1911, he proved himself a prolific novelist whose disciplined work habits and unflagging energy recall Wharton's own, writing a total of twenty-three novels in addition to essays, a play, and journalistic pieces.

In changing modes from nonfiction to fiction, Phillips nonetheless retained his commitment to social criticism. Early novels of business such as *The Cost* (1904) and *The Deluge* (1905) had exposed corruption on Wall Street and in politics, a trend that would continue with *The Plum Tree* (1905), but Phillips gradually turned his investigative talents toward the same topos that Wharton had chosen: the class-bound social world of the American aristocracy and the arrivistes who sought to join its ranks. Published anonymously beginning in February 1905 in *The Saturday Evening Post, The Social Secretary,* Phillips's first foray into the genre, was billed as the "true" account of political and social life in Washington, D.C., as told in the diary of the social secretary to an ambitious Midwestern senator's wife (Filler 84). Despite being characterized as insubstantial—"daintily flavored meringue," according to the *New York Times Saturday Review* for 7 October 1905—it sold over a hundred thousand copies, thus making 1905 a banner year for Phillips as well as for Wharton, whose *House of Mirth* appeared in book form in October. Phillips's book of essays denouncing New York society, *The Reign of Gilt,* was also published in September of that year. Given the sheer number of society-themed works Phillips published in 1905—three novels and a book of essays—it was inevitable that some would be compared with Wharton's *House of Mirth.* In "New York Society Held Up to Scorn in Three New Books: Mrs. Edith Wharton's 'The House of Mirth' a Novel of Remarkable Power—Comedy of Social Life" (*New York Times* 15 Oct. 1905), Phillips's *Reign of Gilt* is described as "forming a *pronunciamento* against American society and its greed of wealth as flamboyant and readable (not as sincere and sensible) as Jeremy Collier's historic 'Short View' in which the amusements of the English Restoration were so vivaciously denounced," while *The House of Mirth* is compared favorably to "a Greek tragedy." The December 1905 issue of Albert Shaw's *Review of Reviews* proclaims a similar judgment on the two authors. Having applauded Wharton's portrait of "the palpable coarseness, the repellent obtrusion, of a blatant, unscrupulous upstart" in *The House of Mirth,* the review blasts Phillips for his positive treatment of the same subject matter in *The Deluge* and pronounces his novel a failure (757). Despite *The House of Mirth*'s positive treatment, such comparative reviews may well have fuelled both Wharton's fear of being thought simply a "society novelist" and her efforts to ensure that her novel not be judged as one more "daintily flavored meringue" for an insatiable but undiscerning public.

Like those of Wharton, Phillips's later novels frequently focus on the role and status of women in society, especially that of the New Woman. With an almost Calvinistic faith in the value of hard work, Phillips drew less than sympathetic portraits of heroines who lazily abandoned all efforts to keep themselves intellectually or physically attractive after marriage, yet his portrayals of clubmen and other male society "parasites" were equally unsparing. His presentation of contemporary social issues shocked readers who were not used to hearing that divorce, exercise, and plastic surgery might improve lives (*Old Wives for New,* 1908) or that an adulterous affair might benefit the restless intellectual woman more than the material comforts of a conventional marriage (*Hungry Heart,* 1909). Like Wharton, Phillips was simultaneously praised and damned for his naturalistic approach. A 1905 review by "E.F.E." of *The House of Mirth* had proclaimed that "Mrs. Wharton out-Howells

Howells; she puts all the realists, all the naturalists, even all the romanticists to shame. Zola may have been more sensational, more gross, more repulsively human, but he was never so exact, so truthful, so absolutely indisputable, as is Mrs. Wharton in 'The House of Mirth.'" The reviewer's recognition of the "bitter taste" beneath the "ice cream soda and marshmallows" of Wharton's society novel matches a similar recognition of the naturalism underlying Phillips's method. In "The Leading American Novelist," an essay for the January 1911 issue of *The Smart Set,* H. L. Mencken praises Phillips for a similar set of naturalistic virtues. Posing the question implied in his title—"Who is he?"—Mencken dismisses Henry James and Wharton from contention with arguments that announce his own critical principles: "James? James is no more an American than the Sultan of Sulu. . . . A lady, perhaps? Mrs. Wharton? See James, Henry." Mencken instead proposes Phillips for the honor:

> Novelists succeed among us in proportion as they keep outside the skin. But Mr. Phillips does not bid for success in that way. He boldly ventures upon hazardous psychological laparotomies; he insists upon making indecent cross sections of the American woman; he looks for the roots of ideals, not in the heart, but in the stomach; he orates vociferously all the while he is at work. (163–64)

Mencken's prejudices aside, the image of the dissecting surgeon searching for truth by reading bodies, not minds, recalls similar images of the projects of naturalistic authors dating back to Zola's medical model in "The Experimental Novel" and looks ahead to Phillips's focus on the body in *Susan Lenox.* Even with this new subject matter, however, Phillips did not abandon the society novel entirely, publishing *The Fashionable Adventures of Joshua Craig* in 1909. The accuracy with which Phillips had "dissected" his well-born female protagonist was tragically borne out by subsequent events, of which Wharton's remark about "poor Phillips" suggests that she had knowledge. On January 23, 1911, a man who thought his sister had been satirized in the book approached Phillips outside the Princeton Club and shot him six times before turning the gun on himself. Despite extensive surgery, Phillips died the following day, January 24, 1911—coincidentally Wharton's forty-ninth birthday.

Finally, Wharton's comments about Phillips must also be placed in the context of their shared association with D. Appleton and Company. Wharton's connection with the company, which began with her sale of *The Reef* to the firm in 1912 (Benstock 250) and continued with the publication of *Summer* in July 1917, marked her debut at the firm at the very moment that it was issuing *Susan Lenox* as the last of Phillips's posthumous publications. Indeed, the dust jacket for *Summer* advertises *Susan Lenox* among Appleton's current offerings as "a courageous picture of American life" (Garrison 196). Wharton's statement that she came upon the work "accidentally" is thus somewhat sur- prising if not altogether disingenuous, although her war work may well have precluded any knowledge of its notorious publication history. After Phillips's death, *Susan Lenox* first appeared serially in a censored version by *Hearst's Mag- azine* from June 1915 to January 1917. Publication of the two-volume unex- purgated version in February of that year brought forth a storm of protest, although, as Phillips's friend Arthur Little wrote in 1931, "Phillips never wrote a dirty thought in his life. He made pen pictures of great realism, but there was always a purpose of worthiness back of his pictures. He could never under- stand why it was necessary in making a picture of dramatic life to give the world the impression that the author believed in Santa Claus."[6]

However, with the *Boston Transcript* calling it "an extremely offensive addition to the literature of pornography" and the February 23, 1917, review in the *New York Times* declaring that "it would have been better for Mr. Phillips' reputation and the reputation of American letters if it had never been pub- lished" (Filler 172), the novel was, as Wharton says, subjected to "grotesque censorship." Forced by John Sumner and his Society for the Suppression of Vice to withdraw the book in April 1917, Appleton and Carolyn Phillips Frevert staved off an impending trial on obscenity charges by bringing out a version acceptable to the Society.[7] In short, the book that Wharton had called a saving grace for "the republic—of letters" was seen by the government and the *New York Times* as contributing to the same republic's destruction.

II

As a retrospective commentary upon *The House of Mirth, Susan Lenox* vindi- cates Wharton's vision in much the same manner that, as Ellen Dupree has argued, "Wharton strongly believed that Loos's depiction of Lorelei 'vindi- cated' her own portrait of Undine Spragg in *The Custom of the Country*" (Dupree 269). Phillips's novel chronicles five years in the life of its heroine, the "natural daughter of Lorella Lenox" (*Susan Lenox* 1:555) whose sexual igno- rance causes her, in one of Phillips's ironic twists on the novel of seduction, to confess to being "betrayed" despite her actual innocence. Forced to marry an uncouth farmer, who rapes her on their wedding night, Susan escapes to Cincinnati on a showboat, where she is befriended by the company manager, Burlingham, and performs as a singer. When Burlingham falls ill, Susan pros- titutes herself to earn the $10 that will ensure his care, only to learn upon her return to the hospital that he has died. Determined to "learn to be strong," Susan alternates between such self-sacrificing stints of prostitution and what Phillips scathingly terms "honest toil" as a factory worker, singer, cloak model, and, like Lily Bart, hat trimmer.

After moving to New York with her lover, Rod Spenser, and then leaving him when she fears that she is responsible for his failure as a playwright, Susan descends into the naturalistic urban hell of the inner city, a territory that Phillips, like Norris, London, and Crane, hypothesizes as an "internal colony" of the defamiliarized and foreign.[8] As Phillips constructs it, the city neutralizes outrage and morality into a simple and practical struggle to exist: alcoholism, opium addiction, incest, prostitution, beatings, and death pale into insignificance compared to a corrupt sociopolitical system that forces the weak to prey upon the weaker to survive. Surviving the emotional brutality of weak men like Spenser, Susan next falls prey to the forces of poverty and her own system of ethics. After spending the night with Gideon, a rich businessman who offers to make her his mistress and gives her good practical advice about getting on in the world, Susan rejects him as decisively as Lily Bart rejects Simon Rosedale's similar proposal in *The House of Mirth*. She continues her descent when she is virtually enslaved by Freddie Palmer, a procurer whose combination of physical abuse and sexual attraction she escapes only when she nearly chokes him to death during a pitched battle. Discovered by Brent, a playwright as strong and successful as Spenser is weak, Susan begins acting lessons, only to give them up when she fears Brent has abandoned her. She again meets Freddie Palmer, by this time enormously rich and determined to succeed socially, and travels abroad with him. Learning that Brent had considered her promising as an actress after all, she decides to take up the stage again, after which a jealous Freddie has Brent killed. Susan is left truly free, ironically not because of her own efforts but because Brent has left her his fortune. Thus the "fall and rise" of the title is a progress through parallel careers as Susan sheds her position as "lady," moves through and beyond the "trade of woman" (2:306) and finally transcends gender altogether through her triumphant career on the stage.

In its essential elements, then, *Susan Lenox* reads like a dark mirror version of *The House of Mirth*. The most central parallels between the works concern the three significant types of men in *Susan Lenox,* types that parallel strikingly those in *The House of Mirth:* the ineffectual "artistic" man whose impossible standards of conduct the heroine can never maintain (Rod Spenser, Lawrence Selden); his opposite number, the brutish man whose participation in the world of exchange endangers the heroine's autonomy (Freddie Palmer,

Gus Trenor); and the cultural outsider whose attempts to aid the heroine are tragically at odds with her circumstances (Robert Brent, Simon Rosedale). Like his counterpart Lawrence Selden, Rod Spenser conceives himself to be aesthetically superior both to his profession, journalism, at which he earns a modest living, and to the culture that supports him. After meeting Susan in flight from her forced marriage, Spenser promises but fails to help her escape to Cincinnati. Like Lawrence Selden, whose hypocrisy about his own affairs does not prevent his "sharp shock of disillusionment" at seeing Lily emerge from the Trenors' house at midnight (146), the womanizing Spenser declares that Susan has "killed" his love by telling him of her prostitution. In both novels, the basic narrative pattern is one of approach toward emotional intimacy followed by male disillusionment, retreat into intellectual rationalization, and flight. For example, this pattern informs Selden's response to his and Lily's "golden afternoon" at Bellomont as well as his reaction to the *tableau vivant* and subsequent episode with Gus Trenor. In a similar fashion, Spenser sends his best friend, Drumley, to tell Susan that being "entangled in an intrigue with a woman he is ashamed to love" has hampered his growth as a playwright, after which Susan promptly leaves him (1:494). Such massive failures on Selden's and Spenser's parts do not dissuade the women in these novels from performing their own rescues, however. At her lowest point, Susan discovers the dissolute Spenser in a dive and determines to rescue him, although he has never understood or acknowledged her sacrifice, much as Selden never intuits Lily Bart's destruction of his letters to Bertha Dorset. Yet the difference between them is telling: Lily's silences, like her sacrifice of both letters and self, allow Selden to retain the illusion that he still lives in the "republic of the spirit" (55) and remains the interpreter of the "word which made all clear" (256). As Candace Waid points out, "Lily . . . cannot stop being a text; Selden has the last word because he is left reading" (43). By contrast, Susan lifts Spenser from utter squalor and encourages his production of plays, but she will neither participate in fictionalizing experience nor permit interpretation: "You've got several false ideas about me. You'll have to get rid of them, if we're to get along. . . . You and I fancied we loved each other for a while. We don't fool ourselves in that way now" (1:337).

Failing to exist as texts in the aesthetic realm, Susan and Lily must reinvent themselves as commodities in the naturalistic world of commerce and "debasing exchange" represented by the novels' businessmen. Brokers of intangibles (the services of women and securities), both Freddie Palmer and Gus Trenor serve as necessary correctives to the destructive fictions of Spenser and Selden, the brutal reality of prostitution that they signal exacting a harsh toll upon women whose education as "ladies" has ill fitted them to enter the marketplace. Introduced into this realm and possessing only themselves as a medium of exchange, Susan and Lily attempt to keep their market value inflated by infinitely deferring the process, implied by their promise of sexuality, of gratifying their purchasers' desires. Susan successfully accomplishes this balancing act by selling herself sexually yet deliberately maintaining a distinction between the commercial self that she barters, signified by her "working name" of Queenie Brown and the "gray of thought and action" that enters her eyes (1:505), and the inner self, the Susan whose eyes shine violet with emotion. As she tells Freddie, "what I sold was no more myself than—than the coat I'd pawned and drunk up before I did it" (2:494). Susan makes this distinction even within her relationship with Freddie, separating her sexual desire from the business relationship in which he beats her: "Had he—this kindly handsome youth—done that frightful thing? No—no. It was another instance of the unreality of the outward life. *He* had not done it, any more than she—her real self—had suffered it" (2:146). Through her experience with Gus Trenor, Lily also comes to understand the real nature of the transaction of "letting Trenor . . . lean a little nearer and rest his hand reassuringly on hers" (68). Her self-justifying thought that "to a clever girl, it would be easy to hold him by his vanity" (68) differs little from the blunt assessment of Ida, one of Susan's prostitute friends, that "Men are just crazy about themselves. Nothing easier than to fool 'em" (2:120). Recalling her actions after Gus has attacked her, Lily confesses to Gerty that she has prostituted herself emotionally if not technically: "I've sunk lower than the lowest, for I've taken what they take, and not paid as they pay" (132). Unlike Susan, however, Lily labors under a double burden of guilt as she strives to integrate the commercial and the inner self. She asks Gerty whether "bad girls . . . always go from bad to worse" and believes that "there's no turning back—your old self rejects you, and shuts you out" (131). Her error, as Susan points out in another context to Clara, lies in believing that these selves are sequential and mutually exclusive: "If you slipped and fell in the mud—or were thrown into it—you wouldn't say, 'I'm dirty through and through. I can never get clean again'—would you?" (2:330). Clinging to her past selves as she clings to the role of lady, Lily strokes the dresses that preserve "an association . . . in every fold" (236); by contrast, Susan gradually frees herself from past lives as she discards the soiled and ragged clothes of her external self throughout the book.

As the extensive symbolic use of clothing as identity suggests, the construction of class and race in these novels exists in a complex double relation to gender. Inherited, immutable, and inimitable, class bestows the sort of ethical character that should ensure success in a just world; however, given the social and economic exchanges necessary to preserve the concept of "lady" in a corrupt society, the position becomes a hindrance, variously imaged by Wharton and Phillips as fetters, burdens, and blinders. As Susan defines the problem, "I wasn't raised right. I was raised as a lady instead of as a human being. So I didn't know how to meet the conditions of life" (2:324). Raised as ladies, Lily and Susan learn that in a market economy they are allowed to function only within a limited and sexualized sphere, are turned into commodities, and are denied access to an authentic self. Their parallel experiences as millinery workers emphasize their unfitness to produce and to survive in a working-class environment, for they have been trained to produce only themselves as ladies. Thus, neither character can accommodate herself easily even to the virtuous "dinginess" of Gerty Farish's small flat, let alone to the greasy, lice-ridden tenement room of Susan's friend Etta Brashear. The awareness of class further exists in the characters' desperate, seemingly perverse refusal to capitalize upon such chances for success as their corrupt societies allow them. In a brutal inversion of the supportive communities of sentimental and local color fiction, the women in these novels confirm rather than resist the exchange values of the dominant culture. As Lorna Sackville or Queenie Brown, her *noms de guerre* for her life as a prostitute, Susan receives counsel from a succession of similarly named confidants—Etta, Ida, Clara—but what they give her is marketing advice, practical methods of packaging the self into ever more commercially available fragments. As has been amply demonstrated by Wai-Chee Dimock, Robert Shulman, Walter Benn Michaels, and Barbara Hochman, Lily encounters much the same situation and advice when she enters the marketplace.[9]

The simple economics of day-to-day survival thus transform themselves into a classic naturalistic dilemma: the Darwinian problem of adaptation and evolution. Both novels reverberate with the language of Darwinian thought, and critical commentary on *The House of Mirth* has extensively discussed the evolutionary flower imagery associated with Lily.[10] As Maureen Howard writes, "Lily Bart is socially unfit, a weak strain, though morally she proves to be a rare subspecies—ultimately an individual, superior to the world that produced her" (152). Noting in addition the much-discussed "hothouse" image, Jennie A. Kassanoff reads a different kind of extinction in Lily's plight, one grounded in race as well as class: "Lily is a hyperevolved specimen whose purity demands a life sheltered from the encroaching dinginess of American democracy. The hothouse with frosted windows thus perfectly captures her evolutionary dilemma: once breeding has become a rarefied art, akin to the skilled horticulture of lilies and orchids, the well-bred can no longer survive in the chill air of a potentially heterogeneous world" (63). The problem of adaptation suggested by the hothouse also suggests its nature: to provide an artificial environment that encapsulates and protects homogeneity requires immersion in the world of commerce. Lily's problem, like Susan's, is that for all her celebrated "pliancy," she can neither escape nor embrace an economic nexus that she at heart despises. The result for both characters is a curiously maladaptive habit of procrastination and refusal, of grasping at the least common denominator and thereby denying the system that commodifies them. In this manner, the heroine subverts the entire system by devaluing herself before those who would own her can devalue her. Thus Lily, in Carry Fisher's memorable phrase, "works like a slave preparing the ground and sowing her seed; but the day she ought to be reaping the harvest she over-sleeps herself or goes off on a picnic" (147–48). Susan likewise avoids calculation in choosing her clients, preferring instead to sell herself cheaply at rare intervals so as not to enrich Freddie and the system that he represents. Their ethos reverses that of ethnic outsiders Simon Rosedale, Gideon, and Freddie Palmer, to whose one-quarter Italian ancestry Phillips attributes his intelligence, ambition, ruthlessness, and sexual power. In a world where such men can succeed, to act like a lady is, quite perversely, to reverse the immigrant's striving and narrative of success: to eschew the art of the deal, to buy high and sell low, and thus to prove oneself genetically and ideologically pure despite the threat of extinction.

In addition to this indictment of economic and social worlds, Phillips extends and intensifies other naturalistic perspectives found in *The House of Mirth*, among them the movement's rejection of conventional sentimental genres and its invocation of the spectator as voyeur and both the city and the female body as spectacle. Like *Susan Lenox* neither pastiche nor parody, *The House of Mirth* nonetheless draws from a number of sources in addition to the society novel. Elaine Showalter has argued that "*The House of Mirth* goes back to adapt the characteristic plot of mid-nineteenth-century 'woman's fiction' and to render it ironic by situating it in the post-matriarchal city of sexual commerce" (137). *Susan Lenox* and its "fall and rise" plot structure also follows and reverses the "woman's fiction" plot described by Nina Baym: in *Susan Lenox,* an orphaned girl confronts the vicissitudes of life by learning to accommodate herself to a truly terrible external environment without becoming degraded by it or allowing it to destroy her essential self. Further, Cynthia Griffin Wolff's assessment that *The House of Mirth* is a *kunstleroman* applies even more cogently to *Susan Lenox*. If, as Jennifer Fleissner has argued, one defining characteristic of the naturalistic novel is its representation of "the female body as a site of constant *work*, work that defines itself in some way 'modern' by virtue of its repetitive, mechanical nature" (82), then Susan's protracted stints of wage slavery, prostitution, and a type of "natural" acting that Brent makes her repeat mechanically all strikingly suggest the body as (working) machine that Fleissner and also Mark Seltzer have described. In addition, the similar episodes of Lily Bart's short-lived career in a workroom and the Nettie Struther subplot of *The House of Mirth* suggest both novels' fleeting debt to serious working-girl novels like Dorothy Richardson's *The Long Day, the Story of a New York Working Girl* (1905) and the rejection of sentimental fare such as Carrie Meeber discards in *Sister Carrie*—Charlotte M. Brame's *Dora Thorne* (1883) or Laura Jean Libbey's *Little Leafy, the Cloakmaker's Beautiful Daughter: A Romantic Story of a Lovely Working Girl in the City of New York* (1891).[11]

The final principal way in which Phillips reaffirms Wharton's vision lies in his complex rearticulation of the relationship between spectacle and spectator. As June Howard demonstrates in *Form and History in American Literary Naturalism,* the concept of the spectator is central to naturalistic form, especially as it allows for both disengagement from and appropriation of the naturalistic scene on the part of audience as well as narrator. Two scenes of spectacle in particular emerge in naturalistic novels from *McTeague* to *Sister Carrie*. The first is that of the focused panoramic gaze at the city, one that takes in squalor as well as splendor. According to Christophe Den Tandt, the former produces not simply the familiar horror ascribed to naturalism but a dual sense of the "oceanic sublime" that is the city's vitality and a "naturalist sublime" of exhilaration and dread that for naturalist protagonists provides "the otherwise exhilarating contact of the metropolis" that is "superseded by pessimistic feelings of ambivalence, expressed in the gothic terms of horror and wonder . . ." (4). Although much of Lily Bart's life is spent in urban interiors, her brief foray into the streets after burning Bertha's letters during the visit to Selden illustrates one version of this feeling:

> Lily walked on unconscious of her surroundings. She was still treading the buoyant ether which emanates from the high moments of life. . . . The melancholy pleasure-ground [of Bryant park] was almost deserted when she entered it, and she sank down on an empty bench in the glare of an electric street-lamp. . . . Night had now closed in, and the roar of traffic in Forty-second Street was dying out. (242)

The heightened and symbolic isolation that Lily experiences amidst what Norris had called the "sullen diapason" of city noises recalls also Susan's similar experience, as Phillips several times presents her gazing across rooms and streets as though recalling the horrors of the city as well as the attributes that made her consider New York her "City of the Sun."

The second such spectacle common to naturalism is the vision of a woman's motionless body, often a violated body, but one that is nonetheless extensively described. Broadly speaking, the murdered women's bodies in *McTeague* (Maria Macapa and Trina McTeague) share this feature of spectacle with Carrie Meeber's silent little frowning Quakeress. Furthermore, both visions converge in a form barely extant during the time when *The House of Mirth* and *Susan Lenox* were written: the white slave narrative. As Marc Connelly describes the form in *The Response to Prostitution in the Progressive Era,* the plot of the white slave involves an innocent country girl who abandons her home when lured to the city, after which "the insidious white slaver would brutally seduce the girl and install her in a brothel, where she became an enslaved prostitute."[12] Thrust into national attention by reports like Clifford G. Roe's *The Great War on White Slavery* (1911), T. P. Curtis's *Traffic in Women* (1912), and Paul Elliot's *White Slavery and What It Is* (1910) as well as novels such as Reginald Wright Kauffman's *House of Bondage* (1910) or *The Girl that Goes Wrong* (1911), the form proposed the bodies of women as a national as well as naturalist spectacle. With the advent of increasing employment opportunities in the cities, the white slave threat also became one way to organize surveillance of daughters and to regulate their behavior. As Clifford Roe exhorts his audience in "The Auctioneer of Souls," one of the essays in Ernest Bell's *Fighting the Traffic in Young Girls* (1910), "Girls, look out for the pitfalls. Mothers and fathers, you can't afford to let your young daughters leave home with strangers unless you want to send them to ruin . . . [;] do not be too anxious to make money, or for the higher position in the social life at the expense of your daughter" (173). Small town families with daughters were advised to be watchful lest their daughters disappear into the hands of "cadets" or procurers, often characterized as foreign born. Although the frequently discussed elegant *tableau vivant* of Lily Bart as Mrs. Lloyd initially seems removed from such scenes,[13] Margit Stange reads *The House of Mirth* and this scene in particular as a not-so-oblique reference to these ideas: "Standing in front of her audience, her female body showing through her white dress, Lily is like the white slave whose body has the capacity to manifest various identities in the eyes of its beholders and owners (or potential owners). And the plot of Wharton's novel shades into the white slavery narrative: like the victim of white slavery, Lily is an unprotected heroine circulating in a market where, if her rightful protector fails to claim her, she falls into the hands of 'alien' marketeers . . ." (96). Stange suggests that on the level of spectacle, at least, the white body and dress create Lily as a text upon which to write one's fantasies. At a more basic level, however, Lily is also, like Susan, an innocent burdened with the persistent innocence of her class, thrust into an unreal and nightmarish city despite her seeming sophistication.

Susan Lenox presents similar spectacles of a woman's motionless body; indeed, the focus on Susan's body generally throughout the novel is incessant and constitutes the novel's major source of signification. Susan herself views it as an instrument and deliberately adorns it in ways that at once announce and mock her choice of profession, adopting a "Broadway" hairstyle, reddened lips, and a clinging, disagreeably sensual perfume that seem at odds with her quiet demeanor. Through these markers that undercut the obvious good breeding that Phillips insists is evident in every gesture, Susan constructs herself as a paradoxical, unreadable text with few cues to her real nature except her eyes—gray for commerce, violet for emotion—and her feet. As the rocking chair with its circular movement comes to signify Carrie's aspirations in *Sister Carrie,* so the images of feet and shoes, described with eroticized, rhapsodic attention by the narrative voice, convey a similar meaning in *Susan Lenox*; linked literally to Susan's incessant walking in quest of clients and figuratively to her movement between worlds, her shoes are never allowed to be down at heel or round-heeled, the latter a slang reference to sexual promiscuity, for she tends to them carefully even in the most desperate circumstances. Despite her almost constant movement as she walks all over New York, Susan is also shown in poses of stillness. The image of Lily posing as a classic work of art for male purchasers is transmuted in the humbler world of *Susan Lenox* into the image of a woman posing for male purchasers as Susan sings before rowdy riverboat crowds and models clothing for Gideon. She recapitulates Lily's experience as an aestheticized object of desire when she tries on Paris fashions for Freddie, who has literally purchased her time as Gus Trenor has sought to do with Lily.

The real *tableaux vivants* in *Susan Lenox,* however, feature quite another presentation of a woman's still body:

> When she came to her senses, she was lying sprawled on the far side of the bed. Her head was aching wildly; her body was stiff and sore; her face felt as if it were swollen to many times its normal size. . . . Her face was indeed swollen, but not to actual disfigurement. Under her left eye there was a small cut from which the

> blood had oozed to smear and dry upon her left cheek. Upon her throat were faint bluish finger marks. . . . "You are as low as the lowest," she said to her image—not to herself but to her image; for herself seemed spectator merely of that body and soul aching and bleeding and degraded. . . . She turned round to look again at the man who had outraged them. His eyes were open and he was gazing dreamily at her, as smiling and innocent as a child. . . . "You *are* a beauty!" said he. (2:142–43)

and

> She awakened in a small, rather dingy room. She was lying on her back with only stockings on. Beyond the foot of the bed was a little bureau at which a man, back full to her, stood in trousers and shirt-sleeves tying his necktie. She saw that he was a rough looking man, coarsely dressed—an artisan or small shop-keeper. Used as she was to the profound indifference of men of all classes and degrees of education and intelligence to what the woman thought—used as she was to this sensual selfishness which men at least in part conceal from their respectable wives, Susan felt a horror of this man who had not minded her unconsciousness. . . . "Hello, pretty!" cried he, genially. "Slept off your jag, have you?" (2:208–9)

The first scene occurs after Freddie has broken Susan's will and forced her into prostituting herself for him. The second, which recalls the white slave tradition, occurs after a "cadet" or recruiter, a "good-looking, darkish youth . . . partly of Jewish blood" (2:205), buys Susan a drugged drink and sells her to the madam of a brothel; in this scene, she discovers that the man who calls her "pretty" is not even the first to have used her body that night when she was unconscious. If *The House of Mirth* alludes to the white slave narrative through delicately allusive tropes of whiteness and figures of economic power, Phillips's use of the conventions is simple, direct, and powerful—the violence, the drugged drinks, the loss of consciousness and even more conspicuous loss of control. The true naturalistic tableau, Phillips suggests, is this scene of the still woman—battered, bruised, raped, and sprawled naked and supine on a bed—subjected to the happy gaze of ownership bestowed by her oblivious and unrepentant purchaser. Significantly, in each case, the man sees not the real Susan but the image he creates; the "beauty" of her body derives from his absolute power over it. Wharton's subtle interweaving of economics and visual ownership thus becomes transformed when potentially viewed through Susan's eyes instead of Lawrence Selden's, Gus Trenor's, and the rest. The tableau motif shifts as if seen in its true colors for the first time, and *Susan Lenox* appears as a kind of unspeakable or unspoken core for understanding Wharton's more sophisticated work, much like the role that the famous "unpublishable" "Beatrice Palmato" fragment was to have served for one of Wharton's more complexly developed stories. It is this sort of retrospective look—the "backward glance" of recognition—that makes *Susan Lenox* such a compelling and suggestive gloss upon *The House of Mirth* and validates Wharton's claims for its greatness.

III

In one sense, then, *Susan Lenox* is a masterpiece for Wharton not only because it encompasses "tremendous vitality" and "almost all the qualities" she most admired in a novel but because it articulates what *The House of Mirth* leaves unspoken. As the central aesthetic image of *The House of Mirth* is high art and melodrama, the representation of conventional and still images, that of *Susan Lenox* is perversely rendered naturalistic theater, with Susan sympathizing with the "wrong" role of Lola in *Cavalleria Rusticana* and Magda in Ernst Sudermann's *Magda*. Phillips explicates the connections for women between acting, prostitution, and the role of the lady, and Susan's ability to see these clearly enables her to be strong at last. If Lily is an artist of the beautiful, Susan is an artist of the real. *Susan Lenox* thus becomes a mediating presence between creator (Wharton) and character (Lily), a reflection, or perhaps Wharton's revisioning, of Lily—specifically, of a Lily that triumphs.

Further, as a parable of the woman artist, *Susan Lenox* functions as a gloss on Wharton's own apprenticeship. For Susan, the most critical juncture in the novel is her decision to abandon the luxurious life of fashion and house decoration that she shares with Freddie Palmer for the rigors of learning to act. Robert Brent, the great playwright whose tutelage she accepts and whose legacy she carries on after his death, forces her to learn *not* to act—that is, to act in a wooden fashion—until she gains control of her body, the medium of her art. The parallels with Wharton's own apprenticeship are clear, for perfecting the art of packaging and selling the self without selling the soul is the task of lady, prostitute, and artist alike. Synthesizing natural taste, a knowledge of real life, and a disciplined approach to practicing her craft, Susan Lenox masters this task and enacts the death of the lady, to use Elaine Showalter's phrase, and the birth of the female artist. Both Wharton's writings and her admiration for *Susan Lenox* proclaim her success in this arena. If, as Donald Pizer has argued, Wharton's 1920 novel *The Age of Innocence* represents her naturalism in its perfected state, then *Susan Lenox,* with its themes of sexual display, economic power, and artistic identity, represents her naturalism not perfected but developed in a different direction—a divergent road, one admired but not taken.

NOTES

1. *Edith Wharton's Argument with America* (Athens: U of Georgia P, 1980), 155. Ammons also says that Wharton did not specify what "the best of Frank Norris" might be (153), although in "The Great American Novel" Wharton lists *McTeague* in company with the other books that she cites.

2. In her letter of 26 Jan. 1926 to John Hugh Smith, Wharton writes, "My dear, I knew you were worthy of "Blondes"! How I wish we could talk that masterpiece over. . . . I've just been reading Ld. Rosebery's Napoleon, for the first time since it appeared, nearly 80 years ago; & I find it even greater than I did then. What a masterpiece, that also. . . . I don't know if the blonde's trick of speech is Southern[?]—but I somehow know it's *all right*—& that Undine at last is vindicated!" (box 26, folder 807, Edith Wharton Collection, Beinecke Library, Yale University).

3. *Edith Wharton's Library: A Catalogue,* compiled by George Ramsden, with a foreword by Hermione Lee (Settrington: Stone Trough Books, 1999), 98. At least two other sets of library records exist: the twenty-six-page inventory "Liste des Livres à Jean-Marie" at the Beinecke Library, and "The Library of Edith Wharton (offered for sale)" at the Huntington Library, a list nearly but not wholly identical with Ramsden's *Catalogue.* The first does not mention Phillips, but the second mentions this edition of *Susan Lenox.*

4. Letter Book, box 167, folder 1, Charles Scribner's Sons Archive, Manuscripts Division, Dept. of Rare Books and Special Collections, Princeton University Library.

5. For a complete account of Phillips as a professional journalist, see Christopher Wilson's *The Labor of Words: Literary Professionalism in the Progressive Era* (Athens: U of Georgia P, 1985).

6. Letter to Isaac Frederick Marcosson, 29 Dec. 1931 (Manuscripts Division C0140, Dept. of Rare Books and Special Collections, Princeton University Library). Marcosson, a critic who had also been a close friend of Frank Norris, used some of Little's lengthy letter in *David Graham Phillips: His Life and Times* (New York: Dodd, Mead, 1932), although Little was less than pleased with Marcosson's interpretation of Phillips.

7. Several critics discuss the publishing history of *Susan Lenox.* See Louis Filler, *Voice of the Democracy* (University Park: Pennsylvania State UP, 1978), 171–82; Laura Hapke, *Girls Who Went Wrong: Prostitutes in American Fiction 1885–1917* (Bowling Green: Bowling Green State U Popular P, 1989), 153–55; Abe Ravitz, *David Graham Phillips* (New York: Twayne, 1966), 141–42; and the introduction to the Gregg Press reprint of the novel (Upper Saddle River, NJ: Gregg Press, 1968). The Gregg Press edition unfortunately does not reproduce the complete title page but lists 1917 as the first edition. In the introduction, however, F.C.S. writes that the novel was issued as a two-volume novel in July 1915 and withdrawn shortly thereafter in response to

John Sumner's suit. However, Ravitz specifies 1917 as the date for the two-volume version (12), and Hapke gives February 1917 as the date of the unexpurgated version (154). The National Union Catalogue lists 1917 as the date of the first edition.

8. On the concept of the "internal colony," see James R. Giles, *The Naturalistic Inner-City Novel in America: Encounters with the Fat Man* (Columbia: U of South Carolina P, 1995), and June Howard, *Form and History in American Literary Naturalism* (Chapel Hill: U of North Carolina P, 1985).

9. See especially Wai-Chee Dimock, "'Debasing Exchange': Edith Wharton's *The House of Mirth,*" *PMLA* 100 (Oct. 1985): 783–92, reprinted in *Edith Wharton,* ed. Harold Bloom (New York: Chelsea House, 1986), 123–38; Robert Shulman, "Divided Selves and the Market Society: Politics and Psychology in *The House of Mirth,*" *Perspectives on Contemporary Literature* 11 (1985): 10–19; and Barbara Hochman, "The Rewards of Representation: Edith Wharton, Lily Bart, and the Writer/Reader Interchange," *Novel* 24 (Winter 1991): 147–61.

10. Wharton's debts to evolutionary theory have been well documented. See especially Bert Bender, *The Descent of Love: Darwin and the Theory of Sexual Selection in American Fiction, 1871–1926* (Philadelphia: U of Pennsylvania P, 1996); Mary Suzanne Schriber, "Darwin, Wharton, and 'The Descent of Man': Blueprints of American Society," *Studies in Short Fiction* 17 (1980): 31–38; and Maureen Howard, "The Bachelor and the Baby," *The Cambridge Companion to Edith Wharton,* ed. Millicent Bell (New York: Cambridge UP, 1995), 137–56.

11. For a full discussion of the genre, see Laura Hapke's *Tales of the Working-Girl: Wage-earning Women in American Literature, 1890–1925* (New York: Twayne, 1992).

12. Marc Connelly, *The Response to Prostitution in the Progressive Era* (Chapel Hill: U of North Carolina P, 1980), 116. See also Barbara Meil Hobson's *Uneasy Virtue: The Politics of Prostitution and the American Reform Tradition* (New York: Basic Books, 1987) and Ruth Rosen's *The Lost Sisterhood: Prostitution in America, 1900–1918* (Baltimore: Johns Hopkins UP, 1982). Laura Hapke has a helpful discussion of the genre in *Girls Who Went Wrong.*

13. For example, as Wai-Chee Dimock has shown, in *The House of Mirth,* Lily Bart constructs herself as aesthetic object but becomes instead "human merchandise" (124) most obviously when, posing for the *tableaux vivants,* she markets not only her charm but her figure in the clinging robes of Reynolds's *Mrs. Lloyd.*

WORKS CITED

Ammons, Elizabeth. *Edith Wharton's Argument with America.* Athens: U of Georgia P, 1980.

Bender, Bert. *The Descent of Love: Darwin and the Theory of Sexual Selection in American Fiction, 1871–1926.* Philadelphia: U of Pennsylvania P, 1996.

Benstock, Shari. *No Gifts from Chance: A Biography of Edith Wharton.* New York: Scribner's, 1994.

Connelly, Marc. *The Response to Prostitution in the Progressive Era.* Chapel Hill: U of North Carolina P, 1980.

Den Tandt, Christophe. *The Urban Sublime in American Literary Naturalism*. Urbana: U of Illinois P, 1998.

Dimock, Wai-Chee. "'Debasing Exchange': Edith Wharton's *The House of Mirth*." *PMLA* 100 (Oct. 1985): 783–92. *Edith Wharton*. Ed. Harold Bloom. Modern Critical Views. New York: Chelsea House, 1986. 123–38.

Dupree, Ellen Phillips. "Wharton, Lewis, and the Nobel Prize Address." *American Literature* 56 (May 1984): 262–70.

E.F.E. "Books of the Day: Mrs. Wharton's Latest Novel." Undated review of *The House of Mirth*. Edith Wharton Collection.

Edith Wharton Collection. Yale Collection of American Literature. Beinecke Rare Book and Manuscript Library, Yale University.

Edith Wharton Papers. Beinecke Library, Yale University.

Filler, Louis. *Voice of the Democracy*. University Park: Pennsylvania State UP, 1978.

Fleissner, Jennifer. "The Work of Womanhood in American Naturalism." *Differences* 8.1 (1996): 57–93.

Garrison, Stephen. *Edith Wharton: A Descriptive Bibliography*. Pittsburgh: U of Pittsburgh P, 1990.

Giles, James R. *The Naturalistic Inner-City Novel in America: Encounters with the Fat Man*. Columbia: U of South Carolina P, 1995.

Goodman, Susan. *Edith Wharton's Women: Friends and Rivals*. Hanover, NH: UP of New England, 1990.

Hapke, Laura. *Girls Who Went Wrong: Prostitutes in American Fiction, 1885–1917*. Bowling Green: Bowling Green State U Popular P, 1989.

———. *Tales of the Working-Girl: Wage-earning Women in American Literature, 1890–1925*. New York: Twayne, 1992.

Hobson, Barbara Meil. *Uneasy Virtue: The Politics of Prostitution and the American Reform Tradition*. New York: Basic Books, 1987.

Hochman, Barbara. "The Rewards of Representation: Edith Wharton, Lily Bart, and the Writer/Reader Interchange." *Novel* 24 (Winter 1991): 147–61.

Howard, June. *Form and History in American Literary Naturalism*. Chapel Hill: U of North Carolina P, 1985.

Howard, Maureen. "The Bachelor and the Baby." *The Cambridge Companion to Edith Wharton*. Ed. Millicent Bell. New York: Cambridge UP, 1995. 137–56.

Jewett, Rutger. Letter to Edith Wharton. 16 Aug. 1920. Box 33, folder 1032, Edith Wharton Papers.

———. Letter to Edith Wharton. 30 Sept. 1920. Box 33, folder 1032, Edith Wharton Papers.

Kassanoff, Jennie. "Extinction, Taxidermy, Tableaux Vivants: Staging Race and Class in *The House of Mirth*." *PMLA* 115 (Jan. 2000): 60–74.

Little, Arthur. Letter to Isaac Frederic Marcosson. 29 Dec. 1931. Manuscripts Division C0140, Dept. of Rare Books and Special Collections, Princeton U Library.

Mencken, H. L. "The Leading American Novelist." *American Mercury* 33 (1911): 163–68.

Michaels, Walter Benn. *The Gold Standard and the Logic of Naturalism: American Literature at the Turn of the Century.* Berkeley: U of California P, 1987.

Nevius, Blake. *Edith Wharton: A Study of Her Fiction.* Berkeley: U of California P, 1953.

"New York Society Held Up to Scorn in Three New Books: Mrs. Edith Wharton's 'The House of Mirth' a Novel of Remarkable Power—Comedy of Social Life." *New York Times* 15 Oct. 1905. Clipping. Edith Wharton Collection.

Phillips, David Graham. *Susan Lenox: Her Fall and Rise.* 1917. 2 vols. Upper Saddle River, NJ: Gregg Press, 1968.

Pizer, Donald. "American Naturalism in Its 'Perfected' State: *The Age of Innocence* and *An American Tragedy.*" *Edith Wharton: New Critical Essays.* Ed. Alfred Bendixen and Annette Zilversmit. New York: Garland, 1992. 127–41.

Ravitz, Abe. *David Graham Phillips.* New York: Twayne, 1966.

Rev. of *The Social Secretary*, by David Graham Phillips. *New York Times Saturday Review* 10 (7 Oct. 1905): 650.

"Review of the Season's Fiction." Rev. of *The Deluge,* by David Graham Phillips, and *The House of Mirth,* by Edith Wharton. *Review of Reviews* 32.6 (Dec. 1905): 757.

Roe, Clifford G. "The Auctioneer of Souls." *Fighting the Traffic in Young Girls.* Ed. Ernest Bell. N.p., 1910. 163–73.

Rosen, Ruth. *The Lost Sisterhood: Prostitution in America, 1900–1918.* Baltimore: Johns Hopkins UP, 1982.

Schriber, Mary Suzanne. "Darwin, Wharton, and 'The Descent of Man': Blueprints of American Society." *Studies in Short Fiction* 17 (1980): 31–38.

Seltzer, Mark. *Bodies and Machines.* New York: Routledge, 1992.

Showalter, Elaine. *Sister's Choice: Tradition and Change in American Women's Writing.* Oxford: Clarendon, 1991.

Shulman, Robert. "Divided Selves and the Market Society: Politics and Psychology in *The House of Mirth.*" *Perspectives on Contemporary Literature* 11 (1985): 10–19.

Stange, Margit. *Personal Property: Wives, White Slaves, and the Market in Women.* Baltimore: Johns Hopkins UP, 1998.

Waid, Candace. *Edith Wharton's Letters from the Underground: Fictions of Women and Writing.* Chapel Hill: U of North Carolina P, 1991.

Wharton, Edith. *A Backward Glance.* New York: Scribner's, 1934. *Edith Wharton: Novellas and Other Writings.* Ed. Cynthia Griffin Wolff. Library of America. New York: Literary Classics of the United States, 1990. 767–1069.

———. "The Great American Novel." *Yale Review* 16 (July 1927): 646–56.

———. *The House of Mirth.* 1905. Ed. Elizabeth Ammons. New York: Norton, 1990.

————. Letter to Rutger Jewett. 28 July 1920. Box 33, folder 1032, Edith Wharton Papers.

————. Letter to Rutger Jewett. 13 Sept. 1920. Box 33, folder 1032, Edith Wharton Papers.

————. Letter to John Hugh Smith. 26 Jan. 1926. Box 26, folder 807, Edith Wharton Papers.

————. *The Letters of Edith Wharton.* Ed. R. W. B. Lewis and Nancy Lewis. New York: Collier-Macmillan, 1989.

Wilson, Christopher P. *The Labor of Words: Literary Professionalism in the Progressive Era.* Athens: U of Georgia P, 1985.

Wilson, Edmund. "Justice to Edith Wharton." *The Wound and the Bow.* New York: Oxford UP, 1947. *Edith Wharton: A Collection of Critical Essays.* Ed. Irving Howe. Englewood Cliffs, NJ: Prentice-Hall, 1962. 19–31.

Wolff, Cynthia Griffin. *A Feast of Words: The Triumph of Edith Wharton.* New York: Oxford UP, 1977.

"**H**UNTING FOR THE REAL" IS THE EXPRESSION THAT THE TWENTY-SIX-YEAR-OLD EZRA POUND USES IN A LETTER OF 22 OCTOBER 1912 (*Letters* 46) to describe his major preoccupation in London at that time. The phrase refers to the problems he encounters in the reception of poetry: "luke-warm praise of the mediocre" and the tendency toward "mildly affirming the opinion of someone who hasn't cared enough about the art to tell what he actually believes." In place of such lackadaisical pretense, Pound longs for an "honest opinion from the firing line."

Pound's affirmation of "the real" carries resonance far beyond the immediate realm to which he applies it. As Lionel Trilling argued in the Norton Lectures at Harvard in 1970, the rise to centrality of the concepts of sincerity and authenticity in moral life coincides with the crystallization of the Romantic Movement at the turn of the eighteenth century. And, Trilling adds, the issue "asserts itself with a new energy when an accelerated social mobility makes right conduct problematical" (82).

Several other factors not adduced by Trilling coalesced in the course of the nineteenth century to turn the spotlight onto the desirability—and the difficulty—of attaining "the real" in art as in conduct. The Romantics' interest in origins and organicity initiated investigations of the past. Bishop Percy's *Reliques* (1765), a collection of folk writings, followed on the startling success throughout Europe of James Macpherson's *Ossian* (1760), presented as translations of a primeval Celtic bard, but certainly in good part recent accretions. In Germany Achim von Arnim and Clemens Brentano published between 1805 and 1808 *Des Knaben Wunderhorn*, a compilation of traditional folk lyrics.

In 1812 the Grimm brothers' *Märchen* appeared. The Grimms were in the forefront of linguistic research too, formulating the sound shifts underlying the transformation of Latin into German. Their work was continued by

Karl Lachmann (1793–1851) who also edited many Greek, Latin, and old German sagas, notably the *Nibelungenlied*. Similarly basic work on French medieval works was carried out by Joseph Bédier (1864–1938). The archeological excavations of Heinrich Schliemann (1821–90) in the late 1860s and early 1870s at Troy not only aroused immense excitement but also drew even greater attention to the significance of "the real." So the naturalists' preoccupation with the authenticity of their portrayal of reality has many precedents reaching beyond the mid- to later-nineteenth-century realists, their accepted precursors, extending as far back as the romantics.

The validation of "the real" became increasingly critical in what Walter Benjamin has called "the age of mechanical reproduction." The daguerreotype, invented in 1839 by Louis Daguerre, together with J. P. Niepce, was an early version of photography, a technique that advanced enormously the capacity to furnish credible simulacra. The mass production of consumer goods consequent to the industrial revolution flooded the market with copies that superseded and threatened to swamp "the real." Benjamin succinctly summarizes the process: "The technique of reproduction detached the reproduced object from the domain of tradition. By making many reproductions it substitutes a plurality of copies for a unique existence" (221). To establish the status of "the real" becomes an ever more formidable task, and authenticity an ever more decisive issue from the intellectual as well as the financial perspective.

The selection, evaluation, and preservation of "objects on the basis of their aesthetic quality— . . . and on their value as single, unique items" (Tonelli 31) was one of the main functions of the art museum as a cultural institution. It is not by chance that the European perception of the art museum as a temple and a treasure house was adopted in the United States too, in the age of mechanical reproduction, for it acts essentially as a counteragent to and a bulwark against the mere copy. With the expertise of the new professional art historians such as Harvard's Charles Eliot Norton, the museum sought to guarantee the authenticity of the objects displayed. As the fine arts were elevated and distinguished from folk art in the last decade of the nineteenth century, there was a boom of activity in the foundation of art societies and schools. The American Historical Association, inaugurated in 1884, was complemented by the formation of the American Association of Museums in 1905. By the first decade of the twentieth century, specialized art museums such as the Museum of Modern Art in New York, the Whitney, the Museum of American Art, and the Boston Institute of Contemporary Art came into existence as an outcome of public and private enthusiasm. Visits to European museums and historical sites also became fashionable in recognition of the civilizing impact of the pursuit of the arts. Just "the *having-been-there* of things" is posited by Roland Barthes as a crucial criterion of reality (15; "*l'avoir-été là*," 88). Evidently, Pound was not alone in "hunting for the real" at the turn of the century. Not surprisingly, the acquisition and possession of "the real" turned into a potent status symbol: "Seeking personal recognition, social status, and cultural sophistication, a few prominent Americans with newly made fortunes in the world of industry and finance became interested in the collecting of fine art, which was defined at that time as European painting and sculpture" (Tonelli 33).

This is the context for rereading Edith Wharton's *Custom of the Country,* which appeared in 1913, the year after Pound coined his striking phrase. Wharton's extensive personal command of the novel's geographic and social environments in both the United States and Europe assured the attainment of her own "real" without need of the deliberate documentation that is one of the hallmarks of naturalism. Born at 14 West Twenty-third Street just off Fifth Avenue and fashionable Madison Square into a family with inherited social standing, baptized in Grace Church which "guaranteed one's place in the social hierarchy of the city" (Benstock 6), she embarked on her first visit to Europe shortly before her fifth birthday. After a year in Italy, the family settled in Paris for two years (1868–70). Throughout her life, even after the establishment of her home, the Mount, in Lenox in the opening years of the twentieth century, Wharton traveled incessantly throughout Europe, particularly in France and Italy, and often lived there for long periods while renting her houses in Massachusetts and New York, as her parents had done. Through her friendship with such eminent men as the French writer Paul Bourget (1852–1935) and the art collector Bernard Berenson (1865–1959), in addition to her own prestige as a novelist, Wharton gained entry into echelons of European society not normally accessible to outsiders. She was thus in a position to see the upper strata of French and American society from the inside. Her familiarity with the activities and conversations at spas is reported to be based partly on the impressions of her husband, Teddy, who had a ready eye and ear for social foibles, as well as on her own (Benstock 187). So Wharton's documentation in *The Custom of the Country* is soundly based primarily on first-hand observations. Her acute awareness not only of class status but also of the intricate interplay of class and money is the fruit of her own experience. It is also worth noting that while relatively affluent, her family was by no means exempt from financial difficulties at various points, especially in her early life before her great success as a novelist.

All the novel's major characters are deliberately or instinctively "hunting for the real," although they pursue this quest in differing ways and with very differing outcomes. And in every instance except one, "the real" is associated and often wholly identified with authentic works of art.

What renders the problem of authenticity so prominent in *The Custom of the Country* is the novel's focus on the theme of social mobility, the factor that, according to Trilling, "makes right conduct problematical" (82). At the turn of the century, both physical and moral changes were taking effect with growing rapidity. The long enforced codes of proper behavior were being stretched as was the geographic horizon with New York's spread northward and with more American visitors to Europe. To participate in the Parisian season—rather than to vacation on Long Island or in the Adirondacks— fuels the desire of all the social climbers and playboys in *The Custom of the Country*. Removed from the constraints of their customary environment, living in hotels, associating in the neutral, sometimes dubious milieu of cafés, and flitting from resort to resort, they feel free to follow their whims with scant heed to the codes of conduct that still reigned back home. This context, too, exacerbates the difficulty of discovering "the real."

In France as in New York, the lines of demarcation among those "hunting for the real" are cultural and often specifically artistic. The fundamental rift is best formulated in *The Custom of the Country* in the terms chosen by Ralph Marvell:

> Ralph sometimes called his mother and grandfather the Aborigines, and likened them to those vanishing denizens of the American continent doomed to rapid extinction with the advance of the invading race. He was fond of describing Washington Square as the "Reservation," and of prophesying that before long its inhabitants would be exhibited at ethnological shows, pathetically engaged in the exercise of their primitive industries. (47)

Despite the unmistakable note of self-irony on Ralph's part, his dichotomization into "Aborigines" and "Invaders" (50) encapsulates the broad divide among the characters as well as the tensions animating the plot.

That plot is essentially the enactment of the Darwinian recognition of the survival of the fittest. The aborigines are like dinosaurs; though not confined to their "Reservation," in practice it is only in certain milieus that they can exist. The lives they lead are limited by their inability—and unwillingness —to adapt to the changing social mores. They cling to old established habits and values, and although *The Custom of the Country* does not seriously question the ideals that determine their conduct, it is obvious that these very ideals, despite their nobility, contribute to their decline and will eventually lead to their displacement by the upstart invaders. Ralph's refusal to contest the custody of his son in order to spare his mother (a previous generation even more wedded to the aborigine creed) and to avoid any public scandal is the most striking instance of a dinosaur's tendency to self-destruct. Likewise, Ralph's ineptitude in his experiments with speculative investment and his poor judgment in this respect are a further expression of his lack of instinct for self-preservation. Raymond de Chelles, too, ultimately has to divest himself of his cherished heirloom tapestries out of sheer financial exigency. In both the United States and Europe, the aborigines are drifting toward extinction. Significantly, de Chelles has no progeny, and Ralph's son is brought up among invaders.

The invaders, on the other hand, are hampered by no scruples whatsoever in their thrust to upward mobility, to the acquisition of the money and possessions that had previously been the aborigines' prerogative. Wharton portrays the invaders as psychologically less complex than the aborigines and for that reason more successful. Having set their sights on certain goals, they pursue them ruthlessly, unimpeded by the ethical considerations that hold the aborigines in check. Notwithstanding their vulgarity and lack of inhibitions—or perhaps precisely *because* of these traits—the invaders are better equipped than the aborigines to deal with the changing economic methods and standards. Because of its alleged cynicism *The Custom of the Country* is reputed to have cost Wharton the Nobel Prize (Benstock 386). However, it is the perception of life as a struggle for survival of the fittest—not the most refined—that places the novel squarely within the parameters of naturalism.

The antithesis between the aborigines and the invaders emerges most clearly in *The Custom of the Country* in the divergent attitudes toward works of art. Among the aborigines, respect for art and understanding of it is an integral facet of their heritage. The leading representatives of this group are Ralph himself and Raymond de Chelles who succeeds Ralph as Undine's husband. Through these two figures the aborigine culture is shown to be as pronounced in France as in the United States, although the vast majority of the invaders do not come into contact with it in Europe and are not even aware of its force. Ralph and Raymond are alike in being strongly bound to their family traditions. They are embedded in ancestral homes, they observe well-defined rituals and conventions, they subscribe to the accepted proprieties of their class, they care for and are also dependent on extended family, and they socialize mostly with their own kind.

Their traditions, conventions, prohibitions, and prejudices definitively shape the Marvell family into which Undine marries, and the failure of that marriage can be ascribed in large measure to her inability to grasp their values. A revealing episode occurs when she is first invited to dinner at the home of the Fairfords, Ralph's sister and brother-in-law. She is disappointed at the smallness and shabbiness of their house:

> There was no gilding, no lavish diffusion of light: the room they
> sat in after dinner, with its green-shaded lamps making faint pools
> of brightness, and its rows of books from floor to ceiling, reminded
> Undine of the old circulating library at Apex, before the new marble
> building was put up. Then, instead of a gas-log, or a polished grate
> with electric bulbs behind ruby glass, there was an old-fashioned
> wood-fire. (21)

Undine thinks the house "dull" and cannot recognize its dignified authenticity, for her ideas, gleaned from the Sunday papers, have led her to expect "to view the company through a bower of orchids and eat pretty *entrées* in ruffled papers" rather than the "plain roasted or broiled meat" served at tables decorated only with a "low centre-dish of ferns" (21). Her attraction to the copy or gloss over "the real" is symbolized by her preference for a gas-log or a simulated electric rather than a wood fire. Similarly, her expectations of the food and table decorations indicate the allure of the showy and pretentious. Her intellectual vacuity and aesthetic insensitivity are comically exposed during the ladies' after-dinner conversation. Undine is confused by "questions as to what pictures had interested her at the various exhibitions of the moment, and which of the new books she had read" (24). Neither has she heard of the current theatrical events, although she recalls having seen "Sarah Burnhard" in a play she calls "Leg-long" and another that she pronounces as "Fade" (25). Naively, she offers the additional information that she has read "When the Kissing Had to Stop" and seen "Oolaloo" fourteen times. The crassness of the disparity between the aborigines' genuine commitment to the arts and the invaders' ignorant indifference is brilliantly conveyed in this scene.

For Ralph the arts hold an importance far greater than for most of the aborigines. He not only delights in visiting museums and old churches in Italy on his honeymoon; he actually aspires to creative activity himself. His nominal profession as a lawyer is no more than an empty ritual: he has "his desk at the office of the respectable firm in whose charge the Dagonet estate had mouldered for several generations" (48). He remains within the parameters of family conventions and interests; yet the phraseology suggests the absence of any enthusiasm or dynamism: he has not worked at "his desk," and the estate "had mouldered." A certain disdain for the mundane concerns of life is characteristic of the gentlemanly stance. Ralph is fully aware of his position: "his profession was the least real thing in his life. The realities lay about him now: the books jamming his old college bookcases and overflowing on chairs and tables; sketches too— . . . and, on the writing-table at his elbow, scattered sheets of prose and verse, charming things also, but, like the sketches, unfinished" (48). Such "desultory dabbling" (48) does not meet with disapproval in the aborigine lifestyle; however, it marks Ralph as an amateur in his artistic endeavors as much as in his profession. His aspiration to "the real" finds expression in the novel he wants to write, but the vague plans he has long nurtured have to be shelved during his marriage to Undine when he has to go into business to make money and is too exhausted to write in the evenings. One of the cardinal paradoxes implicit in *The Custom of the Country* is adumbrated here: the necessity for at least a modicum of money to support the hunt for the aesthetic "real," and simultaneously the barrier to that hunt created by that very prior imperative. Only after the end of his marriage to Undine is Ralph able to give himself to his writing. His deep satisfaction at the promising progress of his novel conveys how much more "real" this activity is to him than anything else he has done.

Yet, despite the note of irony in Ralph's characterization of the aborigines, despite his defiance of family ideals in marrying Undine, despite even his vision for his own life as reaching out beyond mere appreciation of art, he remains loyal to the code in which he was brought up. He refrains from contesting the divorce and the custody of his son on "the strength of the social considerations" (271). He wants at all costs to spare his family embarrassment:

> He recalled all the old family catchwords, the full and elaborate vocabulary of evasion: "delicacy," "pride," "personal dignity," "preferring not to know about such things"; Mrs. Marvell's: "All I ask is that you won't mention the subject to your grandfather," Mr. Dagonet's: "Spare your mother, Ralph, whatever happens," and even Laura's terrified: "Of course, for Paul's sake, there must be no scandal." (273)

Wharton's recourse to quotations here is more than a device to reproduce the family idiom; it also suggests, through repetition of evidently stock phrases, the fixity of the code. In retrospect Ralph, too, realizes the deleterious impact of clinging to "the whole archaic structure of his rites and sanctions" (294): "As he looked back it seemed as though even his great disaster had been conventionalized and sentimentalized by this inherited attitude: that the thoughts he had thought about it were only those of generations of Dagonets, and that there had been nothing real in his life" (274). This bitter insight is repeated and this time stylistically embodied in quotation, reinforced by a parenthetical comment: he "had simply declared that he wanted 'to turn his back on the whole business' (Ralph recognized the phrase as one of his grandfather's)" (274). This mode of verbal presentation implies that the aborigine code, through reiteration and imitation, has forfeited its original strength and reality in the same way as Ralph forfeits his son.

The apparently casual remark noted in parenthesis is crucial once again when Undine thinks: "(it was odd how he [Raymond] reminded her of Ralph)" (301). Raymond de Chelles, in a transatlantic setting, is a more robust version of Ralph Marvell. He is truly an aborigine, committed literally to the reservation in the shape of his ancestral country estate. Its name, Saint Désert, obviously denotes at once its desolation and its sacredness. The castle, where winters are spent, and summers too if repairs are necessary, strikes Undine as "one vast monotonous blur" (307). Although in Paris Raymond had seemed more dashing than Ralph, in the country he becomes totally engrossed in the management and improvement of the estate, especially after his father's death when he becomes head of the family. But this position brings only added responsibility, not wealth; on the contrary, apart from meeting the needs of the estate, he has to settle his profligate brother's debts. The de Chelles' creed of honor in this matter is reminiscent of the solidarity of the Marvells, the Dagonets, and the Fairfords in their readiness to help Ralph in the financial crises into which Undine's extravagances plunge him. The authenticity of the aborigines' willingness to make personal sacrifices contrasts with the invaders' self-aggrandizing opportunism.

In order to be able to maintain the estate in good order, the de Chelles have to reduce their living expenses to a minimum. Such "considerations of economy" (300) result in cramped quarters for the young couple during their brief stays in Paris, and in the country "the most unremitting economy" (338) is practiced in regard even to heating and food. Undine comes up against "a definite and complicated code of family prejudices and traditions" (302), considerably more stringent than that she had encountered among the Marvells and the Dagonets in New York. Like Ralph, Raymond had presumed that Undine would "be gradually subdued to the customs of Saint Désert" (322), but she remains resistant and puzzled. As she sees it, every facet of the de Chelles' life "was only a part of their wholly incomprehensible way of regarding themselves (in spite of their acute personal and parochial absorptions) as minor members of a powerful and indivisible whole, the huge voracious fetish they called The Family" (321–22). Symbolizing that fetish is the old house and its artistic treasures from which, to Undine's mind, "some spell" seems to emanate because it "had so long been the custodian of an unbroken tradition" (323–24).

What Undine cannot begin to comprehend is that the family and the estate are "the real" to Raymond. He sees himself as the guardian of a precious heritage entrusted to him, and he expects Undine to bear him a son to continue the lineage, but another child would interfere with her craving for incessant "amusement" (325). In the face of Undine's blindness to what is most "real" to him, Raymond reacts differently than Ralph: "she was gradually to learn that it was as natural to Raymond de Chelles to adore her and resist her as it had been to Ralph Marvell to adore her and let her have her way" (310). While Ralph allows himself to be destroyed by Undine, Raymond has his priorities firmly set and remains faithful to his principles. On the surface he is courteous to his wife, but he evidently writes her off, stifling all intimacy behind "the barrier of his indifference" (319). Readers are never given access to Raymond's thoughts as they are to Ralph's. We have to deduce them from his sparse utterances and above all from his actions. In his disappointment at his marriage, he devotes himself the more passionately to his estate and to politics. His artistic inclinations are far slighter than Ralph's; he merely paints a little occasionally. Nonetheless, aesthetic concerns inspire his devotion to the family heirlooms, notably the priceless tapestries. To Raymond these objects are "the real" that he is morally obliged to preserve for succeeding generations.

Undine's utter inability to gain any insight into this aborigine outlook culminates in her idea of selling the de Chelles tapestries, as one sees in the following disastrous conversation with Raymond:

> "Why, there's a fortune in this one room: you could get anything you chose for those tapestries. And you stand there and tell me you're a pauper!"
>
> His glance followed hers to the tapestries, and then returned to her face. "Ah, you don't understand," he said.
>
> "I understand that you care for all this old stuff more than you do for me, and that you'd rather see me unhappy and miserable than touch one of your great-grandfather's arm-chairs."
>
> The colour rose slowly back to his face, but it hardened into lines she had never seen. He looked at her as though the place where she stood was empty. "You don't understand," he said again. (330)

Ralph, too, had known that "she would not understand" (139). Undine's barbarously mercantile perception of the tapestries is a repetition of a previous parallel act of vandalism when she commissions a Parisian jeweler to re-set the engagement ring Ralph had given her. She cannot even understand her husband's sense of hurt at what he experiences as a desecration, for the ring was his grandmother's, a Dagonet heirloom. Undine's mother is rather offended that the ring had not been bought specially for her daughter at Tiffany's; it is Mrs. Heeny, the manicurist, the Spragues' mentor in social matters, who explains: "Them's old stones" in a "quaint" setting, "ancestral jewels" (54). An invader, Undine is devoid of values other than a predilection for the showiest, the latest and trendiest, as her cultivation of fashion in clothing and hairstyles testifies. Her preference for gas logs and electric over wood fires prefigured this later absence of good taste and disregard for the authentic in the arts.

Significantly, when Mrs. Heeny, at the very end of the novel, wants to tell Paul about his mother's life, she does so by giving him the "piles and piles of lovely new clippings" (324) she has collected from the newspapers. The metaphor is apt, for Undine's life is no more than an assemblage of fragments. She has no "real." Even her name is, as it were, doubly unreal: Ralph assumes that she is named after the water-sprite, which would suggest her innate fluidity, but in an ironic subversion her mother discloses the truth: "we named her after a hair-wave her father put on the market the week she was born" (51). So the commercial has from the outset taken precedent over the aesthetic in Undine's story. The clippings record a random series of events and actions, themselves imitations of what Undine had read about in those same newspapers. In a sense she, too, is "hunting for the real" without, however, any genuine idea what it might mean, as against the ideals Ralph, Raymond, and their families cherish. The aborigine code may be "completely out-of-date" (279), as Ralph's cousin, Clare, ventures; its current retrenchment is epitomized in Harriet Ray, the girl whom Ralph's family would wish him to marry, who is described as "sealed up tight in the vacuum of inherited opinion" (53). Still, these aborigines have a core identity lacking in Undine, who can only cling to appearances and cobble together a life of clippings—that is, essentially a fragmented copy.

Undine's severe limitations are revealed in the shallowness of her response to the arts quite apart from her faux pas in relation to the ring and the tapestries. Early on, spurred by the ladies' after-dinner conversation at the Fairfords, she decides to go and see the pictures they had been discussing. However, she goes less to view the pictures than in the hope that "she might meet some of the people she had seen at dinner—from their talk one might have imagined that they spent their lives in picture-galleries" (31). Decked out in her handsomest furs and newest hat, she revels in the homage she provokes. At the gallery she sees a lady in black examining the pictures "through a tortoise-shell eye-glass adorned with diamonds and hanging from a long pearl chain. Undine was instantly struck by the opportunities this toy presented for graceful wrist movements and supercilious turns of the head" (31–32). This little cameo is typical of Undine: to imitate, to fasten onto the externals, to focus in a self-absorbed manner on the impression she can make. Incidentally, it never occurs to her that the eyeglass, rather than being a decorative "toy," is an instrument better to view works of art. She then bumps into a young man whose image she has often seen in the newspapers; the copies enable her to identify "the original before her" (32). Distracted and entranced by his casually polite comment, "The crowd's simply awful, isn't it?" (32), she forgets all about the pictures: "When she reached home she found that she could not remember anything about the pictures she had seen . . ." (33). Wharton's suspension points are an invitation to readers to reflect on the light shed on Undine by her behavior in this early incident in the novel.

The fundamental shortcomings in Undine's education and aesthetic sensibility become an increasingly serious handicap to her. Although she continues to be able to attract attention through her beauty and the splendor of her gowns, she cannot hold attention in cultured circles because of the flatness of her talk. Raymond, like Ralph, at first tries "to tell her about what he was reading or what was happening in the world; but her sense of inadequacy made her slip away to other subjects, and little by little their talk died down to monosyllables" (317). Eventually, Madame de Trézac, an American who has married into an aristocratic French family, explains this to her: "they think you beautiful; they're delighted to bring you out at their big dinners, with the Sèvres and the plate. But a woman has got to be something more than good-looking to have a chance to be intimate with them: she's got to know what's being said about things" (339). Mortified at hearing that she is considered a "bore" (339), Undine, with half-hearted thoughts about cultivating herself, goes so far as to spend a morning at the Louvre and attend a couple of lectures by a fashionable philosopher. But she is quickly disconcerted when she finds that everybody appears to know more about the things she has just learned, and "her comments clearly produced more bewilderment than interest" (339). She draws the absolutely wrong conclusion that she had "gone dowdy, and instead of wasting more time in museums and lecture-halls she prolonged her hours at the dressmaker's and gave up the rest of the day to the scientific cultivation of her beauty" (339–40). Art remains impenetrable to Undine just as she remains no more than a decorative possession on a par with the Sèvres and the plate. So, ironically, she herself is commodified as a kind of art object.

But not all invaders prove as impervious to art as Undine. Elmer Moffatt, her first and fourth husband, is a man who rises from utmost obscurity and ignorance to connoisseurship. In contrast to Ralph and Raymond with their illustrious family trees, "no one in Apex knew where young Moffatt had come from, and he offered no information on the subject" (344). He is the archetypal upstart who makes a fortune in business through schemes that, while not technically illegal, are decidedly questionable. When Ralph, in dire need of money, enters into dealings in partnership with Elmer, he is extremely uneasy about the issue of integrity. Although Elmer suffers many financial and social setbacks, he has the dynamism and the fascination with business that lead to success. He also has a level of intelligence and understanding lacking in Undine. When she urges him to retire from business because he already has a more than ample fortune, Elmer uses exactly the same phrase, "you don't understand," as Ralph and Raymond had done, but he confronts her bluntly instead of giving up on her:

> See here, Undine—you're the one that doesn't understand. If I
> was to sell out tomorrow, and spend the rest of my life reading art
> magazines in a pink villa, I wouldn't do what you're asking me.
> And I've about as much idea of dropping business as you have of
> taking to district nursing. There are things a man doesn't do. I
> understand why your husband won't sell those tapestries—till he's
> got to. His ancestors are *his* business. Wall Street's mine. (360)

Elmer here exhibits an insight into aborigine culture and into the significance of the de Chelles tapestries that Undine never attains.

Throughout much of *The Custom of the Country,* it is money that is "the real" for which Elmer is "hunting." He openly equates "cash" with "pull" (293); money is to him the prerequisite to all else. But while he maintains a certain vulgarity that makes him a good match for Undine, he also develops an appreciation of art that goes in tandem with his ascent to respectability. As "a dawning sense of his stability was even beginning to make itself felt on Fifth Avenue" (287), he fills his flat with Chinese porcelains and Persian rugs. In his office, which has an air of opulence through its brass railings and mahogany bookcases, Ralph on two occasions finds him fingering crystal vases: as Elmer himself points out, "I ain't a judge—but now and then I like to pick up a pretty thing" (283). The slangy grammar and unsophisticated phraseology ("a pretty thing") suggest his intermediate position at this stage in his career.

Later Elmer will indeed emerge as "a great collector" (333) with a "growing passion for pictures and furniture" and the "desire to form a collection which should be a great representative assemblage of unmatched specimens" (337). The dealer who comes to Saint Désert to evaluate the tapestries describes him as "the greatest American collector"; he "buys only things that are not for sale" (332). Through his collecting Elmer is thus conforming to a custom of his country at that time, namely the acquisition of European art as a status symbol, but he is also exercising a sort of self-assertive revenge by seeking to extract from the aborigines precisely what they are least willing to yield. As he confides to Undine in one of his usual colloquialisms: "When the swells are hard-up nowadays, they generally chip off an heirloom" (336). At some level, monetary values remain supreme to Elmer; when Raymond initially refuses to sell the tapestries, he can only ask "Why? Didn't I offer him enough?" (350). His characteristic combination of commonness and aestheticism has its incarnation in his living quarters where "a lapis bowl in a Renaissance mounting of enamel and a vase of Phoenician glass that was like a bit of a rainbow caught in cobwebs . . . seemed to be shrinking back from the false colours and crude contours of the hotel furniture" (355–56).

At the end of the novel, Elmer and Undine Moffatt, re-married, are installed in a large apartment in a private Parisian *hôtel* which Elmer has bought. It is described through the eyes of the nine-year-old Paul Marvell who has come from school to visit his mother and stepfather. Since they are, as so often, still away on his arrival, and on their return preoccupied with preparations for a dinner-party, the boy is left to wander through the rooms alone. He is uncomfortable: "the newness and sumptuousness of the room embarrassed him" (362). Everything bespeaks "the showy" (121) that Undine has always favored: "the wonderful lacy bedroom, all pale silks and velvets, artful mirrors and veiled lamps, and the boudoir as big as a drawing-room, with pictures he would have liked to know about, and tables and cabinets holding things he was afraid to touch" (362). This decor has none of the coziness of a home; it is more a showcase, almost a private museum, for expensive and precious objects. Attracted to the library by his habit of reading in his frequently lonely hours, Paul finds rows and rows of books gorgeously bound; "but the bookcases were closed gilt tresilling, and when Paul reached up to open one, a servant told him that Mr. Moffatt's secretary kept them locked because the books were too valuable to be taken down" (363). Here, too, everything is geared to mere display. In this survey of the house, Wharton makes splendid use of the child's innocence to ironic ends. Paul wonders, for instance, "whether the wigged and corseleted heroes on the walls represented

Mr. Moffatt's ancestors, and, why, if they did, he looked so little like them" (363). Yet Paul has inherited aborigine good taste; he is most drawn to a portrait of a boy in gray velvet, which is "the one genuine picture in the house" (Gair 363), the "Vandyck" [*sic*] for which Elmer had paid the largest sum ever for a picture by that artist.

Paul reads about this in the clippings Mrs. Heeny gives him. He also reads about the Moffatts' home at 5009 Fifth Avenue, "an exact copy of the Pitti Palace, Florence" (367). The motif of the copy is important in *The Custom of the Country* as a more or less mechanical reproduction in antithesis to the authentic work of art such as the de Chelles tapestries, the Dagonet ring, or Vandyck's "Grey Boy." Many of the clippings contain photographs of society figures that Undine studies compulsively as models for herself. It is as a result of having seen his photograph in the "Sunday Supplements" that she is able to recognize "the original" (32) of the prominent, wealthy playboy Peter Van Degen, whom she encounters on her one visit to an art gallery. Photographs of Undine festoon Ralph's study, and are tactfully removed by his sister after she absconds. Also more copy than art are the portraits painted by the fashionable society painter, Claud Walsingham Popple. His reputation has been established by the rich patron who declared that Popple "could 'do pearls'" (117). The quotation marks highlight the verdict while leaving its precise meaning open. To Popple's sitters his ability to "do pearls" as well as gowns and skin is clearly a crucial merit; "he always subordinated art to elegance" (117). Again, the quotation marks are a means to present an opinion in a seemingly non-judgmental manner, leaving it to readers to distinguish between those who esteem a painter for his capacity to "'do pearls'" and those who are aware of the superficiality of such an approach. Popple hunts for the apparent reproduction of the real for his own commercial purposes. Undine has, of course, been painted by Popple. Indeed, among Mrs. Heeny's clippings is one "about the last portrait" (366); the adjective "last" supports the inference that Undine has had several portraits painted. By having herself reproduced in this manner, she becomes a willing participant in her commodification as a kind of debased work of art such as she always has been in the eyes of the aborigines.

By the close of *The Custom of the Country,* the Moffatts, in their Parisian *hôtel* and their copy of the Pitti Palace, are making considerable headway in invading aborigine territory. There is a clipping about the pearl necklace Elmer gave Undine the previous Christmas. Mrs. Heeny reads it to Paul: "'The necklace, which was formerly the property of an Austrian Archduchess, is composed of five hundred perfectly matched pearls that took thirty years to collect. It is estimated among dealers in precious stones that since Mr. Moffatt began to buy the price of pearls has gone up over fifty per cent'" (366). Through the appended comment on the financial impact of Elmer's acquisitiveness, the beauty and antiquity of the necklace are linked—and subordinated—to its monetary value. A parallel comment features in the newspaper report about Elmer's bid for the Vandyck: "'Since Mr. Moffatt began to buy extensively it is estimated in art circles that values have gone up at least seventy-five per cent'" (365). A third instance of the close association of an heirloom and money occurs in the account of Elmer's gifts to his bride which include "'a necklace and tiara of pigeon-blood rubies belonging to Queen Marie Antoinette, a million dollar cheque and a house in New York'" (367). The invaders' increasing strength stems from their command of growing fortunes which enable them to despoil the aborigines as they in turn become impoverished. As the monetary balance shifts, so does the ownership of precious objects. The de Chelles tapestries finally fall to Elmer after the financial collapse of General Arlington, the rich American father-in-law of Raymond's brother. Undine will keep the necklace given to her by Elmer, unlike the earlier one she had got from Peter Van Degen and had had to sell for ready cash. Presumably, also, she will not have Marie Antoinette's necklace and tiara re-set, as she had done the Dagonet ring. The purchase of heirlooms and works of art is an endeavor on the invaders' part to put themselves on a par with the aborigines. Nonetheless, the objects the invaders acquire, however high their pecuniary value, can never have the same worth for them as they did to the aborigines because they are not rooted in longstanding family tradition. The "wigged and corseleted heroes" (363) on the walls of the Moffatts' Parisian home are not Elmer's real ancestors. There is an inevitable element of spuriousness or of innate frustration in the invaders' "hunting for the real."

The sole exception to the categorization prevailing in *The Custom of the Country* is Paul Marvell himself. As the offspring of the (temporary) union of an aborigine and an invader, Paul may have the capacity to bridge the opposing strains. To his father he represents not just the continuation of the lineage but the ultimate "real." It is Ralph's recognition that he is losing Paul because of his failure to fight for his custody in compliance with the family code that precipitates his suicide. In his early years Paul has been nurtured in the Marvell-Dagonet environment, and he enters a similar milieu, though in the French countryside, at Saint Désert. Raymond, who wishes for a son of his own, is fond of Paul and teaches him about the estate. His affection for the boy makes Undine realize "what an acquisition" he is (300), quite apart from being the tool to extort money from Ralph by blackmail. To Undine her son is therefore primarily an object whose value can be exploited for her own ends; he has no independent reality for her. On the other hand, Elmer, like Raymond, is attached to the boy. From the moment when he first runs into Undine carrying the child on a New York street while she looks for a cab, he admires Paul's aristocratic appearance and good manners. Elmer shows him a tenderness that Undine never does (she forgets to go to his birthday celebration). When Elmer comes upon the boy sobbing with loneliness in the Parisian *hôtel,* he knows it is "because your mother hadn't time for you." And he adds consolingly: "If we two chaps stick together it won't be so bad—we can keep each other warm, don't you see? I like you first rate, you know; when you're big enough I mean to put you in my business. And it looks as if one of these days you'd be the richest boy in America . . ." (369). Again the suspension points invite reflection. Paul will be the richest boy in America through invader money; but he can ally wealth to fine taste through his aborigine background, as is already implied in his attraction to the best picture in the place.

In the figure of Paul, then, Wharton offers a conciliatory closure to the novel. Undine will never have "the real" despite her overabundant possessions. As a divorced woman, she cannot be an ambassador's wife, "the one part she was really made for" (372). Those are the novel's last words. She is still copying, playing a "part," and a "part," as a role, is the opposite to "the real." There is a cost even for her in this struggle for the fittest to survive.

Works Cited

Barthes, Roland, "L'effet de réel." *Communications* 11 (1968): 84–89. "The Reality Effect." Trans. R. Carter. *French Literary Theory Today.* Ed. Tzvetan Todorov. Cambridge: Cambridge UP, 1982. 11–17.

Benjamin, Walter. "The Work of Art in an Age of Mechanical Reproduction." 1936. *Illuminations.* Ed. Hannah Arendt. New York: Schocken, 1969. 217–51.

Benstock, Shari. *No Gifts from Chance: A Biography of Edith Wharton.* New York: Penguin, 1995.

Gair, Christopher. "The Crumbling Structure of 'Appearances': Representation and Authenticity in *The House of Mirth* and *The Custom of the Country.*" *Modern Fiction Studies* 43.2 (Summer 1997): 349–73.

Pound, Ezra. *The Letters of Ezra Pound.* Ed. D. D. Paige. London: Faber & Faber, 1951.

Tonelli, Edith A. "The Art Museum." *The Museum: A Reference Guide.* Ed. Michael Steven Shapiro. Westport, CT: Greenwood Press, 1990. 31–58.

Trilling, Lionel. *Sincerity and Authenticity.* Cambridge: Harvard UP, 1971.

Wharton, Edith. *The Custom of the Country.* 1913. New York: Oxford UP, 1995.

Turning Zola Inside Out

JANE ADDAMS AND
LITERARY NATURALISM

—*Katherine Joslin*

A S A STUDENT AT ROCKFORD FEMALE SEMINARY IN THE LATE 1870S, JANE
ADDAMS DISTURBED HER TEACHER CAROLINE POTTER BY WRITING A
parody of Victorian essays on social progress. Nineteenth-century college students were encouraged to think about big ideas, and Addams blends notions
of social progress and biological evolution with an inversion of the creation
myth. Turning the biblical narrative inside out, she playfully reverses the story
that God created man in his image, positing instead that nature created the
human soul whose job it was to create the human body: "Man alone seems to
be an exception to the ordinary course of creation, his soul seems to have been
created first entire and complete, it contained immortal life, the forces of
nature trying thier [*sic*] best could not evolve a body which would likewise be
immortal; the soul then must have organized for itself a body of perishable
flesh." The youthful Addams points out the irony that in fashioning his mortal flesh, "man" imprisoned his immortal spirit rather than embodying it. To
illustrate the problem, she takes a prosaic and visceral example: "Still his vexation and chagrin were not complete until he examined his teeth and he
found what a failure they were." Why, if "man" is so smart, does he have cav-
ities? Addams depicts the battle to wrestle back from nature the potent forces
he has unwittingly ceded to her: "reeling onward, falling rising again, stag-
gering forward, a wounded felon daring to escape from his prison." The narrative ends in bathos: "we can still see in all his laws and inventions his efforts
to give his soul a chance to expand in other words his progress in the manufacture of teeth." The reader senses that Addams herself must have known the
pain of a toothache.

As a pragmatic Midwesterner, she shuns the sentimentality of her age,
eyeing the claims of both religion and science skeptically. Creation is a muddle,
she acknowledges, and the best we have to show for human progress against
natural imperfection is false teeth. The essay elicited a "speak to me of this

paper" response from Miss Potter, who, known for her "little sermons" on human responsibilities, must have been pleased to have such a spirited student if troubled by her unconventionality.[1]

Much of Jane Addams—social thinker, settlement house founder, saint of American progressivism, Nobel Peace Prize winner—can be found in her college essays. From her teenage years onward, she had a sharp sense of the frailties of the intellect and remained doubtful of its power to know and, much less, to control the human condition. As a pragmatist, she knew that teeth, disappointing as they are, might be aided by "progress in the manufacture of teeth," inexpert as such devices must have been in the nineteenth century. At the same time, she feared that humans might work "simply for the body" and not for the "soul." Her later writings study the nature of men and women, speculate on the conditions that put stress on their frailties, and suggest ways to ameliorate physical, biological, social, political, cultural, and economic pressures in order to allow people more freedom of time and movement, more opportunities perhaps to dwell on the life of the soul.

Moreover, Addams's college essay "Teeth" provides an early expression of her sense of herself as a literary person. The assignment called for serious exposition, yet the nascent writer felt the pull of imaginative expression. Tension between rational and imaginative prose is the most striking feature, I would argue, of Addams's writing from her teenage essays to her final book, a biography of her friend Julia Lathrop. Her blending of literary genres has made it difficult to categorize her books and essays.[2] Her books are always hard to find in bookstores and libraries. Ought we to look under sociology, the scholarly discipline newly developing in Chicago at the turn of the last century? Would we find her alongside contemporary writers on social work? Perhaps we would find her in the Women's Studies section or on the regional shelves under Midwestern history and culture. Why not think of her simply as a Chicago writer along with Theodore Dreiser, James T. Farrell, and Richard Wright? Her interdisciplinary thinking and her writing give us reason at the turn into the twenty-first century, when so much of our academic and scholarly work has moved across traditional boundaries, to reread Jane Addams's books and to rethink the nature of her prose and its connection to the literature of her day.

This essay looks at Addams's third book, *The Spirit of Youth and the City Streets* (1909), to consider her mode of writing and to explore her link to literary naturalism. What kind of writer is she? The answer lies in Émile Zola's portrait of the writer as an "experimental moralist." Lars Åhnebrink noted that "Zola, especially, had a reformer's zeal. He believed that society was responsible for all the misfortunes that befell the French people." In "The Experimental Novel" (1880), Zola had set out a theory of literary naturalism, urging his generation of writers to replace novels of pure imagination with novels of observation and experiment, a literature that might embody the spirit of an age of scientific investigation. In naturalist novels, as defined by Zola, writers record the links between heredity and environment in stories about the reciprocal influences of society on the individual and the individual on society. The moral task of the writer, in Zola's paradigm, is to expose the conditions that cause human misery. In his essay, he celebrates the physician Claude Bernard, who "says so well, as soon as we can act and do act on the determinism of phenomena, in modifying environment, for example, we are not fatalists" (180). Zola urges the young generation of writers at the end of the nineteenth century to examine, as a scientist does, the human condition in order to gain control, as a social scientist might, over the mechanism that controls fate. "We show the mechanism of the useful or the harmful," Zola claims of the naturalist novelists; "we disengage the determinism of human and social phenomena so that we may one day control and direct these phenomena" (181). The novelist overwhelms nature, or at least may lead the way in the task, and thus is not a fatalist but an experimental moralist, or so his argument goes.

Claude Bernard, or the fact that he was a physician, provides a useful link between Zola and Jane Addams. The doctor as a model of the scientist signals Zola's interest not only in discovering the diseases of society but also in treating them. An experimental moralist, as a doctor would, takes up the burden of curing social ills through progressive social reform. Jane Addams had thought of medicine when she considered becoming a scientist. She had grown up in the small Midwestern town of Cedarville, Illinois, in the shadow of her father John Addams, an entrepreneurial mill owner, banker, state legislator, and political friend of Abraham Lincoln. Largely because of her father's example, she desired a life of public service and sought a way to translate her religious training at Rockford into a secular effort that would allow her a professional life.

As she grew up in the bucolic Illinois landscape, she played with her two stepbrothers in a scientific club; the Haldeman boys would go on to study science, one to become a physician. In her journal begun in 1875 when she was living with her family in Cedarville, Addams wrote about her life as a typical kid—going sliding, having snowball fights, playing hopscotch, and loathing school—revealing little sign of the congenital back malady that supposedly troubled her in her youth. Every bit as eager to learn science and to achieve significant professional recognition as her stepbrothers, the teenage

Jane Addams fought hard with her father over where she would go to college. She preferred Smith College because of its rigorous male-styled curriculum; John Addams, however, preferred that his daughter stay close to home and enrolled her in Rockford in a course of study that, although modeled on male education, still asked the female student to see her life as service, reflecting traditional notions of women as handmaidens to men. Addams, as her essay "Teeth" suggests, rejected much of Christian doctrine, studied Darwin and other scientific thinkers, and urged her classmates toward professional life. Her journal records meetings of the Scientific Society at Rockford, "a sort of club for mutual improvement. The main text book is the Popular Science Monthly." She longed to study medicine at the University of Edinburgh and thus to move into a male profession.

Her argument with her father resolved itself when he died suddenly of appendicitis after she completed her course of study at Rockford, settling the question of who would decide her next step. "The greatest sorrow that can ever come to me has past [sic] and I hope it is only a question of time until I get my moral purpose," she wrote in a letter to her friend Ellen Gates Starr. Depressed by his death and enervated by stress in her dealings with her step-mother, Jane Addams yet insisted on attending Philadelphia Medical College for Women, only to plunge into an eight-year depression that was diagnosed by S. Weir Mitchell as hysteria, the prevailing malady of the first generation of college-educated women in America. Gioia Diliberto, in a new biography of Jane Addams, argues that Addams was disappointed in the education she received in medical school and, especially, in the situation of women in medicine and the dearth of opportunities then open to women doctors (84–86).

Weir Mitchell's "rest cure" gave Addams, perhaps for the first time in life, a "luxurious consciousness of leisure," exactly what her doctor intended, and allowed her the freedom to leave medical school. "I remember opening the first volume of Carlyle's *Frederick the Great* with a lively sense of gratitude that it was not Gray's *Anatomy*," she acknowledged later in *Twenty Years at Hull-House* (1910), "having found, like many another, that general culture is a much easier undertaking than professional study" (65–66). Weir Mitchell, so vilified by Charlotte Perkins Gilman in "The Yellow Wallpaper," seemed not to have troubled Addams, but rather, as Edith Wharton had done, she took books with her for her "rest," and while not being cured, seemed at least not to have been harmed by the treatment.

The eight-year depression she suffered marked her metamorphosis from a would-be physician into what Zola called an experimental moralist. After eight years of idleness, frustration, and depression, Addams found her intellectual and literary home at the age of twenty-nine when she moved with Ellen Gates Starr into Hull House in the Halsted Street neighborhood. In Chicago, she read William James and John Dewey, as well as Leo Tolstoy, W. E. B. Du Bois, George Eliot, H. G. Wells, and John Galsworthy, situating herself always between analytical and imaginative thinking and writing. She admired the naturalist novels of Frank Norris and Upton Sinclair with their blend of preaching and storytelling. In her books, we find remnants of her science club, her college essays, the women's medical school, nineteenth-century fiction, and contemporary sociology.

Jane Addams's method of writing, in a sense, turns Émile Zola's theory inside out. He and the American naturalists who followed him believed that literature ought to become more like science and sought to objectify fiction by infusing it with scientific observation and experimentation. Addams turns the theory inside out by making science (or the social science she was helping to define) more dramatic. Her method is to infuse scientific discourse with fictional episodes. After moving to Chicago, Addams had worked with Florence Kelley and Julia Lathrop to edit *Hull-House Maps and Papers* (1895). Allen Davis in his biography of Addams notes that the scientific study of ethnic groups and income in the poor immigrant neighborhood surrounding the settlement house sold fewer than 1,000 copies (128). Kelley had counseled Addams to adopt the mode of inquiry and analysis being developed by male sociologists at the University of Chicago, based on the Enlightenment regard for empiricism, reason, and logic.[3]

The first book that Addams wrote on her own, *Democracy in Social Ethics* (1902), moved considerably away from the scientific discourse Kelley preferred and toward a more literary style, based on synthetic and impressionistic depiction rather than strict rational argument. She juxtaposed argument with dramatic presentation and, in so doing, established the authority of her public voice.[4] Sales went up strikingly; the book sold 4,500 copies in the first eighteen months and continued to sell well over the next ten years with a total of 10,000 copies. Her use of a more literary discourse has rankled some historians over the years. Jill Conway, in the most notable case, registers her irritation with Addams's refusal to use the logic and statistical data of male discourse and dismisses her work for its lack of rigor: "to base one's social criticism upon the idea that feminine intuition could both diagnose and direct social change was to tie one's identity as a social critic to acquiescence in the traditional stereotype of women."[5]

After the failure of *Hull-House Maps and Papers,* Addams came more and more to doubt the adequacy of scientific writing to hold the human imagination.

In another Rockford essay that debates the affirmative point "Resolved—The Civilization of the Nineteenth Century tends to fetter intellectual life and Expression," Addams discusses the tension between science and literature. In reading Thomas Huxley, she concludes that "the physical and moral laws which govern man" allow us to see "things exactly as they are"; and yet in reading Matthew Arnold, she finds that literature "adds to the scientific theory a moral endeavor." She quotes Carlyle in a passage that seems to sum up her thinking: "The sum of man's misery is even this that he feels himself crushed under the Juggernaut wheels and knows that Juggernaut is no god but a dead mechanical idol." Her philosophical naturalism allows for both scientific and literary expression of the human condition. A decade later, Addams seems to have concluded that a purely scientific study of the Hull House community was not adequate to depict the daily lives of her neighbors.

As she puts it in *Democracy and Social Ethics,* "ideas only operate upon the popular mind through will and character, and must be dramatized before they reach the mass of men" (75). At the same time, she is suspicious of art as a purely imaginative medium because of its power to transport the reader beyond the quotidian world. For the social reformer, transport poses a real problem in that readers quite naturally wander away from the pressing social problems surrounding them. Addams questions the transportive power of art in a discussion of moving pictures: "From a tangle of 'make believe' [people] gravely scrutinize the real world which they are so reluctant to reenter, reminding one of the absorbed gaze of a child who is groping his way back from fairyland whither the story has completely transported him" (75). Movies seem to her a vulgar form of art but art nonetheless, and her suspicion of "make believe" as a costly diversion extends to all forms of art, including writing. In *Twenty Years at Hull-House* (1910), she uses an anecdote about De Quincey, who tells the story of a time when he was trying to recall a line from *The Iliad* as he saw an accident about to happen in front of him, to illustrate her contention that art may stand in the way of action. De Quincy struggled to disentangle his mind from the line of poetry in order to save the hapless couple. "This is what we were all doing," she warns her generation, "lumbering our minds with literature that only served to cloud the really vital situation spread before our eyes" (70). Addams fears the power of the imagination to transport the reader, yet desires a limited transport, a brief journey that would double back and leave the reader with a heightened sense of moral responsibility to reform the flaws of the world.

The Spirit of Youth and the City Streets is, in significant ways, a book about the power and the limitations of art. It opens with a tribute to poets and artists who through art "reveal to others the perpetual springs of life's self-renewal" and laments that literature is unavailable to those who remain illiterate, the working class poor in the Halsted neighborhood. Although literature and high art may be beyond their grasp, the common folk of Chicago and elsewhere experience the "perpetual springs" through the vitality of youth itself. Her contention that youth replicates the artistic impulse comes laden with attitudes about social class. There is no getting around her condescension toward the newly arrived, laboring immigrants, who presumably lack the education necessary to appreciate high art; at the same time, her middle-class readers may be smugly confident that art and nature remain open to them. The poetry of Wordsworth, the essays of Emerson, the plays of Shakespeare and Ibsen record and preserve "the perpetual springs" for the middle and upper-middle classes who have been trained to read and appreciate literature. She further argues that the literal "spring" of nature is a source of expression and delight. Too, her readers have the leisure time and the money to travel beyond the despoiled city of Chicago to restore themselves in the more pristine landscape of nature. Looking around at the immigrant laborers in Chicago, Addams questions how that "spirit" might find its equivalent among the lower classes.

An urban landscape, Addams laments, offers only debased forms of art and nature to its laboring youth. Popular romances, movie theaters, vaudeville shows, gin mills, soda shops, and bawdy songs all signify for her the efforts of commerce to defraud the young. Popular culture clearly frightens Addams: "The newly awakened senses are appealed to by all that is gaudy and sensual, by the flippant street music, the highly colored theater posters, the trashy love stories, the feathered hats, the cheap heroics of the revolvers displayed in the pawn-shop" (27). The ultimate in vulgarity for her is a song with a refrain like "snatching a kiss from her ruby lips"; clearly, every word offends her. One might argue that the very vitality of the city could be found in her portrait of the popular culture of Chicago.

Certainly, the portrait of a twentieth-century Sodom captured the imagination of the middle-class reader, an armchair tourist who might through Addams's books travel into the slums without the risk of an actual encounter with the "dangerous" classes. Addams knew as much as Upton Sinclair or Frank Norris or Theodore Dreiser or Zola himself did about the power of such descriptions to sell books. As an experimental moralist, she exposed the flaws of capitalist culture that put pressure on its most vulnerable members, especially on the poor and the young. To deliver her lecture to her middle-class readers, Addams juxtaposed her didactic message with portraits of those trapped by the city. She advocated public theater, recreation, sports, festivals, parades, concerts, and crafts as wholesome expressions of the "perpetual springs of life's self-renewal." Addams did little to promote class mobility, arguing instead for changes in urban conditions that would ameliorate the problems of harsh poverty and brutalizing labor. Public theater or ethnic crafts might provide the working poor "the foundation for their working moral codes and the data from which they will judge the proprieties of life."

The Spirit of Youth followed the design of Democracy and Social Ethics, offering a meta-narrative about her own life as a social settlement worker interspersed with vignettes of immigrant life. Addams could not resist telling stories and, although she filters them all through her own voice, the pleasure in reading The Spirit of Youth often comes from the exuberance of the street tales themselves, tales that at times subvert the sociological argument. Her book reads much like the muckraking fiction of her day. Upton Sinclair's The Jungle, for example, uses the narrative power of fiction to bring the public to an understanding of the economic and social oppression of immigrant laborers caused by the owners of the meatpacking plants in Chicago. Sinclair's novel, as we know, did little to change labor laws; instead, it frightened middle-class consumers about the cleanliness of the meat they were eating.

The power of fiction to open many questions at once, what Mikhail Bakhtin called its "dialogic" nature, caused Addams to be selective in how she embedded imaginative passages in her social tracts. The Spirit of Youth continues to be popular with readers, I would argue, because we hear in the book the voices of common folks, voices from what Bakhtin called the carnival. These sketches of lower-class life interweave with popular movie plots and scenes from literature in the autobiographical account of Addams's walk along Halsted Street. In the meta-narrative, an upper-middle-class, college-educated, professional woman converses with her middle-class readers about the social conditions of her lower-class neighbors.

Her vignettes read like naturalist fiction, sketching lurid tales of compulsive and destructive sexuality, addiction, and brutality. "Poor little Ophelia," a typical example, might have come from a Zola novel. Ophelia is trapped in an abusive relationship with Pierre, who suffers "from his prolonged debauch of whiskey and opium." "I can see her now," Addams writes, "running for protection up the broad steps of the columned piazza then surrounding Hull-House. Her slender figure was trembling with fright, her tear-covered face swollen and bloodstained from the blows he had dealt her" (40–42). Like Gervaise in L'Assommoir, Ophelia seems to have accepted her fate: "'He is apt to abuse me when he is drunk,'" she tells the social worker, who discovers that they are not married, have no children, and that Pierre has twice tried to kill Ophelia. Addams notes the irony that although the settlement workers have tried to convince the young woman to leave the brute, virtue is no match for vice: "A poor little Ophelia, I met her one night wondering in the hall half dressed in the tawdry pink gown 'that Pierre likes best of all' and groping on the blank wall to find the door which might permit her to escape to her lover." The Hull House workers, horrified and mystified by the power of sexuality, put her in restraints in a hospital, yet after her release she returns to her lover who presses her into prostitution to earn money for his drug habit. Addams acknowledges what many parents know: "we were obliged to admit that there is no civic authority which can control the acts of a girl of eighteen." The spirit of youth itself is the culprit.

The narrative unabashedly employs titillating details: the piazza is columned; the female figure is slender, trembling, and scantily clad; her tears flow; and the villain draws blood. The allusion to the "high" art of Shakespeare comes dressed in melodramatic excess—tawdry pink gown and masochistic desire. Addams's fictionalizing of the account borrows heavily from sentimental literature, the tales of seduction and betrayal so popular in the nineteenth century. Although proper Rockford Female Seminary girls were forbidden to read sentimental novels, Addams humorously recorded in her journal a discussion of *Guy Mannering*: "'My,' she says, 'it is just like those affected scenes that I've read dozens of in cheap novels.' and a warning pinch stop her [*sic*] 'Don't confess it' whispers her neighbor." Jane Addams, the mature writer, is present here in the early journal, especially in the playful way she narrates the scene.

Her hybrid constructions juxtapose sentimental plots with social issues to illustrate her naturalist philosophy. Like Zola and Sinclair and Dreiser and Wright, Addams thought that fate is determined by such things as hormones, poverty, and addiction. Ophelia becomes what was called at the time a "white slave," forced into prostitution by her addicted lover.[6] The fictional episodes in *The Spirit of Youth* are so colorful that one wonders whether the middle-class reader is convinced to take up Ophelia's cause or whether the lurid details set the tainted heroine apart from the community Addams had hoped to establish. In the narrative, Ophelia leaves the Halsted Street neighborhood when she follows Pierre. Addams offers no further hope for the fallen woman, no social reform that might curb her biological urge, and no cure for Pierre's addiction to drugs.

Instead, she gives the reader another tale of the right sort of female behavior. Angelina (not exactly the opposite of Ophelia although the message is clear from their names) inhibits her sex instinct and waits patiently and hopefully for her father to arrange a proper marriage (45). Presumably, the father will be able to detect biological and social imperfections in other males and will not have such imperfections himself. Oddly, arranged marriage emerges as the safest solution to female sexuality in the book. With sex as with art, Addams fears the power of transport.

Another significant feature of Addams's naturalism is that although females are safest in their prelapsarian state, males cannot resist the fall. Her book is full of stories about male juvenile delinquents from eleven to fifteen years old, accounts that she has gathered from court cases and newspaper articles about exploits along the railroad tracks. A typical example depicts a street fight among the toughs in the neighborhood, an obligatory scene in naturalist novels by Dreiser or Farrell and one that Addams has actually clipped from a Chicago newspaper. Thirteen-year-old Daniel O'Brien leads his neighborhood friends in throwing stones at a Polish boy named Nieczgodzki who is goaded by another kid named Pfister into pulling out a revolver: "'Nieczgodzki aimed his revolver at Pfister and fired. The bullet crashed through the top of his head and entered the brain'" (61). In another example, this one in her own words, she tells a sentimental tale of Davie, a country boy from Ohio, who shot and killed a policeman. Addams's story uses the mother's voice to soften the criminality of the son: "'Davie was never a bad boy until about five years ago when he began to go with this gang who are always looking out for fun'" (43), she explains to the settlement worker.

The male instinct for adventure seems to Addams natural and, if redirected by society, a healthy and vital resource for the community. The section of the book on boys is full of exuberance: "It is as though we were deaf to the appeal of these young creatures, claiming their share of the joy of life, flinging out into the dingy city their desires and aspirations after unknown realities, their unutterable longings for companionship and pleasure" (70–71). Her heroes commit petty crimes—they shoot craps, smoke cigarettes, keep bad company, experiment with drugs, hobo around the country—because of their urge to express "the unrecognized and primitive spirit of adventure, corresponding to the old activity of the hunt, of warfare, and of discovery" (53). The expectation is that in his postlapsarian state the boy will become "the steady young man of nineteen who brings home all his wages" (58). How does the hero avoid the fate of the sado-masochistic Pierre whose instinct turned to perversion? Addams never answers that question but rather puts forward a set of social reforms, aimed at redirecting male instinct, that includes athletic programs and industrial education to train the primitive urges into healthy and useful behaviors. Over the years leading up to the writing of *The Spirit of*

Youth, Addams had been working with William James and other pacifists on the prospects for creating what she called in 1903 "A Moral Substitute for War."[7] The idea that society might find what James called "equivalents" for male aggression seemed rational to Addams who spoke along with him in Boston at the thirteenth Universal Peace Conference in the fall of 1904.

In turning Zola's theory inside out, Addams employs fiction to aid social discourse, creating a hybrid literary genre that proved popular with middle-class readers and helped to transform thinking about parks, recreation, athletics, and education in America. Hull House as an institution worked to shorten working hours, open kindergartens, form sports teams, organize trips to natural environments, and provide a community theater and immigrant craft museum. The reforms Addams urged on her readers in *The Spirit of Youth* may have seemed at times no more successful than "progress in the manufacture of teeth." We are all aware in the twenty-first century that the solutions she set into practice at Hull House have not cured the social ills she kept her eye on throughout her career as a social worker. Yet we reread her book today with a clear sense of her as a literary figure, a Chicago writer of the naturalist school.

NOTES

1. Jane Addams was always writing and as a girl kept a journal dated 1875. The journal begins in 1875 but seems to pick up again after Addams goes to Rockford Female Seminary in 1877. The types of questions that Caroline Potter asked her students to consider are suggested in a couplet Addams once recorded: "What am I? whence produced? and for what end? / Whence draw I being to what period tend?" The journal records Addams's own spirit of youth; it is witty, humorous, and lively.

    The writings that I use for this essay can be found in the Jane Addams Memorial Collection, Library, University of Illinois at Chicago. Scholars can also read her papers in a microfilm edition, *Jane Addams Papers Project,* edited by Mary Lynn McCree Bryan, who has also provided a wonderfully detailed and useful guide to the microfilm, *The Jane Addams Papers: A Comprehensive Guide,* ed. Mary Lynn McCree Bryan (Bloomington: Indiana UP, 1996). The University of Illinois Press is publishing *The Selected Papers of Jane Addams, Vol. 1: Preparing to Lead, 1860–81,* edited by Mary Lynn McCree Bryan, Barbara Bair, and Maree de Angury (2002).

2. Two new books consider Addams as a public intellectual, a term that Jean Bethke Elshtain uses in *Jane Addams and the Dream of American Democracy: A Life* (New York: Basic Books, 2002). Louis Menand places Addams in the company of John Dewey and William James in *The Metaphysical Club: A Story of Ideas in America* (New York: Farrar, Straus and Giroux, 2001), making the argument that the two men absorbed her ideas.

3. Mary Jo Deegan, in *Jane Addams and the Men of the Chicago School, 1892–1918* (New Brunswick, NJ: Transaction, 1988), makes the argument that the work of Addams and Kelley in mapping the Hull House neighborhood established the model of sociological investigation that became the "core methodology" in the 1920s of Chicago sociologists. Further, she asserts that their contribution has never been fully acknowledged. "Such a systematic exclusion of the women's work can only be explained as academic dishonesty," she charges (46).

4. I have developed this argument in an earlier essay, "Literary Cross-Dressing: Jane Addams Finds Her Voice in *Democracy and Social Ethics,*" *Femme de conscience: Aspects du feminisme americain (1848–1875)* (Paris: Presses de la Sorbonne Nouvelle, 1994), 217–38.

5. Jill Conway in "Women Reformers and American Culture, 1870–1930," *Journal of Social History* 5.1 (1971): 164–77, gets bogged down in a rigid conception of gender difference and criticizes Addams for not using male discourse. Scientific thought, Conway seems not to understand, blends intuition and reason, hunches and experiments.

6. Janet Beer and I have discussed white slavery and Addams's relationship with Gilman in "Diseases of the Body Politic: White Slavery in Jane Addams's *A New Conscience and an Ancient Evil* and Selected Short Stories by Charlotte Perkins Gilman," *Women in America,* part 1, spec. issue of *Journal of American Studies* 33 (Apr. 1999). In 1912, Addams published a book about white slavery, *A New Conscience and an Ancient Evil.*

7. Allen Davis discusses the relationship between Addams and James, working hard, it seems curious to me, to diminish James's high regard for her as a writer; see pages 140–44. Her second book, *The Newer Ideals of Peace,* was published in 1907.

WORKS CITED

Addams, Jane. *Democracy and Social Ethics.* 1902. Ed. Anne Firor Scott. Cambridge: Harvard UP, 1972.

———. *The Spirit of Youth and the City Streets.* 1909. Urbana: U of Illinois P, 1972.

———. *Twenty Years at Hull-House.* New York: Macmillan, 1910.

Åhnebrink, Lars. *The Beginnings of Naturalism in American Fiction.* Essays and Studies on American Language and Literature 9. Cambridge: Harvard UP, 1950.

Beer, Janet, and Katherine Joslin. "Diseases of the Body Politic: White Slavery in Jane Addams' *A New Conscience and an Ancient Evil* and Selected Short Stories by Charlotte Perkins Gilman." *Women in America,* part 1. Spec. issue of *Journal of American Studies* 33 (Apr. 1999).

Bryan, Mary Lynn McCree, ed. *The Jane Addams Papers: A Comprehensive Guide.* Bloomington: Indiana UP, 1996.

Conway, Jill. "Women Reformers and American Culture, 1870–1930." *Journal of Social History* 5.1 (1971).

Davis, Allen F. *American Heroine: The Life and Legend of Jane Addams.* New York: Oxford UP, 1965.

Deegan, Mary Jo. *Jane Addams and the Men of the Chicago School, 1892–1918.* New Brunswick, NJ: Transaction, 1988.

Diliberto, Gioia. *A Useful Woman: The Early Life of Jane Addams.* New York: Scribner's, 1999.

Jane Addams Memorial Collection. Library. U of Illinois, Chicago.

Joslin, Katherine. "Literary Cross-Dressing: Jane Addams Finds Her Voice in *Democracy and Social Ethics.*" *Femme de conscience: Aspects du feminisme americain (1848–1875).* Paris: Presses de la Sorbonne Nouvelle, 1994.

Zola, Émile. "Le Roman experimental." *Le Roman experimental.* Paris, 1880. *Documents of Modern Literary Realism.* Ed. George J. Becker. Princeton: Princeton UP, 1963.

Oppressive Bodies

VICTORIANISM, FEMINISM, AND NATURALISM
IN EVELYN SCOTT'S *THE NARROW HOUSE*

—Tim Edwards

DONALD PIZER'S RECENT RETHINKINGS OF NATURALISM IN AMERICAN fiction HAVE SUGGESTED FASCINATING POSSIBILITIES FOR HOW WE MIGHT reinvigorate our understanding of the canon. Pizer's suggestions involve reconsidering the narrow definitions of naturalistic fiction as mere "pessimistic determinism," a simplistic but unfortunately resilient label applied by Oscar Cargill in *Intellectual America* (1941). For Pizer, naturalism in American fiction should not be limited to the decade of the 1890s and the work of Crane, Norris, and Dreiser; nor should naturalism be seen as a "school" or even a "movement" (*Theory* 7). Instead, Pizer asserts, we should regard naturalism as a sort of recurring impulse in American fiction which periodically resurfaces throughout the twentieth-century canon—not a historically defined literary era but a longstanding literary tradition, the "ideological core" of which suggests "a sense of man more circumscribed than conventionally acknowledged" (20). What interests Pizer is "the dynamic flexibility and amorphousness of naturalism" (Introduction 13), an "adaptability" which allows naturalistic novelists to inject "fresh currents of idea and expression" into "a core of naturalistic preoccupations" (13). What is important here, of course, is that Pizer's reconsideration of naturalism inherently opens up the naturalistic canon, urging us to reexamine through a naturalistic lens texts and writers not previously associated with this tradition. Among the writers Pizer connects to the naturalistic impulse are women novelists such as Edith Wharton and Kate Chopin, artists whose texts reflect the "central theme of the entrapment of women within social codes and taboos" (14). "Indeed," Pizer observes, "a great deal of fiction by women about women, from Wharton and Kate Chopin onward, can be said to reflect this naturalistic theme" (14).

The long neglected work of Evelyn Scott presents a similar sort of opportunity to inscribe feminist voices into the naturalistic canon. Efforts to retrieve the corpus of Scott's work have typically positioned her fiction within the context of southern literature or, occasionally, within the broader and more pliable borders of modernism. Scott was, in fact, southern, and her literary project, frequently marked by forays into formal experimentation, shares critical connections with those of her modernist contemporaries. But while Scott's work stands astride several important intersections of American literature—realism, expressionism, modernism—her earliest prose texts tap into the vein of literary naturalism shaping the direction of many novelists of the twenties.

Indeed, Scott's early prose works—*The Narrow House,* especially—allow us to consider the naturalistic impulse in American fiction from the more liberating angles Donald Pizer has encouraged us to explore. In Scott's text, we see a brand of naturalism quite apart, in many respects, from the economic determinism of Norris or the unyielding natural world of Crane and London. We encounter, instead, a surprisingly complex and disturbing naturalism in the familiar and deceptively innocuous setting of the domestic sphere, a naturalism that critiques the shallow moral conventionalities and domestic ideologies Evelyn Scott observed around her, one that vigorously attacks the cultural ideals of motherhood and feminine beauty paraded forth by patriarchal constructions of the feminine.

Evelyn Scott's *The Narrow House* was one of the most controversial novels of its day. Eight years before William Faulkner gave us *The Sound and the Fury,* Evelyn Scott explored the same kind of madness, betrayal, and perversion lurking behind the walls of the decaying, vaguely gothic architecture of the Farley home. Now, like its writer, too often relegated to the margins in our discussions of the modern canon, this experimental novel of familial dissolution and spiritual decay shocked contemporaries with its morbid commentary on the state of the American family.

Hailed by H. L. Mencken and Sinclair Lewis as a major literary event, *The Narrow House* clearly emerges from the naturalistic impulse in American fiction, telling the story of the hopeless and loveless Farley clan, a family trapped within a domestic hell of distrust, betrayal, and domination that seems to prefigure the vicious absurdity of later works like Jean-Paul Sartre's *No Exit* and Harold Pinter's *The Homecoming.* Evelyn Scott herself described the naturalistic fibers from which her early texts were woven: "While I was at school in New Orleans," she wrote, "the works of Stephen Crane, Frank Norris, and Theodore Dreiser influenced me far more significantly than my half-creole milieu" (*Background* 286). As with the women novelists Pizer identifies, however, the naturalistic impulse coursing through Scott's earliest work is shaped by a decidedly feminist awareness.

Published in 1921, Scott's novel straddles a number of historical and literary boundaries. On one level, the text considers the decaying standards of the residual Victorianism of early-twentieth-century culture. Convinced that the false refinements of her own late-nineteenth-century southern background had no place in a modern world in which the artist should turn a frank eye to reality, Scott viciously assailed the rigid and dated social codes that still, two decades into the twentieth century, continued to construct a narrow house of imprisonment, of death-in-life, for the individual consciousness. Like her older admirer Sinclair Lewis, Evelyn Scott helped set the rebellious tone for American literature of the 1920s, appropriating a naturalistic framework, as Robert L. Welker has observed, to articulate her critique of domesticity and conventionality, the sorts of residual Victorianism—or Puritanism, as both Scott and H. L. Mencken frequently labeled it—that continued to shape American moral and political attitudes even in the supposedly "modern" era of the early 1920s. In *The Narrow House*, Evelyn Scott works hard to overturn such conventional ideologies. And by deploying both a naturalistic and a feminist critique of those very social codes and conventions, Scott's novel becomes a text of a culture in transition—critiquing the old order from a rebellious, modern perspective; more than this, though, it becomes a text of literature in transition—at least, in the hands of one bold experimenter—as Evelyn Scott strives aggressively to reinvent literary naturalism with a feminist impulse of energetic daring.

The Narrow House arrived on the threshold of a critical decade in American literature—and in literary naturalism, in particular: the 1920s. Donald Pizer sees the 1920s as a transitional period in which naturalistic themes that surfaced during the 1890s meshed with the technical innovations of the emerging modernist movement. James Joyce's *Ulysses*, Sherwood Anderson's *Winesburg, Ohio*, and Theodore Dreiser's *An American Tragedy*, Pizer asserts, all treat the "abstract deterministic ideas" of 1890s naturalistic fiction with a more experimental "oblique expression" (*Theory* 25): "Many of the novelists of the twenties appeared to be saying that we live in a trivial, banal, and tawdry world that nevertheless encloses us and shapes our destinies. We seek to escape from this world into the inner life because only there do we seem to find the richness of feeling denied us in experience" (*Theory* 25).

Pizer's vision of 1920s fiction is a remarkably apt profile of the aims and achievements of *The Narrow House*, particularly when we consider Pizer's further comments about the fiction of this period: "But in fact we do not really escape. The retreat into the inner life transforms us into grotesque exaggerations

of what we wish to be, or causes us (with fatal consequences) to seek the translation of fantasy into reality, or engages us in an endless search for the understanding and love denied us in life" (*Theory* 25). The passage quoted above
could, indeed, easily have been lifted from a contemporary review of Scott's
novel so closely does it reflect the central imagery, themes, and narrative turns
of *The Narrow House.*

Perhaps even more significant, however, is the shift in setting we see in
this hybrid of modernist experimentalism and naturalistic thematics. As Pizer
explains, "By the 1920s, the naturalistic impulse had refined itself into a more
subtle representation of the qualifications placed on man's freedom than was
true of naturalistic work of the 1890s. Rather, the theme of constraint is dramatized within more domesticated and everyday phases of life" (*Theory* 158).
The Narrow House is foremost a domestic narrative focusing on everyday
events, and Evelyn Scott stages her naturalistic plot not upon the Darwinian
landscapes and seascapes characteristic of much of the earlier naturalistic
fiction but rather against the familiar backdrops of the typical bourgeois
home: the kitchen, the parlor, the bedroom.

Although current discussions of Scott's work seldom locate her within
the naturalistic tradition, the first critical reactions to *The Narrow House* commonly characterized that text as an example of a kind of naturalistic fiction, but
critics frequently differed on just what kind of naturalistic fiction the novel
exemplifies. Fred B. Millett, in his *Contemporary American Authors* (1940), calls
Scott's novel highly subjective "psychological naturalism" (33). For Harlan
Hatcher, however, the text exudes a colder, more objective atmosphere, with "a
sharp, scientific eye riveted on truth" (181). Indeed, *The Narrow House,* though
not a commercial success, sparked a considerable debate among critics and
reviewers, many of whom found Evelyn Scott's first novel painful reading.
Scott's work found an important champion in Sinclair Lewis, whose review of
The Narrow House in the *New York Times Book Review and Magazine* hailed the
publication of the novel as "an event": "Salute to Evelyn Scott! It would be an
insult to speak with smug judiciousness of her 'promise.' She has done it!" (18).
The few more recent critics who have written extensively on Scott's life and
work record a more positive shock of recognition in engaging with her first
novel: Mary Wheeling White, for instance, recalls how the work "shocked
and thrilled [her] with its unexpected narrative" (xiii); Mary Carrigg comments on the "stark power" of the novel (92); and Robert L. Welker considers
the work "a remarkably fine presentation," "complete in the record it gives of
the spiritual death of one family generation" (253). Pessimistic, graphic, almost

claustrophobic, Scott's unrelenting vision of a quietly (sometimes quietly, at any rate) disintegrating Farley household is, as Steven Ryan has observed, astonishingly sustained in its brutal tone: "the unity of atmosphere," Ryan writes, "is the novel's most remarkable accomplishment" (36). And, indeed, in an interview in *The Bookman,* Evelyn Scott recalled the writing of the novel as one of the most intense experiences she had ever had (Salpeter 284).

The Narrow House tells the story of three generations of the Farley family: Mr. and Mrs. Farley, their two adult children, Alice and Laurence, Laurence's wife Winnie, and their young children May and Bobby. The central conflicts revolve around the long-term infidelity of Mr. Farley, the ineffectual family patriarch, who has fathered a child with a lover in Kansas City. Despite public knowledge of the affair, the elder Farleys have remained together, primarily to keep up appearances—and the tension emanating from the older couple infects the entire household with a sense of decay and distrust. That the Farleys desperately try to deny the truth of Mr. Farley's sexual infidelity is symptomatic of the family's malaise on a number of levels—for the physical body is a vexing subject for all of the Farleys, so much so that comparisons of Scott's work to that of D. H. Lawrence are almost inevitable (Flora 287).

In *The French Lieutenant's Woman,* John Fowles attempts to explain— or at least to illustrate—the Victorian schizophrenia afflicting his fictional characters. A similar self split against itself stalks the darkened hallways of Scott's *The Narrow House,* for, as Joseph M. Flora has pointed out, "the division between mind and body is apparent everywhere" in Scott's early novels (287). This is certainly true of *The Narrow House,* in which work Evelyn Scott is very much concerned with analyzing, exposing, and finally exploding this sort of schizophrenia—what she would have called unhealthy Puritan repression— primarily by illustrating the dreadful results of this sort of denial. As Mary Wheeling White explains, "Scott's novel reflected a mindset widely held by young experimental artists of the 1920s . . . [who] felt oppressed by an older generation that clung to outmoded Victorian moral codes" (61). In *The Narrow House,* then, Scott squarely confronts issues of morality, physicality, and sexuality that remained anathema to the Puritanical America of the early 1920s, demonstrating how the repression of these issues, while intended to erect some bulwark of virtue and duty and love, in fact served in the end only to rot the foundations beneath the imprisoning narrow house of Victorian domesticity.

The wasteland imagery that marks the opening scene of the narrative establishes the tone of moral, spiritual, and physical decay that led many contemporary readers to decry "the repulsiveness of Scott's artistic vision"

(White 60). The novel's initial sequence opens on the Farley family neighborhood, a "hot, bright street [that] looked almost deserted" (*Narrow House* 1); a "disheveled building" presides ominously over the near empty cityscape, flanked by a "glaring heap" of "broken plaster" (1). The themes of alienation, fragmentation, and decay suggested by this imagery shift soon enough from the deserted terrain of the opening scene to the Farley family members themselves, a transfer of meaning carried through the medium of another crucial image—the Farley house:

> The old-fashioned house next door [the Farley family home] was as badly in need of improvements as the one undergoing alterations. The dingy brick walls were streaked by the drippage from the leaky tin gutter that ran along the roof. The massive shutters, thrown back from the long windows, were rotting away. Below the lifted panes very clean worn curtains hung slack like things exhausted by the heat. (1)

The short passage above bristles with metaphorical energy. The choice of the term "old-fashioned" to capture the architectural detail of the house is a significant one, serving equally well to label the dated and ultimately superficial Victorian morality to which the family so desperately and futilely clings. Indeed, the Farley family proves to be as "dingy," "streaked," and "rotting" as their home. And like the worn curtains hanging "slack" and "exhausted" in their windows, the Farleys' vain efforts to sustain a "clean" facade cannot conceal the decay within. Clearly, then, such a domestic environment, like the dwelling that houses it, is "badly in need of improvements" (7).

Yet the novel is more than simply a tale of family discord, for its title takes on a particular importance when we consider how Scott's approach to naturalism is filtered through a sort of feminist lens. Of course, a "narrow house" is a coffin or casket—clearly an image of both entrapment and death. On a larger level, however, the central metaphor of the house is critical for our understanding of Scott's aims, for the house—the home—is the privileged locus of Victorian domesticity, evident in everything from Coventry Patmore's "The Angel in the House" in England to "The Cult of True Womanhood" Barbara Welter sees shaping nineteenth-century constructions of American femininity. Thus, the title of the work itself suggests the ominous implications of a hopeless entombment within a sort of domestic hell—a fearful setting that nevertheless summons forth all sorts of romanticized portraits of ideal family and ideal femininity.

When Mrs. Farley, the first family member we encounter, steps onto this sterile and rotting stage, we see the transfer of tropes from landscape to house to family. Dressed in a fading but genteel fashion, with "shabby white cotton gloves" and a skirt "too long behind," Mrs. Farley seems the embodiment of the old order. Depleted and devalued, much like her old house, Mrs. Farley "wish[es] that something might be done to improve her home" (8)—and, of course, as the narrative unfolds, that desire takes on an increasingly rich meaning.

But if Scott's characters are trapped metaphorically within the dilapidated home, they are even more dramatically entangled by the narrow houses of their own bodies—bodies that prove to be powerfully constricted by the moral conventions and cultural expectations weighing upon them. Indeed, as Joseph M. Flora's comment suggests, Scott's characters are deeply at odds with their own bodies, with their own physical natures, and with the rigid limitations, expectations, and social conventions their bodies and natures continually threaten to violate. Like so many naturalistic novelists, Scott continually foregrounds the physical, the animal, and the sexual in human nature. Human bodies in Scott's narrative prove, in the final analysis, to be traps—though different sorts of traps for different sorts of characters. Equally entrapping, of course, are those various cultural and social expectations we have mentioned, a set of ideologies that shape and determine how these bodies must be regarded and valued—or devalued.

The mind-body division Flora foregrounds is particularly evident in the adult males of the Farley household—Mr. Farley and his son Laurence. Both men are powerfully disturbed not only by their own sexual desires but also by the female sexuality around them—and both try desperately to ignore these issues. Laurence Farley seems obsessed by women, yet he clearly fears the sexual power they seem to hold over him: "He felt suffocated by women," we are told (92). The houses of his street "were secret and filled with women. . . . Laurence felt crowded between the bodies of women and houses. He walked quickly with his head bent" (66). Later, he laments that, despite his best efforts, "women were [still] troubling him, [and] he had not actually eliminated them from his desires" (211).

Similarly, Laurence's father is deeply troubled by his secret—and not so secret—sins of sexual desire. One particularly powerful moment involves Mr. Farley and his daughter-in-law, the beautiful but manipulative Winnie: "Again and again, as if in spite of himself, he [Mr. Farley] allowed his gaze to rest on Winnie. His daughter-in-law disturbed him and if he could avoid it he never looked her in the eye" (30–31). Here, ocular imagery plays a central role as Mr. Farley tries desperately to deny his sexual impulses: "If he could keep from noticing the throats and breasts and arms of women he was usually all right. . . . Sex had invariably placed him in the wrong, so sex must be the expression of a perverse impulse" (30–31). For a bohemian and liberated Greenwich Village artist like Evelyn Scott, such characters as the Farley men would personify, in her view, the worst of Victorian prudery. More than this, however, they also signify how the cornerstones of Victorian morality are cemented by the mortar of hypocrisy; that Mr. Farley, for instance, as well as his wife, tries so vigorously to deny the truth of sexual infidelity and marital betrayal is, ultimately, as tragic as it is absurd.

With the two primary women characters in the text, we see Scott's critique shift toward a more specifically feminist angle of attack. Winnie Farley and her sister-in-law, Alice Farley, are, in very different ways, illustrative of the troubling varieties of naturalistic entrapment that threaten all women. In the case of these women characters, the denial of sexual impulses—so prominent in the portrayal of the male Farleys—is overshadowed by a different trajectory of dangers, dangers built primarily around culturally constructed notions of ideal femininity. Winnie suffers through a complicated pregnancy, finally dying shortly after giving birth. Her terrifying ordeal seems to elaborate on the critique of the mother-woman offered in Kate Chopin's *The Awakening* in that, in scenes rendered with unsettling detail, Scott's Winnie suffers the horrifying fate Chopin suggests more indirectly in the account of Madame Ratignolle's pregnancy near the conclusion of *The Awakening*. The maternal anxiety Adele suffers in Chopin's novel is supplanted in *The Narrow House* by a fearful and full-blown crescendo of terror as Winnie's complicated pregnancy reaches its fatal and inevitable end.

Alice, Winnie's unmarried sister-in-law, suffers from a different kind of entrapment. Struggling with a disturbing awareness of the "otherness" of her own female body, Alice is haunted by the cultural ideals of feminine beauty which her own ungainly and unlovely body inevitably violates. Driven to despair, indeed to the brink of suicide, Alice Farley illustrates with frightening clarity the darkest implications of women's entrapment in the naturalistic web of "social codes and taboos."

Of particular interest is how the image of the woman's body figures into Scott's particular angle on the naturalistic tradition. Women's bodies are agents of oppression in the text—agents of oppression, most importantly, against women themselves. For feminist critics such as Mary Russo and Sidonie Smith, subjectivity—particularly female subjectivity—is inherently rooted in the body.

Of course, this determination carries with it a special significance regarding marginal subjects, those whose bodies are marked by difference. And a woman's body is, in fact, such a body marked by difference, an issue Scott's early naturalistic texts consider from a variety of provocative vantage points. An awareness of the body and how characters in fiction are embodied is crucial for understanding what is at stake in *The Narrow House,* and critics such as Smith and Russo provide an essential critical apparatus for considering the intersection of naturalism and feminism in Evelyn Scott's novel.

Sidonie Smith has contributed groundbreaking insights into the nature of women's autobiography by examining how the notion of subjectivity is shaped by cultural and biological constructions of the body. Smith sees the woman as an "encumbered" self, identified by social roles, yes, but also powerfully shaped by a sort of biological entrapment: for Smith, a woman's anatomy, in part, shapes her destiny (*Subjectivity* 12). In much women's autobiography, Smith observes, the autobiographical voice is molded in significant ways by an awareness of the differentness of the female body: and because of the differentness of their bodies, these women writers frequently "find themselves partitioned in their bodies, culturally embodied" ("Identity's Body" 269)—a marginalized position which then becomes a central concern of the autobiographical woman writer.

As critic Harlan Hatcher has noted, *The Narrow House* shares significant stylistic and thematic connections with Evelyn Scott's experimental autobiography, *Escapade,* published two years after the novel (180). The narrator of Scott's *Escapade,* in turn, provides an astonishing example of the sort of autobiographical voice Smith theorizes. A young, pregnant American isolated in the androcentric environment of World War I–era Brazil, the narrator develops a painfully acute awareness of how her body—her pregnant body, in particular—marks her as different, as Other. Once pregnancy "has so altered [her] figure" that she requires a new wardrobe, the narrator endures a disturbing sequence at the local atelier's shop: "While he [the male atelier] was measuring me, he talked volubly and pressed his hand carelessly and caressingly over my hips and breasts. I felt like an animal being examined for good points. . . . I was conscious of my flesh as of some horrible garment" (18–19).

The pregnant condition of Scott's narrator in the early segments of *Escapade* is of crucial significance. Among the most critical of the feminine ideals constructing the image of the "True Woman," Barbara Welter tells us, is motherhood, maternity, a happy state of "usefulness" and "prestige" (38) that locates the mother-woman at the nucleus of the idealized domestic cosmos. Feminist critics, of course, see these issues in a different light: Mary Jacobus, for instance, regards "the representation and ideology of motherhood" (144) as the primary foundation for the systematic oppression of women. We find similar critiques of ideal motherhood in the works of women writers such as Kate Chopin and, indeed, in the work of Evelyn Scott, who felt that the most stringent restrictions on a woman's liberty centered on her body, particularly in terms of reproductive freedom (Callard 137–38). We see, for instance, in *Escapade* a clear sense that the pregnant narrator is hopelessly trapped in her maternal body, which seems to move forward inexorably, impelled by its own reproductive momentum. As the moment for delivery approaches, Scott's narrator begins to perceive herself as a veritable biological/maternal machine, a mere vehicle for reproduction: "I knew that I was caught up in a mechanism of some kind that had to go on and on to the end—even if the end were death" (52). *Escapade,* then, relentlessly undercuts any idealized notions of maternity, exposing instead the very real dangers masked beneath these conventional ideals: "Horrible to be a part of flesh," Scott's narrator reflects, "from which there is no escape" (203–4).

 The Narrow House confronts these same sorts of issues but in a fictional rather than an autobiographical context. Maternity, marginality, and the confining conventions and ideals that play upon the female body and the feminine consciousness—all are issues central to *The Narrow House,* much as they are to Scott's experimental autobiography. As we have seen, both Winnie and Alice embody—quite literally—the sorts of entrapment theorized by feminist critics from Barbara Welter to Sidonie Smith. In fact, Winnie and Alice are antipodes of a sort: Winnie demonstrates the dangers of conforming to ideal notions of the feminine, while Alice suggests the equally dangerous possibilities of violating these ideals.

 In the character of Winnie, Mary Carrigg contends, Scott targets "the cult of the beautiful woman which is so important to the mythification of the home" (100). Winnie is a particularly interesting character, especially when we consider the typical role of the Victorian woman—whether English or American. Robert D. Altick has identified the role of the "weaker sex" during Victorian times as a sort of "domestic priestess"—fragile, passionless with regard to sex, a dutiful, pious, and obedient wife, and, all too frequently, a prolific child bearer (50–59). Barbara Welter's discussion of "The Cult of True Womanhood" indicates similar sorts of expectations urged upon American women of the nineteenth century—piety, purity, submissiveness, and domesticity.

 Winnie Farley, Laurence's wife, both confounds and confirms these expectations. Fragile and strikingly beautiful, Winnie nonetheless proves to be less than pious, pure, or submissive. Her relationships to the other family members are defined by power. She clearly seeks to dominate the household, primarily by playing upon the guilt of the other Farleys, even her own children, whom she frequently confronts with aggressive demands for love: "You must love me. . . . Then you love Papa best? Oh, May, that's cruel! You mustn't love him best!" (15). Part of Winnie's dominance of the household centers on her maternal role—although, in the end, her fulfillment of this maternal role, so important for the sorts of domestic myths Scott relentlessly interrogates in the novel, actually destroys Winnie. Despite her doctor's warnings that another pregnancy may well kill her, Winnie seems driven to reinsert herself into the critical maternal slot in the Farley home. In contradiction to the pure and submissive demeanor expected of her, Winnie actively and repeatedly tries to seduce Laurence, who finally submits, becoming, in the narrator's words, "the death-giver, glad, in spite of himself, of the drunkenness of moving with the unseen" (98). The resulting pregnancy finds Winnie stepping into the maternal role despite its clear dangers—"keenly dramatizing herself," affecting a "Madonna look," and drinking in her own idealized maternal image as she "glanc[es] stealthily at the mirror" (160).

Indeed, throughout the first half of Scott's novel, Winnie's transfixing charms establish her as the embodiment of ideal feminine beauty, and Winnie fully accepts this role, lingering narcissistically over her own mirror image, as we have seen. Later in the narrative, however, as her body begins to alter, Winnie is deeply disturbed by the image the mirror reflects: "As she walked she was obliged to sway grotesquely backward to balance the weight she carried before her. When she passed the long mirror in the little-used parlor, and saw herself hideous and inflated, she burst into tears" (166). More importantly, however, like that of the narrator of *Escapade,* Winnie's pregnant body becomes a kind of deterministic maternal mechanism, and, indeed, she comes to hate "her family for dedicating her to this sordid thing every minute of her life" (167).

The idealized motherhood steeped in "usefulness" and "prestige" (38), as Barbara Welter explains, descends even more dramatically into the troubling reality of a life-threatening childbirth when Winnie goes into labor. With a mixture of brutal realism and expressionistic obliqueness, Scott forces the reader, along with Winnie and the other Farleys, to confront the frightening dangers of the real veiled behind the ideal: "Suddenly Winnie clutched at the nurse's hands, and, with eyes open and unseeing, uttered shriek after shriek. . . . She saw the bright things in the doctor's bag. Then long claws of steel. . . . The joy refused her. At the instant she knew it entirely, she ceased to be" (174–75).

Scott's narrative voice here deploys a studied lack of sentimentality in attempting to narrate maternity: "Its life had become definite and independent of her. It lay in her, complete, as though it had no right there. . . . It seemed to Winnie that her life was being taken away and given to the child" (167). When the child finally arrives "to wrestle with her" (171), Winnie becomes a victim of her maternal destiny: "something leaped angrily upon her and dragged her to earth. Hot claws sank into her" (173). Note the animalistic imagery here, typical of so much naturalistic fiction. Moreover, like the flat indifference of nature in a Stephen Crane or Jack London story, the birthing process ruthlessly absorbs and blots out Winnie's individual existence (she dies in childbirth), while the narrative voice blankly reports, "The child passed from the torture which went on without it" (174).

Perhaps an even more troubling figure is Alice Farley, Winnie's unmarried sister-in-law. Alice deeply resents her beautiful sister-in-law, even as she is similarly victimized by the ensnaring conventions surrounding domesticity and femininity. Much as Winnie personifies many of the conventional domestic ideals, though, as we have seen, in problematic ways, Alice embodies one of the great fears of Victorian women—spinsterhood. An outcast from the cult of beauty, "[a]n old maid barricaded behind ridicule" (61), as she herself thinks, Alice grows to hate her body, regarding it as a sort of trap: "She did not want her body. If she could only make Horace Ridge [a man whom she secretly loves] understand that she had no body" (36).

Not surprisingly, Alice loathes mirrors, just as she loathes her own image, her own body, and the "ridiculing eyes" of the patriarchy (32). This awareness of her "Other" body, in fact, is most graphically portrayed in her deeply rooted ocularphobia. Whereas Winnie is infatuated with her mirror image, Alice is repulsed and terrified by hers: "She dared not see herself in the glass opposite," we read (32). With a "homely rugged face," "coarse sallow skin and large hands and feet" (25), Alice has long since given up "[trying] to make herself into something men would like" (32).

Clearly, too, Alice bitterly resents the more culturally ideal examples of the feminine surrounding her, both within and without the walls of her narrow house: "When she met a pretty woman in the streets Alice had a sense of outrage. A self-righteous flame burnt in her" (32–33). And Alice plainly sees her own failures to achieve the ideals of feminine beauty as a sort of entrapment: "Where will my light go to?" she reflects, "Ugly old maid. Emancipation of women" (138–39). Notice the juxtaposition of "Ugly old maid" and "Emancipation of women." Alice's fragmented thoughts seem here to be weighing the possibilities of a woman's freedom against the entrapment imposed by cultural ideals of feminine beauty.

Significantly, much of Alice's hatred of her body centers on her breasts, a bodily site inherently associated with the maternal: "Why did it hurt to see her breast?" she wonders at one point (34). Later, she seems to link her childlessness with the revulsion she feels toward her own body: "Alice felt her body harsh like the moon. . . . They [her breasts] make me ugly, because unmeaning" (197). Clearly, Alice recognizes that her failure to achieve the cultural ideal of femininity stems not only from her unattractiveness but also from her childlessness, and this arouses in her a sort of ambivalence toward the maternal ideal, an ambivalence in which she is both repelled by the maternal yet, at the very same time, desperately attracted to it: "There seemed something secret and awful in maternity—some desecration" (34), Alice reflects; "Winnie's maternity. Bobby seemed slimed all over with Winnie. To wash Bobby clean—clean of Winnie!" (36). Her own childlessness, then, much like her lack of physical beauty, relegates Alice to the margins of "The Cult of True Womanhood": "Cool ache of being outside life," she thinks; "Clothes made her virgin when she was a mother. If she could undress herself he [again, Horace Ridge] would know that she was a mother" (36).

Over the course of the narrative, Alice mounts increasingly desperate efforts to overcome the corporeal trap in which she is ensnared: "She wanted to tear away her flesh, but it seemed to resist her. . . . Life sucked at her like a wild beast. . . . Her body oppressed her" (35). In some of the most unnerving scenes in the narrative, Alice begins to attack her own body, first biting her own flesh angrily, and, later, wielding a more formidable weapon: "She . . . picked up a pair of scissors, plunging the points twice into her flesh with quick stabs" (109). Certain that her body must be destroyed in order to set her self free, she ritually removes her clothing in the darkness of her room, symbolically shedding her encumbered bodily self much as Edna Pontellier strips away her old self when she sheds her garments before entering the water: "She began to pull her clothes off. . . . Take this body away from me. I do not know it. I can no longer bear the company of this unknown thing" (*NH* 196).

Indeed, the power of the domestic ideals and conventions we have been considering is perhaps most forcefully illustrated in the harrowing despair of Alice Farley's tortured thoughts. Unlike Winnie, Alice survives Scott's narrative—she ultimately resists her suicidal urges—but in some respects, her fate seems the more tragic, for despite the fatal endgame of Winnie's quest for the feminine ideal, Alice remains, throughout the novel— and, we presume, throughout her life—ruthlessly haunted by her own inability to achieve the feminine ideals forever dangled before her.

Our discussion of Alice's entrapment brings us again to the issue of naturalism in Scott's novel, for the "unknown thing" Alice wishes so desperately to escape reminds us of the implacable and unknowable universe typical of naturalistic works such as "The Open Boat" or "To Build a Fire." What is important here, of course, is that the uncaring, inexorable cosmos of Crane or London is supplanted by the woman's body, by Alice Farley's body, in our final example— a body straining under the enormous pressures of cultural expectations, cultural ideals, cultural coercions. The narrow house enclosing the Farleys, as most critics have noted, is in fact a domestic prison for the entire family. For the Farley women, too, the house is a sort of prison or trap, but the woman's body, in the cases of Winnie and Alice, becomes a trap within a trap, a narrow house of flesh. If, as Donald Pizer claims, the foundational assumption of naturalistic fiction is that "man is more circumscribed than ordinarily assumed" (Introduction xi), certainly Evelyn Scott's work suggests that woman, burdened by a physicality upon which a plethora of confining forces is hard at work, is more circumscribed still. Indeed, Evelyn Scott's contribution to our redefinitions of naturalism is one that seems timelier now, perhaps, than even in Scott's own era. With the emergence of feminist theory and the vocabulary it provides, works like *The Narrow House* serve to indicate the possibilities of rereading naturalism through feminism—and, in turn, of rereading feminism through naturalism.

I began this study by asserting that *The Narrow House* is spun from the threads of naturalistic fiction that Donald Pizer sees informing so many of the major novelists of the 1920s. The effort—or sometimes the unintentional effect—of many naturalistic novelists was not so much to describe a deterministic universe from which no escape is possible but, rather, to enact change, to protest, to expose to public scrutiny the fatal flaws of the systems and hegemonies at work around them. Consider Upton Sinclair's *The Jungle* or even a later work such as Richard Wright's *Native Son*. Like much of Matthew Arnold's poetry, Scott's earliest fiction examines a society in transition, a liminal state between two worlds—one dead, the other—seemingly, at least— powerless to be born. Part of Evelyn Scott's project in *The Narrow House,* it seems to me, is to urge into existence a new kind of world, one that replaces the dead Victorianism suggested by the title of the novel itself and the death-in-life this world assures for its inhabitants. By baring the insidious devices and artificialities of Victorian morality and domesticity, Evelyn Scott hopes to dismantle those conventions and the moral prison they have erected, clearing a space for newer, freer, and more honest definitions of gender, of sexuality, and of human beings, beyond the imprisoning walls and entrapping architecture of *The Narrow House.*

WORKS CITED

Altick, Robert D. *Victorian People and Ideas: A Companion for the Modern Reader of Victorian Literature*. New York: Norton, 1973.

Callard, D. A. *"Pretty Good for a Woman": The Enigmas of Evelyn Scott*. New York: Norton, 1985.

Carrigg, Mary Ethel. "Escape from *The Narrow House*: The Autobiographies and Fiction of Evelyn Scott." Diss. U of Wisconsin–Madison, 1978.

Flora, Joseph M. "Fiction in the Twenties: Some New Voices." *The History of Southern Literature*. Ed. Louis D. Rubin Jr. et al. Baton Rouge: Louisiana State UP, 1985. 279–90.

Hatcher, Harlan. *Creating the Modern American Novel*. New York: Russell, 1935.

Jacobus, Mary. *Reading Woman: Essays in Feminist Criticism*. New York: Columbia UP, 1986.

Millett, Fred B. *Contemporary American Authors: A Critical Survey and 219 Bio-Bibliographies*. New York: Harcourt, Brace, 1940.

Pizer, Donald. "Introduction: Defining the Problem." *The Cambridge Guide to American Realism and Naturalism: Howells to London*. Ed. Pizer. Cambridge: Cambridge UP, 1995. 1–18.

———. *The Theory and Practice of American Literary Naturalism: Selected Essays and Reviews*. Carbondale: Southern Illinois UP, 1993.

———. *Twentieth-Century American Literary Naturalism: An Interpretation*. Carbondale: Southern Illinois UP, 1982. ix–xiii.

Ryan, Steven J. "The Terroristic Universe of *The Narrow House*." *Southern Quarterly* 28.4 (1990): 35–44.

Salpeter, Harry. "Portrait of a Disciplined Artist." *Bookman* 71 (1930): 281–86.

Scott, Evelyn. *Background in Tennessee*. New York: Robert M. McBride, 1937.

———. *Escapade*. 1923. Charlottesville: UP of Virginia, 1995.

———. *The Narrow House*. 1921. New York: Shoreline, 1977.

Smith, Sidonie. "Identity's Body." *Autobiography and Postmodernism*. Ed. Kathleen Ashley, Leigh Gilmore, and Gerald Peters. Amherst: U of Massachusetts P, 1994. 266–92.

———. *Subjectivity, Identity, and the Body: Women's Autobiographical Practices in the Twentieth Century*. Bloomington: Indiana UP, 1993.

Welker, Robert L. "Evelyn Scott: A Literary Biography." Diss. Vanderbilt U, 1958.

Welter, Barbara. *Dimity Convictions: The American Woman in the Nineteenth Century*. Athens: Ohio UP, 1976.

White, Mary Wheeling. *Fighting the Current: The Life and Work of Evelyn Scott*. Baton Rouge: Louisiana State UP, 1998.

Fear, Consumption, and Desire

NATURALISM AND ANN PETRY'S
THE STREET

—Kecia Driver McBride

A T THE END OF THE NOVEL *THE STREET,* THE HEROINE, LUTIE JOHNSON, GETS ON A TRAIN WITH A ONE-WAY TICKET TO CHICAGO. SHE HAS JUST murdered Boots Smith, who tried to rape her, in a blind rage and is now reluctantly abandoning her son, who is being unjustly held in juvenile detention. As the train starts to move, Lutie traces a design on the window with her finger, a "series of circles that flowed into each other." She remembers

> When she was in grammar school the children were taught to get the proper slant to their writing, to get the feel of a pen in their hands, by making these same circles.
>
> Once again she could hear the flat, exasperated voice of the teacher as she looked at the circles Lutie had produced. "Really," she said, "I don't know why they have us bother to teach your people to write." (435)

As Lutie moves her finger over the glass, making circles that show up clearly in the dust on the window, she thinks, "The woman's statement was correct. . . .What possible good has it done to teach people like me to write?" (436).

The placement of this memory at the end of the text emphasizes an important point: there is no place within this language in which Lutie can create meaning. Like many naturalist heroes, she is often rendered inarticulate; she cannot find the words to express what she needs and wants. Instead, Lutie is always already constructed as a subject, not as an individual, within the dominant discourse. Her beauty, which should logically be an asset in this culture, becomes a tremendous liability because the men who see her immediately desire and want to possess her; furthermore, as we shall see, Lutie will not capitalize on her beauty, a fact which will eventually destroy her. Unlike most of the other characters in the text, Lutie does not find a way to commodify desire, and because she continues to invest in a language that limits her in terms of race, class, and gender, she is destined to fail within this economically determined system.

In telling the story of Lutie Johnson, a single black mother who struggles unsuccessfully to create a better life for herself and her son in Harlem in the 1940s, *The Street* reveals the artifice of the American dream for many hardworking, highly motivated Americans. Although Lutie wants financial gain and social advancement, she cannot see that this desire is socially constructed. She believes that she can determine a self through acquisition: a nicer home, better furniture, nicer clothes.[1] Although she does not view herself as a materialistic person, she accepts the trappings of capitalism and the myth of the Protestant work ethic, influenced by the time she spends in domestic labor to the Chandlers, a wealthy white family in Connecticut. Like many women of this time, Lutie allows her desire to be mediated through consumerism, especially through the conflicted pleasure she takes in consuming various forms of the media. Thus, while Lutie often intuitively grasps the limitations that race and gender place on her ability to succeed, her investment in the American dream is sometimes overpowering. The social institutions in the text shape Lutie's expectations in contradictory and ultimately irreconcilable ways. As long as she accepts these messages at face value, she feels protected by the law and the police, confident in her abilities, and determined to better her economic situation. However, when she is repeatedly confronted by the gap between these (ideologically imposed) expectations and her actual material experiences, she realizes that her feelings of safety and hope are illusions, and her life is actually shaped instead by hunger, longing, and fear. This essay will focus on the interpellation by various institutions of Lutie as a consumer and as a commodity, and her inability ultimately to accommodate this positioning. Her alienation from the dominant discourse is demonstrated in the marked difference between Lutie's private, silent thoughts and what she chooses to vocalize: the public construction of a self that she hopes to fit within the dominant discourse. Struggling in a hostile social environment, Lutie is distanced from the natural rhythms of her own body and has lost contact with what she needs; her instincts have become unreliable, interrupted by the commodity culture in which she is immersed.

Like many other naturalist writers, Ann Petry learned about working-class life as a journalist. Born into a comfortable middle-class family in Connecticut, Ann Petry moved to New York in her thirties and worked for two Harlem newspapers. It was during this time that she came to know the horrors of tenement housing: domestic violence, overcrowding, frequent fires, broken families, inadequate childcare, street gangs, high death rates. She also worked for nine months with an after-school program for elementary school children, which assignment showed her firsthand the problems of latchkey children in Harlem. In an interview conducted not long after the 1946 publication of *The Street,* Petry explained that she wanted

> to show how simply and easily the environment can change the course of a person's life. . . . I try to show why the Negro has a high crime rate, a high death rate, and little or no chance of keeping his family unit intact in northern cities. . . . I am of the opinion that most Americans regard Negroes as types—not quite human—who fit into a special category and I wanted to show them as people with the same capacity for love and hate . . . and the same instincts for survival possessed by all men. (199–200)

Petry's focus on the effects of the environment as well as her interest in passion and the instinct for survival clearly situates this text within the naturalistic tradition. As many recent critics have suggested, this emphasis on the dual effects of biology and environment has been employed in problematic and sometimes superficial ways by traditional naturalist writers (such as Crane, Dreiser, and especially Norris) to support stereotypes based on race, gender, and ethnicity. Petry instead uses naturalistic techniques and themes to examine the limitations of social positioning in 1940s Harlem. Certainly, Lutie is an appropriate representative of what Donald Pizer labels "the myth of the autonomous self," a character who believes that she can affect real change in her life and achieve great things despite her difficult circumstances (164).[2] Within classic naturalist texts, that "self" is most often both white and male (whether character, author, or both). Here, strikingly, that already overdetermined self is a beautiful black woman.

The Street was an enormously successful first novel, selling over a million copies and earning Petry both critical and popular success, and critics have speculated that much of the appeal of *The Street* came in the wake of the positive response to Richard Wright's *Native Son* (1940), another text that can be successfully read as a product of the naturalist tradition more than that of the Harlem Renaissance. Both novels were crossover successes, both focus on the oppressive effects of racism and poverty on African Americans, and both end with a violent act and an escape to Chicago.[3] As Barbara Christian writes, "[Petry's] novel poses a perennial question of contemporary black literature: given the harshness of racism, to what extent can each individual control his or her fate?" (67). In *The Street,* the "harshness of racism" is complicated by the fact that the language of racism becomes less obvious and thus potentially more dangerous, as we will see. For black feminist critics, however, *The Street* offers another dimension to Wright's work: a focus on the intersections of race, class, and gender.[4] It also thus significantly rewrites the typical naturalist project.

I am particularly concerned with the connections between naturalism and a materialist approach to *The Street*. Louis Althusser's discussion of "the *imaginary* relationship of subjects to their real conditions of existence" echoes Pizer's definition of a naturalist text, wherein the aesthetic tension depends upon the subject's continuing investment in the illusion of autonomy. The subject must believe that individual agency can determine outcome and that language can produce meaning. This capitalist ideology is produced through the languages employed by each of the various ideological state apparatuses (referred to hereafter as ISAs—the school, the legal system, the church, the media). As Chris Weedon writes, "Each ideological state apparatus contributes to the reproduction of capitalist relations of exploitation in 'the way proper to it' and the means by which it determines dominant meanings is *language*" (29). The idea that these institutions gain power through the manipulation of language can, then, enrich a reading of this text as naturalistic. According to Althusser, ideology functions such that it "recruits" subjects through hailing;[5] his most famous example is of the police officer calling out "Hey, you there" to the subject in the street, at which point the subject recognizes the hailing and turns around, thus accepting the subject position that is offered. Althusser writes, "[W]hat thus seems to take place outside of ideology (to be precise, *in the street*), in reality takes place in ideology" (301, emphasis mine). As we shall see, Althusser's example of the street as the space of everyday, commonplace, naturalized activities, as well as the site for the hidden work of ideological production and the display of interpellated subjects, yields rich meanings for Petry's novel.

One way to approach the naturalistic tendencies in the text—and to do justice to the multiple concerns of race, class, and gender—is to use a materialist feminist focus on language. In a move recalling Pizer's myth of the autonomous self, Catherine Belsey defines the goal of capitalist ideology as follows: "to suppress the role of language in the construction of the subject, and its own role in the interpellation of the subject, and to present the individual as a free, unified, autonomous subjectivity" (662). Belsey goes on to make the point that the rise of classic realism "roughly coincides chronologically with the epoch of industrial capitalism. It performs . . . the work of ideology, not only in its representation of a world of consistent subjects who are the origin of meaning, knowledge and action, but also in offering the reader, as the position from which the text is most readily intelligible, the position of subject as

the origin both of understanding and of action in accordance with that understanding" (663). I would argue that naturalism, long seen as subsumed within
the "more important" movement of realism, also produces texts that "perform
the work of ideology" through the objective and detached study of human
experience. Focusing on the extent to which humans are motivated by instincts,
naturalist writers employ the same close attention to detail that the realists use,
but for a "scientific" purpose, the investigation of determinism, be it biological,
environmental, or economic. Like the subjects of realism, the subjects of naturalism believe themselves to be both "consistent" and "the origin of meaning,
knowledge, and action"; the difference is that the subjects of naturalism are
rarely allowed to maintain this belief through the end of the text. These texts
do not, then, provide a mimetic picture of "reality" but, instead, display the
ideologies in which they find themselves inscribed.

Lutie becomes fully invested in the ideology of the work ethic after her
husband loses his job and she spends a year away in domestic service to the
Chandlers. She comes to accept the belief that

> anybody could be rich if he wanted to and worked hard enough and
> figured it out carefully enough. . . . She and Jim could do the same
> thing, and she thought she saw what had been wrong with them
> before—they hadn't tried hard enough, worked long enough, saved
> enough. There hadn't been any one thing they wanted above and
> beyond everything else. These people had wanted only one thing—
> more and more money—and so they got it. (43)

Not only do the Chandlers understand how to make money, they know how
to capitalize on the desires of others; Mr. Chandler owns a business (paper
products) that will make money despite economic flux. Lutie doesn't seem
troubled by the fact that the Chandlers, despite their "perfect" home and
money, are not happy. From the Chandlers she learns the "new philosophy"
that through hard work and focused effort, any American citizen can achieve
success. The problem before, she now understands, was her own fault.

Despite her will to succeed, however, Lutie does not find a way to commodify desire so that she can turn a profit and thus ensure her success, as the
Chandlers and many of the other characters do. Mrs. Hedges, for example,
who runs a brothel from the first floor of Lutie's building, clearly capitalizes
on the desires of men and the hopelessness of young girls. She first comes to
the city from a small town in Georgia, hoping she would be "inconspicuous"
and that she would find a man to love her, even if she has to buy one. (As with
most madams, the title of Mrs. does not truly apply in this case but is an empty

signifier.) Despite her aspirations, she remains unemployed because the white people at the agencies "let her see what a monstrosity they thought she was" (241). Soon "her big body . . . fill[s] with a gnawing, insatiable hunger" that has her prowling the streets, picking through garbage. Mrs. Hedges has a fierce will to survive, however, and is willing to manipulate the system in order to support herself.

After she is trapped in a burning building, Mrs. Hedges finds that her skin and hair have been literally consumed by fire; she is left bald, scarred, and blackened. In direct contrast to Lutie, Mrs. Hedges is able to alter, although not to escape, her categorization in terms of race and gender by redefining her connections to those categories. Clearly marked now as outside the realm of conventional feminine beauty, she responds by becoming a subject rather than the object she will not ever be: she manipulates the desires of others in order to profit from and protect the pretty but weak girls of the street. Mrs. Hedges understands the effects of supply and demand. She knows there will be lots of customers, men "who knew vaguely that they hadn't got anything out of life and knew clearly that they never would get it, even though they didn't know what it was they wanted . . . [,] men who had to find escape from their hopes and fears, even if it was for just a little while" (250). Her working girls, in contrast, have "seen too many movies and didn't have the money to buy all the things they wanted" (252). The role she creates for herself involves bringing these two groups together, in some ways meeting the needs of each but also making a profit for herself in the process.

Interestingly, Mrs. Hedges is the first to "hail" Lutie when she arrives to look at the apartment. As Lutie stands in the street, looking up at the tenement and guessing about the room, she hears someone clear "his or her throat" very distinctly, "as though someone had said, 'hello'" (5). Mrs. Hedge calls the apartment a "nice little place" and encourages Lutie to ring the Super's bell. Lutie immediately dislikes Mrs. Hedges because of her eyes, which wander "over her body, inspecting and appraising her from head to foot" (6). Mrs. Hedges's assessment of Lutie (who has also seen a lot of movies) is that she could turn a profit because of her beauty; however, despite repeated attempts throughout the text to recruit her, Lutie continues to resist. Unlike Mrs. Hedges or her "girls," Lutie is neither able to indulge in the pleasures of her sexuality nor to profit from it.

Through the dominant discourse, Lutie is thus positioned as both a consumer and a commodity. In her interactions with black men, especially, Lutie finds herself viewed as consumable. For example, when she first examines the apartment with Jones, her initial feelings are fear, although she is not sure what exactly frightens her, and this unnamed fear will return again at the end of the text. She sees in his eyes "a hunger so urgent that she was instantly afraid of him and afraid to show her fear" (10). The fact that she experiences this desire as a fear of consumption or of being consumed is clearly illustrated in the dream she has in which the Super and his dog become one: a man with a dog's mouth and teeth, who whines and pants, chained to the building which he drags along behind him. In her dream, he thinks she has the key that will free him, and, when she tries to help him, he closes his fangs on her hand and chews off her arm. She screams and the windows to the buildings open, spilling millions of people out into the street; they immediately turn into rats, each with a building chained to its back. Lutie experiences this terror in and through her body; she is afraid of men like Jones who are so starved for life they would devour the women beside them. She senses a desire in him that is likely to erupt in dangerous and potentially violent actions; cut off from his own needs and practically invisible in the community, Jones constructs an elaborate fantasy of physically overpowering Lutie in order to ease his pain.

Boots Smith, in turn, is the most explicit in his weighing of her value to him when his boss, Junto, warns him to keep away because he has "other plans for her." In a long interior monologue, he remembers his past experiences as a porter, of being called

> Boy. George. Nameless.... Niggers steal. Lock your bag. Niggers lie. Where's my pocketbook? Call the conductor. That porter— Niggers rape. Cover yourself up. Didn't you see that nigger looking at you? . . . Balance Lutie Johnson. Weigh Lutie Johnson. Long legs and warm mouth. Soft skin and pointed breasts. Straight slim back and small waist. Mouth that curves over white, white teeth. Not enough. She didn't weigh enough when she was balanced against a life of saying "yes sir" to every white bastard who had the price of a Pullman ticket. (264–65)

Like Jones, Boots is only too familiar with the narrow self-definition that race gives him, the silences he is forced to assume in order to make a living in a white culture, yet his own oppression does not stop him, in turn, from limiting Lutie in terms of her gender. Further, whereas he resents being called a thief, a liar, and a rapist, he also comes to fulfill all of these terms in the text. In the end he decides to commodify Lutie, to pimp her out to his boss, and even to beat and rape her in order to keep the limited social power that Junto has extended to him.

Boots's boss Junto, a newly affluent white man who used to pick garbage off the streets, along with Mrs. Hedges now exploits the carnal desires of the people in Harlem. Although Junto commodifies desire in several ways throughout the text, for Lutie the most vital is his bar, the Junto Bar and Grill on 116th Street, an important space for young working people; they rush home from work, eager to move from producing commodities to becoming consumers. What Junto's place has to sell in this case is not merely alcohol: "The beer was incidental and unimportant. It was the other things that the Junto offered that [Lutie] sought: the sound of laughter, the hum of talk, the sight of people and brilliant lights, the sparkle of the big mirror, the rhythmic music from the juke-box" (145). As many critics have pointed out, Lutie makes a mistake in not developing stronger support through the community; particularly as a single mother of color, she is predestined to need significant help in order to survive. Yet in going to the bar for solace, she demonstrates her loneliness and, more significantly, her willingness to purchase a comforting illusion. Just as she turns on the radio so that she won't feel alone in the apartment, she enjoys going to Junto's for the soft lights and warm feeling of companionship, even though she sits alone: "No matter what it cost them, people had to come to places like the Junto, she thought. They had to replace the haunting silences of rented rooms and little apartments with the murmur of voices, the sound of laughter; they had to empty two or three small glasses of liquid gold so they could believe in themselves again" (147). Junto has become a wealthy man because he identified a particular need and found a way to capitalize on it; for a price, these people can soothe their loneliness and blunt the sharpness of their despair. What Lutie does not realize is that this illusion also keeps her complicit, within the dominant system, by selling her a false sense of community and escape. Lutie perceives what motivates people to come to Junto's and how artificial this setting is, and yet this understanding in no way modifies her own desire to participate. She is eager to purchase this illusion, even though she cannot afford it, because it helps to fuel her determination to somehow escape the street (even as the purchase of the beer eats up her savings and pushes her that much further away from escaping). The bar functions in much the same way as do the movies that she sends her son Bub to see in that both are temporary and cheap forms of escape, illusions of a brighter, happier reality that lull the inmates of Harlem into a contentment in their belief that tomorrow will be better and today is not so bad.

The movies that Bub views are just one example of how the media control the characters and shape their expectations. Social norms are created and supported through the daily workings of social institutions, such as the media. Although these institutions appear to be relatively autonomous, they all perform similar ideological work in that they encourage subjects to focus on material acquisition, individual achievement, and competition between peers. Although these social norms are slanted in favor of a particular group, they are naturalized and therefore accepted as commonplace by all subjects, even when such acceptance affects some subjects adversely. Furthermore, despite their appearance of autonomy, the different ISAs are all related by what John Fiske calls "an unspoken web of ideological interconnections, so that the operation of any one of them is 'overdetermined' by its complex, invisible network of interrelationships with all the others. Thus the educational system, for example, cannot tell a story about the nature of the individual different from those told by the legal system, the political system, the family, and so on" (287). The constant need for the reproduction of ideology in people requires careful attention to the role of language in the construction of subjects, particularly (for Fiske) the language of media.

The media, like all ISAs, depend upon appearing so fluid, comfortable, and "natural" that the characters (and the reader) barely notice their own complicity in their construction as subjects. In this novel, various forms of print and visual media shape the perceptions of the characters, and yet it is through engaging these media-generated representations that Lutie eventually begins to notice their inadequacy. Stuart Hall writes in "The Rediscovery of Ideology" that the media "become part and parcel of that dialectical process of the 'production of consent'—shaping the consensus while reflecting it— which orientates them within the field of force of the dominant social interests represented within the state" (87). This dialectical process is made apparent in *The Street* through repeated references to the reading of newspapers, which aggressively shape their readers to participate fully in consumer culture.[6] At the Chandler house, the men are all college educated, and yet the only thing they read is the newspaper; even then, they merely glance at the front page, then turn straight to the financial pages, and perhaps the sports page. Their priority (getting "filthy rich") is clearly represented in their daily reading habits; that is, the mirror they seek to reflect the world will show them only the elements they find valuable, so they are concerned only with the financial page instead of local politics or other matters of broader social concern. In contrast, Lutie describes her husband Jim, who is out of work, as spending a lot of time sitting in waiting rooms reading old newspapers with out-of-date information. He grows increasingly bitter and alienated after he loses his job and his ability to provide for his family; there is no need for him to look at the financial page, and he cannot, in any case, afford to buy a newspaper each day.

The most significant example of how newspapers shape perceptions about the people on the street occurs in the middle of the novel. In flashback, Lutie recalls one afternoon in the spring when she came upon a crowd outside of a bakery, gathered around the figure of a thin, shabbily dressed boy who has been stabbed and lies dead on the sidewalk. She recalls,

> The next day's papers said that a 'burly Negro' had failed in his effort to hold up a baker shop, for the proprietor had surprised him by resisting and stabbed him with a bread knife. She held the paper in her hand for a long time, trying to follow the reasoning by which that thin ragged boy had become in the eyes of a reporter a 'burly Negro.' And she decided that it all depended on where you sat how these things looked. If you looked at them from inside the framework of a fat weekly salary, and you thought of colored people as naturally criminal, then you didn't really see what any Negro looked like. You couldn't, because the Negro was never an individual. He was a threat, or an animal, or a curse, or a blight, or a joke. . . .
>
> The reporter saw a dead Negro who had attempted to hold up a store, and so he couldn't really see what the man lying on the sidewalk looked like. He couldn't see the ragged shoes, the thin, starved body. He saw, instead, the picture he already had in his mind: a huge, brawny, blustering, ignorant, criminally disposed black man who had run amok with a knife on a spring afternoon in Harlem and who had in turn been knifed. (199)

The silent black body of the boy in the street is a blank page that requires a narrative, and the reporter constructs his story about the "burly Negro" for the Chandlers and people like them; this is the story they expect to read, and their prejudices are reaffirmed each time they do. The reporter himself undoubtedly read countless similar stories during his apprenticeship, so the pattern of this story suggests itself to him even as he bends over the body. It does not occur to him to question the pattern nor to wonder if deadly violence is an appropriate response for (alleged, attempted) robbery.

Lutie, however, considers this boy with the holes in his shoes, walking on the hot pavement of the city, and does not condemn him; she recognizes instead the inequities of the capitalist system and how such forces can shape one's destiny. While the newspaper reporter depicts the boy as threatening,

Lutie sees him differently: as hungry and frightened and manipulated by the desire to shape an identity through the acquisition of products that are out of his grasp. Lutie is all too familiar with the inferior goods available to the residents of Harlem. She notes the poor scraps of meat, cheap fabric, imitation leather and coarse lace, the withered and wilting vegetables, the bruised, rotten fruit: "All of [the stores] sold the leavings, the sweepings, the impossible unsaleable merchandise, the dregs and dross that were reserved especially for Harlem" (153). Even after she sees this dead boy, though, and reads between the lines of the newspaper story, Lutie continues to believe in her own agency. In fact, she becomes that much more resolved that the only way she and Bub will escape the inevitable violence of the street is through money.

Lutie's perceptions are also shaped more subtly and more powerfully by another form of media in the text: advertisements. Whereas Lutie is able to reach a point where she observes for herself the gap between the newspaper story and the event it supposedly depicts, she allows herself to be interpellated repeatedly by advertisements as a subject who accepts the value system of the dominant culture. The night that Boots Smith, a smooth-talking jazz musician, tells her she won't get paid for singing at the club, Lutie climbs the long flights of stairs to her apartment and repeatedly hears the radio soap jingle "Buy Shirley Soap and Keep Beautiful" (312). It is significant that she hears this ad right after the dream of becoming a nightclub singer has been taken from her because her immediate response is to blame herself. She speculates as to what has squelched Smith's desire for her, wonders at her own inadequacies, and is then confronted with an ad from a radio soap opera promising physical beauty. Another example of her willingness to be seduced or determined by the media is an advertisement she finds in a Negro newspaper: "Singers needed Now for Broadway Shows. Nightclub Engagements. Let Us Train You Now for High-Paying Jobs" (318). When she responds to the ad, she is told that she will need six weeks' worth of training (at a cost of $125), and then she will be guaranteed high-paying singing jobs. When she protests that she cannot come up with this amount of money, the agent responds, "They all say that. . . . It sounds out of the question because most people don't know what it takes to be a singer. They don't want it bad enough" (321). He then suggests that they might be able to work out an arrangement, an exchange of sex for his fee. Although she is repulsed by this man and violently rejects his offer (hurling a pot of ink at him in the process), his rhetoric here is a version of her own earlier conceptualization of the work ethic, formulated at the Chandlers: the reason she will not succeed is that she doesn't want "it" enough and hasn't tried hard enough.

The most pervasive and subtle influence of advertisements is constructed in the space of the train, where the passengers "settled down into small private worlds, thus creating the illusion of space between them and their fellow passengers. The worlds were built up behind newspapers and magazines, behind closed eyes or while staring at the varicolored show cards that bordered the coaches" (27). The reading materials clutched by these commuters from Harlem distinguish them from their unemployed counterparts on the street, marking them as literate, middlebrow consumers. These newspapers and magazines are also full of advertisements. During her train ride, Lutie stares at an ad on a showcard, mounted on the wall of the train, of a girl with "incredible blonde hair" and a man in a navy uniform standing in a beautiful kitchen, a "miracle of a kitchen" (28). This woman in no way resembles Lutie, and this room is nothing like the kitchen of her new apartment but "almost exactly like the one she had worked in in Connecticut" (28). The picture of this kitchen evokes for her the problem at the center of the breakdown of the black family: because black women are performing domestic labor in white homes, their own families suffer. Nevertheless, Lutie hopes that someday she will own such a kitchen herself. She does not recognize the ad as a depiction of a completely false expectation, nor does she recall the unhappiness of the Chandler household despite their beautiful kitchen.

In addition to these advertisements, Lutie's expectations and desires are shaped by various other forms of media: magazines, radio, and popular films. At the Chandler house, Lutie learns about "Country Living" from the "fat sleek magazines" Mrs. Chandler receives but never reads: *Vogue, Town and Country, Harper's Bazaar, House and Garden, House Beautiful.* Mrs. Chandler passes them on, along with "all the newest books" to Lutie, who decides "it was almost like getting a college education free of charge" (50). Clearly, the glossy pages of these magazines have shaped Lutie's perception of physical beauty (including the consumption of cosmetics, lotions, and fashion), as well as her expectations of "home": a place filled with costly, well-chosen objects. In addition, like the girls who work for Mrs. Hedges and the other girls who work in her office, Lutie likes to see movies occasionally for entertainment, and it is clear that these cinematic images have influenced her. In fact, the first night that she goes riding with Boots Smith, she immediately thinks, "This is the kind of car you see in the movies" (155), inserting herself in a fantasy position of glamorous screen star while he drives her around and she imagines wearing a mink coat and a sable scarf. Lutie also unwittingly encourages her son to get pleasure from a similar combination of escapism and acculturation by repeatedly sending Bub to the movies for entertainment to watch detective thrillers and police dramas, while at night he listens to spy hunts or cowboy stories on the radio. She often listens to the radio herself, especially when she is alone in the apartment: "The radio was on full blast, but under it there was a stillness that crept through all the rooms" (78).

As the novel progresses, though, she comes to realize that these media messages are empty and potentially disturbing. On the day that she kills Boots, the final day of the text, she tries to distract herself by going to see a film, but "the picture didn't make any sense. It concerned a technicolor world of bright lights and vast beautiful rooms. . . . The glitter on the screen did nothing to dispel her sense of panic. She kept thinking it had nothing to do with her, because there were no dirty little rooms, no narrow crowded streets, no children with police records, no worries about rent and gas bills" (412). She ends up leaving in the middle of the picture, profoundly disturbed at the disjunction between the imaginary and her lived experience.

Lutie's resistance to this film late in the text highlights the extent to which ideology depends upon remaining invisible and feeling "natural"; it is much easier to control subjects when they experience pleasure in the very images that shape their social positioning and limit their power. Subjects who resist these conventions must be forced to comply against their will. Whereas ISAs encourage the tendency of subjects to behave and think in support of social conventions, Althusser believed that repressive state apparatuses, such as the police and the law, coerce subjects into such behavior. Furthermore, these social conventions work to naturalize the sites of power already in place, which serve white, male, middle-class interests. Lutie begins the text with a firm belief that the police will protect her if her rights are threatened. When Lutie first considers whether or not to rent the apartment, she thinks to herself that should Jones attack her (a situation she does not really believe possible), she could scream and "a cop will eventually rescue [me]" (19). Ironically, though, when Jones later does attack her, she is rescued instead by Mrs. Hedges. In addition, the police officers who arrest her son, although unaware that he has been duped, will ultimately initiate Bub into the penal system and rob him of his innocence. In fact, the clash between Bub's media-influenced perceptions of the police and their actual behavior can be noted in his eagerness to fall for Jones's scheme. Earlier in the novel, he tells Jones about seeing a film in which a police officer pretends to be a gangster in order to fight crime (103). Later, when Jones tells him that the police need Bub to catch the bad guys, he honestly believes that he is assisting the law.[7] His fondness for thrillers and police films featuring secret agents and undercover cops enables him to create a narrative in which he himself fulfills this role; he simply inserts himself into the preexisting cultural pattern, not understanding all the ways in which that pattern was not cut for him and will never represent his reality.

The legal system is another instance of a repressive state apparatus that, despite her expectations, does not offer Lutie any solace; because she cannot afford a lawyer, she must stay legally married to Jim even though they are separated. Nonetheless, at the beginning of the text, she blames herself for the breakup of her marriage and sees the legal system as protecting the image of the nuclear family that she still wishes she had. Gradually, she comes to believe that her own family fell apart because Jim was prevented from remaining the primary wage earner and she could not stay within the traditional definition of mother and wife. Her belief in the legal system has remained so strong that, when her son is arrested, she immediately goes to see a lawyer, assuming both that she needs one and that he will protect her son's rights. When she sees the words "children's court," she immediately assumes "court means lawyer" (387), acting through her vague, media-influenced perceptions of the criminal justice system. While the lawyer appears to listen to her story, "all the time he was trying to figure out how much she would be able to pay." He also wonders idly why she doesn't know that she doesn't need a lawyer for this case. "It was like picking two hundred bucks up in the street. 'And who am I to leave it there kicking around?'" he says (391). He has learned how to sell his ability to listen, to appear attentive, and to offer hope, and Lutie is all too willing to buy.

The characters who will survive in this system are all able to find ways to manipulate the institutions enough to meet their most basic needs, even at the cost of exploiting others, and to establish some sense of community, even if that sense has to be purchased. The Prophet David in some ways stands in for organized religion, especially in his ability to commodify the power of religious symbols. Although many critics view the fact that Min, the abused mistress of Jones, turns to him in the text as an affirmation of cultural difference (as representative of root doctors and voodoo) and of forming community ties, he is also a peddler of desires and wishes. Like the white lawyer, his appeal lies in his ability to listen closely to women who are starved for attention. Min believes after their encounter that he has given her "the means of controlling Jones," and in a way he has: he has given her a renewed sense of self-confidence and satisfaction, based on his ability to listen and appear interested. Whereas Lutie's purchase of a movie theatre ticket or a beer merely buys her a few hours of escape and further implicates her into the system of the street, Min's purchase of a cross to place above her bed quite effectively limits Jones's power to hurt her. Just as the cheap domestic objects the women of Harlem buy mark their rented spaces as homes, Min's purchase of the cross, powder, and red liquid allows her to have the illusion of control over her environment. Jones neither believes in religion nor goes to church, and feels contempt for those who do, yet "to him a cross was an alarming and unpleasant object, for it was a symbol of power. It was mixed up in his mind with the evil spirits and the powers of darkness it could invoke against those who outraged the laws of the church" (138). The symbol of the cross interpellates Jones such that he cannot behave violently towards Min, however furious he becomes. The purchase of the cross and the placement of it as a symbol above their bed afford Min more protection than her active participation in organized religion; in fact, she chooses not to go and seek counsel from her pastor because she senses that he doesn't listen to her.

The intersections of race, gender, class, and violence here are powerful in that the biological and environmental components each work to (over)-determine the other. What happens to Bub and to Lutie is the result of the system that Fiske calls "the unspoken web of ideological interconnections" (287). A powerful example of Fiske's (and Althusser's) theory of overdetermination is presented in the chapter that focuses on Mrs. Rinner, Bub's white schoolteacher, who represents the institution of public education in the text. This early acculturation through the public schools ensures the perpetuation of ideological conventions, introducing the children of Harlem to the limitations they can expect throughout their lives. Mrs. Rinner dreams of being transferred to a school district filled with blonde, blue-eyed, well-fed, silent, carefully starched children who will sit still and "look at her with adoration" (33). By comparison, she finds these children from Harlem dirty, impudent, wriggling, and frightening: "There was a sudden reckless violence about them and about their parents that terrified her. Just like Lutie's memory of her own childhood teacher, Mrs. Rinner regards teaching the children of Harlem anything as a hopeless task, so she devotes most of the day to maintaining order and devising ingenious ways of keeping them occupied" (330). Because Mrs. Rinner doesn't see any point in encouraging independent thought or schooling these children in articulation, Bub will become a product of the same sort of limiting and limited education that his mother received. Furthermore, Mrs. Rinner's anticipation of a "sudden reckless violence" in all black people suggests that, for some residents of Harlem, this belief becomes a self-fulfilling prophecy, as it does for Lutie. This violence is not a biological trait, as racist ideology would suggest, but rather a direct product of a racist environment.

For Lutie, as for many characters in naturalist texts, her growing sense of hopelessness in a hostile environment is compounded by her inability to express herself, and her frustration eventually explodes into violent action.

Despite Lutie's interpellation by the various institutions, the text clearly demonstrates the fact that the language of the dominant ideology is inadequate to her needs. Many critics have commented on the fact that Lutie seems unable to understand the extent to which the value system of the Protestant work ethic, of Ben Franklin and the Chandlers, excludes her. In many ways I would agree, and yet Lutie also demonstrates repeatedly her awareness of the limitations of the white value system and its attempt to exclude and limit her decisions. Although in her public voice she continues to support the ideals of the dominant discourse, her private voice often lets the reader know that she is a sophisticated reader of codes. This split consciousness is clearly indicated in the text in the first chapter, when Lutie's internal monologue reflects a strong sense of foreboding and an intuitive grasp of the deleterious limitations of the environment. For instance, she is able, despite the harsh wind, to read the sign advertising the apartment and, beyond that, to interpret the words once she is able to read the description (three rooms, steam heat, parquet floors, respectable tenants, reasonable) and the actual conditions she will find in the apartment. She is savvy about the way the apartment is advertised: she knows the gaps between the descriptive words used and the true meanings of those words. When she actually sees the apartment, then, "it was no better and no worse than she had anticipated" (16).

The moments in the text when Lutie struggles to express herself indicate her growing awareness of the contradictions of this system, but this struggle does not always produce positive results. When she finds Bub shining shoes on the street, for example, she becomes furious and unable to speak, so she slaps him. Falteringly, she tries to articulate her fears that if he starts shining shoes at eight he will grow up and fulfill the white expectation that he is not good enough to do anything better. His expression afterwards worries her; she is not sure she has expressed herself well, but she can't rephrase the thought, and so she pats him on the shoulder and starts dinner. Finally, he asks her, "'Why do white people want colored people shining shoes?' She turned toward him, completely at a loss as to what to say, for she had never been able to figure it out for herself" (71). Instead, she examines her own strong, brown hands, wondering if it is just a shock for white people to see brown skin: "It must be hate that made them wrap all Negroes up in a neat package labeled 'colored'; a package that called for certain kinds of jobs and special kinds of treatment. But she really didn't know what it was" (72). She does not share with him her thoughts as she looks at her hands, but finally she admits to him that she doesn't know why. As he turns away, she wonders what he is thinking.

Lutie arrived at a similar conclusion about the characterization of black bodies while living with the Chandlers. There, all of the wealthy white women immediately assume she is promiscuous and sexually available to white men. She at first wonders if it is because she is a maid but notices that they don't draw the same conclusions about the white girl who comes to help with big parties, and Mrs. Chandler is downright friendly, even in public, to the white man who cuts their grass and weeds the garden: "Apparently it was an automatic reaction of white people—if a girl was colored and fairly young, why, it stood to reason she had to be a prostitute. If not that—at least sleeping with her would be just a simple matter, for all one had to do was make a request. In fact, white men wouldn't even have to do the asking because the girl would ask them on sight" (45).[8] She remembers as well "the friends of the Chandlers who had thought of her as a nigger wench; only, of course, they were too well-bred to use the word 'nigger'" (323). Their breeding does not, on the other hand, keep them from feeling the prejudices implied by the open use of that word; they just choose not to label their attitudes as racist because they do not like the way this word reflects them. Lutie's awareness of the slippage between idea and word, in her own language as well as in the language of others, indicates that her construction as a subject is not as complete as it might sometimes appear to be. This awareness, however, does not prevent her from investing in the capitalist ideology of progress and hope.

For much of the text, Lutie Johnson believes in the illusion that she can control her conditions of existence and, through hard work, triumph over her poverty. She is a virtuous, hardworking, chaste, and beautiful woman, and yet she gradually comes to understand that she will not be successful. Furthermore, much of her experience cannot be spoken within the dominant system; there is no language in which to declare that she has been raped, lied to, cheated, abandoned, and manipulated. All during the last day in the text, she is conscious of an "awful creeping silence" that follows her everywhere; this silence represents her growing awareness of the hollowness of language, the inadequacy of expression for her desires, and the overdetermination of her subjection. Language, she has learned, reflects the interests of the dominant ideology, and "[s]treets like the one she lived on were no accident. They were the North's lynch mobs . . . [,] the method the big cities used to keep Negroes in their place" (323). Like the language used by Mrs. Chandler's friends, who are too polite to articulate their own prejudice, "the street" points to a different sort of racism which is more subtle, insidious, and dangerous, designed to keep people like Lutie in an ever-narrowing space. At the end, Lutie can no longer maintain the illusion of a fully functioning (and consuming) public self, is unable to reconcile the fear and longing of her private self, and so she responds with violence, destroying the image of the men who would consume her. As she sits on the train, reflecting back on her life, Lutie finally understands that the circles she has been taught to trace and call language are a pattern with no progression.

NOTES

1. Her materialistic tendencies here can be compared to Dreiser's Carrie. As Blanche Gelfant writes in her article on *Sister Carrie,* "the ways of consuming women in naturalistic fiction appear to be static, impervious to the historical changes effected by a seemingly radical change of setting, of time and place. . . . Seeing what others have and [Carrie] lacks, this unconsummated and consuming woman believes that she must have *more*, and that having *more* will allow her to become . . . more and more the person she is capable of becoming" (192).
2. Pizer is discussing *The Age of Innocence* and *An American Tragedy,* not *The Street.*
3. These texts in some ways challenged their literary heritage. As Barbara Christian points out, Petry's novel "strikes a heavy blow at one of the major tenets of many Renaissance writers—that you can make it if you try. . . . No matter how conventional and no matter how American a poor black person may be, she will be defeated by her environment" (65–67). See also Nellie McKay, "Ann Petry's *The Street* and *The Narrows*: A Study of the Influence of Class, Race, and Gender of Afro-American Women's Lives."
4. Henry Louis Gates, among others, has pointed out the importance of Petry as an influence for contemporary African American women writers like Toni Morrison and Gloria Naylor.
5. According to John Fiske, "Hailing is the process by which language identifies and constructs a social position for the addressee. Interpellation is the larger process whereby language constructs social relations for both parties in an act of communication and thus locates them in the broader map of social relations in general" (308).
6. Newspapers have a strong metaphorical representation in the text as well. For example, when Lutie first comes to the street to look for an apartment, the wind is blowing all kinds of paper around, and she especially notices that old newspapers are "wrapped around their feet, entangling them" (2). Old newspapers are part of the junk of the street that Junto gathers and ties into neat bundles. In addition, when Lutie goes to the office of the corrupt lawyer, he is reading a newspaper, and the agent who attempts to solicit sex in exchange for voice training has stacks of newspapers in his office. The girls who work in the office with Lutie spend their evenings reading newspapers, "mostly the funnies and the latest murders" (396).
7. In an interview, Ann Petry stated that the novel "was built around a story in a newspaper—a small item occupying perhaps an inch of space. It concerned the superintendent of an apartment house in Harlem who taught an eight-year-old boy to steal letters from mail boxes" (qtd. in Ivy 160).
8. The grand irony, of course, is that Lutie has been taught by her grandmother never to let a white man put his hands on her, and she would prefer to go to bed with a rattlesnake than a white man.

WORKS CITED

Althusser, Louis. "Ideology and Ideological State Apparatuses." *Lenin and Philosophy and Other Essays.* Trans. Ben Brewster. London: New Left Books, 1971.

Belsey, Catherine. "Constructing the Subject: Deconstructing the Text." 1985. *Feminisms: An Anthology of Literary Theory and Criticism.* Ed. Robyn Warhol and Diane Price Herndl. 2nd ed. New Brunswick, NJ: Rutgers UP, 1997. 657–73.

Christian, Barbara. *Black Women Novelists: 1892–1976.* Westport, CT: Greenwood Press, 1980.

Fiske, John. "British Cultural Studies and Television." *Channels of Discourse: Television and Contemporary Criticism.* Ed. Robert C. Allen. 2nd ed. Chapel Hill: U of North Carolina P, 1992. 284–326.

Gelfant, Blanche H. "What More Can Carrie Want? Naturalistic Ways of Consuming Women." *The Cambridge Companion to American Realism and Naturalism.* Ed. Donald Pizer. New York: Cambridge UP, 1995. 178–210.

Hall, Stuart. "The Rediscovery of Ideology." *Culture, Society, and the Media.* Ed. Michael Gurevitch, Tony Bennett, James Curran, and Janet Woollacott. New York: Methuen, 1982. 56–90.

Ivy, James. "Ann Petry Talks about First Novel." *Sturdy Black Bridges.* New York: Doubleday, 1979. 197–200.

Macherey, Pierre. *A Theory of Literary Production.* London: Routledge and Kegan Paul, 1978.

McKay, Nellie Y. "Ann Petry's *The Street* and *The Narrows*: A Study of the Influence of Class, Race, and Gender of Afro-American Women's Lives." *Women and War: The Changing Status of American Women from the 1930s to the 1950s.* Ed. Maria Diedrich and Dorothea Fischer-Hornung. New York: Berg, 1990. 127–40.

O'Brien, John, ed. *Interviews with Black Writers.* New York: Liveright, 1973.

Petry, Ann. *The Street.* Boston: Houghton Mifflin, 1946.

Pizer, Donald. "American Naturalism in Its 'Perfected' State: *The Age of Innocence* and *An American Tragedy*." *The Theory and Practice of American Literary Naturalism.* Carbondale: Southern Illinois UP, 1993. 153–66.

Weedon, Chris. *Feminist Practice and Poststructuralist Theory.* 2nd ed. Oxford: Blackwell, 1997.

Naturalism's Middle Ages

THE EVOLUTION OF THE
AMERICAN TRUE-CRIME NOVEL,
1930–1960

—*Lana A. Whited*

A FTER THE 1925 PUBLICATION OF *AN AMERICAN TRAGEDY*, IT IS WIDELY BELIEVED THAT NATURALISM WENT INTO REMISSION. DONALD PIZER, the leading scholar of American naturalism, notes that by the 1940s, eminent critics such as Malcolm Cowley and Lionel Trilling were heralding the movement's death (85). Evidence to support naturalism's reported demise was readily available. In 1925, Jack London had been dead for nine years, Frank Norris for twenty-three, and Stephen Crane for twenty-five. Over the remaining twenty years of his life, Dreiser published no more novels,[1] and by the late thirties, people were often surprised to learn that he was still alive. Even Dreiser doubted the longevity of his own achievement. Confident that *An American Tragedy* would win the 1926 Pulitzer Prize, the author was dismayed and somewhat surprised when Sinclair Lewis won instead, and declined, for *Arrowsmith*. This suggested to Dreiser and others that naturalism had never really displaced realism as the dominant mode in American letters.

But just as reports of Dreiser's own death in the 1930s were, to use Mark Twain's famous phrase, "greatly exaggerated," the swan songs for naturalism were also premature. During the 1930s, 40s, and 50s, a strain of the *American Tragedy* brand of naturalism continued to appear in American novels: the protagonist who, through a combination of biological and environmental factors, is driven to homicide. At least four prominent examples exist: William Faulkner's *Light in August* (1932), James M. Cain's *The Postman Always Rings Twice* (1934), Richard Wright's *Native Son* (1940), and Meyer Levin's *Compulsion* (1955). These novels provide a transition from the classic phase of American literary naturalism as exemplified by *An American Tragedy* to Truman Capote's 1965 book *In Cold Blood,* a work whose publication marks a renaissance of what might be termed the naturalistic homicide novel tradition.

In this middle period, three basic elements of the naturalistic homicide novel are foregrounded. First, the naturalistic homicide novel in the United

States was created by writers who apprenticed as reporters; thus, it retains a strong journalistic element. Second, the writer chooses as his protagonist the murderer himself, as if following Thomas De Quincey's dictum from "On the Knocking at the Gate in *Macbeth*" that anyone writing about murder "must throw the interest on the murderer. [I]n the murderer . . . there must be raging some great storm of passion . . . and into this hell we are to look" (733). Third, this "storm" has clear deterministic causes; the protagonist is presented as a person whose free will is severely limited, if not eradicated, by a combination of economic, biological, psychological, and sociological factors.

All the early American naturalists had extensive training as journalists, and both *An American Tragedy* and *McTeague* are based on actual cases, Dreiser's novel on the 1905 murder of Grace Brown by Chester Gillette in upstate New York and Norris's on an 1893 case widely publicized in the *San Francisco Examiner*. Both Dreiser and Norris were heavily indebted to newspaper accounts in the crafting of these two books. In the middle naturalistic period, news stories of squalid murders continued to stimulate novelists' imaginations.

For example, the murder which is the central violent act in *Light in August* was not a product of William Faulkner's imagination but most likely derived from a 1908 homicide committed outside Oxford. Nelse Patton, a black "trusty" from the county jail in Oxford, went to the home of Mrs. Mattie McMillan, a white woman, on an errand from Mrs. McMillan's husband, an inmate. When Mrs. McMillan apparently spurned his advances, Patton slit her throat with a razor. Arrested after a mob pursuit, Patton was killed the same night by a local posse who, according to some accounts, cut off his genitals and hung his stripped body from a tree in the public square. This crime is detailed in at least three Faulkner sources: Joseph Blotner's *Faulkner: A Biography* (113–14); *Old Times in the Faulkner Country,* a collaboration of John Cullen and Floyd C. Watkins; and, more recently, Joel Williamson's *William Faulkner and Southern History.* Both the Cullen-Watkins and the Williamson accounts are based on original newspaper articles from the *Jackson Daily Clarion-Ledger* of September 1908. Details of the Nelse Patton affair were also readily available to ten-year-old Billy Falkner, not only in the newspaper stories but also in the accounts of his friends John and Jencks Cullen, sons of the deputy sheriff. According to available sources, the Cullen boys played key roles in the pursuit and capture of Patton. Additionally, Williamson notes, young Falkner's house was located "not more than a thousand yards" from the town square, and if he did not witness the events himself, he probably heard them in progress (159).

A second crime which Blotner offers as a potential source was the 1919 murder, again just outside Oxford, of a black woman by her husband, Leonard Burt. Burt was apprehended four months later and was shot to death in an escape attempt en route from the Oxford jail to the courthouse (he was not castrated). Although Nelse Patton's crime resembled Joe Christmas's killing of Joanna Burden more closely than did Burt's, Blotner points out two important details of the Burt case: first, Burt's wife's body was badly mutilated, reminding one of Joanna Burden, with her head nearly severed and facing a direction different from the rest of her body; and second, leaving the house, Burt had set a fire in an attempt to hide the murder (762–63).

Despite his success in fiction, James M. Cain insisted that he be described in *Who's Who* as "a newspaper man" (qtd. in Hoopes 199). Like the early naturalists, Cain was a journalist by training. He described how he got the idea for *Postman* from a gas station he patronized regularly: "Always this bosomy-looking thing comes out—commonplace, but sexy, the kind you have ideas about. We always talked while she filled up my tank. One day I read in the paper where a woman who runs a filling station knocks off her husband. Can it be this bosomy thing? . . . I inquire. Yes, she's the one—this appetizing but utterly commonplace woman" (225).

Cain also claimed that the Ruth Snyder/Judd Gray case in New York, a high-profile murder trial which, according to biographer Roy Hoopes, "dominated" newspapers in 1927, served as an important source (232). Cain realized that just as in the Snyder/Gray story, the true tension in his story lay in the conspirators' relationship. He told a friend the key idea was to be that "no two people can share this terrible secret and live on the same earth. They turn against each other, as Judd and Ruth did" (qtd. in Hoopes 233). Thus Cain conceived the tense scenes in which Frank and Cora ask themselves, "if you could kill Nick, what's to stop you from killing me?"

Richard Wright said that Bigger Thomas was based on several models from his childhood. Wright's autobiographical *Black Boy* suggests one of those sources. When he was nine, young Richard's aunt Maggie and a man called "uncle" fled in the middle of the night because "uncle" had robbed a woman and set her house on fire. Quizzed by Wright's mother, "uncle" defended his actions: "If they found her, she'd tell. I'd be lost. . . . But if she burns, nobody'll ever know" (*Black Boy* 76–77). Wright must have recalled this rationalization when writing Bigger's realization: "[H]e would *burn* her! That was the safest thing of all to do" (*Black Boy* 89). Aunt Maggie's fussing with her trunk is also significant, as it brings to mind Bigger's concealment of Mary Dalton's body in her own half-packed trunk (*Native Son* 87).

In May 1938, the character Wright had been viewing as a composite of figures like "uncle" and the young men he met during his work at Chicago's South Side Boys' Club appeared fully formed in the Chicago news pages. Robert Nixon and Earl Hicks, both young, illiterate black men, were charged with the rape and murder of a white woman, Florence Johnson, whose head was smashed, apparently with a brick, the same weapon with which Bigger would murder his girlfriend Bessie. Wright, living in Brooklyn, sent two air-mail special delivery letters to his friend Margaret Walker in Chicago request-ing clippings about the case. Walker later recalled that she sent enough for Wright to cover his bedroom floor and that "he was using them in the same way Dreiser had done in [An] American Tragedy. He would spread them all out and read them over and over again and then take off from there in his own imagination" (Alexander 60). Of particular significance in the press accounts was the racist nature of the *Tribune*'s description of Robert Nixon in an article headlined "Brick Slayer Likened to Jungle Beast." Wright acknowledges in *How "Bigger" Was Born* that "[m]any of the newspaper items and some of the incidents in *Native Son* are but fictionalized versions of the Robert Nixon case and rewrites of news stories from the *Chicago Tribune*" (38).

In November 1938, Wright traveled to Chicago with the goal of match-ing his novel to the city terrain. His agenda, now contained in the Wright Archives at Yale, includes selecting key sites, tracing Bigger's flight through five blocks of Indiana Avenue, obtaining copies of official documents from the Nixon case, and visiting the Cook County jail, the courtroom where Robert Nixon had been tried, the death house at the Statesville penitentiary, and, if pos-sible, Nixon himself, on death row. Wright also planned to check libraries for accounts of the Leopold-Loeb case[2] and to find the homes of principals in that crime (Kinnamon 28). Wright's curiosity about the Leopold-Loeb material con-firms that he was working in a journalistic—and sensationalized—tradition.

Compared to *Native Son,* Meyer Levin's novel *Compulsion* might be called "How the Other Half (of Chicago) Lives." *Compulsion* (1940) is a liter-ary oddity: a novel which borrows the outline, details, and some of the actual reporting of a real 1924 murder case but fictionalizes names and alternates first- and third-person points of view. The book does not fit neatly into the naturalistic homicide novel tradition, but it does fulfill most of the major requirements.

Levin followed a noteworthy succession of writers, most tellingly Dreiser, through the doors of the *Chicago Daily News,* and his involvement there proved fortuitous: *Daily News* reporters had provided a critical clue in the

Leopold-Loeb case when they matched a ransom note to documents produced on Nathan Leopold's typewriter. The reporters subsequently won a Pulitzer prize (Rubin 85), and Levin had near-proprietary access to this material, some of which he had originally written himself.

Despite Levin's providing fictional names for the characters, he adheres closely to fact. He interviewed the families and friends of Leopold, Loeb, and the victim Bobby Franks, and Levin had Leopold's full cooperation (Loeb was killed in prison in the 1930s [Rubin 87–88]). The proceedings of Loeb and Leopold's trial closely follow the court records, and the speech of attorney "Jonathan Wilk" is reproduced verbatim and attributed, in the novel's foreword, to its "real author, Clarence Darrow" (ix).

When murder cases such as those fictionalized in these novels are reported in the American media, the culprit quickly emerges as protagonist. We remember Ted Bundy, Jeffrey Dahmer, and David Berkowitz, but how many of us can name a single victim of these killers? Our curiosity about the unfamiliar feeds our fascination with murderers, especially serial killers; their victims tend to lead lives very much like our own, and we consequently find them less interesting. When novelists use real cases as their subjects, their narratives reflect this same preoccupation, focusing on the "great storm of passion" raging within the murderer. In such novels, the naturalistic recipe requires more than a "look" into this "hell"; the novelist encourages us to look *with sympathy* into the "storm." The result is a virtual apologia for the protagonist's acts.

Despite his two factual models, William Faulkner did not focus *Light in August* on Joe Christmas right away. He insisted that the novel began in his mind with the image of the pregnant Lena Grove walking along a dirt road. Manuscripts confirm that the first character to appear on paper was Gail Hightower, about whom Faulkner had begun a novel (Millgate 6–7). But Joe Christmas quickly came to dominate the story in Faulkner's mind, with Lena Grove serving as "counterpoint for the obsessed and doomed Christmas," as Joseph Blotner notes (761). Faulkner added the long flashback section which comprises the story of Joe's youth (chapters 6–9) late in the novel's composition, a creative act motivated by the same impulse that led Dreiser, in inventing book 1 of *An American Tragedy,* to give Clyde a past to lead up to the present Dreiser already knew from his nonfiction models.

Drawing on the Patton and Burt cases, Faulkner supplied an original motive for Joe Christmas's murder of Joanna Burden, creating a clearly deterministic drama.[3] Like Norris and Dreiser, Faulkner was interested in the circumstances which led his protagonist to murder; in *Light in August,* those factors are largely religious and racial, and both involve dichotomies. Joe Christmas grew up in a society where everyone was either black or white, and race was often both identity and destiny. Unable to confirm his own racial heritage, Christmas is, as many critics have noted, a displaced person (Brooks; Williamson 405–6). The second dichotomy results from a society characterized by an absolutist Calvinism, illustrated by his grandfather, his "adoptive" father Simon McEachern, and Joanna Burden and her ancestors. The Calvinist's world is thus ordered and predictable but does not allow for gradations of human behavior. The legacy of Calvinism for Joe Christmas is that it causes him to polarize experience and to agonize over anyone or anything that does not fit neatly into a category. Calvinism's central dichotomy is a strong belief in predestination, the notion that one's lot in life has already been determined as elect or damned. This concept permeates the novel and applies to every major character *except* Lena Grove, whose fortunes are determined more by her offspring—i.e., her pregnancy—than her past.

For instance, Joe's attitude toward and his appetites for food, women, and sex are determined by a formative experience in the orphanage where his grandfather left him. While gulping sweet toothpaste, Joe watches a dietician have sex with a doctor; when the dietician flings back the curtain concealing the young boy and exclaims "you little nigger bastard," the concepts of taste, women, and sex become fixed as a juxtaposition in his mind, and, thenceforth, he feels a disgust for all three (114).

The dietician's epithet is linked to the other major determinant in Joe's life: his mixed racial heritage. In the orphanage, a black gardener explains that the other children call the five-year-old Christmas "nigger" because "don't nobody but God know what you is" (363). This notion of Joe's "nobody"-ness, his imprecise racial heritage, then haunts him for the rest of his life and remains unresolvable, as both his parents are dead. Faulkner said that "the tragic, central idea of [Joe's] story is that he didn't know what he was, and there was no way possible in life for him to find out" (qtd. in Blotner 762). Indeed, not knowing his racial heritage devastates Joe. His tragedy, like that of Oedipus, is one of identity, except that in *Light in August* it is not knowledge but *lack* of knowledge that destroys. In a culture polarized as black and white, Joe's ambiguous status leaves him feeling very much a pariah, as Cleanth Brooks has argued. Christmas murders Joanna Burden in an attempt to exercise control, to forge an identity. Burden represents the forces which have haunted Christmas throughout his life: she is female, she is religious, and she insists on seeing Joe as black so that she can "improve" him. By murdering her, Joe seeks to kill the nobody she reminds him that he is.

Perhaps the most remarkable aspect of *Light in August* is Faulkner's presentation of Christmas as both victim and victimizer. Asked why he would impose Christ symbolism onto "such a sort of bad man as Joe Christmas," Faulkner replied that Christmas seemed to him "tragic" rather than "bad" (Gwynn and Blotner 118), noting also that "man is the victim of himself, or his fellows, or his own nature, or his environment" (qtd. in Welsh 125). Blotner writes that Faulkner "presented Christmas in his maturity as thinking he acted out of something like free will, though his history made it clear that he had largely been shaped by his environment" (763–64).

The deterministic scope of *Light in August* extends beyond Joe Christmas to include every other major character, as scores of critics have noted. Perry Westbrook contends that "not one of them is a free agent in the sense of having the ability to break out of the fated groove of his will" (180). For Faulkner's characters, the factors which have determined the grooves of characters' wills are predominantly historical. Joanna Burden, like Christmas, is a victim of a Calvinist past. She has inherited the family cause of helping black Americans, a cause whose cost was the life of Joanna's grandfather and her half-brother Calvin. Joanna's father tells her these family members were killed "not by one white man but by the curse which God put on a whole race before your grandfather or your brother or me or you were even thought of" (239). Gail Hightower is a victim of his inability to reconcile his grandfather's ignominious death in a chicken coop with his otherwise idealized portrait of that ancestor. Faulkner writes that the minister "grew to manhood among phantoms, and side by side with a ghost" (449). Even Lena Grove feels that her reunion with Lucas Burch, father of the child she carries, is foreordained. She tells Martha Armstid, "a family ought to be all together when a chap comes. Specially the first one. I reckon the Lord will see to that" (18). Lena is, at the same time, the only character in *Light in August* who shapes her own destiny to any significant extent; indeed, the most significant action in her past is not that of her forebears but her own: she had sex with Burch and became pregnant (and, of course, the earlier naturalists would point out the biological determinism here). In turn, her pregnancy has determined that she search for Burch.

Perry Westbrook argues that just as "the orthodox Christian ascribes the perverted will of man to the sin in the Garden of Eden, Faulkner relates the sorry plight of his doomed characters to family histories of violence and crime" (179)—and, we might add, illicit sex. *Light in August* is an extended dramatization of the past living in the present, a reminder that, as Gavin Stevens tells his nephew Chick in *Intruder in the Dust,* "[y]esterday won't be over until tomorrow and tomorrow began ten thousand years ago" (194).

Some critics have asserted that Faulkner's novel cannot accurately be viewed as naturalistic because the forces which act on his characters are not scientific or biological forces. For example, in *The Myth of Southern History,* F. Garvin Davenport Jr. holds that Faulkner's determinant is "the force of history and not the force of glands and hostile universes" (118). And Westbrook notes that the characters' "bondage will not seem so great as that presented in a strictly naturalistic novel where the characters are the playthings of environment and biochemistry" (178). Two responses are necessary. First, Davenport's contention that biological forces do not influence the characters is an overstatement, if not an outright falsehood. Obviously, the factor of Joe's biological identity weighs very heavily in his predicament, just as Lena Grove's pregnancy weighs heavily in hers. Faulkner is also interested in the clash between human and more primitive tendencies in both Christmas and Joanna Burden; arriving for a sexual encounter, for example, Joe "hunts" Joanna in her house: "sometimes he would have to seek her about the dark house until he found her, hidden . . . waiting, panting, her eyes in the dark glowing like the eyes of cat. Now and then . . . he would find her naked, or with her clothing half torn to ribbon upon her, in the wild throes of nymphomania" (245). A second response to Davenport's and Westbrook's contentions would be that naturalism has never concerned itself purely with biological causes. Rather, it has preoccupied itself, following a Darwinian model, with man's environment; that environment might just as easily present economic or social determinants as biological ones. Even in the work of the early naturalists who emphasized biology most heavily—Zola, Norris, and London—economic and social determinants are always present. Faulkner's recurring use of "the Player" who moves Percy Grimm and Joe Christmas around like chessmen (an analogy also present in Dreiser's *Jennie Gerhardt*) makes clear that the novelist saw man as characterized by an essential lack of freedom. Faulkner's determinism may begin with different causes, but it ends with the same effect.

In the last twenty-five years, considerable critical space has been devoted to showing that Faulkner and Richard Wright were mining a similar vein. If Joe Christmas's problem is not knowing his racial identity, Bigger Thomas's is that he knows his all too well. Bigger is trapped within the narrow range of possibilities that a predominantly white power structure allowed poor young black men in the 1930s. He takes his job with the Dalton family because, otherwise, his family's "relief" will be cut off (12). He places the pillow over Mary

Dalton's face because he does not see another alternative to being caught in her room by her mother. Cutting off Mary's head and putting her corpse into the basement furnace is a loathsome task for Bigger, but, again, he sees no other option. With Roberta Alden's drowning in *An American Tragedy* in mind, Joseph T. Skerrett Jr. calls Mary Dalton's death "Dreiserian, determined by Bigger's social conditioning and the terrible pressure of the moment" (134). Later, in the rape and murder of his girlfriend Bessie, Bigger continues to act on impulse and instinct in response to his sense of total entrapment. Wright invokes the medieval concept of the *rota fortuna* or wheel of fortune when he describes Bigger during the rape as feeling as if he were "on some vast turning wheel that made him want to turn faster and faster" (219). Clearly, Bigger kills Bessie out of a sense of entrapment: "What about Bessie? He could not take her with him and he could not leave her behind" (221). Even Bigger's choice of a weapon is presented in deterministic terms; his gun would make noise and draw attention, so he decides that he "would have to use a brick" (221). Still, Bigger struggles until he convinces himself that he is in a corner, like the rat in the novel's opening scene. Three times in the next two paragraphs, he reminds himself that he "could not take [Bessie] and he could not leave her." The third time, he adds, "It was his life against hers" (221–22). Wright's description of Bigger in *How "Bigger" Was Born* as "a hot and whirling vortex of undisciplined and unchannelized impulses" is borne out in these pages.

That Richard Wright was well versed in the naturalistic tradition is a matter of record.[4] In his famous description in *Black Boy* of using a white friend's library card and a forged note to borrow books from the Memphis library, Wright lists the many literary acquaintances he subsequently made. At least a third of them are naturalists or writers who felt a strong naturalistic influence: Sherwood Anderson, Dostoevsky, Tolstoy, Hardy, Crane, Zola, Norris, Ibsen, Balzac, Turgenev, Dreiser (272). He was especially drawn to Dreiser, writing that *Jennie Gerhardt* and *Sister Carrie* evoked memories of his mother's suffering. Of his reading at that time, Wright wrote, "I was overwhelmed. . . . It would have been impossible for me to have told anyone what I derived from these novels, for it was nothing less than a sense of life itself. All my life had shaped me for the realism, the naturalism of the modern novel, and I could not read enough of them" (274).

True to the naturalistic tradition, Wright ultimately indicts society for Bigger Thomas's entrapment and its consequences. Wright pointed to two specific factors which caused Bigger's "revolt": his estrangement from "the religion and folk culture of his race" and the overwhelming effect of "the dominant civilization whose glitter came to him through newspapers, magazines, radios, movies, and the mere imposing sight and sound of daily American life" ("*Bigger*" 27). In the first respect, Bigger is Joe Christmas; in the second, he is Clyde Griffith. In both, he is more acted upon than acting. Like Clyde, Bigger drifts between where he came from and a place he can never get to, a place to which his culture has nevertheless taught him to aspire. Like Dreiser, Wright works to mitigate a reader's condemnation of Bigger. Harold Bloom says that Bigger "can be apprehended only as we apprehend Dreiser's Clyde and Carrie, which is under the sign of suffering . . . [;] there is something maternal in Wright's stance toward Bigger, even as there [is] in Dreiser's towards Clyde or Carrie" (1).

Wright's description of his method for *Native Son* also places him squarely in the naturalistic tradition. His comments in *How "Bigger" Was Born* about the approach he planned to take could have been lifted directly from the pages of Zola's "Le roman experimental":

> Why should I not try to work out on paper the problem of what will happen to Bigger? Why should I not, like a scientist in a laboratory, use my imagination and invent test-tube situations, place Bigger in them, and, following the guidance of my own hopes and fears, what I had learned and remembered, work out in fictional form an emotional statement and resolution of this problem? (33)

Just how familiar Wright was with the work of the French naturalists is unclear, though he does mention Zola in *Black Boy*. (In fact, if he was *not* familiar with "Le roman experimental," his comment in *How "Bigger" Was Born* would be all the more striking.) Whatever his familiarity with the Frenchman's work, Wright shared his aims.

As Irving Howe has argued, Wright's real achievement in *Native Son* is the novel's double-barreled approach to racial problems in the United States; it forced white Americans "to recognize [themselves] as the oppressor" while also forcing black Americans "to recognize the cost of [their] submission" ("Black" 7). Wright made clear, Baldwin says, that "the oppressed and the oppressor are bound together within the same society" ("Protest" 5). Howe writes that "[t]he day *Native Son* appeared, American culture was changed forever" because the novel "[a]ssaulted the most cherished of American vanities: the hope that the accumulated injustice of the past would bring with it no lasting penalties" ("Black" 7). We want to think, with the *Chicago Tribune* reporter, that a Bigger Thomas is a monster, an alien; we must realize, Wright reminds us, that he is a "native son."

The proletarian or protest novel was almost certainly the dominant mode of American literature in the 1930s, and *The Grapes of Wrath* is its foremost

example. *Native Son* has been termed by Seymour Gross "the culmination of
the protest tradition . . . [,] its finest example" (18). Richard Wright thus
extended proletarian ideology to include the experience of the American
Negro, who was, Gross says, "the most dislocated and deprived figure on the
American economic landscape" (16). Of course, the social protest writers had
merely adapted the methods of the turn-of-the-century naturalists to the social
conditions of the Great Depression. In mining the same vein, Wright helped
determine the course of African American literature at mid-century; as Blyden
Jackson has argued, because Wright "cut his writer's teeth on naturalism,"
"most black writers for more than twenty years seemed decidedly more akin to
Frank Norris than to Henry James" (447–48).

While Richard Wright's reputation has remained unquestionably strong,
two factors have tended to reduce James M. Cain's literary stature. First, Cain
suffered from the knee-jerk critical response that a writer's popular success
signaled the absence of real literary merit in his work. Three of his novels—
The Postman Always Rings Twice, Mildred Pierce, and *Double Indemnity*—each
sold over two million hardcover copies (Madden 121). The motion picture
industry's enthusiasm for Cain's work only compounded this problem. *Postman* alone spawned six film versions (Skenazy 195–96). A second factor
which has reduced Cain in stature is critics' labeling of him as a genre writer,
a member of the "tough guy" school of writing. Cain does have much in
common with Raymond Chandler, Dashiell Hammett, and other writers of
this school, particularly the gritty realism of his characters and landscapes, but
placing him in the "tough guy" camp has limited critical consideration of his
work and, particularly, his ties to the naturalistic writers. *The Postman Always
Rings Twice,* for instance, provides a clear transition in homicide novels from
the classic explicit naturalism of Norris and Dreiser to Truman Capote's more
implicit, detached style.

Despite James M. Cain's initial interest in "the bosomy-looking thing"
whom he transformed into Cora Papadakis, he began his novel with the voice
of Frank Chambers. And, notably, from the very first line, Chambers presents
himself as acted upon rather than acting: "They threw me off the hay truck
about noon" (3). Cain then takes the reader on the roller coaster ride which is
Frank and Cora's fortune. On the surface, their story looks more like luck
than determinism. For instance, just when it looks as though they will be
caught trying to murder Nick, they and a suspicious policeman are distracted
by a cat who steps onto a fuse box, causing a power outage. After Frank and
Cora murder Nick, just when it looks as though the prosecution has frightened Chambers into turning state's witness, Frank's shyster lawyer (whose

name, Katz, echoes the nine-lives motif) talks Nick's insurance company out of aiding the prosecution. Frank is taken to Katz's office expecting to learn when Cora will be hanged and finds instead that she has not only been freed but also awarded ten thousand dollars from Nick's insurance policy. Much later, after Frank and Cora have re-established their trust, married, and declared their commitment to each other and to the child Cora is carrying, Cora is killed instantly when Frank slams into a culvert wall while attempting to pass a truck. Ironically, at the end of the novel, Frank awaits execution for the death he did not mean to cause, having gotten away with the one that was intentional, recalling a similar scenario in *Native Son*, wherein Bigger is executed not for Bessie's death, which he caused, but for the accidental killing of Mary Dalton.

But the determinism of *Postman* is more complicated than simple luck. Frank's attraction to Cora is powerful and animalistic. W. M. Frohock has said that Chambers's "response to stimuli [is] automatic and completely physical," noting a scene in which Frank vomits because he cannot have sex with Cora (19). In other moments, Frank is rough and forceful with Cora. After Nick's murder, he socks Cora in the eye to make her look injured, and they both find his aggression stimulating (46). That Frank is a creature of appetites is verified by his repeated references to food, and the food motif is as central to this novel as it is to *Light in August,* although the offering of food repulses Joe Christmas but stimulates Chambers. For instance, in an opening chapter less than 750 words long, Frank catalogs his first meal at Nick and Cora's, a breakfast consisting of "orange juice, corn flakes, fried eggs and bacon, enchilada, flapjacks, and coffee" (4). In fact, Frank's relationship with Cora is equated throughout with consumption. They make their sexual overtures in Cora's kitchen. During their first sexual encounter, Frank bites her lip hard, drawing blood. As Paul Skenazy notes, Frank and Cora engage in "a kind of consumerism of each others' bodies," a "cannibalism [which] is a caricature of their culture's materialist hungers" (31).

The socioeconomics of *Postman* is also recognizably that of the naturalistic novel. Tom Reck's comment that the main characters are "Anglo-Saxon whites descended from traditions of economic, educational and moral poverty" who lead "a life of misery, drunkenness, adultery, violence, of economic and emotional woe" might just as accurately describe Crane's *Maggie* (381). Despite the differences between urban New York and rural California, the garbage piles on which Jimmy Johnson conducts his "warfare" in *Maggie* were not foreign to Cain. Several critics have suggested that Cain "worked a literary lode bordering a trash heap" (Madden 123). His characters live a gritty, tarnished existence. Both Frank and Cora work in an atmosphere of grease—his auto-motive, hers culinary, theirs sexual.

Recalling Dreiser's central figures, Cain's principal characters are on the outside of the American dream peeping in, as if through a knothole in a fence. Cora's Hollywood dream, fueled by her victory in an Iowa beauty contest, died during her first screen test, when she realized that she came across as "a Cheap Des Moines trollop, that had as much chance in pictures as a monkey has" (12). The automobile is an appropriate symbol for Frank, a creature of impulses and drives, and his restlessness makes him an apt precursor of Capote's Dick Hickock and Perry Smith, who spend weeks on the road eluding police. Throughout the novel, Frank and Cora seem for the most part the passive vic-tims of circumstances over which they have no control. They come to realize that even their most willful act, Nick's murder, has inextricably determined their own fate: Frank says, "We're chained to each other, Cora. We thought we were on top of a mountain. That wasn't it. It's on top of us, and that's where it's been ever since that night" (108). While, as David Fine argues, the lovers "beat a murder rap," they are finally "unable to escape each other" (28).

The tone of inevitability in the novel is reinforced by its tempo, what Tom Wolfe has called its "momentum" or "acceleration" (v). Frank and Cora meet on page four, have sex for the first time on page eleven, begin plotting Nick's murder on page fourteen, attempt it for the first time on page eighteen, and accomplish it on page forty-three. As Skenazy writes, by page forty-six (of the paperback) "the lovers' wish has come true" (22). The novel begins in motion, as Frank is thrown off the hay truck, and never slows down. This pace underscores the sense of an inevitability which Frank and Cora neither control nor perceive. It is also a major shift from the slower, more methodical pacing of Dreiser and Norris. In addition, the economy of Cain's sentences, reflecting the terse, newspaper style, contrasts sharply with Dreiser's verbosity, and Cain's closest parallel among the early naturalists might be Crane, who had the most facility with language. That is, *The Postman Always Rings Twice* has much more in common, stylistically, with *Maggie* or *In Cold Blood* than with *An American Tragedy*. The style they share is, in large part, responsible for the book's momentum and its overwhelming atmosphere of inevitability.

When Meyer Levin's biographer Steven J. Rubin wrote that, after the 1940 publication of *Citizens*, Levin left behind the writing of social novels, he must have forgotten *Compulsion*. Before *Compulsion*, Levin had written two novels using distinctly naturalistic methods. In *The Old Bunch* (1937), Levin explores how a second-generation Jewish community on Chicago's West Side preserves its cultural values. Rubin notes that *The Old Bunch* has a distinctly naturalistic orientation, his claim based on the meticulousness of Levin's cultural details and the focus on individuals who are "overwhelmed by the forces of environment and the grinding weight of a capitalistic economy" (38). In *Citizens* (1938), Levin attempted the documentary mode to tell the story of the 1937 Memorial Day confrontation between members of a local steelworkers' union and the Chicago police in which ten workers were killed. Levin's research for *Citizens* is reminiscent of Zola's research for some of the Rougon-Macquart novels, especially *Germinal*; he spent months studying the workers in their environments of the mill, the boarding house, and union meetings. His goal was not so much to achieve an accurate narrative but "to understand the meaning of the workers' lives, their relationship to the economic system, and their role in the class struggle . . . taking place in America" (Rubin 54).

In *Compulsion,* Levin turned to the "fittest" in the struggle of the American classes for survival. Like Dreiser with Chester Gillette, Meyer Levin was able to evoke understanding of his murderers, Nathan Leopold and Richard Loeb, whom he calls Judd Steiner and Artie Straus, largely because of his identification with them. The murderers were Levin's age and, like him, were students at the University of Chicago. In addition, Leopold, Loeb, and Levin were all from the same predominantly Jewish neighborhood. Levin wrote that he understood Leopold and Loeb's feeling of "being strangers to our parents and our past, unsure of our place in society" (*In Search* 21), and Steven Rubin suggests that Levin identified with the teen-age murderers' "alienation from their parents, their pathological intellectual curiosities, and their obsessive need for experience" (85). Levin clearly wanted readers to understand the killers' motives; in his foreword, he explains his goal of achieving "the increase of understanding of such crimes that has come, during these years [since 1924], and . . . of drawing from it some further increase in our comprehension of human behavior" (ix).

The Leopold-Loeb case was, in fact, "one of the earliest . . . in which a psychoanalytical study of the defendants had been attempted" (Rubin 86), due largely to the affluence of the defendants' families. Levin's narrator/reporter intimates that the boys "would virtually be taken apart, to see what made them tick" (307). Two psychiatrists, reportedly getting $1,000 a day, would interview first family members, then the young men themselves, and an even more prominent psychiatrist would synthesize the results. The philosophy of these specialists was essentially deterministic: they felt that "[t]he entire aim of psychiatry was to unravel the causes of behavior. And if all behavior had a cause, where was guilt?" (342). Thus, the determinism which factors in Judd

Steiner and Artie Straus's crime is rather more that of Sigmund Freud rather than of Émile Zola.

The Straus and Steiner family situations follow the same blueprint: both boys are raised in an atmosphere of affluence and parental detachment. Artie's father is too busy for his son, and Mrs. Straus characterizes her husband as "not a demonstrative man" (312). When young Artie wants to talk to someone about his brother's birth, he reminds himself that "you never ask your father" (331). Although she prides herself on being "a new woman, a leader," with "advanced knowledge of child care," Mrs. Straus, through her civic involvements, puts the welfare of other children before that of her own (310). The arrival of a baby brother only compounds Artie's alienation and may help account for why he later kills a younger boy. When psychiatrists ask why the family never sought help when Artie exhibited symptoms of abnormality, Mrs. Strauss explains that the family "simply hoped [he] would grow out of it, as boys do" (313).

During the psychiatric interviews, Judd Steiner never mentions his father, a person of little consequence to him. Instead, Judd is preoccupied with the memory of his mother, whose inherited kidney disease worsened after Judd's birth and eventually caused her death. Of his mother, Judd tells a psychiatrist, "I used to picture her as the Madonna. I still do" (321). In his wife's absence, Judah Steiner indulges his son. When Judd is caught without a fishing license and has his expensive equipment confiscated, his father simply buys him more (314). Judah Steiner believes "nothing should stand in the way" of a boy as gifted as his son, an attitude which is conveyed to the boy.

In both families, a nanny is employed to compensate for the parents' neglect, and, in both cases, she compounds the boy's suffering rather than relieving it. Judd's nanny sexually abuses him while he is small; Artie's is prudish about sexual matters, and he finds her refusal to explain where his little brother came from particularly frustrating. Not surprisingly, both young men grow up deviating from prescribed norms and without an adequate sense of what is morally and sexually acceptable.

Both Judd and Artie also suffer from a superiority/inferiority paradox. Their affluence conveys a sense of entitlement. Their remarkable intelligence contributes to this problem; like his model Loeb, Artie is the youngest student ever to enter the University of Chicago, and Judd's intelligence is off the Stanford-Binet scale. Thus, when the boys encounter the Nietzschean Superman in philosophy class, they convince themselves that the German philosopher was writing about them. As was the case with London's Wolf Larsen, it is not difficult to see how Nietzsche's elitist, anti-democratic arguments would appeal to two boys who had always been told they were exceptional. Judd and Artie then convince themselves that committing the "perfect crime" will verify that they *are* Supermen.

The boys' preoccupation with Nietzschean philosophy might seem to obscure a naturalistic reading of their actions, but it is important to remember that, despite Nietzsche's harsh criticism of evolution theory, the Superman concept is entirely consistent with Darwinism. The Superman can be viewed as the inevitable victor in the selection process, he who survives because of his superiority. The dimensions of that superiority, as spelled out by Will Durant in *The Story of Philosophy,* are

> that in this battle we call life, what we need is not goodness but strength, not humility but pride, not altruism but resolute intelligence; that equality and democracy are against the grain of selection and survival; that not masses but geniuses are the goal of evolution; that not "justice" but power is the arbiter of all differences and all destinies. (301–2)

Subscribing to this philosophy, Judd and Artie convince themselves that committing the "perfect crime"—determining the destiny of another human being and exerting their intelligence and perceived power over the police—would verify that they *are* Supermen. The fact that the two are apprehended underscores the failure of their theory. In "determining" Paulie Kessler's fate, they have also determined their own; the one sense in which they are genuinely "Supermen"—their families' money—does not spare them the inevitable consequences of their actions.

Like Dreiser, Levin employs powerful courtroom scenes featuring an eloquent apologist to advocate sympathy for his rich young defendants. The closing argument of defense attorney Jonathan Wilk, Clarence Darrow's fictional counterpart, is an argument grounded in pure determinism. The speech, reprinted verbatim from court records of the Leopold-Loeb trial (Rubin 91), takes two days to deliver, and Levin's description of it is laudatory. Wilk's appeal is rooted in two basic principles: that crime is a disease, and that whether it is caused by heredity or environment (or both), the individual can do nothing to prevent contracting it. In the course of the speech, Wilk refers repeatedly to his clients as "these two unfortunate boys" who killed Paulie Kessler "because somewhere in the infinite processes that go to the making up of the boy or the man something slipped" (431). His belief that Straus and Steiner are victims with whom we should empathize is verified by his conviction that "any mother might be the mother of Artie Straus, of Judd Steiner" (432).

Levin makes no pretense to the accuracy Truman Capote claims in the preface to *In Cold Blood*. For instance, he admits in his foreword that some of his episodes are "total interpolations, and some of [the] personages have no correspondence to persons in the case in question" (ix). However, it is often exactly at the point where Levin departs from journalistic accuracy that he leans in the direction of the naturalistic novel. For example, early in book 1, the body of "Paulie Kessler" (Bobby Franks) is found stuffed in a drainage pipe in an outlying marsh by a character whose identity is never developed in the original newspaper accounts. In *Compulsion,* however, this character is Peter Wrotzlaw, a steel worker who has fortuitously veered off his usual path to work to run an errand. Wrotzlaw notices a foot sticking out of the pipe and realizes on a level which Levin stresses is purely instinctual that something is wrong: "It was even said to be providential that Wrotzlaw had once lived on a farm, for in a submerged way his nature sense knew something strange was there, neither animal nor fish" (22). Because he can detect the unnatural, Wrotzlaw is also able to find a stocking and the glasses which eventually help to convict the killers. Levin's characterization of the steel worker as a person who interacts instinctually with the world is clearly naturalistic; Wrotzlaw might be McTeague in the California mountains.

Ultimately, *Compulsion* is most valuable, as Levin realized, for its portrayal of a particular philosophical mindset in twentieth-century America. Levin wrote in the foreword that "[c]ertain crimes seem to epitomize the thinking of their era"; just as *Crime and Punishment* and *An American Tragedy* arose out of their particular times and places, *Compulsion* is to be taken as a period document (ix). The era of Richard Loeb and Nathan Leopold's crime was the pre-Depression 1920s, a period which F. Scott Fitzgerald described as "one long party." For readers of McTeague's and Clyde Griffiths's stories, Levin's novel warns of danger at the other end of the social scale, implying that like poverty, prosperity, too, has its costs, and that excessive wealth can determine a person's fate just as certainly as poverty.

Taken together, *Light in August, Native Son, The Postman Always Rings Twice,* and *Compulsion* make clear that the flame of naturalism was not extinguished after the 1925 publication of *An American Tragedy.* Rather, that flame seems to have been re-routed into several smaller blazes, each focusing on a different aspect of the naturalistic formula. The thread of determinism takes its most religious turn in Faulkner's novel and its most social in Wright's. Wright's novel fits the prescription for documentary accuracy more closely than do the other three books, although Cain's most exemplifies the journalistic prose style. Cain's and Levin's novels are particularly colored by the dark philosophy of nihilism, though Wright's work also evokes existential questions concerning the human condition. And while Levin's protagonists are inhabitants of a social world far removed from that of the "bottom-dog literature" of John Steinbeck and James T. Farrell, his indictment of society is perhaps the most scathing of the four authors discussed here.

These four novels and others carried forward the naturalistic preoccupation with social misfits, outcasts, and nobodies well past the mid-century mark. In *Native Son* and *Light in August,* Wright and Faulkner introduced into the tradition issues of racial identity and equality which would reappear in *In Cold Blood,* with Perry Smith's struggle over his biraciality, and, three years later, in *The Algiers Motel Incident,* with John Hersey's examination of violence fueled by racial prejudice. Levin's dramatizing his reporter, Sid Silver, prefigures the I-centered "gonzo" journalism of the New Journalism. And Cain's carefully crafted, minimalist prose provides a stylistic transition between the prolixity of Norris and Dreiser and Capote's more crafted style.

Some important variation exists among the four novels I have discussed: for example, *Compulsion* follows the facts of an actual case far more closely than do the other three, and in *Postman* the deterministic element often seems to be pure chance, whereas in the other three, determinism is a complex of social, psychological, and historical circumstances. *Light in August* and *Native Son* are very much within the literary mainstream, while *Postman* has had a more commercial reputation, and *Compulsion* is now somewhat obscure. But variation from author to author and work to work has always characterized naturalism. Donald Pizer was well aware of such variations, and in the penultimate sentence of *Twentieth-Century American Literary Naturalism,* he predicts that naturalism might experience yet another transformation in the "documentary narrative" (152). The example Pizer cites, Truman Capote's 1965 masterpiece *In Cold Blood,* is, however, less a transformation than a renaissance of the naturalism practiced in *McTeague* and *An American Tragedy,* tied to the naturalistic tradition via strands that continued to be present in these four masterful novels of homicide.

NOTES

1. *The Bulwark* and *The Stoic* were both published posthumously, the former in 1946 and the latter in 1947. Dreiser died in 1945.
2. On May 22, 1924, the body of fourteen-year-old Bobby Franks was found in a culvert in Chicago. A pair of eyeglasses found near the body was traced to nineteen-year-old Nathan Leopold, a neighbor of the Franks boy and the son of a prominent businessman. A ransom note was subsequently traced to Leopold's typewriter, and

he and eighteen-year-old Richard Loeb, son of a Sears vice-president, were arrested. Leopold and Loeb were convicted and probably only spared a death sentence by the passionate arguments of their attorney, Clarence Darrow. Both received life sentences. Leopold and Loeb told authorities they were motivated by the desire to commit an undetectable crime.

3. The subject of determinism in Faulkner's work and particularly in *Light in August* has been very thoroughly explored and consequently will not be examined at length in this study. Particularly useful sources on that subject include Perry Westbrook's *Free Will and Determinism in American Literature,* Donald Pizer's *Twentieth Century American Literary Naturalism: An Interpretation,* F. Garvin Davenport Jr.'s *The Myth of Southern History,* Michael Millgate's *New Essays on* Light in August, and Cleanth Brooks's essay "The Community and the Pariah."

4. See especially Seymour Gross and John Edward Hardy's *Images of the Negro in American Literature,* Harold Bloom's *Bigger Thomas,* Keneth Kinnamon's *New Essays on* Native Son, James Baldwin's essay "Everybody's Protest Novel," Irving Howe's essay "Black Boys and Native Sons," Wright's own *How "Bigger" Was Born,* and Yoshinobu Hakutani's work on naturalism in *Native Son,* especially *American Literary Naturalism: A Reassessment.*

WORKS CITED

Alexander, Margaret Walker. *Richard Wright: Impressions and Perspectives.* Ann Arbor: U of Michigan P, 1973.

Baldwin, James. "Everybody's Protest Novel." *Partisan Review* (1949). Bloom 5–6.

———. "Many Thousands Gone: Richard Wright's *Native Son.*" *Notes of a Native Son.* By Baldwin. Boston: Beacon, 1955. Gross and Hardy 233–48.

Bloom, Harold, ed. *Bigger Thomas.* Major Literary Characters Series. New York: Chelsea, 1990.

Blotner, Joseph. *Faulkner: A Biography.* 2 vols. New York: Random House, 1974.

Broeske, Pat H. "Serial Killers Claim Movies as Their Prey." *New York Times* 13 Dec. 1992: 18–19H.

Brooks, Cleanth. "The Community and the Pariah." *William Faulkner: The Yoknapatawpha Country.* By Brooks. New Haven: Yale, 1963. 47–74.

Cain, James M. *The Postman Always Rings Twice.* 1934. Vintage Crime/Black Lizard. New York: Knopf, 1992.

Cullen, John B., with Floyd C. Watkins. *Old Times in the Faulkner Country.* Chapel Hill: U of North Carolina P, 1961.

Davenport, F. Garvin, Jr. *The Myth of Southern History.* Nashville: Vanderbilt UP, 1970.

De Quincey, Thomas. "On the Knocking at the Gate in *Macbeth.*" 1823. *Romantic Poetry and Prose.* Ed. Harold Bloom and Lionel Trilling. New York: Oxford UP, 1973. 731–35.

Faulkner, William. *Intruder in the Dust.* Modern Library College Editions. New York: Random House, 1948.

———. *Light in August.* 1932. Modern Library College Editions. New York: Random House, 1959, 1968.

Fine, David, ed. *Los Angeles in Fiction: A Collection of Original Essays.* Albuquerque: U of New Mexico P, 1984.

Frohock, Wilbur Merrill. *The Novel of Violence in America.* 2nd ed. Dallas: Southern Methodist UP, 1957.

Gross, Seymour, and John Edward Hardy, eds. *Images of the Negro in American Literature.* Chicago: U of Chicago P, 1966.

Gwynn, Frederick L., and Joseph L. Blotner. *Faulkner in the University.* Charlottesville: UP of Virginia, 1959.

Hakutani, Yoshinobu, and Lewis Fried, eds. *American Literary Naturalism: A Reassessment.* Heidelberg: Winter, 1975.

Hoopes, Roy. *Cain: The Biography of James M. Cain.* New York: Holt, 1982.

Howe, Irving. "Black Boys and Native Sons" (excerpt). *A World More Attractive: A View of Modern Literature and Politics.* New York: Horizon, 1963. Bloom 6–9.

Jackson, Blyden. "Richard Wright." *The History of Southern Literature.* Ed. Louis D. Rubin et al. Baton Rouge: Louisiana State UP, 1985. 443–49.

Kinnamon, Keneth, ed. *New Essays on* Native Son. Cambridge: Cambridge UP, 1900.

Levin, Meyer. *Compulsion.* New York: Simon and Schuster, 1956.

———. *In Search.* New York: Horizon, 1950. New York: Pocket, 1973.

Madden, David. *James M. Cain.* Twayne United States Authors Series. New York: Twayne, 1970.

Marling, William. "James M. Cain, Journalist." *The American Roman Noir: Hammett, Cain, and Chandler.* By Marling. Athens: U of Georgia P, 1995. 148–87.

Millgate, Michael. "A Novel, Not an Anecdote: Faulkner's *Light in August.*" Millgate, *New Essays* 31–53.

———, ed. *New Essays on* Light in August. Cambridge: Cambridge UP, 1987.

Mitchell, Lee Clark. "Naturalism and the Languages of Determinism." *Columbia Literary History of the United States.* Ed. Emory Elliott et al. New York: Columbia UP, 1988. 525–45.

Pizer, Donald. *Twentieth-Century American Literary Naturalism: An Interpretation.* Crosscurrents/Modern Critiques. Ed. Harry T. Moore and Matthew J. Bruccoli. Carbondale: Southern Illinois UP, 1982.

Rahv, Philip. "Notes on the Decline of Naturalism." *Partisan Review* 9 (1942): 483–93. *Documents of Modern Literary Realism.* Ed. George J. Becker. Princeton: Princeton UP, 579–90.

Reck, Tom S. "J. M. Cain's Los Angeles Novels." *Colorado Quarterly* 22 (1974): 375–87.

Rubin, Steven. *Meyer Levin.* Boston: Twayne, 1982.

Skenazy, Paul. *James M. Cain*. New York: Continuum, 1989.

Skerrett, Joseph T., Jr. "Composing Bigger: Wright and the Making of *Native Son*." Bloom 125–42.

Welsh, Alexander. "On the Difference between Prevailing and Enduring." Millgate, *New Essays* 123–47.

Westbrook, Perry. *Free Will and Determinism in American Literature*. Cranbury, NJ: Associated UP, 1979.

Williamson, Joel. *William Faulkner and Southern History*. New York: Oxford UP, 1993.

Wolfe, Tom. Introduction. *Cain x 3: The Postman Always Rings Twice, Mildred Pierce, Double Indemnity*. By James M. Cain. New York: Knopf, 1969. v–viii.

Wright, Richard. *Black Boy: A Record of Childhood and Youth*. 1945. New York: Harper, 1966.

———. *How "Bigger" Was Born*. New York: Harper, 1940. Bloom 23–42.

———. *Native Son*. New York: Perennial-Harper, 1940.

From Determinism to Indeterminacy

CHAOS THEORY, SYSTEMS THEORY,
AND THE DISCOURSE OF NATURALISM

—*Mohamed Zayani*

> Systems always remain incommensurable.
>
> — Claude Levi-Strauss,
> *Introduction to the Works*
> *of Marcel Mauss*

TRADITIONALLY, NATURALISTIC fiction HAS BEEN firmly YOKED WITH THE LANGUAGE AND PHILOSOPHY OF DETERMINISM, PROMINENT IN THE United States at the end of the nineteenth century. Naturalism thrived during an age when evolutionary theory was virtually the official philosophy. Naturalists were heavily influenced by social Darwinism which, being anchored in the belief that heredity determines human character, appealed to struggle as the agent that shapes biological and social evolution at the level of race. According to Lars Åhnebrink, one of the first critics to write about this turn-of-the-century movement, naturalism "portrays life as it is in accordance with the philosophical theory of determinism" (vi). Recently, this same perspective has been reiterated in a prominent revisionist critical anthology. Thus, in his contribution to the *Columbia Literary History of the United States,* Lee Clark Mitchell observes that "the concept of determinism inspired new narrative conceptions of setting and character, and by the turn of the century, American authors have incorporated these possibilities in their work" (535). The naturalistic writings of such novelists as Dreiser, London, Norris, and Crane dramatize the vast forces that control man and emphasize a deficit of agency, a lack of autonomy, and an absence of motivation. Characters are caught up in the struggle for survival in a hostile environment over which they have little or no control. The lack of agency and the thinness of representation of inner life in naturalism are held to reveal the author's belief in the animalistic basis of human behavior. In this perspective, human beings are animals lacking free will and, being such, have no power to resist the conditions which press upon them. Characters act the way they do because the forces of heredity and environment act upon them and eventually defeat them: as Åhnebrink writes, "a naturalist believes that man is fundamentally an animal deprived of free will and subjected to an irresistible compulsion of inner physical drives. To a naturalist, man can be explained in terms of the forces, usually hereditary and environmental, which operate upon him" (vii). In naturalism, human beings are unable to control their destinies; they are victims of indifferent forces and subjects of dictated events. In the words of Charles Child Walcutt, naturalist characters are typical people "whose 'choices' entangle them in nets of circumstances from which they cannot be extricated" (74).

Jack London's "To Build a Fire" offers a classic example of the ways the subject in naturalism is conceived as determined by forces beyond his or her control. The story dramatizes the futile attempt of an unnamed man to reach a companion's camp over three miles away. At the end, the man is hampered and defeated. Failing to take into account the old-timer's warning not to travel alone and especially not to undermine the forces of nature, the man eventually freezes and is left to die, survived by his dog, who is clearly better adapted to this hostile environment than human beings. The animal imagery is equally dramatic in Upton Sinclair's *The Jungle.* Describing the dehumanizing effect of the expanding meat industry, Sinclair does not fail to infuse his novel with episodes that are reminiscent of the animalism and bestiality in London's writings. The death of Little Stanislova, Ona's son, is one such example: "rats had killed him and eaten him nearly up when he fell asleep in the corner of a factory" (278). In the instance of Norris, animalism is intimately connected with what Donald Pizer calls "atavistic ferocity" (71). The images of degeneration and primitivism are often indistinguishable from images of eating and devouring. In *Vandover and the Brute,* for instance, the main character undergoes a phenomenal degeneration whereby he succumbs to the brute within and is eventually eaten up by the sexual disease he contracts. Such animalism carries over to Norris's unfinished epic of the wheat. The predatory theme is evident not only in *The Pit,* where bulls and bears engage in fierce competition and ferocious games, but also in *The Octopus,* where Behrman, the railroad agent and speculator, is buried alive beneath the wheat. Stephen Crane's "The Open Boat" further dramatizes nature's indifference to man's struggles and the futility of understanding the meaning and absurdity of the whole incident. The cruel force that is the sea is not only unpredictable but also menacing. In Crane's other writings, the opposition between man and nature is often translated into an opposition between man and society. In "The Blue Hotel," for instance, Crane reiterates the same view that man does not control his destiny.

The Swede, an Easterner, is destroyed by a social environment he is unable to understand. He is trapped by his *idée fixe* about the wild West, which eventually brings about his death. Located in the midst of a snowstorm, and not unlike the boat under the mercy of the waves, the hotel is as much a refuge and a shelter as it is an isolating and threatening place. In both stories, the frailty of the characters is unmistakable. If in "The Open Boat" the strongest man in the group drowns, in "The Blue Hotel" the smallest man kills the burly and violent Swede. This sense of helplessness, powerlessness, and weakness is also at the heart of *Maggie*. The story, as Charles Walcutt puts it, "shows that nothing can be done for Maggie and her family, for they are lost" (72).

Although increasingly critics are trying to disengage naturalism from the early confining conceptions of the movement as a form of pessimistic determinism, the conventional understanding of this movement still draws on the theory of determinism. At least, much of the early criticism on the period (as is epitomized in the writings of Charles Walcutt, Donald Pizer, and John Condor) amounts to little more than an effort to explore the question of free will and determinism. While the often invoked philosophy of determinism cannot be easily disputed as influential—since Zola, a naturalist novelist who dominated the literary scene in France during the last decades of the nineteenth century, often used it and referred to it explicitly in his own works and programmatic vision, and since man's lack of free will and his subjection to powerful forces is a recurrent motif in many naturalistic novels—naturalism cannot be reduced to a philosophy of determinism. Subscribing to the view that characters are not accountable for having acted out of desire does not do justice to the complexity of naturalistic fiction. All that would be needed to explain any action would be a set of conditions, not a responsive self. Take, for instance, Dreiser's *The Financier*. Although the novel opens with one of the most straightforward and stark versions of determinism, and although Dreiser is clear about the impact of the scene of the struggle in the fish tank between a squid and a lobster on the young Frank Cowperwood— namely, the realization that life is essentially a battle between the strong and the weak—the novel cannot be reduced to a treatise about determinism or be read solely and simply in those terms. Although Dreiser tells us that Cowperwood "was a financier by instinct" (11), he does not present him as someone caught up in his instincts or victim of his racial past but as a manipulative, shrewd, and determinate character. His passion for money is not a hereditary acquisition but an interest and a curiosity: "gold interested him. . . . He was curious about stocks and bonds" (11). In a reading of Crane's *Maggie*, Marston La France pursues this argument further:

If "environment" means external living conditions, *Maggie* in no way proves that environment is a tremendous force which "frequently shapes lives regardless." All the characters in this novel, including Maggie herself, are free to choose their own course of action within the usual limitations provided by the particular situation, or else Crane's intense irony is gratuitous. Maggie cannot be determined by heredity because she in no way resembles her mother, brother, or what little is shown of her father. And she cannot be determined by her external environment simply because the novel's structure places her *and* her slum environment in exactly the same position relative to the other characters: both are alike passive, inert, acted upon, actually shaped by the twisted values and hypocritical actions of Mrs. Johnson, Jimmie, and Pete; and Maggie's downfall at the hands of Pete, as predictable as the fate of a roomful of new furniture in the hands of drunken Mrs. Johnson because Maggie chooses to resist Pete about as much as the furniture resists her mother, "is inevitable only under the precondition of human irresponsibility." But again Crane's irony, in all the Bowery works, proclaims that he does not believe human irresponsibility is ever inevitable or determined by anything other than the wilful dishonesty of human beings. (40–41)

Likewise, the structure of desire in *Sister Carrie* resists a one-dimensional, predictable, deterministic reading, although traditionally the novel has been fit squarely within a deterministic formula. According to this formula, Carrie and her lovers are shown as victims of forces; they are blameless because the forces of desire determine the liaisons they form. However, desire seems to act ambiguously on the main character. On the one hand, Carrie is portrayed as the victim of her desires: individuals, objects, and circumstances act on her; she is a passive object for whom Drouet and Hurstwood compete, and eventually the stronger of the two competitors wins her over. On the other hand, Carrie is the epitome of desire; she is a desired and desiring woman; she is a woman who is determined to rise and succeed. New Historicists have pursued the latter line of analysis with a relative emphasis on the question of desire, thus giving fresh impetus to naturalistic fiction. Walter Benn Michaels's *The Gold Standard and the Language of Naturalism* is one such example. For Michaels, the insatiability at the heart of Carrie's desire exemplifies the continual need for expansion at the heart of capitalism. In assessing Dreiser's project, Michaels rightly rejects a schema that makes literature a privileged "outside" to culture, but he does so by ignoring the heterogeneity of culture. In arguing that desire is not a destabilizing force that threatens the system but one that caters to the dominant economic mode, Michaels weaves contradictions into a monolith he calls the market. The consequences of the schema of "belief" he proposes is that the subject is not a constituent but a product of the market. The axiomatic effects he vindicates seem to undermine both the unevenness of the market and the unpredictability of desire. What this means, in part, is that Michaels's new historicism fails to transcend the traditional deterministic model that has for a long time been yoked to naturalism. Whether the overpowering determinant is called the market or hereditary forces, the consequences are one and the same—an undermining of the complexity of the inner life and consciousness of the naturalistic character.

In order to rid the concept of the system that Michaels proposes of its totalitarian bent, one has to recognize that an inexorable part of the system's logic is its potential to develop contradictory tendencies which suggest the existence of limits to the capacity of society to be over-organized. An emphasis on the openness of the system makes it possible to propose a more viable understanding of capitalism, namely that capitalism has not only a tendency to envelop the entirety of the social body but also a proclivity to develop dysfunctionalities, create deficiencies, provoke deviations, and generate counterprocesses that are more tendentious and more momentous than Michaels is willing to admit. As Henri Lefebvre points out,

> reproduction does not occur without changes. This excludes both the idea of an automatic reproductive process internal to the constituted mode of production (as system) and that of the immediate efficacy of a "generative nucleus." The contradictions themselves reproduce, and not without changes. Former relations may degenerate or dissolve. . . . Others are constituted within reproduction. . . . These new relations emerge from within those which are dissolving: they first appear as the negation of the latter, as destroyers of the antecedents and conditions which hold them back. This is the specific behavior of the enlarged contradictions. (90–91)

The deployment of the system produces unpredictable conditions which call for a special attention not only to the reproduction of the system but also to the movement of its elements. The structural imbalance that characterizes capitalism bolsters it up but at the same time alters it. At the very least, systems theory teaches us that the continuity of the system does not reside in its identity but in the relation of its elements to their environment. Capitalism is an inherently unstable system which engenders a continuous interplay of its elements. This play of elements is not, however, without consequences. In attuning its internal contradictions and replacing its elements, the system transforms itself and reconfigures itself at a higher level of complexity. The system feeds, as it were, on its own problems, but in the process it evolves and changes.

The attention to complex, self-organizing, self-renewing structures, which are at the basis of both systems theory and chaos theory, has ushered in a postmodern science that is unpredictable and therefore unknowable to the degree of precision and exactness demanded by modern science. The behavior of a system—whether it be an atom, a person, or a society—cannot be fully predicted; it cannot be known completely, perfectly, and precisely. More importantly, the imperfection of and contradiction within the system can no longer be considered conjunctural or exceptional; they can no longer be dismissed as a sign of imperfection—one that is often relegated to the realm of errors, glitches, gremlins, gaps, and deviancies. Rather, imperfection is inherent, immanent, and integral. As Margaret Wheatley aptly puts it in *Leadership and the New Science,*

> dissipative structures that *disorder* can be a source of *order,* and that growth is found in disequilibrium, not in balance. The things we fear most in organizations—fluctuations, disturbances, imbalances—need not be signs of an impending disorder that will destroy us. Instead, fluctuations are the primary source of creativity. Scientists in this newly understood world describe the paths between disorder and order as "order out of chaos" or "order through fluctuation." These are new principles that highlight the dynamics between chaos and creativity, between disruptions and growth. (20)

At the core of the new science is what may be termed an anti-scientific attitude. Increasingly, scientists harbor an unconscious resistance to determinism and assert a conscious conviction of the necessity of chance in the creation of forms. Chance, noise, complexity, bifurcation, and fluctuation become matters of attention and interest partly because they defy our understanding of systems as having a controllable evolution. As formalism continues to lose its efficacy for describing these notions, science is more and more interested in the amorphous syntax of forms and systems. It studies the changing relationship between order and disorder, chance and necessity, determinacy and randomness, permanence and change, organic and inorganic forms, consistency and inconsistency, entropy and neg-entropy, linear and non-linear dynamics in both natural and social systems. The argument that these opposite strains are more complementary than they seem to be calls for the need to leave behind the ontological opposition of chance and necessity. Deterministic systems allow for a variety of virtual states of a system to exist, at least latently, with a particular realization resulting from the conditions of the limits imposed by a given environment. Within such a perspective, the existing constraints of a system allow for a better understanding of the dynamics of its change. The principle of order through fluctuation assumes that there is a non-equilibrium ordering principle of organization that governs dynamic aspects of evolving systems at various levels. What defines a living system, as Antoine Danchin argues in "Permanence and Change," is in great part its ability to undergo the effects of various contingencies without being destroyed—in other words, its ability to adapt and to subsist in a changing environment. In fact, evolution in living systems is more related to progress and complexification than it is associated with deterioration and disintegration.

If with the translation from French of Ilya Prigogine and Isabelle Stengers's *Order out of Chaos* (1984) and the publication of James Gleick's *Chaos: Making a New Science* (1987) chaos theory started to gain eminence in scientific circles, with the appearance of Katherine Hayles's *Chaos Bound* (1990) chaos started to provide the perspective and even the methodology for an *avant-garde* theory of literature. Chaos theory is increasingly used to inform our reading and understanding of literary texts. The implications of such a theory on the study of literature are exciting, to say the least. By refusing to ascribe origins, to draw centers, and to construct identities to and for texts and their authors, literary deconstructionism has brought a wave of anti-causality to the way of literary analysis. The pursuit of chaos within the context of naturalism is all the more exciting because the literary movement under consideration has been traditionally associated with and deeply entrenched in the philosophy of determinism. Chaos makes it possible to explore certain themes and concepts in naturalistic fiction which are obfuscated by the emphasis on determinism. Although these chaotic tendencies have not escaped the attention of some critics of the period, they have not been duly analyzed. In *Form and History in American Literary Naturalism,* for instance, June Howard foregrounds a number of prominent themes in turn-of-the-century American literature which continue to preoccupy historians of the period because they constitute powerful elements of the ideology of that period. At the heart of the discourse of naturalism are such issues as populism, proletarianization, uncontrolled economic forces, reform, class warfare, immigration, and nativism, to name but a few. Focusing primarily on determinism, sensationalism, and reformism in general, and the vocabulary of savagery within a hegemonic ideology that reproduced tensions of assimilation in particular, Howard turns the inquiry from themes *per se* to "the fundamental conceptual opposition that informs and structures these themes" (40). In her view, the terror of the brute, which is hard to ignore in the novels of Jack London, for instance, does not simply reflect a fear of "the mob and the criminal"; it bespeaks a deeper anxiety about "revolution and chaos" (95). Recognizing these tensions is central to Howard's conception of history—namely, that history does not forego uncertainty:

> It is my hope that this study will bring my readers, as it has me, to a recognition of the irrevocable openness of any historical moment and an apprehension of naturalism not as an exhibit in a gallery of literary types but as a dynamic solution to the problem of generating narrative out of the particular historical and cultural materials that offered themselves to these writers. This recognition is in some sense the discovery that our own history is contingent, that our world really was not a foregone conclusion. (x–xi)

According to Christophe Den Tandt, this openness is precisely what distinguishes naturalism from realism. Naturalism relies heavily on documentary discourse but also draws on areas that go beyond the limits of such positivistic discourse. For the author of *The Urban Sublime in American Literary Naturalism,* realism is invested in a "logic of exclusion" (27) which annihilates what it cannot represent; it conceals the heterogeneity of its narrative discourse by domesticating the Other. Unlike realism, naturalism unleashes the discursive heterogeneity inherent in the text. This point is of utter importance to Den Tandt's overall argument because it enables him to avoid the shortcomings of *The Social Construction of American Realism* in which Amy Kaplan identifies elements that seem to be antithetical to and incompatible with the realist ethos only to reabsorb them within an enlarged definition of realism. By using a mixture of documentary and romantic discourses, naturalists have produced what Den Tandt calls a pseudo-totalizing spectacle of the urban scene. That is, they have doubts about the very possibility of portraying the city—with both its familiar and uncanny spaces—as a social totality that is comprehensible in human terms. At its core, the naturalists' conception of life in the great strange city bespeaks a paradoxical experience of wonder and terror, of delight and fear, of pleasure and peril, of fascination and dread. Accordingly, the metropolis is painted as an immensely large and unfathomably mysterious field, the apprehension of which can only be fragmented—whence the importance of such naturalistic themes as the mysterious netherworld of instincts and life forces that cannot be objectified in realist discourse. There is no need to push

the analysis further; one need only point out the brute in London, the insur-
rectionary mob in Dreiser, and the animal within in Norris.

No one has, probably, explored this chaotic strain in naturalism more
fully and more elaborately than Patrick Brady. He has both revised and
refined our understanding of naturalism not simply by moving it away from
the deterministic perspective with which it has long been associated and from
which it has been unable to dissociate itself, but by capitalizing on the presence
and significance of chaos in various naturalistic writings. Although naturalism
is very much informed by the philosophy of determinism, it is not void of the
element of indeterminacy either. For Brady, chaos theory is worthy of attention because it identifies unsuspected aspects of naturalism, the examination of
which enhances our appreciation of this movement and complicates our
understanding of the period during which it thrived. Before exploring the
scope and complexity of Brady's argument about the specificity of naturalism,
a brief overview of Brady's own understanding of the theory of chaos is in
order. Chaos, Brady writes,

> is, firstly, complexity, turbulence, discontinuous process; secondly,
> it is disunity, fragmentation, and non-linearity; thirdly, chaos is
> constrained randomness, or relative uncertainty, and centrally
> engages the parameters of predictability. Chaos may be defined as
> low-level deterministic non-linear dynamics. It involves both
> determinacy and indeterminacy; determinacy because its random-
> ness is limited and indeterminacy because it has only a few vari-
> ables or factors. Chaos theory casts doubt on (undermines) real
> randomness (total predictability) on the one hand and exact pre-
> dictability on the other hand; it denies the possibility of unified
> order. ("Transactional Analysis" 184)

Based on this definition, Brady extrapolates six formal principles which are
highly operative within chaos theory:

1. *Concealed order*: an order that is dissimulated beneath an apparent disorder. Thus, while in appearance the reverse side of a
   carpet may be disorderly, in reality it hides an order. Likewise,
   chaotic processes may produce orderly patterns, which is tantamount to saying that within chaotic systems, there is a pattern
   of limited predictability.
2. *Constrained randomness*: an erratic or random movement within
   set boundaries.

3. *Non-linearity*: a disproportion between cause and effect which is best represented by the butterfly effect—an effect whereby initial conditions and trivial incidents can play a determining role and insignificant causes can produce great effects. Such exponential repercussions are based on sensitive dependence on initial conditions.

4. *Self-similarity, typified in fractals*: the repetition, in different registers, of the principle of fragmentation in an endless proliferation or a *mise-en-abîme* structure. Accordingly, irregular shapes or number sequences can repeat themselves on varying scales (as is the case with trees, branches, twigs, etc.).

5. *Entropy*: a measure for the degradation of energy in a closed system.

6. *Feedback (or retroaction)*: a principle which calls for the output of a system to be re-inscribed in the system.

Unlike what many critics tend to think, Brady argues, these six principles of chaos are not confined to modernist writings, nor are they a privilege of postmodern literature: "While it is tempting to see as 'historically-conditioned' the twentieth-century conjunction between modern art and literature and chaos theory, the truth is more complex. Many of the central tendencies of modernism, which was born from late-nineteenth-century Impressionism, are to be found in the rococo art and literature of the early eighteenth century" (Brady, "Transactional Analysis" 186). For Brady, rococo art and literature contain clear examples of the kind of indeterminacy, fractals, strange attractors, and butterfly effects that are usually associated with chaos. The inconsistency and incoherence in Marivaux's *La vie de Marianne* provide a poignant illustration of chaos in rococo literature. The novel contains different, even contradictory stylistic tendencies (what Brady calls *un mélange de tons*). The fragmentation and dissonance that characterize the style of the novel are worthy of attention partly because they point to a break with classicism and neo-classicism. Chaotic tendencies in the literature of the eighteenth (and nineteenth) century are particularly significant because they highlight "anti-classical aesthetics" (Brady, "Théorie du chaos et structure narrative" 51). The principle of order which is so central to neo-classical literature, at least as exemplified in the unity of tone and the continuity of movement in the writings of Montesquieu, is abandoned in the rococo novel. This is not to say, however, that a text like *La vie de Marianne* is void of the element of order. The novel has a peculiar order—one that has to do with the voice of the character. In fact, the apparent disorder that characterizes the novel conceals a principle of order which provides the narrative with a kind of unity. Breaking the novel into levels of discourse enables Brady to identify a number of passages, comparable in length and similar in tone, that point to a progression in the story. Such a progression gives the work a solid structure that is often unsuspected because of its apparently chaotic style. This line of analysis enables Brady to explain why the rococo aesthetic pays a special attention and lends a great importance to seemingly insignificant things, meticulous details, and miniscule events. He acknowledges that one may object to his argument on the basis that it can be applied to almost every type of aesthetic, but he insists that in rococo, the element of chaos is privileged and naturally invites a chaos analysis. In Brady's words, the rococo aesthetic "is based on spontaneity and caprice . . . [and as such] can profit from a chaos analysis more than any other aesthetic" ("Chaos et structure narrative" 45–46).

These chaotic tendencies are even more pointed in modernism. In "Chaos Theory, Control Theory, and Literary Theory," Brady observes that "the spontaneity of the Impressionists who revolutionized painting and music a century ago and so opened the door to modern art, was viewed by their contemporaries as anarchistic and chaotic" (72). Stéphane Mallarmé's famous poem "Un coup de dés jamais n'abolira le hasard" is a case in point. Unlike what appearances suggest, the movement of the dice is subject to a pattern, albeit a concealed one. When sufficiently multiplied, the result of casting conforms to a highly ordered pattern, which is tantamount to saying that dice throwing does not involve randomness but chaos. A few decades later, with André Gide and Marcel Proust, the presence and role of indeterminacy becomes even more prominent. Gide, in particular, "dismantled the traditional ideal model of psychological consistency in the portrayal of fictional characters. Gide preached moral and experiential flexibility or availability and spontaneity (unpredictability). He also showed a character acting in a manner not only independent of Fate, Providence, and heredity but even independent of any motivation on his own part" (Brady, "Transactional Analysis" 186).

This type of analysis can arguably be extended to naturalism, and, in fact, many critics have started to question the rigid distinction between modernism, on the one hand, and realism and naturalism, on the other. According to Brian Lee, realism (a term he uses interchangeably with naturalism) has evaporated precisely because its cause has been taken up by modernism (28). The naturalism of Stephen Crane lends support to Lee's argument. Crane's fiction can be considered realism, psychological realism, naturalism, regionalism, symbolism, and impressionism. In the words of Charles Swann, Crane is "a master of the contradictory effect" (98). Crane's fiction is fragmented, to say the least. *Maggie,* as Swann explains, is "not so much an experiment in life as an experiment in style—a language game" (103). These comments further justify the rapprochement Brady envisions between modernism and naturalism. Brady extends chaos analysis to naturalism, which, in a peculiar way, is presented as a kind of bridge between rococo literature and postmodern literature: "impressionism, much like rococo, which it recalls in more than one way, is a complex aesthetic genre which readily lends itself to a chaos analysis" ("La théorie du chaos et *L'Œuvre"* 111), and he finds the same principles of chaos insistently operative in the writings of Émile Zola. *L'Œuvre,* for instance, lends itself almost perfectly to a "chaos type of analysis" ("Théorie du chaos et structure narrative" 51). It is a novel that throbs with "pathological disorder" ("Chaos et naturalisme" 203), "psychological disorder," "aesthetic incoherence" ("La théorie du chaos et *L'Œuvre"* 107, 109) and, as such, provides several variations on different aspects of chaos theory.

Although invigorating, Brady's project leaves the reader with a number of questions. One of the insistent problems with the kind of analysis Brady provides is that chaos theory is a tool rather than a way of thinking. Because Brady contents himself with pointing out manifestations of chaos theory in literary works, his analysis runs the danger of slipping into a cookie-cutter approach. In article after article, we are reminded that what is at stake is merely an attempt to "provide illustrations" ("Chaos et naturalisme" 202), to "apply" or "verify" (Théorie du chaos et structure narrative" 43, 45) the presence of a number of principles operative in chaos theory within either the rococo or the naturalistic aesthetic. Accordingly, Brady observes that certain stylistic aspects of *Les liaisons dangereuses* are "reminiscent" of fractals in chaos theory ("Théorie du chaos et structure narrative" 50). In this instance, Brady's depiction of chaos strikes the reader as somewhat anecdotal. The same can be said about Brady's exemplification of the principle of non-linearity in Zola's *L'Œuvre.* In this novel, we are told, an apparently insignificant or banal incident proves to have profound ramifications on the unfolding of events. Were it not for the late arrival of the train to Paris at the outset of the novel, Christine would not have met Claude, which means that her life would have taken a different course. Overall, Brady's discussion of chaos is not purposive and, as such, risks being nothing more than a checklist. For each of the above-mentioned principles of chaos, Brady provides an example from naturalist texts. The emphasis throughout is almost exclusively on the manifestation of chaos in naturalist works of literature. Little, if anything, is said about the larger implication of such moments of chaos on naturalism as a movement.

These shortcomings should not undermine Brady's achievement. The questions he raises are certainly not to be rejected. In fact, they call for a more sophisticated engagement with the theory of chaos. In the following, I propose to take Brady's argument a step further by focusing on the language as well as the narrative strategy of the naturalistic novel. Brady's argument is particularly interesting because it stands in marked distinction to prominent works which treat the language of naturalism. In *Determined Fiction,* for instance, Lee Clark Mitchell embraces the understanding of naturalism as "a mode characterized by determinism" (30), but moves the attention away from scientific determinism to linguistic determinism. In his view, naturalism is far from being a deficient literary movement plagued with the tendentiousness and heavy-handed extravagance of verbal effort. Nor are the abundant recurrences, the repetitive stylistic patterns, and the verbal reiterations in naturalism signs of bad writing. The form of the naturalist novel is functional in the sense that it enhances its content. According to Mitchell, determinism can be observed not just at the story level but also at the level of the language, not just at the level of narrative plot but also at the level of syntactic structure and verbal style: "the 'mechanisms' of literary naturalism belong less to some physical 'universe of force' than to the grammatical pressures of distinctively verbal realms" (*Determined Fiction* xv). Naturalists are committed to a deterministic belief through their verbal constructs, which is tantamount to saying that philosophy and style converge, and, further, that fiction does not so much argue for a certain philosophy as it embodies a metaphysics in its very syntax: "Not only plot and events but aspects of style seem uncontrollably repeated depriving both characters and readers of an otherwise comforting sense of autonomy. . . . Naturalist characters repeat themselves with little variation, in narrative whose advance notices undercut suspense to enforce a 'plot of predestination'" (21–26). Seen from this vantage point, the plodding, graceless paragraphs are a source of vigor for naturalism and its language rather than an index of artistic failings. The soggy repetitiveness that marks the naturalist novel leaves the reader with a sense of helplessness. Irving Howe concurs. In his view, the main literary problem of the naturalist novel is that of pacing: "The naturalist novel moves along at a steady march, from one demonstration to another, usually on a downward path. It is hard to imagine a short naturalistic novel—heaviness seems part of its very being. After a time, an experienced reader learns to anticipate the inexorable slippage of the characters, and may grow impatient with the writer's insistence that it is all a matter of necessity. The form tends to tire itself out" (227).

Howe's argument is, however, much more sophisticated than Mitchell's. For the author of "Naturalism and Taste," repetition in naturalism is far from being steady and fully anticipated: "If pushed to an extreme, naturalism has a way of turning into something other than itself, often into a kind of gross expressionist nightmare or an autonomous grotesquerie" (227). The repetition that characterizes the naturalistic novel is often accelerated, leading to a kind of a runaway. Frank Norris has alluded to this trend in his theoretical writings when arguing that realism has a tendency to turn into melodrama: "Terrible things must happen to the characters of the naturalistic tale. They must be twisted from the ordinary, wrenched from the quiet, uneventful round of everyday life and flung into the throes of a vast terrible drama that works itself out in unleashed passions, in blood and sudden death" (qtd. in Howe 228). These observations suggest that although the naturalistic text seems to be a closed and redundant narrative, it is not void of a random and incomprehensive succession of events. Stated differently, the naturalistic text is not a closed and predictable text but an open and creative one; or, at least, one may say that the naturalist text has an unsuspected capacity to incorporate incomprehensible and random elements, thus spawning unfinished, non-teleological narratives.

But what does it mean to talk about a non-teleological narrative? In "Chance, Complexity, and Narrative Explanation," William Paulson argues that narrative is inherently a mode of representing the incomprehensible and the random. A narrative does not give explanations as much as it follows the unfolding of events. In order to explain the outcome of a particular event, whether it be historical or fictional, one has to follow the narrative rather than compress it into "explanatory schemata" or reduce it to a "set of generative principles" (Paulson 9):

> In general, the recourse to narrative (as opposed to analytic or theo-retical) explanation implies . . . contingency and incomprehensibil-ity. . . . In effect, the data has to be listed, rather than summarized, and so there is no valid substitute for a narrative recounting of events. Narrative explanation is the mode of understanding appro-priate to a largely open, contingent, unpredictable world. For that part of the world in which events are repeatable and determined, where knowledge can attain closure, narrative explanation becomes superfluous. (9)

Paulson critically probes the nature of narrative (as well as its explanatory function), and he objects to the conception of narrative as a mode of knowledge.
Narrative, he argues, imposes an *a priori* pattern which does not do justice to
the intrinsic structure of events or account for their contingency: "Perhaps the
most fundamental form of narrative order is that of closure" (12). Narrative
does imply a recognizable pattern which gives a sense of coherence and organization to the events, but such a pattern is far from being either rigid or inflexible: "The notion of narrative includes this kind of comprehensibility as much
as it does a certain incomprehensibility due to which only the story itself and
not its mere principle can be satisfying" (12). In *Games Authors Play,* Peter
Hutchinson goes a step further. He argues that literature has an intrinsic ludic
characteristic—that literature is inherently playful. Literary games play a
significant role in structuring the relationship between the reader and the text.
These games entail a playfulness by means of which "an author situates his
reader to deduce or speculate, by which he encourages him to see a relationship
between different parts of the text" (14). From the standpoint of Hutchinson,
then, playfulness is an integral part of the literary text. Nancy Morrow concurs.
Every novelistic text, she argues, "plays a particular kind of game with the readers; by encouraging them to participate in the play of language and ideas, by
making them believe in the imagined world of the text, or even challenging
them to solve a particular problem or puzzle" (22). Realism seems to be the
exception because realist representation tends to resist playfulness. In fact, playfulness is a feature that realist and naturalist writers often strive to suppress. For
instance, proponents of realist discourse maintain that realist fiction is more
associated with fact (i.e., reality) than it is with fiction (i.e., a fictional version of
reality): "just as the realist must convince readers that the fictional world is factual, she or he must persuade them that the characters are faithful reproductions of 'real' people, typical and exemplary, case studies that illustrate some
'fact' about contemporary life" (Morrow 29–30).

Philippe Hammon's "The Major Features of Realist Discourse" provides the ground for testing these elaborations on the nature of narrative
within the context of realist fiction. Hammon is totally opposed to the notion
that realism copies reality. In his view, literary forms have to be conceived of
as modes of discourse. The realist, and by extension the naturalist, discourse
obeys a set of heterogeneous criteria. Naturalism is marked, among other
things, by the coherence of its statements. The text either refers us back to
something that has already been said (such as memory, family line, heredity,
tradition, and cycle) or allows a preview of what is to come (such as prediction,
program, presentiment, order, and contract). In naturalism, "the text constructs

itself as foreseeable. . . . [It] is characterized by a marked redundancy and fore-seeability of its content" (Hammon 167–73) insofar as it privileges the profane and avoids the sacred, which means that references to an elsewhere (something sacred, exotic, or otherworldly) are very minimal: "Realist discourse is simply a discourse *ostentatious with knowledge* (the descriptive mode) which it wants to *show* (to the reader by *circulating* it) in and through narrative" (172). As such, the realist text is accessible and readable; it permits itself to unfold and to be understood (which means that there is no room for the unnamable and the indescribable). The realist discourse thus has "a (utopian) thrust towards monosemesis" (177). It strives to reduce the ambiguity of the text through the fullness of description, the refusal to play on words, the presentation of precise facts, the listing of exact numbers, the use of technical language, and the atten-tion to the banal, the simple, the mundane, and the prosaic. The realist's keen-ness on being exhaustive—on offering an inventory, accounting for and explaining everything—further supports this point.

It is clear that Hammon's argument is much more sophisticated than Lee Clark Mitchell's. The major feature Hammon outlines in the realist dis-course is to a large extent a matter of effect, which is tantamount to saying that the realist text is not void of maneuvers or free from contours. The realist dis-course is one characterized by the "mirage of reproducibility and of verifiabil-ity" (Hammon 178) whereby the novelist strives to reduce the imbalance that exists between the *being* and the *appearance* of objects and characters, among other things. In a line of analysis that is reminiscent of the argument Roland Barthes puts forth in "L'Effet de réel," Hammon argues that although the real-ist text is readable and although it tends to unfold smoothly, much of the real-ity it conveys is nothing more than an effect; what is conveyed is not reality *per se* but an intimacy with the real: "The reality effect is thus, quite often, only the reader's euphoric recognition of a certain vocabulary. It is therefore normal to come across, in someone like Zola, at the opening of a series of denominations or of a descriptive 'segment', an extraordinary frequency of verbs such as *to explain* or *to name*" (174). The realist discourse—with its proffered aversion to ambiguity—is less a reflection of reality than it is an attempt to prevent "a 'deflation' of the realist illusion" (177). The absence of reference to the act of storytelling in the realist novel further maintains the appearance of a trans-parent mode of writing: "Realist discourse will in general reject reference to the process of articulation, and move instead towards a 'transparent' writing dominated only by the transmission of information. This leads to what could be called a neutralization or a *detonalization* of the message" (175). The latter observation is quite significant: for Hammon, realist discourse is marked by two complementary and, to some extent contradictory, tendencies; it is as much "an aesthetic of discontinuity" as it is "an aesthetic of continuity" (181). Beneath the apparent flatness, coherence, and unity of the realist discourse are masked, latent, and insidious disruptions. The absence of disruptions and discordances in the text (such as narrative traps, slow-downs, distortions, and awaits) does not necessarily mean the absence of indeterminacy. It suggests that indeterminacy is there but is unthinkable. In realist discourses, there is an unsettling anxiety and a strong desire not to let anything fall beyond control—hence what Hammon calls the hurriedness of the text and its haste to fulfill the reader's horizon of expectations:

> The realist text is a text 'in a hurry', characterized by what might be called the *accelerated semanticisation,* by a maximum of the journey and the distance between the functional kernels of the narration. . . . Realist discourse rejects [narrative traps, slow-downs, distortions, and awaits]: the appearance of a new character, manifested by the appearance of a proper name, i.e. of an 'asemanteme', will immediately be followed by the information to which it will refer in the rest of the text: biography, physical or psychological descriptions, characteristic act, programme of action; the outline will be followed by its realization; the appearance of a blacksmith by the description of the smith and the blacksmith at work; etc. Hence a certain flattening of the text in its haste to fulfill the horizons of expectation created by the appearance of every new indeterminacy. It could be said that realist discourse has a horror of the informational gap, and that it will in general reject dilatory procedures: nothing more alien to realist discourse than any intrigue that involves 'suspense' or 'deceptiveness', any structural layout 'in parts', 'in strands', etc. or any 'elliptical' structures that would skip a necessary step in the logical overall cohesion of the discourse. (180–81)

Hammon's discourse analysis reveals a new perception of realism—namely, that realism is far from being a simple and artless mode: it is not void of indeterminacy, inconsistency, and variability; it is not merely descriptive but is also and primarily performative. The above description suggests as well that it is impossible to construct a special "type" of realist discourse. Realist discourse is only a product of a constructed theoretical type. At the heart of realist discourse is a set of contradictions, and it is through these specific contradictions that realist and, by extension, naturalist discourse can best be characterized.

Norris's playful novel *Vandover and the Brute* is a case in point. Although the novel deals with some of the major themes and motifs in naturalism, it does so in ways that complicate these themes and motifs rather than merely reproduce them. Reduced to its most basic story line, the novel relates the gradual decline and the inevitable disintegration of a phenomenal character from being a genteel artist with a promising talent to a debased animal. Under the spell of the animal within, Vandover degenerates physically, mentally, and socially; he squanders his money, loses his artistic talent, and is ultimately reduced to being an impoverished brute. Subject to the unsolicited prompting of instinct and a victim of moral weakness, he succumbs to the forces of evil. His sexual indulgence and recklessness not only dramatize the fall of a virtuous character from innocence to sin but also highlight the deterministic theme that runs throughout naturalism, namely the existence of vast forces over which individuals have little or no control. However, *Vandover and the Brute* cannot be reduced to this predictable story line. At times, one cannot help feeling that Norris is losing control over his prose. Certain developments in Vandover's life resist explanation so much so that, toward the end, the novel becomes grotesque and veers toward a creative and even ludic destabilization of explanation. Yet, to assume that these moments of literary disorientation or derailment are blemishes and to dismiss them as weaknesses in the narrative unity is to overlook an interesting strain in the book. The novel contains a set of narrative strategies, textual maneuvers, unpredictable developments, and rhetorical strategies that complicate its unfolding rather than undermine its achievement. Within this ludic dimension, the kind of determinism one expects in such a naturalist novel is continuously deconstructed.

A convenient starting point for analysis is the playfulness that characterizes the relationship between Vandover and his old chum Geary. The numerous exchanges between the two characters are marked by a consistent ambiguity. Throughout the novel, Geary takes advantage of his friend. The success of his machinations depends on his rare ability to develop discursive ploys and to construct recondite arguments. Geary intentionally and repeatedly misleads Vandover: for example, in one episode, "Vandover had often wondered at Geary's persistence in the matter, and had often asked what he could possibly want of the block. But Geary was very vague in his replies, generally telling Vandover that here was money in the investment if one could and would give the proper attention to pushing it" (251). His vagueness is far from being incidental. Vandover himself uses the same strategy of incommunicability in dealing with Geary. This is particularly evident in an exchange between the two

characters right after Vandover gambles away all his money. Hungry, impoverished, and desolate, Vandover pays an unexpected visit to Geary to seek some
money. Vandover is, in fact, playing a game on Geary. To his inquiry about the
fate of Vandover's bonds, Geary receives no definite answer. What he gets
instead are perplexing stories: "'bonds?' replies Vandover, dazed and bewildered. 'I ain't never had any bonds. What bonds? Oh, yes—well, I—those—
those, I had to sell those bonds—had some debts, you see, my board and my
tailor's bill. They got out some sort of paper after me. Yet, I had forgotten
about my bonds. I lost every damned one of them playing cards—gambling
'em all away'" (331). Geary's inquiry is met with a series of claims that confuse
more than they clarify; in fact, Vandover's statements are more ludic than lucid.
What we end up with is a string of excuses, a series of stories, and a number of
possible scenarios: "Well first I began to pawn things when my money got
short—the Old Gentleman's watch that I said I never would part with, then my
clothes" (332). Interestingly enough, even when Vandover insists that he is
being sincere, the apparent sincerity of his admission is diffused with a baffling
story that claims to crystallize the truth while in reality it further adds to its
concealment: "'I don't want to run any bunco game. I'm an honest man—I'm
honest. I gave money to help another duck; gave him thousands; he was good
to me when I was on my uppers and I mean to repay him. I was grateful. I
signed a paper that gave him everything I had. I was in Paris. There's where
my bonds went to'" (332). To say that the relationship between Vandover and
Geary is ludic is to say that it is inconceivable outside these discursive ploys.
Vandover manages to extort money from his friend precisely because the latter
fails to understand him: "I couldn't keep away from the cards. Of course, you
can't understand that" (332). It is interesting that although readers are provided
with clues about certain key episodes in the novel, they are deprived of absolute
certainty. In fact, the reader is constantly called upon to verify, interpret, and
evaluate the reality that the novel presents. The unrevealed fate of the bonds
can further illustrate this point. Geary consents to help Vandover through his
financial crisis without fully knowing how the latter really lost his bonds. At the
end, however, he seems to settle for Vandover's contention that "somehow, they
all went" (332). Even the narrator's comments on the fate of the bonds lacks
specificity; in fact, they, too, are more ludic than revelatory: "Of the many different stories that Vandover had told about the disappearance of his bonds, the one
that was probably truest was the one that accounted for the things by his passion for gambling" (336–37). Even the narrator, then, is playing games with the
reader. We never get a clear-cut explanation as to how Vandover squandered
his money; instead, we are left only with possible scenarios.

Vandover's mendacity compels the reader to make speculations, to formulate hypotheses, and to enact choices. Gaining an insight into Vandover's real character necessitates imagining an expanded world of possibilities, evaluating a number of alternatives, and considering a set of variables. Faced with Vandover's unpredictability, the reader must turn into a player-reader, for to read Norris's novel is to face the challenge of deciphering the main character. This challenge can be pointed out as early as the first chapter of the novel: "Little by little, the crude virility of the young man began to develop in him. It was a distressing, uncanny period; had Vandover been a girl, he would have been subject to all sorts of abnormal vagaries, such as eating his slate pencil, nibbling bits of chalk, wishing he were dead, and drifting into states of unseasoned melancholy" (98–99). Behind the depiction of the pliable character of Vandover lies a counter-factual game, one which goes counter to and even undermines the proclaimed realism of the novel. The unpredictability of the protagonist is not without effect: it induces a textual predilection toward equivocality whereby the reader slides into the reality of the uncertain, if not the unreal. This is not to say, however, that Vandover is not a realist character. The transmogrification of Vandover is phenomenal but neither improbable nor unreal. The unpredictable unfolding of the events does not undermine the consistency of the character. To put it somewhat differently, the realism of Vandover's character emanates from his inconsistencies. In fact, it is his unexpectedness that makes him a credible character: Vandover's only consistency is his inconsistency. In turn, Vandover's inconsistency reflects the complexity of reality itself. Such is at least the nature of the real as Norris explains it in his *Literary Criticism*: "the story writer must go to real life for his story. You can never think out or invent or imagine a tale that will be half so good as the things that have 'really happened.' The complications of real life are infinitely better, stronger, more original than anything you can make up" (51). Norris's fiction stands out not as a portrayal of the real but as an experiencing of reality. To represent reality in its full complexity is to capture the real in its elusiveness and playfulness, which is tantamount to saying that the central question that Norris's naturalism poses is not how the text copies reality but how it convinces the reader that it does. *Vandover and the Brute,* as Miles Orvell has eloquently put it, "raises in dramatically unexpected form the question of how real realism could be. Or, perhaps, how *unreal* realism could be?" (116). With Norris, we are no longer in the realm of referential reality (i.e., mimetic realism) but in the realm of performative reality (i.e., ludic realism).

The pursuit of ludic elements and chaotic trends in naturalism is exciting insofar as it opens up lines of analysis which are unthinkable within a traditional perspective anchored exclusively in the philosophy of determinism. Although suggestive work has already been done in this area, the canonical understanding of naturalism remains, to large extent, unchallenged. Michaels's *The Gold Standard and the Language of Naturalism*—a work which has received tremendous critical attention—epitomizes the limits of revisionism in its most vigorous moments. Michaels foregoes the classical view of naturalism as biological determinism only to embrace a peculiar type of economic determinism. He struggles with what may be termed, after Fredric Jameson, the dilemma of getting out of the system only to affirm the futility of such an endeavor. What is missing in his reading of the period is the theoretical necessity to account for those moments, trends, or impulses that escape reification. Other critics have tried to avoid the shortcomings that are inherent to the conception of naturalism as an all-encompassing totality or a total system but have not succeeded in profoundly altering our basic conception of this movement partly because the attention to indeterminacy is more a methodological posture than a polemic stance. One can certainly sense in June Howard's emphasis on the need to acknowledge the openness of any historical moment, and especially her recognition that history is contingent, a sophisticated conception of history as a system that is constituted by the conjunctural overlapping of disparate tendencies—what Raymond Williams calls dominant, residual, and emergent. Likewise, Patrick Brady's serious attempt to bring chaos theory to bear on the study of naturalism can hardly be ignored by any serious study of the period. Both initiatives do more than pay lip service to the presence of indeterminacy in naturalism, and they both are good as far as they go, but they do not go far enough. This essay suggests that when taken further, chaos theory can offer more than a checklist. When used more systematically, a chaos-oriented type of analysis—with its emphasis on the aleatory, the stochastic, and the contingent—affords rich possibilities for the study of naturalism. Using chaos theory and systems theory cautiously can both refine and complicate our understanding of naturalism.

WORKS CITED

Åhnebrink, Lars. *The Beginning of Naturalism: A Study of the Works of Hamlin Garland, Stephen Crane, and Frank Norris, with Special References to Some European Influences, 1891–1903.* New York: Russell and Russell, 1961.

Barthes, Roland. "L'Effet de réel." *Communications* 11 (1968): 84–89.

Brady, Patrick. "Chaos et naturalisme." *Les cahiers naturalistes* 67 (1993): 201–9.

———. "Chaos Theory, Control Theory, and Literary Theory: Or, A Story of Three Butterflies." *Modern Language Studies* 20.4 (1990): 65–48.

————. "From Transactional Analysis to Chaos Theory: New Critical Perspectives." *Australian Journal of French Studies* 26.2 (1989): 176–93.

————. "Mutilation, Fragmentation, Creation: Zola's Ideology of Order." *Émile Zola and the Arts.* Ed. J.-M. Guieu and A. Hilton. Washington: Georgetown UP, 1988. 115–22.

————. "La théorie du chaos et le texte naturaliste." *Les cahiers naturalistes* 65 (1992): 89–103.

————. "La théorie du chaos et *L'Œuvre*: peinture, structure, thématique." *Les cahiers naturalistes* 66 (1992): 105–12.

————. "Théorie du chaos et structure narrative." *Eighteenth-Century Fiction* 4.1 (1991): 43–51.

Conder, John J. *Naturalism in American Fiction: The Classical Phase.* Lexington: UP of Kentucky, 1984.

Danchin, Antoine. "Permanence and Change." *Substance* 40 (1983): 61–71.

Den Tandt, Christophe. *The Urban Sublime in American Literary Naturalism.* Urbana: U of Illinois P, 1998.

Dreiser, Theodore. *The Financier.* New York: New American Library, 1967.

Hammon, Philippe. "On the Major Features of Realist Discourse." *Realism.* Ed. Lilian R. Furst. London: Longman, 1992. 166–85.

Howard, June. *Form and History in American Literary Naturalism.* Chapel Hill: U of North Carolina P, 1985.

Howe, Irving. "Naturalism and Taste." *A Critic's Notebook.* Ed. Nicholas Howe. New York: Harcourt Brace, 1994. 216–28.

Hutchinson, Peter. *Games Authors Play.* London: Methuen, 1983.

La France, Marston. *A Reading of Stephen Crane.* Oxford: Clarendon, 1971.

Lee, Brian. *American Fiction, 1865–1940.* London: Longman, 1987.

Lefebvre, Henri. *The Survival of Capitalism: Reproduction of the Relations of Production.* Trans. Frank Bryant. London: Allison & Busy, 1976.

Michaels, Walter Benn. *The Gold Standard and the Logic of Naturalism: American Literature at the Turn of the Century.* Berkeley: U of California P, 1987.

Mitchell, Lee Clark. *Determined Fictions: American Literary Naturalism.* New York: Columbia UP, 1989.

————. "Naturalism and the Language of Determinism." *Columbia Literary History of the United States.* Ed. Emory Elliot. New York: Columbia UP, 1988. 524–45.

Morrow, Nancy. *Dreadful Games: The Play of Desire in the Nineteenth-Century Novel.* Kent: Kent State UP, 1988.

Norris, Frank. *The Literary Criticism of Frank Norris.* Ed. Donald Pizer. New York: Russell and Russell, 1976.

————. *Vandover and the Brute.* Lincoln: U of Nebraska P, 1978.

Orvell, Miles. *The Real Thing: Imitation and Authenticity in American Culture, 1880–1940*. Chapel Hill: U of Carolina P, 1989.

Paulson, William. "Chance, Complexity, and Narrative Explanation." *Substance* 74 (1994): 5–21.

Pizer, Donald. *The Novels of Frank Norris*. New York: Haskell, 1973.

Sinclair, Upton. *The Jungle*. New York: Viking, 1946.

Suwala, Halina. *Autour de Zola et le naturalisme*. Paris: Honoré Champion, 1993.

Swann, Charles. "Stephen Crane and a Problem of Interpretation." *Literature and History* 7.1 (1981): 91–123.

Walcutt, Charles Child. *American Literary Naturalism: A Divided Stream*. Minneapolis: U of Minnesota P, 1956.

Weiss, Allen S. "Ideology and the Problem of Style: The Errant Text." *Enclitic* 2 (1983): 17–23.

Wheatley, Margaret J. *Leadership and the New Science: Learning about Organization from an Orderly Universe*. New York: Berrett Koehler, 1992.

Whither Naturalism?

—*Philip Gerber*

We try to choose our life.

—W. D. Snodgrass

FOR MANY YEARS NOW A SPECIAL SLOT ON MY BOOKSHELF HAS BEEN OCCU-
PIED BY A VOLUME THAT'S BEEN OF REMARKABLE VALUE TO ME, fiRST IN
my study of naturalism and then in my teaching. Most of the traditional figures
are represented in the pages of this handbook: those late-nineteenth-century
scientist-philosophers whose ideas were the inspiration, from Darwin and
Spencer to Marx and Huxley, Tyndall and Schopenhauer. Here as well are
gathered the young American writers of the era who followed the gleam,
from the early Hamlin Garland through Stephen Crane and Jack London to
Frank Norris. And Zola, whose stories got the ball underway as a literary
thing and who gave a new name to it, "Naturalism," which he counted on
absolutely to distinguish his severe and frank studies of French society from
the imagination-fed romanticism of his times.[1] By emphasizing links with
Balzac and Flaubert, he provided us gratis with an invaluable tradition when
we had none of our own. Dreiser is represented, naturally—the noisiest
young naturalist on the block. Somewhat surprisingly, Herman Melville. The
book offers a fine and useful collection; it's the title that seems all wrong: *What
Was Naturalism?*[2] That word *Was* is striking. It labels naturalism as an
"event," something akin to Prohibition, an era come and gone and unregretted,
or perhaps more like a circus that has played out its exciting run, loaded its
acrobats and elephants on the train, folded its tent, and departed, lodging
indelible dream-state memories in the brain.

That's a mistake, it seems to me—to think of naturalism as some nine-
day wonder that's served its purpose and bowed out. I'd much rather think of

it as something possessed of a good deal more permanence, something evolving, surely, but nevertheless lodged in our tradition and here to stay, at least as long as the novel itself remains with us. The day when young Frank Norris strolled the green campus walks of Berkeley with a well-thumbed copy of Zola tucked under his arm is a thing of the vanished past, of course. Now that we've entered the twenty-first century, no time perhaps seems more distant, more quaint, and even to be despised than the nineteenth century; and that Zola novel, if under any arm at all (or loaded into a khaki bookbag, a thick paper-back?), is more likely just now to be a copy of, say, Tom Wolfe's *A Man in Full* or maybe E. Annie Proulx's millennial version of *U.S.A., Accordion Crimes,* that compendium of present-day death and survival in America, that updated, vastly expanded *Winesburg,* hyperactive scene of ethnic/racial mayhem and social disaster. Both books harken rather directly back to Zola.[3]

That naturalism *was* we surely know. That it *has been* is not really in dispute. However, what naturalism *is* not all of us can agree, I'm sure. And that it *will be* is a point disputed, I'd wager, by even a greater number of dis-heartened chroniclers than during the course of the past half-century were moved to announce the sad demise of the novel itself. The novel had enjoyed a certain preeminence among literary forms well before Norris declared it to be the supreme genre for expressing contemporary life, superior in that regard to architecture, painting, poetry, and even to music (Norris 256). The shape of the novel has altered considerably since the time of *Pamela* or the Victorian triple-decker, but, *plus çe change,* its focus on the middle range of human soci-ety has held pretty firm, I'd say. The novel is possessed of an inherent resilience that will see it through, greatly altered as its sway may be under stress of with-ering attention span and expanding digital technology. Despite the competition, I see no reason to doubt its survival any more than I question the expectation that a form of literary naturalism will play a significant role in the fiction of the future.

One reason for my confidence is that naturalism in its earliest days struck certain emotional chords to which readers responded strongly, know-ing their truth. Those chords resonate in our lives today and seem ever more crucial to those of us who by necessity are bundled closely together into social groups—which in the year 2001 includes most of us. The struggle for survival, as one instance of those chords of truth, sticks with us always, whether we mean by it the sheer physical stamina required merely to "last it out" in good stoical fashion or whether we refer to a surplus of psychic energy that can pro-pel us forward not merely to endure but perhaps even to prevail. And the entire survival affair is less likely now to be confined to any sheerly physical realm. Fiction writers today show less interest in pugilistic slugfests staged by such as Jack London—all those sleek muscles, glowing white bodies pummeling each other. "Survival" as the twenty-first century begins is much more likely to be given a social, economic, political or psychological spin. Also, the significant battle waged as group society seeks always and everywhere to dominate the lonely soul does not appear likely to succumb to entropy at any date in the foreseeable future: Thoreau surely was on the mark when he declared society to be forever in conspiracy against individualism. And what doubt can there be that mankind—and writers, especially writers—will persist until the day of doom itself to debate elusive niceties concerning freedom of the will? Is there any greater question?

These centers hold, although with time we can expect a considerable alteration in writers' targets, and American naturalists seem always to require solid targets for the wrath that fires their pens. When the naturalist doctrines were first offered to our writers during the 1880s and 1890s, they manifested themselves at once in works whose angry centers focused on primeval forces antagonistic to man: drouth, blaze, flood, plague, and blizzard. Some of the early Hamlin Garland is sufficiently elemental to be important here, and a great deal of London, whose story "To Build a Fire" is a pure example. That even the popular versifiers could be caught up in the excitement, the Arctic poems of Robert W. Service stand as witness: "This is the law of the Yukon, that only the strong shall thrive; / That surely the Weak shall perish, and only the Fit survive" (25). Poetry aside, was truth ever more baldly stated? Like Service, the other American naturalists scarcely questioned the new philosophers' central dictum. Put metaphorically, as Dreiser and others were quick in doing, the lesson is this: the human being accosted by invincible forces at play throughout the universe counts for no more than a wisp of leaf tossed this way and that by capricious winds of chance. All else is illusion. To believe that the world fundamentally is a dangerous and hostile place is to state a conviction whose roots sank deep into human thinking during the long sadness of the twentieth century. That conviction grew ever stronger during our endless wars and their attendant unspeakable horrors, death camps, and political terrorism. The grim specter of individual helplessness clamps down hard on all of us; the beast's jaws tighten, the knifelike teeth refuse to loosen their hold on our collective psyche. So pervasive has been this apprehended vision of our lives that it no longer needs to be stated or argued. In a sense, each of us now comes into the world not half so much a tabula rasa as a true-faith believer in the powerlessness of any human agency really to alter the fundamental scheme of things. It's become, you might say, instinctive.

Fast on the heels of the elemental naturalistic lessons first preached by such as London and Norris, the arsenal of naturalistic weapons was co-opted for use as cudgels to wield against runaway capitalism, whose satanic side was already showing clearly in the savage greed of industrial dinosaurs that rampaged society during the wide-open Jurassic age of Big Business. The unholy linkage of money with power commanded our writers' rage. The result was a pack of angry novels that today are said to constitute a "classic" era: Norris's *Octopus* challenged the railroad oligarchy; Sinclair's *Jungle* anatomized the evils of the meatpackers; Dreiser's *Financier* stripped bare the insatiable appetites of the moneychangers. There were a host of others, not excluding the angry exposés conducted by the novelists' first cousins, the journalistic muckrakers of the Progressive Era (for then as now the wall separating fact from fiction could be tissue thin). Poets were not unmoved by the spirit of the time; Edwin Arlington Robinson's brave sonnet "Zola" is uncompromising in its praise, while Crane's "The trees in the garden rained flowers" not only epitomizes gilded-era Social Darwinism but serves as well to define the phenomenon.

The twin forces of heredity and environment, for most of the twentieth century, served to shape a common basis undergirding the labors of serious American novelists. Belief in those forces and acceptance of the consequences implicit in such a belief helped to shape the rock-hard infrastructure upon which were erected innumerable houses of fiction. But it must be said that tales of environmental control have comprised the vast majority of these fictions. Investigative forays into the dark world of heredity have lagged. What is passed along from generation to generation—the force of the heritable, so powerful in concept but difficult to depict, too much a tantalizing mystery. Meanwhile, decade after decade, the question of environment has continued to inspire hundreds, no doubt thousands, of novels, stories, and plays in the realist tradition—continues to do so for the simple reason that the environments in which we find ourselves mired are inherently fascinating. The world around us, its physicality, its solid quality, lends itself so naturally to portrayal via language. Words connect so very readily with the five senses of our everyday existence. We respond to the mystery of heredity, yes, but we have lacked vocabulary. We have not had the tools that were suited to things "impalpable to form."

Even so, it may be said that since 1900 most, if not all, of the American writers engaged in the "realistic" portrayal of life have by necessity been to one extent or another purveyors of the naturalistic view of things. When we hear the postmodern poet Anne Sexton declare that ". . . I have a body / and I cannot escape from it. . . . / I am stuck here in this human form," we are likely to respond absolutely and at once. We know what she means; we've been there, too. But when, as she sometimes does, Sexton attempts to open the knotty question of her compulsion toward suicide, especially when she approaches the notion that the tendency to kill oneself might relate to some traceable family weakness, then words fail her.[4] The impulse is a brave one, and it reminds us that only intermittently has an American writer felt capable of grappling seriously with the difficult question of inherited traits. Eugene O'Neill and the vexation of alcoholism comes to mind, as well as Dreiser's *The Hand of the Potter* with its message that a man can't help being what he is any more than a fly can help (or avoid) being a fly. Also Sherwood Anderson's brave and early efforts in *Winesburg, Ohio,* where in certain tales he appears directly on the verge of daring to take a plunge beyond the sphere of matter.[5] John Steinbeck, Anderson's most immediate descendant, perhaps because he was a generation younger, perhaps because improved tools were available—and certainly in consequence of his strong bias toward the biological sciences—was equipped to be considerably more explicit. Hence the better success with his *Pastures of Heaven,* which appeared a dozen years after the debut of *Winesburg.*[6] But *Pastures,* loaded as it is with psychic grotesques and standing tall among Steinbeck's finest efforts, has never enjoyed the comprehension and popularity of some of his slighter efforts. By way of contrast, *The Grapes of Wrath,* given physical immediacy via its irresistible story of a tenant-farming family's struggle to survive the vicissitudes of weather and poverty, became an immediate and enduring success.

Therein, pretty much, rests the story of American naturalistic fiction during the century just ended. Making space for sub-genres worthy but not mentioned yet—the strike novel and the war novel come to mind at once— that fecund century must encompass the bulk of the nation's serious fiction, and its best and most memorable has been naturalistic, although some writers and critics cling to the allied descriptive *realist* (which in another sense is what Zola meant by his invented word *Naturalism* to label stories that were tough enough to face the harsh truths about existence on the planet and not flinch in the process). Our serious fiction has, by all odds, been dominated by the environmentalists, many of whom individually, and all of whom severally, brought our national literature out of the parish and into global prominence. Before they appeared on the scene, we were nowhere, really.

These writers have done exemplary work, beginning with Theodore Dreiser, whose *Sister Carrie,* serendipitously published in 1900, ushered the twentieth century in on a strongly naturalistic note. The book, cried an exultant Randolph Bourne, "fairly soaks in environment"; as Dreiser drenches his untutored heroine "in the sights and sounds that flow from the glittering, ugly city [readers] feel impressions impinging upon her" (8). Plunged into the swelling American cityscapes of Chicago and New York with the Darwinian command to sink or swim, adapt or die, Carrie not only survives but prospers. That the girl fares so well is due essentially to a set of instinctive reactions to people and events. She seems empowered intuitively to distinguish between those phenomena that tend to promote life and those that will surely lead her deathward. The American city is an indispensable portion of Carrie's story; it is the environment set up for her testing. Among Dreiser's greatest contributions was his early recognition that the important proving ground for Americans was not to be agrarian and rural so much as it was to be technological and urban. Farm life as a center was finished; he saw that, and also that the future of the small town was a mirage. Largely through Dreiser's persistent example, the city achieved a literary preeminence it has never surrendered. Among those following Dreiser from the deathly quiet of the only sometimes savage countryside into the compulsive hammer-beating heart of the metropolis have been such as John Dos Passos, James T. Farrell, Richard Wright, James M. Cain, Saul Bellow, Willard Motley, Henry Roth, Nelson Algren, Joyce Carol Oates, E. Annie Proulx, Robert Stone, and the two Wolfes—the earlier Thomas (*You Can't Go Home Again, Time and the River*) and the later Tom (*The Bonfire of the Vanities, A Man in Full*). And there is a legion of others, great and small.

Where American naturalists have managed to establish reputations with materials from beyond the limits of the city center, they usually have succeeded by replacing the frenzied and controlling urban landscape with some great and fiery issue. *The Grapes of Wrath* is surely the defining example here; but William Faulkner, writing about the Siamese-twin topics of race and the Civil War surely has been the great name in non-urban naturalism. Others also, in their own ways, have managed to prosper in pursuing the rural theme; in *God's Little Acre* and *Tobacco Road,* Erskine Caldwell turned the eroded hills of the southeast into significant naturalistic territory, but only by peopling his tenant farms with Andersonian grotesques, out-Heroding Herod. William Styron has been an important exception, locating naturalistic materials in significant historical events (*The Confessions of Nat Turner*) and in stories connected with wartime social upheaval (*Sophie's Choice*). Scratch Willa Cather, and you will rouse a naturalist. Not for nothing was she vitally connected early on with the greatest of the muckraking magazines, *McClure's.* Read her early stories—"A Wagner Matinée," "Paul's Case," and "The Sculptor's Funeral." *My Ántonia* is no romance of the plains, by any stretch of the imagination, nor do many happy things occur in either *Death Comes for the Archbishop* or *The Professor's House*. *My Mortal Enemy* is dark, dark, dark—every bit as black as it is brief. Among later novelists, the versatile Oates has sometimes managed to have it both ways, focusing at one moment on the city center (*them*), at another returning to her rural Eden County roots (*I Lock My Door upon Myself*) or even, given American mobility, managing to alternate between metropolis and meadow (*Wonderland*). But Oates is exceptional; for most writers, the city has provided the indispensable battleground. As Robinson Jeffers might have it, we have been diligent at gathering a universe of human sardines into luminescent nets called cities; now let the great catastrophes begin.

The urban novel by definition involves a social story, and where people multiply, we can expect multiplication also of the interactions, the chance encounters, that inevitably alter lives. American readers have long been receptive to the knowledge that however deterministic life may prove to be, it is not at all *pre*deterministic—that is, not Calvinistic, *not* written in the stars. Always there remains the possibility, indeed the likelihood, that a toss of the dice might swing one's affairs around full circle, reverse a man's fortunes (to rise or to sink as the case may be) and in the process initiate a new line of determined action destined to remain in place—until he is caught in the next accident of circumstance. From Monopoly to the Lottery, we do love our games of chance. And why not? Isn't that what America at bottom is all about, a flip of the coin, heads or tails? Why else all those cosmic gambles taken by millions of immigrants happily inebriated by the possibility of "changing their luck"? Lacking essential trust in the notion that life *could* change, also that, given an alteration of environment, it *would* change, what point could there possibly be in enduring those endless and arduous sea voyages? Why else was this hemisphere dubbed the New World? Jack London well understood the renewing possibilities involved in environmental change, and while removing his people to the Arctic laboratory where he could observe their every reaction to minus-fifty-degree temperatures, he simultaneously introduced a wide range of chance elements into his fiction; happenstance regularly locks people into deterministic chains. Even so, London's potent man/nature theme remained somewhat overly one-note: man against the storm, little more. What worked like magic for him did not work so well for others, his extravagant arctic theme being too atypical, too unvaried to encourage any army of disciples to follow the path he blazed into the frigid wild.

The city, on the other hand, has provided an unending variety of modes and situations. *Sister Carrie* is a novel of two cities, Chicago and New York, and its heroine's rise is marked by a remarkable succession of unplanned encounters. Call them coincidental, if you wish (and of course they are; the naturalist does not shrink from coincidence but encourages it, recognizing it as a fundamental proof that chance predominates). Carrie's "luck" begins with her first, utterly unpredictable meeting with Charles Drouet on the day coach traveling from Columbia City to Chicago, followed by her fortuitous re-encounter with the drummer on the city streets when, cold and out of work, she desperately needs a helping hand. Then we are witness to Carrie's world-shaking introduction via Drouet to George Hurstwood, the latter's easy "abduction" of her, and their passage by train to New York, where Hurstwood ends disastrously and she becomes famous, largely because a musical-comedy actor spontaneously departs for a moment from his script. For Carrie, such chance events become the mechanism for a dramatic rise—and were there nothing more to it, the novel would likely have been little more than another, somewhat bittersweet Cinderella story. Surely it could never have endured to become a naturalistic classic. *Except that there is Hurstwood.* And because of Hurstwood, the picture of life in urbanized, industrialized American is vastly, decisively different. With Hurstwood the novel leaves the universe of wish fulfillment wholly in its wake as it enters the world we all recognize as true.

The "accidents" that direct George Hurstwood's life in a direction different from Carrie's, toward tragedy, became archetypal for later twentieth-century naturalists. His "fate" cut a sharp template for many others to follow. The unlucky stroke that initiates that unhappy man's fall occurs, all unsuspectingly, at the moment he has reached his zenith. ("Some men," confides Dreiser, "never recognize the turning in the tide of their abilities" [362]. Would that he had written *most*.) Well-placed socially and economically, just a step or two from the upper rungs of the socioeconomic ladder, Hurstwood when he meets Carrie has achieved pretty much what he is able to achieve in America given his age, talents, and opportunities. The manner in which he blows it provides a cautionary tale for all of us. As a "greeter" for a posh downtown Chicago saloon (the first public relations man in American fiction), a clotheshorse of sorts, suave and polished, well spoken, a man of fine manners, he moves all evening among celebrities, nodding and smiling. Hurstwood has been more fortunate than most men—and he is far from comprehending the immense fragility of his position. He loves his place—but he is not a good caretaker. The trait for which Dreiser most praises Carrie, her invincible sense of self-interest (not always of benefit to others but a fine tool for personal survival), is Hurstwood's weakness. The long sad slide that will take him to suicide gets underway on the not otherwise noteworthy evening when, stressed by a lack of domestic tranquility and besotted by his infatuation with

Carrie, Hurstwood toys with the night's receipts, trying to decide whether to become a thief, whether he can resist the deterministic force that is already deciding for him. While he ponders, the safe closes and locks shut, his employer's money in his hands. Did he nudge that iron door shut? No one will ever know—least of all Hurstwood. He decides on impulse to take the cash and talk Carrie into running away with him to begin an idyllic life together—somewhere—he knows not where—in some safe haven, in a figment of his imagination far from any problem, away from the arm of the law. He awakens in Fool's Paradise. The dominoes are already toppling. Beginning with that first click! his run of bad luck does not finish until, pockets empty, out of work, a bum dragging the streets in soiled remnants of his fine wardrobe, he reaches the Bowery flophouse room where all that is left for him is to mutter "What's the use?" and turn on the gas.

What happened to Hurstwood could so very easily happen to any success-minded, stressed-out American; that's what's so terrifying. The message, so extremely suitable for our fiction, has been persuasive. In the receptive reader, it still causes involuntary shivers that resonate with Greek-like fear and trembling. If Carrie represents American dream fulfillment, Hurstwood represents its terror. Throughout the twentieth century this ironic, unforeseen (but utterly predictable), and absolutely American turnabout has been repeated by one novelist after another, the more expert repetitions infused with a fresh originality of particulars that has provided them with the sheen of something brand new. James M. Cain recycled the Hurstwood debacle time after time. What, after all, is *The Postman Always Rings Twice* if not Hurstwood done once again, for the 1930s, this time in the guise of a sharp but dumb drifter, a supposed survivor, falling for a "dame" and on her account making a fatal misstep? *Double Indemnity* the same, with a savvy insurance agent playing the goof. Neither novel may be "literature" in any transcendent sense (would "delightful trash" do?), but both stories, with their laconic, "tough-guy" surfaces, were *new,* and their cutting-edge modernity made for exciting, engrossing reading—they still retain an ability to affect one's pulse.

A glance at a pair of superior examples will tell us something of the pervasive spread of the Hurstwood story and the permutations rung upon it during the course of twentieth-century fiction. What is surely the finest early-century version of Hurstwood's fate arrived simultaneously with Cain's art deco ventures into crime and punishment: John O'Hara's *Appointment in Samarra.* Here the role of Hurstwood is assigned to Julian English, debt-plagued proprietor of the Cadillac agency in Gibbsville, Pennsylvania. On Christmas Eve, 1930—not a good moment for rocking the economic boat, with the Great Depression just hitting its stride—Julian, on a sudden impulse, yields to his imp of the perverse and does something he has longed to do; he throws a drink in the face of a man he has reason to detest, a wealthy bootlegger named Harry Reilly. Out of this simple, direct, and unmistakably public act of violence (it occurs at the Lantenango Country Club before scores of guests), Julian's tragedy is born. The dominoes of disaster are lined up again. Once triggered, they drop, one bringing down the next, momentum building until the last has fallen.

On the morning after the fateful drink is tossed, Caroline English suggests to Julian that he had better return her expensive Christmas bracelet to the jewelers because they're going to need every penny they possess; she sees economic retaliation from Reilly less as a threat than a certainty. Caroline understands better than Julian just how loudly money roars in Gibbsville. All of their friends owe money to Harry Reilly; Julian can expect no overt support from them. On top of this, he is in debt to Reilly himself to the tune of $20,000, borrowed to save his Cadillac agency from bankruptcy. Christmas day brings a futile effort at damage control. Harry Reilly, his eye blackened, refuses to see Julian, and that night a local comic entertains the social elite with a gag about throwing drinks at people. A friend reminds Julian of something that he should have known to beware of, that Reilly is not only rich but a mover and shaker among the newly empowered Irish population. And while every Irishman knows that Reilly is "a horse's ass," still, he is *their* horse's ass, and the ethnics will stick by him. It is clear that English's surname will not be an asset here in this Irish-Catholic stronghold.

That night, reaching for surcease via his twin anodynes of liquor and sex, Julian impulsively invites a nightclub singer out to his car in the parking lot of the Stage Coach, thereby humiliating his wife before all of Gibbsville. His most prominent ally is lost as Caroline withdraws from him. The first domino has fallen. The second begins to topple when, next day, a local Catholic undertaker cancels his order for a Cadillac limousine. The auto-agency salesman reminds his boss that the singer he seduced is the mistress of the Stage Coach's owner, who not only is a rich Irish bootlegger but has in the past regularly steered customers to Julian's showroom. The knowledge that Julian English cannot possibly repay his loan to Reilly and probably has lost his chance to borrow elsewhere, Gibbsville being the tightly knit and financially pressured community that it is, chills the Cadillac dealer. With an ominous sense of dread, he reviews his financial books for 1930: a disaster. He is going to need another loan of at least $5,000 to keep his sinking business afloat, and it strikes him that he has managed to alienate the two men most likely to have such a sum available. As with Hurstwood, Julian English is working with money belonging to another, and the alienated "other" will do everything he can to get it back from him. Social friendships snap under economic strain. The fragile English marriage is collapsing, the bankruptcy of the Cadillac agency predictable. Himself clearly *persona non grata* in Gibbsville, Julian now comprehends an axiom that had bewildered him during his college days: *Don't buck the system; you're liable to gum up the works.* Like Hurstwood, he dies a suicide by gas, not in a flophouse but sitting in his personal Cadillac in his closed garage.

Half a century after *Samarra,* there appeared another novelist cast in the mold of Zola. The majority of novelists are not theorists, but Tom Wolfe has been willing to declare himself publicly a social novelist and, in fact, to declare (even at a time when requiems are being sung for The Book itself) that the novel of society—and naturalism itself—both retain their vigor. In his essay "Stalking the Billion-Footed Beast," which he does not shrink from dubbing a literary manifesto, Wolfe sets himself up as an "old fashioned" realist of the Sinclair Lewis stamp, an investigator-documenter such as Zola had been, a *reporter.* "I wanted to prove [the] point," he says, speaking of his *Bonfire of the Vanities* (1987), "that the future of the fictional novel would be in a highly detailed realism based on reporting, a realism more thorough than any currently being attempted, a realism that would portray the individual in intricate and inextricable relation to the society around him" (50). New York City would be his turf, Manhattan from the Bronx to the Battery, with all of its diversity and contrasts, the "astonishing metropolis" which had served Dreiser and Dos Passos and Wolfe the first and so many others so well. He would cram as much of its highs and lows between covers as he could, he promised himself, "the most tempting, the most challenging, and the most obvious idea an American writer could possibly have" (45). He would document the city as it had never been documented before, using this archetypal urban environment to demonstrate his inevitable theme, "the city always in the foreground, exerting its relentless pressure on the souls of its inhabitants," displaying "the influence of society on even the most personal aspects of the life of the individual" (46, 51).

The person Wolfe selects as his smart-dumb protagonist is Sherman McCoy, bond salesman par excellence. We meet him as he is in the act of committing the impulsive and ill-considered gesture that will send him reeling. McCoy in his hubris styles himself a "Master of the Universe." But in a story where irony runs high, this delusion is a fruit ripe for picking. The night on Park Avenue is dark and rain-spattered. Despite the weather, Sherman McCoy is out in this driving storm, walking his reluctant dachshund. Why? So that he can pause at a pay phone to make a private call to his mistress, Maria Ruskin. Not a good idea. Inadvertently perhaps (out to prove Freud right on the question of accidents?), Sherman by mistake dials his home number. His wife, Judy, answers, and Sherman hastily hangs up the receiver—but not before he has asked for Maria. Not before Judy has recognized his voice and inquired, "Sherman? Is that you?" (16).

How to explain? He wants to regard his faux pas as a triviality, but it is not. "All you did was make a telephone call," commiserates his lover Maria. Sherman comprehends his jeopardy somewhat better: "I don't know how I can go out at 9:30 at night and say I'm walking the dog and then call up and say, 'Oh, I'm sorry. I'm really out here calling Maria Ruskin'" (22). Unable to dream up a plausible alibi for Judy, Sherman goes into denial: he didn't call home; he doesn't even know anyone called Maria. But he and his wife both know better, and his lie is crucial because, as with Julian English, his wife is his greatest potential ally in the difficulties that are about to descend upon him. At stake is his domestic life, his social shield. Add to this Sherman's financial jeopardy: a mortgage for nearly two million dollars on his Park Avenue apartment. The payments depend absolutely on the continuation of favorable financial conditions in society and, as with Hurstwood, his ability to maintain an impeccable façade of reputation among his fastidious clientele. This "Master of the Universe" is highly vulnerable and is skating on exceedingly thin ice.

The cold war on Park Avenue continues. Some nights later, Sherman calls Judy from his office to say that he will be working late. Actually, he is on his way to Kennedy Airport to meet Maria, flying home from a trip abroad. The pair set off for Manhattan in Sherman's bright new Mercedes. Coming off the Triborough Bridge, Sherman's ego soars as he contemplates the toiling millions who undoubtedly envy his exalted social position on the magic Island of Manhattan, that bright cliff of brick and glass. His vainglorious thoughts overwhelm him:

> There it was, the Rome, the Paris, the London of the twentieth century, the city of ambition, the dense magnetic rock, the irresistible destination of all those who insist on being *where things are happening*—and he was among the victors! He lived on Park Avenue, the street of dreams! He worked on Wall Street, fifty floors up, for the legendary Pierce and Pierce, overlooking the world! He was at the wheel of a $48,000 roadster with one of the most beautiful women in New York. . . . He was of that breed whose natural destiny it was . . . to have what they wanted! (77)

Ironies being what they are in life and in naturalism, this is Sherman McCoy's tallest moment; the deluge is about to begin. As he boasts, inflated with pride, he misses his proper exit into Manhattan. Another trivial "accident." Not to worry. But then he finds himself swept in a current of traffic toward the toll plaza leading into the Bronx, unknown and dangerous territory for such as himself. For the moment his hubris supports him; he will simply turn and retrace his steps. He's where he never planned to go, doesn't want to go—but how bad can such a tiny misstep possibly be?

Sherman is about to discover how bad it can get for a man whose foot slips on the shaky social ladder. His Mercedes is stopped when it strikes a tire lying on the unlighted street, an obstacle whose placement may not be wholly accidental. A pair of young black men emerge from the lonely, enclosing darkness of the unfamiliar neighborhood. Sensing a threat, Sherman and Maria panic. In making a hasty retreat, he hits one of the men with his car. No question of notifying the police—Sherman is determined that no one shall ever know. Publicity inevitably would mean the destruction of his domestic well-being, for there is no way on earth that he can explain Maria's presence in his Mercedes and still preserve any vestige of the marriage to Judy which is so important to his standing at conservative Pierce and Pierce and among his well-heeled clientele. As with Hurstwood, his reputation is close to being his all in all.

Because Manhattan is a considerably larger stage than Gibbsville, PA, the social ruination of Sherman McCoy requires a good deal more than the rapid, pervasive word-of-mouth messages that suffice to destroy Julian English. Naturally, it is the mass media which is called upon. First, the newspapers and tabloids. Wolfe provides us with "facsimiles" of the sensationalized press reports about a supposedly respectable (and high-income-bracket) citizen who has struck an innocent pedestrian—a black man, yet—and who then cravenly fled the scene in a damaged Mercedes, newly discovered in a repair shop. The ubiquitous paparazzi who feed photographs to the tabloids are hot on Sherman's trail, and he loses every shred of personal privacy. We might recall that the newspapers also played an important role in the destruction of Hurstwood who, too late, realized that if news of his infidelity with Carrie were to come out in the press he would be ruined; if his name so much as appeared in the papers in any disparaging sense, Fitzgerald and Moy would discharge him from his sensitive public-relations post at the saloon. As it happens, it is the exposure not of his love life but of his theft that is Hurstwood's ruination. Very soon after absconding to Montreal with Carrie, it occurs to him that copies of the Chicago newspapers surely will be arriving on the local newsstands with accounts of his theft and flight. And they do. His romantic coup is overshadowed by the dark realization that he is being unmasked publicly as "a safe breaker," a white-collar embezzler and no better than a common burglar.

Technological progress being what it is in America, Wolfe has a more powerful weapon to unleash: television. Like the eye of God, its camera sees all. In the author's hands, the television acts upon people as a social "force" every bit as invincible as those suggested by Herbert Spencer and reflected so strongly in the works of Dreiser and London and other early naturalists. Sherman McCoy almost instantly is obsessed with a constant and pervasive dread of the camera's invasive eye. Mustering his bravado, he attends a dinner on Fifth Avenue given by his (not-yet-lost) friends the Bavardages, and on the foot journey to their apartment he encounters naked fear: "He reached the sidewalk. *Whuh?* Just to the left, in the gloaming, a figure—a *photographer*— *right over* there—Sheer terror! *My picture in the paper!*" (330). Then he realizes that the shadow world has done him in: it's no more than a man walking a dog! This little paranoid episode only hints at the real thing. Later, having been taken to the Criminal Courts Building in a police car and identified as the probable hit-and-run driver, Sherman as he leaves the building during a driving rainstorm spots a huddle of people wrapped in ponchos and mistakes them for a welfare line at a soup kitchen. He has inverted his earlier experience at confusing reality and artifice but doesn't realize it until he becomes aware of the television cameras. The crews spot him and come running, rain-soaked people everywhere, threatening, closing in on him.

Sherman and his police escorts attempt to return to the building, but they must run the gauntlet, the mob of reporters and cameramen swarming, shouting as if in a riot; they seem out to get him. A camera is shoved rudely in his face: "'Sherman!' 'Over here, Sherman!' 'Hey, Sherman!'" The cameras are rolling. A microphone appears before him. Another. And another: "'Hey, Sherman! Hey, shitface!'" He realizes that he is theirs. They have taken him in, usurped his given name, stripped him of any formality or respect and delivered him naked to a million living rooms: "'That's it, shitface, look right here!'" (453). It gets worse, of course, in macabre scenes any contemporary reader can relate to. Whatever the degree of his guilt or innocence, Sherman as *the accused* finds himself dehumanized, thrown to the wolves and shredded.

In expressing confidence in the durability of naturalism as a major path for modern fiction, I have come face to face with the inevitable question: if this way of writing is to continue, what changes (if any) will occur? To ask this is not to imply that the uses of environment might be altered. Nor is it to suggest that the environmental theme might diminish in importance. Its uses have been many, its influence massive, and in its name novelists have escorted us on exciting journeys into just about every realm connected with modern society.

Literary predictions, like political forecasts, are tricky, as loaded with hazards as a tar pit, yet if encouraged I would rush onward to suggest that the next great opportunity for American novelists to stake claims will, in all likelihood, be retrograde, revisiting naturalism's original impetus. But not, this time, to explore environmental impact; rather, to take on the challenge of its inviting but baffling counterpart, heredity. The desire to explore inland, beyond the shoreline, has been a strong temptation. Those hints first thrown out by biologists, then by chemists, joined soon by physicists and eventually by mathematicians have always been a challenge. And if heredity is to be accepted fully as the determining force that our eyes assure us it is, our novelists will be catapulted into dealing with it in ways scarcely dreamed of hitherto. They have never been unwilling, that should be said, but they have been unable. Soon, provided with legitimate means, there is promise that they will rise to the challenge.

Certain preliminaries have already occurred, some of the most retrospectively interesting steps having been taken during the opening decades of the twentieth century by Dreiser, who very early on was convinced that considerably more than mere environment was involved in the exterior influences acting on the human personality, massive as that shaping determinant clearly was. As he began his career in fiction, not yet out of his twenties, Dreiser eagerly served as a lightning rod for scientific nods and becks that hinted at a physico-chemical explanation for life, all in an effort satisfactorily to replace the religious authority he had jettisoned under the tutelage of such as Spencer, Tyndall, and Huxley. In composing *Sister Carrie* in 1899, he allowed himself to be overwhelmed by appealing but semi-formed enthusiasms that stood poised on the lunatic fringe of scientific progress, and he then allowed his indiscretions to stand on the printed page where they would remain, apparently forever, as quirky speculations bent on haunting him, youthful indiscretions he could not erase.

Dreiser stepped out a considerable distance onto philosophical thin ice as he groped in the dark for answers. Building on the evolutionary truism suggested by Spencer that any organism—say a human being—is either "growing stronger, healthier, wiser" or, having reached its zenith, it is declining, its temporary equilibrium giving way to "a sagging to the grave side," he declares that Hurstwood's morbid dwelling upon the ever more apparent contrast between his earlier status in the social group and his later produces "a constant state of gloom or, at least, depression."

So far so good. Then Dreiser acquiesces to powerful temptation and attributes the man's disastrous personality change to the magic of chemistry, and, for most readers of his time (not to exclude our own), he crosses a border into the occult:

> Now, it has been shown experimentally that a constantly subdued frame of mind produces certain poisons in the blood, called katastates, just as virtuous feelings of pleasure and delight produce helpful chemicals called anastates. The poisons generated by remorse inveigh against the system, and eventually produce marked physical deterioration. To these Hurstwood was subject [and] left to brood. (362)

Grant Dreiser a few years, and he would invoke the name, theories, and terminology of Sigmund Freud, but in the America of 1899, Freud did not yet exist. Always striving to rebuild the shattered structure of his ethical life, to raise a new authority in place of that blown away by Spencer and company in Pittsburgh in 1894, Dreiser wholeheartedly—one might without hyperbole say *desperately*—pursued a range of scientific thinkers, including scientists at the Woods Hole Laboratory. He managed to strike up a correspondence with Robert A. Millikan, the physicist who in 1923 was awarded the Nobel Prize for isolating and measuring the electron. It might be said that the smaller the particle of matter the greater the interest Dreiser took in it, for that path appeared to lead directly to the essential sameness of all things. By 1938 his long-held belief in a mechanistic universe allowed him to declare that "a flower is as much a mechanism as a sewing machine; a rainbow as a dynamo" (Fadiman 355). He had already investigated the works of an important and boldly outspoken mechanistic biologist, Jacques Loeb.[7] Like the novelist, Loeb was passionate about establishing a physico-chemical basis for existence. He had declared that the major job for scientists pursuing questions of heredity would be to locate and identify the chemical substances in the chromosomes that govern the transmission of qualities from one generation to another. (It was, said historian Donald Fleming some decades later, "a plea for the discovery of DNA" [Loeb xli].) Reading Loeb's 1912 volume *The Mechanistic Conception of Life,* Dreiser came upon phrases such as "the riddle of life" that closely approximated the phraseology of his own struggle to understand the mysteries of existence:

> Our wishes and hopes, disappointments and sufferings have their source in instincts which are comparable to the light instinct of the heliotropic animals. The need of and the struggle for food, the sexual instinct with its poetry and its chain of consequences, the

maternal instincts . . . [,] the instinct of workman-ship . . . [,] are the roots from which our inner life develops. For some of these instincts the chemical basis is at least sufficiently indicated to arouse the hope that their analysis, from the mechanistic point of view, is only a question of time. (32)

The novelist was stunned by the "miraculous" manner in which Loeb achieved fertilization of sea urchin eggs merely by adding the appropriate chemicals. Dreiser had long been ready to believe that life was at bottom a matter of chemicals, and after observing Loeb, the belief became an obsession, a "mania" that haunted him so that "he was always seeing mountains as men and men as atoms, and men and mountains and atoms as transitory bubbles in an unfathomable flood of Being, of which there was neither beginning nor end" (Moers 246).

During most of Dreiser's life, to hold such a belief was considered an aberration if not a cop-out by a man who knew nothing about science but wished to leave the impression that he knew much indeed. Today, in the age of miracle drugs, when, for example, everyone seems aware of the huge difference a tiny dose of Lithium can make in regulating the "madness" wrought by manic depression, such knowledge is elementary. Equally well established is the effect of dopamine, a shortage of which chemical results in the "indecisive and frozen personality" which in its most extreme form we know as Parkinson's disease, and an excess of which renders one "highly exploratory and adventurous [and] may be the immediate cause of schizophrenia" (Ridley 162).

Most of the commotion to date regarding the uses of genetics has concerned the use of our gathering knowledge for medical purposes, and the information disseminated in the popular press has centered on the great favor that genetics seems in the process of bestowing upon the race, granting its wish to control natural forces, especially those of disease and disorder. The empowering belief that we can control life has as its natural corollary the strong conviction that we exist as free agents. It is easy to think that whatever we need to do and want to do, we can do, just as soon as geneticists show us the way. In that sense, a brave new world seems to be unfolding. How accurate is that belief? How free *are* we?

Dreiser died in 1945, just as the great mysteries of genetic science were about to be solved. The diligent effort to establish as fact the principle that all life is one is what gives meaning to the labors of Jacques Loeb and other lonely investigators of his era, hewing to their laboratories, manipulating genetic substances in their petri dishes. In 1953 a threshold was crossed at the

Eagle pub in Cambridge, England, when physicist Francis Crick announced to his friend and co-worker James Watson "We've discovered the secret of life" (Ridley 49). Their revelation was that the code of DNA was written along a filament shaped to resemble an intertwined staircase—a double helix—of infinite length. DNA was microscopic and coiled, its twin spirals worked in pairs, and its secrets were embedded in four-letter codes. With such tools, the book of life was opened.

The revelation constituted a major breakthrough in confirming the chemical basis for life. From that moment the race was on to achieve the full decoding of DNA—ultimately to decode the human genome. Somewhat like the Rosetta Stone but infinitely more complicated and portentous, DNA was to provide the key to endowing the human race with great power over its future. Any reader of newspapers has been privy to the advances in cloning, which bypasses the usual path taken in sexual reproduction. And who has not been flooded with the news of the power of DNA in establishing guilt and innocence in determining questions of paternity? The genetic connections with disorders such as early onset dystonia, kidney cancer, and Alzheimer's, once discovered, have affected the predictability of those disorders. The inevitable course of Huntington's, a disease invariably ending in madness and caused by a genetic mutation, is described in *Genome* as a chilling sequence:

> It does not matter if you smoke, or take vitamin pills, if you work out or become a couch potato. The age at which madness will appear depends strictly and implacably on the number of repetitions of the "word" CAG in one place in one gene. If you have thirty-nine you have a ninety per cent probability of dementia by the age of seventy-five and will on average get the first symptom at sixty-six; if forty, on average you will succumb at fifty-nine; if forty-one, at fifty-four; if forty-two, at thirty-seven; and so on until those who have fifty repetitions of the "word" will lose their minds at roughly twenty-seven years of age. (56)

No horoscope in any sense approaches the accuracy of such a prophecy, author Matt Ridley reminds us; it predicts with greater precision than any theory of causality: "This is determinism, predestination and fate on a scale of which Calvin never dreamed" (56). If true, that is a major blow to the notion that genetics will place the human being handily in the driver's seat.

For those who write fiction, no development seems more vital than Richard Dawkins's theory of the "selfish gene." His intention to examine "the biology of selfishness and altruism" plunges Dawkins by necessity into the larger context of evolution and his disagreement with traditional writers on the topic, who assume that the significance of evolution has to do with the good of the species rather than the good of the individual (in Dawkins's lexicon, for *species* read "group"; for *individual* read "gene"). Most writers have gotten evolution all wrong, says Dawkins. It is simply a process "by which some genes become more numerous and others less numerous in the gene pool" (48). Out of the primal biological "soup" containing the chemical raw materials of water, carbon dioxide, methane, and ammonia, there developed by some quirk of alchemy certain molecules capable of making copies of themselves. Dawkins labels these "replicators." Those replicators that managed to survive did so because they built organisms to house and protect them: "survival machines." Certain of these machines for survival operate under the label *human beings:* "The replicators are in you and me; they created us, body and mind; and their preservation is the ultimate rationale for our existence. They have come a long way, those replicators. Now they go by the name of genes, and we are their survival machines" (22). We share this origin in common with all bacteria, viruses, plants, and animals. We are all survival machines, all housing the same kind of replicators, the molecules we now call DNA. Dawkins is not alone in believing that genes are the "replicating currency" of natural selection and that what is important to them is to cause behavior that enhances their survival. So, then, we are designed not to take actions favorable to our species so much as to our individual genes. We operate at their command; they program us. Says Dawkins, "The predominant quality to be expected in a successful gene is ruthless selfishness" (2). Hence the term *selfish gene.* The genes are past masters at programming: their lives are at stake. In the court of survival, they are judged by the success of those programs as their machines cope with the untold hazards that life launches against them. The survival machines (bodies) are highly ephemeral; an individual may not live very long—it generally doesn't—but genes have the potential for extremely long life, during which they undoubtedly pass through an extended series of human lives.

In the role of gene as determinist of human life lies the significance to literature of current genetic research. Yes, we already possess genetically manipulated foods, new strains of corn and rice and wheat (not without resultant controversy, of course). But what are the implications for people? And what will our writers make of this newest revolution, this latest overturning of orthodoxies? Perhaps criticism will be the first genre to be affected (surely the notion of the selfish gene by itself invites reinterpretations of a novel such as *Sister*

Carrie). That must be the focus of our attention here—the ways in which our writers will utilize the discoveries and the new slants on life that they stimulate. Ridley reminds us that "determinism, whether of the genetic or environmental kind, is a depressing prospect for those with a fondness for free will" (75).

How will the literary art be affected? Ridley reprises a note of cynicism expressed by other scientists: when one sees an animal doing something to benefit another, one must assume either that (1) the first is manipulating the other or that (2) it is being subtly selfish. A humiliating blow to human self-importance is dealt by those who demonstrate that a human being is no more than "the disposable plaything and tool of a committee of self-interested genes" (18–19). The continuing discoveries of science do not shake but bolster the bedrock assumptions of literary naturalism. A general recognition that "it's all in the genes," a goal anticipated with keen delight by science, is already stirring up controversy—it would be a miracle if it did not.

To date most of the public dither about genomics has centered upon the immense and unqualified boon it will be to medicine, but the shadier side of the prospect will undoubtedly swing into greater prominence as attitudes shape up and the word spreads. The debate will undoubtedly become as tense and highly pitched as the turmoil that followed in the wake of Darwinian concepts during the fourth quarter of the nineteenth century. Even such outspoken champions of everything genetic as Matt Ridley admit that the great book of the genome, once fully opened, "may give us the bleakest kind of self-knowledge: the knowledge of our destiny" (64).

That debate, in fact, has simmered in a semi-subterranean way for years, but now it is coming to a boil; the battle is being joined. The question "What is Man?" has never seemed more critical or puzzling or more divisive. Are we human beings free agents (and to what degree)? Or are we in thrall to blind chance (and to what degree)? Most importantly, when may we expect a surge of serious, new fictioneers sufficiently fired by the revolution in genetics to begin presenting us with their candidates for the Great American Novel? Not to hold our breaths, I think. We must remember that a full generation born "After Darwin," as one might put it, passed before American literary radicals such as Crane and Norris and Dreiser first put pen to paper. But the generation of 1870 did become the big names of 1900, especially as viewed in retrospect, for with them arrived the fresh literary expression, new thoughts for a new day. Their successors have possibly just been born, perhaps have only now toddled off to kindergarten. Even allowing for the speedup that seems to characterize life now, we probably will not be reading the books of the future tomorrow morning. But they will arrive.

NOTES

1. An important light is shed on the term "Naturalism" by the art critic Jack Lindsay in his volume *Cézanne: His Life and Art* (1969). Investigating the friendship of Zola with Paul Cézanne and their close association as artists, Lindsay has delved into the friends' correspondence, where they speak to each other rather more frankly and forthrightly man to man than either—but particularly Zola—might speak in a formal essay. Lindsay is able to demonstrate rather convincingly that "the deceptive name of Naturalism" was consciously invented both to distance Zola from the prevailing idealistic spirit (which we later called Romanticism) and to define "the strangeness of actuality" produced by the collision of our human dreams with the stark reality we observe on every hand. And so, in Zola's thinking, Naturalism clearly is little more than a contrived term (with a pseudo-scientific connotation) for that literature which emphasizes a harshly realistic concept of existence.

2. Edward Stone, ed. *What Was Naturalism?* New York: Appleton, 1959.

3. In his *Garden of Zola* (1978), Graham King is adamant in declaring that "Without Zola . . . there could not have been a Steinbeck, a James Jones or an Arthur Hailey . . . [;] naturalism is not a literary aberration" (423).

4. In *Anne Sexton* (1991), Diane Wood Middlebrook comments on suicide among the poet's forebears including her father's sister Frances, who attempted suicide while in her twenties and who shot herself not long after Anne's death; also, Anne's sister Jane, like herself, was a suicide in middle age.

5. Of special interest are tales such as "Hands," "Respectability," and "The Philosopher."

6. Steinbeck approaches the questions raised by genetics particularly in writing of the idiot savant Tularecito (story 4). Stories 5, about the demented Hilda Van Deventer; 8, about Molly Morgan's fears concerning family traits; and 11, about the Whiteside dynasty, are rewarding. The novel *Of Mice and Men* is pertinent, surely, as is *East of Eden*. In fact, whenever Steinbeck writes of two or more generations, he seems tempted to dip into materials that concern heritable qualities. His deep interest in things scientific is relevant here.

7. During the 1920s Loeb became a well-known figure on the scientific front, in part through publicity generated by his disciple Paul De Kruif, a writer for popular magazines like *Harper's* and *Century*. Sinclair Lewis engaged De Kruif as a scientific resource person in composing his novel *Arrowsmith,* in which the figure of the idealistic scientist Max Gottlieb is based to a large extent on Loeb and his work.

WORKS CITED

Anderson, Sherwood. *Winesburg, Ohio.* New York: Liveright, 1919.

Bourne, Randolph. "Theodore Dreiser." *New Republic 11* (17 Apr. 1915): 7–8.

Brill, Abraham A. *Psychoanalysis: Its Theories and Practical Application.* 1912. New York: Arno, 1972.

Cain, James M. *Double Indemnity. Three of a Kind.* New York: Knopf, 1943.

———. *The Postman Always Rings Twice.* New York: Knopf, 1934.

Caldwell, Erskine. *God's Little Acre.* New York: Duell-Sloan, 1932.

————. *Tobacco Road*. New York: Modern Library, 1940.

Cather, Willa. *Death Comes for the Archbishop*. New York: Knopf, 1927.

————. *My Ántonia*. New York: Houghton, 1918.

————. *My Mortal Enemy*. New York: Knopf, 1926.

————. *The Professor's House*. New York: Knopf, 1925.

————. *Youth and the Bright Medusa*. New York: Knopf, 1921.

Crane, Stephen. *The Poems of Stephen Crane*. New York: Cooper Square, 1971.

Dawkins, Richard. *The Selfish Gene*. New York: Oxford UP, 1976.

Dos Passos, John. *U.S.A.* Boston: Houghton, 1963.

Dreiser, Theodore. *An American Tragedy*. New York: Liveright, 1925.

————. *The Financier*. New York: Harper's, 1912.

————. *The Hand of the Potter*. New York: Liveright, 1918.

————. *Sister Carrie*. New York: Doubleday, Page, 1900.

Fadiman, Clifton, ed. *I Believe*. New York: Simon and Schuster, 1939.

Loeb, Jacques. *The Mechanistic Conception of Life*. Cambridge: Harvard UP, 1964.

Moers, Ellen. *Two Dreisers*. New York: Viking, 1969.

Norris, Frank. *The Octopus*. New York: Doubleday, Page, 1903.

Oates, Joyce Carol. *I Lock My Door upon Myself*. New York: Ecco, 1990.

————. *them*. New York: Vanguard, 1969.

————. *Wonderland*. New York: Vanguard, 1971.

O'Hara, John. *Appointment in Samarra*. New York: Harcourt, 1934

Proulx, E. Annie. *Accordion Crimes*. New York: Scribner's, 1996.

Richardson, Samuel. *Pamela*. New York: Dutton, 1914.

Ridley, Matt. *Genome*. New York: Harper Collins, 1999.

Robinson, Edwin Arlington. *Collected Poems of Edwin Arlington Robinson*. New York: Macmillan, 1937.

Service, Robert W. *The Spell of The Yukon and other Verses*. New York: Barse, 1907.

Sexton, Anne. *The Complete Poems*. Boston: Houghton, 1981.

Sinclair, Upton. *The Jungle*. New York: Doubleday, Page, 1906.

Spencer, Herbert. *First Principles*. New York: H. M. Caldwell, 1880.

Steinbeck, John. *The Grapes of Wrath*. New York: Viking, 1939.

————. *The Pastures of Heaven*. New York: Viking, 1963.

Stone, Edward, ed. *What Was Naturalism?* New York: Appleton, 1959.

Styron, William. *The Confessions of Nat Turner*. New York: Random, 1967.

————. *Sophie's Choice*. New York: Random, 1979.

Wolfe, Thomas. *Of Time and the River.* New York: Scribner's, 1935.

———. *You Can't Go Home Again.* New York: Harper's, 1941.

Wolfe, Tom. *The Bonfire of the Vanities.* New York: Farrar, 1987.

———. *A Man in Full.* New York: Farrar, 1998.

———. "Stalking the Billion-Footed Beast." *Harper's* 279 (Nov. 1989): 45–56.

Is American Literary Naturalism Dead?

A FURTHER INQUIRY

—Donald Pizer

I SUBTITLE THIS EFFORT TO DETERMINE WHETHER ANY TRACES OF NATU-
RALISM REMAIN IN CONTEMPORARY AMERICAN WRITING "A FURTHER
inquiry" because the question has been asked and answered at several other
moments in American literary history since the initial flourishing of the movement in the 1890s. Many younger writers and critics of the 1920s and 1930s
welcomed the onset of modernism because it seemed to represent a return to a
seriousness and intensity of artistic endeavor in fiction after what they believed
was the simplistic thinking and mindless documentation of the naturalistic
novel. This attitude was confirmed in the 1940s and 1950s by the significant
presence during the 1930s of leftist beliefs in the work of a group of social novelists with naturalistic tendencies (notably Farrell, Steinbeck, and Dos Passos),
beliefs which came to be identified with the intellectual and moral bankruptcy
of Stalinist policy. Thus, Philip Rahv, in a widely commented-upon essay of
1942, announced both the emptiness of naturalism and its death as a continuing force in American writing, a position echoed later in the decade in equally
widely read essays by Lionel Trilling and Malcolm Cowley.

Academic criticism of American naturalism since the 1950s has, with
some notable exceptions, accepted the premise that naturalism is a spent force
and has confined itself largely to the study of a group of canonical naturalists
of the late nineteenth and early twentieth centuries—earlier chiefly Dreiser,
Crane, and Norris; and, in recent years, London, Wharton, and Chopin as
well. The exceptions fall into several groups: The effort, for the most part
rejected by the scholarly community, to locate naturalistic tendencies in such
major figures as Hemingway and Faulkner;[1] the attempt, handicapped by the
stigma of the association between naturalism and communism in the 1930s, to
identify much of the important social fiction of the decade as naturalistic in
character;[2] and the more recent effort, sporadic in nature, to locate pockets of
naturalistic expression in modern urban fiction[3] and in specific moments of
"hard times" since World War II.[4]

I don't wish in this paper to challenge the conventional notion that naturalism, as a fictional method most familiar to us through the novels of Dreiser, Crane, and Norris in the 1890s, is dead. It indeed is. We no longer have a fiction in which a slum is an allegorical equivalent of an environment which "shapes lives regardless" (Crane 132) or in which parental alcoholic degeneracy produces children whose "foul stream of hereditary evil" (Norris 22) leads to a life of violent crime. But we do have, as I hope to show by examining works by three of our most frequently studied contemporary writers, a fiction which, like that of the naturalists of the 1890s, desires to render the circumstances of American life which severely condition and determine the fate of most Americans. In characteristic works by Raymond Carver, Paul Auster, and Don DeLillo, I will argue, we find neither the sensationalistic exploitation of themes derived from contemporary scientism nor the detailed documentation usually cited as among the most distinguishing characteristics of early American literary naturalism. Each writer, indeed, can more readily be identified with particular strains of postmodernism in form and technique than with conventional naturalistic devices. But there nevertheless runs through the works by these writers which I will examine—Carver's *Where I'm Calling From,* Auster's *New York Trilogy,* and DeLillo's *White Noise*—a deep vein of naturalistic assumption that man is not only inseparable from the material, social, and intellectual world in which he lives but is deeply and often irrevocably limited in his actions and beliefs by that world. These works also reveal a tendency to place the fictional dramatization of this assumption within the traditional naturalistic contexts of mediocre and unfulfilled lives, alcoholism, crime, and violence. By the conclusion of the paper I will therefore offer both a positive and negative reply to the question posed by its title, borrowing, in doing so, from the historiography of English romanticism. The romanticism of Coleridge, Keats, and Shelley was indeed dead by the close of the nineteenth century, but romanticism nevertheless lived on, expressed in new themes and forms responsive to the conditions of its own time, in Swinburne, Stevenson, and Yeats.

Since Raymond Carver's *Where I'm Coming From: New and Selected Stories* (1988) contains thirty-seven stories, I can best deal with the naturalistic strain in his fiction by initially discussing it as a general characteristic and by then taking it up more specifically in several stories. Carver's fictional world is principally that of working-class people on the margins of material and emotional survival. His characters are not the bums and prostitutes of naturalism at its most "degraded," but they do resemble McTeague, Hurstwood, or Maggie,

toward the end of the novels in which they appear, in being close to the end of
their tether. Typically waitresses, salesmen, mechanics, or secretaries in their
early forties, life for them is now in its downhill stage. They live in shabby
homes in dingy neighborhoods and are either unemployed or locked into dull
and unrewarding jobs. Their family life has either disintegrated, with absent
spouses and children, or is dysfunctional, with anger, recrimination, and bitterness the operative emotions. Always there is the question of money—where
the next car or rent payment is coming from in the face of mounting debt and
unending obligation. The need for some sort of escape from the realization of
what their lives have descended to drives these figures into drink, chain smoking, TV addiction, and, most of all, into a mindless and empty chatter which
masks their deep and inexpressible malaise of the spirit. The archetypal scene
in a Carver story is thus one in which a couple no longer young—he out of
work, she in a dead-end job—are discovered in their shabby living room. He
is drinking and watching TV, she is doing household chores and complaining,
and both are filled with an unutterable angst at the realization of dreams and
hopes unfulfilled and of where their lives have brought them. Carver is not
concerned, as were some of the early naturalists, in tracing the precise cause of
this angle of descent. Rather, his fiction assumes both a body of generic human
inadequacy and the limitations placed on human endeavor by social reality
and then dramatizes the discovery by his characters, in early middle age, that
they have already reached the near-bottom of this slope.

Thus, the ambience and tone of a typical Carver story often resembles
that of Dreiser at his most saturnine. In Dreiser's "The Second Choice," for
example, a young girl locked into the prisons of a dull secretarial job and a
restrictive home is deserted by a lover who had appeared to represent a more
exciting and fulfilling life and settles for her "second choice," a man who constitutes all she had hoped to escape from. This, too, is Carver's world and
theme—the dull aching pain of realizing that life has passed one by and that
what remains is a thin existence of meaningless and repetitive tasks which
will culminate in a complete emptiness of spirit. The naturalism of fiction of
this kind is not that of the sensationalistic collapse of a life into crime and violence, as in Norris's *McTeague,* but rather that of the grinding down of an
existence by its minutia, as in Dreiser's account of Hurstwood and Carrie in
New York. There, Hurstwood's slow material decline is almost an exact
equivalent of his psychic disintegration, while Carrie and Hurstwood in their
life together have moved from their shared expectations for a better existence
in the Chicago portion of the novel to the distance and recriminations of a
couple going through the motions of a relationship. Carver's naturalism, in

brief, is that of the slow crumbling of mind and spirit within a setting in which seedy homes, unfulfilling work, and empty relationships are the physical analogues of what the inner life has descended to.

Three of Carver's most striking stories in *Where I'm Calling From*— "Are These Actual Miles?," "Why Don't You Dance?," and "Intimacy"— express his naturalistic theme of the movement of weak and flawed figures from an initial vision of the promise of life to a realization of what a shabby existence they have led and will continue to lead. And all of the stories, each in its own way, make the contrast between falsely based earlier expectation and present understanding the source of the distinctive tone of Carver's stories of an alternating bitterness, resignation, and anger arising from his characters' dim perception that life for them has been a cheat.

"Are These Actual Miles?" is the clearest example of this theme. Leo and Toni are out of work and about to be declared bankrupt. To prevent having their convertible, a relic of earlier, better days in their marriage, seized, Toni, with Leo's approval, tarts herself up and goes in search of a susceptible used car sales manager. Torn between his need for a good price for the car and the realization of what he and Toni must do to get it, Leo drinks, watches TV, thinks bitterly of his failed life, and contemplates suicide. Toni returns at dawn, having sold the car and slept with the sales manager. The circumstances of the story, and the manager's question to Leo about the convertible's speedometer reading, create the story's central metaphor of life as a wearing and empty journey. All the miles of Leo and Toni's life have indeed been actual, and have left indelible scars on their spirits. "Bankrupt," Toni screams self-defensively at Leo when she arrives home. And later, in the closing passage of the story, in bed with the sleeping Toni, Leo

> runs his fingers over her hip and feels the stretch marks there. They are like roads, and he traces them in her flesh. He runs his fingers back and forth, first one, then another. They run everywhere in her flesh, dozens, perhaps hundreds of them. He remembers waking up in the morning after they bought the car, seeing it, there in the drive, in the sun, gleaming. (103)

"Why Don't You Dance?" uses a different shape and central metaphor to express a similar theme of a character's realization of the dispiriting decline and failure of his life. The no-longer-young central figure of the story, having been deserted by his wife, places all their household belongings in their front yard and offers them for sale. A young couple, in love and just furnishing their first apartment, comes by. The older man, in an expression of resigned bitterness and cynicism at the difference between his and their position on the incline of life, sells them the appliances and furniture for what they are willing to pay and also joins them in a kind of party, drinking and dancing in the front yard. The man has said nothing about himself, but the girl dimly senses the implication of his actions and state of mind for her own relationship. As she and he dance, she says, "'You must be desperate or something'" (121). And weeks later, she is still telling her friends about the man and his sale: "She kept talking. She told everyone. There was more to it, and she was trying to get it talked out. After a time, she quit trying" (121).

"Intimacy" is basically a monologue. A writer in his mid-forties who had broken up with his wife some years ago visits her. Both are remarried, but the story consists of the recreation of the emotional texture of their marriage in the form of her outpouring of anger, bitterness, and recrimination toward him. (Most of the paragraphs in the story begin, "She says.") They had been deeply in love. "'We were so *intimate* once upon a time I can't believe it now'" (332), she tells him. He, under her barrage of excoriation, eventually falls to his knees and touches the hem of her skirt in an instinctive effort both to recapture that lost sense of intimacy and to ask forgiveness for his part in its loss. Grudgingly and half-cynically she does forgive him, but they separate again with an incomplete sense of reconciliation. As he departs, he notes piles of leaves everywhere: "I can't take a step without putting my shoe into leaves. Somebody ought to make an effort here. Somebody ought to get a rake and take care of this" (337).

"So Much Water So Close to Home," one of Carver's longer stories, offers a more complex and wide-ranging dramatization of the theme of an awakening to a sense of the unutterable emptiness and loneliness of one's existence. Here the setting is more conventionally middle class than most of Carver's stories. Claire and Stuart are comfortably well off and live a traditional family life, he the hard-working engineer, she the housewife looking after the home and a child. Stuart and his fishing buddies go off for a weekend in the mountains and stumble across the nude body of a murdered young girl in a river. Unwilling to give up their trip, they let the body float in the river for a day and a half before coming down and reporting their find to the police. For Claire, who has had earlier, inexplicable periods of anxiety about her life, the incident serves as a bleak epiphany. The young girl, she senses, dead in the cold river and not considered important enough by the men to interrupt their plans, is both herself and the human condition in general. Life has been reduced to routine and ritual at the expense of individual human need. The men in the hills, unwilling to interrupt their drinking and fishing expedition, her own world expecting her to perform within unending and unchanging roles—all human existence has been reduced to a vast systemization and thus a corresponding anomie and isolation of the individual human spirit. Claire thinks, "Two things are certain: 1) people no longer care what happens to other people; and 2) nothing makes any real difference any longer" (167). Making her own futile gesture toward caring and difference, Claire drives 120 miles over a difficult mountain road to attend the murdered girl's funeral. Stuart, on the other hand, responds to Claire's troubled spirit with a ritualized masculine belief that what she requires is more sexual attention. The story closes with Claire locking herself in a bedroom, a moment that, though not in Norris's sensationalistic mode, mimics, in its image of the outsider hounded into isolation by his world, the scene of McTeague alone and forlorn in Death Valley.

Paul Auster's fiction has, in recent years, become a favorite site for critics seeking to describe the nature of literary postmodernism, with his *The New York Trilogy* receiving the bulk of this attention. Auster's preoccupations with the fluidity of personal identity, with the significance of the trope of surveillance in modern life, and with the indeterminacy of language have struck responsive chords among such readers. I would like in my discussion of *The New York Trilogy* as a work which maintains several characteristics of American literary naturalism not to dismiss Auster's obvious participation in these postmodern concerns but rather to suggest that there is no incompatibility between the two strains. Just as John Dos Passos in his *U.S.A.* trilogy was able to combine a 1920s experimental ethos with naturalistic themes of the imprisoning of the individual by his or her class origins, so Auster should be allowed a comparable density in his fiction.

Auster's principal tie to naturalism in *The New York Trilogy* lies in the relationship of its first two novels, *City of Glass* and *Ghosts,* to the major naturalistic theme of the destructive isolation of the individual within a great metropolis. (Since the third novel, *The Locked Room,* does not contain this theme, I will not discuss it.) As Richard Lehan has documented well in his recent *The City in Literature,* many of the major nineteenth-century novelists, from Dickens and Balzac to Zola, depicted in their fiction the paradox of personal isolation, both in social relationships and in spirit, within a mass urban culture. Zola in *L'Assommoir* dramatized this theme by means of the compelling trope of a large block of flats in which the occupants of individual flats are ostensibly linked by their common dwelling but in reality move downward toward fates unrealized and unshared by others in their block. Frank Norris picks up this theme in his *McTeague* (subtitled by Norris *A Story of San Francisco*), where the seemingly thriving communal life of Polk Street is reduced first to McTeague and Trina's building, where the various occupants know each other only superficially, and then to their own flat, where the drama of their incompatible and self-destructive temperaments is played out largely in isolation. Dreiser also exploits this theme toward the second half of *Sister Carrie,* when Carrie feels detached from her world in the flat she and Hurstwood occupy in the upper West Side and then, later, when Hurstwood, reduced to the role of an unnoticed beggar on the swarming New York streets, embraces the ultimate expressive act of urban isolation by committing suicide in a bare room in a crowded Bowery flophouse. That Dreiser continued to be haunted by these images of urban anomie—the apartment cell and the death of the derelict—is revealed by two of his later sketches, "The Loneliness of the City" (1905) and "The Man on the Sidewalk" (1909). In the first, Dreiser describes an apartment house on Mott Street in the Bronx where he and his wife were living. He begins by noting that "One of the most painful results of modern congestion in cities . . . is the utter isolation and loneliness of heart forced upon the average individual" (157). In his apartment house, for example, the occupants "live in small, comfortably furnished and very convenient apartments, but they live alone. No one ever sees any exchange of courtesies between them. . . . You might live there a year, or ten years, and I doubt if your next-door neighbor would even so much know of your existence" (157–58). In the second sketch, Dreiser reprints a brief newspaper account of the death of an emaciated and shabbily dressed man on a New York Street. To Dreiser, the scarcely noticed and tersely reported death is "so characteristic of the city, and of life as a whole. Nature is so grim. The city, which represents it so effectively, is also so grim. It does not care at all. It is not conscious. The passing of so small an organism as that of a man or a woman is nothing to it" (165–66).

Much of this naturalistic theme of the city as the modern analogue of the "grimness" of nature is present in Auster's *City of Glass* and *Ghosts.* His central figures, the detective novelist Quinn in *City of Glass* and the detective Blue in *Ghosts,* live alone in small apartments or single rooms. They know little of the other dwellers of their buildings, and they have few friends or even acquaintances. When they venture out of their homes, it is to wander through the city on foot—as Quinn does in a notable passage (160–62)—derelicts in mind and spirit if not in actuality. "New York," Quinn reflects, "was an inexhaustible space, a labyrinth of endless steps, and no matter how far he walked, no matter how well he came to know its neighborhoods and streets, it always left him with a feeling of being lost" (10). "Wandering," he later concludes, was thus "a kind of mindlessness" (96). Theirs is a world of the human jetsam and flotsam of the city, of poor neighborhoods and cheap luncheonettes and of meaningless chatter with strangers. They are therefore defined from the outset as isolatos within the teeming life of the city. And because they have received little self-identification from others or their worlds, they have fluid and uncertain identities. Quinn writes under a pseudonym, is attracted by the identity of his fictional detective, and adopts, when it is offered, the identity of the "detective" Paul Auster. In *Ghosts,* Auster gives all his characters the names of colors (Blue, Black, Brown, and White) to signify their depersonalization.

The two novels are constructed on the model of the *film noir* detective story. A stranger appears or calls and engages a detective ("Auster" and Blue) in an act of surveillance. "Auster" is to follow Peter Stillman's father to ensure he does not again harm his son, as he had done years ago, and Blue is to spy on Black, a writer, for reasons not explained to him. Both works, however, almost immediately push the conventions of the detective story genre beyond their normal limits into the allegorical mode. The fluid, uncertain, and isolated self who is the spy wanders the labyrinths of the city in search of meaning and identity and comes to believe it lies in the identity of the lonely, isolated, and (for Stillman's father) derelict figure whom he has been hired to spy on. Blue, spying on Black from the window of his room, realizes that "it is as though [he] were looking into a mirror, and instead of merely watching another, he finds that he is also watching himself " (217).

The surveillances thus become obsessions. Quinn spends "weeks . . . perhaps even months" (170) of twenty-four-hour days outside Peter Stillman's apartment, waiting for the elder Stillman to appear, and Blue spends a year-and-a-half observing Black from his own room across the street, even though he soon realizes that Black's life is an unchanging routine of writing, reading, and walking. Gradually, both spies become symbolic reflections both of the city itself, in all its emptiness of spirit, and of the figures they are spying upon, in their emptiness of spirit. Quinn, at his post outside Peter Stillman's apartment house, observes that "remarkable as it seems, no one ever noticed [him]. It was as though he had melted into the walls of the city" (175–76).

In both novels, this confirmation of the absence of selfhood within the city is disastrous. Quinn finally breaks into Peter Stillman's apartment and finds it vacant and emptied of belongings. He takes possession of the apartment as a squatter and soon descends to a level of minimal existence; eventually "the story [of his fate] grows obscure. The information has run out . . ." (198). Both Quinn and his narrative have diminished into nothingness. He has not, as Hurstwood had done after much lonely wandering in the city, made a final retreat to a cheap Bowery flophouse and turned on the gas, but he has undergone a similar degeneration and dissolution within the anonymity and indifference of the city. Blue is also reduced "to almost no life at all" by his act

398

Is American Literary Naturalism Dead? A Further Inquiry

of surveillance (254). Like Quinn, he is eventually driven to bring the matter to a conclusion and breaks into Black's room. He finds that it was Black, disguised as White, who hired him to spy on Black—that Black, wishing to write about the loneliness and death in life of the city and especially of the writer in the city, has used Blue as a concrete objectification of that reality, which he also felt within himself. Blue, mimicking a writer as he prepared his reports in his room, has thus become the living model of the isolation of mind and spirit within the city which Black wishes to record. Infuriated both by Black's deception and by what this deception has revealed about his own nature and life, Blue viciously assaults Black and then, like Quinn, disappears.

Don DeLillo's *White Noise* differs from Carver's *Where I'm Calling From* and Auster's *New York Trilogy* in that its potential naturalistic strain is not immediately suggested by its characters and setting. Rather than Carver's out-of-work salesmen in run-down homes and shabby neighborhoods or Auster's urban derelicts, DeLillo's Gladneys are a well-off academic couple living a comfortable life in an idyllic New England college town. He is a full professor and department head, she a housewife and worker in the community. They and their children resemble the active, noisy, and sometimes quarrelsome family of TV situation comedy and thus appear to be far distant from the psychic collapses, deep angst, and physical violence of Carver's and Auster's worlds. DeLillo, however, quickly introduces into this seeming middle-class Eden— the rich foliage of early autumn, the students arriving fresh for a new school year, the satisfying family life—the basic human condition of the fear of death. Both Jack Gladney and his wife Babette are afflicted with this malady. They talk to each other about their fear, they have nightmares about it, and they have sought to build defenses against it.

There is, of course, little about the fear of death as a theme that can be traced directly to the specific conventions of literary naturalism. The topic is inherent to consciousness and has been addressed within varying religious, philosophical, and literary contexts, with varying conclusions, since the beginning of expression. Nevertheless, DeLillo's particular exploration of the theme does contain a significant naturalistic element in that his dramatization of its presence in the Gladneys relates the condition directly to the modern American culture in which they live. Like most Americans of their class, they are embedded, with little or no opportunity for conscious choice, in a society in which technology and popular culture condition every aspect of their existence. DeLillo's object in representing this reality is not only to show how these aspects of our culture seek, in their various but interrelated ways, to allay our fear of death, but—in the central ironic and naturalistic turn of the novel—how they in fact play the major roles in causing that fear because of their threat to our existence. Although DeLillo's New England college town is not Jack London's Yukon or Crane's East Side slum, he will demonstrate that environment, even when perceived as safe and protective, can indeed still be dangerous and therefore still "shapes lives regardless." Environment, for the Gladneys and for most middle-class Americans, is thus not the slum alcoholism, prostitution, and violence of the Johnson family in Crane's *Maggie;* nor is it the ice and cold of London's Northland. It exists, rather, in the form we now call a "culture"—that is, as a pervasive determining force of interrelated material conditions, unconscious assumptions, and social codes, all of which indirectly but deeply and often negatively affect the way we live and thus how we feel about life. As Jack Gladney's friend Murray says, we remain "fragile creatures surrounded by a world of hostile facts" (81).

The principal "hostile fact" in *White Noise* is the technologically based civilization which we have created both in order to prolong life and to make it more comfortable. Jack and Babette participate fully and gladly in this civilization. Their home is dominated by TV and household gadgets, their life outside the home centers on the automobile and the gleaming and efficient neighborhood supermarket, and they take full advantage of modern medicine. But despite the assurances implicit in these technological "advances" that life is better and less open to danger, the Gladneys instinctively sense that this is not true, that they are indeed threatened in some ineffable way by the life they lead—hence their angst. In a long speech, Murray, who plays the role throughout the novel of sardonic chorus on the plight of the Gladneys, sums up this paradox, in which the very safeguards we have created to thwart death are accompanied by its increased threat to our well-being:

> "This is the nature of modern death. . . . It is growing in prestige and dimension. It has a sweep it never had before. We study it objectively. We can predict its appearance, trace its path in the body. We can take cross-section pictures of it, tape its tremors and waves. . . . We know it intimately. But it continues to grow, to acquire breadth and scope, new outlets, new passages and means. The more we learn, the more it grows." (150)

Although *White Noise* is permeated with instances in which technology, in its various guises, illustrates the truth of this paradox, DeLillo devotes his fullest attention to two seemingly disparate but related examples—the "toxic event" which causes the temporary evacuation of the town, and the dominance of TV in the Gladney household. The first constitutes a striking and obvious

400

Is American Literary Naturalism Dead? A Further Inquiry

overt physical threat to well-being and to life itself, the second a more pervasive but less immediately apparent threat to the life of the mind and spirit.

In "The Airborne Toxic Event" (the title of the second book of the
novel), a large poisonous cloud is released after a railroad freight car accident
and transforms the entire town, including the Gladneys, into refugees. The
poisonous gas, we are reminded several times, is a byproduct in the manufacture of insecticide; what our technological knowledge has created to make life
more secure and comfortable can also, in its "byproducts," kill us. Even more
ominous is the relationship between the event and the Holocaust, where poison gas was used to achieve a more technologically advanced and therefore
more efficient means of mass killing. DeLillo makes the allusion to the Holocaust contained within the toxic event almost painfully evident by the transformation which Heinrich, one of the Gladney's children, undergoes while it
is occurring. Earlier a passive and shy teenager, he is absorbed by the event,
brings to it a good deal of technical expertise, and begins asserting an unexpected authority of tone and manner. The emotional resonance of the fact that
he and his family and the entire population of the town face death evades him
entirely. As a consequence of all the poison clouds we have created, the allegorical symbolism of the toxic event suggests, we have all become Jews seeking
to escape extermination, while the Nazi mentality of pride in the technological efficiency of a process, regardless of its consequences, is itself another
"byproduct" of our technological civilization.

Television is a less immediately ominous but a more insidious and omni-
present instance of the relationship between technology and a fear of death.
The initial book of *White Noise* is entitled "Waves and Radiations," a reference to the technological wonder which duplicates pictorially almost every
aspect of human existence in almost every American household. On the one
hand, television, with its constant and overwhelming reportage of disasters
throughout the globe, creates "brain fade" (67), a condition in which the mind
is incapable of absorbing and understanding the true import of the disasters
reported. On the other hand, it offers, as Murray explains, "incredible amounts
of psychic data" which, in its "coded messages and endless repetitions, like
chants, like mantras," cast us back into the innocence of primal responses to
experience (51). The result of both of these effects is the emergence of TV as
the white noise of our civilization, the meaningless but soothing background
sound which appears to blot out our awareness of the dangers inherent in that
civilization but which in fact increases our malaise.

These two technological phenomena—the toxic event and high-tech
communication—come together strikingly in a passage describing the poisonous

cloud and its attendant culture of reportage. The Gladneys are attempting to outrun the cloud in their car, but find it almost overhead and sit transfixed as it passes nearby:

> We sat in the car, in the snowy woods, saying nothing. The great cloud, beyond its turbulent core, was silver-tipped in the spotlights. . . . In its tremendous size, its dark and bulky menace, its escorting aircraft, the cloud resembled a national promotion for death, a multimillion-dollar campaign backed by radio spots, heavy print and billboards, TV saturation. (157–58)

Death, it would seem, has been "domesticated" and made less threatening by its neutralizing association with technological advance and by being absorbed within the familiar cultural contexts of advertising and reporting. But death is still death, as Jack and Babette instinctively realize, and the popular culture created to disguise that reality, the white noise of our civilization, only heightens their fear, since that which mankind once addressed openly is now disguised or hidden and thus made even more fearful.

Seeking to alleviate their fear, Jack and Babette seek out specific anodynes. Babette is a devotee of strenuous exercise, and, more ominously, makes herself available as a human guinea pig in the secret testing of a drug specifically designed to combat the fear of death. Jack, as Murray explains, was attracted to Hitler Studies because of the presumed protective magic of the subject: "'Helpless and fearful people are drawn to magical figures, mythic figures, epic men. . . . Some people are larger than life. Hitler is larger than death. You thought he would protect you'" (287). Both Babette and Jack, however, are led into self-betrayal by these attempts. Babette, in order to be selected as a test site for the experimental drug, agrees to sleep with the scientist in charge. Jack, who believes he must learn to speak German despite the instinctive revulsion he feels for the language, has disguised throughout his career the fact that he does not know the language. Indeed, when toward the close of the novel he attempts to act out a principle of the fascist ideology of power—that to kill another is to gain a renewal of life for oneself—he botches the effort. He is a better man—and Babette is a better woman—than the false roles into which they have been forced by their fear of death.

The novel ends with nothing resolved. Jack and Babette continue to live within an environment dominated by technology and pop culture which, because it threatens life, will continue to trigger their fear of death. The final scene of *White Noise* is of Jack at the supermarket, where there is much confusion among the patrons because the stock has been rearranged. But it "doesn't matter what they see or think they see. The terminals are equipped with holographic scanners, which decode the binary secret of every item, infallibly. This is the language of waves and radiation. . . . And this is where we wait together, regardless of age, our carts stocked with brightly colored goods" (326). Few conventional naturalists have rendered as suggestively or powerfully the bleak reality of mankind in the grip of the mechanistic civilization which it itself has created.

As I noted at the outset, I do not wish in this examination of naturalistic tendencies in selected works by Carver, Auster, and DeLillo to make the claim that naturalism, as written in the 1890s, is still a living force among American writers. We no longer have a fiction in which environment is allegorized or in which characteristics of temperament are linked to specific chemical or biological causation. Nor does the contemporary writer of fiction render his beliefs with the mix of detailed social documentation and melodramatic violence which was Frank Norris's principal contribution to the seemingly permanent reputation of naturalism as crude and inept. Instead, contemporary writers of fiction are deeply implicated in the various sophistications of fictional method, which themselves constitute indirection and complexity in fictional theme, that are the products of the century of modern and postmodern expression since the late nineteenth century. Nevertheless, a powerful thread of continuity between the past and the present can be discerned. Carver's minimalist portraits of suburban angst, Auster's ghost-like cities of mysteries and surveillance, and DeLillo's surreal college town—all still seek to render the ways in which experience is deeply and usually negatively conditioned by the circumstances within which we live. Leaving aside the question of whether it is profitable for literary history to designate this continuing thread with the explicit term "naturalism," it is nevertheless necessary to acknowledge the presence of the thread.

NOTES

"Is American Literary Naturalism Dead? A Further Inquiry" by Donald Pizer originally appeared in his *American Literary Naturalism: Recent and Uncollected Essays* (Bethesda, MD: Academia Press, 2002). It is reprinted here by permission of the publisher.

1. Although both writers are occasionally discussed as naturalists, Hemingway has received the most attention in this regard. See the sections devoted to Hemingway in Thorp, Walcutt, and Civello.
2. See "The 1930s" (Farrell, Dos Passos, and Steinbeck) in Pizer, *Twentieth-Century*.

3. See the essays on Wright, Farrell, and Algren in Hakutani and Fried and the chapters on Gold, Wright, Algren, Selby, and Oates in Giles.

4. See "The Late 1940s and Early 1950s" (Mailer, Styron, and Bellow) in Pizer, *Twentieth-Century,* and "Contemporary American Literary Naturalism" in Pizer, *Theory.* The most useful wide-ranging effort to locate naturalistic tendencies in American fiction since World War II remains Graham.

Works Cited

Auster, Paul. *The New York Trilogy: City of Glass, Ghosts, The Locked Room.* Los Angeles: Sun & Moon, 1994.

Carver, Raymond. *Where I'm Calling From: New and Selected Stories.* New York: Atlantic Monthly, 1988.

Civello, Paul. *American Literary Naturalism and Its Twentieth-Century Transformations.* Athens: U of Georgia P, 1994.

Cowley, Malcolm. "'Not Men': A Natural History of American Naturalism." *Kenyon Review* 9 (1947): 414–35. Pizer, *Documents.*

Crane, Stephen. *Maggie: A Girl of the Streets.* Ed. Thomas A. Gullason. New York: Norton, 1979.

DeLillo, Don. *White Noise.* New York: Viking, 1985.

Dreiser, Theodore. "The Loneliness of the City." 1905. *Theodore Dreiser: A Selection of Uncollected Prose.* Ed. Donald Pizer. Detroit: Wayne State UP, 1977.

————. "The Man on the Sidewalk." 1909. *Theodore Dreiser: A Selection of Uncollected Prose.* Ed. Donald Pizer. Detroit: Wayne State UP, 1977.

Giles, James R. *The Naturalistic Inner-City Novel in America: Encounters with the Fat Man.* Columbia: U of South Carolina P, 1995.

Graham, Don. "Naturalism in American Fiction: A Status Report." *Studies in American Fiction* 10 (1982): 1–16.

Hakutani, Yoshinobu, and Lewis Fried, eds. *American Literary Naturalism: A Reassessment.* Heidelberg: Carl Winter, 1975.

Lehan, Richard. *The City in Literature: An Intellectual and Cultural History.* Berkeley: U of California P, 1998.

Norris, Frank. *McTeague: A Story of San Francisco.* Ed. Donald Pizer. 2nd ed. New York: Norton, 1997.

Pizer, Donald. *The Theory and Practice of American Literary Naturalism: Selected Essays and Reviews.* Carbondale: Southern Illinois UP, 1993.

————. *Twentieth-Century American Literary Naturalism: An Interpretation.* Carbondale: Southern Illinois UP, 1982.

————, ed. *Documents of American Realism and Naturalism.* Carbondale: Southern Illinois UP, 1998.

Rahv, Philip. "On the Decline of Naturalism." *Partisan Review* 9 (1942): 483–93. *Image and Idea*. New York: New Directions, 1949.

Trilling, Lionel. "Reality in America." *The Liberal Imagination*. New York: Viking, 1950. 3–21. Pizer, *Documents*.

Walcutt, Charles C. *American Literary Naturalism, A Divided Stream*. Minneapolis: U of Minnesota P, 1956.

Contributors

DONNA M. CAMPBELL is Associate Professor of English at Gonzaga University. She is author of *Resisting Regionalism: Gender and Naturalism in American Fiction, 1885–1915* (Ohio University Press, 1997) and the introduction to a new edition of Edith Wharton's *The Fruit of the Tree* (Northeastern University Press, 2000). Her articles on Frank Norris, Edith Wharton, Sarah Orne Jewett, and other turn-of-the-century writers have appeared in essay collections and in *Studies in American Fiction, American Literary Realism, Legacy,* and *Frank Norris Studies.*

BRANNON W. COSTELLO is a doctoral candidate at the University of Tennessee specializing in American literature from the late nineteenth century to the contemporary period. His primary interests are in southern literature, particularly the interrelationship of race and class in the formation of identity in twentieth-century southern fiction, and in late-nineteenth and early-twentieth-century social protest fiction. He has published essays on Eudora Welty, Richard Wright, Lewis Nordan, and Walker Percy.

WILLIAM DOW is Assistant Professor of English at The American University of Paris and a Maître de conférences at the University of Valenciennes. He has published articles in the fields of American nineteenth-century literature and American twentieth-century fiction in such journals as *PMLA, The Emily Dickinson Journal, Twentieth-Century Literature, ESQ: A Journal of the American Renaissance, Critique, The Hemingway Review, MELUS, Revue Françaises D'Etudes Américaines, Actes Sud, Profils américains,* and *Annales du monde.* His current projects include a book, *Remappings: Sources, Senses, and American Literary Traditions,* and the editing of an anthology on American nostalgia.

ROBERT M. DOWLING received his M.A. in American studies from California State University, Fullerton, and his Ph.D. in English and American studies from the Graduate Center of the City University of New York. He is currently a Lecturer in English at the U.S. Coast Guard Academy.

TIM EDWARDS is Assistant Professor of English at the University of the Ozarks in Clarksville, Arkansas. His previous publications include essays on Evelyn Scott's *Escapade* and on her unpublished novel *Before Cock Crow* as well as an article on Harry Crews's *A Feast of Snakes.* His current projects include a book-length study of Evelyn Scott's major prose works.

LILIAN R. FURST is Marcel Bataillon Professor of Comparative Literature at the University of North Carolina at Chapel Hill. She has published extensively on nineteenth-century literature, mainly European but also American. Recently she has been working in the field of literature and medicine. Her monograph *Naturalism* (1971; 1976) is now out of print. Her study *"All is True": The Claims and Strategies of Realist Fiction* appeared in 1995 (Duke University Press), and her latest work, *Medical Progress and Social Reality: A Reader in Nineteenth-Century Medicine and Literature,* was published in 2001 (SUNY Press).

PHILIP GERBER, Distinguished University Professor at SUNY-Brockport, is the author of *Willa Cather* (rev. ed., 1995) and *Theodore Dreiser Revisited* (1992). A major interest in American poetry has resulted in *Robert Frost* (1966) and, underway, a study of E. E. Cummings. An appreciation of the skill with which ordinary Americans have communicated through personal messages has led to a volume of homesteading letters, *Bachelor Bess* (1990), and a three-year sequence of Civil War letters is forthcoming. Gerber has begun editing another series of letters, these exchanged between husband and wife during World War II.

A member of the Department of English at Northern Illinois University in DeKalb, JAMES R. GILES is the author of *Violence in the Contemporary American Novel; Understanding Hubert Selby, Jr.; The Naturalistic Inner-City Novel in America: Encounters with the Fat Man; The Novels of Nelson Algren;* and *Irwin Shaw: A Study of the Short Fiction.* He is also the author of the Twayne U.S. Authors Series volumes on Claude McKay, James Jones, and Nelson Algren.

SARA BRITTON GOODLING is a doctoral candidate at the University of Delaware. Her doctoral work interrogates long-held convictions concerning American literary naturalism's beginnings, developments, and practitioners. In particular, Ms. Goodling uses the works of nineteenth-century American women writers such as Elizabeth Stuart Phelps and Rebecca Harding Davis to argue for earlier, more American, more feminine roots of American literary naturalism than have previously been acknowledged.

LAURA HAPKE is Professor of English at the Dyson College of Arts and Sciences of Pace University in New York City, where she teaches the literature of U.S. labor. The winner of two *Choice* Outstanding Academic Book Awards, she is the author of *Daughters of the Great Depression: Women, Work, and Fiction in the American 1930s.* Her most recent publication, which signals the shift in her scholarly emphasis, is *Labor's Text: The Worker in American Fiction* (Rutgers University Press, 2001). The first book-length study to cover 150 years of novels and short fiction on U.S. labor, it is a revisionist history of labor representation that approaches the topic from a multicultural perspective and employs an interdisciplinary integration of working-class and literary history.

DAVID K. HECKERL is Assistant Professor of English at St. Mary's University in Halifax, Nova Scotia. His research in American fiction and culture reflects an ongoing interest in relating literary texts to the history of liberalism in philosophy and political thought. He is currently preparing material for a book on the eclipse of politics by culture in Anglo-American literary criticism from Arnold to the present day.

BARBARA HOCHMAN teaches American literature at Ben Gurion University in Israel. She has published widely on nineteenth-century American fiction. Her most recent book is *Getting at the Author: Reimagining Books and Reading in the Age of American Realism* (University of Massachusetts Press, 2001). Her current project—Uncle Tom's Cabin *and the Reading Revolution*—explores the relation between fiction and reading practices in antebellum America.

HILDEGARD HOELLER is Assistant Professor of English at the College of Staten Island–CUNY, where she teaches nineteenth-century American literature and culture. This essay is part of a larger study entitled *From Gift to Commodity: The Economics of Nineteenth-Century American Fiction;* the project traces the central tensions between gifts and commodities in fiction by Foster, Child, Warner, Melville, Howells, and Norris. She is the author of *Edith Wharton's Dialogue with Realism and Sentimental Fiction* (University Press of Florida, 2000).

KATHERINE JOSLIN is the author of *Edith Wharton* in the Macmillan Women Writers Series and a coeditor of *Wretched Exotic: Essays on Edith Wharton in Europe.* Her work includes essays on Willa Cather, Kate Chopin, Theodore Dreiser, Charlotte Perkins Gilman, and Virginia Woolf. She is currently completing a literary biography, *Jane Addams: A Writer's Life,* and coediting *Documents in the History of American Feminism,* a four-volume collection. Joslin is Professor of English at Western Michigan University, where she directs American studies and has received the Alumni Teaching Excellence Award. Over the past three years, she has directed Fulbright Summer Institutes in American studies for international professors.

KECIA DRIVER MCBRIDE is Assistant Professor of English at Ball State University in Muncie, Indiana, where she teaches and publishes in American literature, women's studies, American cultural studies, and film. She is currently completing her first book manuscript, which examines silence as narrative space in the works of early-twentieth-century American women writers. Her most recent publication examines the folk plays of the Carolina Playmakers at the University of North Carolina from 1918 to 1930.

MARY E. PAPKE, Associate Professor of English at the University of Tennessee, is the author of *Verging on the Abyss: The Social Fiction of Kate Chopin and Edith Wharton* (1990) and *Susan Glaspell: A Research and Production Sourcebook* (1993), both from Greenwood Press. In addition, she has published essays on feminist theory, postmodern women writers, the unpublished drama of Evelyn Scott, the political theater of Sean O'Casey, and Marxist literary criticism in early twentieth-century America, among other topics. All of these projects have focused significantly on issues of gender and class ideologies as well as the process of ethical and aesthetic evaluation.

DONALD PIZER is Pierce Butler Professor of English at Tulane University, where he has taught since 1957. He has published widely on American literature between 1865 and 1945, including many studies and editions bearing directly on American literary naturalism. Among his books are *Realism and Naturalism in Nineteenth-Century American Naturalism* (1966; 2nd ed., 1984), *Twentieth-Century American Literary Naturalism: An Interpretation* (1982), and *The Theory and Practice of American Literary Naturalism: Selected Essays and Reviews* (1993).

DANIEL SCHIERENBECK is Assistant Professor of English at Central Missouri State University. Though his primary specialization is British Romanticism, his broader interest in cultural and literary authority has led him to investigate these subjects in a wide range of texts and contexts.

NANCY VON ROSK received her Ph.D. from the University of New Hampshire where she teaches courses in writing and American literature. Her essay is adapted from a chapter in her dissertation, "Private Lives and Public Spectacles: Cultural Transformation and the American Urban Novel, 1852–1925." She has also published scholarly articles in *Southwestern American Literature, Studies in the Novel, Mosaic,* and *Prospects: An Annual of American Cultural Studies;* and her travel writing on Morocco was included in the anthology *An Inn Near Kyoto: Writing by American Women Abroad* (New Rivers Press, 1998).

LANA A. WHITED began her study of naturalism when she read *Sister Carrie* as an undergraduate. Searching for an approach to analyzing novels about homicide several years later, she recognized a naturalistic influence. She subsequently wrote a dissertation on how nonfiction novels such as *In Cold Blood* and *The Executioner's Song* evolved from the naturalistic tradition. She earned degrees at Emory and Henry College, The College of William and Mary, Hollins University, and the University of North Carolina at Greensboro. She teaches English and journalism at Ferrum College in Virginia's Blue Ridge Mountains and recently edited *The Ivory Tower and Harry Potter: Critical Perspectives on a Literary Phenomenon* (Missouri, 2002).

ADAM H. WOOD is currently completing his doctoral work at Georgia State University where his primary interests are in American naturalism and materialist and historicist critical theory. His current project involves a historical and political investigation into the issues of closure and resolution in American naturalism, particularly in the texts of Frank Norris and Theodore Dreiser.

MOHAMED ZAYANI has a Ph.D. in English from Indiana University. He is the author of *Reading the Symptom: Frank Norris, Theodore Dreiser, and the Dynamics of Capitalism* and numerous scholarly articles. He is currently Associate Professor of literature and critical theory at the American University of Sharjah in the United Arab Emirates.

Index

Twisted from the Ordinary was designed and typeset on a Macintosh computer system using QuarkXPress software. The body text is set in 10.5/14 Granjon and display type in Edwardian Script. This book was designed and typeset by Cheryl Carrington and manufactured by Thomson-Shore, Inc.